A
Harmony
of the
Four Gospels
in
Delaware

The translation by
Ira D. Blanchard and James Conner (1837-1839)

Volume II

Edited and Translated by
Ives Goddard

Mundart Press

2021

Copyright © 2021 by Joshua Jacob Snider
Mundart Press, 807 Howard Street, Petoskey MI 49770

All rights reserved. No part of this book may be reproduced or transmitted in any form or by any means, electronic or mechanical, including photocopying, recording, or by any information storage and retrieval system, without permission in writing from the publisher.

The publisher hereby grants such permission to the Delaware Tribe of Indians and the Delaware Nation of Western Oklahoma for any tribal educational or cultural purpose.

A publication of the Recovering Voices Program of the Smithsonian Institution, supported in part by a gift from the Shoniya Fund.

Publisher's Cataloguing-in-Publication Data

Names: Blanchard, Ira D., 1808-1872, translator. | Conner, James, 1817-1872, translator. | Goddard, Ives, 1941- editor, translator.
Title: A harmony of the four Gospels in Delaware : the translation by Ira D. Blanchard and James Conner / edited and translated by Ives Goddard.
Other titles: Bible. Gospels. Delaware.
Description: Petoskey, MI : Mundart Press, 2021. | Includes bibliographical references.
Identifiers: ISBN: 978-0-9903344-4-6 (v.1) | 978-0-9903344-5-3 (v.2) | LCCN: 2021902981
Subjects: LCSH: Bible. Gospels--Harmonies. | Delaware language--Texts. | Delaware Tribe of Indians--Missions. | Delaware Nation, Oklahoma--Missions.
Classification: LCC: BS345.D4 2021 | DDC: 226.1/0597345--dc23

Blanchard's Harmony of the Gospels

(continued)

          /b   tuh vuh ct ntclsen rli qelu vatao cntxi kejekif?
          /p   'tá=č=háč=ét ntə́lsi·n, é·li-kwí·la-hát·aɔ éntxi-ki·š·í·k·ink?'
          /t   'I wonder what I shall do, as I have no place to put all the crops?'
          /k   What shall I do, because I have no room where to bestow my fruits?

Lk 12.18 /b   Letrvr b kch ntclsen;
          /p   li·t·é·he·, 'yú=ké=č ntə́lsi·n.
          /t   He thought, 'Well, this is what I'll do.
          /k   And he said, This will I do:

          /b   lwkunimunh cvatrk ntunhih lukveqetwn;
          /p   llo·kənə́mən=č ehháte·k, ntánči-=č -ləkhikwí·to·n.
          /t   I'll take down the barn for them, and I'll build it bigger.
          /k   I will pull down my barns, and build greater;

          /b   nuh nc ntatwn cntxi kejekif, ok wrmi cntxi nevlatamu.
          /p   ná=č nə́ ntá·to·n éntxi-ki·š·í·k·ink, ɔ́·k wé·mi éntxi-nihəlá·t·ama.
          /t   That's where I'll put all the crops and everything I own.
          /k   and there will I bestow all my fruits and my goods.

Lk 12.19 /b   Nuh ntclan ntunaprokun, Mrhi xrli lahrswakun kwlvatw,
          /p   ná=č ntə́la·n ntənna·p·e·ɔ́·k·an, 'mé·či xé·li lač·e·s·əwá·k·an ko·lhátu.
          /t   Then I will say to my soul, 'You now have many possessions.
          /k   And I will say to my soul, Soul, thou hast much goods laid up

          /b   xrlih kavtunri knakatamun;
          /p   xé·li=č kahtəné·i kəna·ká·t·amən.
          /t   You will rely on them for many years.
          /k   for many years;

          /b   bqc alaxemwi tcxi jwq mevmetsi, ok mevmunc, ok wlrluntu.
          /p   yúkwe ala·x·í·mwi, téxi šúkw mihəmí·tsi, ɔ́·k míhəmənə, ɔ́·k wəle·lə́nta.'
          /t   Now rest, and do nothing but eat, drink, and be happy.'
          /k   take thine ease, eat, drink, and be merry.

Lk 12.20 /b   Jwq Krtanitwet tclao, Kwphav,
          /p   šúkw ke·tanət·ó·wi·t təlá·ɔ, 'kkə́pča,   [⟨-v⟩ implies /kkə́pča[h]/]
          /t   But God said to him, 'You are foolish.
          /k   But God said unto him, Thou fool,

          /b   pcxw peskrkc ktunaprokun paleh wunhi wcnhema;
          /p   péxu pi·ské·k·e ktənna·p·e·ɔ́·k·an palí·i=č wə́nči-wenčí·ma·.
          /t   Tonight your soul shall be called to go away.
          /k   this night thy soul shall be required of thee:

	/b	nuh vuh awrn wnevlatamun nrl lahrswakunu?
	/p	ná=č=háč awé·n wənihəlá·t·amən né·l lač·e·s·əwá·k·ana?'
	/t	Then who will own those possessions?'
	/k	then whose shall those things be, which thou hast provided?

Lk 12.21 /b Jr nuni tclsen awrn rvopret nevlahi, jwq ta rvopret tali Krtanitwetif.
/p šé· nəni tə́lsi·n awé·n ehɔ·p·é·i·t nihəláči, šúkw tá=á· ehɔ·p·é·i·t táli ke·tanət·o·wí·t·ink."
/t That is what someone does who is rich for himself, but not rich in God."
/k So is he that layeth up treasure for himself, and is not rich toward God.

Lk 12.22 /b Nu tclan rkrkematpani, Nuni wunhi lilrq,
/p ná tə́la·n e·k·e·ki·ma·tpáni, "nə́ni wə́nči-lə́le·kw,
/t Then he said to his disciples, "That's why I say to you,
/k And he said unto his disciples, Therefore I say unto you,

/b Kahi punarluntufvrq wcntawserq, krkw meherq, ok rqerq.
/p káči pəna·elətánkhe·kw wenta·wsíe·kw, kéku mí·č·ie·kw, ɔ́·k é·k·wie·kw.
/t Don't think about what you live from, the things you eat, or what you wear.
/k Take no thought for your life, what ye shall eat; neither for the body, what ye shall put on.

Lk 12.23 /b Lclrxrokun alwe lr mehwakun rlrk,
/p lehəle·x·e·ɔ́·k·an aləwí·i-lé· mi·č·əwá·k·an é·le·k,
/t Life is more than food,
/k The life is more than meat,

/b ok wavtwvrpi alwe lr rvaqif rlrk.
/p ɔ́·k wahtuhé·p·i aləwí·i-lé· éhahkwink é·le·k.
/t and the body is more than clothing.
/k and the body is more than raiment.

Lk 12.24 /b Punarlumw, ‖ wifrovqrok;
/p pənaé·ləmo· winke·ɔhkwé·ɔk.
/t Think of the ravens.
/k Consider the ravens:

(p. 120) /b rli takw evakevreok, ok mutu wewlataeok
/p é·li takó· i·haki·he·í·ɔk, ɔ́·k máta wi·wəla·ta·í·ɔk,
/t For they never plant and never put up food for themselves,
/k for they neither sow nor reap; which neither have storehouse nor barn;

/b jwq Krtanitwet texamao;
/p šúkw ke·tanət·ó·wi·t tihxamá·ɔ.
/t but God feeds them.
/k and God feedeth them:

Text, Transcription, and Translation

/b mutu vuh ktalwe lusewunroek hwlunsuk?
/p máta=háč ktaləwí·i-ləs·i·wəne·ɔ́·i·k čo·lə́nsak?
/t Are you not superior to the birds?
/k how much more are ye better than the fowls?

Lk 12.25
/b Awrn vuh a kelwu kuski unhi mujaqsw eli kwti srksetuf lukveqi letrvatc?
/p awé·n=háč=á· ki·ló·wa káski-ánči-məšá·kwsu ílli kwə́t·i se·ksí·t·ank ləkhíkwi-li·t·e·há·t·e?
/t Who of you could attain a greater height by thinking even as much as one foot?
/k And which of you with taking thought can add to his stature one cubit?

Lk 12.26
/b Tufenako krkw poi luserqc,
/p tanki·ná·k·ɔ kéku pɔ́·i-ləs·ié·k·we,
/t If you are unable to do the small sort of thing,
/k If ye then be not able to do that thing which is least,

/b krkw vuh a wunhi musi krkw punarluntamrq.
/p kéku=háč=á· wə́nči- mə́si kéku -pəna·elə́ntame·kw.
/t why would you think about everything else?   [*lit.*, all kinds of things]
/k why take ye thought for the rest?

Lk 12.27
/b Punarluntamwq otarsu, rlkeqi wlekif;
/p pəna·elə́ntamo·kw ɔ·taé·s·a, e·lkí·kwi-wəlí·k·ink.
/t Think about the flowers, how beautifully they grow.
/k Consider the lilies how they grow:

/b takw mekumosweeo, ok mutu pemunatrbweeo;
/p takó· mi·kəmɔ·s·o·wi·í·ɔ, ɔ́·k máta pi·məna·te·yo·wi·í·ɔ.
/t They do not work, and they do not spin thread,
/k they toil not, they spin not;

/b jwq ktclwvmw,
/p šúkw ktəllúhəmɔ,
/t but I tell you,
/k and yet I say unto you,

/b Salumunu taoni xifwiluswp, takw telukveqi owulavqewunrp.
/p †sa·lamána, tá·ɔni xínkwi-lə́s·o·p, takó· tilləkhíkwi-ɔwəlahkwí·wəne·p.
/t Solomon, even though he was great, was never dressed so well.
/k that Solomon in all his glory was not arrayed like one of these.

Lk 12.28
/b Krtanitwet a avkonifc skeko, bqc kejqek wlekifi,
/p ke·tanət·ó·wi·t=á· ahkɔnínke skí·kɔ, yúkwe kí·škwi·k wəli·k·ínki,
/t If God clothes the grass, which today grows nicely,
/k If then God so clothe the grass, which is to day in the field,

/b tamsc a alupu lwsaswu
/p tá·mse=á· aláp·a lo·s·á·s·əwa,
/t and perhaps tomorrow it will be burned up,
/k and to morrow is cast into the oven;

/b mutu vuh ct alwe kwlevkwewu?
/p máta=háč=ét aləwí·i ko·lihko·wíwwa?
/t don't you think he will treat you better?
/k how much more will he clothe you,

/b O tufrtw knakrwswakunwu!
/p ó·, tanké·t·u kəna·ke·wsəwa·k·anúwa.
/t Oh, your faith is small.
/k O ye of little faith?

Lk 12.29 /b Kahi ntwnufvrq; krkw a meherq, jitu mrnrrq,
/p káči nto·nánkhe·kw kéku=á· mí·č·ie·kw, ší=tá me·né·e·kw.
/t Don't seek what you would eat or drink.
/k And seek not ye what ye shall eat, or what ye shall drink,

/b kahi jwrlumotufvrq.
/p káči šhwe·ləmɔ·t·ánkhe·kw,
/t Don't be doubtful about it,
/k neither be ye of doubtful mind.

Lk 12.30 /b Rli wrmi awrn cntxet nunul li nrl ntwnuf;
/p é·li- wé·mi awé·n éntxi·t nanáli né·l -ntó·nank.
/t for those things are what everyone that exists seeks after.
/k For all these things do the nations of the world seek after:

/b kwxwu nu watwn ktcli krpwu kavtatumunro.
/p kó·x·əwa nɔ́ o·wá·to·n ktə́li- ké·pəwa -kahta·t·aməné·ɔ.
/t Your father knows that you also desire that.
/k and your Father knoweth that ye have need of these things.

Lk 12.31 /b Jwq wlava ntwnamwq sokemaokun Krtanitwet;
/p šúkw wəláha ntó·namo·kw sɔ·k·i·ma·ɔ́·k·an ke·tanət·ó·wi·t.
/t But rather seek the kingdom of God.
/k But rather seek ye the kingdom of God;

/b wrmih bl kmujinumunro.
/p wé·mi=č yó·l kəməš·ənəməné·ɔ.
/t You shall obtain all these things.
/k and all these things shall be added unto you.

Lk 12.32 /b Kahi alumevrq tatxeterq,
/p káči a·ləmí·he·kw, ta·txí·t·ie·kw,
/t Do not be afraid, you few.
/k Fear not, little flock;

/b rli nu kwxwu wifi luset kmelkwnro sokemaokun.
/p é·li- ná kó·x·əwa -wínki-ləs·i·t kəmi·lko·né·ɔ sɔ·k·i·ma·ó·k·an.
/t For your father is glad to give you his kingdom.
/k for it is your Father's good pleasure to give you the kingdom.

Lk 12.33 /b Mvalumakrq krkw wrlvatarq, melw krtumaksehek;
/p mhalamá·k·e·kw kéku we·lhátae·kw, mí·lo· ke·t·əma·ksí·č·i·k.
/t Sell the things you have and give to the poor.
/k Sell that ye have, and give alms;

/b yimwq vcmsenwtyu, ta vuji xwrki, ok lathrswakunu osavkamc
/p ayəmo·kw hempsi·nó·t·aya, tá=á· háši xuwé·k·i, ó·k lač·e·s·əwá·k·ana ɔ·s·áhkame,
/t Obtain cloth bags that will never become old, and possessions in heaven,
/k provide yourselves bags which wax not old, a treasure in the heavens [that faileth not],

/b cntu ta vuji krvkumwtkrt pat, ok mwxwrsuk cntu ta paletwvtet,
/p énta- tá=á· háši kehkəmó·tke·t -pá·t, ó·k mo·x·wé·s·ak énta- tá=á· -pali·túhti·t.
/t where a thief will never come, and where bugs will never destroy them.
/k where no thief approacheth, neither moth corrupteth.

Lk 12.34 /b rli ktrvwu nanc avpet.
/p é·li- ktéhəwa ná=nə -ahpí·t.
/t For that is where your hearts are.
/k For where your treasure is, there will your heart be also.

Lk 12.35 /b Fumri kulumapeseq, ok kosulrnekunwu fumri naxqsetch;
/p nkəmé·i kəlama·pí·s·i·kw, ó·k kɔ·s·əle·ni·k·anúwa nkəmé·i naxkwsí·t·eč.
/t Always have your belt on, and let your lantern always be lit.
/k Let your loins be girded about, and your lights burning;

Lk 12.36 /b liseq linwuk rvrlusevtet prvavtetc nrvlalqevtehi,
/p ləs·i·kw lənəwak ehələs·íhti·t pe·hahtí·t·e nehəla·lkwihtí·č·i,
/t And do as men do when they wait for their master,
/k And ye yourselves like unto men that wait for their lord,

/b apaheletc wunhi cntu metsavtif,
/p a·p·a·č·i·lí·t·e wənči énta-mi·tsáhtink,
/t when he is coming back from a feast,
/k when he will return from the wedding;

/b   tcli a paletc pwpwvetcmuletc, jac twfjrnumaonro.
/p   tə́li-=á·, pa·lí·t·e, pəp·uhhitehəməlí·t·e, šá·e -tunkše·nəmaɔ·né·ɔ.
/t   so that, when he comes and knocks on the door, they may immediately open the door for him.
/k   that when he cometh and knocketh, they may open unto him immediately.

Lk 12.37
/b   Punu, wrli nwtekrvtetc alwkakunuk wlapcnswuk praletc nrvlalqevtehi.
/p   pənáh, wé·li-no·t·i·k·ehtí·t·e alo·ká·k·anak wəla·p·énsəwak, pe·a·lí·t·e nehəla·lkwihtí·č·i,
/t   Now, blessed are the servants when they were carefully watching the house when their master came.
/k   Blessed are those servants, whom the lord when he cometh shall find watching:

/b   Kvehe ktclwvmw, nrkumuh qulamapeswlao vokyu,
/p   khičí·i ktəllúhəmɔ, né·k·əma=č kwəlama·pi·s·o·lá·ɔ hókaya.
/t   Truly I say to you that *he* shall put on *his* belt.
/k   verily I say unto you, that he shall gird himself,

/b   nuh tclan lumutavpeq, ok metseq
/p   ná=č tə́la·n, 'ləmátahpi·kw ɔ́·k mí·tsi·kw.'
/t   Then he shall say to them, 'Sit and eat.'
/k   and make them to sit down to meat,

/b   ok wifih ajitc krnavkevao cntu ‖ metselet.
/p   ɔ́·k wwínki-=č a·šíte -ke·nahki·há·ɔ énta-mi·tsí·li·t.
/t   And *he* will willingly take care of *them* at their meal.
/k   and will come forth and serve them.

Lk 12.38
(p. 121)
/b   Taoni a lai tpwkw paletc. jitu alweihi
/p   tá·ɔni=á· lá·i-tpó·ku pa·lí·t·e, ší=tá aləwi·íči,
/t   Even though it is midnight when he comes, or a little later,
/k   And if he shall come in the second watch, or come in the third watch,

/b   nrvqevtetc tcli nuni lisenro, eaphi a wlapcnswuk.
/p   ne·ykwihtí·t·e tə́li- nəni -ləs·i·né·ɔ, i·á·pči=á· wəla·p·énsəwak.
/t   when he sees them doing that, they would still be blessed.
/k   and find them so, blessed are those servants.

Lk 12.39
/b   Kwatwnro, wreket a wataqc tclih pan krvkumwtkrt,
/p   ko·wa·to·né·ɔ, we·í·k·i·t=á· wwa·tá·k·we tə́li-=č -pá·n kehkəmó·tke·t,
/t   You know, that if a house-owner knows that a thief is going to come,
/k   And this know, that if the goodman of the house had known what hour the thief would come,

/b   wli a krnavketwn weket wcnhi a mutu paletakwk;
/p   ó·li-=á· -ke·nahkí·to·n wí·k·i·t, wénči-=á· máta -pali·tá·k·uk.

/t   he will watch over his house, so that one will not break into it.
/k   he would have watched, and not have suffered his house to be broken through.

Lk 12.40 /b   krpwu nc lukveqi kejanaqseq;
/p   ké·pəwa nə́ ləkhíkwi-ki·š·əná·kwsi·kw,
/t   You, too, be ready to that extent,
/k   Be ye therefore ready also:

/b   rlih pat Wrqesif linw nrli ta letrvarq.
/p   é·li=č -pá·t we·k·wí·s·ink lə́nu, né·li- tá=á· -li·t·e·há·e·kw."
/t   for the man who is the Son shall come when you do not think (he will)."
/k   for the Son of man cometh at an hour when ye think not.

Lk 12.41 /b   Nu Petul tclanrp, Nrvlalerf, nelwnu vuh nc jwq ktclenrn rnwnvakrokun
/p   ná †pí·təl təlá·ne·p, "nehəlá·lienk, ni·ló·na=háč nə́ šúkw ktəlí·ne·n e·nunthake·ó·k·an,
/t   Then Peter said to him, "Master, do you tell that parable just to us,
/k   Then Peter said unto him, Lord, speakest thou this parable unto us,

/b   ji vuh wrmi awrn?
/p   ší=háč wé·mi awé·n?"
/t   or to everyone?"
/k   or even to all?

Lk 12.42 /b   Nu Nrvlalwrt tclwrn, Awrn vuh et nu wrliliset wejiki wli nwtekrt
/p   ná nehəlá·ləwe·t tə́ləwe·n, "awé·n=háč=ét ná wé·li-lə́s·i·t, wi·šíki-wə́li-no·t·í·k·e·t?
/t   Then the Lord said, "Who do you think is that one who did right (or 'the good one'), working hard at watching the house?
/k   And the Lord said, Who then is that faithful and wise steward,

/b   nulh nu nrvlalkwki qejemkw
/p   nál=č ná nehəla·lkúk·i kwi·š·í·mku
/t   *He* is who his master (obv.) shall appoint
/k   whom his lord shall make ruler over his household,

/b   tclih aphi cji tpisqevlak xaman cntxi nevlalalehi?
/p   tə́li-=č á·pči éši-tpəskwíhəla·k -xáma·n éntxi-nihəla·la·lí·č·i.
/t   to feed those he (obv. = the master) is master of whenever it is the right time.
/k   to give them their portion of meat in due season?

Lk 12.43 /b   Wulapcnswh nc rlset alwkakun paletc nrvlalkwki.
/p   wəla·p·énsu=č nə́ é·lsi·t alo·ká·k·an, pa·lí·t·e nehəla·lkúk·i.
/t   Blessed shall be the servant who is doing that when his master comes.
/k   Blessed is that servant, whom his lord when he cometh shall find so doing.

Lk 12.44 /b Kvehei ktclwvmw,
/p khičí·i ktəllúhəmɔ,
/t Truly I say to you,
/k Of a truth I say unto you,

/b qejemkwh nrvlalkwki tclih nevlalan cntxi nevlalalehi.
/p kwi·š·í·mku=č nehəla·lkúk·i tə́li-=č -nihəlá·la·n éntxi-nihəla·la·lí·č·i.
/t his master shall appoint him to be master of all those *he* is master of.
/k that he will make him ruler over all that he hath.

Lk 12.45 /b Jwq tamsc alwkakun vwtrvif tali lwr, nrvlalet ta jac pri,
/p šúkw tá·mse alo·ká·k·an wté·hink táli-lúwe·, 'nehəlá·li·t tá=á· šá·e pé·i.'
/t But perhaps the servant says in his heart, 'My master won't come right away.'
/k But and if that servant say in his heart, My lord delayeth his coming;

/b nu tcli alumi puvkaman wehe-alwkakunu, linwu ok xqro,
/p ná təli-áləmi-pahkáma·n wíči-alo·ká·k·ana, lə́nəwa ɔ́·k xkwé·ɔ,
/t And then he proceeds to start beating his fellow servants, men and women,
/k and shall begin to beat the menservants and maidens,

/b ok metsen, ok munrn, ok kewsen.
/p ɔ́·k -mí·tsi·n, ɔ́·k -məné·n, ɔ́·k -kí·wsi·n.
/t and to eat, and drink, and be drunk.
/k and to eat and drink, and to be drunken;

Lk 12.46 /b Wexkaohih paletc nrvlalkwki
/p wi·xkaɔ́či=č pa·lí·t·e nehəla·lkúk·i
/t If his master comes unexpectedly,
/k The lord of that servant will come in a day

/b nrli mutu prvat ok nrli mutu punarlumat;
/p né·li- máta -pé·ha·t, ɔ́·k né·li- máta -pənaé·ləma·t.
/t while he is not waiting for him, and while he is not concerned about him,
/k when he looketh not for him, and at an hour when he is not aware,

/b nuh qeskhujwkwn, ekuh tclanrvmalkw rhifxahek rpevtet.
/p ná=č kwi·skčaš·ó·k·o·n, íka=č tələnehəmá·lku e·č·inkxá·či·k e·p·íhti·t.
/t then he shall cut him up and throw him where the disobedient are.
/k and will cut him in sunder, and will appoint him his portion with the unbelievers.

Lk 12.47 /b Alwkakunh wrotaq nrvlalkwki rletrvalet, jwq mutu nuni lsetc,   [⟨ls-⟩ for ⟨lus-⟩]
/p alo·ká·k·an=č we·ɔ́·ta·kw nehəla·lkúk·i e·li·t·e·há·li·t, šúkw máta nəni ləs·í·t·e,
/t The servant who knows what his master wants done but does not do it
/k And that servant, which knew his lord's will, and [prepared not himself], neither did according to his will,

/b aveh pupavkuma,
/p áhi=č pəpahkáma·.
/t shall be severely beaten.
/k shall be beaten with many stripes.

Lk 12.48 /b kahih nu mutu wrotaq taoni hanawsw. krxitih jwq pupavkuma,
/p káč·i=č ná máta we·ó·ta·kw, tá·ɔni čaná·wsu, ke·xíti=č šúkw pəpahkáma·.
/t But the one who does not know, even though he does wrong, shall only be beaten a little,
/k But he that knew not, and did commit things worthy of stripes, shall be beaten with few stripes.

/b rli awrn xrli krkw meluntc anvwqi xrli mrkuk. [⟨rli awrn⟩ for ⟨rli a awrn⟩]
/p é·li-[á·], awé·n xé·li kéku mi·lənte, a·nhúkwi -mé·k·ək.
/t For if someone is given many things, he [should] give them away in turn.
/k For unto whomsoever much is given, of him shall be much required: ...

Lk 12.49 /b Rli pau, wunhi naxqtr cntu lawsif,
/p é·li-pá·a wənči-náxkwte· entalá·wsink.
/t For I come in order that the world catch fire.
/k I am come to send fire on the earth;

/b tuh vuh ct ntclsen bqc mrhi alumi skutr.
/p tá=č=háč=ét ntəlsi·n? yúkwe mé·či áləmi-skát·e·.
/t What shall I do, I wonder? Now the fire has already started burning.
/k and what will I if it be already kindled?

Lk 12.50 /b Heh kwtrnaoki hvopwununtwakun ntclih hvopwunukrn,
/p čí·č kwət·ennáɔhki čhɔ·pwənəntəwá·k·an, ntəli-=č -čhɔ·pwənək·e·n.
/t There is still one more kind of baptism for me to be baptized with.
/k But I have a baptism to be baptized with;

/b kxunkih keji nc lr ntavrluntumh eku pchi.
/p kxántki=č kíši- nə -lé·; ntahe·ləntam=č íka péči.
/t In the end that will be done; until then I will be in distress.
/k and how am I straitened till it be accomplished!

Lk 12.51 /b Ktetrvavmw vuh rli pau wlafwntwakunwh b cntu lawsif.
/p kti·t·e·háhəmo=háč, é·li-pá·a, wəlankuntəwá·k·anu=č yú entalá·wsink.
/t Do you think that because I come there will be peace on earth?
/k Suppose ye that I am come to give peace on earth?

/b Ktclwvmw taa; jwq tclih prpavsevlanro.
/p ktəllúhəmɔ, tá=á·, šúkw təli-=č -pe·pahsihəla·né·ɔ.
/t I tell you, 'No,' but so that they will be divided from each other.
/k I tell you, Nay; but rather division:

Lk 12.52 /b Bqch lr
/p yúkwe=č lé·.
/t It will now happen.
/k For from henceforth

/b tamsc kwti wekwavmif palrnuxk awrnek avpevtetc
/p tá·mse kwə́t·i wi·k·əwáhəmink palé·naxk awé·ni·k ahpihtí·t·e,
/t If perhaps five people are living in one house,
/k there shall be five in one house

/b prpavsevlreoh,   [⟨-reoh⟩ for ⟨-reokh⟩, for /-é·ɔk=č/]
/p pe·pahsihəlé··ɔk=č.
/t they will be divided from each other.
/k divided,

/b nuxuh vwhwprlumawao neju, okh neju vwhwprlumawao nrl nuxu.
                                                                                   [⟨neju vw-‖hwpr-⟩]
/p naxá=č wčəp·e·ləmawwá·ɔ ní·š·a, ɔ́·k=č ní·š·a wčəp·e·ləmawwá·ɔ né·l naxá.
/t Three will exclude two, and two will exclude those three.
/k three against two, and two against three.

Lk 12.53 /b Kvekwenwh, vwhwprlumao qesu, okh wrqeseif vwhwprlumao wxo;
(p. 122) /p khikəwínnu=č wčəp·e·lamá·ɔ kkwí·s·a, ɔ́·k=č we·k·wí·s·ink wčəp·e·ləmá·ɔ ó·x·ɔ,
/t The older man shall exclude his son, and the son shall exclude his father,
/k The father shall be divided against the son, and the son against the father;

/b okh kvekybxqc vwhwprlumao tonu, okh wrtanif vwhwprlumao kovrsu,
/p ɔ́·k=č khikayúxkwe wčəp·e·ləmá·ɔ tó·na, ɔ́·k=č we·t·á·nink wčəp·e·ləmá·ɔ kɔhé·s·a,
/t and the older woman shall exclude her daughter, and the daughter shall exclude her mother,
/k the mother against the daughter, and the daughter against the mother;

/b okh kvekybxqr vwhwprlumao xwmav,   [⟨xwmav⟩ for /xúma[h]/]
/p ɔ́·k=č khikayúxkwe wčəp·e·ləmá·ɔ xúma,
/t and the older woman shall exclude her daughter-in-law,
/k the mother in law against her daughter in law,

/b okh wrxumif vwhwprlumao vwswqesu.
/p ɔ́·k=č wé·x·əmink wčəp·e·ləmá·ɔ wsuk·wí·s·a."
/t and the daughter-in-law shall exclude her mother-in-law."
/k and the daughter in law against her mother in law.

Lk 12.54 /b Ok tclapani,
/p ɔ́·k təlá·p·ani,
/t And he said to them,
/k And he said also to the people,

/b nrmrqc vufq kwmvoq li cvli vwsekak li pchi uspwxwrbw,
/p "ne·mé·k·we=hánkw kɔ́mhɔkw lí- éhəli-wsí·ka·k -lí-péči-aspo·x·we·yó·u,
/t "When you see a cloud come rising up in the west,
/k When ye see a cloud rise out of the west,

/b ktclwcvmw vufq kavtu swkulan;
/p ktələwéhəmɔ=hánkw, 'káhta-só·k·əla·n.'
/t you always say, 'It's going to rain.'
/k straightway ye say, There cometh a shower; [and so it is.]

Lk 12.55 /b ok vufq nrmrqc li pcpaxaqrk wuntuxun, ⟨wuntuxun⟩ for ⟨wuntxun⟩]
/p ó·k=hánkw ne·mé·k·we lí- †pehpa·xhákwe·k -wə́ntxən,
/t And when you see the wind blow from the south,
/k And when ye see the south wind blow,

/b ktclwcvmw vufq kavtu kjuluntr.
/p ktələwéhəmɔ=hánkw, 'káhta-kšəlánte·.'
/t you always say, 'It's going to be hot.'
/k ye say, There will be heat; [and it cometh to pass.]

Lk 12.56 /b Kevakevokcvmw, knunamunro vufq rlenako vwqrbf, ok b vakif;
/p †kkihahki·hɔkéhəmɔ; kənənaməné·ɔ=hánkw e·li·ná·k·ɔ hukwé·yunk ó·k yú hák·ink.
/t You are hypocrites; you recognize what it is like in the sky and here on earth.
/k Ye hypocrites, ye can discern the face of the sky and of the earth;

/b krkw vuh wcnhi mutu nunamwrq bqc krtu lrk?
/p kéku=háč wénči- máta -nənamó·we·kw yúkwe ké·t·a-lé·k?
/t Why do you not recognize what is going to happen now?
/k but how is it that ye do not discern this time?

Lk 12.57 /b Ok krkw vuh wunhi mutu nevlahi watwrq krkw wrlexif?
/p ó·k kéku=háč wə́nči- máta nihəláči -wwa·tó·we·kw kéku we·lí·x·ink?
/t And why do you not know the things of your own that are right?
/k Yea, and why even of yourselves judge ye not what is right?

Lk 12.58 /b Jifalkon nejwxwrrqc li krkyimvrtif wlufwmwmc naohei,
/p šinká·lkɔn ni·š·o·x·we·é·k·we lí ke·kayəmhé·t·ink, wəlanko·mó·me naɔč·í·i,
/t When you and your adversary go together to the ruler, be on good terms with him on the way,
/k When thou goest with thine adversary to the magistrate, as thou art in the way, give diligence that thou mayest be delivered from him;

| | /b | rli a tamsc kpavwkrun eku prjwkonc krkw rlenwavkusehek rpevtet.
| | /p | é·li-=á· tá·mse -kpaho·k·é·an, íka pe·š·ó·k·ɔne kéku e·linnuwahkəs·í·č·i·k e·p·íhti·t.
| | /t | for you could perhaps be imprisoned if he takes you to where those with some official authority are.
| | /k | lest he hale thee to the judge, and the judge deliver thee to the officer, and the officer cast thee into prison.

Lk 12.59 /b Ktclil, ta kwnhi khewun navle kcnh pavkuntrnvanc.   [⟨-nvanc⟩ for *e.g.* ⟨-nvranc⟩]
         /p ktə́ləl, tá=á· kúnči-kčí·wən nahəlí·i kə́nč pahkante·nhé·ane."
         /t I tell you, you would not get out of there in any case until you paid in full."
         /k I tell thee, thou shalt not depart thence, till thou hast paid the very last mite.

Chapter 68 (pp. 122-123). (Luke 13.1-9.)

Lk 13.1 /b Nu nckc lukveqi lan rlenamevtetup Faluleetpanek,
         /p ná-néke ləkhíkwi lá·n e·li·namihtí·t·əp †nka·lali·i·tpáni·k,
         /t Then at that time he was told about what had happened to the people from Galilee
         /k There were present at that season some that told him of the Galilaeans,

         /b nukavkc Pylutu nrvlatpani, nrli wevwfrletup.
         /p nəkáhke †pailát·a nehəla·tpáni, né·li-wi·hunke·lí·t·əp.
         /t that Pilate had killed while they were sacrificing.
         /k whose blood Pilate had mingled with their sacrifices.

Lk 13.2 /b Nhesus tclao; Ktetrvavmw vuh, alwe ct nukavkc lukeqi muvtawswpanek
         /p nčí·sas təlá·ɔ, "kti·t·e·háhəmɔ=háč, aləwí·i=ét nəkáhke ləkhíkwi-mahta·wsó·p·ani·k
         /t Jesus said to them. "Do you think, those people must have been worse sinners
         /k And Jesus answering said unto them, Suppose ye that these Galilaeans were sinners above

         /b wrmi Faluleehek rlkeqi muvtawsevtet?
         /p wé·mi †nka·lali·í·č·i·k e·lkí·kwi-mahta·wsíhti·t?
         /t than all the Galileans?
         /k all the Galilaeans, [because they suffered such things]?

Lk 13.3 /b Ktclwvmw takw,
         /p ktəllúhəmɔ, 'takó·.'
         /t I tell you, 'No.'
         /k I tell you, Nay:

         /b Krpwuh nanc ktclenamunro mutu quluperqc.
         /p ké·pəwa=č ná=nə ktəli·naməné·ɔ, máta kwələp·ié·k·we.
         /t You shall also have the same thing happen to you if you do not repent.
         /k but, except ye repent, ye shall all likewise perish.

Lk 13.4 /b   Kahi nukavkc tclcn ok xaj, rvalwkalint e ntaopwekaon krlvwqvetetup,
            [⟨-lint e⟩ for ⟨-linte⟩, for /-lənti·i/]
         /p   káč·i nəkáhke télən ɔ́·k xá·š ehalo·ka·ləntí·i-ntaɔ·p·əwi·k·á·ɔn ke·lho·khwití·t·əp,
         /t   Or those eighteen that the watchtower of the messenger fell on,
         /k   Or those eighteen, upon whom the tower in Siloam fell, and slew them,

         /b   ktetrvavmw vuh alwe ct nukavkc lukveqi muvtawswpanek
         /p   kti·t·e·háhəmɔ=háč, aləwí·i=ét nəkáhke ləkhíkwi-mahta·wsó·p·ani·k
         /t   do you think those people must have been worse sinners
         /k   think ye that they were sinners above

         /b   wrmi Nhelwsulum rpehek rlkeqi muvtawsevtet?
         /p   wé·mi †nči·ló·sələm e·p·í·č·i·k e·lkí·kwi-mahta·wsíhti·t?
         /t   than all those that lived in Jerusalem?
         /k   all men that dwelt in Jerusalem?

Lk 13.5 /b   Ktclwvmw takw,
         /p   ktəllúhəmɔ, 'takó·.'
         /t   I tell you, 'No.'
         /k   I tell you, Nay:

         /b   Krpwuh nanc ktclenamunro mutu quluperqc. ‖
         /p   ké·pəwa=č ná=nə ktəli·naməné·ɔ, máta kwələp·ié·k·we."
         /t   You shall also have the same thing happen to you if you do not repent."
         /k   but, except ye repent, ye shall all likewise perish.

Lk 13.6 /b   Lupi rnwnvakrokun tclao;
(p. 123) /p   lápi e·nunthake·ɔ́·k·an təlá·ɔ:
         /t   He told them another parable:
         /k   He spake also this parable;

         /b   Linwu mu tokevakunif vetko jwkulepwko wcvcnhi kejekif.
         /p   "lənəwa=máh tɔ·ki·há·k·anink hítkɔ šo·k·əli·pó·k·ɔ wehə́nči-ki·š·í·k·ink.
         /t   "In a certain man's field was a tree on which sweet fruit grew.
         /k   A certain man had a fig tree planted in his vineyard;

         /b   Nu tamsc moi punaon, letrvr kaxunch krkw kejekun,
         /p   ná tá·mse mói-pənáɔ·n, li·t·é·he·, 'ká·xəne=č kéku ki·š·í·k·ən.'
         /t   Then sometime he went to look at it, thinking, 'I wonder whether something will grow.'
         /k   and he came and sought fruit thereon,

         /b   jwq mutu krkw muxkumwi.
         /p   šúkw máta kéku maxkamó·wi.
         /t   But he found nothing.
         /k   and found none.

Lk 13.7 /b Nu tclan tokevakun krnavketwlet,
/p ná tə́la·n tɔ·ki·há·k·an ke·nahki·tó·li·t,
/t Then he said to the one watching his field,
/k Then said he unto the dresser of his vineyard,

/b Mrhi nuxi kavtin nwhi mavmaipunao wu vetwq
/p 'mé·či náxi-kahtə́n nnúči-máhəmai-pənáɔ wá hít·ukw,
/t 'I have been coming to look at this tree for three years now,
/k Behold, these three years I come

/b rli letrvau kaxunch krkw kejekun;
/p é·li-li·t·e·há·a, 'ká·xəne=č kéku ki·š·í·k·ən.'
/t because I thought, 'I wonder whether something will grow.'
/k seeking fruit on this fig tree, and find none:

/b Kesvov, nwhqc qwsqekamun b vake.   [⟨sv⟩ for ⟨skv⟩]
/p kí·skhɔw. nó·čkwe kwəskwí·kamən yú hák·i.'
/t Chop it down. It's pointless for it to burden this land.'
/k cut it down; why cumbereth it the ground?

Lk 13.8 /b Jwq tclao, Nrvlaleun konu lenaw kwti kavtifc svaki,
/p šúkw təlá·ɔ, 'nehəlá·lian, kɔ́na lí·naw kwə́ti-kahtínke sháki.
/t But he said to him, 'My lord, leave it alone for one year.
/k And he answering said unto him, Lord, let it alone this year also,

/b okaih ntcli mwnvo, okh wrltuk krkw eku ntatw.
/p ɔ·ká·i=č ntə́li-mó·nhɔ, ó·k=č wé·ltək kéku íka ntá·tu.
/t I'll dig around it, and I'll put something good there.
/k till I shall dig about it, and dung it:

Lk 13.9 /b Tamsc a puna, krkw eku wunhi kejekun;
/p tá·mse=á· pənáh kéku íka wə́nči-ki·š·í·k·ən.
/t Sometime something may even grow on it.
/k And if it bear fruit, well:

/b jwqh mutu kejekifc krkw, nuh fesvon.   [⟨sv⟩ for ⟨skv⟩]
/p šúkw=č máta ki·š·i·k·ínke kéku, ná=č nkí·skhɔ·n.'"
/t But if nothing grows, then I will chop it down.'"
/k and if not, then after that thou shalt cut it down.

Chapter 69 (pp. 123-124). (Luke 13.10-21.)

Lk 13.10 /b Alaxemwre kejqekc, avkrkifrp tali cvcntu mamacvluf. [⟨ma-|macv-⟩ for ⟨macv-⟩]
/p ala·x·i·məwe·í·i-ki·škwí·k·e, ahke·kínke·p táli ehə́nta-ma·éhəlank.

| | /t | When it was the day of rest, he taught in the synagogue. |
| | /k | And he was teaching in one of the synagogues on the sabbath. |

Lk 13.11 /b Avpwp xqr ktumuki palset,
/p ahpó·p xkwé· ktəmáki-pá·lsi·t.
/t There was a woman who was miserably sick.
/k And, behold, there was a woman which had a spirit of infirmity

/b mrhi nckc tclcn ok xaj txi kavtinri palswp,
/p mé·či néke télən ɔ́·k xá·š txí-kahtəné·i pá·lso·p.
/t She had then been sick for eighteen years.
/k eighteen years,

/b avi okvakrp, takw keski apaqeep. [⟨keski⟩ for ⟨kekski⟩]
/p áhi-ɔ·kháke·p, takó· kí·kski-a·p·a·kwí·i·p.
/t She was severely bent over and was never able to straighten up.
/k and was bowed together, and could in no wise lift up herself.

Lk 13.12 /b Nhesus nrotc notwmapani, tclao,
/p nčí·sas ne·ɔ́·t·e, nɔt·o·má·p·ani, təlá·ɔ,
/t When Jesus saw her, he called for her to come and said to her,
/k And when Jesus saw her, he called her to him, and said unto her,

/b xqr, mrhi kluxi wunhi kpalswakunif,
/p "xkwé·, mé·či kəláx·i wə́nči kpa·lsəwá·k·anink."
/t "Woman, you are now set free from your sickness."
/k Woman, thou art loosed from thine infirmity.

Lk 13.13 /b nu eku tonan,
/p ná íka tɔ́nna·n.
/t Then he put his hand on her.
/k And he laid his hands on her:

/b nu jac topaqen ok moxifokuneman Krtanitwelehi.
/p ná šá·e tɔ·p·á·kwi·n, ɔ́·k mɔx·inkɔhkəní·ma·n ke·tanət·o·wi·lí·č·i.
/t Then immediately she straightened up and praised God.
/k and immediately she was made straight, and glorified God.

Lk 13.14 /b Nu nekanexif tali cntu macvluf, tolumi krkw lwrn
/p ná ni·k·a·ní·x·ink táli énta-ma·éhəlank tɔ́ləmi- kéku -lúwe·n,
/t Then the leader in the synagogue began speaking,
/k And the ruler of the synagogue answered

/b rli mutu wulrluntuf;
/p é·li- máta -wəle·ləntank.
/t as he was not pleased.
/k with indignation, [because that Jesus had healed on the sabbath day,]

/b lwr aphi vufq kwtaj txi kejqc jwq mekumosen;
/p lúwe·, "á·pči=hánkw kwət·a·š txí-kí·škwe šúkw mi·kəmɔ́·s·i·n.
/t He said, "Always only for six days do people work.
/k and said unto the people, There are six days in which men ought to work:

/b ok a palset nunc lukveqi my kekrva, jwq a alaxemwre-kejqekc mutu.
/p ɔ́·k=á· pá·lsi·t ná=nə ləkhíkwi mái-ki·k·é·ha·, šúkw=á· ala·x·i·məwe·í·i-ki·škwí·k·e máta."
/t And that's the time when a sick person should go to be healed, but not on the day of rest."
/k in them therefore come and be healed, and not on the sabbath day.

Lk 13.15
/b Nhesus tclapani, kevakevokc;
/p nčí·sas təlá·p·ani, "kkihahki·hɔ́ke.
/t Jesus said to him, "You are a hypocrite.
/k The Lord then answered him, and said, Thou hypocrite,

/b Mutu vuh vufq kelwu awrn, qutwxolaeo tolumwnsu wunhi wekwaumif
⟨aum⟩ for ⟨avm⟩
/p máta=háč=hánkw ki·ló·wa awé·n kwət·o·x·ola·í·ɔ tɔləmúnsa wə́nči wi·k·əwáhəmink,
/t Don't any of you take out their animals from the house
/k doth not each one of you on the sabbath loose his ox or his ass from the stall,

/b mowsumwkrwunu alaxemwre-kejqekc?
/p mɔwo·s·əmo·ké·wəna ala·x·i·məwe·í·i-ki·škwí·k·e?
/t and take them to water on the day of rest?
/k and lead him away to watering?

Lk 13.16
/b Punu wuni Rplivamif wunheyb,
/p pənáh, wáni †e·pəlihámink wənčí·ayu
/t Now, this one comes from Abraham.
/k And ought not this woman, being a daughter of Abraham,

/b mavtuntw koxpelao mrhi tclcn ok xaj kavtinri,
/p mahtánt·u kɔxpi·lá·ɔ mé·či télən ɔ́·k xá·š kahtəné·i.
/t The devil has bound her for eighteen years now.
/k whom Satan hath bound, lo, these eighteen years,

/b mutu vuh wlexunwi luxunan nrli alaxemwre-kejqek?
/p máta=háč wəli·x·ənó·wi laxəna·n né·li-ala·x·i·məwe·í·i-kí·škwi·k?

	/t	Is it not right for her to be unbound during the day of rest?
	/k	be loosed from this bond on the sabbath day?

Lk 13.17 /b Keji nc lwrtc, mexaniswpanek jifalatpanek,
/p kíši- nə́ -luwé·t·e, mi·x·anəs·ó·p·ani·k šinka·la·tpáni·k.
/t After he said that, his enemies were ashamed.
/k And when he had said these things, all his adversaries were ashamed:

/b ok xrli awrn wlrluntamwp wunhi tolweluswakun. ‖
/p ɔ́·k xé·li awé·n wəle·lə́ntamo·p wə́nči tɔləwí·i-ləs·əwá·k·an.
/t And many people rejoiced because of his power.
/k and all the people rejoiced for all the glorious things that were done by him.

Lk 13.18 /b Nu tclwrnrp, Ta vuh mulaji lenakot Krtanitwet sokemaokun?
(p. 124) /p ná tələwé·ne·p, "tá=háč málahši li·ná·k·ot ke·tanət·ó·wi·t sɔ·k·i·ma·ó·k·an?
/t Then he said, "What is God's kingdom like?
/k Then said he, Unto what is the kingdom of God like?

/b krkwnifh vuh ntclwc lenakot?
/p kéku=nínk=č=háč ntə́ləwe li·ná·k·ot?
/t What shall I say it is like?
/k and whereunto shall I resemble it?

Lk 13.19 /b Lenakot, mulaji mustute mifqtut, linw xkumatc tali tokevakunif,
/p li·ná·k·ot málahši †mɔstatí·i-mínkwtət, lə́nu xkəmá·t·e táli tɔ·ki·há·k·anink.
/t It is like a little mustard seed, if a man plants it in his garden.
/k It is like a grain of mustard seed, which a man took, and cast into his garden;

/b sakifc vufq tvakartw amufetvwnrr,
/p sa·k·ínke=hánkw, †thakaé·t·u amanki·thwəné·e·,
/t When it grows up, in a short time it has large branches,
/k and it grew, and waxed a great tree;

/b wunhi hwlunsuk eku naovlavtet?   ["?" is an error]
/p wə́nči- čo·lə́nsak íka -naɔhəláhti·t."
/t because of which, birds land there."
/k and the fowls of the air lodged in the branches of it.

Lk 13.20 /b Nu lupi tclwrnrp, krkwnifh vuh ntclwc lenakot Krtanitwet sokemaokun?
/p ná lápi tələwé·ne·p, "kéku=nínk=č=háč ntə́ləwe li·ná·k·ot ke·tanət·ó·wi·t sɔ·k·i·ma·ó·k·an?
/t Then again he said, "What shall I say God's kingdom is like?
/k And again he said, Whereunto shall I liken the kingdom of God?

Lk 13.21 /b Lrw mulaji pcpastrk, tamsc xqr lwkavtif vataqc, kxunki wrmi pastr.
/p léˑw málahši pehpáˑsteˑk, táˑmse xkwéˑ lóˑkahtink hatáˑkˑwe, kxántki wéˑmi páˑsteˑ."
/t It is like yeast: if a woman maybe puts it in flour, eventually (the bread) all rises."
/k It is like leaven, which a woman took and hid in three measures of meal, till the whole was leavened.

Chapter 70 (p. 124). (Luke 13.22-30.)

Lk 13.22 /b Nrlwxwrtc li Nhelwsulumif, cntxun wtrnif patc aphi pumutwnvrp.
/p neˑloˑxˑwéˑtˑe lí †nčiˑloˑsələmink, éntxən- oˑtˑéˑnink -páˑtˑe, áˑpči pəmətˑóˑnheˑp.
/t As he journeyed to Jerusalem, he always preached in every town he came to.
/k And he went through the cities and villages, teaching, and journeying toward Jerusalem.

Lk 13.23 /b Nu mawsw linw tclan, Nrvlaleun, Tatxetwukh vuh osavkamc rlwxolunhek?
/p ná máˑwsu lónu tóla·n, "nehəláˑlian, taˑtxíˑtˑəwak=č=háč ɔˑsˑáhkame eˑloˑxˑɔlə́nčiˑk?"
/t Then one man said to him, "My lord, will there be few that are taken to heaven?"
/k Then said one unto him, Lord, are there few that be saved?

/b Tclao,
/p təláˑɔ,
/t He said to him,
/k And he said unto them,

Lk 13.24 /b qhi li punheq tavhrk skontrf.
/p "kwčí-lí-pə́nčiˑkw tahčéˑk skɔ́ntenk.
/t "Try to enter in the narrow door.
/k Strive to enter in at the strait gate:

/b Rli ktclwvmw, xrlih krtu tumekrhek, jwqh qelaluswuk.
/p éˑli ktəllúhəmɔ, xéˑli=č kéˑtˑa-təmiˑkˑéˑčˑiˑk, šúkw=č kwíˑla-lə́sˑəwak.
/t For, I tell you, there will be many who desire to enter, but they will not be able to.
/k for many, I say unto you, will seek to enter in, and shall not be able.

Lk 13.25 /b Wreketh pavswqetc, ok kpavufc weket,
/p weˑíˑkˑiˑt=č pahsukˑwíˑtˑe, ɔ́ˑk kpahánke wíˑkˑiˑt,
/t When the owner of the house gets up and closes the door of his house,
/k When once the master of the house is risen up, and hath shut to the door,

/b nuh ktalumi pwpwvetcvmunro kpavwn kohumif wunhi,
/p náˑč ktáləmi-pəpˑuhhitehəməné·ɔ kpáhoˑn kóčəmink wə́nči,
/t then you will start knocking on the door from outside.
/k and ye begin to stand without, and to knock at the door,

/b okh ktclawu Nrvlalerf, Nrvlalerf, twfjrnumaenrn;
/p ɔ́·k=č ktəláwwa, 'nehəlá·lienk, nehəlá·lienk, tunkše·nəmaí·ne·n.'
/t And you will say to him, 'Master, master, open the door for us.'
/k saying, Lord, Lord, open unto us;

/b jwqh ktclkwu takw kwavlwvwmw ok wcnheaerq.
/p šúkw=č ktəlkúwa, 'takó· ko·wahəlo·húmɔ, ɔ́·k wenči·aíe·kw.'
/t But he will say to you, 'I don't know you, or where you're from.'
/k and he shall answer and say unto you, I know you not whence ye are:

Lk 13.26 /b Ktclawuh nmetsevnap, ok nmunrvnap tali rlifwrxenun,
/p ktəláwwa=č, 'nəmi·tsíhəna·p, ɔ́·k nəmənéhəna·p táli e·linkwe·x·í·nan,
/t You will say to him, 'We have eaten and drunk in your presence,
/k Then shall ye begin to say, We have eaten and drunk in thy presence,

/b ok ktckrkifrvwmp tali ntwtrnynanif;   [⟨ktck-⟩ for /ktak·-/]
/p ɔ́·k ktak·e·kinké·həmp táli nto·t·e·nayəná·nink.'
/t and you have taught in our towns.'
/k and thou hast taught in our streets.

Lk 13.27 /b jwqh amunhei ktclkwu, takw kwavlwvwmw, ok wcnheaerq.
/p šúkw=č amənčí·i ktəlkúwa, 'takó· ko·wahəlo·húmɔ, ɔ́·k wenči·aíe·kw.
/t But he will persist in saying to you, 'I don't know you, or where you're from.
/k But he shall say, I tell you, I know you not whence ye are;

/b Paleaq wrmi mrtawserq.
/p palí·i á·kw, wé·mi me·t·a·wsíe·kw.'
/t Go away, all you sinners.'
/k depart from me, all ye workers of iniquity.

Lk 13.28 /b Nuh kmumxavolamwenro, ok kukumwkuntamunro kepetwao;
/p ná=č kəməmxahɔla·mwi·né·ɔ, ɔ́·k kkək·amo·kantaməné·ɔ ki·p·i·t·əwá·ɔ,
/t Then you will scream loudly and 'gnash' your teeth,
/k There shall be weeping and gnashing of teeth,

/b nrrqc Rplivemu, ok Ysuku, ok Nhrkupu,   [⟨-vemu⟩ for ⟨-vcmu⟩]
/p ne·é·k·we †e·pəlihéma, ɔ́·k †aisáka, ɔ́·k †nče·kə́pa,
/t when you see Abraham, and Isaac, and Jacob,
/k when ye shall see Abraham, and Isaac, and Jacob,

/b ok wrmi ncvnekanewrwsetpanifu li Krtanitwet sokemaokunif;
/p ɔ́·k wé·mi nehəni·k·a·ní·i-we·wsi·tpanínka lí ke·tanət·ó·wi·t sɔ·k·i·ma·ɔ́·k·anink,
/t and all the ancient prophets going to God's kingdom,
/k and all the prophets, in the kingdom of God,

	/b	kahi kelwu pale ktclskakrvmw.
	/p	káč·i ki·ló·wa palí·i ktəlska·k·éhəmɔ.
	/t	but you are driven away.
	/k	and you yourselves thrust out.

Lk 13.29 /b Okh prok wunhi wcvcnhi khifwclak, ok cvli vwsekak, ok lwunrbf, ok jaonrbf
/p ɔ́·k=č pé·ɔk wə́nči wehə́nči-kčinkwéhəla·k, ɔ́·k éhəli-wsí·ka·k, ɔ́·k lo·wané·yunk, ɔ́·k ša·ɔné·yunk.
/t And they shall come from the east, and the west, and the north, and the south.
/k And they shall come from the east, and from the west, and from the north, and from the south,

/b ekuh wihi lumutuvpwuk krtanitwet sokemaokunif.
/p íka=č wíči-ləmatahpúwak ke·tanət·ó·wi·t sɔ·k·i·ma·ɔ́·k·anink.
/t They shall sit down together there in God's kingdom.
/k and shall sit down in the kingdom of God.

Lk 13.30 /b Aluntch bqc nekanehek wvtcfh avpwuk;
/p a·lə́nte=č yúkwe ni·k·a·ní·č·i·k wténk=č ahpúwak,
/t Some who are now in the lead shall be behind,
/k And, behold, there are last which shall be first,

/b okh aluntc bqc wvtcf rpehek nekaneh avpwuk. ‖
/p ɔ́·k=č a·lə́nte yúkwe wténk e·p·í·č·i·k, ni·k·a·ní·i=č ahpúwak."
/t and some who are now behind shall be in front."
/k and there are first which shall be last.

Chapter 71 (p. 125). (Luke 13.31-35.)

Lk 13.31 /b Nu nckc kejqek aluntc Paluseok wtxawapani,
(p. 125) /p ná-néke kí·škwi·k a·lə́nte †pa·ləsi·í·ɔk o·txawwá·p·ani.
/t That same day some of the Pharisees came to him.
/k The same day there came certain of the Pharisees,

/b tclawapani, khel b wunhi, ok pale al, rli Vclut pcxw knevlwq,
/p təlawwá·p·ani, "kčí·l yú wə́nči, ɔ́·k palí·i á·l, é·li †hélat péxu kəníhəlukw."
/t They said to him, "Get out of here, and go away, for Herod is going to kill you."
/k saying unto him, Get thee out, and depart hence: for Herod will kill thee.

Lk 13.32 /b tclao my lw nu oqus;
/p təlá·ɔ, "mái-ló· ná ɔ́·k·wəs,
/t He said to them, "Go tell that fox,
/k And he said unto them, Go ye, and tell that fox,

/b	Futskaokh mavtuntwuk okh fekcwc rlumi kejqek ok alupu,
/p	'nkətskaɔ́·ɔk=č mahtant·ó·wak, ɔ́·k=č nki·k·éhəwe é·ləmi-kí·škwi·k ɔ́·k aláp·a,
/t	'I shall drive out devils and shall heal people during this day and tomorrow,
/k	Behold, I cast out devils, and I do cures to day and to morrow,

/b	ok ekali opufc kwti kejqc nuh fejunaqsen.
/p	ɔ́·k íkali ɔ·p·ánke kwə́t·i kí·škwe, ná=č nki·š·əná·kwsi·n.'
/t	and one day later, then I shall have finished my work and be ready.
/k	and the third day I shall be perfected.

Lk 13.33
/b	Bqc wunhi heh nuxi kejqc nsaki b pumenen;
/p	yúkwe wə́nči čí·č náxi-kí·škwe nsá·ki- yú -pəmínni·n,
/t	Starting from now I remain here three more days,
/k	Nevertheless I must walk to day, and to morrow, and the day following:

/b	rli ta kuski ufuluk ncnekanewrwset pale tali, kcnh Nhelwsulumif.
/p	é·li- tá=á· -káski-ánkələk nehəni·k·a·ní·i-wé·wsi·t palí·i táli kə́nč †nči·lo·səlómink.
/t	for it would not be possible for a prophet to die anywhere else but in Jerusalem.
/k	for it cannot be that a prophet perish out of Jerusalem.

Lk 13.34
/b	O, Nhelwsulum, Nhelwsulum! nrnekane wrwselehi ncnvelat,
/p	"ó·, †nči·ló·sələm, †nči·ló·sələm, nehəni·k·a·ní·i-we·wsi·lí·č·i nenhíla·t,
/t	"O Jerusalem, Jerusalem, who kills prophets
/k	O Jerusalem, Jerusalem, which killest the prophets,

/b	ok rvalwkalunhi yeave pupavkumat avsunu!
/p	ɔ́·k ehalo·ka·lə́nči a·yáhi-pəpahkáma·t ahsə́na.
/t	and formerly threw stones at messengers.
/k	and stonest them that are sent unto thee;

/b	Tumeki vufq futu macvook ktumemunsumuk;
/p	təmí·ki=hánkw nkát·a-ma·ehɔ́·ɔk ktami·mə́nsəmak,
/t	I have often wanted to gather your children together,
/k	how often would I have gathered thy children together,

/b	mulaji tepas cvlukveqi macvot wnehanu li rqulwfonc,
/p	málahši típa·s ehələkhíkwi-ma·éhɔ·t wəni·č·á·na lí e·k·wəlúnkɔne,
/t	like a hen at the times she gathers her chicks (lit., children) under her wings,
/k	as a hen doth gather her brood under her wings,

/b	jwq kjifi lrlumi.
/p	šúkw kšínki-lé·ləmi.
/t	but you refused to let me.
/k	and ye would not!

Lk 13.35 /b Puna, wekerqih xwvrtro.
/p pənáh, wi·k·ié·k·wi=č xo·he·té·ɔ.
/t Behold, your houses will be abandoned.
/k Behold, your house is left unto you desolate:

/b Kvehe ktclwvmw, ta knrevwmw kcnh tpisqevlakc ktclih lwrnro,
/p khičí·i ktəllúhəmɔ, tá=á· kəne·i·húmɔ kə́nč tpəskwihəlá·k·e, ktə́li-=č -luwe·né·ɔ,
/t Truly I tell you, you won't see me until the time comes for you to say,
/k and verily I say unto you, Ye shall not see me, until the time come when ye shall say,

/b nwlapcnswvalwq nu pchi nuxpwxwrt tclswakun Krtanitwet.
/p 'no·la·p·enso·há·lukw, ná péči-naxpó·x·we·t təlsəwá·k·an ke·tanət·ó·wi·t.'"
/t 'He blesses me, the one that comes having the power of God.'"
/k Blessed is he that cometh in the name of the Lord.

Chapter 72 (pp. 125-127). (Luke 14.1-24.)

Lk 14.1 /b Alaxemwe kejqekc ekali tumekrp Paluse krkyimvrt weket,
/p ala·x·i·məwí·i-ki·škwí·k·e, íkali təmí·k·e·p †pa·ləsi·í·i-ke·kayə́mhe·t wí·k·i·t,
/t On the day of rest he went into the house of a Pharisee ruler,
/k [And it came to pass, as] he went into the house of one of the chief Pharisees [to eat bread] on the sabbath day,

/b my metswp.
/p mái-mí·tso·p.
/t going to eat.
/k to eat bread [on the sabbath day],

/b Qrnavkifomawapani,
/b Qrnavkifomawapani,
/p kwe·nahkinkɔ·mawwá·p·ani,
/t And they kept an eye on him,
/k that they watched him.

Lk 14.2 /b rli eku avpet ave palset.
/p é·li- íka -ahpí·t áhi-pá·lsi·t.
/t as there was one who was very sick there.
/k And, behold, there was a certain man before him which had the dropsy.

Lk 14.3 /b Nu Nhesus notwxtaon lupwrenwu ok Paluseu tclao,
/p ná nčí·sas nɔt·o·xtáɔ·n ləpwe·innúwa ó·k †pa·ləsi·í·ɔ, təlá·ɔ,
/t Then Jesus asked the learned men and Pharisees a question, saying to them,
/k And Jesus answering spake unto the lawyers and Pharisees, saying,

/b Wulexun vuh kekcvwrn alaxemwre kejqekc?
/p "wəlí·x·ən=háč ki·k·éhəwe·n ala·x·i·məwe·í·i-ki·škwí·k·e?"
/t "Is it right to heal people if it is the day of rest?"
/k Is it lawful to heal on the sabbath day?

Lk 14.4 /b jwq hetkwswuk.
/p šúkw či·tkwə́s·əwak.
/t But they kept silent.
/k And they held their peace.

/b Nu kcnh eku tonan ok qekrvan nrl palselehi.
/p ná kə́nč íka tónna·n, ó·k kwi·k·é·ha·n né·l pa·lsi·lí·č·i.
/t At that he put his hand on the sick person and healed him.
/k And he took him, and healed him, [and let him go;]

Lk 14.5 /b Nu lupi tclan, Awrn kelwu punhevlaletc tolumwnsu li olavkwf,
/p ná lápi tə́la·n, "awé·n ki·ló·wa pənčihəla·lí·t·e toləmúnsa lí ó·lahkunk,
/t Then again he said to them, "Who of you, if his animal falls into a pit,
/k And answered them, saying, Which of you shall have an ass or an ox fallen into a pit,

/b mutu vuh a qwtunaeo taoni alaxemwe kejkw?
/p máta=háč=á· kwət·əna·í·ɔ, tá·ɔni ala·x·i·məwí·i-kí·šku?"
/t would not haul it out, even if it is the day of rest?"
/k and will not straightway pull him out on the sabbath day?

Lk 14.6 /b qeluluswuk takw koski krkw laewao.
/p kwí·la-ləs·əwak, takó· kóski- kéku -la·iwwá·ɔ.
/t They were at a loss and had nothing they could say to him.
/k And they could not answer him again to these things.

Lk 14.7 /b Mrhi nrotc wepwmahi tcli pepenumulen wrwultuki lclumutuvpifi,
/p mé·či ne·ó·t·e wi·po·má·č·i tóli-pi·p·i·namə́li·n we·wəltə́k·i lehələmatahpínki,
/t And after he saw ones he was eating with selecting the good seats,
/k And [he put forth a parable] to those which were bidden, when he marked how they chose out the chief rooms; [RSV "the places of honor"]

/b nu krkw tclan.
/p ná kéku tə́la·n,
/t he then spoke to them,
/k saying unto them,

Lk 14.8 /b Tamsc ‖ awrn wcnhemkonc wunhi cntu metsavtif,
/p "tá·mse awé·n wenči·mkóne wə́nči énta-mi·tsáhtink,
/t "If someone maybe invites you to a feast,
/k When thou art bidden of any man to a wedding,

(p. 126) /b kahi vapavpevun rlwe wlituk lclumutuvpif;
/p káč·i hapahpí·han e·ləwí·i-wələt·ək lehələmátahpink,
/t don't sit on the best seat,
/k sit not down in the highest room; [RSV "in a place of honor"]

/b rli tamsc awrn pr rlweliset,
/p é·li tá·mse awé·n pé· e·ləwí·i-lə́s·i·t.
/t for perhaps someone comes who is greater.
/k lest a more honourable man than thou be bidden of him;

Lk 14.9 /b nc tamsc wcnhemqrq ktclkwn, bvli; [⟨nc⟩ for ⟨nu⟩]
/p ná tá·mse wenčí·mkwe·kw ktə́lko·n, 'yúh lí.'
/t Then perhaps the one that invited you both says to you, 'Move over here.'
/k And he that bade thee and him come and say to thee, Give this man place;

/b na a kmexanesen ktapavpen nwntae nako lclumutavpif.
  [⟨-nesen⟩ for ⟨-nisen⟩; ⟨nwntae nako⟩ for ⟨nwntaenako⟩]
/p ná=á· kəmi·x·anəs·i·n, ktá·pahpi·n nunta·i·ná·k·ɔ lehələmátahpink.
/t Then you would be ashamed to sit on a lesser seat.
/k and thou begin with shame to take the lowest room. [RSV "the lowest place"]

Lk 14.10 /b Wcnhemkreunc a, ktapavpen a nwntae nako lclumutavpif;
  [⟨reu⟩ for /é·a/; ⟨nwntae nako⟩ for ⟨nwntaenako⟩]
/p wenči·mké·ane=á·, ktá·pahpi·n=á· nunta·i·ná·k·ɔ lehələmátahpink.
/t When you are invited, you should sit on the lesser seat.
/k But when thou art bidden, go and sit down in the lowest room; [RSV "place"]

/b nrvkonc a nu wcnhemkon ktclwq a rlwenako nhw vapavpi,
/p ne·ykóne=á· ná wenčí·mkɔn, ktə́lukw=á·, 'e·ləwi·ná·k·ɔ, nčú, hápahpi.'
/t When your host sees you, he would say to you, 'Sit on a better seat, my friend.'
/k that when he that bade thee cometh, he may say unto thee, Friend, go up higher:

/b nuh wepwmuthek kmuxifwrlumwkwn.
/p ná=č wi·po·máč·i·k kəmax·inkwe·ləmúk·o·n.
/t Then the ones you are eating with will think highly of you.
/k then shalt thou have worship in the presence of them that sit at meat with thee.

Lk 14.11 /b Rli awrn xifwrlumatc nevlahi vokyu, tufrlumwqswh;
/p é·li awé·n xinkwe·ləmá·t·e nihəláči hókaya, tanke·ləmúkwsu=č
/t For if anyone thinks highly of himself, he shall be thought little of,
/k For whosoever exalteth himself shall be abased;

/b okh awrn tufrlunsetc, xifwrlumwkswh.
/p ɔ́·k=č awé·n tanke·lənsí·t·e, xinkwe·ləmúkwsu=č."
/t and if anyone is humble, he shall be thought highly of."
/k and he that humbleth himself shall be exalted.

Lk 14.12 /b   Nu krkw tclan wcnhemkwki; Tclao,
/p   ná kéku təla·n wenči·mkúk·i, təláˑɔ,
/t   Then he spoke to the one that invited him, saying,
/k   Then said he also to him that bade him,

/b   kejextaonch li a xifwi metsavten,
/p   ki·š·i·xtaóne lí-=áˑ -xínkwi-mi·tsáhti·n,
/t   "If you arrange for there to be a big feast,
/k   When thou makest a dinner or a supper,

/b   kahi wcnhemerkuh ketesuk, jitu kemevtisuk, jitu rlufwmuhek, jitu rvoprehek,   [⟨kemevt-⟩ for ⟨kemavt-⟩]
/p   káči wenči·miéˑk·ač ki·t·í·s·ak, ší=tá ki·mahtə́s·ak, ší=tá e·lanko·máč·i·k, ší=tá ehɔ·p·e·í·č·i·k,
/t   don't invite your friends, or your brothers, or your relatives, or rich people,
/k   call not thy friends, nor thy brethren, neither thy kinsmen, nor thy rich neighbours;

/b   rli a tamsc nrkumao nr wcnhmkon.   [⟨wcnhmk-⟩ for ⟨wcnhemk-⟩]
/p   é·li-=áˑ tá·mse ne·k·əmáˑɔ néˑ -wenčí·mkɔn.
/t   as *they* would perhaps also invite *you*.
/k   lest they also bid thee again, and a recompence be made thee.

Lk 14.13 /b   Kejextaonch li a xifwi metsavten,
/p   ki·š·i·xtaóne lí-=áˑ -xínkwi-mi·tsáhti·n,
/t   If you arrange for there to be a big feast,
/k   But when thou makest a feast,

/b   wcnhemwmc krtumaksehek, ok mrtamalsehek, ok kwqelwqevlahek, ok krkrpifohek;   [⟨kwqelwq-⟩ for ⟨kwqulwq-⟩ 2x]
/p   wenči·móˑme ke·t·əma·ksí·č·i·k, ɔ́·k me·t·amalsí·č·i·k, ɔ́·k kuk·wəluk·wihəláˑč·i·k, ɔ́·k ke·k·e·p·inkɔ́·č·i·k.
/t   invite the poor, and those in bad condition, and the crippled, and the blind.
/k   call the poor, the maimed, the lame, the blind:

Lk 14.14 /b   nch luseanc kwlvatrnamih,
/p   nə́=č ləs·iáne, ko·lhaténami=č,
/t   If you do that, you will be happy,
/k   And thou shalt be blessed;

/b   rli ta kuski nrkumao nr ajitc wcnhekwun;   [⟨wcnhek-⟩ for ⟨wcnhemk-⟩]
/p   é·li- tá=áˑ -káski- ne·k·əmáˑɔ néˑ a·šíte -wenči·mkóˑwan,
/t   because *they* would not be able to also invite *you* in turn,
/k   for they cannot recompense thee:

/b okh rli lapvatakrun amwevtetc jaxakwsetpanek.
/p ó·k=č é·li-la·phata·k·é·an a·mwihtí·t·e šaxahka·wsi·tpáni·k."
/t and because you will be paid back when those who had been righteous rise."
/k for thou shalt be recompensed at the resurrection of the just.

Lk 14.15
/b Nuni puntufc mawsw wepwmat tclao,
/p nə́ni pəntánke, má·wsu wi·pó·ma·t təlá·ɔ,
/t When he heard that, one who ate with him said to him,
/k And when one of them that sat at meat with him heard these things, he said unto him,

/b Wlapcnswh awrn methetc avpon tali sokemaokunif Krtanitwet.
/p "wəla·p·énsu=č awé·n mi·č·í·t·e ahpɔ́·n táli sɔ·k·i·ma·ɔ́·k·anink ke·tanət·ó·wi·t."
/t "Blessed shall be anyone when he eats bread in God's kingdom."
/k Blessed is he that shall eat bread in the kingdom of God.

Lk 14.16
/b Nu tclan, Linwu mu kejextwp li xifwi metsavten,
/p ná tə́la·n, "lə́nəwa=máh ki·š·í·xto·p lí-xínkwi-mi·tsáhti·n,
/t Then he said to him, "There was a man who arranged for a great feast,
/k Then said he unto him, A certain man made a great supper,

/b xrli awrn ni wcnhemrp;   [⟨awrn ni⟩ for ⟨awrni⟩]
/p xé·li awé·ni wenčí·me·p.
/t and he invited many people.
/k and bade many:

Lk 14.17
/b mrhi tpisqevlakc nu tolwkakunu tolwkalan,
/p mé·či tpəskwihəlá·k·e, ná tɔlo·ká·k·ana tɔlo·ká·la·n,
/t When the time came, he sent his servant,
/k And sent his servant at supper time

/b tclih lwrlen, Wuntux aq, mrhi wrmi krkw kejexun.
/p tə́li-=č -luwé·li·n, 'wə́ntax á·kw; mé·či wé·mi kéku ki·š·í·x·ən.'
/t for him to say, 'Come; everything is now ready.'
/k to say to them that were bidden, Come; for all things are now ready.

Lk 14.18
/b Jwq wrmi wcnhemuntpanek lwrok konuh mutu.
/p šúkw wé·mi wenči·məntpáni·k luwé·ok, 'kɔ́na=č máta.'
/t But all who had been invited said, 'I guess I won't be able to.'
/k And they all with one consent began to make excuse.

/b Mawsw lwr nmavlum vake, futu my punamun,
/p má·wsu lúwe·, 'nəmáhəlam hák·i, nkát·a-mái-pənámən;
/t One said, 'I bought some land and want to go and look at it;
/k The first said unto him, I have bought a piece of ground, and I must needs go and see it:

	/b	kwlaptwnaluh.
	/p	ko·la·pto·ná·la=č.
	/t	you must make polite excuses to him.'
	/k	I pray thee have me excused.

Lk 14.19 /b Mawsw lwr palrnaxk txrnaoki aksunuk nmavlao,
/p má·wsu lúwe·, 'palé·naxk txennáɔhki a·ksə́nak nəmáhəlaɔ.
/t And one said, 'I have bought five teams of oxen.
/k And another said, I have bought five yoke of oxen,

/b futu my qhevlalaok,
/p nkát·a-mái-kwčihəlalá·ɔk.
/t I want to go and try them out.
/k and I go to prove them:

/b kwlaptwnaluh.
/p ko·la·pto·ná·la=č.
/t you must make polite excuses to him.'
/k I pray thee have me excused.

Lk 14.20 /b Kahi mawsw lwr, nwskjeluntum ta fuski eku ai.
/p káč·i má·wsu lúwe·, 'no·skši·lə́ntam; tá=á· nkáski- íka -á·i.'
/t While one said, 'I'm newly married; I wouldn't be able to go there.'
/k And another said, I have married a wife, and therefore I cannot come.

Lk 14.21 /b Nu alwkakun apahetc tclahemwlxan nrvlalkwki wrmi rlrk.
/p ná alo·ká·k·an a·p·a·č·í·t·e, təla·č·i·mó·lxa·n nehəla·lkúk·i wé·mi é·le·k.
/t Then when the servant got back, he recounted for his master everything that had happened.
/k So that servant came, and shewed his lord these things.

/b Nu wreket mutu wlrluntumwun; tclao tolwkakunu, alumskal   [⟨wlrlun-‖tumwun⟩]
/p ná we·í·k·i·t máta wəle·ləntamó·wən, təlá·ɔ tɔlo·ká·k·ana, 'alə́mska·l.
/t Then the master of the house was not pleased, and he said to his servant, 'Go.
/k Then the master of the house being angry said to his servant, Go out quickly

(p. 127) /b tumakunif wunhi prjwv krtumaksehek, mrhumaleshek   [⟨-leshek⟩ for ⟨-lsehek⟩]
/p təmá·k·anink wə́nči pé·š·əw ke·t·əma·ksí·č·i·k, me·č·amalsí·č·i·k,
/t Bring from the streets poor people, ones in bad condition,
/k into the streets and lanes of the city, and bring in hither the poor, and the maimed,

/b kwqulwqevlahek ok krkrpifohek.
/p kuk·wəluk·wihəlá·č·i·k, ɔ́·k ke·k·e·p·inkɔ́·č·i·k.'
/t ones who are crippled, and ones who are blind.'
/k and the halt, and the blind.

Lk 14.22 /b Tamsc nu alwkakun tclan,
/p tá·mse ná alo·ká·k·an tóla·n,
/t At some point then the servant said to him,
/k And the servant said,

/b Nrvlaleun mrhi keji lr cntxi leun, ok qeaqi taolavkut.
/p 'nehəlá·lian, mé·či kíši-lé· éntxi-lían, ó·k kwiá·kwi taó·lahkat.'
/t 'Master, everything you told me has been done, and still there is room.'
/k Lord, it is done as thou hast commanded, and yet there is room.

Lk 14.23 /b Nu wreket tclan tolwkakunu,
/p ná we·í·k·i·t tóla·n tɔlo·ká·k·ana,
/t Then the master of the house said to his servant,
/k And the lord said unto the servant,

/b Bv tu lupi ntwnaw ok amunhe kavtu prjw,
/p "yúh=tá, lápi ntó·naw, ó·k amənčí·i káhta-pé·š·əw,
/t "Alright, look for more of them, and seek to bring them regardless,
/k Go out into the highways and hedges, and compel them to come in,

/b tclih hwexenunro wekeu.
/p tóli-=č -čuwi·x·i·nəné·ɔ wí·k·ia.
/t so that they may fill up my house.
/k that my house may be filled.

Lk 14.24 /b Rli ktclul wcnhemukpanek, takw nuxpunc kwti qwtuntumwun nmehwakun.
/p é·li któlal, wenči·makpáni·k, takó· náxpəne kwót·i kwət·antamó·wən nəmi·č·əwá·k·an."
/t For I say to you, of the ones I invited, let not even one taste my food."
/k For I say unto you, That none of those men which were bidden shall taste of my supper.

Chapter 73 (p. 127-128). (Luke 14.25-35.)

Lk 14.25 /b Xrli awrnek nolawapani,
/p xé·li awé·ni·k nɔ·ɔlawwá·p·ani,
/k Many people followed him,
/t And there went great multitudes with him:

/b ekali qwlwpep, tclapani;
/p íkali kwəlóp·i·p, təlá·p·ani.
/k and he turned to them and said to them,
/t and he turned, and said unto them,

Lk 14.26 /b Awrn naoletc, mutu alwe avoletc, rlkeqi avolat wxo, kovrsu,
/p "awé·n na·ɔlí·t·e, máta aləwí·i ahɔ·lí·t·e e·lkí·kwi-ahɔ́·la·t ó·x·ɔ, kɔhé·s·a,
/t "If anyone follows me and does not love me more than his father and mother,
/k If any man come to me, and hate not his father, and mother,

/b ok wehrohi, ok wnehanu ok wemavtisu, ok vwtwxqrbmu,
/p ɔ́·k wi·č·e·ɔ́·č·i, ɔ́·k wəni·č·á·na, ɔ́·k wi·mahtə́s·a, ɔ́·k wtuxkwé·yəma,
/t and his wife, and his children, and his brothers, and his sisters,
/k and wife, and children, and brethren, and sisters,

/b kovun, ok nevlahi vokyu,
/p kɔhán, ɔ́·k nihəláči hɔ́kaya,
/t yes, and his own self,
/k yea, and his own life also,

/b ta fuski tomeminsumewun.
/p tá=á· nkáski-tɔmi·mənsəmí·wən.
/t he would not be able to be my pupil.   [*lit.*, child]
/k he cannot be my disciple.

Lk 14.27 /b Ok awrn naoletc, wcvrmwalintc, mutu amunhe naoletc,
/p ɔ́·k awé·n na·ɔlí·t·e, wehe·məwa·lə́nte, máta amənčí·i na·ɔlí·t·e,
/t If anyone follows me and is mocked, and does not follow me anyway,
/k And whosoever doth not bear his cross, and come after me,

/b ta fuski tomeminsumewun.
/p tá=á· nkáski-tɔmi·mənsəmí·wən.
/t he would not be able to be my pupil.
/k cannot be my disciple.

Lk 14.28 /b Awrn kelwu kavtu qrnaku wekwam manetaqc,
/p "awé·n ki·ló·wa, káhta- kwe·ná·k·a wí·k·əwam -manni·tá·k·we,
/t "Who of you, if he desires to build a tall building,
/k For which of you, intending to build a tower,

/b mutu vuh a vetami pwunarluntamwun tclih kvehe tcpi kejetwn,
/p máta=háč=á· hítami pwəna·eləntamó·wən, tə́li=č khičí·i -tépi-ki·š·í·to·n,
/t would not first consider whether he will truly succeed in finishing it,
/k sitteth not down first, and counteth the cost,

/b rli a tamsc alumi wekvrtc qeluliset, mutu nc lusetc?
/p é·li=á·, tá·mse áləmi-wi·khé·t·e, -kwí·la-lə́s·i·t, máta nə́ ləs·í·t·e?
/t since, if he were to begin building, he'd be at a loss what to do if he did not do that?
/k whether he have sufficient to finish it?

Lk 14.29 /b rli a qelulisetc cntxi a nrfek wcvrmwalawao,
         /p é·li=á·, kwí·la-ləs·í·t·e, éntxi-=á· -nénki·k wwehe·məwa·lawwá·ɔ.
         /t For, if he were at a loss what to do, everyone that saw it would mock him.
         /k Lest haply, after he hath laid the foundation, and is not able to finish it, all that behold it begin to mock him,

Lk 14.30 /b lwrok a, jr wu linw wekvr jwq aly kejekvr.
         /p luwé·ok=á·, 'šé· wá lónu wí·khe·, šúkw á·lai-ki·š·í·khe·.'
         /t They would say, 'This man here built but couldn't finish the building.'
         /k Saying, This man began to build, and was not able to finish.

Lk 14.31 /b Sakemu a tclcn txun tclcn txapxki txeletc vwsohulumu kavtu ntwpaletc,
         /p sa·k·í·ma=á·, télən txə́n télən txá·pxki txi·lí·t·e wsɔ·čələ́ma, káhta-nto·p·alí·t·e,
         /t A king, if he had ten thousand soldiers and wanted to go to war,
         /k Or what king, going to make war [against another king, sitteth not down first, and consulteth whether he be able] with ten thousand

         /b mutu vuh a luvupu ahemwasei pwunarluntamwun   [⟨-mwas-⟩ for ⟨-mwls-⟩]
         /p máta=háč=á· lahápa a·č·i·mo·lsí·i, pwəna·eləntamó·wən,
         /t would he not take the time to hold a council and consider
         /k sitteth not down first, and consulteth

         /b tcli a trpi lusen nokeskaon sakemao
         /p tə́li-=á· -tépi-ləs·i·n, nɔk·í·skaɔ·n sa·k·i·má·ɔ
         /t whether he would be able to meet a king
         /k whether he be able ... to meet him that cometh against him

         /b nejenxkc txun tclcn txapxki cntxelet vwsohulumu;
         /p ni·š·í·nxke txə́n télən txá·pxki entxí·li·t wsɔ·čələ́ma.
         /t who had twenty thousand soldiers?
         /k with twenty thousand?

Lk 14.32 /b jvwvrlumwetc,   [⟨jvwvr-⟩ for /šhwe·-/]
         /p šhwe·ləmwí·t·e,
         /t If he has doubts,
         /k Or else,

         /b mutu vuh a nrli ovlumupelet awrni eku lalwkalri,
         /p máta=háč=á·, né·li-ɔhələmap·í·li·t, awé·ni íka lalo·ka·lé·i,
         /t wouldn't he, while the other (king) is far off, send someone to him,
         /k while the other is yet a great way off, he sendeth an ambassage,

         /b tcli a wulafwmkwn.
         /p tə́li-=á· -wəlankó·mko·n?
         /t so that the other (king) would make peace with him?
         /k and desireth conditions of peace.

Lk 14.33 /b   Nuni tpisqi lr
/p   "ná=ní tpə́skwi lé·,
/t   "It is like that,
/k   So likewise,

/b   awrn naoletc, mutu futifc wrmi cntxi krkw nevlatuf,
/p   awé·n na·ɔlí·t·e, máta nkat·ínke wé·mi éntxi- kéku -nihəlá·t·ank,
/t   if someone follows me and does not leave behind everything he has,
/k   whosoever he be of you that forsaketh not all that he hath,

/b   ta fuski tomemisumewun.
/p   tá=á· nkáski-tɔmi·mənsəmí·wən.
/t   he would not be able to be my pupil.
/k   he cannot be my disciple.

Lk 14.34 /b   Laprmkot sekvy;   [Mk 9.50: adds nə́]
/p   la·p·é·mkɔt sí·khay.
/t   Salt is useful.
/k   Salt is good:

/b   jwq a nc sekvrokun mutu vatrkc, ta vuh a wunhi jwan?   [⟨va-‖trkc⟩]
/p   šúkw=á· nə́ si·khe·ɔ́·k·an máta hat·é·k·e, tá=háč=á· wə́nči-šəwán?
/t   But if the saltiness is gone, what would make it be salty?
/k   but if the salt have lost his savour, wherewith shall it be seasoned?

Lk 14.35 /b   Ta laprmkotwi;
(p. 128) /p   tá=á· la·p·e·mkɔt·ó·wi.
/t   It would not be useful.
/k   —

/b   ta nuxpunc vuke wunhi wulitwi;
/p   tá=á· náxpəne hák·i wə́nči wələt·ó·wi.
/t   It would not even be good for the land.
/k   It is neither fit for the land, [nor yet for the dunghill;]

/b   tcpi a jwq pavktwn.   [⟨pavk-‖twn⟩ for ⟨pavketwn⟩]
/p   tépi-=á· šúkw -pahkí·t·o·n.
/t   It would only be fit to be thrown away.
/k   but men cast it out.

/b   Cntxi awrn vwetaoket puntufch.
/p   éntxi- awé·n -hwitaók·i·t pəntánkeč."
/t   Let everyone who has ears hear it."
/k   He that hath ears to hear, let him hear.

Chapter 74 (pp. 128-130). (Luke 15.1-32.)

Lk 15.1 /b   Nu moni mrvmarnifpanek ok wrmi mrtawsetpanek,
          /p   ná móni mehəma·e·ninkpáni·k ó·k wé·mi me·t·a·wsi·tpáni·k
          /t   Then the tax-collectors and all the sinners
          /k   Then [drew near unto him] all the publicans and sinners

          /b   tolumi prxwsvekaonrop rli kavtu puntaovtetup.
          /p   tóləmi-pe·x·o·shikaɔ·né·ɔ·p, é·li-káhta-pəntaɔhtí·t·əp.
          /t   began to come near him, as they desired to hear him.
          /k   [Then] drew near unto him [all the publicans and sinners] for to hear him.

Lk 15.2 /b   Nu Palusewfu ok rvlrkvekrtpanifu mutu wlrluntumwnrop,
          /p   ná †pa·ləsi·i·yúnka ó·k ehəle·khi·k·e·tpanínka máta wəle·ləntamo·wəné·ɔ·p.
          /t   Then elsewhere the Pharisees and scribes were not pleased.
          /k   And the Pharisees and scribes murmured,

          /b   lwrpanek, wuni linw wlufwmao mrtawselehi, ok wepwmao.
          /p   luwé·p·ani·k, "wáni lónu o·lanko·má·ɔ me·t·a·wsi·lí·č·i ó·k wwi·po·má·ɔ."
          /t   They said, "This man is friendly with sinners and eats with them."
          /k   saying, This man receiveth sinners, and eateth with them.

Lk 15.3 /b   Nu trnwntvakrn, tclao.
          /p   ná te·nuntháke·n, təlá·ɔ,
          /t   Then he told a parable, saying to them,
          /k   And he spake this parable unto them, saying,

Lk 15.4 /b   Awrn a kelwu kwtapxki mrkesu tolwmwnsetc.
          /p   awé·n=á· ki·ló·wa kwət·á·pxki mekí·s·a tɔləmunsí·t·e,
          /t   If anyone of you has a hundred sheep,
          /k   What man of you, having an hundred sheep,   (Cf. Mt 18.12-13.)

          /b   Mawselw pvaqclalete, tali trkunu,
          /p   ma·wsí·lu phakwehəla·lí·t·e táli té·kəna
          /t   and if one of them runs away someplace in the wilderness,
          /k   (1) if he lose one of them ... (3) in the wilderness,   [numbers = sequence in L.]

          /b   mutu vuh a wunukalaeo nrl prjkwf txenxkc ok prjkwf
          /p   máta=háč=á· wənək·ala·í·ɔ né·l pé·škunk txí·nxke ó·k pé·škunk,
          /t   won't he leave the ninety-nine,
          /kl (2) doth not leave the ninety and nine ...,

          /b   notwnaeo nrl pwlkwki ave tcli a kxunki muxkaon?
          /p   nɔt·o·naɔ·í·ɔ né·l po·lkúk·i áhi, təli-=á· kxántki -máxkaɔ·n?
          /t   and look for the one that escaped from him intently, until he finds it?
          /kl and go after that which is lost, until he find it?

Lk 15.5 /b muxkaotc wtkcvwenu a rli a wulrluntuf;
         /p maxkaɔ́·t·e, o·tkihhwí·na=á·, é·li-=á· -wəle·lə́ntank.
         /t And when he finds it, he would put it on his shoulders, as he would be happy.
         /k And when he hath found it, he layeth it on his shoulders, rejoicing.

Lk 15.6 /b eku a prjwatc, nu a wcnheman wrmi wetsu, [⟨wetsu⟩ for ⟨wetesu⟩]
         /p íka=á· pe·š·əwá·t·e, ná=á· wwenčí·ma·n wé·mi wi·t·í·s·a,
         /t When he brings him back, then he would call all his friends to come,
         /k And when he cometh home, he calleth together his friends and neighbours,

         /b tclao a wihi wulrluntumwemeq, rli muxkaok nmrkesum pwletup.
         /p təlá·ɔ=á·, 'wíči-wəle·lə́ntaməwí·mi·kw, é·li-máxkaɔk nəmekí·s·əm po·lí·t·əp.
         /t saying to them, 'Rejoice with me, as I've found my sheep that escaped from me.'
         /k saying unto them, Rejoice with me; for I have found my sheep which was lost.

Lk 15.7 /b Ktclwvmw, nuni tclsenro osavkamc rpehek
         /p ktəllúhəmɔ, nə́ni təlsi·né·ɔ ɔ·s·áhkame e·p·í·č·i·k,
         /t I tell you, those in heaven do that,
         /k I say unto you, that likewise [joy shall be] in heaven

         /b nrovtetc eli kwti mrtawselehi tcli qulupelen
         /p ne·ɔhtí·t·e ílli kwə́t·i me·t·a·wsi·lí·č·i, tə́li-kwələp·í·li·n.
         /t when they see even one sinner repent.
         /k over one sinner that repenteth,

         /b xifwi vufq alwe wulrluutamwk, [⟨wulrluut-⟩ for ⟨wulrlunt-⟩]
         /p xínkwi=hánkw aləwí·i wəle·lə́ntamo·k,
         /t They rejoice much more
         /k joy shall be ... more

         /b rlkeqi wlrluntmevtet wunhi rli prjkwf txenxkc ok prjkwf jaxukawsehek.
                                                                   [⟨rli⟩ for ⟨eli⟩]
         /p e·lkí·kwi-wəle·ləntamíhti·t wə́nči ílli pé·škunk txí·nxke ɔ́·k pé·škunk
             šaxahka·wsí·č·i·k.
         /t than they do because of even ninety-nine of the righteous.
         /k than over ninety and nine just persons, [which need no repentance].

Lk 15.8 /b Ok a xqr, tclcn monetitu wulatatqc, kwti afvetaqc, [⟨-atatqc⟩ for ⟨-ataqc⟩]
         /p "ɔ́·k=á· xkwé· télən mɔni·t·ə́t·a wəla·tá·k·we, kwə́t·i ankhitá·k·we,
         /t "And a woman, if she has ten coins and loses one of them,
         /k Either what woman having ten pieces of silver, if she lose one piece,

         /b mutu vuh a osulrnekunu naxqsri ok wli hekvamwun wekwam,
         /p máta=háč=á· ɔ·s·əle·ní·k·ana naxkwsé·i, ɔ́·k ó·li-či·khamó·wən wí·k·əwam,
         /t would she not light a candle, and sweep the house well,
         /k doth not light a candle, and sweep the house,

/b   tovi ntwnamwun tcli a kxunki muxkamun?
/p   tə́hi-nto·namó·wən, tə́li-=á· kxántki -máxkamən?
/t   and look for it carefully, until she finds it?
/k   and seek diligently till she find it?

Lk 15.9
/b   muxkufc, mutu vuh a wcnhemaeo rlafwmahi, ok tclaeo
/p   maxkánke, máta=háč=á· wwenči·ma·í·ɔ e·lanko·má·č·i, ɔ́·k təla·í·ɔ,
/t   If she finds it, would she not call her friends and neighbors and say to them,
/k   And when she hath found it, she calleth her friends and her neighbours together, saying,

/b   wehi wulrluntamwemeq, rli muxkamu rfvetaonup.
/p   'wíči-wəle·ləntaməwí·mi·kw, é·li-máxkama enkhitaɔ́·nəp'?
/t   'Rejoice with me, for I have found what I had lost'?
/k   Rejoice with me; for I have found the piece which I had lost.

Lk 15.10
/b   Nu vufq ok nc ktclwvmw eku rpehek Krtanitwet rlifwrxif, tclkeqi wulrluntumunro
/p   ná=hánkw ɔ́·k nə́, ktəllúhəmɔ, íka e·p·í·č·i·k ke·tanət·ó·wi·t e·linkwé·x·ink təlkí·kwi-wəle·ləntaməné·ɔ,
/t   And that, I tell you, is also how much those that are in the presence of God rejoice
/k   Likewise, I say unto you, there is joy in the presence of the angels of God

/b   eli kwti mrtawset qrlpetc.
/p   ílli kwət·i me·t·á·wsi·t kwe·lpí·t·e."
/t   when even one sinner repents."
/k   over one sinner that repenteth.

Lk 15.11
/b   Tclao, linw mu, nejelwpani qesu;
/p   təlá·ɔ, "lə́nu=máh ni·š·i·ló·p·ani kkwí·s·a.
/t   He said to them, "A man had two sons.
/k   And he said, A certain man had two sons:

Lk 15.12
/b   tcfsesetup wxo tclapani, Nwxa melel cntxi a apcnseu,
/p   tenksi·sí·t·əp ó·x·ɔ təlá·p·ani, 'núxa·, mí·li·l éntxi-=á· -a·p·énsia.'
/t   The younger one said to his father, 'Father, give me everything I would inherit.'
/k   And the younger of them said to his father, Father, give me the portion of goods that falleth to me.

/b   nu ‖ pwrpavsinumaon wrmi cntxi krkw wulataq.
/p   ná pwe·pahsənəmáɔ·n wé·mi éntxi- kéku -a·lá·ta·kw.
/t   Then he divided up for them everything he had.
/k   And he divided unto them his living.

Lk 15.13
(p. 129)
/b   Mutu qune, na nu tcfseset wlwalvrn wrmi krkw nrvlatuf,
/p   máta kwəní·i, ná ná tenksí·si·t o·ləwálhe·n wé·mi kéku nehəlá·t·ank.

	/t	Not long after that, the younger one bundled up everything he owned.
	/k	And not many days after the younger son gathered all together,
	/n	⟨na nu⟩ /ná ná/: ⟨nunu⟩ (Blanchard 1834b:28.6), which must be /nána/ 'then'.

/b nu ovlumi ton,
/p ná óhələmi tɔ́·n.
/t And then he went far away.
/k and took his journey into a far country,

/b nanc wrmi tuntu amyuketwn rli kpithrvoset.
/p ná=nə wé·mi tə́nta-amayahkí·to·n, é·li-kpəč·e·hɔ́·s·i·t.
/t And there he wasted everything because he did foolish things.
/k and there wasted his substance with riotous living.

Lk 15.14 /b Mrhi wrmi paletaqc,
/p mé·či wé·mi pali·tá·k·we,
/t After he had squandered everything,
/k And when he had spent all,

/b tamsc nu alumi ave kavtwpvotenrp nc tali,
/p tá·mse ná áləmi-áhi-kahto·phɔtí·ne·p nə́ táli.
/t at some point then there began to be a serious famine there.
/k there arose a mighty famine in that land;

/b nu tolumi qelu lusen.
/p ná tɔ́ləmi-kwí·la-lə́s·i·n.
/t And then he began to be at a loss what to do.
/k and he began to be in want.

Lk 15.15 /b Na moi mekumosuntamaon kwti wtrnyupelehi,
/p ná mɔ́i-mi·kəmɔ·s·əntamáɔ·n kwə́t·i o·t·e·nayap·i·lí·č·i.
/t Then he went to work for a certain town-dweller.
/k And he went and joined himself to a citizen of that country;

/b vakevakunif lalwkala, tcli a ixaman kwjkwju.
/p haki·há·k·anink lalo·ká·la·, təli-=á· -ihxáma·n kwəškwə́š·a.
/t He was sent into the fields to have the job of feeding hogs.
/k and he sent him into his fields to feed swine.

Lk 15.16 /b Qwkavti nrkanr mehenu rxamat kwjkwju,
/p kwə́kahti- né·k·a né· -mi·č·í·na ehxáma·t kwəškwə́š·a.
/t He, too, would almost eat what he was feeding to the hogs.
/k And he would fain have filled his belly with the husks that the swine did eat:

/b takw eli awrn toxamaepani.
/p takó· ílli awé·n tɔx·ama·í·p·ani.
/t No one even gave him food.
/k and no man gave unto him.

Lk 15.17 /b Mrhi oxpavlatc, lwr,
/p mé·či ɔxpahəlá·t·e, lúwe·,
/t After he came to his senses, he said,
/k And when he came to himself, he said,

/b Krvlu xrli rlwkalunhek nwxif, wrmi, weuki mehwuk avpon
/p 'kéhəla xé·li e·lo·ka·lə́nči·k nó·x·ink wé·mi wiáki-mí·č·əwak ahpɔ́·n,
/t 'A great many hired hands at my father's all have plenty of bread to eat,
/k How many hired servants of my father's have bread enough

/b menaohi alwevlr;
/p †mi·naóči aləwíhəle·.
/t and there is some left over, also.
/k and to spare,

/b kuhi ne, njaolamwi!
/p káč·i ní· nšaɔlá·mwi.
/t But *I* am starving.
/k and I perish with hunger!

Lk 15.18 /b bv tu mpusqen, nwxif ntan,
/p yúh=tá, mpáskwi·n, nó·x·ink ntá·n.
/t Alright, let me get up and go to my father's.
/k I will arise and go to my father,

/b ntcluh, Nwxa nhanelarvap Krtanitwet, ok krpc.
/p ntəla=č, "núxa·, nčani·laé·ha·p ke·tanət·ú·wi t ɔ́·k ké·pc.
/t I will say to him, "Father, I have offended God and also you.
/k and will say unto him, Father, I have sinned against heaven, and before thee,

Lk 15.19 /b Takw heh ntclsewun ktcli a lwevlen fwes,
/p takó· čí·č ntəlsí·wən, ktə́li-=á· -luwíhəli·n, 'nkwí·s.'
/t I am no longer such as to have you call me your son.
/k And am no more worthy to be called thy son:

/b lrlumel ktalwkakunuk rlrlumut.
/p lé·ləmi·l ktalo·ká·k·anak e·lé·ləmat.'"
/t Think of me the way you think of your servants.'"
/k make me as one of thy hired servants.

Lk 15.20 /b Nu posqem, wxifton;   [⟨posqem⟩ for ⟨posqen⟩; ⟨wxif-|ton⟩ for ⟨wxif ton⟩]
          /p ná póskwi·n, ó·x·ink tó·n.
          /t Then he got up, and went to his father's.
          /k And he arose, and came to his father.

          /b jwq nrlumu myai eku prat, nu wrqeset wunron
          /p šúkw né·ləma mayá·i íka pé·a·t, ná we·k·wí·s·i·t wəné·ɔ·n.
          /t But before he had gotten all the way there, his father saw him.
          /k But when he was yet a great way off, his father saw him,

          /b nu ok tolumi ktumakrluman,
          /p ná ó·k tóləmi-ktəma·k·é·ləma·n.
          /t Then he also started to feel pity for him.
          /k and had compassion,

          /b nu topvesvekaon qekxqrnao ok mwstwnamao.
          /p ná tɔ·phishíkaɔ·n, kwi·kxkwe·ná·ɔ, ó·k mmo·sto·na·má·ɔ.
          /t Then he went to meet him as he came, and he touched his neck and kissed him.
          /k and ran, and fell on his neck, and kissed him.

Lk 15.21 /b Nu qesu tclkwn, Nwxa, nhanelarvap Krtanitwet ok krpc.
          /p ná kkwí·s·a tólko·n, 'núxa·, nčani·laé·ha·p ke·tanət·ó·wi·t ó·k ké·pe.
          /t Then his son said to him, 'Father, I have offended God and also you.
          /k And the son said unto him, Father, I have sinned against heaven, and in thy sight,

          /b Takw heh ntclsewun ktcli a lwevlen fwes.
          /p takó· čí·č ntəlsí·wən, ktə́li-=á· -luwíhəli·n, "nkwí·s.'"
          /t I am no longer such as to have you call me your son.'
          /k and am no more worthy to be called thy son.

Lk 15.22 /b Jwq nu wrqeset, tclao tolwkakunu,
          /p šúkw ná we·k·wí·s·i·t təlá·ɔ tɔlo·ká·k·ana,
          /t But the father said to his servants,
          /k But the father said to his servants,

          /b wuntax lwxotwq nc wrltuk avqeun, avkonw,
          /p 'wə́ntax lúxɔhto·kw nə́ wé·ltək ahkwí·an, ahkóno·.
          /t 'Bring here the good robe and dress him in it.
          /k Bring forth the best robe, and put it on him;

          /b ok japwulunhrvwlw, ok hepavqrvwlw.
          /p ó·k ša·p·wələnčehó·lo·, ó·k čipahkwehó·lo·.
          /t And put a ring on his finger, and put shoes on his feet.
          /k and put a ring on his hand, and shoes on his feet:

Lk 15.23 /b   Ok prjw nu weset wejumwetut, knevlaowuh
                              [⟨wej-⟩ for ⟨wcj-⟩; ⟨-laowu⟩ for ⟨-lawu⟩ /-láwwa/]
/p   ɔ́·k pé·š·o· ná wí·s·i·t wehšəmwí·t·ət, kənihəláwwa=č
/t   And bring a fat calf, and you must kill it.
/k   And bring hither the fatted calf, and kill it;

/b   kmovonrn, okh kwlrluntumwvnu.
/p   kəmuhɔ́·ne·n, ɔ́·k=č ko·le·ləntamúhəna.
/t   Let us eat it, and we shall be joyful.
/k   and let us eat, and be merry:

Lk 15.24 /b   Rli wu fwes rfulukup, bqc lclrxrt,
/p   é·li- wá nkwí·s enkəlɔ́k·əp yúkwe -lehəlé·x·e·t.
/t   For my son here, who was dead, is now alive.
/k   For this my son was dead, and is alive again;

/b   taofulwp jwq bqc pr.
/p   taɔ́nkəlo·p, šúkw yúkwe pé·.'
/t   He was lost, but now he has come back.'
/k   he was lost, and is found.

/b   Nu tolumi wulrluntamunro.
/p   ná tɔ́ləmi-wəle·ləntaməné·ɔ.
/t   And then they began to be joyful.
/k   And they began to be merry.

Lk 15.25 /b   Nu krkyet wrqesif vakevakunif avpwp;
/p   "ná ké·kai·t we·k·wí·s·ink haki·há·k·anink ahpɔ́·p.
/t   "The older son was in the field.
/k   Now his elder son was in the field:

/b   apahetc mrhi kexki pratc wekwuvmif,
/p   a·p·a·č·í·t·e, mé·či kí·xki pe·á·t·e wi·k·əwáhəmink,
/t   When he returned, after had had come near the house,
/k   and as he came and drew nigh to the house,

/b   nu pwuntamun li aswen, ok li kuntkan.
/p   ná pwɔ́ntamən lí-a·s·ó·wi·n ɔ́·k lí-kɔ́ntka·n.
/t   he heard singing and dancing.
/k   he heard musick and dancing.

Lk 15.26 /b   Nu notwman alwkakunu; tclao, Krkw vuh lr?
/p   ná nɔt·ó·ma·n alo·ká·k·ana, təlá·ɔ, 'kéku=háč lé·?'
/t   Then he called over a servant and said to him, 'What is going on?'
/k   And he called one of the servants, and asked what these things meant.

Lk 15.27 /b Tclkw kxesumus pr,
/p tálku, 'kxí·s·əməs pé·.
/t He (the other) said to him, 'Your younger brother has come.
/k And he said unto him, Thy brother is come;

/b kwx nvelr weselehi wcjwmwetutu, rli nrot tcli wulumalselen.
/p kó·x nhíle· wi·s·i·lí·č·i wehšəmwi·t·ə́t·a, é·li-né·ɔ·t táli-wəlamalsí·li·n.'
/t Your father killed a fat calf, because he saw him in good health.'
/k and thy father hath killed the fatted calf, because he hath received him safe and sound.

Lk 15.28 /b Nu monwfsen, takw wifi ‖ tumekri;
/p ná mɔnúnksi·n, takó· wínki-təmi·k·é·i.
/t Then he was angry and was unwilling to go in.
/k And he was angry, and would not go in:

(p. 130) /b nuni wunhi wxo toxkwn, kotu wulelarmkw.
/p nə́ni wwə́nči- ó·x·ɔ -tóxko·n, kɔ́t·a-wəli·laé·mku.
/t His father therefore came to him, desiring to appease him.
/k therefore came his father out, and intreated him.

Lk 15.29 /b Jwq tclao wxo, jr mrhi xrli kavtinri kmekumosuntamwl,
/p šúkw təlá·ɔ ó·x·ɔ, 'šé· mé·či xé·li kahtəné·i kəmi·kəmɔ·s·ə́ntamo·l.
/t But he said to his father, 'I have worked for you for many years now.
/k And he answering said to his father, Lo, these many years do I serve thee,

/b ok aphi krkw rleunc mutu ktuhifxrtwlwi,
/p ó·k á·pči kéku e·liáne máta ktač·inkxe·to·ló·wi.
/t And always, when you told me to do something, I did not disobey you.
/k neither transgressed I at any time thy commandment:

/b jwq mutu vuji, kmelei qrnetwnyat mrketut, wunhi a wulrluntumevtet rlufwmukek;
/p šúkw máta háši kəmi·lí·i kwe·ni·tó·naya·t mekí·t·ət wə́nči-=á· -wəle·ləntamíhti·t e·lanko·mák·i·k.
/t But you never gave me a kid so that my friends and neighbors could be joyful.
/k and yet thou never gavest me a kid, that I might make merry with my friends:

Lk 15.30 /b jwq nu qes, nu rli pat, prletaq wcntawseunup li neskawswakunif,
/p šúkw ná kkwí·s, ná é·li-pá·t, pe·lí·ta·kw wenta·wsiánəp lí ni·ska·wsəwá·k·anink,
/t But for your son there, as soon as *he* arrived, the one who squandered what you lived off in foul behavior,
/k But as soon as this thy son was come, which hath devoured thy living with harlots,

	/b	jac knetamao weselehi wcjwmwetutu.
	/p	šá·e kəni·tamáɔ wi·s·i·lí·č·i wehšəmwi·t·ə́t·a.'
	/t	you right away killed a fat calf for him.'
	/k	thou hast killed for him the fatted calf.

Lk 15.31 /b Jwq tclkw, Fwes, fumri ke qetarmi,
/p šúkw tə́lku, 'nkwí·s, nkəmé·i kí· kəwi·t·aé·mi,
/t But he said to him, 'My son, *you* are always with me,
/k And he said unto him, Son, thou art ever with me,

/b ok wrmi cntxi nevlatamu knevlatamun.
/p ɔ́·k wé·mi éntxi-nihəlá·t·ama kənihəlá·t·amən.
/t and everything I have belongs to you.
/k and all that I have is thine.

Lk 15.32 /b Jwq a ktcpi wulrluntamwvnu,
/p šúkw=á· ktépi-wəle·ləntamúhəna,
/t But we should be able to rejoice,
/k It was meet that we should make merry, and be glad:

/b rli kxesmus rfulukup lupi lclrxrt, trofulukup lupi pat.
/p é·li- kxí·s·əməs enkələ́k·əp lápi -lehəlé·x·e·t, te·ɔnkələ́k·əp lápi -pá·t.'"
/t since your younger brother who was dead lives again, and the one who was lost has come back.'"
/k for this thy brother was dead, and is alive again; and was lost, and is found.

Chapter 75 (pp. 130-132). (Luke 16.1-31.)

Lk 16.1 /b Nu tclanrp rkrkematpani, Avpwp rvopretup linw ok wehumwqkpani.
/p ná təlá·ne·p e·k·e·ki·ma·tpáni, "ahpó·p ehɔ·p·e·í·t·əp lə́nu, ɔ́·k wi·č·əmukwpáni.
/t Then he said to his disciples, "There was a rich man, and his helper.
/k And he said also unto his disciples, There was a certain rich man, which had a steward;

/b Tamsc nu lanrp mwmyuketwnu ktcluhrswakunu wehumwkon.
/p tá·mse ná lá·ne·p, 'mumayak·i·tó·na ktəlahče·s·əwá·k·ana wi·č·əmúk·ɔn.'
/t Then at some point he was told, 'Your helper wastes your possessions.'
/k and the same was accused unto him that he had wasted his goods.

Lk 16.2 /b Nu wcnhemanrp; tclapani; Ta vuh ktulsen wcnhi nc listumu?
/p ná wwenči·má·ne·p, təlá·p·ani, 'tá=háč ktə́lsi·n, wénči- nə́ -ləstáma?'
/t The he called him and said to him, 'What are you doing, the reason I hear that?
/k And he called him, and said unto him, How is it that I hear this of thee?

/b   Wlextwl cntu wehumeun, rli ta heh wehumeon.
/p   wəlí·xto·l énta-wi·č·əmían, é·li- tá=á· čí·č -wi·č·əmí·ɔn.'
/t   Put the place where you help me in order, as you will no longer be my helper.'
/k   give an account of thy stewardship; for thou mayest be no longer steward.

Lk 16.3
/b   Na nu wehumat tolumi punarluntumun, letrvr, tuh vuh ct ntclsen?
/p   ná ná wí·č·əma·t tóləmi-pəna·elə́ntamən, li·t·é·he·, 'tá=č=háč=ét ntə́lsi·n?
/t   Then that one that helped him began to consider, thinking, 'What shall I do?
/k   Then the steward said within himself, What shall I do?

/b   rli rlwkalet ta kuski mekumosuntumaook,
/p   é·li- e·lo·ká·li·t tá=á· -káski-mi·kəmɔ·s·əntamaó·ɔk.
/t   For I will not be able to work for my employer.
/k   for my lord taketh away from me the stewardship:

/b   ok a nmexunisen nwevenwrn.
/p   ó·k=á· nəmi·x·anə́s·i·n nəwihí·nəwe·n.
/t   And I would be ashamed to beg.
/k   [I cannot dig;] to beg I am ashamed.

Lk 16.4
/b   Mrhi nmuxkamun rnimuh,
/p   mé·či nəmáxkamən ennə́ma=č,
/t   I have now found what I shall do,
/k   I am resolved what to do,

/b   wcnhih pavkeletc peli awrnek wrtunevtet.
/p   wénči-=č pahki·lí·t·e pí·li awé·ni·k -we·t·əníhti·t.'
/t   so that when I am dismissed other people will accept me.'
/k   that, when I am put out of the stewardship, they may receive me into their houses.

Lk 16.5
/b   Nu wcnheman wrmi cntxi lrkvamalehi;
/p   "ná wwenčí·ma·n wé·mi éntxi-le·khama·lí·č·i.
/t   "Then he summoned every one of those that had debts.
/k   So he called every one of his lord's debtors unto him,

/b   mawselw tclao, ta vuh ktuntxrkvamaon rlwkalet?
/p   ma·wsí·lu təlá·ɔ, 'tá=háč ktəntxe·khamáɔ·n e·lo·ká·li·t?'
/t   To one he said, 'How much do you owe my employer?'
/k   and said unto the first, How much owest thou unto my lord?

Lk 16.6
/b   tclkw avpami ct xaj txapxki frluntif pumi rlaovtek.
/p   tə́lku, 'ahpá·mi=ét xá·š txá·pxki nkelántink pəmí e·lá·ohti·k.
/t   The other one said to him, 'I guess the amount of about 800 gallons of oil.'
/k   And he said, An hundred measures of oil.

	/b	Nu tclan jac lumutavpi ktulrkvekunif tali lrkva nropxki.
	/p	ná tála·n, 'šá·e lamátahpi, ktəle·khí·k·anink táli-lé·kha ne·ó·pxki.'
	/t	Then he said to him, 'Sit down quickly and write 400 on your paper.'
	/k	And he said unto him, Take thy bill, and sit down quickly, and write fifty.

Lk 16.7 /b Nu ok takoki tclan, ta vuh ke ktcntxrkvamaon?
/p ná ó·k takó·ki tála·n, 'tá=háč kí· ktəntxe·khamáɔ·n?'
/t Then he said to another one, 'How much do *you* owe him?'
/k Then said he to another, And how much owest thou?

/b Tclkw avpami ct tclintxapki mpwjilif vwet rlaovtek.
/p tálku, 'ahpá·mi=ét télən txá·pxki †mpúšəlink hwí·t e·lá·ɔhti·k.
/t The other one said to him, 'I guess the amount of about a thousand bushels of wheat.'
/k And he said, An hundred measures of wheat.

/b Nu tclan, jac lumutavpi, ktulrkvekunif tali lrkva xaj txapxki.
/p ná tála·n, 'šá·e lamátahpi, ktəle·khí·k·anink táli-lé·kha xá·š txá·pxki.'
/t Then he said to him, 'Sit down quickly and write 800 on your paper.'
/k And he said unto him, Take thy bill, and write fourscore.

Lk 16.8 /b Nu rlwkalatup wlavkunemapani nrl mchi wehumwqki rli lupolet. [⟨rlwkala-‖tup⟩]
/p ná e·lo·ka·lá·t·əp o·lahkəni·má·p·ani né·l méči-wi·č·əmúkwki, é·li-ləpó·li·t.
/t The one who employed the one who behaved badly in helping him spoke well of him for being wise.
/k And the lord commended the unjust steward, because he had done wisely:

(p. 131) /b Wuni vaki tomeminsumu alwei lupwrok
/p "wáni hák·i tɔmi·mánsəma aləwí·i ləpwé·ɔk
/t "The children of this earth are wiser
/k for the children of this world are in their generation wiser

/b rlkeqi lupolet oxrrk tomemunsumu.
/p e·lkí·kwi-ləpó·li·t ɔ·x·é·e·k tɔmi·mánsəma.
/t than the children of light.
/k than the children of light.

Lk 16.9 /b Ktclwvmw, wlufwnswvalqrqch ktavoprokunwu,
/p ktəllúhəmɔ, wəlankunso·ha·lkwé·k·weč ktahɔ·p·e·ɔ·k·anúwa,
/t I tell you, let your wealth make you be neighborly,
/k And I say unto you, Make to yourselves friends of the mammon of unrighteousness;   [RSV "by means of unrighteous mammon"]

/b wcnhih krpwu tamsc qeluluserqc, eku lwxolukrrq
/p wénči-=č ké·pəwa, tá·mse kwí·la-ləs·ié·k·we, íka -lo·x·ɔlək·é·e·kw

/t so that you also, when at some point you are no more, will be brought to
/k that, when ye fail, they may receive you

/b tutu a heme rperq.
/p tə́ta=á· či·mí·i é·p·ie·kw.
/t wherever you will be forever.
/k into everlasting habitations.

Lk 16.10 /b Awrn a wli krnavketaqc, tatxiti, taoni a xrli wli a krnavketwn
/p awé·n=á· wə́li-ke·nahki·tá·k·we ta·txíti, tá·ɔni=á· xé·li, ó·li-=á· -ke·nahkí·to·n.
/t If someone takes good care of a little, he would take good care of even a lot.
/k He that is faithful in that which is least is faithful also in much:

/b ok awrn wifi hani luset krxiti, ok a wifi xifwi hani lusw.
/p ɔ́·k awé·n wínki-čáni-lə́s·i·t ke·xíti, ɔ́·k=á· wínki-xínkwi-čáni-lə́s·u.
/t And someone inclined to do wrong a little would also willingly do a big wrong.
/k and he that is unjust in the least is unjust also in much.

Lk 16.11 /b Mutu myai luserqc mekintamrqc lunei avoprokun,
/p máta mayá·i-lə·sié·k·we mi·kəntamé·k·we lə·ní·i-ahɔ·p·e·ɔ́·k·an,
/t If you do not do right when you work for ordinary wealth,
/k If therefore ye have not been faithful in the unrighteous mammon,

/b awrn vuh a kmelkwu myaei avoprokun?
/p awé·n=háč=á· kəmi·lkúwa maya·í·i-ahɔ·p·e·ɔ́·k·an?
/t who would give you true wealth?
/k who will commit to your trust the true riches?

Lk 16.12 /b Mutu wli krnavketwrqc peli awrn ncvlatuf,
/p máta wə́li-ke·nahki·to·wé·k·we pí·li awé·n nehəlá·t·ank,
/t If you do not take good care of what another person owns,
/k And if ye have not been faithful in that which is another man's,

/b awrn vuh a kmelkwu krkw a nrvlatamrq?
/p awé·n=háč=á· kəmi·lkúwa kéku=á· nehəlá·t·ame·kw?
/t who would give you what you would own?
/k who shall give you that which is your own?

Lk 16.13 /b Taa awrn kuski mekumosintamari neju awrni;
/p tá=á· awé·n káski-mi·kəmɔ·s·əntamaé·i ní·š·a awé·ni,
/t No one can work for two people,
/k No servant can serve two masters:

/b rli a jifalat mawselw, ok mawselw aholat;
/p é·li-=á· -šinká·la·t ma·wsí·lu ɔ́·k ma·wsí·lu -ahɔ́·la·t,
/t for he would hate one and love the other,
/k for either he will hate the one, and love the other;

/b ok tamsc wlsitao mawselw kuthi mawselw tothifxrtao.
/p ɔ́·k tá·mse o·lsət·aɔ́·ɔ ma·wsí·lu, káč·i ma·wsí·lu tɔč·inkxe·taɔ́·ɔ.
/t or else he listens to one but disobeys the other.
/k or else he will hold to the one, and despise the other.

/b Taa kuski mekumosuntamaoewu Krtanitwet nuxpi avoprokun.
/p tá=á· kkáski-mi·kəmɔ·s·əntamaɔ·íwwa ke·tanət·ó·wi·t náxpi ahɔ·p·e·ɔ́·k·an."
/t You (pl.) will not be able to work for God along with wealth."
/k Ye cannot serve God and mammon.

Lk 16.14
/b Krtaohrswrhek Paluseok mrhi nc puntamevtetc,
/p ke·t·aɔč·e·s·əwé·č·i·k †pa·ləsi·í·ɔk mé·či nə́ pəntamihtí·t·e,
/t After the covetous ones, the Pharisees, heard that,
/k And the Pharisees also, who were covetous, heard all these things:

/b nu wcvrmwalanro.
/p ná wwehe·məwa·la·né·ɔ.
/t they made fun of him.
/k and they derided him.

Lk 16.15
/b Tclapani,
/p təlá·p·ani,
/t And he said to them,
/k And he said unto them,

/b ktclsenro kwluvkunwtumunro nevluhi kvakybu tali rlifwrxenvetet awrnek.
/p "ktəlsi·né·ɔ, ko·lahkəno·t·əməné·ɔ nihəláči khak·ayúwa táli e·linkwe·x·i·nhíti·t awé·ni·k.
/t "You are ones who speak well of yourselves in the presence of people.
/k Ye are they which justify yourselves before men;

/b Jwq Krtanitwet wavao ktrvwao.
/p šúkw ke·tanət·ó·wi·t o·wa·há·ɔ ktehəwá·ɔ.
/t But God knows your hearts.
/k but God knoweth your hearts:

/b Rli Krtanitwet vwjifatumun, b cntu lawset rvotuf.
/p é·li ke·tanət·ó·wi·t wšinká·t·amən yú entalá·wsi·t ehɔ́·t·ank.
/t For God hates what man loves.
/k for that which is highly esteemed among men is abomination in the sight of God.

Lk 16.16 /b Xwi aptwnakun ok nrvnekanewrwsetpanek avpwpanek eku pchi Nhanu rpetc;
/p xúwi-a·pto·ná·k·an ɔ́·k nehəni·k·a·ní·i-we·wsi·tpáni·k ahpó·p·ani·k íka péči nčá·na e·p·í·t·e.
/t The law and the prophets were until when John was.
/k The law and the prophets were until John:

/b nu nckc wunhi wuntax li Krtanitwet toptwnakun jwq wuntamasen,
/p ná-néke wənči wəntax lí ke·tanət·ó·wi·t tɔ·pto·ná·k·an šúkw wəntamá·s·i·n.
/t From then to now only the word of God is taught.
/k since that time the kingdom of God is preached,

/b ok xrli awrn kotu nc li lclrxrn.
/p ɔ́·k xé·li awé·n kɔ́t·a- nə́ -lí-lehəlé·x·e·n.
/t And many people want to live that way.
/k and every man presseth into it.

Lk 16.17 /b Bl xwi aptwnakunu, ta eli kwti vuji mrhevlri;
/p yó·l xúwi-a·pto·ná·k·ana, tá=á· ílli kwə́t·i háši me·čihəlé·i.
/t As for the laws, not even one will ever pass away.
/k [And it is easier for heaven and earth to pass,] than one tittle of the law to fail.

/b alweh b vaki ok vwqrbf apwi mrhevlr.
/p aləwí·i=č yú hák·i ɔ́·k hukwé·yunk á·p·əwi-me·číhəle·.
/t More easily will the earth and heaven pass away.
/k [And] it is easier for heaven and earth to pass, [than one tittle of the law to fail].

Lk 16.18 /b Awrn pavkelatc wehrohi, peli wehrotc, hanih lusw;
/p awé·n pahki·lá·t·e wi·č·e·ɔ́·č·i, pí·li wi·č·e·ɔ́·t·e, čáni-=č -lə́s·u.
/t If anyone divorces his wife and marries another, he will do wrong.
/k Whosoever putteth away his wife, and marrieth another, committeth adultery:

/b ok prkelun awrni wehrotc nrkuh nr hani lusw.   [⟨-un⟩ for ⟨-unt⟩ Mt 19.9]
/p ɔ́·k pe·k·í·lənt awé·ni wi·č·e·ɔ́·t·e, né·k·a=č né· čáni-lə́s·u.
/t And if one who was divorced marries anyone, they, too, do wrong.
/k and whosoever marrieth her that is put away from her husband committeth adultery.

Lk 16.19 /b Avpwp mu avoprenw owulavkwq, fumri   [⟨-kwq⟩ for ⟨-kwp⟩]
/p "ahpó·p=máh ahɔ·p·e·ínnu, ɔwə́lahko·p nkəmé·i.
/t "There was a rich man, and he always dressed in fine clothing.
/k There was a certain rich man, which was clothed in purple and fine linen,

/b ok owuli metswp cji kejqek.
/p ɔ́·k ɔ́wəli-mí·tso·p éši-kí·škwi·k.
/t And he also ate well every day.
/k and fared sumptuously every day:

Lk 16.20 /b Ok avpwp wcvenwrt ‖ lwcnswp Laslus;
/p ɔ́·k ahpó·p wehí·nəwe·t, luwénso·p †lá·səlas.
/t And there was a beggar named Lazarus.
/k And there was a certain beggar named Lazarus,

(p. 132) /b nul nuku eku vwtuskontrbmif jcfexenwp
/p nál náka íka wtəskɔnté·yəmink šenki·x·í·no·p,
/t And it was he who lay at his door.
/k which was laid at his gate,

/b mukebp msihri rlkeluk;
/p məkí·yo·p məsəč·é·i e·lkí·lək.
/t And he had sores all over his body.
/k full of sores,

Lk 16.21 /b kotatuminrp xaman preontasek wunhi nuku avoprenwu tcvcntu lepwifumif;
[⟨preont-⟩ for ⟨peont-⟩ 4x]
/p kɔt·a·t·amə́ne·p xáma·n pi·ɔntá·s·i·k wə́nči náka ahɔ·p·e·innúwa tehəntali·p·wínkəmink.
/t He wanted to be fed the leftover scraps from that rich man's table.
/k And desiring to be fed with the crumbs which fell from the rich man's table:

/b ta tamsc vufq morkunro vwheskuntamakwnrp mwukeu.
/p ta·tá·mse=hánkw mwe·k·ané·ɔ wči·skantama·k·ó·ne·p mwə́k·ia.
/t At times dogs licked his sores.
/k moreover the dogs came and licked his sores.

Lk 16.22 /b Nu tamsc tofulun nu wcvenwrt,
/p ná tá·mse tɔ́nkələn ná wehí·nəwe·t.
/t Then at some point that beggar died.
/k And it came to pass, that the beggar died,

/b nu rvalwkalunhek eku tulwxolanro Rplivcm wulwfwif,
/p ná ehalo·ka·lə́nči·k íka təlo·x·ɔla·né·ɔ †e·pəlíhem wəlúnkwink.
/t Then angels took him to the fold of Abraham's robe.
/k and was carried by the angels into Abraham's bosom:

/b tamsc nu ok tofulun nu avoprenw, ok pokvakcvo.
/p tá·mse ná ɔ́·k tɔ́nkələn ná ahɔ·p·e·ínnu, ɔ́·k phɔkhakéhɔ·.
/t And then at some point the rich man also died and was buried.
/k the rich man also died, and was buried;

Lk 16.23 /b Eku tali uspifwrxenwp ufulwakunif rli amuxavrluntuf,
/p íka táli-aspinkwe·x·í·no·p ankələwá·k·anink, é·li-amax·ahe·lə́ntank.
/t He looked up in "death," as he was suffering torments.
/k And in hell he lift up his eyes, being in torments,

Text, Transcription, and Translation

/b ovlumi tcli nropani Rplivcmu ok Laslusu eku wlwfwif;
/p óhələmi táli-ne·ó·p·ani †e·pəlihéma ó·k †la·səlás·a íka wəlúnkwink.
/t And he saw in the distance Abraham, and Lazarus in the fold of his robe.
/k and seeth Abraham afar off, and Lazarus in his bosom.

Lk 16.24 /b nu wulupavketaon tclao, Nwxa Rplivcm ktumakrlumel!
/p ná wələpahkí·taɔ·n, təlá·ɔ, 'núxa·, †e·pəlíhem, ktəma·k·é·ləmi·l.
/t Then, weeping as he did so, he said to him, 'Father Abraham, have mercy on me!
/k And he cried and said, Father Abraham, have mercy on me,

/b alwkal Laslus, hvopwunifch tulwvekun li mpif, tvwpavtaetch nelanwv,
/p aló·ka·l †lá·səlas; čhɔ·pwənínkeč təlo·hí·k·an lí mpínk, thupahtaí·t·eč ní·lanu,
/t Send Lazarus; let him dip his forefinger in water, and let him cool my tongue,
/k and send Lazarus, that he may dip the tip of his finger in water, and cool my tongue;

/b rli nmumxavrluntum b tali cntu wifulrk.
/p é·li nəməmxahe·ləntam yú táli énta-wínkəle·k.
/t for I am suffering torments in this blazing fire.'
/k for I am tormented in this flame.

Lk 16.25 /b Jwq Rplivcm tclao Fwes, mujatu
/p šúkw †e·pəlíhem təlá·ɔ, 'nkwí·s, məšá·t·a,
/t But Abraham said to him, 'My son, remember,
/k But Abraham said, Son, remember that

/b cntu lclrxranc kwlilenamwvwmp, kahi Laslus mavhi lenamwp;
/p énta-lehəle·x·é·ane kó·li-li·namúhump, káč·i †lá·səlas máhči-lí·namo·p.
/t when you were alive you had good fortune, while Lazarus had bad fortune.
/k thou in thy lifetime receivedst thy good things, and likewise Lazarus evil things:

/b jwq bqc wli lenam, kahi ke ktave lenam.
/p šúkw yúkwe wə́li-lí·nam, káč·i kí· ktáhi-lí·nam.
/t But now he has good fortune, while *you* are suffering severely.
/k but now he is comforted, and thou art tormented.

Lk 16.26 /b Ok lupi, trtae xifwi keskalavkut,
/p ó·k lápi te·t·aí·i xínkwi-ki·ská·lahkat.
/t And in addition there is a large trench in between.
/k And beside all this, between us and you there is a great gulf fixed:

/b nuni wunhi ta kuski awrn b wunhi nata pat
/p nə́ni wə́nči- tá=á· -káski- awé·n yú wə́nči ná·ta -pá·t,
/t Because of that no one would be able to get to where you are from here,
/k so that they which would pass from hence to you cannot;

443

/b ok nata wunhi na b pat.
/p ɔ́·k ná·ta wə́nči ná=yú -pá·t.'
/t or to come here from where you are.'
/k neither can they pass to us, that would come from thence.

Lk 16.27
/b Nu tclan
/p "ná tə́la·n,
/t "Then he said to him,
/k Then he said,

/b Nwxa, nani wunhi qulu eku ktulalwkalan nwx weket;   [⟨nani⟩: nə́ni]
/p 'núxa·, nə́ni wə́nči kwə́la íka ktəlalo·ká·la·n nó·x wí·k·i·t,
/t 'Father, therefore I wish you would send him to my father's house,
/k I pray thee therefore, father, that thou wouldest send him to my father's house:

Lk 16.28
/b rli palrnaxk nemavtisuk; tcli a wuntamaon;
/p é·li palé·naxk ni·mahtə́s·ak, tə́li-=á· -wəntamáɔ·n,
/t as I have five brothers, in order that he could explain to them,
/k For I have five brethren; that he may testify unto them,

/b wunhih mutu nrkumao nr na b pavtet cntu ave lenama.
/p wə́nči-=č máta ne·k·əmá·ɔ né· ná=yú -páhti·t énta-áhi-lí·nama.'
/t so that they, too, will not come here to where I am suffering severely.'
/k lest they also come into this place of torment.

Lk 16.29
/b Rplivcm tclao, Mwjiju ok ncnekanewrwsetpanifu toptwnakunwu eku vatr,
/p ṭe·pəlíhem təlá·ɔ, 'mo·šə́š·a ɔ́·k nehəni·k·a·ní·i-we·wsi·tpanínka tɔ·pto·na·k·anúwa íka hát·e·.
/t Abraham said to him, 'They have the law of Moses and the ancient prophets.
/k Abraham saith unto him, They have Moses and the prophets;

/b nuni a qwlsitamunro.
/p nə́ni=á· kwəlsət·aməné·ɔ.
/t They should listen to *that*.'
/k let them hear them.

Lk 16.30
/b Tclkw taa nwxa Rplivcm;
/p tə́lku, 'tá=á·, núxa· ṭe·pəlíhem.
/t He said to him, 'No, they wouldn't, father Abraham.
/k And he said, Nay, father Abraham:

/b jwq a rfululetup toxqevtetc, qwlupeok a.
/p šúkw=á· enkələlí·t·əp tɔxkwihtí·t·e, kwələp·í·ɔk=á·.'
/t But if one who had died comes to them, they would repent.'
/k but if one went unto them from the dead, they will repent.

Lk 16.31 /b Nu tclan; mutuh klistaotetc Mwjiju ok ncnekanewrwseletpanifu;
/p ná tə́la·n, 'máta=č kələstaɔhtí·t·e †mo·šə́š·a ɔ́·k nehəni·k·a·ní·i-we·wsi·li·tpanínka,
/t Then he said to him, 'If they do not listen to Moses and the ancient prophets,
/k And he said unto him, If they hear not Moses and the prophets,

/b taoni a rfululetup toxkwk taa qwlsitaoewao. ‖
/p tá·ɔni=á· enkələ́lí·t·əp tɔ́xko·k, tá=á· kwəlsət·aɔ·iwwá·ɔ.'"
/t even though one who had died comes to them, the would not listen to him.'"
/k neither will they be persuaded, though one rose from the dead.

Chapter 76 (p. 133). (Luke 17.1-10.)

Lk 17.1 /b Nu tclanrp rkrkematpani, qelulr hanelacntwakunh vatr,
(p. 133) /p ná təlá·ne·p e·k·e·ki·ma·tpáni, "kwí·la-lé·, čani·laentəwá·k·an=č hát·e·.
/t Then he said to his disciples, "There's no avoiding that there will be temptations to sin,"
/k Then said he unto the disciples, It is impossible but that offences will come:
[RSV "temptations to sin"]

/b jwqh ktumaksw awrn hanelacfrtc,
/p šúkw=č ktəmá·ksu awé·n čani·laenké·t·e.
/t but if anyone tempts people to sin he will be in a bad way.
/k but woe unto him, through whom they come!

Lk 17.2 /b Alwe a wli lenum xifwi asun wxqrkufunif wuntaptwfc
/p aləwí·i=á· wəli-lí·nam, xínkwi-ahsə́n uxkwe·k·ánkanink wənta·ptúnke,
/t It would be better for him if a large stone were tied from his neck
/k It were better for him that a millstone were hanged about his neck,

/b nali munwprkwf lanivifc,   [presumably ⟨nali⟩ for ⟨nrli⟩ /né·li/]
/p né·li mənəp·é·k·unk lanihínke.
/t and he were thrown out into the sea,
/k and he cast into the sea,

/b rlkeqi a ave lenuf hanelarmatc mawselw tcfrlunselehi.
/p e·lkí·kwi-=á· -áhi-lí·nank, čani·lae·má·t·e ma·wsí·lu tenke·lənsi·lí·č·i.
/t compared to how severe it would be for him if he causes one of the humble ones to do wrong.
/k than that he should offend one of these little ones.   [RSV "cause .. to sin"]

Lk 17.3 /b Jwq bni mjatamwq, Kemavtus hanelackonc, qetuluh,
/p šúkw yó·ni məšá·t·amo·kw: kí·mahtəs čani·laehkɔ́ne, kkwí·təla=č.
/t But remember this: If your brother offends against you, you must admonish him.
/k Take heed to yourselves: If thy brother trespass against thee, rebuke him;

	/b	jerluntufc, pavketatumwmc.
	/p	ši·e·ləntánke, pahki·t·a·t·amó·me.
	/t	If he is sorry, forgive him.
	/k	and if he repent, forgive him.

Lk 17.4
- /b Nejaj txun hanelackonc kwti kejqc
- /p ní·š·a·š txə́n čani·laehkóne kwə́t·i kí·škwe,
- /t If he offends against you seven times in one day
- /k And if he trespass against thee seven times in a day,

- /b ok nunc txun lwkonc njerluntumun
- /p ó·k ná=nə txə́n lúk·ɔne, 'nši·e·ləntamən,'
- /t and tells you he's sorry that same number of times,
- /k and seven times in a day turn again to thee, saying, I repent;

- /b pavketatamwmc.
- /p pahki·t·a·t·amó·me."
- /t forgive him."
- /k thou shalt forgive him.

Lk 17.5
- /b Nu rlwkalunhek tclanrop; Nrvlalerf, unhi melenrn nvakatamwrokun.
- /p ná e·lo·ka·lə́nči·k təla·né·ɔ·p, "nehəlá·lienk, ánči-mi·lí·ne·n nhaka·t·amwe·ó·k·an."
- /t Then the apostles said to him, "Master, give us more faith."
- /k And the apostles said unto the Lord, Increase our faith.

Lk 17.6
- /b Tclkwao, mostute mifqtut rlrk lrkc knakatamwrokunwu,
- /p təlkəwá·ɔ, "†mɔstatí·i-mínkwtət é·le·k lé·k·e kəna·ka·t·amwe·ɔ·k·anúwa,
- /t He said to them, "If your faith was like a little mustard seed,
- /k And the Lord said, If ye had faith as a grain of mustard seed,

- /b lrqc a wu xuxaq mwnevla lawunwprqc mai nepai,
- /p lé·k·we=á· wá xáx·a·kw, 'mo·níhəla, la·wənəp·é·k·we mái-ní·p·ai,'
- /t and if you said to this sycamore tree, 'Uproot and go stand in the middle of the sea,'
- /k ye might say unto this sycamine tree, Be thou plucked up by the root, and be thou planted in the sea;

- /b na nc lr.
- /p ná=á· nə́ lé·.
- /t that's what would happen.
- /k and it should obey you.

Lk 17.7
- /b Jwq awrn vuh a kelwu tolwkakunetc tuluxakerletc jitu xumatc wcjwmwesu;
- /p "šúkw awé·n=háč=á· ki·ló·wa tɔlo·ka·k·aní·t·e, talaxhakie·lí·t·e ší=tá xamá·t·e wehšəmwí·s·a,

Text, Transcription, and Translation 447

/t   "But which of you, if he has a servant and he plows or feeds cattle,
/k   But which of you, having a servant plowing or feeding cattle,

/b   upi mekumoseletc, tclao vuh a, my lumutavpi metsi?
/p   ápi-mi·kəmɔ·s·i·lí·t·e, təlá·ɔ=háč=á·, 'mái-ləmátahpi, mí·tsi'?
/t   when he comes from his work, would say to him, 'Go sit down and eat'?
/k   will say unto him by and by, when he is come from the field, Go and sit down to meat?

Lk 17.8 /b   Mutu vuh a tclaeo wlextwl mcvmethif, ntclih metsen ok munrn,
/p   máta=háč=á· təla·í·ɔ, 'wəlí·xto·l mehəmí·č·ink, ntə́li-=č -mí·tsi·n ɔ́·k -məné·n.
/t   Would he not say to him, 'Prepare food so that I shall eat and drink.
/k   And will not rather say unto him, Make ready wherewith I may sup,

/b   okh krnavkeve kwehumi pchi alu metseanc ok munranc;
/p   ɔ́·k=č kke·nahkí·hi, kəwí·č·əmi, péči ála-mi·tsiá·ne ɔ́·k -məne·á·ne.
/t   And you must take care of me and help me until I'm through eating and drinking.
/k   and gird thyself, and serve me, till I have eaten and drunken;

/b   nuh kcnh ajitc kmetsen ok munrn.   [⟨munrn⟩ for ⟨kmunrn⟩ after /-k/]
/p   ná=č kə́nč a·šíte kəmí·tsi·n ɔ́·k kəmə́ne·n'?
/t   *Then* it will be your turn to eat and drink'?
/k   and afterward thou shalt eat and drink?

Lk 17.9 /b   Qrnamao vuh a kejiluseletc rlat?
/p   kwe·na·má·ɔ=háč=á· kíši-ləs·i·lí·t·e é·la·t?
/t   Would he thank him if he has done what he told him to?
/k   Doth he thank that servant because he did the things that were commanded him?

/b   Ntitc taa.
/p   ntíte, tá=á·.
/t   I don't think he would.
/k   I trow not.

Lk 17.10 /b   Nanc tpusqi ktclsenro kelwu, pavkunhi luserqc rlvkrrq b luseq,
/p   ná=nə tpə́skwi ktəlsi·né·ɔ ki·ló·wa, pahkánči-ləs·ié·k·we e·lké·e·kw, 'yú ləs·i·kw.'
/t   *You* do likewise, when you complete doing what you are told to do.
/k   So likewise ye, when ye shall have done all those things which are commanded you,

/b   lwrrq, takw krkw rlaprmkwsehek alwkakunuk nvakynanuk;   [⟨-rrq⟩ for ⟨-rq⟩]
/p   lúwe·kw, 'takó· kéku e·la·p·e·mkwəs·í·č·i·k alo·ká·k·anak nhak·ayəná·nak;
/t   Say, 'We are not servants who are good for anything.   [misunderstood]
/k   say, We are unprofitable servants: [RSV "unworthy servants"]

    /b   nanc jwq fuski lusenrn.
    /p   ná=nə šúkw nkáski-ləsˑíˑneˑn.'"
    /t   That's just what we were able to do.'"
    /k   we have done that which was our duty to do.

                                                                     [RSV "we have only done what was our duty."]

Chapter 77 (pp. 133-135). (Luke 17.11-37.)

Lk 17.11 /b   Nrlwxwrt li Nhelwsulum lovomunrp Sumrliewf ok Falulewf.   [⟨l-⟩ for /wəl-/]
           /p   neˑlóˑxˑweˑt lí †nčiˑlóˑsələm, wəloˑhómaneˑp †sameˑlííˑyunk óˑk †nkaˑlalíˑyunk.
           /t   As he journeyed to Jerusalem, he passed through Samaria and Galilee.
           /k   And it came to pass, as he went to Jerusalem, that he passed through the midst of Samaria and Galilee.

Lk 17.12 /b   Tamsc kwti wtrnrtutif preatc feskar tclcn linwu neskufululehi,
           /p   táˑmse kwóˑti oˑteˑneˑtˑətˑink peˑáˑtˑe, nkíˑskaeˑ télən lónəwa niˑskankələlíˑčˑi.
           /t   At one point when he came to one village he met ten men with the nasty disease.
           /k   And as he entered into a certain village, there met him ten men that were lepers,

           /b   ovlumihi nu nokevlalen;
           /p   ɔhələmíči nó nɔkˑihəláˑliˑn.
           /t   They stopped some distance away from it.
           /k   which stood afar off:

Lk 17.13 /b   amufexswuk, tclawao, Nhesus Nrvlalerf ktumakrlumenrn.   [⟨ktu-‖makrlumenrn⟩]
           /p   amankiˑxsúwak, təlawwáˑɔ, "nčíˑsas, nehəláˑlienk, ktəmaˑkˑeˑləmíˑneˑn."
           /t   They raised their voices and said to him, "Jesus, our master, take pity on us."
           /k   And they lifted up their voices, and said, Jesus, Master, have mercy on us.

Lk 17.14 /b   Mrhi prnaotc, tclao, mai punwntulw kvakybu wcvevwfrhek.
(p. 134)   /p   méˑči peˑnaóˑtˑe, təláˑɔ, "mái-pənúntəloˑ khakˑayúwa wehiˑhunkéˑčˑiˑk.
           /t   After he had seen them, he said to them, "Go show yourselves to the priests."
           /k   And when he saw them, he said unto them, Go shew yourselves unto the priests.

           /b   Mrhi rlumskavtetc nu pwelsenro.
           /p   méˑči eˑləmskahtíˑtˑe, ná pwiˑlsiˑnéˑɔ.
           /t   After they had started on their way, they became clean.
           /k   And it came to pass, that, as they went, they were cleansed.

Lk 17.15 /b   Mawsw mrhi nrfc tcli kekrn, nu tolumi qtuken,
           /p   máˑwsu méˑči nénke tóli-kíˑkˑeˑn, ná tóləmi-kwtókˑiˑn.
           /t   One of them, after he saw that he was healed, started back.
           /k   And one of them, when he saw that he was healed, turned back,

/b amufexsw moxifovkunemao Krtanitwelehi,
/p amankí·xsu, mɔx·inkɔhkəni·má·ɔ ke·tanət·o·wi·lí·č·i.
/t He raised his voice and praised God.
/k and with a loud voice glorified God,

Lk 17.16 /b ekali alwlavtcvlr wsetelet Nhesusu qrnamao.
/p íkali a·lo·lahtéhəle· wsi·t·í·li·t nči·sás·a, kwe·na·má·ɔ.
/t He threw himself face-down at Jesus's feet and thanked him.
/k And fell down on his face at his feet, giving him thanks:

/b Sumrlie linw nuni.
/p †same·lií·i-lənu náni.
/t He was a Samaritan man.
/k and he was a Samaritan.

Lk 17.17 /b Nhesus tclao, Mutu vuh tclcntxeeok pelevunhek?
/p nčí·sas təlá·ɔ, "máta=háč télən txi·í·ɔk pi·li·hənči·k?
/t Jesus said to him, "Weren't there ten that were made clean?
/k And Jesus answering said, Were there not ten cleansed?

/b ta vuh nukavkc prjkwf?
/p tá=háč nəkáhke pé·škunk?
/t Where are the other nine?
/k but where are the nine?

Lk 17.18 /b Takw wavkotwi tuli qtukenro, ok xifovkunemanro Krtanitwelehi,
/p takó· wwahkot·ó·wi təli-kwtək·i·né·ɔ ó·k -xinkɔhkəni·ma·né·ɔ ke·tanət·o·wi·lí·č·i,
/t It is not known that they came back and praised God,
/k There are not found that returned to give glory to God,

/b nuni jwq pale wunheyetup.
/p náni šúkw palí·i wənči·aí·t·əp."
/t only that one who had come from another place."
/k save this stranger.

Lk 17.19 /b Tclapani, Amwel alumskal, knakatamwrokun kwlamalswvalkwn.
/p təlá·p·ani, "á·mwi·l, aləmska·l; kəna·ka·t·amwe·ó·k·an ko·lamalso·há·lko·n."
/t And he said to him, "Stand up and go; your faith has made you well."
/k And he said unto him, Arise, go thy way: thy faith hath made thee whole.

Lk 17.20 /b Paluseok tclawao, Hifch vuh prerw Krtanitwet sokemaokun?
/p †pa·ləsi·í·ɔk təlawwá·ɔ, "čínke=č=háč pe·yé·yu ke·tanət·ó·wi·t sɔ·k·i·ma·ó·k·an?"
/t The Pharisees asked him, "When will God's kingdom come?"
/k And when he was demanded of the Pharisees, when the kingdom of God should come,

/b Tclao Krtanitwet sokemaokun prerekc ta xifwenavkotwi.
                                                              [⟨-navkot-⟩ for ⟨-nakovt-⟩]
/p təlá·ɔ, "ke·tanət·ó·wi·t sɔ·k·i·ma·ɔ́·k·an pe·ye·í·k·e, tá=á· xinkwi·nakɔhtó·wi.
/t He said to them, "When God's kingdom comes, it will not appear to be great.
/k he answered them and said, The kingdom of God cometh not with observation:
                                                       [RSV "not .. with signs to be observed"]

Lk 17.21 /b Okh ta lwrwun, Jr b vatr, jitu wlc nc vatr,
/p ɔ́·k=č tá=á· luwé·wən, 'šé· yú hát·e·,' ší=tá, 'wəlé nə́ hát·e·',
/t And people will not say, 'Here it is!' or 'It's over there!',
/k Neither shall they say, Lo here! or, lo there!

/b rli Krtanitwet sokemaokun wetavpemqrq.
/p é·li- ke·tanət·ó·wi·t sɔ·k·i·ma·ɔ́·k·an -witahpí·mkwe·kw."
/t for God's kingdom is with you."
/k for, behold, the kingdom of God is within you.

Lk 17.22 /b Tclapani rkrkematpani, prerekch kejqeki,
/p təlá·p·ani e·k·e·ki·ma·tpáni, "pe·ye·í·k·e=č ki·škwí·k·i,
/t He said to his disciples, "When the days come,
/k And he said unto the disciples, The days will come,

/b ktavih letrvavmw, qwlu nrmunrn kwti kejqeq, Linw wrqesif qejkwbm,
                                                                                                    [⟨-qeq⟩ for ⟨-qek⟩]
/p ktáhi·=č -li·t·e·háhəmɔ, 'kwə́la nné·məne·n kwə́t·i kí·škwi·k, lə́nu we·k·wí·s·ink kwi·škó·yəm.'
/t you shall very much wish to see one day, the day of the man who is the Son.
/k when ye shall desire to see one of the days of the Son of man,

/b jwq taa knrmwunro.
/p šúkw tá=á· kəne·mo·wəné·ɔ.
/t But you will not see it.
/k and ye shall not see it.

Lk 17.23 /b Ktclkwaokh, Jr bni, jitu jr nc wlc;
/p ktəlkəwá·ɔk=č, 'šé· yó·ni,' ší=tá, 'šé· nə́ wəlé.'
/t They will say to you, 'This is it,' or 'That's it over there.'
/k And they shall say to you, See here; or, see there:

/b jwq kahi wlamvetawerkrq, ok naolerkrq.
/p šúkw káči wəla·mhitawié·k·e·kw ɔ́·k na·ɔlié·k·e·kw.
/t But don't believe them or follow them.
/k go not after them, nor follow them.

Lk 17.24 /b Rvrlukveqi vufq wexkaohi sasapulclak wunhi vokwf ok wrmi b tali oxclak,
/p ehəlkhíkwi-=hánkw wi·xkaɔ́či sa·sa·p·əléhəla·k wə́nči hɔ́kunk
wé·mi yú -táli-ɔ·x·éhəla·k,
/t As brightly as lightning from the sky suddenly shines everywhere here,
/k For as the lightning, that lighteneth out of the one part under heaven, shineth unto the other part under heaven;

/b nunih lukveqi wexkaohi prerw Linw wrqesif qejkwbm.
/p nə́ni=č ləkhíkwi- wi·xkaɔ́či -pe·yé·yu lə́nu we·k·wí·s·ink kwi·škó·yəm.
/t that will be how brightly the day of the man who is the Son will suddenly come.
/k so shall also the Son of man be in his day.

Lk 17.25 /b Jwqh vetami xrlrnaoki krkw wunhi amuxavrluntum
/p šúkw=č hítami xe·lennáɔhki kéku wə́nči-amax·ahe·lə́ntam,
/t But first he shall suffer torments of many kinds, [lit., 'many kinds of things']
/k But first must he suffer many things,

/b okh puvkelkwsw b tali cntu lawsif.
/p ɔ́·k=č pahki·lkwə́s·u yú táli entalá·wsink.
/t and he shall be rejected in this world.
/k and be rejected of this generation.

Lk 17.26 /b Tpisqih lr rlrkup Norsu rpetc Linw wrqesif lupi patc.
/p tpə́skwi=č lé· e·lé·k·əp †no·wé·s·a e·p·í·t·e, lə́nu we·k·wí·s·ink lápi pá·t·e.
/t When the man who is the Son comes again, it will be as it was when Noah lived.
/k And as it was in the days of Noe, so shall it be also in the days of the Son of man.

Lk 17.27 /b Metswpanek, ok munrpanek, ok wjelintamwpanek, ok ovjelintamwrvoltwpanek,
/p mi·tsó·p·ani·k, ɔ́·k məné·p·ani·k, ɔ́·k wši·ləntamó·p·ani·k, ɔ́·k ɔwši·ləntamwe·hɔ·ltó·p·ani·k,
/t They ate, and they drank, and they married, and they gave each other in marriage,
/k They did eat, they drank, they married wives, they were given in marriage,

/b eku pchi nc kejqek rlkeqi Norsu pwsetup li mwxwlif;
/p íka péči nə́ kí·škwi·k e·lkí·kwi- †no·wé·s·a -po·s·í·t·əp mux·ó·link.
/t up until the day when Noah boarded the ship.
/k until the day that Noe entered into the ark,

/b nu prtaqexunwp wrmi ufulwpanek.
/p ná pe·t·a·kwí·x·əno·p, wé·mi ankəlɔ́·p·ani·k.
/t Then a flood came, and everyone died.
/k and the flood came, and destroyed them all.

Lk 17.28 /b Okh tpisqi lr rlrkup, Latu rpetc.
/p ó·k=č tpə́skwi lé· e·lé·k·əp †lá·ta e·p·í·t·e
/t And it will also be as it was when Lot lived.
/k Likewise also as it was in the days of Lot;

/b Metswpanek, munrpanek, mumvalumaovwtpanek,   [⟨mumvalumao-‖vwtpanek⟩ for ⟨mumvalumaovtwpanek⟩]
/p mi·tsó·p·ani·k, məné·p·ani·k, məmhalama·ohtó·p·ani·k,
/t They ate, they drank, they bought and sold,   [*lit.*, they bought from each other]
/k they did eat, they drank, they bought, they sold,

(p. 135) /b vakevrpanek, ok wekvavtwpanek.
/p haki·hé·p·ani·k ó·k wi·khahtó·p·ani·k.
/t they planted and all built houses.
/k they planted, they builded;

Lk 17.29 /b Jwq na nckc kejq ek Latu krhetc wunhi Satumif,   [⟨kejq ek⟩ for ⟨kejqek⟩]
/p šúkw ná-néke kí·škwi·k †lá·ta ke·č·í·t·e wə́nči †sá·tamink,
/t But the very day that Lot left Sodom,
/k But the same day that Lot went out of Sodom

/b swkulanevlrp tunty, ok wesark avsun wrmevkwnrop,
/p so·k·əla·níhəle·p tə́ntay ó·k wi·s·á·e·k ahsə́n, wwe·mihko·né·ɔ·p.
/t it rained fire and yellow stone, and it killed them all.
/k it rained fire and brimstone from heaven, and destroyed them all.

Lk 17.30 /b nunih lr rlkeqi Wrqesif linw upi nrvkwset.
/p nə́ni=č lé· e·lkí·kwi- we·k·wí·s·ink lə́nu -ápi-ne·ykwə́s·i·t.
/t That is what will happen at the time when the man who is the Son has appeared.
/k Even thus shall it be in the day when the Son of man is revealed.

Lk 17.31 /b Nunih lukveqi awr̃n xqetakc avpetc,
/p nə́ni=č ləkhíkwi awé·n xkwi·t·á·k·e ahpí·t·e,
/t At that time, if someone is on top of the house
/k In that day, he which shall be upon the housetop,

/b tulavhrswakunu lumekwavmc vatrkc,   [⟨lum-⟩ for ⟨lam-⟩]
/p təlahče·s·əwá·k·ana la·mi·k·əwáhəme hat·é·k·e,
/t and his possessions are inside the house,
/k and his stuff in the house,

/b kahi lexeveh my pale lwxovtwveh;
/p káči li·x·í·hi·č, mái- palí·i -luxɔhtó·hi·č.
/t he must not come down and go to take them away.
/k let him not come down to take it away:

/b   ok awrn tutu mvehe avpetc, kahi kuvtu maheveh.
/p   ɔ́·k awé·n tətá mhičí·i ahpí·t·e, káči káhta-ma·č·í·hi·č.
/t   And if someone is somewhere out in the open, let him not seek to go home.
/k   and he that is in the field, let him likewise not return back.

Lk 17.32 /b   Mujalw Latu wehrotpani.
              /p   məšá·lo· ṭlá·ta wi·č·e·ɔ·tpáni.
              /t   Remember Lot's wife.
              /k   Remember Lot's wife.

Lk 17.33 /b   Awrnh ntwnufc b tali lclrxrokun tofvetwnh wulclrxrokun,
              /p   awé·n=č nto·nánke yú táli lehəle·x·e·ɔ́·k·an, tɔnkhíto·n=č wəlehəle·x·e·ɔ́·k·an.
              /t   If anyone seeks life here, he shall lose his life.
              /k   Whosoever shall seek to save his life shall lose it;

              /b   Kahih awrn afvetaqc wulclrxrokun b tali, lupih moxkumun.
              /p   káč·i=č awé·n ankhitá·k·we wəlehəle·x·e·ɔ́·k·an yú táli, lápi=č mɔ́xkamən.
              /t   But if someone loses his life here, he shall find it again.
              /k   and whosoever shall lose his life shall preserve it.

Lk 17.34 /b   Ktclwvmw nunih trpvwqek nejuh linwuk wepcntwuk,
              /p   ktəllúhəmɔ, nə́ni=č te·phúkwi·k, ní·š·a=č lə́nəwak wi·péntəwak,
              /t   I tell you, on that night two men will be sleeping in the same bed,
              /k   I tell you, in that night there shall be two men in one bed;

              /b   mawswh alumwxola okh mawsw fala.
              /p   má·wsu=č aləmó·x·ɔla·, ɔ́·k=č má·wsu nkála·.
              /t   and one shall be taken and the other shall be left.
              /k   the one shall be taken, and the other shall be left.

Lk 17.35 /b   Okh neju xqrok nejikovokrok,
              /p   ɔ́·k=č ní·š·a xkwé·ɔk níši-kɔhɔ·k·é·ɔk,
              /t   And two women will be pounding corn in a mortar together,
              /k   Two women shall be grinding together;

              /b   mawswh alumwxola okh mawsw fala.
              /p   má·wsu=č aləmó·x·ɔla·, ɔ́·k=č má·wsu nkála·."
              /t   and one shall be taken and the other shall be left."
              /k   the one shall be taken, and the other left.

Lk 17.37 /b   Nu notwxtaonro, tclawao, Tanih vuh tali Nrvlalerf?
              /p   ná nɔt·o·xtaɔ·né·ɔ, təlawwá·ɔ, "tá·ni=č=háč táli, nehəlá·lienk?"
              /t   Then they asked him a question, saying to him, "Where will it be, Master?"
              /k   And they answered and said unto him, Where, Lord?

/b Tclao, wews vufq tutu jrfexifc opalanrok vufq eku marvlrok.
/p təláˑɔ, "wióˑs=hánkw tətá šenkiˑxˑínke, ɔˑpˑalanéˑɔk=hánkw íka maˑehəléˑɔk."
/t He said to them, "If flesh is lying somewhere, bald eagles gather there."
/k And he said unto them, Wheresoever the body is, thither will the eagles be gathered together.

Chapter 78 (pp. 135-136). (Luke 18.1-14.)

Lk 18.1
/b Rnwnvakrokun tclapani
/p eˑnunthakeˑóˑkˑan təláˑpˑani,
/t He told them a parable
/k And he spake a parable unto them to this end,

/b rli a wejiki patamuf, ok mutu lwkavlaif,
/p éˑli-=áˑ -wiˑšíki-pátamank, óˑk máta -loˑkahəláˑink.
/t of how one should work hard at praying and not give up.
/k that men ought always to pray, and not to faint;

Lk 18.2
/b lwr, Avpwp kwti wtrnif krkyimvrt,
/p lúweˑ, "ahpóˑp kwə́tˑi oˑtˑéˑnink keˑkayə́mheˑt.
/t He said, "There was in a certain town a ruler.
/k Saying, There was in a city a judge,

/b takw koxaepani Krtanitwelehi ok mutu krkw tulrlumaepani navkoi linwu,
/p takó kɔxˑaˑíˑpˑani keˑtanətˑoˑwiˑlíˑčˑi, óˑk máta kéku təleˑləmaˑíˑpˑani nahkóˑi lə́nəwa.
/t He did not fear God and had no regard for any mere man.
/k which feared not God, neither regarded man:

Lk 18.3
/b ok nuni wtrnif tcpenrp kotvwetup xqr;   [⟨tcp-⟩ for ⟨top-⟩]
/p óˑk nə́ni oˑtˑéˑnink təpˑíˑneˑp kɔˑthoˑwíˑtˑəp xkwéˑ.
/t And in that town there was a widowed woman.
/k And there was a widow in that city;

/b wtxapani, tclapani, Wetavrmel wcnhih pwnemet jifalet.
/p oˑtxáˑpˑani, təláˑpˑani, "wiˑtˑahéˑmiˑl, wénči-=č -poˑnímiˑt šinkáˑliˑt."
/t She went to him and said to him, "Help me, so my enemy will stop talking about me."
/k and she came unto him, saying, Avenge me of mine adversary.
                                    [RSV "vindicate me against my adversary"]

Lk 18.4
/b Jwq nakri mutu wifi.
/p šúkw naˑkˑéˑi máta wínki.
/t But for a while he was unwilling.
/k And he would not for a while:

/b Oweri prnarluntufc letrvr,
/p ɔ·wié·i pe·na·eləntánke, li·t·é·he·,
/t Later on when he considered it, he thought,
/k but afterward he said within himself,

/b taonih mutu foxai Krtanitwet ok mutu krkw ntulrlumai navkoi linw;
/p 'tá·ɔni=č máta nkɔx·á·i ke·tanət·ó·wi·t, ó·k máta kéku ntəle·ləmá·i nahkó·i lə́nu,
/t 'Although I do not fear God, and have no special regard for any man,
/k Though I fear not God, nor regard man;

Lk 18.5
/b jwq nuni kotvwxqr somi luxaevwq, bv tu nwetavrman,
/p šúkw náni kɔ·thó·xkwe só·mi llax·aí·hukw, yúh=tá nəwi·t·a·hé·ma·n,
/t yet that widow annoys me so much, alright, I'll help her,
/k Yet because this widow troubleth me, I will avenge her,

/b rli a tumeki patc nsukwelarvwq a.
/p é·li-=á· təmí·ki -pá·t·e, nsak·wi·laé·hukw=á·.'"
/t as, if she comes often, she would torment me.'"
/k lest by her continual coming she weary me.

Lk 18.6
/b Nrvlalwrt lwr, Puntamwq nuku mutu wrlilisetup krkyimvrsu rlwrtup.
/p nehəlá·ləwe·t lúwe·, "pə́ntamo·kw náka máta wé·li·ləs·í·t·əp ke·kayəmhé·s·a e·ləwé·t·əp.
/t And the Lord said, "Listen to what that unrighteous ruler said.
/k And the Lord said, Hear what the unjust judge saith.

Lk 18.7
/b Mutu vuh ct ok Krtanitwet wetavrmaeo pepenaohi
/p máta=háč=ét ó·k ke·tanət·ó·wi·t wwi·t·a·he·ma·í·ɔ pi·p·i·naó·č·i,
/t Don't you think God also helps those he chooses,
/k And shall not God avenge his own elect,

/b qwni kejwq ok kwnetpwq nvakalkwkc, taoni mutu jac?   [⟨kej-‖wq⟩]
/p kwə́ni-kí·š·ukw ó·k kwə́ni-tpó·kw nhaka·lkúk·e, tá·ɔni máta šá·e?
/t if they need his help day and night, even if not immediately?
/k which cry day and night unto him, though he bear long with them?

Lk 18.8
(P. 136)
/b Ktclwvmw, kvehei wexkaohih wetavrmao.
/p ktəllúhəmɔ, khičí·i, wi·xkaóči=č wwi·t·a·he·má·ɔ.
/t I tell you, truly, that he will speedily help them.
/k I tell you that he will avenge them speedily.

/b Alwt lupi patc Linw wrqesif
/p alóʼt lápi pá·t·e lə́nu we·k·wí·s·ink,
/t When the man who is the Son comes again, however,
/k Nevertheless when the Son of man cometh,

	/b	muxkumh vuh nvakatamwrokun b tali cntu lawsif.
	/p	máxkam=č=háč nhaka·t·amwe·ó·k·an yú táli entalá·wsink?"
	/t	will he find faith in this world?"
	/k	shall he find faith on the earth?

Lk 18.9	/b	Bqc bni rnwnvakrokun, tclanrp rletrvaletup nwli lclrxc
	/p	yúkwe, yó·ni e·nunthake·ó·k·an təlá·ne·p e·li·t·e·ha·lí·t·əp, "nó·li-lehəlé·x·e,"
	/t	Now, this parable he told to ones who had thought, "I live a righteous life,"
	/k	And he spake this parable unto certain which trusted in themselves that they were righteous,

	/b	ok mrtrlumaletup alintc awrni.
	/p	ó·k me·t·e·ləma·lí·t·əp a·lə́nte awé·ni.
	/t	and who had thought badly of some others.
	/k	and despised others:

Lk 18.10	/b	Neju linwfu eku rpanek patamwrekaonif my patamapanek;
	/p	"ní·š·a lənúnka íka é·p·ani·k pa·tamwe·i·k·á·ɔnink, mái-pa·tamá·p·ani·k.
	/t	"Two men went to the temple, going to pray.
	/k	Two men went up into the temple to pray;

	/b	mawswu Paluse linwu, kahi mawswu moni mcmrnifup. [⟨mcmrn-⟩ for ⟨mcmarn-⟩]
	/p	ma·wsúwa †pa·ləsi·í·i-lə́nəwa, káč·i ma·wsúwa mɔ́ni mehəma·e·nínkəp.
	/t	One was a Pharisee, while the other was a tax-collector.
	/k	the one a Pharisee, and the other a publican.

Lk 18.11	/b	Nu Paluse linw nepwp patamap, lwrp,
	/p	ná †pa·ləsi·í·i-lə́nu ní·p·o·p, pá·tama·p, lúwe·p,
	/t	The Pharisee stood and prayed, saying,
	/k	The Pharisee stood and prayed thus with himself,

	/b	Krtanitweun, wuneji ntcli mutu lusewun, wrmi awrn rlset,
	/p	'ke·tanət·ó·wian, wanə́š·i ntə́li- máta -ləs·í·wən wé·mi awé·n é·lsi·t,
	/t	'O God, thank you that I am not the way everyone else is,
	/k	God, I thank thee, that I am not as other men are,

	/b	cvamunhevwrthek mutu juxavkawsehek, wceukski wekifrhek,
	/p	ehamənčihəwé·č·i·k, máta šaxahka·wsí·č·i·k, †weyákski-wi·k·inké·č·i·k,
	/t	ones who force people to do things, are not righteous, or are promiscuous,
	/k	extortioners, unjust, adulterers,

	/b	ok wuni rlset moni mcmarnif.
	/p	ó·k wáni é·lsi·t mɔ́ni mehəma·é·nink.
	/t	or the way this tax-collector is.
	/k	or even as this publican.

Lk 18.12 /b Aphi ntclsen, nejaj txi kejqc nejun vufq mutu nmetsei
/p á·pči ntə́lsi·n; ní·š·a·š txí-kí·škwe, ní·š·ən=hánkw máta nəmi·tsí·i.
/t I am always so; in seven days, I do not eat twice.
/k I fast twice in the week,

/b wrmi krkw cntxi wlatao krkrxiti vufq eku nwnhi nuxpufwnsi.
/p wé·mi kéku éntxi-wəlá·taɔ, ke·ke·xíti=hánkw íka núnči-naxpankúnsi.
/t Of everything I have, I always give a little as gifts.
/k I give tithes of all that I possess.

Lk 18.13 /b Nuni moni mcmarnif ovlumi nepwp, takw nuxpunc uspwqrep,
/p náni móni mehəma·é·nink ɔ́həlami ní·p·o·p, takó· náxpəne asphukwé·i·p.
/t The tax-collector stood at a distance and did not even lift up his head.
/k And the publican, standing afar off, would not lift up so much as his eyes unto heaven,

/b jwq pokuntamun vwtwlvy, lwrp, Krtanitweun ktumakrlumi mrtawseu.
/p šúkw pɔk·ántamən wtó·lhay, lúwe·p, 'ke·tanət·ó·wian, ktəma·k·é·ləmi me·t·a·wsía.'
/t He only struck his chest and said. 'O God, take pity on me, a sinner.'
/k but smote upon his breast, saying, God be merciful to me a sinner.

/b Ktclwvmw nu linw nvakrlintamwp rlumi mahetc; kahi nu takok mutu;
/p ktəllúhəmɔ, ná lónu nhake·e·ləntamo·p é·ləmi-ma·č·í·t·e, káč·i ná tákɔ·k máta,
/t I tell you, that man was hopeful when he went home, but the other one was not,
/k I tell you, this man went down to his house justified rather than the other:

/b rli cntxi awrn xifwrlintuf voky, tufrlumwqset,
/p é·li- éntxi- awé·n -xinkwe·ləntank hók·ay -tanke·ləmúkwsi·t,
/t for everyone who thinks highly of himself is thought little of,
/k for every one that exalteth himself shall be abased;

/b kahi awrn tufrlintuf voky xifwrlumwqsw.
/p káč·i awé·n tanke·ləntank hók·ay xinkwe·ləmúkwsu."
/t while anyone who thinks little of himself is thought a lot of."
/k and he that humbleth himself shall be exalted.

Chapter 79 (pp. 136-137). (Matthew 19.1-12, Mark 10.1 [part], 10-12.)

Mt 19.1 /b Mrhi Nhesus kejaptunrtc bl aptwnukunu, [⟨-tun-⟩ for ⟨-twn-⟩; ⟨-nuk-⟩ for ⟨-nak-⟩]
/p mé·či nčí·sas ki·š·a·pto·né·t·e yó·l a·pto·ná·k·ana,
/t After Jesus had finished these talks,
/k ... when Jesus had finished these sayings,

Mk 10.1 /b nu posqenrp,
/p ná pɔskwí·ne·p,
/t he arose
/kl ... he arose from thence, ...

Mt 19.1 /b alumskrp eku wunhi Faluleuf, eku prp Nhwtei vakif, Nhutunif kamif.
/p alə́mske·p íka wə́nči †nka·lalí·yunk, íka pé·p †nčo·ti·í·i-hák·ink, †nčátanink ká·mink.
/t and departed from Galilee, and went to the land of Judaea across the Jordan.
/k he departed from Galilee, and came into the coasts of Judaea beyond Jordan;

Mt 19.2 /b Ave xrli awrn noolapani.
/p áhi-xé·li awé·n nɔ·ɔlá·p·ani.
/t A great many people followed him.
/k And great multitudes followed him;

Mk 10.1 /b Lupi xrli awrn wtxapani, jac lupi avkrkifrp
/p lápi xé·li awé·n o·txá·p·ani, šá·e lápi ahke·kínke·p,
/t And again many people came to him, and right away again he taught them,
/kl and the people resort unto him again; and, as he was wont, he taught them again.

Mt 19.2 /b ok kekrvwrp.
/p ɔ́·k ki·k·éhəwe·p.
/t and he healed people.
/kl ... and he healed them there.

Mt 19.3 /b Ok Paluseok wtxawapani, koqrhevawapani, tclawapani,
/p ɔ́·k †pa·ləsi·í·ok o·txawwá·p·ani, kɔk·we·č·i·hawwá·p·ani, təlawwá·p·ani,
/t And Pharisees also came to him and tested him, saying to him,
/k The Pharisees also came unto him, tempting him, and saying unto him,

/b wlexun vuh linw pokelan wehrohi navkoi krkw wunhi?
/p "wəlí·x·ən=háč lə́nu pok·í·la·n wi·č·e·ɔ́·č·i nahkɔ́·i kéku wə́nči?"
/t "Is it right for a man to divorce his wife for anything at all?"
/k Is it lawful for a man to put away his wife for every cause?

Mt 19.4 /b Tclao, mutu vuh vuji ktukuntamwnro,
/p təlá·ɔ, "máta=háč háši ktak·əntamo·wəné·ɔ,
/t He said to them, "Haven't you ever read
/k And he answered and said unto them, Have ye not read,

/b tcli Kejrlumatup kejrlumanrp linwu ok xqro, [⟨Kej-‖rlumatup⟩]
/p tə́li- ki·š·e·ləmá·t·əp -ki·š·e·ləmá·ne·p lə́nəwa ɔ́·k xkwé·ɔ,
/t that he who made them made a man and a woman,
/k that he which made them at the beginning made them male and female,

Mt 19.5	/b	ok lwrn
(p. 137)	/p	ɔ́·k -lúwe·n,
	/t	and said,
	/k	And said,

/b nunih wunhi linw pwnrluman wxov ok kovrsu, xqrbf li psukwen,   [⟨-ov⟩: /-ɔ/]
/p 'nə́ni=č wwə́nči- lə́nu -po·né·ləma·n ó·x·ɔ ɔ́·k kɔhé·s·a, xkwé·yunk -lí-psák·wi·n.
/t 'For that reason a man will forsake his father and mother and adhere to a woman.
/k For this cause shall a man leave father and mother, and shall cleave to his wife:

/b nuh nrk neju maot vokybu,
/p ná=č né·k ní·š·a má·ɔt hɔk·ayúwa.'?
/t Then those two shall have a single body.'?
/k and they twain shall be one flesh?

Mt 19.6	/b	ta hek nejeeok, maoth vokybu. [⟨hek⟩ for ⟨heh⟩]
	/p	tá=á· čí·č ni·š·i·í·ɔk, má·ɔt=č hɔk·ayúwa.
	/t	They will no longer be two; their bodies will be one.
	/k	Wherefore they are no more twain, but one flesh.

/b Puna krkw Krtanitwet trqextaq, kahi awrn hpunifveh.
/p pənáh kéku ke·tanət·ó·wi·t te·k·wí·xta·kw; káči awé·n čpənínkhi·č."
/t See what God has joined together; let no one break it apart.
/k What therefore God hath joined together, let not man put asunder.

Mt 19.7	/b	Tclawao, Krkw vuh wunhi Mwjiju lwrtup,
	/p	təlawwá·ɔ, "kéku=háč wə́nči- †mo·šə́š·a -luwé·t·əp,
	/t	They said to him, "Why did Moses say,
	/k	They say unto him, Why did Moses then command

/b Lrvekunitituh awrn melintc konu pokelao wehrohi?   [⟨Lrvek-⟩ for ⟨Lrkvek-⟩]
/p 'le·khi·k·anət·ɔ́t·a=č awé·n mi·lə́nte, kɔ́na pɔk·i·lá·ɔ wi·č·e·ɔ́·č·i'?"
/t 'If someone is given a document, he is free to divorce his wife'?"
/k to give a writing of divorcement, and to put her away?

Mt 19.8	/b	Tclao Mwjiju wunhi nc lwrnrp rli hetanisevtet ktcvwaok.
	/p	təlá·ɔ, "†mo·šə́š·a wwə́nči- nə́ -luwé·ne·p é·li·či·t·anəs·íhti·t ktehəwá·ɔk.
	/t	He said to them, "Moses said that because your hearts were hard.
	/k	He saith unto them, Moses because of the hardness of your hearts suffered you to put away your wives:

/b Jwq vetami mutu ncni lexunwep.
/p šúkw hítami máta nə́ni li·x·ənó·wi·p.
/t But at first that was not the law.
/k but from the beginning it was not so.

Mt 19.9 /b Ktclwvmw, awrnh pavkelatc wehrohi
/p ktəllúhəmɔ, awé·n=č pahki·lá·t·e wi·č·e·ɔ́·č·i,
/t I tell you, if anyone divorces his wife,
/k And I say unto you, Whosoever shall put away his wife,

/b mutu keme wekifrokun wunhi, peli wehrotc, avih hani lusw;
/p máta ki·mí·i-wi·k·inke·ɔ́·k·an wə́nči, pí·li wi·č·e·ɔ́·t·e, áhi=č čáni-lə́s·u,
/t not because of fornication, and marries someone else, he will do something very wrong.
/k except it be for fornication, and shall marry another, committeth adultery:

/b ok prkelunt awrni wehotc avih hani lusw.   [⟨wehotc⟩ for ⟨wehrotc⟩]
/p ɔ́·k pe·k·í·lənt awé·ni wi·č·e·ɔ́·t·e, áhi=č čáni-lə́s·u."
/t And if one who was divorced marries anyone, they do something very wrong."
/k and whoso marrieth her which is put away doth commit adultery.   (Cf. Lk 16.18.)

Mk 10.10 /b Mrhi wekwavmif pratc,
/p mé·či wi·k·əwáhəmink pe·á·t·e,
/t After he came to the house,
/k And in the house

/b nul nc lupi rkrkematpani ajitc notwtumakwnrp.
/p nál nə́ lápi e·k·e·ki·ma·tpáni a·šíte nɔt·o·t·əma·k·ó·ne·p.
/t his disciples again asked him about the same thing.
/k his disciples asked him again of the same matter.

Mk 10.11 /b Tclao, Linwh puvkelatc wehrohi, ok peli wehrotc
/p təlá·ɔ, "lə́nu=č pahki·lá·t·e wi·č·e·ɔ́·č·i, ɔ́·k pí·li wi·č·e·ɔ́·t·e,
/t He said to them, "If a man divorces his wife and marries a different one,
/k And he saith unto them, Whosoever shall put away his wife, and marry another,

/b avih hane lusw;
/p áhi=č čáni-lə́s·u.
/t he will do something very wrong.
/k committeth adultery against her.

Mk 10.12 /b okh xqr puvkelatc wehrohi avih hane lusw.
/p ɔ́·k=č xkwé· pahki·lá·t·e wi·č·e·ɔ́·č·i, áhi=č čáni-lə́s·u."
/t And if a woman divorces her husband, she will do something very wrong."
/k And if a woman shall put away her husband, and be married to another, she committeth adultery.

Mt 19.10 /b Rkrkemahi tclkw, nuni kvehe lrkc,
/p e·k·e·ki·má·č·i tə́lku, "nə́ni khičí·i lé·k·e,
/t His disciples said to him, "If that is truly so,
/k His disciples say unto him, If the case of the man be so with his wife,

          /b   tcxi a wlexun alikc mutu awrn wewvjeluntumwun.
          /p   téxi=á· wəlí·x·ən, álike máta awé·n wi·wši·ləntamó·wən."
          /t   it would be an altogether good thing for a person never to get married anyway."
          /k   it is not good to marry.

Mt 19.11 /b   Jwq tclao, Alintc awrn mutu koski wlatwun b aptwnakun,
           /p   šúkw təlá·ɔ, "a·lə́nte awé·n máta kɔ́ski-wəla·tó·wən yú a·pto·ná·k·an,
           /t   But he said to them, "Some people are not able to keep this word,
           /k   But he said unto them, All men cannot receive this saying,

          /b   jwq krski lusehek,
          /p   šúkw ké·ski-ləs·í·č·i·k.
          /t   only those who can do it.
          /k   save they to whom it is given.

Mt 19.12 /b   rli alintc qelu luswuk nckc kejeketetc nwhi,
           /p   é·li a·lə́nte kwí·la-lə́s·əwak néke ki·š·i·k·ihtí·t·e núči,
           /t   For some are unable (to marry) from the time when they are born,
           /k   For there are some eunuchs, which were so born from their mother's womb:

          /b   ok aluntc qela luswuk rli nevlalkwsevtet,
          /p   ɔ́·k a·lə́nte kwí·la-lə́s·əwak é·li-nihəla·lkwəs·íhti·t,
          /t   and some are unable to because they are not free to act,   [*lit.*, they are owned]
          /k   and there are some eunuchs, which were made eunuchs of men: [RSV "by men"]

          /b   ok aluntc qela luswuk osavkamre sakemaokun wunhi.
          /p   ɔ́·k a·lə́nte kwí·la-lə́s·əwak ɔ·s·ahkame·í·i-sa·k·i·ma·ɔ́·k·an wə́nči.
          /t   and some are unable to because of the heavenly kingdom.
          /k   and there be eunuchs, which have made themselves eunuchs for the kingdom of heaven's sake.

          /b   Jwqh awrn trpi luset, pwuntamunh.
          /p   šúkw=č awé·n tépi-lə́s·i·t, pwə́ntamən=č.
          /t   But anyone who is able to must listen to it."
          /k   He that is able to receive it, let him receive it.

Chapter 80 (pp. 137-138). (Matthew 19.13-15, Mark 10.13-15, Luke 18.15-17)

Mt 19.13 /b   Nu eku prjwanrp memuntituk,
           /p   ná íka pe·š·əwá·ne·p mi·məntə́t·ak,
           /t   Then little children were brought to him,
           /k   Then were there brought unto him little children,

/b tcli a eku a lunan ok patamwrlxan;   [⟨a lunan⟩ for ⟨alunan⟩]
/p tə́li-=á· íka -alə́na·n, ə́·k -pa·tamwé·lxa·n.
/t so that he would put his hand on them and pray for them.
/k that he should put his hands on them, and pray:

Lk 18.15, Mk 10.13
/b rkrkemunhek nc rlenumevtetc, qetulawapani prjwalehi.
/p e·k·e·ki·mə́nči·k nə́ e·li·namihtí·t·e, kkwi·təlawwá·p·ani pe·š·əwa·lí·č·i.
/t When the disciples saw that, they admonished those that brought them.
/l but when his disciples saw it, they rebuked those that brought them.

Mk 10.14 /b Nhesus nc rlenufc tove mutu li wulrluntamwunrp,
/p nčí·sas nə́ e·li·nánke, tóhi- máta -lí-wəle·ləntamó·wəne·p.
/t When Jesus saw that, he was very much not pleased in doing so.
/kl But when Jesus saw it, he was much displeased,

Lk 18.16 /b notwmapani, lwrp,
/p nɔt·o·má·p·ani, lúwe·p,
/t He called them over and said,
/k But Jesus called them unto him, and said,

Mk 10.14 /b konulenw nrk memuntituk nwtxwkwn,
/p "kə́na lí·no· né·k mi·məntət·ak no·txúk·o·n.
/t "Let the little children come to me.
/kl Suffer the little children to come unto me,   (Cf. Lk 18.16, without "the".)

/b kahe qvetvekrvrq;
/p káči khwithiké·he·kw,
/t Do not forbid anyone,
/kl and forbid them not: (Also Lk 18.16.)

/b rli nuni rlsehek krtanitwet sokemaokunif avpevtet.   [⟨sokema-‖okunif⟩]
/p é·li- nə́ni e·lsí·č·i·k ke·tanət·ó·wi·t sɔ·k·i·ma·ɔ́·k·anink -ahpíhti·t.
/t for ones like that are in God's kingdom.
/kl for of such is the kingdom of God.   (Also Lk 18.16.)

Lk 18.17 /b Kvehe ktclwvmw,
(p. 138) /p khičí·i ktəllúhəmɔ,
/t Truly, I say to you,
/k Verily I say unto you,   (Cf. Mk 10.15.)

/b Awrnh, mutu memuntutif lukveqi nwntarlunsetc Krtanitwet sokemaokun
/p awé·n=č máta mi·məntət·ink ləkhíkwi-nuntae·lənsí·t·e ke·tanət·ó·wi·t
    sɔ·k·i·ma·ɔ́·k·an,
/t if someone is not as humble towards God's kingdom as a little child
/k Whosoever shall not receive the kingdom of God as a little child

/b ta tcxi ekali tumekri.
/p tá=á· téxi íkali təmi·k·é·i.
/t there is no way he will enter it.
/k shall in no wise enter therein.

Mk 10.16 /b Nu wrtunanrp, nu tcli welelet alunanrp, nu potamwrlxanrp,
/p ná wwe·t·əná·ne·p, ná təli- wi·lí·li·t -aləná·ne·p, ná pɔ·tamwe·lxá·ne·p.
/t Then he picked them up and put his hand on their heads, and he prayed for them.
/k And he took them up in his arms, put his hands upon them, and blessed them.

Mt 19.15 /b nu eku wunhi alumskanrp.
/p ná íka wwə́nči-aləmská·ne·p.
/t Then he departed from there.
/kl ... and departed thence.

Chapter 81 (pp. 138-141). (Mark 10.17, 19-21, 23-24, 26-27, 29-31; Matthew 19.16-18, 21-25, 27-28; Luke 18.18, 20, 24, 27)

Mk 10.17, Luke 18.18, Mt 19.20
/b Tumakunif pratc, krkaimvrtit skenw eku jevlrp,
(p. 138) /p təmá·k·anink pe·á·t·e, ke·kayəmhé·t·ət skínnu íka šíhəle·p
/t When he came to the road, a young man of the ruling class ran up to him
/l And when he was gone forth into the way, behold, a certain ruler came running, [*who was a young man*]

/b wnejetqetaopani notwxtao,   [⟨-ao⟩ for /-aɔ́·ɔ/]
/p wəni·š·i·tkwi·taɔ́·p·ani, nɔt·o·xtaɔ́·ɔ,
/t and he knelt down to him and asked him,
/l and kneeled to him, and asked him,

Mt 19.16, Mk 10.17
/b tclao, Wrleluseun Nrvlaleun, ta vuh nc wrlvik rlseu a
/p təlá·ɔ, "wé·li-lə́s·ian nehəlá·lian, tá=háč nə́ wé·lhik e·lsía=á·,
/t saying to him, "My good master, what good thing should I do,
/l saying, Good Master, what good thing shall I do,

/b wcnhi a patatao rvalumakumek pumawswakun?
/p wə́nči-=á· -pa·tá·taɔ ehaləmá·kami·k pəma·wsəwá·k·an?"
/t by which I would earn eternal life?"
/l that I may inherit eternal life?

Mt 19.17 /b Nhesus tclao, Krkw vuh wcnhi lwevleun wrli luset?
/p nčí·sas təlá·ɔ, "kéku=háč wénči-luwíhəlian 'wé·li-lə́s·i·t'?
/t Jesus said to him, 'Why do you call me 'good'?
/k And he said unto him, Why callest thou me good?

	/b	mawsw jwq wrli luset, nul nu Krtanitwet.
	/p	má·wsu šúkw wé·li-lə́s·i·t, nál ná ke·tanət·ó·wi·t.
	/t	There is only one who is good; that is God.
	/k	there is none good but one, that is, God:

	/b	Jwqh kutu tumekrunc rvalumakumek pumawswakunif,
	/p	šúkw=č káhta-təmi·k·é·ane ehaləmá·kami·k pəma·wsəwá·k·anink,
	/t	But if you want to enter eternal life,
	/k	but if thou wilt enter into life,

	/b	kulrluntumuh nc xwi aptwnakun.	[⟨-umuh⟩ for ⟨-umunh⟩]
	/p	kkəle·lə́ntamən=č nə́ xúwi-a·pto·ná·k·an."	
	/t	you must keep the commandments."	[singular form]
	/k	keep the commandments.	

Mt 19.18	/b	Tulkw ta vuh rlenako?	
	/p	tə́lku, "tá=háč e·li·ná·k·ɔ?"	
	/t	He said to him, "Which ones?"	['ones': *lit.*, 'one', as in Mt 19.17]
	/k	He saith unto him, Which?	

	/b	Nhesus tclao,
	/p	nčí·sas təlá·ɔ,
	/t	Jesus said to him,
	/k	Jesus said, ...

Mk 10.19.	/b	Kwatwn ct nc qvetulitwakun.
	/p	"ko·wá·to·n=ét nə́ khwitələt·əwá·k·an.
	/t	"You must know the law.
	/k	Thou knowest the commandments,

Mt 19.18	/b	Kahi nvelwrvun, Kahi manwxqrrvun,
	/p	'káči nhiləwé·han; káči manuxkwe·é·han;
	/t	'Do not commit murder; do not take another man's wife;
	/k	... Thou shalt do no murder, Thou shalt not commit adultery,

	/b	Kahi kumwtkrvun, kahi kulwnrvun…
	/p	káči kəmo·tké·han; káči kəlo·né·han;
	/t	do not steal; do not lie;
	/k	Thou shalt not steal, Thou shalt not bear false witness,

Mk 10.19	/b	Kahi kevokrvun,
	/p	káči ki·hɔké·han;
	/t	do not cheat people;
	/k	Defraud not,

Mt 19.19 /b Xifwrlum kwx ok kavrs,
/p xinkwé·ləm kó·x ɔ́·k kkáhe·s;
/t respect your father and your mother.
/k Honour thy father and mother:

Mt 19.19 /b ktulkeqih avolan rlafwmut rlkeqi avolut kvaky.
/p ktəlkí·kwi-=č -ahɔ́·la·n e·lankó·mat, e·lkí·kwi-ahɔ́·lat khák·ay.'"
/t You must love your relative as much as you love yourself.'"
/k and, Thou shalt love thy neighbour as thyself.

Mt 19.20 /b Nu skenw tclapani Nrvlaleun, wrmi ncni ntclsen trfteteanc nwhi;
/p ná skínnu təláp·ani, "nehəlá·lian, wé·mi nɔ́ni ntɔ́lsi·n tenkti·t·iá·ne núči.
/t The young man said to him, "Master, I have done all of that since I was little.
/k The young man saith unto him, All these things have I kept from my youth up:

/b krkw vuh heh nrsko ntclsei?
/p kéku=háč čí·č né·skɔ ntəlsí·i?"
/t What have I still not yet done?"
/k what lack I yet?

Mk 10.21 /b Nhesus nuni puntufc pwunaopani, ok tolumi avolapani, talao,
/p nčí·sas nɔ́ni pəntánke, pwənaɔ́·p·ani, ɔ́·k tɔ́ləmi-ahɔ·láp·ani, təlá·ɔ,
/t When Jesus heard it, he looked at him, and he began to love him, and said to him,
/k Then Jesus beholding him loved him, and said unto him,

Lk 18.22 /b heh kwtrnaoki, nrlumu ktclsei.
/p "čí·č kwət·ennáɔhki né·ləma ktəlsí·i.
/t "There is still one thing you have not yet done.
/k Yet lackest thou one thing:

Mt 19.21 /b Kavtu pavkunhi luseanc kmyh mvalumakrn wrmi cntxi krkw wlataon,
/p káhta-pahkánči-ləs·iáne, kəmái-=č -mhalamák·e·n wé·mi éntxi- kéku -wəlá·taɔn.
/t If you want to be perfect, you must go and sell everything you have.
/k ... If thou wilt be perfect, go and sell that thou hast,

/b ktukvamaonh krtumaksehek,
/p ktakhamáɔ·n=č ke·t·əma·ksí·č·i·k.
/t You must distribute it to the poor.
/k and give to the poor,

/b nuh kpan, kwrtunimunh ktajwetrvasekum
/p ná=č kpá·n; kəwe·t·ənɔ́mən=č †kta·š·əwi·teha·sí·k·əm.
/t Then you must come, and you shall get your recompense(?).
/k and thou shalt have treasure in heaven:

/b knaolih.
/p kəná·ɔli=č."
/t You must follow me."
/k and come and follow me.

Mt 19.22, Lk 18.23
/b Jwq nu skenw nc rlsitufc, ave jerluntumwp
/p šúkw ná skínnu nɔ́ e·lsət·ánke, áhi-ši·e·lɔ́ntamo·p,
/t But when the young man heard that, he was very upset
/l But when the young man heard that saying he was very sorrowful,

/b alumi mavtrluntumwxwr,   [⟨mwx⟩ for ⟨mwwx⟩ (Lk 10.17)]
/p áləmi-mahte·ləntaməwó·x·we·,
/t and went away feeling bad,
/l and went away grieved;

/b rli ave avopretup ok xifwi nevlatamwp.
/p é·li-áhi-ahɔ·p·e·í·t·əp, ɔ́·k xínkwi-nihəlá·t·amo·p.
/t for he was very rich and owned a great deal.
/l for he was very rich, and had great possessions.

Lk 18.24 /b Nhesus nrfc tcli avi jerluntumulen,
/p nčí·sas nénke tɔ́li-áhi-ši·e·ləntamɔ́li·n,
/t When Jesus saw that he was very upset,
/k And when Jesus saw that he was very sorrowful, ...

Mk 10.23 /b nu okai tulifwrxenun, tclao rkrkemahi,
/p ná ɔ·ká·i təlinkwe·x·í·nən, təlá·ɔ e·k·e·ki·má·č·i,
/t he then looked around and said to his disciples,
/l he looked round about, and saith unto his disciples, ...

Mt 19.23 /b Kvehei ktclwvmw,
/p "khičí·i ktəllúhəmɔ,
/t "I tell you truly,
/kl Verily I say unto you,

/b krvlu avhifih tumekrn osavkamrei sakemaokun.   [⟨osav-‖kamrei⟩]
/p kéhəla ahčínki=č təmí·k·e·n ɔ·s·ahkame·í·i-sa·k·i·ma·ɔ́·k·an."
/t It will be really difficult to enter the kingdom of heaven."
/kl That a rich man shall hardly enter into the kingdom of heaven.

Mk 10.24 /b Rkrkemahi kanjrluntamwpanek rli nc lwrlet.
(p. 139) /p e·k·e·ki·má·č·i kanše·ləntamɔ́·p·ani·k é·li- nɔ́ -luwé·li·t.
/t His disciples were astonished because he said that.
/k And the disciples were astonished at his words.

Text, Transcription, and Translation

/b Jwq Nhesus lupi tclapani,
/p šúkw nčí·sas lápi təlá·p·ani,
/t But Jesus again said to them,
/k But Jesus answereth again, and saith unto them,

/b Meminstwq, Ta vuh if lu lukveqi avot
/p "mi·mə́nsto·kw, tá=háč=ínk=láh ləkhíkwi-áhɔt
/t "Children, how hard do you imagine it is
/k Children, how hard is it

/b nrkatufek avoprokun vwtumekrnro li Krtanitwet sokemaokunif?
/p ne·ka·t·ánki·k ahɔ·p·e·ɔ́·k·an wtəmi·k·e·né·ɔ lí ke·tanət·ó·wi·t sɔ·k·i·ma·ɔ́·k·anink?
/t for those who depend on wealth to enter God's kingdom?
/k for them that trust in riches to enter into the kingdom of God!

Mt 19.24 /b Luvupu ktulunro, alwe a apwi kcmil punhe li rjkunj cntu pqwset
/p lahápa ktəlləné·ɔ, aləwí·i á·p·əwi- kéməl -pə́nči· lí é·škanš énta-pkwə́s·i·t
/t Suppose I tell you: it is easier for a camel to enter the eye ("hole") of a needle
/k And again I say unto you, It is easier for a camel to go through the eye of a needle,

/b rlkeqi apwatuk rvopret vwtumekrn li Krtanitwet sokemaokunif,
/p e·lkí·kwi-a·p·əwát·ək ehɔ·p·é·i·t wtəmí·k·e·n lí ke·tanət·ó·wi·t sɔ·k·i·ma·ɔ́·k·anink."
/t than (how easy) it is for a rich man to enter God's kingdom."
/k than for a rich man to enter into the kingdom of God.

Mt 19.25 /b rkrkematpani puntamuletc ave unhi kanjrluntumwpanek,
/p e·k·e·ki·ma·tpáni pəntaməlí·t·e, áhi-ánči-kanše·ləntamó·p·ani·k.
/t When his disciples heard it, they were even more astonished.
/k When his disciples heard it, they were exceedingly amazed, ...
/k And they were astonished out of measure, ... (Mk 10.26)
/l ... they were exceedingly amazed, and astonished out of measure, ...

Mk 10.26 /b nevlahi litwpanek, awrn nc va mct kuski eku pr?
/p nihəláči lət·ó·p·ani·k, "awé·n=néh=á·m=ét káski- íka -pé·?"
/t They said among themselves, "Who would possibly be able to get there?"
/k ... saying among themselves, Who then can be saved?

Mk 10.27 /b Jwq Nhesus eku rlvwqrtc tclapani,
/p šúkw nčí·sas íka e·lhukwé·t·e, təlá·p·ani,
/t But when Jesus turned to them, he said to them,
/k And Jesus looking upon them saith,

Lk 18.27 /b Krkw b cntu lawset aly luset, Krtanitwet ta toly lusewun.
/p "kéku yú entalá·wsi·t á·lai-lə́s·i·t, ke·tanət·ó·wi·t tá=á· tɔ́·lai-ləs·í·wən.
/t "Things mankind is unable to do, God would not be unable to do.
/k The things which are impossible with men are possible with God.

Mk 10.27 /b B cntu lawset ta koski nevlahi nc lisewun
/p yú entalá·wsi·t tá=á· kóski- nihəláči nə́ -ləs·í·wən,
/t Mankind would not be able to do it by themselves,
/k With men it is impossible,

/b jwq Krtanitwet mutu nc tclsewun,
/p šúkw ke·tanət·ó·wi·t máta nə́ təlsí·wən,
/t but God is not that way,
/k but not with God:

/b rli Krtanitwet kuski wrmi krkw luset.
/p é·li- ke·tanət·ó·wi·t -káski- wé·mi kéku -ləs·i·t."
/t since God can do everything."
/k for with God all things are possible.

Mt 19.27 /b Nu Petul tclan,
/p ná †pí·təl tə́la·n,
/t Then Peter said to him,
/kl Then [answered] Peter [and] said unto him,

/b nelwnu wrmi krkw nukavtumunrn, naolilrf,
/p "ni·ló·na wé·mi kéku nnəkahtəmə́ne·n, na·ɔlə́lenk.
/t "*We* left everything when we followed you.
/kl [Behold,] we have forsaken all, and followed thee;

/b krkwh vuh nmjinumvwmnu?   [⟨nmjin-⟩ for ⟨nmijin-⟩]
/p kéku=č=háč nəməš·ənəmhúmənа?"
/t What will we get?"
/k what shall we have therefore?

Mt 19.28 /b Tclao
/p təlá·ɔ,
/t He said to them,
/k And Jesus said unto them,

/b kelwu cntxi naolerq li wuski kejekwakunif; ktclwvmw,
/p "ki·ló·wa éntxi-na·ɔlíe·kw lí wə́ski-ki·š·i·k·əwá·k·anink, ktəllúhəmɔ,
/t "All you who follow me to the new birth, I tell you,
/k Verily I say unto you, That ye which have followed me, in the regeneration

/b Wrqesif Linw lumutavpetc cntuh xifwrlumwkset,
/p we·k·wí·s·ink lə́nu ləmatahpí·te énta-=č -xinkwe·ləmúkwsi·t,
/t when the man who is the Son sits in the place where he will be glorified,
/k when the Son of man shall sit in the throne of his glory,

/b krpwuh tclcn ok neju lclumutuvpifi ktapavpevmw,

/p ké·pəwa=č télən ɔ́·k ní·š·a lehələmatahpínki kta·pahpíhəmɔ.
/t you also will sit on twelve seats.
/k ye also shall sit upon twelve thrones,

/b ktuntuh krnavkevanro nrk tclcn ok neju cntxakrehek Isliluk.
/p ktə́nta-=č -ke·nahki·ha·né·ɔ né·k télən ɔ́·k ní·š·a entxa·ke·í·č·i·k †isəlɔ́lak.
/t There you shall oversee the twelve tribes of Israelites.
/k judging the twelve tribes of Israel.

Mk 10.29 /b Ok kvehe ktclwvmw, awrnh futifc wekehi, jitu wemavtu,
/p ɔ́·k khičí·i ktəllúhəmɔ, awé·n=č nkat·ínke wi·k·í·č·i, ší=tá wí·mahta,
/t And I tell you truly, if anyone shall leave his houses, or his brothers,
/k ... Verily I say unto you, There is no man that hath left house, or brethren,

/b jitu vwtwxqrbmu, jitu kovrsu, jitu wehrohi jitu wunehanu, jitu toke,
/p ší=tá wtuxkwé·yəma, ší=tá kɔhé·s·a, ší=tá wi·č·e·ɔ́·č·i, ší=tá wəni·č·á·na, ší=tá tɔ́·ki,
/t or his sisters, or his mother, or his wife, or his children, or his land,
/k or sisters, or father, or mother, or wife, or children, or lands,

/b wunhi ne ok ntaptwnakun,
/p wə́nči ní· ɔ́·k nta·pto·ná·k·an,
/t because of me and my word,
/k for my sake, and the gospel's,

Lk 18.29 /b ok rli Krtanitwet sokemaokun,
/p ɔ́·k é·li ke·tanət·ó·wi·t sɔ·k·i·ma·ɔ́·k·an,
/t and for the sake of God's kingdom,
/k ... for the kingdom of God's sake,

Mk 10.30 /b ta kuski mutu mjinamwi, kwtapxki txun nuni txi b tali cntu lawsif,
/p tá=á· káski- máta -məšənəmó·wi kwət·á·pxki txɔ́n nə́ni txí yú táli entalá·wsink,
/t he would not fail to get a hundred times the amount in this world,
/k But he shall receive an hundredfold now in this time,

/b wekwavmul, ok wemavtul, ok vwtwxqrbmul, ok kovrsul, ok wunehanul,
/p wi·k·əwáhəmal, ɔ́·k wí·mahtal, ɔ́·k wtuxkwé·yəmal, ɔ́·k kɔhé·s·al, ɔ́·k wəni·č·á·nal,
/t of houses, and his brothers, and his sisters, and his mother, and his children,
/k houses, and brethren, and sisters, and mothers, and children,

/b ok vaki, vapi sukwelacntwakun   [⟨cnt⟩ for ⟨cvt⟩]
/p ɔ́·k hák·i, hápi sak·wi·laehtəwá·k·an.
/t and land, along with persecutions.
/k and lands, with persecutions;

	/b	okh ekali li nevlatum mutu weqrk pumawswakun.
	/p	ó·k=č íkali lí-nihəlá·t·am máta wí·kwe·k pəma·wsəwá·k·an.
	/t	And going there he shall have life that has no end.
	/k	and in the world to come eternal life.
Mk 10.31.	/b	Jwq xrli nekanexifek vwtcfh avpwuk;
	/p	šúkw xé·li ni·k·a·ni·x·ínki·k wténk=č ahpúwak,
	/t	But many that are ahead shall be behind,
	/k	But many that are first shall be last;
	/b	ok vwtfc rpehek nekaneh avpwuk. [⟨vwtfc⟩ for ⟨vwtcf⟩]
	/p	ó·k wténk e·p·í·č·i·k ni·k·a·ní·i=č ahpúwak.
	/t	and ones behind shall be ahead.
	/k	and the last first.
Mt 20.1	/b	Rli lro osavkamri sokemaokun, mulaji linw ‖ cvakevrt, [⟨sok-⟩ ('his') for ⟨sak-⟩]
	/p	é·li lé·w ɔ·s·ahkamé·i-sa·k·i·ma·ó·k·an málahši lə́nu ehhakí·he·t.
	/t	For the kindom of heaven is like a man who is a farmer.
	/k	For the kingdom of heaven is like unto a man that is an householder,
(p. 140)	/b	alupae khetc my alwkalatc mcmekumoselehi li tokevakunif.
	/p	alap·a·í·i kčí·t·e, mái-alo·ka·lá·t·e mehəmi·kəmɔ·s·i·lí·č·i lí tɔ·ki·há·k·anink.
	/t	when he goes out early in the morning, going to hire workers for his field.
	/k	which went out early in the morning to hire labourers into his vineyard.
Mt 20.2	/b	Mrhi keji nuxkwntetetc tclih kwti monetut melan kwti kejqc,
	/p	mé·či kíši-naxkuntihtí·t·e, tə́li-=č kwə́t·i mɔní·t·ət -mí·la·n kwə́t·i kí·škwe,
	/t	After he has agreed with them that he will give them one "penny" for one day,
	/k	And when he had agreed with the labourers for a penny a day,
	/b	nu tolwkalan li tokevakunif.
	/p	ná tɔlo·ká·la·n lí tɔ·ki·há·k·anink.
	/t	he then sends them to his field to work.
	/k	he sent them into his vineyard.
Mt 20.3	/b	Avpami lrlai li spevlr nu lupi quthen,
	/p	ahpá·mi le·lá·i lí-spíhəle·, ná lápi kwə́č·i·n.
	/t	The sun goes about halfway up, and then he goes out again.
	/k	And he went out about the third hour,
	/b	peli nrr li rvcntu mvalumaotif mutu krkw mekintumulehi,
	/p	pí·li né·e· lí ehə́nta-mhalamá·ɔhtink máta kéku mi·kəntaməlí·č·i.
	/t	He sees some others in the marketplace who are not doing any work.
	/k	and saw others standing idle in the marketplace,

Mt 20.4
/b tclao krpwu ok vakevakunif aq,
/p təláˑɔ, "képəwa ɔ́ˑk hakiˑháˑkˑanink áˑkw.
/t He says to them, "You also, go to the field.
/k And said unto them; Go ye also into the vineyard,

/b kwlrnvwlvwmwh.
/p koˑleˑnhoˑlhúmɔ=č."
/t I'll pay you well."
/k and whatsoever is right I will give you.

/b Nu eku tonro.
/p ná íka tɔˑnéˑɔ.
/t Then they go there.
/k And they went their way.

Mt 20.5
/b Lupi paxaqrkc, ok lrlai cntakc lupi nanc tclsen.
/p lápi paˑxhakwéˑkˑe, ɔ́ˑk leˑláˑi entáˑkˑe lápi, ná=nə tálsiˑn.
/t Again at noon, and when the sun was halfway (down) again, he does the same thing.
/k Again he went out about the sixth and ninth hour, and did likewise.

Mt 20.6
/b Lupi mrhi ave loqetekc krhetc, lupi peli nrr mutu krkw mekuntumulehi;
/p lápi méˑči áhi-lɔˑkˑwiˑtˑíˑkˑe, keˑčˑíˑtˑe, lápi pɪ́ˑli néˑeˑ máta kéku miˑkəntaməlɪ́ˑčˑi.
/t Again after it was late in the early evening, when he went out, he saw still others who were not doing any work.
/k And about the eleventh hour he went out, and found others standing idle,

/b Tclao, Krkw vuh wcnhi kwti kejqc b nepyerq?
/p təláˑɔ, "kéku=háč wénči- kwəti-kɪ́ˑškwe yú -niˑpˑaɪ́eˑkw?
/t He says to them, "Why are you standing here all day?"
/k and saith unto them, Why stand ye here all the day idle?

Mt 20.7
/b Tclawao, rlik mutu awrn alwkalkwrf.
/p təlawwáˑɔ, "éˑli-=k máta awéˑn -aloˑkaˑlkóˑwenk."
/t They say to him, "Well, because no one hired us."
/k They say unto him, Because no man hath hired us.

/b Tclao, krpwu, ok eku aq vakevakunif,
/p təláˑɔ, "képəwa ɔ́ˑk íka áˑkw hakiˑháˑkˑanink.
/t He says to them, "You, too, go to the field also.
/k He saith unto them, Go ye also into the vineyard;

/b wlrnvaovtwakunh kmujinumvwmw.
/p wəleˑnhaˑɔhtəwáˑkˑan=č kəməšˑənəmhúmɔ."
/t You shall receive good pay.
/k and whatsoever is right, that shall ye receive.

Mt 20.8 /b Mrhi rlumi peskrkc, nu wrtvakevakunet, tulan rvlrkvekaqki,
/p mé·či é·ləmi-pi·ské·k·e, ná we·thaki·há·k·ani·t tóla·n ehəle·khi·k·á·kwki,
/t After it was getting dark, then the owner of the field said to his bookkeeper,
/k So when even was come, the lord of the vineyard saith unto his steward,

/b Ntwm mekumosehek, ok rnvaw
/p "ntó·m mi·kəmɔ·s·í·č·i·k, ó·k é·nhaw,
/t "Call the workers and pay them,
/k Call the labourers, and give them their hire,

/b Vwtcf wunhi mekumosehek vetami Kxunkih nrtami mekumosehek.
/p wténk wə́nči-mi·kəmɔ·s·í·č·i·k hítami; kxántki=č né·tami-mi·kəmɔ·s·í·č·i·k.
/t the ones that worked last, first; and finally the first workers.
/k beginning from the last unto the first.

Mt 20.9 /b Nrk loqunei nwhi mekumosehek pravtetc,
/p né·k lɔ·k·wəní·i núči mi·kəmɔ·s·í·č·i·t·e,
/t When those who began working in the evening came,
/k And when they came that were hired about the eleventh hour,

/b wrmi monetutu mujinamwk.
/p wé·mi mɔni·t·ɔ́t·a məšə́nəmo·k.
/t they all got small coins.
/k they received every man a penny.

Mt 20.10 /b Jwq pravtetc nrk vetami mekumosehek,
/p šúkw pe·ahtí·t·e né·k hítami mi·kəmɔ·s·í·č·i·k,
/t But when the first workers came,
/k But when the first came,

/b letrvrok alweh ntuntxi mjinumwvnu,
/p li·t·e·hé·ɔk, "aləwí·i=č ntə́ntxi-məšənəmúhəna."
/t they thought they would get more (lit., "We will get more.").
/k they supposed that they should have received more;

/b jwq wrmi kwtrnaovki txi monetutu mjinumwk.
/p šúkw wé·mi kwət·ennáɔhki txí mɔni·t·ɔ́t·a məšə́nəmo·k.
/t But they all got the same amount of small coins.
/k and they likewise received every man a penny.

Mt 20.11 /b Mrhi mrjinumvetetc, honemawao wrtvakevaokunelehi,   [⟨-vaok-⟩ for ⟨-vak-⟩]
/p mé·či me·š·ənəmhití·t·e, čɔni·mawwá·ɔ we·thaki·ha·k·ani·lí·č·i,
/t After they received it, they criticized the owner of the field,
/k And when they had received it, they murmured against the goodman of the house,

Mt 20.12 /b tclawao,
/p təlawwá·ɔ,
/t saying to him,
/k Saying,

/b Bk vwtcf wcnhi mekumosehek kwti awlif jwq svaki mekumoswuk
/p "yó·k wténk wénči-mi·kəmɔ·s·í·č·i·k kwə́t·i á·wəlink šúkw sháki-mi·kəmɔ́·s·əwak,
/t "These who worked last only worked for one hour,
/k These last have wrought but one hour,

/b na wrnu ktupsqrluman nelwnu rlrlumerf,
/p ná wé·na ktəpskwé·ləma·n ni·ló·na e·le·ləmíenk,
/t but still you consider them equal to *us*,
/k and thou hast made them equal unto us,

/b taoni kwti kejqc cntu kjluntrk ntuntu wejuksevnu.   [⟨kjluntrk⟩ for ⟨kjuluntrk⟩]
/p tá·ɔni kwə́ti-kí·škwe énta-kšəlánte·k ntə́nta-wi·šəksíhəna."
/t although we worked hard all day in the heat."
/k which have borne the burden and heat of the day.

Mt 20.13 /b Tclao, Nhwterstwq, takw tu keolilwvwmw;
/p təlá·ɔ, "nčo·t·ié·sto·kw, takó·=tá kki·ɔləlo·húmɔ.
/t He said to them, "My friends, I didn't cheat you.
/k But he answered one of them, and said, Friend, I do thee no wrong:

/b mutu vuh knaxkwmevwmwp nanvkwti monetut tu wunhi?
/p máta=háč kənaxko·mi·húmɔ·p ṭnənk·wə́ti moní·t·ət=tá wə́nči?
/t Did you not each agree with me for one penny?
/k didst not thou agree with me for a penny?

Mt 20.14 /b Wrtunimwq nrvlatamrq, alumskaq;
/p we·t·ənə́mo·kw nehəlá·t·ame·kw, aləmska·kw.
/t Take what belongs to you and go.
/k Take that thine is, and go thy way:

/b rli nrk vwtcf wunhi pahek, kwtrnaoki ktuntxi melwvmw.
/p é·li né·k wténk wə́nči-pá·č·i·k kwət·ennáɔhki ktə́ntxi-millúhəmɔ.
/t For I give you and those that came last the same amount.
/k I will give unto this last, even as unto thee.

Mt 20.15 /b Mutu vuh wlexunwi lclpeu ntcletwn nrvlatumu?
/p máta=háč wəli·x·ənó·wi lelpía ntəlí·to·n nehəlá·t·ama?
/t Is it not right for me to do what I please with what I own?
/k Is it not lawful for me to do what I will with mine own?

	/b	Kmuhi vuh punarlumevmw, rli ne wletrvau?
	/p	kəmáči-=háč -pənae·ləmíhəmɔ, é·li- ní· -wəli·t·e·há·a?
	/t	Do you think ill of me because I am good-hearted?
	/k	Is thine eye evil, because I am good?

Mt 20.16 /b Puna vwtcf rpehek nekaneh avpwuk, ⟨ne-‖kaneh⟩
　　　　 /p pənáh, wténk e·p·í·č·i·k, ni·k·a·ní·i=č ahpúwak,
　　　　 /t Well, as for the last, they shall be first,
　　　　 /k So the last shall be first,

Mt 20.16　/b ok nekane rpehek vwtcfh avpwuk;
(p. 141)　 /p ɔ́·k ni·k·a·ní·i e·p·í·č·i·k, wténk=č ahpúwak.
　　　　　/t and the first, they shall be last.
　　　　　/k and the first last:

	/b	rli xrli wcnhemunhek jwq tatxetwuk pepenwnhek.
	/p	é·li xé·li wenči·mə́nči·k, šúkw ta·txí·t·əwak pi·p·i·núnči·k."
	/t	For many are the ones called, but few are the ones chosen."
	/k	for many be called, but few chosen.

Chapter 82 (pp. 141-144). (John 11.1-57)

Jn 11.1　/b Linw mu palswp, lwcnswp Lasulus. Pctuni wtrnif tali,
　　　　 /p lə́nu=máh pá·lso·p, luwénso·p †lá·səlas, †pétəni o·t·é·nink táli.
　　　　 /t There was a man who was sick, named Lazarus, in the town of Bethany.
　　　　 /kl Now a certain man was sick, named Lazarus, of Bethany,

	/b	ok eku avpelwp vwtwxqrbmu Mrlesu ok xwesumusu masesu.
	/p	ɔ́·k íka ahpí·lo·p wtuxkwé·yəma, me·lí·s·a ɔ́·k xwi·s·əmə́s·a, ma·sí·s·a.
	/t	And his sisters also lived there, Mary and her younger sister Martha.
	/kl	the town of Mary and her sister Martha.

Jn 11.2　/b (Nul nuni Mrles mpeswn eku rvli jwvmaotup vwsetelet Nhesusu
　　　　 /p (nál náni mé·li·s mpí·s·o·n íka ehəli-šuhəmaɔ́·t·əp wsi·t·í·li·t nči·sás·a,
　　　　 /t (It was the same Mary that had rubbed medicine on Jesus's feet
　　　　 /k (It was that Mary which anointed the Lord with ointment, and wiped his feet with her hair,

	/b	tcli xonsu palselenrp.)
	/p	təli- xɔ́nsa -pa·lsi·lí·ne·p.)
	/t	whose older brother was sick.)
	/k	whose brother Lazarus was sick.)

Jn 11.3　/b Xwesumusu Nhesusif lalwkrmwelw,
　　　　 /p xwi·s·əmə́s·a nči·sás·ink lalo·ke·mwí·lu,

/t His sisters sent a message to Jesus,
/k Therefore his sisters sent unto him,

/b lwrlw, Rvolut palsw.
/p luwé·lu, "ehɔ́·lat pá·lsu."
/t saying, "The one you love is sick."
/k saying, Lord, behold, he whom thou lovest is sick.

Jn 11.4
/b Nhesus nc puntufc lwrp.
/p nčí·sas nə́ pəntánke, lúwe·p,
/t When Jesus heard that, he said,
/k When Jesus heard that, he said,

/b Ta ncni palswakun wunhi ufulwun,
/p "tá=á· nə́ni pa·lsəwá·k·an wwə́nči-ankəló·wən,
/t "The sickness is not because he is dying,
/k This sickness is not unto death,

/b jwqh wunhi nrvkot Krtanitwet tcli xifwi lusen
/p šúkw=č wə́nči-né·ykɔt ke·tanət·ó·wi·t tə́li-xínkwi-lə́s·i·n,
/t but so that it shall be seen that God has great power,
/k but for the glory of God,

/b tclih Krtanitwet Qesu ncni wunhi xifwrlumwqsen.
/p tə́li-=č ke·tanət·ó·wi·t kkwí·s·a nə́ni -wə́nči-xinkwe·ləmúkwsi·n."
/t so that the son of God shall be thought great because of that."
/k that the Son of God might be glorified thereby.

Jn 11.5
/b Nhesus tovolapani Masesu ok xwesumuselct, ok Lasulusu.
/p nčí·sas tɔhɔ·lá·p·ani ma·sí·s·a ɔ́·k xwi·s·əməs·í·li·t, ɔ́·k †la·səlás·a.   (Cf. Jn 11.1.)
/t Jesus loved Martha and her younger sister, and Lazarus.
/k Now Jesus loved Martha, and her sister, and Lazarus.

Jn 11.6
/b Mrhi puntufc tcli palselen;
/p mé·či pəntánke tə́li-pa·lsí·li·n,
/t After he heard that he (the other one) was sick,
/k When he had heard therefore that he was sick,

/b qeaqi nejwquni nanc topen;
/p kwiá·kwi ni·š·ó·k·wəni ná=nə tɔ́p·i·n.
/t he stayed in the same place for two more days.
/k he abode two days still in the same place where he was.

Jn 11.7 /b nu kcnh tclan rkrkemahi, Lupi tu eku atamwq Nhwtewf.
         /p ná kə́nč tə́la·n e·k·e·ki·má·č·i, "lápi=tá íka á·t·amo·kw †nčo·tí·yunk."
         /t Only then did he say to his disciples, "Let's all go again to Judaea."
         /k Then after that saith he to his disciples, Let us go into Judaea again.

Jn 11.8 /b Rkrkemahi tclkw,
         /p e·k·e·ki·má·č·i tə́lku,
         /t His disciples said to him,
         /k His disciples say unto him,

         /b Nrvlalerf kcnh bqc Nhwuk kutu asunu puvkumkwpanek   [⟨Nrvla-|erfkcnhbqc⟩]
         /p "nehəlá·lienk, kə́nč yúkwe nčó·wak kkát·a- ahsə́na -pahkamkó·p·ani·k.
         /t "Master, the Jews here lately wanted to throw stones at you.
         /k Master, the Jews of late sought to stone thee;

         /b lupih vuh eku ktav?
         /p lápi=č=há́č íka ktá?"
         /t Will you go there again?"
         /k and goest thou thither again?

Jn 11.9 /b Nhesus tclao mutu vuh tclcn ok neju awlif svesvaki kejqei?   [⟨svesv-⟩ for ⟨sesv-⟩]
         /p nčí·sas təlá·ɔ, "máta=háč téŀən ɔ́·k ní·š·a á·wəlink sisháki-ki·škwí·i?
         /t Jesus said to them, "Isn't it always day for twelve hours?
         /k Jesus answered, Are there not twelve hours in the day?

         /b awrn kejqune pumuskatc, taa mujexenwi rli oxrrk;
         /p awé·n ki·škwəní·i pəməská·t·e, tá=á· məši·x·i·nó·wi, é·li-ɔ·x·é·e·k.
         /t If someone walks during the day, he won't stumble, because it is light.
         /k If any man walk in the day, he stumbleth not, because he seeth the light of this world.

Jn 11.10 /b Awrn a pumuskatc peskrwune mumjexena,
         /p awé·n=á· pəməská·t·e pi·ske·wəní·i, məmší·x·i·n=á·,
         /t If someone walks at night, he would stumble,
         /k But if a man walk in the night, he stumbleth,

         /b rli mutu vokrf vatrk oxrrk;
         /p é·li- máta hɔ́k·enk -hát·e·k ɔ·x·é·e·k."
         /t because there is no light in his body."
         /k because there is no light in him.

Jn 11.11 /b mrhi nc keji latc
         /p mé·či nə́ kíši-lá·t·e,
         /t After he said that to them,
         /k and after that he saith unto them,

	/b	nu tclan ketesunu Lasulus kae,
	/p	ná tə́la·n, "ki·t·í·s·əna †lá·sələs kaí·,
	/t	then he said to them, "Our friend Lazarus is sleeping,
	/k	Our friend Lazarus sleepeth;

	/b	jwq nmy twkunu rli kaet.
	/p	šúkw nəmái-tó·kəna é·li-kaí·t."
	/t	but I go to wake him up as he sleeps."
	/k	but I go, that I may awake him out of sleep.

Jn 11.12	/b	Nu tclkwn rkrkemahi, wlih lr kaetc.
	/p	ná tə́lko·n e·k·e·ki·má·č·i, "wə́li-=č -lé· kaí·t·e."
	/t	Then his disciples said to him, "It will be good if he sleeps."
	/k	Then said his disciples, Lord, if he sleep, he shall do well.

Jn 11.13	/b	Nukcx rli ufululet wunhi nc lwrn;	[lwrn; / jwq: ⟨lwrnijwq⟩ (but ⟨i⟩ unclear)]
	/p	nə́=ké=x é·li-ankələ́li·t wwə́nči- nə́ -lúwe·n;	
	/t	Well, in fact it was because he (obv.) was dead that he said that;	
	/k	Howbeit Jesus spake of his death:	

	/b	jwq, letrvrok lune ct kae.
	/p	šúkw li·t·e·hé·ɔk, "ləní·i=ét kaí·."
	/t	but they thought he was sleeping in the ordinary way.
	/k	but they thought that he had spoken of taking of rest in sleep.

Jn 11.14	/b	Nu kcnh Nhesus tclan ufulu ta Lasulusu.
	/p	ná kə́nč nčí·sas tə́la·n, "ánkəla=tá †la·səlás·a.
	/t	Only then did Jesus say to them, "Lazarus is dead.
	/k	Then said Jesus unto them plainly, Lazarus is dead.

Jn 11.15	/b	Ok nwlrluntam rli kelwu wunhi, mutu eku avpeo
	/p	ɔ́·k no·le·lə́ntam é·li- (ki·ló·wa wə́nči) máta íka -ahpí·ɔ,
	/t	And I am glad that (because of you) I was not there,
	/k	And I am glad for your sakes that I was not there,

	/b	rli futatumun kwlamvetaenro,
	/p	é·li nkat·á·t·amən ko·la·mhitai·né·ɔ.
	/t	for I want you to believe in me.
	/k	to the intent ye may believe;

	/b	eku tu rtamwq.	[⟨rtamwq⟩ for ⟨atamwq⟩]
	/p	íka=tá á·t·amo·kw."	
	/t	Let's all go there."	['there': or 'to him']
	/k	nevertheless let us go unto him.	

Jn 11.16 /b Nu Tamus rlwcnset kavprs tulan wetesu,
          /p ná †támas, e·ləwénsi·t 'kahpé·s,' tóla·n wi·tí·s·a,
          /t Then Thomas, who was called 'the Twin,' said to his friends,
          /k Then said Thomas, which is called Didymus, unto his fellowdisciples,

          /b bv eku tu atamwq ktclih wimpunrmanrn.   [⟨at-‖amwq⟩]
          /p "yúh, íka=tá á·t·amo·kw, któli-=č -wimpəne·má·ne·n."
          /t "Alright, let's all go there, so that we shall die with him."
          /k Let us also go, that we may die with him.

Jn 11.18 /b Avpami neju mylif Nhelwsulumif wunhi tali lwcntaswp Pctuni.
(p. 142) /p (ahpá·mi ní·š·a máilink †nči·lo·sələmink wónči táli-luwentá·s·o·p †pétəni.) [syntax]
          /t (About two miles from Jerusalem was the place called Bethany.)
          /k Now Bethany was nigh unto Jerusalem, about fifteen furlongs off:

Jn 11.19 /b Krxu Nhwuk wtxawapani Masesu ok Mrlesu rli ufululet xonswao.
          /p ké·x·a nčó·wak o·txawwá·p·ani ma·sí·s·a ó·k me·lí·s·a, é·li-ankəléli·t xɔnsəwá·ɔ.
          /t Several Jews visited Martha and Mary because their older brother was dead.
          /k And many of the Jews came to Martha and Mary, to comfort them concerning their brother.

Jn 11.17 /b Nhesus eku pratc mrhi nrbqunakut li pvokvakrvon.
          /p nčí·sas íka pe·á·t·e, mé·či ne·yo·k·wənák·at lí-phɔkhakéhɔ·n.
          /t When Jesus got there, it had already been four days that he had been buried.
          /k Then when Jesus came, he found that he had lain in the grave four days already.

Jn 11.20 /b Mase mrhi puntufc tcli Nhesus eku pan,
          /p má·si mé·či pəntánke tóli- nčí·sas íka -pá·n,
          /t When Martha heard that Jesus was coming there,
          /k Then Martha, as soon as she heard that Jesus was coming,

          /b jac topesvekaoo,
          /p šá·e tɔ·phishikaó·ɔ.
          /t she went imediately to meet him.
          /k went and met him:

          /b jwq Mrles klumavpwp tali wekwavmif.
          /p šúkw mé·li·s kəlámahpo·p táli wi·k·əwáhəmink.
          /t But Mary sat quietly in the house.
          /k but Mary sat still in the house.

Jn 11.21 /b Masi tclao Nhesusu,
          /p má·si təlá·ɔ nči·sás·a,
          /t Martha said to Jesus,
          /k Then said Martha unto Jesus,

	/b	Nrvlaleun avpeunpanc a, ta ufulwep nuxansu,	[-p n-: ⟨-pn-⟩]
	/p	"nehəlá·lian, ahpianpáne=á·, tá=á· ankəló·wi·p naxánsa.	
	/t	"Master, if you had been there, my older brother would not have died.	
	/k	Lord, if thou hadst been here, my brother had not died.	

Jn 11.22 /b jwq nwatwn
          /p šúkw no·wá·to·n,
          /t But I know,
          /k But I know,

          /b eli bqc wenwumatc Krtanitwet krkw kmelkwn a.
          /p ílli yúkwe wi·nəwamát·e ke·tanət·ó·wi·t kéku, kəmí·lko·n=á·."
          /t that if you ask God for something even now, he would give it to you."
          /k that even now, whatsoever thou wilt ask of God, God will give it thee.

Jn 11.23 /b Nhesus tclao Kxunsh tu amwe.   [-tu am-: ⟨tuam⟩]
          /p nčí·sas təlá·ɔ, "kxáns=č=tá á·mwi·."
          /t Jesus said to her, "Your older brother shall rise up."
          /k Jesus saith unto her, Thy brother shall rise again.

Jn 11.24 /b Masi tclao,
          /p má·si təlá·ɔ,
          /t Martha said to him,
          /k Martha saith unto him,

          /b nwatwn tu tclih amwen amwltifc mukuni kejqekc.
          /p "no·wá·to·n=tá təli-=č -á·mwi·n a·mo·ltínke məkə́ni-ki·škwí·k·e."
          /t "I know that he shall rise up when people all rise up on the last day."
          /k I know that he shall rise again in the resurrection at the last day.

Jn 11.25 /b Nhesus tclao, ne tu amweokun ok pumawswakun;
          /p nčí·sas təlá·ɔ, "ní·=tá a·mwi·ó·k·an ó·k pəma·wsəwá·k·an.
          /t Jesus said to her, "I am resurrection and life.
          /k Jesus said unto her, I am the resurrection, and the life:

          /b awrn wrlamvetaet taonih eufulwp,
          /p awé·n we·la·mhítai·t, tá·ɔni=č i·ánkəlo·p,
          /t Anyone who believes in me, even though they died some time ago,
          /k he that believeth in me, though he were dead,

          /b jwqh lupi lclrxr;
          /p šúkw=č lápi lehəlé·x·e·.
          /t still they shall live again.
          /k yet shall he live:

Jn 11.26 /b ok awrn bqc lclrxrt, wulamvetaetc ta vuji ufulwi.
/p ɔ́·k awé·n yúkwe lehəlé·x·e·t wəla·mhitaí·t·e, tá=á· háši ankəlóʼwi.
/t And if anyone living now believes in me, they shall never die.
/k And whosoever liveth and believeth in me shall never die.

/b Kwlamvetamun vuh nuni?
/p ko·la·mhítamən=háč nə́ni?"
/t Do you believe that?"
/k Believest thou this?

Jn 11.27 /b Tclao, kovun Nrvlaleun, nwlamvetamun ktcli Klysten
/p təlá·ɔ, "kɔhán, nehəlá·lian, no·la·mhítamən ktə́li-kəláisti·n,
/t She said to him, "Yes, master, I believe that you are Christ,
/k She saith unto him, Yea, Lord: I believe that thou art the Christ,

/b ktcli Qesumwkwn Krtanitwet rvlwrfup prwh.
/p ktə́li-kkwi·s·əmúk·o·n ke·tanət·ó·wi·t, ehələwénkəp, 'pé·w=č.'"
/t and that you are the son of God, who has always been said to be going to come."
/k the Son of God, which should come into the world.

Jn 11.28 /b Keji nc lwrtc alumskr moi lan mwesu Mrlesu kemei,
/p kíši- nə́ -luwé·t·e, alə́mske·, mɔ́i-lá·n mwí·s·a me·lí·s·a ki·mí·i,
/t After saying this, she left, and she went a told her older sister Mary in secret,
/k And when she had so said, she went her way, and called Mary her sister secretly,

/b tclao Nrvlakofq mrhi pr kwcnhemwq.   [⟨Nrvlakofq⟩ for ⟨Nrvlalkofq⟩]
/p təlá·ɔ, " nehəlá·lkɔnkw mé·či pé·, kəwenčí·mukw."
/t saying to her, "Our master has come and is asking for you."
/k saying, The Master is come, and calleth for thee.

Jn 11.29 /b Nc puntufc jac paswkwep eku rp.
/p nə́ pəntánkc, šá·e pahsúk·wi·p, íka é·p.
/t When she heard that, she immdeiately got up and went to him.
/k As soon as she heard that, she arose quickly, and came unto him.

Jn 11.30 /b Nhesus nrlumu myai wtrnif prep
/p nčí·sas né·ləma mayá·i o·t·é·nink pé·i·p,
/t Jesus had not yet come all the way into the town.
/k Now Jesus was not yet come into the town,

/b qeaqi nanc topenrp Masi cntu feskaotup.
/p kwiá·kwi ná=nə tɔp·í·ne·p má·si énta-nki·skaɔ́·t·əp.
/t He was still in the same place where Martha had met him.
/k but was in that place where Martha met him.

Jn 11.31 /b Nrk Nhwuk wrtxatpanek nrovtetc,
/p né·k nčó·wak we·txa·tpáni·k ne·ɔhtí·t·e,
/t When the Jews that had come to visit her saw
/k The Jews then which were with her in the house, and comforted her, when they saw Mary,

/b tcli Mrles pavswqen alumi khen noolawao,
/p tə́li- mé·li·s -pahsúk·wi·n, -áləmi-kčí·n, nɔ·ɔlawwá·ɔ.
/t Mary get up and start out, they followed her.
/k that she rose up hastily and went out, followed her,

/b lwrok, eku ct r mavhekamekwf my ct eku tali lupuq.
/p luwé·ɔk, "íka=ét é· mahči·k·amí·k·unk; mái-=ét íka -táli-ləpákw."
/t They said, "She must be going to the grave; she must be going to weep there."
/k saying, She goeth unto the grave to weep there.

Jn 11.32 /b Mrles eku Nhesusif pratc
/p mé·li·s íka nči·sás·ink pe·á·t·e,
/t When Mary came to where Jesus was,
/k Then when Mary was come where Jesus was, and saw him,

/b vwsetelet li vakif levlr;
/p wsi·t·í·li·t lí hákink líhəle·.
/t she fell down at his feet.
/k she fell down at his feet,

/b tclao Nrvlaleun, avpeunpanc a ta ufulwep nuxansu.
/p təlá·ɔ, "nehəlá·lian, ahpianpáne=á·, tá=á· ankəló·wi·p naxánsa."
/t She said to him, "Master, if you had been there my brother would not have died."
/k saying unto him, Lord, if thou hadst been here, my brother had not died.

Jn 11.33 /b Nhesus nrotc tcli lupukulen, ok Nhwu.
/p nčí·sas ne·ó·t·e tə́li-ləpák·əli·n, ó·k nčó·wa,
/t When Jesus saw her weeping, and also the Jews,
/k When Jesus therefore saw her weeping, and the Jews also weeping which came with her,

/b Vwtrvif tali muntum ok sukwrluntum.
/p wté·hink táli-mə́ntam, ó·k sak·we·ləntam.
/t he moaned in his heart and was distressed.
/k he groaned in the spirit, and was troubled,

Jn 11.34 /b Tclao, tavuh ktavlan?
/p təlá·ɔ, "tá=háč ktáhəla·n?"
/t He said to her, "Where have you (sg.) put him?"
/k And said, Where have ye laid him?

	/b	Tclkw wuntux al puna.
	/p	tə́lku, "wə́ntax á·l; pənáh."
	/t	She said to him, "Come along and see."
	/k	They said unto him, Lord, come and see.

Jn 11.35
- /b Nhesus lupuq.
- /p nčí·sas ləpákw.
- /t Jesus wept.
- /k Jesus wept.

Jn 11.36
- /b Nhwuk lwrpanek punw, tulkeqi avolan!
- /p nčó·wak luwé·p·ani·k, "pənó· təlkí·kwi-ahɔ́·la·n.
- /t The Jews said, "See how much he loved him.
- /k Then said the Jews, Behold how he loved him!

Jn 11.37
- /b Mutu vuh wuni linw aeavi taxkifwrnat krkrpifolehi,
- /p máta=háč wáni lə́nu, a·yáhi-ta·xkinkwé·na·t ke·k·e·p·inkɔ·lí·č·i,
- /t Wouldn't this man, who previously opened the eyes of blind people,
- /k And some of them said, Could not this man, which opened the eyes of the blind,

- /b mutu vuh a ok vwtrpi lusewun wunhi a mutu ufulwkup nuku linwu? [⟨lu-‖sewun⟩]
- /p máta=háč=á· ɔ́·k wtépi-ləs·í·wən wə́nči-=á· máta -ankəlɔ́·k·əp náka lə́nəwa?"
- /t wouldn't he also be up to making it so that this man wouldn't die?"
- /k have caused that even this man should not have died?

Jn 11.38
(p. 143)
- /b Nc wunhi Nhesus lupi muntamun tali vwtrvif,
- /p nə́ wwə́nči- nčí·sas lápi -mə́ntamən táli wté·hink.
- /t Hearing that, Jesus again moaned in his heart.   [*lit.*, 'Because of that']
- /k Jesus therefore again groaning in himself

- /b eku pr mavhekamekwf.
- /p íka pé· mahči·k·amí·k·unk.
- /t And he went to the grave.
- /k cometh to the grave. [It was a cave, and a stone lay upon it.]

Jn 11.39
- /b Nhesus lwr, Pale linumwq b avsun.
- /p nčí·sas lúwe·, "palí·i lə́nəmo·kw yú ahsə́n."
- /t Jesus said, "You people, take away this stone."
- /k Jesus said, Take ye away the stone.

- /b Masi wrxasetup nrl rfululehi, tclao   [⟨wrxasetup⟩ for ⟨wrxansetup⟩]
- /p má·si, we·x·ansí·t·əp né·l enkələlí·č·i, təlá·ɔ,
- /t Martha, the younger sister of the man who was dead, said to him,
- /k Martha, the sister of him that was dead, saith unto him,

/b Nrvlaleun mrhi ct hemaqsw rli mrhi nrbqwnakut.
/p "nehəlá·lian, mé·či=ét či·má·kwsu, é·li mé·či ne·yo·k·wənák·at."
/t "Master, he must already be stinking, as it has been four days."
/k Lord, by this time he stinketh: for he hath been dead four days.

Jn 11.40
/b Nhesus tclao Mutu vuh ktclwi
/p nčí·sas təlá·ɔ, "máta=háč ktəlló·wi,
/t Jesus said to her. "Didn't I tell you,
/k Jesus saith unto her, Said I not unto thee,

/b wlamvetaeunch knrmunh Krtanitwet moxifwrlumwqswakun?
/p 'wəla·mhitaiáne=č, kəné·mən=č ke·tanət·ó·wi·t mɔx·inkwe·ləmukwsəwá·k·an'?"
/t 'If you believe in me, you shall see God's glory'?"
/k that, if thou wouldest believe, thou shouldest see the glory of God?

Jn 11.41
/b Nu pale totwnro nc avsun.
/p ná palí·i tɔ·to·né·ɔ nə́ ahsə́n.
/t Then they moved the stone away.
/k Then they took away the stone [from the place where the dead was laid].

/b Nu Nhesus tospifwrxenun
/p ná nčí·sas tɔspinkwe·x·í·nən.
/t Then Jesus lifted up his eyes.
/k And Jesus lifted up his eyes,

/b lwr, Nwxa krnamul wuniji ktcli puntaen;
/p lúwe·, "núxa·, kke·ná·məl; wanə́š·i ktə́li-pə́ntai·n.
/t He said, "Father, I give thanks to you; thank you for listening to me.
/k and said, Father, I thank thee that thou hast heard me.

Jn 11.42
/b ok nenwhi nwatwn ktcli nenkumri puntaen;
/p ɔ́·k ni·núči no·wá·to·n ktə́li- nink·əmé·i -pə́ntai·n.
/t And I have long known that you always listen to me.
/k And I knew that thou hearest me always:

/b jwq bk nepaehek nwnhi nc lwrn,
/p šúkw yó·k ni·p·aí·č·i·k núnči- nə́ -lúwe·n,
/t It was just because of the people standing here that I said that,
/k but because of the people which stand by I said it,

/b wunhi a wulamvetamevtet ktcli prtalwkalen.
/p wə́nči-=á· -wəla·mhitamíhti·t, ktə́li-pe·t·alo·ká·li·n."
/t so that they would believe that you sent me."
/k that they may believe that thou hast sent me.

Jn 11.43 /b Mrhi nc lwrtc amufexsw; lwr, Laslus pchi khel!
/p mé·či nə́ luwé·t·e, amankí·xsu, lúwe·, "†lá·səlas, péči-kčí·l!"
/t After saying that, he spoke with a loud voice, saying, "Lazarus, come out!"
/k And when he thus had spoken, he cried with a loud voice, Lazarus, come forth.

Jn 11.44 /b Nu eku tcli khen rfulukup
/p ná íka tə́li-kčí·n enkələk·əp.
/t Then the one that had been dead came out there.
/k And he that was dead came forth,

/b nuxpunc noxul, ok vwsetul kaxpeswu rli wexqrxumuntup, [⟨noxul⟩ for ⟨noxkul⟩]
/p náxpəne nóxkal ó·k wsí·t·al kaxpi·s·əwa, é·li-wi·xkwe·x·əmə́ntəp.
/t His hands and his feet were even tied, as he had been wrapped up.
/k bound hand and foot with graveclothes:

/b kahi wel hetanrk vcmpus wexqrptekrn.
/p káč·i wí·l čí·t·ane·k hémpəs wi·xkwe·ptí·k·e·n.
/t But he had his head tied around with a thick cloth.
/k and his face was bound about with a napkin.

/b Nhesus tclao luxunw, wunhih pumuskat.
/p nčí·sas təlá·ɔ, "laxə́no·, wə́nči-=č -pəmə́ska·t."
/t Jesus said to them, "Untangle him, so that he can walk."
/k Jesus saith unto them, Loose him, and let him go.

Jn 11.45 /b Xrli Nhwuk wrtxatpanek Mrlesu
/p xé·li nčó·wak we·txa·tpáni·k me·lí·s·a,
/t Many Jews that had come to visit Mary,
/k Then many of the Jews which came to Mary,

/b nc rlenumevtetc rlsetup Nhesus, wlamvetaowapani.
/p nə́ e·li·namihtí·t·e e·lsí·t·əp nčí·sas, o·la·mhitaɔwwá·p·ani.
/t when they saw what Jesus did, believed in him.
/k and had seen the things which Jesus did, believed on him.

Jn 11.46 /b Jwq aluntc eku wtxawapani Paluseok,
/p šúkw a·lə́nte íka o·txawwá·p·ani †pa·ləsi·í·ɔk,   [prox. pl. for obv.]
/t But some went to the Pharisees
/k But some of them went their ways to the Pharisees,

/b tohemwlxawapani wrmi rlsetup Nhesus.
/p tɔ·č·i·mo·lxawwá·p·ani wé·mi e·lsí·t·əp nčí·sas.
/t and reported to them everything that Jesus had done.
/k and told them what things Jesus had done.

Jn 11.47
/b Nu wcvevwfrhek, ok Paluseok wcnhemanro cvahemwlselehi,
/p ná wehi·hunké·č·i·k ó·k †pa·ləsi·í·ɔk wwenči·ma·né·ɔ eha·č·i·mo·lsi·lí·č·i.
/t Then the priests and Pharisees called in the members of the council.
/k Then gathered the chief priests and the Pharisees a council,

/b lwrok, Krkwh vuh ntclsevnu?
/p luwé·ɔk, "kéku=č=háč ntəlsíhəna?
/t They said, "What shall we (exc.) do?
/k and said, What do we?

/b rli nu linw xrlrnaoki kanjacvosw?
/p é·li ná lənu xe·lennáɔhki kanšaehó·s·u.
/t For that man does many miracles.
/k for this man doeth many miracles.

Jn 11.48
/b konu a lenaofwc wrmi a awrn wlamvctaoo;
/p kóna=á· li·naónkwe, wé·mi=á· awé·n o·la·mhitaó·ɔ,
/t If we (inc.) leave him alone, everyone would believe him,
/k If we let him thus alone, all men will believe on him:

/b ok a Lomunsuk prok
/p ó·k=á· lo·mánsak pé·ɔk,
/t and the Romans would come
/k and the Romans shall come

/b tobmunro rpeufq ok knevlatamwrokununu.
/p tɔyəməné·ɔ é·p·iankw ó·k kənihəla·t·amwe·ɔ·k·anəna.
/t and take the place where we are and our autonomy.
/k and take away both our place and nation.   [RSV: "our holy place and our nation"]

Jn 11.49
/b Nu mawsw lwcnswp Krupus nul nu nekanexif wcvevwfrs;
/p ná má·wsu luwénso·p †ke·ápas, nál ná ni·k·a·ní·x·ink wehi·húnke·s.
/t The one of them named Caiaphas was the one who was the head priest.
/k And one of them, named Caiaphas, being the high priest that same year,

/b na nckc tclao, Takw tcxi krkw kwatwvwmw
/p ná-néke təlá·ɔ, "takó· téxi kéku ko·wa·to·húmɔ,
/t He said to them at that time, "You know nothing at all.
/k said unto them, Ye know nothing at all,

Jn 11.50
/b ok takw kpunarluntumwunro
/p ó·k takó· kpəna·eləntamo·wəné·ɔ
/t and you do not understand
/k Nor consider

/b li wlexun kwti linw tofuln wunhi vwtunaprebmu [⟨tofuln⟩ for ⟨tofulun⟩]
/p lí-wəlí·x·ən kwə́t·i lə́nu tə́nkələn wə́nči wtənna·p·é·yəma
/t that it is a good thing for one man to die for his people,
/k that it is expedient for us, that one man should die for the people,

/b wunhi a bk rlvakrehek wrmi ufulevtet.
/p wə́nči-=á· yó·k e·lhake·í·č·i·k [máta] wé·mi -ankəlíhti·t." [/máta/ NEG missing]
/t so that these tribes would [not] all perish."
/k and that the whole nation perish not.

Jn 11.51 /b Bni bqc takw nevlahi tclwrwunrp;
/p yó·ni yúkwe takó· nihəláči tələwé·wəne·p,
/t This he did not say on his own,
/k And this spake he not of himself:

/b jwq rli nekanexif wevevwfrs na nckc luveqi [⟨weve-‖vwfrs⟩ for ⟨wcvevwfrs⟩]
/p šúkw é·li-ni·k·a·ní·x·ink wehi·húnke·s ná-néke ləkhíkwi,
/t but as he was the head priest at that time,
/k but being high priest that year,

(p. 144) /b wunhi nekane wuntamunrp tclih Nhesus ufulun wunhi nrl rlvakrelehi
/p wwə́nči- ni·k·a·ní·i -wəntamə́ne·p, tə́li-=č nčí·sas -ánkələn wə́nči né·l e·lhake·i·lí·č·i.
/t thereby prophesying that Jesus would die for that nation.
/k he prophesied that Jesus should die for that nation;

Jn 11.52 /b ok mutu jwq ncni rlvakrelehi,
/p ó·k máta šúkw nə́ni e·lhake·i·lí·č·i, [nə́ni (inan. sg.) s.b. né·li (obv.) (Jn 11.51)]
/t And not only that nation,
/k And not for that nation only,

/b jwq morvooh wrmi tomeminsumu Krtanitwet
/p šúkw mɔ·ehɔ́·ɔ=č wé·mi tɔmi·mə́nsəma ke·tanət·ó·wi·t,
/t but he will gather all the children of God,
/k but that also he should gather together in one the children of God

/b tclih mawswelen tuk tu rpelet. [⟨tuk|tu⟩]
/p tə́li-=č -ma·wso·wí·li·n, tákta e·p·í·li·t.
/t for them to be one, wherever they are.
/k that were scattered abroad.

Jn 11.53 /b Nanc kejqek wunwhi ahemwlscnro tcli a nvelanro.
/p ná=nə kí·škwi·k wənúči-a·č·i·mo·lsi·né·ɔ, tə́li-=á· -nhila·né·ɔ.
/t From that very day on they counseled together in order to kill him.
/k Then from that day forth they took counsel together for to put him to death.

Jn 11.54
/b Nuni wunhi Nhesus mutu heh tumeki nrvkwsewunrp Nhwif prpamskatc,
/p nə́ni wə́nči- nčí·sas máta čí·č təmí·ki -ne·ykwəs·í·wəne·p nčó·wink pep·a·mská·t·e.
/t For that reason Jesus was no longer often seen when walking among the Jews.
/k Jesus therefore walked no more openly among the Jews;

/b pale rp nc wunhi eku rp kexki trkunu
/p palí·i é·p nə́ wə́nči, íka é·p kí·xki té·kəna.
/t He went away from there, going near the wilderness.
/k but went thence unto a country near to the wilderness,

/b vatrp wtrny lwcntasw Eplum,
/p hát·e·p o·t·é·nay luwentá·s·u †í·pələm.
/t There was a town named Ephraim.
/k into a city called Ephraim,

/b nunc toeavpenrp ok rkrkematpani.
/p ná=nə tɔ·yahpí·ne·p, ɔ́·k e·k·e·ki·ma·tpáni.
/t that is where he stayed, along with his disciples.
/k and there continued with his disciples.

Jn 11.55
/b Nhwe lwen, pcxwhevlrp.
/p nčo·wí·i-ló·wi·n pe·x·o·č·íhəle·p.
/t The time for the Jews' Passover was near.
/k And the Jews' passover was nigh at hand:

/b Xrli palc rpehek eku rok Nhelwsulumif
/p xé·li palí·i e·p·í·č·i·k íka é·ɔk †nči·lo·sələmink.
/t Many who lived elsewhere went to Jerusalem.
/k and many went out of the country up to Jerusalem

/b my pelarvoswpanek, nrlumu nc rlrk.
/p mái-pi·laehɔ·s·ó·p·ani·k né·ləma nə́ é·le·k.
/t They went to perform acts of purification before it took place.
/k before the passover, to purify themselves.

Jn 11.56
/b Nu notaopamanro Nhesusu.
/p ná nɔt·aɔ·p·ama·né·ɔ nči·sás·a.
/t Then they looked around for Jesus.
/k Then sought they for Jesus,

/b Nrli nc avpevtet patamwre-kaonif, lutwuk,
/p né·li- nə́ -ahpíhti·t pa·tamwe·i·k·á·ɔnink, lə́t·əwak,
/t While they were in the temple, they said to each other,
/k and spake among themselves, as they stood in the temple,

/b Ktetrvavmw vuh, prwh pcxw cntu metsavtif?
/p "kti·t·e·háhəmɔ=háč, 'pé·w=č péxu énta-mi·tsáhtink?'"
/t "Do you think he will he be coming to the feast?"
/k What think ye, that he will not come to the feast?

Jn 11.57
/b Wcvevwfrhek ok Paluseok mrhi keji lwrpanek
/p wehi·hunké·č·i·k ɔ́·k †pa·ləsi·í·ɔk mé·či kíši-luwé·p·ani·k,
/t The priests and the Pharisees had already said,
/k Now both the chief priests and the Pharisees had given a commandment,

/b awrnh wavatc tutu rpelet, prtahemwh, wunhih tvwnunt.
/p "awé·n=č wwa·há·t·e tətá e·p·í·li·t, pe·t·a·č·í·mu=č, wə́nči-=č -thwə́nənt."
/t "If anyone knows where he is, he must report it, so that he will be arrested."
/k that, if any man knew where he were, he should shew it, that they might take him.

Chapter 83 (pp. 144-145). (Mark 10.32, 35, 36-41; Luke 18.31, 32-33 part, 34; Matthew 20.18-19 part, 20, 23 end, 24 end, 25-28)

Mk 10.32, Lk 18.31
/b Nu Nhesus ok rkrkemahi eku tonro Nhelwsrlum, Nhesus nekanep.
/p ná nčí·sas ɔ́·k e·k·e·ki·má·č·i íka tɔ·né·ɔ †nči·ló·sələm, nčí·sas ni·k·á·ni·p.
/t Then Jesus and his disciples went to Jerusalem, and Jesus went in the lead.
/l And they were in the way going up to Jerusalem; [*Jesus with his disciples,*] and Jesus went before them:

/b Kanjrluntumwpanek nrli naolavtet, ok wejaswpanek.
/p kanše·ləntamó·p·ani·k né·li-na·ɔláhti·t, ɔ́·k wi·š·a·s·ó·p·ani·k.
/t They were amazed as they followed him, and they were afraid.
/l and they were amazed; and as they followed, they were afraid.

/b Nu tamsc nrl tclcn ok neju rkrkematpani pale tulwxolan keme,
/t ná tá·mse né·l télən ɔ́·k ní·š·a e·k·e·ki·ma·tpáni palí·i təló·x·ɔla·n ki·mí·i.
/p Then at some point he took his twelve disciples aside secretly.
/l And he took unto him the twelve disciples apart in the way,

/b nu tolumi lan krkwh rlenuf;
/t ná tóləmi-lá·n kéku=č e·lí·nank.
/p Then he began to tell them what things would happen to him.
/l and began to tell them what things should happen unto him,

Lk 18.31
/b lwr, Puna Nhelwsulumif Ktavnu;
/p lúwe·, "pənáh, †nči·lo·səlɔ́mink ktáhəna.
/t He said, "Now, we are going to Jerusalem.
/l *saying*, Behold, we go up to Jerusalem,

	/b	ekuh paufwc wrmih krkw rlrkvekrvtetup nrvnekanewrwsetpanifu,
	/p	íka=č pa·ánkwe, wé·mi=č kéku e·le·khi·k·ehtí·t·əp nehəni·k·a·ní·i-we·wsi·tpanínka
	/t	When we get there, everything the ancient prophets have written
	/kl	and all things that are written by the prophets

	/b	wunhi linw Wrqesif, pavkunhih lri,
	/p	wə́nči lə́nu we·k·wí·s·ink, pahkánči-=č -lé·.
	/t	about the man who is the Son shall be fulfilled.
	/k	concerning the Son of man shall be accomplished.

Mt 20.18	/b	Rlih melunt wcvevwfrhek ok rvlrkvekrhek,
	/p	é·li-=č -mí·lənt wehi·hunké·č·i·k ó·k ehəle·khi·k·é·č·i·k.
	/t	For he shall be handed over (*lit.*, given) to the priests and the scribes.
	/l	For he shall be delivered unto the chief priests and unto the scribes,

	/b	nrkumaoh qwntrlumawao tclih ufulun.
	/p	ne·k·əmá·ɔ=č kwənte·ləmawwá·ɔ tə́li-=č -ánkələn.
	/t	*They* shall condemn him to die.
	/kl	and they shall condemn him to death,

Mt 20.19	/b	Mwrkunroih Lomunsuk mwelanro
	/p	mwe·k·əne·ó·i=č, lo·mánsak mwi·la·né·ɔ. [prox. pl. for obv.]
	/t	They shall hand him over, giving him to the Romans.
	/kl	And shall deliver him to the Gentiles, ... [B. rearranges these lines from L.]

Lk 18.32	/b	Nuh oesavkevan, ok muvhevan, ok siswkvolan,
	/p	ná=č ɔwisahkí·ha·n, ó·k mahčí·ha·n, ó·k səs·ukhó·la·n,
	/t	Then he shall be mocked, and badly mistreated, and spat upon,
	/l	And he shall be mocked, and spitefully entreated, and spitted on:

	/b	tclih owesavkevanro ok srsrkycvonro,
	/p	tə́li-=č -ɔwisahki·ha·né·ɔ ó·k -se·s·e·k·ayehɔ·né·ɔ,
	/t	for them to mock and whip him,
	/k	to mock, and to scourge,

	/b	okh tcli psuqvetcvonro.
	/p	ó·k=č tə́li-psakhwitehɔ·né·ɔ,
	/t	and for them to crucify him,
	/k	and to crucify him: ...

Lk 18.33	/b	ok srsrkycvon, ok nvelan;
	/p	ó·k -se·s·e·k·ayéhɔ·n, ó·k -nhíla·n.
	/t	and for him to be whipped and killed.
	/kl	And they shall scourge him, and put him to death:

	/b	jwqh ‖ nuxwqunakvakc amwe
	/p	šúkw=č naxo·k·wənakháke, á·mwi·."
	/t	But after three days he shall rise up."
	/kl	and the third day he shall rise again.

Lk 18.34 /b Takw tufiti wnunwstamwunro;
(p. 145) /p takó· tankíti wənəno·stamo·wəné·ɔ.
/t They did not understand even a little of this.
/kl And they understood none of these things:

/b takw kuski eku pchi lupwreok,
/p takó· káski- íka péči -ləpwe·í·ɔk,
/t That degree of intelligence was beyond their abilities,
   (*lit.*, They were unable to be intelligent that far.)
/kl and this saying was hid from them,

/b ok mutu watwunro wcnhi nc lwrt.
/p ó·k máta o·wa·to·wəné·ɔ wénči- nə́ -lúwe·t.
/t and they did not know why he said that.
/kl neither knew they the things which were spoken.

Mt 20.20, Mk 10.35
/b Nu wtxan Srputes wunwnjrbmu ok qeswao, Nhim ok Nhan;
/p ná ó·txa·n †sé·pati·s wənunšé·yəma ó·k kkwi·s·əwá·ɔ, nčím ó·k nčá·n,
/t Then there came to him the mother of Zebedee's children (*lit.*, his child-bearer) and their sons, Jim and John,
/l Then came to him the mother of Zebedee's children with her sons James and John, the sons of Zebedee,

Mt 20.20 /b wenwumao.
/p wwi·nəwamá·ɔ,
/t and one (of them) entreated him,
/l worshipping him, and desiring a certain thing of him:

Mk 10.35 /b Tulao, Qwlu ktulevenrn rli nvakalun.
/p təlá·ɔ, "kwə́la ktəli·hí·ne·n é·li-nhakállan."
/t saying to him, "I wish you would do for us what I need you to do."
/kl saying, Master, we would that thou shouldest do for us whatsoever we shall desire.

Mk 10.36 /b Tulkw Krkw vuh ktetrvuvmw qwlu ntulevkwnrn?
/p tə́lku, "kéku=háč kti·t·e·háhəmɔ, 'kwə́la ntəlihkó·ne·n?'"
/t He said to him, "What do you (pl.) wish for me to do for you?"
/k And he said unto them, What would ye that I should do for you?

Mk 10.37 /b   Tulao, Melenrn wunhih kuski kwti ktunavaonif lumutavpet
/p   təláˑɔ, "miˑlíˑneˑn wə́nči-=č -káski- kwə́tˑi ktənnaˑháˑɔnink -ləmátahpiˑt,
/t   He said to him, "Grant us the means for one of us to be able to sit on your right,
/k   They said unto him, Grant unto us that we may sit, one on thy right hand,

/b   ok kwti kmununheonif tali cntu xifwrlumwqseun.
/p   ɔ́ˑk kwə́tˑi kəmənančíˑɔnink táli énta-xinkweˑləmukwsían."
/t   and the other on your left in the place where you are glorified."
/k   and the other on thy left hand, in thy glory.   [B. omits the mother's repetition.]

Mk 10.38 /b   Jwq Nhesus tulao, Takw kwatwunro krkw wenwrrq.
/p   šúkw nčíˑsas təláˑɔ, "takóˑ koˑwaˑtoˑwənéˑɔ kéku wiˑnəwéˑeˑkw.
/t   But Jesus said to them, "You don't know what you're asking for.
/k   But Jesus said unto them, Ye know not what ye ask:

/b   Ktrpih vuh munrnro neh mrnru,
/p   ktépi-=č=háč -məneˑnéˑɔ níˑ=č meˑnéˑa?
/t   Will you be able to drink what *I* shall drink?
/k   can ye drink of the cup that I drink of?

/b   okh vuh ktrpi li hvopwunukrnro neh rli hvopwunif?
/p   ɔ́ˑk=č=háč ktépi-líˑčɔˑpwənəkˑeˑnéˑɔ níˑ=č éˑli-čhɔ́ˑpwənink?"
/t   And will you be able to be baptized the way *I* shall be baptized?"
/k   and be baptized with the baptism that I am baptized with?

Mk 10.39 /b   tulawao, Ntcpi tu lusenrn.
/p   təlawwáˑɔ, "ntépi-=tá -ləsˑíˑneˑn."
/t   They said to him, "We can."
/k   And they said unto him, We can.

/b   Nhesus tulao. Kveheh tu kmunrnro, mrnruh,
/p   nčíˑsas təláˑɔ, "khičíˑi=č=tá kəməneˑnéˑɔ meˑnéˑa=č,
/t   Jesus said to them, "Truly you shall drink what I shall drink
/k   And Jesus said unto them, Ye shall indeed drink of the cup that I drink of;

/b   ok ktuli hvopwunukrnro neh rli hvopwunif;
/p   ɔ́ˑk ktə́li-čhɔˑpwənəkˑeˑnéˑɔ níˑ=č éˑli-čhɔ́ˑpwənink.
/t   and be baptized the way *I* shall be baptized.
/k   and with the baptism that I am baptized withal shall ye be baptized:

Mk 10.40 /b   jwq a wunhi lumutavpif ntunavaonif ok nmununheonif
/p   šúkw=áˑ wə́nči-ləmátahpink ntənnaˑháˑɔnink ɔ́ˑk nəmənančíˑɔnink,
/t   But the means whereby one sits on my right and on my left
/k   But to sit on my right hand and on my left hand

/b   takw nevlatamwun ntuli a mrkun,
/p   takó· nnihəla·t·amó·wən ntə́li-=á· -mé·k·ən,
/t   I would not have the authority to give,
/k   is not mine to give; ...

Mt 20.23 /b   jwq Nwx cntxi kejextaot.
/p   šúkw nó·x, éntxi-ki·š·i·xtáɔ·t."
/t   but only my father, to as many as he prepares it for."
/kl   ... but *it shall be given to them* for whom it is prepared of my Father.

Mk 10.41 /b   Mrhi nrk tclcn puntumevtetc
/p   mé·či né·k télən pəntamihtí·t·e,
/t   When the (other) ten heard (this),
/kl   And when the ten heard it,

/b   nu tolumi avevkwnro Nhimu ok Nhanu,
/p   ná tóləmi-ahihko·né·ɔ nčíma ó·k nčá·na.
/t   they began to be angered by Jim and John.
/kl   they began to be much displeased with James and John,

Mt 20.24 /b   alumi mutu wulrluntumweok rli nrl neju wemavtwao.
/p   áləmi- máta -wəle·ləntamo·wí·ɔk é·li né·l ní·š·a wi·mahtəwá·ɔ.
/t   They began to be displeased because of their two brothers.
/l   and were moved with indignation against the two brethren.

Mk 10.42 /b   Nu Nhesus notwman wrmi tulao, kwatwnro,
/p   ná nčí·sas nɔt·ó·ma·n wé·mi, təlá·ɔ, "ko·wa·to·né·ɔ,
/t   Then Jesus called them all over and said to them, "You know
/kl   But Jesus called them to him, and saith unto them, Ye know

Mt 20.25 /b   sakemaok b cntu lawsif tolwe luswakunwu torkrnro,
/p   sa·k·i·má·ɔk yú entalá·wsink tɔləwí·i-los·ɔwa·k·anúwa tɔe·ke·né·ɔ,
/t   that the princes of the world use their power,
/kl   that the princes of the Gentiles exercise dominion over them,

/b   ok xifwrlumwqsehek torkrnro lenwavkuswakun.
/p   ó·k xinkwe·ləmukwsí·č·i·k tɔe·ke·né·ɔ linnuwahkəs·əwá·k·an.
/t   and noblemen exercise authority.
/kl   and they that are great exercise authority upon them.

Mt 20.26 /b   Jwq kelwu cntxerq,
/p   šúkw ki·ló·wa entxíe·kw,
/t   But among all of *you*,
/kl   But it shall not be so among you:

/b   awrn kavtu xifwrlumwqsetc tolwkakunenh;
/p   awé·n káhta-xinkwe·ləmukwsí·t·e, tɔlo·ká·k·ani·n=č.
/t   if anyone wants to be a nobleman, he must be a servant,
/kl but whosoever will be great among you, let him be your minister;

Mk 10.44
/b   ok awrn kavtu xwvu alwelusetc, kmaonih tolwkakunenro.
/p   ó·k awé·n káhta- xó·ha -aləwí·i-ləs·í·t·e, kəmá·wəni-=č -tɔlo·ka·k·ani·né·ɔ.
/t   and if anyone wants to have power alone, you must all have him as your servant.
/kl And whosoever of you will be the chiefest among you, shall be servant of all:

Mt 20.28
/b   Rli puna linw Wrqesif, takw wunhi pat tcli a awrn wetavrman,
/p   é·li pənáh lə́nu we·k·wí·s·ink, takó· wə́nči-pá·t tə́li-=á· awé·n -wi·t·a·hé·ma·n,
/t   For, look, the man who is the Son did not come in order for someone to serve him,
/k   Even as the Son of man came not to be ministered unto,

/b   jwq tcli a awrni wetavrman,
/p   šúkw tə́li-=á· awé·ni -wi·t·a·hé·ma·n,
/t   but to serve people,
/k   but to minister,

/b   okh mwrkun wulclrxrokun tclih xrli awrn khwvalkwn.
/p   ó·k=č mwé·k·ən wəlehəle·x·e·ó·k·an, tə́li-=č xé·li awé·n -kčo·há·lko·n.
/t   and he shall give his life so that many will be saved by him.
/k   and to give his life a ransom for many.

Chapter 84 (pp. 145-147). (Luke 19.1-27)

Lk 19.1
/b   Nhesus pratc Nhclikwif, rlumskatc nc wunhi, ‖
/p   nčí·sas pe·á·t·e †nčelikó·wink, e·ləmská·t·e nə́ wə́nči,
/t   When Jesus came to Jericho and went on from there,
/k   And Jesus entered and passed through Jericho.

Lk 19.2
(p. 146)
/b   linw lwcnswp Sakeus,
/p   lə́nu luwénso·p †sa·kí·as.
/t   there was a man named Zacchaeus.
/k   And, behold, there was a man named Zacchaeus,

/b   nul nu nekanexif wrmi cntxevtet moni mcvmarnifek,
/p   nál·ná ni·k·a·ní·x·ink wé·mi entxíhti·t mɔ́ni mehəma·e·nínki·k,
/t   He was the leader among all the tax-collectors,
/k   which was the chief among the publicans,

	/b	ave avoprbp;
	/p	áhi-ahɔ·p·é·yo·p.
	/t	and he was very rich.
	/k	and he was rich.

Lk 19.3 /b tove kavtu nropani Nhesusu rlenaqselet,
　　　　 /p tóhi-káhta-ne·ɔ·p·ani nči·sás·a e·li·na·kwsí·li·t,
　　　　 /t He very much wanted to see what Jesus was like,
　　　　 /k And he sought to see Jesus who he was;

　　　　 /b jwq mutu kuski rli xrli awrn okrkaot ok rli tvakoqtetet.
　　　　 /p šúkw máta káski, é·li- xé·li awé·n -ɔ·ké·kaɔ·t, ɔ́·k é·li-thakɔ·kwtí·t·i·t.
　　　　 /t but he could not, since many people surrounded him, and since he was short.
　　　　 /k and could not for the press, because he was little of stature.

Lk 19.4 /b Nu nekane tujevlan ralet xuxakwf li kuntavkwswv.
　　　　 /p ná ni·k·a·ní·i təš·íhəla·n e·á·li·t, xax·á·kunk lí, kəntahkó·s·u.
　　　　 /t Then he ran on ahead the way he was going, to a sycamore tree, and climbed up.
　　　　 /k And he ran before, and climbed up into a sycomore tree to see him: for he was to pass that way.

Lk 19.5 /b Nhesus eku pratc uspvwqr wunroo.
　　　　 /p nčí·sas íka pe·á·t·e, asphúkwe·, wəne·ɔ́·ɔ,
　　　　 /t When Jesus got there, he looked up and saw him,
　　　　 /k And when Jesus came to the place, he looked up, and saw him, and said unto him,

　　　　 /b Tulao, Sakeus, lavpi lexel.
　　　　 /p təlá·ɔ, "†sa·kí·as, láhpi lí·x·i·l.
　　　　 /t and he said to him, "Zaccheus, hurry up and get down!
　　　　 /k Zacchaeus, make haste, and come down;

　　　　 /b rli rlumih kejqek, eku ntaeavpi wekeun.
　　　　 /p é·li é·ləmi-=č -kí·škwi·k íka ntá·yahpi wí·k·ian."
　　　　 /t For later today I will be staying at your house."
　　　　 /k for to day I must abide at thy house.

Lk 19.6 /b Nu qwji lexen, tovi wulelarmkwv.
　　　　 /p ná kwə́ši-lí·x·i·n, tóhi-wəli·laé·mku.
　　　　 /t Then he quickly came down, and he was very pleased by his words.
　　　　 /k And he made haste, and came down, and received him joyfully.

Lk 19.7 /b Nc rlenumevtetc alumi mutu wulrluntamweok,
　　　　 /p nə́ e·li·namihtí·t·e, áləmi- máta -wəle·ləntamo·wí·ɔk,
　　　　 /t When they saw that, they began to be displeased,
　　　　 /k And when they saw it, they all murmured,

	/b	lwrok, Kotu wepwmao mrtawselehi.
	/p	luwé·ɔk, "kɔ́t·a-wi·po·má·ɔ me·t·a·wsi·lí·č·i."
	/t	saying, "He wants to eat with a sinner."
	/k	saying, That he was gone to be guest with a man that is a sinner.

Lk 19.8
	/b	Sakeus eku nepw, tulao Nhesusu,
	/p	†sa·kí·as íka ní·p·o·, təlá·ɔ nči·sás·a,
	/t	Zacchaeus stood there and said to Jesus,
	/k	And Zacchaeus stood, and said unto the Lord;

	/b	Nrvlaleun, punu, pavsei cntxi nevlatumu nmelan vufq krtumaksehek,
	/p	"nehəlá·lian, pənáh, pahsí·i éntxi-nihəlá·t·ama nəmí·la·n=hánkw ke·t·əma·ksí·č·i·k.
	/t	"Master, look, half of what I own I regularly give to the poor.
	/k	Behold, Lord, the half of my goods I give to the poor;

	/b	ok vufq awrn nwhqe krkw wrtunumaokc
	/p	ɔ́·k=hánkw awé·n nó·čkwe kéku we·t·ənəmaɔ́k·e,
	/t	And if I take anything from someone for no just reason,
	/k	and if I have taken any thing from any man by false accusation,

	/b	nrwun vufq nc txi nmelav.
	/p	né·wən=hánkw nə́ txí nəmí·la."
	/t	I always give him four times that amount."
	/k	I restore him fourfold.

Lk 19.9
	/b	Nhesus tulao, Bqc kejqek, lclrxrmvaltwakun prerw b wekwavmif,
	/p	nčí·sas təlá·ɔ, "yúkwe kí·škwi·k lehəle·x·e·mha·ltəwá·k·an pe·yé·yu yú wi·k·əwáhəmink.
	/t	Jesus said to him, "Today salvation has come to this house.
	/k	And Jesus said unto him, This day is salvation come to this house,

	/b	punav, wuni Rplivcmu wqesumwkwv.
	/p	pənáh wáni †e·pəlihéma o·k·wi·s·əmúk·u.
	/t	Even this (man) is a son of Abraham.
	/k	forsomuch as he also is a son of Abraham.

Lk 19.10
	/b	Rli linw Wrqesif wunhi pat, tulih lclrxrmvrn trofululehi.
	/p	é·li lə́nu we·k·wí·s·ink wə́nči-pá·t, tə́li-=č -lehəle·x·é·mhen te·ɔnkələlí·č·i."
	/t	For the reason the man who is the Son comes is to save the lost."
	/k	For the Son of man is come to seek and to save that which was lost.

Lk 19.11
	/b	Nrli nc listaovtet tonhi rnwntvakrokun lao,
	/p	né·li- nə́ -ləstaɔ́hti·t, tɔ́nči- e·nunthake·ɔ́·k·an -lá·ɔ,
	/t	As they listened to him say that, he told them a parable in addition,
	/k	And as they heard these things, he added and spake a parable,

/b rli mrhi kexki avpevtet Nhelwsulum,
/p é·li- mé·či kí·xki -ahpíhti·t †nči·ló·sələm,
/t as they were already near Jerusalem,
/k because he was nigh to Jerusalem,

/b ok rli letrvalet Krtanitweth sokemaokun nrvkot eku patc.
/p ó·k é·li-li·t·e·há·li·t, "ke·tanət·ó·wi·t=č sɔ·k·i·ma·ó·k·an né·ykɔt íka pá·t·e."
/t and as they thought, "God's kingdom will appear when he (Jesus) arrives there."
/k and because they thought that the kingdom of God should immediately appear.

Lk 19.12 /b Tulao, Linw mu xifwrlumwqsetpanu ovlumi rp,
/p təlá·ɔ, "lə́nu=máh, xinkwe·ləmukwsi·tpána, ɔ́həlɔmi é·p,
/t He said to them, "There was a man, a nobleman, and he went far away,
/k He said therefore, A certain nobleman went into a far country

/b my mjinumwp nevlahi sakemaokun, kavtu lupi prp.
/p mái-məšə́nəmo·p nihəláči sa·k·i·ma·ó·k·an, káhta- lápi -pé·p.
/t going to acquire for himself a kingdom, and intending to come back.
/k to receive for himself a kingdom, and to return.

Lk 19.13 /b Wcnhemao tclcn tolwkakunu, tclcn pwntif tokvamaoo,
/p wwenči·má·ɔ télən tɔlo·ká·k·ana, télən púntink tɔkhamaɔ́·ɔ,
/t He called in his ten servants and distributed ten pounds to them,
/k And he called his ten servants, and delivered them ten pounds,

/b tulao, Knevlatamunroh srkvakreu.   [⟨reu⟩ for /é·a/]
/p təlá·ɔ, 'kənihəla·t·aməné·ɔ=č se·khaké·a.'
/t saying to them 'You will be in charge of it for as long as I am away.'
/k and said unto them, Occupy till I come.
        [RSV "trade with these"; NSOED: *occupy* 'do business, work, trade, deal']

Lk 19.14 /b Jwq wctwtrnyuvrmahek vwjifalawao,
/p šúkw wi·t·o·t·e·nayahe·má·č·i·k wšinka·lawwá·ɔ.
/t But his fellow townsmen hated him.
/k But his citizens hated him,

/b nu tolwkrmwenro li naolan tclih my lwrlen,
/p ná tɔlo·ke·mwi·né·ɔ lí-ná·ɔla·n, tɔ́li-=č -mái-luwé·li·n,
/t Then they sent someone to follow after him, for them to go and say,
/k and sent a message after him, saying,

/b Takw ntcli wulrluntamwunrn qekyimvrn.
/p 'takó· ntə́li-wəle·ləntamó·wəne·n kwi·kayə́mhe·n.'
/t 'We are not happy for him to be the ruler.'
/k We will not have this man to reign over us.

Lk 19.15 /b Mrhi mrjinif nc sakemaokun, nu lupi pon.
/p mé·či mé·š·ənink nə́ sa·k·i·ma·ɔ́·k·an, ná lápi pó·n.
/t After he had obtained the kingdom, he came back.
/k And it came to pass, that when he was returned, having received the kingdom,

/b Nu tulwrn wcnhemw ntalwkakunuk, melukpanek moni,
/p ná tə́ləwe·n, 'wenčí·mo· ntalo·ká·k·anak, mi·lakpáni·k móni,
/t Then he said, 'Call my servants, the ones I gave money to,
/k then he commanded these servants to be called unto him, to whom he had given the money,

/b wcnhih wataov cntxi patatwvtet nuni wunhi.
/p wénči-=č -wwá·taɔ éntxi-pa·ta·túhti·t nə́ni wə́nči.'
/t so that I may know how much they earned from it.'
/k that he might know how much every man had gained by trading.

Lk 19.16 /b Nrtami pat, tulao.
/p né·tami-pá·t təlá·ɔ,
/t The one who came first said to him,
/k Then came the first, saying,

/b Nrvlaleun, Kpwntum patatw tclcn pwntif,
/p 'nehəlá·lian, kpúntəm pa·tá·to· télən púntink.'
/t 'Master, your pound earned ten pounds.'
/k Lord, thy pound hath gained ten pounds.

Lk 19.17 /b Tulkwv, Wulit, wrliluset ntalwkukun;   [⟨-kukun⟩ for ⟨-kakun⟩]
/p tə́lku, 'wələ́t, wé·li-lə́s·i·t ntalo·ká·k·an.
/t The other one said to him, 'It is good, my good servant.
/k And he said unto him, Well, thou good servant:

/b rli wli krnavketaon nuni tufiti, tclcnh wtrnif ktuntu kvekybmvc.   [⟨krnav-‖ketaon⟩]
/p é·li-wə́li-ke·nahkí·taɔn nə́ni tankíti, télən=č o·t·é·nink ktə́nta-khikayə́mhe.'
/t Because you took good care of that small thing, you shall rule in ten towns.'
/k because thou hast been faithful in a very little, have thou authority over ten cities.

Lk 19.18 /b Nu lupi peli pon, tulao, Nrvlaleun, Kpwntum palrnuxk pwntif patatw.
(p. 147) /p ná lápi pí·li pó·n, təlá·ɔ, 'nehəlá·lian, kpúntəm palé·naxk púntink pa·tá·to·.'
/t Then another one came and said to him, 'Master, your pound earned five pounds.'
/k And the second came, saying, Lord, thy pound hath gained five pounds.

Lk 19.19 /b Ok nuni nanc tulkwn; palrnuxkh wtrnif ktuntu kvekybmvc.
/p ɔ́·k náni ná=nə təlko·n, 'palé·naxk=č o·t·é·nink ktə́nta-khikayə́mhe.'
/t And that one he told the same thing, 'You shall rule in five towns.'
/k And he said likewise to him, Be thou also over five cities.

Lk 19.20	/b	Nu lupi peli pon, tulao,
	/p	ná lápi pí·li pó·n, tǝlá·ɔ,
	/t	Then another one came and said to him,
	/k	And another came, saying,

/b Nrvlaleun, Punav kpwntum, nwli krnavketwn,
/p 'nehǝlá·lian, pǝnáh, kpúntǝm nó·li-ke·nahkí·to·n;
/t 'Master, look, I took good care of your pound;   [B. punctuates differently]
/k Lord, behold, here is thy pound, which I have kept

/b hetanu vcmpsif nwexqrptwnrp.
/p či·t·anahémpsink nǝwi·xkwe·ptó·ne·p.
/t I wrapped it up in a thick cloth.
/k laid up in a napkin:

Lk 19.21 /b Koxul rli kwavul rmuntapret linw kvaky;
/p kkóx·ǝl, é·li ko·wá·hǝl e·mǝnta·p·é·i·t lǝ́nu khák·ay.
/t I was afraid of you, as I knew you to be a high-handed man.
/k For I feared thee, because thou art an austere man: [RSV "severe"]

/b kwrtunumun vufq mutu vuji krkw tutu rtwun,
/p kǝwe·t·ǝnǝ́mǝn=hánkw máta háši kéku tǝtá e·tó·wan,
/t You take up things you never put down anywhere,
/k thou takest up that thou layedst not down,

/b ok vufq ktumjimun mutu vuji ke rkevreon.
/p ó·k=hánkw ktǝmšǝ́mǝn máta háši kí· e·ki·hé·ɔn.'
/t and you reap what *you* never planted.'
/k and reapest that thou didst not sow.

Lk 19.22 /b Nu tulkwn,
/p ná tǝlko·n,
/t Then the other said to him,
/k And he saith unto him,

/b nevlahi ktwn kwnhi kuntrlumul mrtapret alwkakun.
/p 'nihǝláči któ·n kúnči-kǝnté·lǝmǝl, me·ta·p·é·i·t alo·ká·k·an.
/t 'From your own mouth I condemn you, wicked servant.
/k Out of thine own mouth will I judge thee, thou wicked servant.

/b Kwatwn ntcli amuntapren
/p ko·wá·to·n ntǝ́li-amǝnta·p·é·i·n,
/t You know that I am a high-handed man,
/k Thou knewest that I was an austere man,

Text, Transcription, and Translation

/b ntcli wrtunimun krkw mutu ne tutu rtwu,
/p ntə́li-we·t·ənəmən kéku máta ní· tətá e·tó·wa,
/t that I take up things that *I* didn't put down anywhere,
/k taking up that I laid not down,

/b ok ntcli tumijimun mutu ne rkevreo.
/p ɔ́·k ntə́li- gəmən máta ní· e·ki·hé·ɔ.
/t and that I reap what *I* never planted.
/k and reaping that I did not sow:

Lk 19.23
/b Krkw vuh wunhi mutu eku lwxovtwun numoneum cvcntu ajwntrnasek
/p kéku=háč wə́nči- máta íka -luxɔhtó·wan nəmɔní·yəm ehə́nta-a·š·unte·ná·s·i·k,
/t Why didn't you take my money to the place where it is exchanged,
/k Wherefore then gavest not thou my money into the bank,

/b ntcli a paanc mjinumun ok vupi cntxi patataon?
/p ntə́li-=á· pa·á·ne -məšə́nəmən, ɔ́·k hápi éntxi-pa·tá·taɔn.'
/t so that when I came back I would receive it and with it the amount you earned.'
/k that at my coming I might have required mine own with usury?

Lk 19.24
/b Nu tulan, eku nepyelehi,
/p ná tə́la·n íka ni·p·ai·lí·č·i,
/t Then he said to some standing there,
/k And he said unto them that stood by,

/b Hekunw nc kwti pwntif, melw nu tclcn pwntif wrlvataq.
/p 'čí·k·əno· nə́ kwə́t·i púntink, mí·lo· ná télən púntink we·lháta·kw.'
/t 'Take the pound away from him, and give it to the one that has ten pounds.'
/k Take from him the pound, and give it to him that hath ten pounds.

Lk 19.25
/b Tulawao, Nrvlalerf, wuni tclcn pwntif wrlvataq.
/p təlawwá·ɔ, 'nehəlá·lienk, wáni télən púntink we·lháta·kw.'
/t They said to him, 'Master, he is one who has ten pounds.'
/k (And they said unto him, Lord, he hath ten pounds.)

Lk 19.26
/b Tulao, Ktulwvmw cntxi awrn wulataq unhih mela;
/p təlá·ɔ, 'ktəllúhəmɔ, éntxi- awé·n -wəlá·ta·kw ánči-=č -mí·la·,
/t He said to them, 'I say to you, that everyone that has some shall be given more,
/k For I say unto you, That unto every one which hath shall be given;

/b ok cntxi awrn mutu wulataq hekunanh eli cntxi wulataq.
/p ɔ́·k éntxi- awé·n máta -wəlá·ta·kw, čí·k·əna·n=č ílli éntxi-wəlá·ta·kw.
/t and from everyone that doesn't have any even all they have shall be taken away.
/k and from him that hath not, even that he hath shall be taken away from him.

Lk 19.27 /b Kuhi nrk jifalehek mutu krtatufpanek fekybmvrn,
/p káč·i né·k šinka·lí·č·i·k máta ke·t·a·t·ankpáni·k nki·kayə́mhe·n,
/t But as for the enemies of mine that don't want me to rule,
/k But those mine enemies, which would not that I should reign over them,

/b prjw. Ok nvelw tali rlifwrxenu.
/p pé·š·o·, ɔ́·k nhílo· táli e·linkwe·x·í·na.'"
/t bring them, and kill them in front of me.'"
/k bring hither, and slay them before me.

Chapter 85 (pp. 147-148). (Mark 10.46, 48-50; Matthew 20.29-34; Luke 18.36-39, 40, 42-43)

Mk 10.46 /b Nhclikwif wcnhi alumskatc ok rkrkemahi
/p †nčelikó·wink wénči-aləmská·t·e, ɔ́·k e·k·e·ki·má·č·i,
/t When he went out of Jericho along with his disciples,
/kl And as he went out of Jericho with his disciples

Mt 20.29 /b xavrli awrnek noolawao.
/p xahé·li awé·ni·k nɔ·ɔlawwá·ɔ.
/t many people followed him (or them).
/kl a great multitude followed him.

Mt 20.30, Lk 18.35
/b Punu, kexki Nhclekw joexkunac lumutavpwpanek krkrpifohek neju linwuk
/p pənáh, kí·xki †nčéliku šɔi·xkanáe ləmatahpó·p·ani·k ke·k·e·p·inkɔ́·č·i·k ní·š·a lə́nəwak,
/t Now, near Jericho by the side of the road two blind men were sittimg
/l And, behold, nigh unto Jericho, two blind men *were* sitting by the high-way side,

Mk 10.46 /b tevcntu wenwrnro; mawsw lwcnselw wxo Timeus.
/p tihə́nta-wi·nəwe·né·ɔ; má·wsu luwcnsí·lu ó·x·ɔ †təmí·as.
/t and they would beg there; the father of one of them was named Timaeus.
/l begging. [*And one of them was*] blind Bartimaeus, the son of Timaeus.

Lk 18.36 /b Rmamavtetc xrli awrni, nul nu lwr, krkw vuh lr?
/p e·mamahtí·t·e xé·li awé·ni, nál ná lúwe·, "kéku=háč lé·?"
/t When they became aware of many people, that one said, "What's happening?"
/kl And hearing the multitude pass by, he asked what it meant.

Lk 18.37 /b La, Nhesus Nasulutif wcnheyet b pwmskan.
/p lá·, "nčí·sas †nasəlát·ink wenčí·ai·t yú pwə́mska·n.
/t He was told, "Jesus of Nazareth is going by here."
/kl And they told him, that Jesus of Nazareth passeth by.

Mt 20.30 /b Mrhi puntamevtetc ‖ tuli Nhesus nc pumuskan, amuxavolamwuk lwrok,
/p mé·či pəntamihtí·t·e tə́li- nčí·sas nə́ -pəmə́ska·n, amax·ahɔlá·məwak, luwé·ɔk,
/t When they heard that Jesus was going by there, they shouted, saying,
/l And when they [*both*] heard that Jesus passed by, *they* cried out, saying,

(p. 148) /b Ktumakrlumenrn, O Nrvlalerf Ntrpitu wrqesumwkon!
/p "ktəma·k·e·ləmí·ne·n, ó· nehəlá·lienk, †nte·pít·a we·k·wi·s·əmúk·ɔn.
/t "Have mercy on us, O Master, son of David!
/kl Have mercy on us, O Lord, thou Son of David.

Lk 18.38 /b Nhesus Ntrpitu wrqesumwkon ktumakrlumenrn.
/p nčí·sas, †nte·pít·a we·k·wi·s·əmúk·ɔn, ktəma·k·e·ləmí·ne·n."
/t Jesus, you son of David, have mercy on us."
/kl Jesus, thou Son of David, have mercy on me.

Lk 18.39 /b Nekanehek qetulawao,
/p ni·k·a·ní·č·i·k kkwi·təlawwá·ɔ,
/t The ones in the lead admonished them,
/k And they which went before rebuked him, ...

Mk 10.48, Mt 20.31
/b ok xrli peli awrnek tulawao hetkwseq.
/p ɔ́·k xé·li pí·li awé·ni·k təlawwá·ɔ, "či·tkwə́s·i·kw."
/t and many other people said to them, "Be quiet!"
/l And many charged them that they should hold their peace:

Mt 20.31, Mt 10.48
/b Jwq avalwei amuxavolamwuk, lwrok
/p šúkw ahaləwí·i amax·ahɔlá·məwak, luwé·ɔk,
/t But they shouted all the more, saying,
/l but they cried the more a great deal, saying,

/b Ktumakrlumenrn, O Nrvlalerf Ntrpitu wrqesumwkon!
/p "ktəma·k·e·ləmí·ne·n, ó· nehəlá·lienk, †nte·pít·a we·k·wi·s·əmúk·ɔn!"
/t "Have mercy on us, O Master, son of David!"
/l Have mercy on us, O Lord, thou Son of David.

Mt 20.32, Mk 10.49
/b Nu Nhesus nokevlan,
/p ná nčí·sas nɔk·íhəla·n,
/t Then Jesus stopped where he was,
/kl And Jesus stood still, (L. "and called them" omitted.)

Lk 18.40 /b ok lwr wuntux lwxolw.
/p ó·k lúwe·, "wə́ntax ló·x·ɔlo·."
/t and said, "Bring them here."
/l and commanded *them* to be brought unto him.

Mk 10.49 /b Nu wcnhemanro nrk krkrpifohek,
/p ná wenči·ma·né·ɔ né·k ke·k·e·p·inkó·č·i·k.
/t Then those blind men were called over.
/l And they call the blind,

/b laok nvakrrluntamwq, pavswqeq kwcnhemkwu.
/p lá·ɔk, "nhake·e·lə́ntamo·kw; pahsúk·wi·kw; kəwenči·mkó·wa.
/t They were told, "Have hope; get up; he's calling you to come."
/l saying unto *them*, Be of good comfort, rise; he calleth *you*.

Mk 10.50 /b Nu poketwnro rqevtet pavswqeok eku rok Nhesusif.
/p ná pɔk·i·t·o·né·ɔ e·k·wíhti·t, pahsuk·wí·ɔk, íka é·ɔk nči·sás·ink.
/t Then they threw down their garments, and they got up and went to Jesus.
/l And *they*, casting away their garment, rose, and came to Jesus.

Mt 20.32 /b Nhesus tulao, Krkw vuh ktetrvavmw qwlu ntclevkwnrn?
/p nčí·sas təlá·ɔ, "kéku=háč kti·t·e·háhəmɔ, 'kwə́la ntəlihkó·ne·n?'"
/t Jesus said to them, "What do you (pl.) wish for me to do for you?"
/l And Jesus said, What will ye that I shall do unto you?

Mt 20.33 /b Tulkwv, Nrvlalerf taxkifwrnenrn.
/p tə́lku, "nehəlá·lienk, ta·xkinkwe·ní·ne·n."
/t They said to him, "Master, open our eyes."
/l They said unto him, Lord, that our eyes may be opened.

Mt 20.34 /b Nu Nhesus qutumakrluman, eku tonao wujkifwelet,
/p ná nčí·sas kwət·əma·k·é·ləma·n, íka tɔnná·ɔ wəškinkwí·li·t.
/t Then Jesus had pity on them, and he touched them on their eyes.
/kl So Jesus had compassion *on them*, and touched their eyes: ...

Lk 18.42, Mk 10.52
/b tulao Taxkifwrq; alumskaq knakatamwrokunwu kwlevkwnro.
/p təlá·ɔ, "ta·xkínkwe·kw, alə́mska·kw; kəna·ka·t·amwe·ɔ·k·anúwa ko·lihko·né·ɔ."
/t He said to them, "Open your eyes and go; your faith has made you well."
/l and said unto *them*, Receive your sight: go *your* way, *your* faith hath made *you* whole.

Mt 20.34 /b Nu jac toxkifwrnro,
/p ná šá·e tɔ·xkinkwe·né·ɔ,
/t Then immediately their eyes were open.
/l And immediately their eyes received sight,

Lk 18.43 /b ok tolumi naolawao, moxifovkunemawao Krtanitwelehi.
/p ɔ́·k tɔ́ləmi-na·ɔlawwá·ɔ, mɔx·inkɔhkəni·mawwá·ɔ ke·tanət·o·wi·lí·č·i.
/t And they began following him, praising God.
/l and followed him in the way, glorifying God:

/b Ok wrmi nc rlenufek moxifovkanemawao Krtanitwelehi.
/p ɔ́·k wé·mi nə́ e·li·nánki·k mɔx·inkɔhkəni·mawwá·ɔ ke·tanət·o·wi·lí·č·i.
/t And all those who saw it praised God.
/kl and all the people, when they saw it, gave praise unto God.

Chapter 86 (pp. 148-149). (John 12.1-7, 9-11; Matthew 26.6, 8-8; Mark 14.3, 5-9)

Jn 12.1 /b Kwtaj txwquni nrsko xifwi metsavtebf, nu Nhesus eku pon Pctunebf;
/p kwə́t·a·š txó·k·wəni né·skɔ xínkwi-mi·tsahtí·yunk, ná nčí·sas íka pɔ́·n †petəní·yunk,
/t Then, six days before the big feast, Jesus came to Bethany,
/l Six days before the passover Jesus came to Bethany, [KJV: "Then Jesus ..."]

/b Laslusu rpetup, aeavi amwekununtup wunhi mavhekamekwf.
/p †la·səlás·a e·p·í·t·əp, a·yáhi-a·mwi·kənə́ntəp wə́nči mahči·k·amí·k·unk.
/t where Lazarus lived, who had earlier been raised up from the grave.
/kl where Lazarus was [which had been dead], whom he raised from the dead.

Jn 12.2 /b Nc tali loqwne kejextaopanek mehwakun
/p nə́ táli lɔ·k·wəní·i ki·š·i·xtaɔ́·p·ani·k mi·č·əwá·k·an
/t There in the evening a meal was prepared for them
/kl There they made him a supper;

Mt 26.6 /b tali Symun weket, nul nuni aeavi neskufulukup,
/p táli †sáiman wí·k·i·t; nál náni a·yáhi-ni·skankələ́k·əp.
/t at the house of Simon; it was he who had previously had the nasty disease.
/kl in the house of Simon the leper, ... (also Mark 14.3)

Jn 12.2 /b Masi tcli mekuntamaonrp, kahi Laslus wepwmapani.
/p má·si tə́li-mi·kəntamaɔ́·ne·p, káč·i †lá·səlas wwi·po·má·p·ani.
/t Martha was the one that served them, but Lazarus ate with them.
/kl and Martha served: but Lazarus was one of them that sat at the table with him.

Mt 26.7, Mk 14.3, Jn 12.3
/b Nu Mrles wtxan, kulinum opasune vakvaq
/p ná mé·li·s ó·txa·n, kəlɔ́nəm ɔpahsəní·i-hákhakw.
/t Then Mary came to him carrying a white-stone bottle.
/l There came Mary unto him, having an alabaster box

	/b	kwti pwntif eku vatr ave wrltuk jrmrk mpeswn, ave rvoovtek,
	/p	kwə́t·i púntink íka hát·e· áhi wé·ltək šé·me·k mpí·s·o·n, áhi ehɔ́·ɔhti·k.
	/t	In it was a pound of very fine ointment, which was very expensive.
	/l	with a pound of ointment of spikenard, very precious,

Jn 12.3
/b eku tcli jwvmaon vwsetelet Nhesusu, ok wvheskvamaon mweluxk torkrn.
/p íka tə́li-šuhəmáɔ·n wsi·t·í·li·t nči·sás·a, ɔ́·k wči·skhamáɔ·n, mwí·laxk tɔé·ke·n.
/t She rubbed it on Jesus's feet and wiped them using her hair.
/kl and anointed the feet of Jesus, and wiped his feet with her hair.

Mk 14.3
/b Ok pokvetcvmun nc vakvaq, nu wrmi eku vwswkvamaon welelet,   [⟨swk-‖vam⟩]
/p ɔ́·k ppɔ·khitéhəmən nə́ hákhakw, ná wé·mi íka wsɔ·khamáɔ·n wi·lí·li·t.
/t And she broke the bottle and then poured all of it on his head.
/l And [*afterward*] she brake the box, and poured it [*entirely*] on his head ... ;

Jn 12.3
(p. 149)
/b hwemakot nc wekwavmif nc wifemako mpeswn.
/p čuwi·má·k·ɔt nə́ wi·k·əwáhəmink nə́ winki·má·k·ɔ mpí·s·o·n.
/t The odor of that sweet-smelling medicine filled the house.
/kl and the house was filled with the odour of the ointment.

Jn 12.4
/b Nu mawsw rkrkemunt, rlwcnsetup Nhwtus Iskaliot Symunu qesu, tulwrn,
/p ná má·wsu e·k·e·kí·mənt, e·ləwensí·t·əp †nčó·tas-iská·liɔt, †sáimana kkwí·s·a, tə́ləwe·n,
/t Then one disciple, whose name was Judas Iscariot, Simon's son, said,
/kl Then saith one of his disciples, Judas Iscariot, Simon's son, ...

Jn 12.5
/b koh vuh mutu mvalasek rli xenxkc laovtek
/p "kɔ́č=háč máta mhalá·s·i·k é·li- xí·nxke -lá·ɔhti·k,
/t "Why wasn't it sold, as it is worth thirty dollars,
/kl Why was not this ointment sold for three hundred pence,

/b li a melan krtumaksehek?
/p lí-=á· -mí·la·n ke·t·əma·ksí·č·i·k?"
/t to be given to the poor?"
/kl and given to the poor?

Jn 12.6
/b Mutu xunr krvlu pwunarlumaeo krtumakselehi
/p máta=xánne· kéhəla pwənae·ləma·í·ɔ ke·t·əma·ksi·lí·č·i,
/t He did not, however, think a lot about the poor,
/k This he said, not that he cared for the poor;

/b jwq rli kevkumwtkrt wunhi nc lwrn,
/p šúkw é·li-kihkəmó·tke·t wwə́nči- nə́ -lúwe·n,
/t but it was because he was a thief that he said that,
/k but because he was a thief,

	/b	ok rli kulunif monee nwtrswu ok tuktu krkw eku rtrk.
	/p	ɔ́·k é·li-kəlánink mmɔnií·i-no·t·é·s·əwa, ɔ́·k tákta kéku íka é·te·k.
	/t	and because he carried their money bag and whatever was in it.
	/k	and had the bag, and bare what was put therein.

Mt 26.8
- /b Ok takokek rkrkemunhek aluntc mutu tuli wulrluntamwunro, lwrok,
- /p ɔ́·k takɔ́·ki·k e·k·e·ki·mə́nči·k a·lə́nte máta tə́li-wəle·ləntamo·wəné·ɔ, luwé·ɔk,
- /t And some of the other disciples were not happy with it, saying,
- /k But when his disciples saw it, they had indignation, saying,

- /b Nwhqc amyuketwn;
- /p "nó·čkwe amayahkí·to·n.
- /t "It is wasted for no purpose.
- /k To what purpose is this waste?

Mt 26.9
- /b rli nc mpeswn tcpi a mu xrli rlaovtek wunheybp,
- /p é·li nə́ mpí·s·o·n, tépi-=á·=máh xé·li e·lá·ɔhti·k -wənčí·ayo·p,
- /t For from that medicine, a large amount (of money) could have come,
- /k For this ointment might have been sold for much,

- /b li a melanrop krtumaksehek;
- /p lí-=á· -mi·la·né·ɔ·p ke·t·əma·ksí·č·i·k."
- /t to have been given to the poor."
- /k and given to the poor.

Mk 14.5
- /b honemawao nrl xqro.
- /p čɔni·mawwá·ɔ né·l xkwé·ɔ.
- /t They admonished the woman.
- /k ... And they murmured against her.

Mt 26.10
- /b Nhesus puntaotc, tulao,
- /p nčí·sas pəntaɔ́·t·e, təlá·ɔ,
- /t When Jesus heard them, he said to them,
- /k When Jesus understood it, he said unto them,

Mk 14.6
- /b Konu lenw,
- /p "kɔ́na lí·no·.
- /t "Leave her alone.
- /k Let her alone;

Mt 26.10
- /b koh vuh suqelarvrq wu xqr?
- /p kɔ́č=háč sak·wi·laé·he·kw wá xkwé·?
- /t Why do you torment this woman?
- /k Why trouble ye the woman?

       /b   rli wulumekumosuntamaet.
       /p   é·li-wəlami·kəmɔ·s·əntamái·t.
       /t   For she has done a good service for me.
       /k   for she hath wrought a good work upon me.

Mk 14.7   /b   Rli krtumaksehek aphih qetavpemkwaok,
       /p   é·li ke·t·əma·ksí·č·i·k á·pči=č kəwitahpi·mkəwá·ɔk.
       /t   As the poor will be with you always.
       /k   For ye have the poor with you always,

       /b   navkoi a lukveqi letrvarqc kuski wetavrmawaok.
       /p   nahkɔ́·i=á· ləkhíkwi li·t·e·ha·é·k·we kkáski-wi·t·a·he·mawwá·ɔk.
       /t   You could help them anytime you want.
       /k   and whensoever ye will ye may do them good:

       /b   Kahi ne, taa aphi.
       /p   káč·i ní·, tá=á· á·pči.
       /t   But in my case, it will not always be.
       /k   but me ye have not always.

Mk 14.8   /b   Nanc tulsen jevkunh krski luset;
       /p   ná=nə tə́lsi·n šíhkanč ké·ski-lə́s·i·t.
       /t   She did the best she could.
       /kl   She hath done what she could:

Jn 12.7, Mt 26.12, Mk 14.8
       /b   rli wlvatwnrp nc mpeswn
       /p   é·li o·lható·ne·p nə́ mpí·s·o·n,
       /t   For she had kept this ointment ("medicine"),
       /l   for in that she hath kept this ointment,

       /b   nvakrf wvswkvamun, wunhi nc lusen,
       /p   nhák·enk wso·khámən, wwə́nči- nə́ -lə́s·i·n.
       /t   and she poured it on my body, which is why she did so.
       /l   and poured it on my body, she did it

       /b   nekane njumunwq rlih pvokvakrvaseu.
       /p   ni·k·a·ní·i nšámənukw, é·li-=č -phɔkhakehá·s·ia.
       /t   She anointed me ahead of time the way I shall be buried.
       /l   to anoint me aforehand to my burying.

Mk 14.9   /b   Kvehe kulwvmw,
       /p   khiči·i ktəllúhəmɔ,
       /t   I tell you truly,
       /k   Verily I say unto you,

/b Tutuh tali b avpami xqetvakameqc avkunwtasekc bl ntaptwnakunu,
/p tə́ta=č táli yú ahpá·mi xkwi·thakamí·k·we ahkəno·t·a·s·í·k·e yó·l nta·pto·ná·k·ana,
/t anywhere all over on this earth when these words of mine are told about,
/k Wheresoever this gospel shall be preached throughout the whole world,

/b aphih ok vapi avkunwtasw wu xqr rlacvoset wunhih mjalan.
/p á·pči=č ɔ́·k hápi ahkəno·t·á·s·u wá xkwé· e·laehɔ́·s·i·t, wə́nči-=č -məšá·la·n."
/t what this woman did will also always be told about, for her to be remembered.
/k this also that she hath done shall be spoken of for a memorial of her.

[Section 87 begins here in L.1 and L.2.]

Jn 12.9 /b Nu tamsc xrli Nhwok wrotwvtetc tcli nc avpen, eku prok,
/p ná tá·mse xé·li nčó·wak we·ɔ·tuhtí·t·e tə́li- nə́ -ahpí·n, íka pé·ɔk,
/t Then at some point many Jews, when they knew he was there, went there,
/k Much people of the Jews therefore knew that he was there: and they came

/b alwt mutu jwq wunhi Nhesusu,
/p aló·t máta šúkw wə́nči nči·sás·a,
/t yet not only because of Jesus,
/k not for Jesus' sake only,

/b jwq ok tuli a nronro Laslusu, amweletup wunhi muvhekamekwf.
/p šúkw ɔ́·k tə́li-=á· -ne·ɔ·né·ɔ †la·səlás·a, a·mwi·lí·t·əp wə́nči mahči·k·amí·k·unk.
/t but also to see Lazarus, who had risen from the grave.
/k but that they might see Lazarus also, whom he had raised from the dead.

Jn 12.10 /b Jwq nekanexifek wcvewfrhek tokunwtumunrop   [⟨wcvew⟩ for ⟨wcvevw⟩]
/p šúkw ni·k·a·ni·x·ínki·k wehi·hunké·č·i·k tɔk·əno·t·əməné·ɔ·p
/t But the head priests had talked about
/k But the chief priests consulted

/b wcnhi a nevlavtet Laslusu,   [⟨nevl-⟩ for ⟨nvel-⟩]
/p wénči-=á· -nhiláhti·t †la·səlás·a,
/t how they might kill Lazarus,
/k that they might put Lazarus also to death;

Jn 12.11 /b rli nrkumu wunhi xrli Nhwok alumi wlamvetaonro Nhesusu. ‖
/p é·li nék·əma wwə́nči- xé·li nčó·wak -áləmi-wəla·mhitaɔ·né·ɔ nči·sás·a.
/t as because of him many Jews began to believe in Jesus.
/k Because that by reason of him many of the Jews went away, and believed on Jesus.

Chapter 87 (pp. 150-151). (L. section 88.) (L.: Matthew 21.1-11, Mark 11.1-11, Luke 19.28-46, John 12.12-19.)

Lk 19.29, Jn 12.12
(p. 150) /b   Lrp rluvparkc rlumskavtetc nc wunhi;
/p   lé·p, e·lahpa·é·k·e e·ləmskahtí·t·e nə́ wə́nči,
/t   It happened, after they left there the next morning,
/l   And it came to pass, on the next day,

Lk 19.29, Mk 11.1
/b   Pctuni ok Mpetprh, kexki pravtetc Nhelwsulumif,   [⟨Mpet-⟩ for ⟨Mpct-⟩]
/p   †pétəni ɔ́·k †mpétpe·č kí·xki pe·ahtí·t·e, †nči·lo·sələ́mink,
/t   and after they had come near Bethany and Bethphage, (near) Jerusalem,
/l   when they drew nigh unto Jerusalem, and were come to Bethphage and Bethany,...

Mk 11.1 /b   neju rkrkemahi tolwkalao,
/p   ní·š·a e·k·e·ki·má·č·i tɔlo·ka·lá·ɔ,
/t   that he sent two of his disciples,
/l   Jesus sendeth forth two of his disciples,

Lk 19.30, Mt 21.2
/b   tulao, Eku aq b nukveqiti wtrnrtutif,
/p   təlá·ɔ, "íka á·kw yú nəkhikwíti o·t·e·ne·t·ə́t·ink.
/t   saying to them, "Go to the small town a short distance from here.
/l   saying unto them, Go your way into the village over against you;

/b   ekuh parqc knrovmwh qrkonxatut krxpeset
/p   íka pa·é·k·we, kəne·ɔ́həmɔ=č kwek·ɔ·nxá·t·ət ke·xpí·s·i·t,
/t   When you get there, you will see a little donkey tied up,
/l   and as soon as ye be entered into it, ye shall find an ass tied,

/b   ok wunehantutu, nrlumu carkrebf,   [⟨-rebf⟩ for /-é·yunk/]
/p   ɔ́·k wəni·č·a·nt·ə́t·a, né·ləma i·ae·ké·yunk.
/t   and her young one, which has never yet been ridden.
/l   and a colt with her, whereon yet never man sat:

Lk 19.30 /b   kluxunawuh, kprtaenroh.
/p   kəlax·ənáwwa=č, kpe·t·ai·né·ɔ=č.
/t   You must untie it, and you must bring it to me.
/k   loose him, and bring him hither.
/l   loose *them*, and bring *them* hither unto me.

Mk 11.3 /b   Awrnh lwqrqc, koh vuh nc luserq?
/p   awé·n=č luk·wé·k·we, 'kɔ́č=háč nə́ ləs·ie·kw?'
/t   If anyone says to you, 'Why are you doing that?'
/k   And if any man say unto you, Why do ye this?

/b   ktulawuh, Nrvlalwrt kotalao,
/p   ktəláwwa=č, 'nehəlá·ləwe·t kɔt·a·lá·ɔ.'
/t   you must say to him, 'The master wants it.'
/l   thus shall ye say unto him, The Lord hath need of them.

                                                            [Mk 11.3, Lk 19.31: "of him"]

/b   nuh jac qunhhinan.
/p   ná=č šá·e kwənččəna·n."
/t   Then he will send it off immediately."
/l   and straightway he will send them hither.   [Mk 11.3: "send him"]

Jn 12.12   /b   Xrli awrnek macvlrok krtu tavqepwehek,
             /p   xé·li awé·ni·k ma·ehəlé·ɔk ké·t·a-tahkwi·p·wí·č·i·k.
             /t   Many people gathered who wanted to take part in the feast.
             /k   ... much people that were come to the feast,

/b   puntamevtetc tcli Nhesus eku an,
/p   pəntamihtí·t·e təli- nčí·sas íka -á·n,
/t   When they heard that Jesus was going there,
/k   when they heard that Jesus was coming to Jerusalem,

Jn 12.13   /b   wrtunumwk pame-twvnututu, moi apvesvekaowao.
             /p   we·t·ənə́mo·k pa·mí·i-tuhənət·ə́t·a, mɔ́i-a·phishikaɔwwá·ɔ.
             /t   they took palm branches and went to meet him on the way.
             /k   Took branches of palm trees, and went forth to meet him,

Mt 21.6   /b   Nrl rkrkemahi rlwkalahi eku rok, nanc tclsenro Nhesus rlat,
            /p   né·l e·k·e·ki·má·č·i e·lo·ka·lá·č·i íka é·ɔk, ná=nə təlsi·né·ɔ nčí·sas é·la·t.
            /t   The disciples he sent went there, and they did what Jesus told them to.
            /l   And the disciples that were sent went their way, and did as Jesus commanded them,

Mk 11.4, Lk 19.32

        /b   moxkaowao nrl wuskxwmtutu, wuluki rlatup,
        /p   mɔxkaɔwwá·ɔ né·l wəskxəmtə́t·a, wəláki e·lá·t·əp.
        /t   They found the colt just as he had told them.
        /l   and found the colt even as he had said unto them.

        /b   kohumif kexi skontc kaxpesw cntu tavkokrxif;   [⟨kexi⟩ for ⟨kexki⟩]
        /p   kóčəmink kí·xki skónte kaxpí·s·u énta-tahkɔ·ké·x·ink.
        /t   It was tied outside near the door at a place where paths came together.
        /l   tied by the door without in a place where two ways met; ...

Lk 19.33, Mk 11.5

    /b   rlumi luxunavtetc, wrtalumwnset eku nepwv.
    /p   é·ləmi-laxənahtí·t·e, we·t·aləmúnsi·t íka ní·p·o·.
    /t   When they set about untying it, the owner stood there.
    /l   And as they were loosing the colt, the owners thereof that stood there

    /b   Tulkwao, Krkw vuh wcnhi luxunrq wu wuskxwmtut?
    /p   təlkəwá·ɔ, "kéku=háč wénči-laxəne·kw wá wəskxə́mtət?"
    /t   He said to them, "Why are you untying this colt?"
    /l   said unto them, Why loose ye the colt?

Mk 11.6 /b   Tulawao, Rli Nhesus li lwqrf,
    /p   təlawwá·ɔ, "é·li- nčí·sas -lí-lúk·wenk.
    /t   They said to him, "Because Jesus told us to.
    /k   And they said unto them even as Jesus had commanded:

Lk 19.34 /b   Nrvlalwrt kotalao.
    /p   nehəlá·ləwe·t kɔt·a·lá·ɔ."
    /t   The master wants it."
    /k   The Lord hath need of him.

Mk 11.6 /b   Nu konu tulenakwnro tolumwxolanro.
    /p   ná kɔ́na təli·na·k·o·né·ɔ, tɔləmo·x·ɔla·né·ɔ.
    /t   Then he let them go, and they took it with them.
    /k   and they let them go.

Mt 21.7, Lk 19.35

    /b   Eku pwrjwawao nrl qrkonxatutu ok wnehanelet Nhesusif.
    /p   íka pwe·š·əwawwá·ɔ né·l kwek·ɔ·nxa·t·ə́t·a ɔ́·k wəni·č·a·ní·li·t nči·sás·ink.
    /t   They brought the little donkey and her foal (*lit.*, child) to Jesus.
    /l   And they brought the ass and the colt to Jesus,

    /b   Nu rvavqivtehi eku totaonro,
    /p   ná ehahkwihtí·č·i íka tɔ·taɔ·né·ɔ,
    /t   Then they put their clothing on it for him,
    /l   and they cast their garments upon the colt;

    /b   nu tcli eku valanro Nhesusu,
    /p   ná tə́li- íka -hala·né·ɔ nči·sás·a.
    /t   and they proceeded to set Jesus on it,
    /l   and they set Jesus thereon,

    /b   nu torkrlen.
    /p   ná tɔe·ké·li·n.
    /t   and then he rode it.
    /l   and he sat upon him.

Mt 21.8, Mk 11.7-8, Lk 19.36

    /b   Nrlwxwctet avi xrli wlunakrnro rvavqevtehi li rli alet,
    /p   ne·lo·x·wéhti·t, áhi-xé·li o·lana·ke·né·ɔ ehahkwihtí·č·i lí é·li-á·li·t.
    /t   As they went, a great many spread their clothing on the ground in their way.
    /l   And as he went, a very great multitude spread their garments in the way;

Mt 21.8   /b   ok aluntc twvnututu keskvamwk wlunakrnroi.
    /p   ɔ́·k a·lə́nte tuhənət·ə́t·a ki·skhámo·k, o·lana·ke·ne·ɔ́·i.
    /t   And some cut branches and spread them on the ground.
    /l   and others cut down branches off the trees, and strawed them in the way.

Lk 19.37   /b   Mrhi kexki preavtetc rlumi punusevtetc wunhi Olipe ovhwf,
    /p   mé·či kí·xki pe·ahtí·t·e, é·ləmi-pənas·ihtí·t·e wə́nči †ɔlipí·i-ɔhčúnk,
    /t   When they had gotten near and started down from Olive Mountain,
    /k   And when he was come nigh, even now at the descent of the mount of Olives,

    /b   nu tolumi rkrkemunhek tavqe aswenro,
    /p   ná tɔ́ləmi- e·k·e·ki·mə́nči·k tahkwí·i -a·s·o·wi·né·ɔ.
    /t   then the disciples began singing together,
    /k   the whole multitude of the disciples began to rejoice

    /b   ok mcxifovkunemawao Krtanitwelehi, ave amufalamwuk   [⟨mcx-⟩ for ⟨mox-⟩]
    /p   ɔ́·k mɔx·inkɔhkəni·mawwá·ɔ ke·tanət·o·wi·lí·č·i, áhi-amankalá·məwak
    /t   and they praised God at the very top of their voices,
    /k   and praise God with a loud voice

    /b   wunhi wrmi xiforvoswakun rlenamevtet.
    /p   wə́nči wé·mi xinkɔehɔ·s·əwá·k·an e·li·namíhti·t.
    /t   because of all the great deeds they had seen.
    /k   for all the mighty works that they had seen;

Mt 21.9   /b   Xavrli nekanehek ok vwtcf wcfek wrmi amufalamwuk,
    /p   xahé·li ni·k·a·ní·č·i·k ɔ́·k wténk wénki·k wé·mi amankalá·məwak,
    /t   Many going in the lead and coming behind all shouted with loud voices,
    /kl   And the multitudes that went before, and that followed, cried,

    /b   lwrok Krtanitweun aphi ‖ lclrxrmvrl Ntrpitu wrqesumwkwk,
    /p   luwé·ɔk, "ke·tanət·ó·wian, á·pči lehəle·x·émhe·l †nte·pít·a we·k·wi·s·əmúk·wək.
    /t   saying, "O God, let the son of David live forever.
    /kl   saying, Hosanna to the Son of David!   [H. taken as 'save, I beseech thee'.]

Mt 21.9, Lk 19.38, Jn 12.13

(p. 151)   /b   wrlapcnset, maeai sakema, prat wunhi tulswakun Nrvlalkofq.
    /p   we·la·p·énsi·t mayá·i-sa·k·í·ma, pé·a·t wə́nči təlsəwá·k·an nehəlá·lkɔnkw.
    /t   Blessed is the king who comes acting for our lord.
    /l   blessed is he, a king, that cometh in the name of the Lord:

Mt 21.9 /b Krtanitweun aphi lclrxrmvrl!
         /p ke·tanət·ó·wian, á·pči lehəle·x·é·mhe·l.
         /t O God, let him live forever.
         /k Hosanna in the highest.   [See Mt 21.9.]

Mk 11.10 /b Wlapcnswvalqrfch sokemaokun nwxunanu Ntrpitu,
         /p wəla·p·enso·ha·lkwénkeč, sɔ·k·i·ma·ó·k·an no·x·əná·na †nte·pít·a,
         /t May he bless us, the kingdom of our father David,
         /kl Blessed be the kingdom of our father David,

         /b prat wunhi tulswakun Nrvlalkofq.
         /p pé·a·t wə́nči təlsəwá·k·an nehəlá·lkɔnkw.
         /t who comes by the power of our lord.
         /kl that cometh in the name of the Lord:

         /b Krtanitweun aphi lclrxrmvrl wunhi vwqrbf.
         /p ke·tanət·ó·wian, á·pči lehəle·x·é·mhe·l wə́nči hukwé·yunk.
         /t O God, let him live forever on high.
         /kl Hosanna in the highest.   [See Mt 21.9.]

Lk 19.38 /b Wlufwntwakunekch osavkamc,
         /p wəlankuntəwa·k·aní·k·eč ɔ·s·áhkame,
         /t Let there be peace in heaven,
         /kl Peace in heaven,

         /b ok xifovkunemkwswakunekch vwqrbf.
         /p ó·k xinkɔhkəni·mkwəs·əwa·k·aní·k·eč hukwé·yunk."
         /t and let there be praise on high."
         /kl and glory in the highest!

Mt 21.4 /b Wunhi nuni lrp, lih pavkunhi lr rlwrtup nrvnekanewrwsetpanu,
         /p wə́nči- nə́ni -lé·p, lí-=č -pahkánči-lé· e·ləwé·t·əp nehəni·k·a·ní·i-we·wsi·tpána,
         /t That happened so that it would happen exactly as the ancient prophet said,
         /k All this was done, that it might be fulfilled which was spoken by the prophet,

Mt 21.5 /b rlwrtup, Lw, Nsaeun tonu,
         /p e·ləwé·t·əp, "ló· †nsá·yən tó·na,
         /t when he said, "Tell the daughter of Zion (you pl.),
         /k saying, Tell ye the daughter of Sion,

         /b Punaw preat ksakemaeum,
         /p 'pənáw pé·a·t ksa·k·i·má·yəm.
         /t 'Look at your king coming.
         /k Behold, thy King cometh unto thee,

/b   tufrlunsw, qrkonxatutu arkr;
/p   tanke·lə́nsu, kwek·ɔ·nxa·t·ɔ́t·a aé·ke·,
/t   He is humble, riding on a donkey,
/k   meek, and sitting upon an ass,

/b   ok wunehanelet wunaolwkw.
/p   ɔ́·k wəni·č·a·ní·li·t wəna·ɔlúk·u.'"
/t   and her foal (*lit.*, child) is following her.'"
/k   and a colt the foal of an ass.

Jn 12.16   /b   Rkrkemunhek vetami mutu watwunrop wcnhi nc lrk;
             /p   e·k·e·ki·mə́nči·k hítami máta o·wa·to·wəné·ɔ·p wénči- nə́ -lé·k.
             /t   The disciples did not know at first why that happened.
             /k   These things understood not his disciples at the first:

             /b   jwq Nhesus mrhi xifovkunemkwsetc
             /p   šúkw nčí·sas mé·či xinkɔhkəni·mkwəs·í·t·e,
             /t   But after Jesus was glorified (*lit.*, praised),
             /k   but when Jesus was glorified,

             /b   nu mwjatumunro rlaptwnrtup nrvnekanewrwsetpanu,
             /p   ná mwəš·a·t·amə́né·ɔ e·la·pto·né·t·əp nehəni·k·a·ní·i-we·wsi·tpána,
             /t   then they remembered what the ancient prophet had said,
             /k   then remembered they that these things were written of him,

             /b   ok tcli mrhi nc lusenrp.
             /p   ɔ́·k tə́li- mé·či nə́ -ləs·í·ne·p.
             /t   and that he had done that.
             /k   and that they had done these things unto him.

Chapter 88 (pp. 151-152). (No new section in L.1, p. 176, and L.2, top of p. 196.) (John 12.17-19; Luke 19.39-44; Matthew 21.10-12, 14-16; Mk 11.11)

Jn 12.17   /b   Eku rpetpanek nckc wcnhematc Lasulusu li mavhekamekwf,
             /p   íka e·p·i·tpáni·k néke wenči·má·t·e †la·səlás·a lí mahči·k·amí·k·unk,
             /t   The people that had been there when he called Lazarus from the grave,
             /k   The people ... that was with him when he called Lazarus out of his grave,

             /b   cntu amwekunatc rfululetc, tulahemwenrop.
             /p   énta-a·mwi·kəná·t·e enkələlí·t·e, təla·č·i·mwi·né·ɔ·p.
             /t   when he raised him up after he died, told what had happened.
             /k   and raised him from the dead, bare record.

Jn 12.18 /b Nuni wunhi apvesvekaonro,
/p nə́ni wwə́nči-a·phishikaɔ·né·ɔ,
/t For that reason they went to meet him as he came,
/k For this cause the people also met him,

/b puntamevtetc tuli ncli kanjacvosenrp.
/p pəntamihtí·t·e tə́li- nə́ -lí-kanšaehɔ·s·í·ne·p.
/t having heard that he had done that miracle.
/k for that they heard that he had done this miracle.

Jn 12.19 /b Paluseok lutwpanek,
/p †pa·ləsi·í·ɔk lət·ó·p·ani·k,
/t The Pharisees said to each other,
/k The Pharisees therefore said among themselves,

/b krvlu qelu lusevnu,
/p "kéhəla kkwí·la-ləs·íhəna.
/t "There's really nothing we can do.
/k Perceive ye how ye prevail nothing?

/b jr wrmi awrn noolao.
/p šé· wé·mi awé·n nɔ·ɔlá·ɔ."
/t See how everyone follows him."
/k behold, the world is gone after him.

Lk 19.39 /b Aluntc Paluseok wihi naolahek, tulawao;
/p a·lə́nte †pa·ləsi·í·ɔk wiči-na·ɔlá·č·i·k təlawwá·ɔ,
/t Some Pharisees among those that followed him said to him,
/k And some of the Pharisees from among the multitude said unto him,

/b Qvetul Nrvlalerf rkrkemuthek.
/p "khwítəl, nehəlá·lienk, e·k·e·ki·máč·ɪ·k."
/t "Master, admonish your disciples."
/k Master, rebuke thy disciples.

Lk 19.40 /b Tulao, Hetkwvsetetc a jac a avsunuk kunhemwuk.   [⟨-kwvset-⟩ for ⟨-kwsevt-⟩]
/p təlá·ɔ, "či·tkwəs·ihtí·t·e=á·, šá·e=á· ahsə́nak kənčí·məwak."
/t He said to them, "If they are silent, the stones would immediately cry out."
/k And he answered and said unto them, I tell you that, if these should hold their peace, the stones would immediately cry out.

Lk 19.41 /b Kexki pratc wtrnif eku lifwrxen, ok lupuq,
/p kí·xki pe·á·t·e o·t·é·nink, íka linkwé·x·ɪ·n, ɔ́·k ləpákw.
/t When he got near the city, he turned his gaze to it and wept.
/k And when he was come near, he beheld the city, and wept over it,

Lk 19.42 /b lwr, O jeki a muv kwatwnrp, kwpunc ke, eli b kejkwbm
/p lúwe·, "ó·, ší·ki=á·=máh ko·wa·tó·ne·p, kó·pəne kí·, ílli yú kki·škó·yəm,
/t He said, "Oh, it would have been good for you, at least, to know, even this day of yours,
/k Saying, If thou hadst known, even thou, at least in this thy day,

/b krkw a wcnhi wulafwmkreun! [⟨-reun⟩ for /-é·an/]
/p kéku=á· wénči-wəlanko·mké·an.
/t the things that are the reason for your peace.
[*lit.*, 'for why people are at peace with you']
/k the things which belong unto thy peace!

/b Jwq bqc mrhi kuntvataswv ktulih taa nrmwun.
/p šúkw yúkwe mé·či kanthatá·s·u, któli-=č tá=á· -ne·mó·wən.
/t But now they are hidden so that you cannot see them.
/k but now they are hid from thine eyes.

Lk 19.43 /b Rlih jifalkonek okai li mwnvakcvtet rpeun,
/p é·li-=č šinka·lkóni·k ɔ·ká·i -lí-mo·nhakéhti·t é·p·ian,
/t For your enemies shall dig a trench around the place where you are,
/k For ... thine enemies shall cast a trench about thee,

/b okh kokrkakwk,
/p ɔ́·k=č kɔ·ke·ká·k·o·k,
/t and they shall surround you,
/k and compass thee round,

/b okh kunwtumalkwk wcnhih mutu kuski kheon
/p ɔ́·k=č kəno·t·əmá·lko·k, wénči-=č máta -káski-kčí·ɔn.
/t and they shall guard you so that you will not be able to get out.
/k and keep thee in on every side,

Lk 19.44 /b okh kjcfexumwkwk mvehe vakif, okh navle knehanuk, [⟨kneh-‖anuk⟩]
/p ɔ́·k=č kšenki·x·əmúk·o·k mhičí·i hák·ink, ɔ́·k=č nahəlí·i kəni·č·á·nak.
/t And they shall lay you down even with the ground, along with your children.
/k And shall lay thee even with the ground, and thy children within thee;

(p. 152) /b ok taa nuxpunc ktusunum petaexunwi,
/p ɔ́·k tá=á· náxpəne [kwə́t·i] ktás·ənəm pi·tai·x·ənó·wi,
/t And not even [one] stone of yours will lie upon another, ['one' missing]
/k and they shall not leave in thee one stone upon another;

/b rli mutu watwun ktcli toxkrnrp.
/p é·li- máta -wwa·tó·wan któli-tɔxké·ne·p."
/t because you do not know that you are having visitors."
/k because thou knewest not the time of thy visitation.

Mk 11.11 /b   Nu Nhesus eku tuli tumekrn Nhelwsulumif,
/p   ná nčí·sas íka táli-təmí·k·e·n †nči·lo·sələmink.
/t   Then Jesus entered Jerusalem.
/kl   And Jesus entered into Jerusalem,

Mt 21.10 /b   mrhi trmekrtc wrmi wrtwtrnyehek salaxkevlrok
/p   mé·či te·mi·k·é·t·e, wé·mi we·t·o·t·e·naí·č·i·k salaxkihəlé·ɔk.
/t   After he entered, all the townspeople were agitated,
/l   and when he was come into Jerusalem, all the city was moved,

/b   lwrok, Awrn vuh wuv?
/p   luwé·ɔk, "awé·n=háč wá?"
/t   saying, "Who is this?"
/kl   saying, Who is this?

Mt 21.11 /b   Wehrohek tulawao,
/p   wi·č·e·ɔ́·č·i·k təlawwá·ɔ,
/t   His companions told them,
/kl   And the multitude said,

/b   Nul tu wu Nhesus Nasulute nrvnekanewrwset tali Falulebf.
/p   "nál=tá wá nčí·sas, †nasəlat·í·i-nehəni·k·a·ní·i-wé·wsi·t táli †nka·lalí·yunk."
/t   "This is Jesus, the prophet of Nazareth in Galilee."
/kl   This is Jesus the prophet of Nazareth of Galilee.

Mt 21.12 /b   Nhesus ekali tumekrp Krtanitwetei patamwrekaonif,
/p   nčí·sas íkali təmí·k·e·p ke·tanət·o·wi·t·í·i-pa·tamwe·i·k·á·ɔnink,
/t   Jesus went into the temple of God,
/kl   And Jesus went into the temple of God,

Mk 11.11 /b   wrmi krkw pwunamun tali lamekwavmc.
/p   wé·mi kéku pwɔ́namən táli la·mi·k·əwáhəme.
/t   and he looked at everything inside.
/l   and looked round about upon all things;

Mt 21.14 /b   Nrli nc wekwavmif avpet kckrpifohek ok kwqulwqevlahek, wtxawao
/p   né·li- nə́ wi·k·əwáhəmink -ahpí·t, ke·k·e·p·inkɔ́·č·i·k ɔ́·k kuk·wəluk·wihəlá·č·i·k o·txawwá·ɔ,
/t   While he was in the building, blind and lame people came to him,
/kl   and the blind and the lame came to him in the temple;

/b   qekrvao, nanc tali.
/p   kwi·k·e·há·ɔ ná=nə táli.
/t   and he healed them in that very place.
/kl   and he healed them.

Mt 21.15 /b Mrhi nekanexifek wcvevwfrhek ok rvlrkvekrhek nc rlenamevtetc
/p mé·či ni·k·a·ni·x·ínki·k wehi·hunké·č·i·k ó·k ehəle·khi·k·é·č·i·k nə́ e·li·namihtí·t·e,
/t After the head priests and scribes saw that,
/k And when the chief priests and scribes saw

/b rli xifwi krkw luset,
/p é·li- xínkwi-kéku -ləs·i·t,
/t how he did a great thing,
/k the wonderful things that he did,

/b ok nrk memunsuk rli wekwavmif tali xawvetaqsevtet
/p ó·k né·k mi·mə́nsak é·li- wi·k·əwáhəmink -táli-xa·whita·kwsíhti·t,
/t and how the children were shouting in the building,
/k and the children crying in the temple,

/b rli lwcvtet, Krtanitweun aphi lclrxrmvrl wu Ntrpitu wrqesumwkwk;
/p é·li-luwéhti·t, "ke·tanət·ó·wian, á·pči lehəle·x·é·mhe·l wá †nte·pít·a we·k·wi·s·əmúk·wək,"
/t and saying, "O God, let this son of David live forever,"
/k and saying, Hosanna to the Son of David; [See Mt 21.9.]

/b ave mutu wulrluntamweok.
/p áhi máta wəle·ləntamo·wí·ɔk.
/t they were very much displeased.
/k they were sore displeased,

Mt 21.16 /b Tulawao, Kpuntaook vuh bk rlwcvtet?
/p təlawwá·ɔ, "kpəntaɔ́·ɔk=háč yó·k e·ləwéhti·t?"
/t They said to him, "Do you hear what these are saying?"
/k And said unto him, Hearest thou what these say?

/b Tulkwao, kovun. Mutu vuh vuji ktukintamwunro, cntu lwcf,
/p təlkəwá·ɔ, "kɔhán; máta=háč háši ktak·əntamo·wəné·ɔ énta-lúwenk,
/t He said to them, "Yes: have you never read where it says,
/k And Jesus saith unto them, Yea; have ye never read,

/b Meminsuk ok nwnrhek vwtwnwawf nwnhi puvkunhextwn wlukunemkwswukun?
/p 'mi·mə́nsak ó·k no·né·č·i·k wto·nəwá·unk núnči-pahkančí·xto·n wəlak·əni·mkwəs·əwá·k·an'?"
/t 'I have perfected praise from the mouths of children and nursing infants'?"
/k Out of the mouth of babes and sucklings thou hast perfected praise?

[Chapter 89] (pp. 152-154). (L. section 89.) (John 12.20-43)

Jn 12.20 /b Aluntc Fleksuk eku wetavpwuk
        /p a·lə́nte nkəlí·ksak íka witahpúwak
        /t Some Greeks were there among them
        /k And there were certain Greeks among them

        /b krtu wehi patamahek ok tavqepwehek,
        /p ké·t·a-wíči-pa·tamá·č·i·k ɔ́·k -tahkwi·p·wí·č·i·k.
        /t who desired to join in the prayer and the feast.
        /k that came up to worship at the feast:

Jn 12.21 /b nulek nrk wtxawao Pilupsu Mpctsryti wcnheyelehi Fululebf;   [⟨Ful-⟩ for ⟨Fal-⟩]
        /p náli·k né·k o·txawwá·ɔ †pilápsa, †mpetse·áiti wenči·ai·lí·č·i, †nka·lalí·yunk.
        /t It was they who came to Philip, who was from Bethsaida in Galilee.
        /k The same came therefore to Philip, which was of Bethsaida of Galilee,

        /b tulawao Nhwv, futu nrowunu Nhesus.
        /p təlawwá·ɔ, "nčú, nkát·a-ne·ɔ́·wəna nčí·sas."
        /t They said to him, "Friend, we want to see Jesus."
        /k and desired him, saying, Sir, we would see Jesus.

Jn 12.22 /b Nu Pilups anvwqi tulan Antlwsu,
        /p ná †pílaps a·nhúkwi tóla·n †antəló·s·a.
        /t Then Philip, in turn, told Andrew,
        /k Philip cometh and telleth Andrew:

        /b Antlws ok Pilups tulanro Nhesusu.
        /p ántəlo·s ɔ́·k †pílaps təla·né·ɔ nči·sás·a.
        /t and Andrew and Philip told Jesus.
        /k and again Andrew and Philip tell Jesus.

Jn 12.23 /b Nhesus tulao,
        /p nčí·sas təlá·ɔ,
        /t Jesus said to them,
        /k And Jesus answered them, saying,

        /b Mrhi tpisqevlr li Wrqesif linw xifovkuneman.
        /p "mé·či tpəskwíhəle· lí- we·k·wí·s·ink lə́nu -xinkɔhkəní·ma·n.
        /t "The time has come for the man who is the Son to be glorified (*lit.*, praised).
        /k The hour is come, that the Son of man should be glorified.

Jn 12.24 /b Kvehe ktulwvmw,
        /p khičí·i ktəllúhəmɔ,
        /t I tell you truly,
        /k Verily, verily, I say unto you,

Text, Transcription, and Translation 519

/b Kwti a vwet e mifq mutu homvakec muvtrxifc ok alutkc,
/p kwə́t·i=á· hwi·tí·i-mínkw máta †čɔ·mhákie mahte·x·ínke ɔ́·k alə́tke,
/t if one grain ('seed') of wheat does not fall into the ground and decay,
/k Except a corn of wheat fall into the ground and die,

/b aphi a maot.
/p á·pči=á· má·ɔt.
/t it would always be (only) one.
/k it abideth alone:

/b Jwq a alutkc xrli a eku wunheyb.
/p šúkw=á· alə́tke, xé·li=á· íka wənčí·ayu.
/t But if it decays, much would come from it.
/k but if it die, it bringeth forth much fruit.

Jn 12.25
/b Awrnh rvotuf wulclrxrokun, ufulh.
/p awé·n=č ehɔ́·t·ank wəlehəle·x·e·ɔ́·k·an, ánkəl=č.
/t Anyone who loves their life shall die.
/k He that loveth his life shall lose it;

/b Kahih awrn jifatuf wulclrxrokun b tali cntu lawsif;
/p káč·i=č awé·n šinká·t·ank wəlehəle·x·e·ɔ́·k·an yú táli entalá·wsink
/t But anyone who hates their life in this world
/k and he that hateth his life in this world

/b ekuh tulawsw cntu mutu ealu pumawsif.
/p íka=č talá·wsu énta- máta -i·ála-pəmá·wsink.
/t shall live where life is eternal (*lit.*, 'where one never stops living').
/k shall keep it unto life eternal.

Jn 12.26
/b awrn mekumosuntamaetc, naoletch. [⟨mekumo-‖suntamaetc⟩]
/p awé·n mi·kəmɔ·s·əntamaí·t·e, na·ɔlí·t·eč.
/t If anyone serves (*lit.*, works for) me, let him follow me.
/k If any man serve me, let him follow me;

(p. 153)
/b Tutuh rpeu, nrkuh nr nanc topen.
/p tə́ta=č é·p·ia, né·k·a=č né· ná=nə tɔ́p·i·n.
/t Wherever I shall be, he, too, shall be in the same place.
/k and where I am, there shall also my servant be:

/b Awrnh mekumosuntamaetc nrkuh Nwx wlelarva. [⟨-a⟩ for /-á·ɔ/ (perhaps /-á·a/)]
/p awé·n=č mi·kəmɔ·s·əntamaí·t·e, né·k·a=č nó·x o·li·lae·há·ɔ.
/t If anyone serves me, my father himself will please him.
/k if any man serve me, him will my Father honour.

Jn 12.27 /b Bqc mrhi ntrvif nsukwrluntum, krkwh vuh ntulwc?
/p yúkwe mé·či nté·hink nsak·we·lə́ntam; kéku=č=háč ntə́ləwe?
/t Now I am distressed in my heart; what shall I say?
/k Now is my soul troubled; and what shall I say?

/b Nwxa pale lunel nrlumu tpisqevlak;
/p 'núxa·, palí·i lə́ni·l né·ləma tpəskwíhəla·k.'
/t 'Father, remove me before the time comes.'
/k Father, save me from this hour:

/b alwt nanc nwnhi pan.
/p aló·t ná=nə núnči-pá·n.
/t Yet that is the very reason why I came.
/k but for this cause came I unto this hour.

Jn 12.28 /b Nwxa xifovkunemvatu ktulwcnswakun!
/p núxa·, xinkɔhkəni·mhá·t·a ktələwensəwá·k·an."
/t Father, 'glorify' your name."
/k Father, glorify thy name.

/b Nu vwqrbf wuntvetakot lwrokun lwrtakot,
/p ná hukwé·yunk wənthitá·k·ɔt luwe·ɔ́·k·an, luwe·tá·k·ɔt,
/t Then a voice was heard from on high, being heard to say,
/k Then came there a voice from heaven, saying,

/b Memrhi nmuxifovkunemvatumunrp, okh ntunhi xifovkunemvatamun.
/p "mi·mé·či nəmax·inkɔhkəni·mha·t·amə́ne·p, ɔ́·k=č ntánči-xinkɔhkəni·mhá·t·amən."
/t "I have glorified it in the past, and I shall glorify it over again."
/k I have both glorified it, and will glorify it again.

Jn 12.29 /b Eku nepaehek puntamevtetc, lwrok, Prtvakvon!
/p íka ni·p·aí·č·i·k pəntamihtí·t·e, luwé·ok, "pe·thákhɔn."
/t When the ones standing there heard it, they said, "There was thunder."
/k The people therefore, that stood by, and heard it, said that it thundered:

/b Jwq aluntc lwrok osavkamre cvalwkalunt krkw tulao.
/p šúkw a·lə́nte luwé·ɔk, "ɔ·s·ahkame·í·i-ehalo·ká·lənt kéku təlá·ɔ."
/t But others said, "An angel ('heavenly messenger') spoke to him."
/k others said, An angel spake to him.

Jn 12.30 /b Nhesus tulao, Takw ne wunhi nc puntavkovtwi,   [⟨puntavk⟩ for ⟨puntak⟩]
/p nčí·sas təlá·ɔ, "takó· ní· wə́nči- nə́ -pəntakɔhtó·wi,
/t Jesus said to them, "I was not the reason that was heard;
/k Jesus answered and said, This voice came not because of me,

/b kelwu tu wunhi.
/p ki·ló·wa=tá wə́nči.
/t it was because of you.
/k but for your sakes.

Jn 12.31
/b Bqc wulava lr kuntrlumwqswakun vatr cntu lawsif;
/p yúkwe wəláha lé·, kənte·ləmukwsəwá·k·an hát·e· entalá·wsink.
/t Now, rather, it is happening, and there is condemnation in the world.
/k Now is the judgment of this world:

/b bqch sakemu b cntu lawsif pavkelqwsw.
/p yúkwe=č sa·k·í·ma yú entalá·wsink pahki·lkwə́s·u.
/t Now the prince (chief, king) of this world shall be thrown out.
/k now shall the prince of this world be cast out.

Jn 12.32
/b Ne uspunifc b wunhi vakif wrmih awrn eku mprjwu.
/p ní· aspənínke yú wə́nči hák·ink, wé·mi=č awé·n íka mpé·š·əwa."
/t And *I*, when I am lifted up from this earth, will bring everyone there."
/k And I, if I be lifted up from the earth, will draw all men unto me.

Jn 12.33
/b Nuni tulwrn, wuntamasen rlih ufuluk.
/p nə́ni tə́ləwe·n, wwəntamá·s·i·n é·li-=č -ánkələk.
/t He said that explaining how he was going to die.
/k This he said, signifying what death he should die.

Jn 12.34
/b Eku rpehek tulawao,
/p   íka e·p·í·č·i·k təlawwá·ɔ,
/t   The people there said to him,
/k   The people answered him,

/b mpuntamunrnap wunhi xwi aptwnakun, tulih Klyst aphi avpen;
/p "mpəntaməné·na·p wə́nči xúwi-a·pto·ná·k·an, tə́li-=č kəláist á·pči -ahpí·n.
/t "We have heard from the law ('old word') that Christ will be forever.
/k We have heard out of the law that Christ abideth for ever:

/b ta vuh kwnhi lwrn, linwh Wrqesif uspuna?
/p tá=háč kúnči-lúwe·n, 'lə́nu=č we·k·wí·s·ink áspəna·'?
/t Why do you say, 'The man who is the Son will be lifted up'?
/k and how sayest thou, The Son of man must be lifted up?

/b Awrn vuh nu linw wrqesif?
/p awé·n=háč ná lə́nu we·k·wí·s·ink?"
/t Who is the man who is the Son?"
/k who is this Son of man?

Jn 12.35 /b Nu Nhesus tulan,
          /p ná nčí·sas tə́la·n,
          /t Then Jesus said to them,
          /k Then Jesus said unto them,

          /b Heh tvakiti oxrrk qetavpemkwnro.
          /p "čí·č thakíti ɔ·x·é·e·k kəwitahpi·mko·né·ɔ.
          /t "The light is with you (pl.) for a short while longer.
          /k Yet a little while is the light with you.

          /b Wulwxwrq nrli oxrrk, wunheh mutu peskrnamerq;
          /p wəló·x·we·kw né·li-ɔ·x·é·e·k, wə́nči-=č máta -pi·ske·namíe·kw.
          /t Walk well while there is light, so that you are not overtaken by the dark.
          /k Walk while ye have the light, lest darkness come upon you:

          /b rli awrn cntu peskrk prmskat, mutu watwun tutu reat.
          /p é·li awé·n énta-pí·ske·k pé·mska·t máta o·wa·tó·wən tə́ta é·a·t.
          /t For someone who walks in the dark does not know where he is going.
          /k for he that walketh in darkness knoweth not whither he goeth.

Jn 12.36 /b Srki vatrk oxrrk, nvakatamwq; wcnhih oxrrkumerq.
          /p sé·ki-hát·e·k ɔ·x·é·e·k, nhaká·t·amo·kw, wénči-=č -ɔ·x·e·e·k·amíe·kw."
          /t As long as there is light, rely on it, so that you shall have light."
          /k While ye have light, believe in the light, that ye may be the children of light. ...

          /b Nhesus keji nc lwrtc, palerp konjepvapani.
          /p nčí·sas kíši- nə́ -luwé·t·e, palí·i é·p, kɔnši·phá·p·ani.
          /t After Jesus finished saying that, he went somewhere else and hid from them.
          /k These things spake Jesus, and departed, and did hide himself from them.

Jn 12.37 /b Jwq mutu wlamvetaoewapani,
          /p šúkw máta o·la·mhitaɔ·iwwá·p·ani,
          /t But they did not believe him,
          /kl (1) But ... (3) yet they believed not on him: [numbers = sequence in L.]

          /b taoni xrlrnaovki li kanjacvoselwp tali rlifwrxenvetet;
          /p tá·ɔni xe·lennáɔhki lí-kanšaehɔ·s·í·lo·p táli e·linkwe·x·i·nhíti·t.
          /t even though he had performed many kinds of miracles before their eyes.
          /kl (2) though he had done so many miracles before them, ...

Jn 12.38 /b nu pavkunhi lrp rlwrtup nrvnekanewrwsetpanu Esyusu rlwrtup;
          /p ná pahkánči-lé·p e·ləwé·t·əp nehəni·k·a·ní·i-we·wsi·tpána ✝i·sayə́s·a, e·ləwé·t·əp,
          /t Then was fulfilled what was said by the ancient prophet Esaias, when he said,
          /k That the saying of Esaias the prophet might be fulfilled, which he spake,

Text, Transcription, and Translation

/b Nrvlaleun awrn vuh wlamvetamun ntaptwnakununu!
/p "nehəlá·lian, awé·n=háč o·la·mhítamən nta·pto·na·k·anə́na?
/t "My lord, who believed our report ('words')?
/k Lord, who hath believed our report?

/b awrni vuh pwunwntulan Nrvlalwrt wunaxk?
/p awé·ni=háč pwənúntəla·n nehəlá·ləwe·t wənáxk?"
/t Who did the Lord show his hand to?"
/k and to whom hath the arm of the Lord been revealed?

Jn 12.39
/b Puna wunhi mutu kuski wulamvetaowunro, rli Esyusu lupi lwrtup,   [⟨tao-‖wunro⟩]
/p pənáh, wwə́nči- máta -káski-wəla·mhitao·wəné·ɔ, é·li- †i·sayə́s·a lápi -luwé·t·əp,
/t Now, they were not able to believe him because Esaias said again,
/k Therefore they could not believe, because that Esaias said again,

Jn 12.40
(p. 154)
/b Kokrpifwrvalkwao ok vwhetanetakwnro vwtrvwao;
/p "kɔk·e·p·inkwe·ha·lkəwá·ɔ ɔ́·k wči·t·ani·ta·k·o·né·ɔ wtehəwá·ɔ,
/t "He (obv.) blinded them and hardened their hearts,   [translated literally]
/k He hath blinded their eyes, and hardened their heart;   [i.e., 'made them obtuse']

/b tulih mutu nrmwunro, ok mutu nunwstamwunro vwtrvwaif
/p tə́li-=č máta -ne·mo·wəné·ɔ, ɔ́·k máta -nəno·stamo·wəné·ɔ wtehəwá·ink,
/t so that they would not see it and would not understand it in their hearts,
/k that they should not see with their eyes, nor understand with their heart,

/b okh tuli mutu qulupewunro wunhi a kekrvuk.
/p ɔ́·k=č tə́li- máta -kwələp·i·wəné·ɔ, wə́nči-=á· -ki·k·é·hak."   [B. adds 'not']
/t and so that they would not be converted, in order that I would cure them."
/k and be converted, and I should heal them.   [RSV: "and turn for me to heal them."]

Jn 12.41
/b Esyusu bni tulwrnrp,
/p †i·sayə́s·a yó·ni tələwé·ne·p,
/t Esaias said this,
/k These things said Esaias,

/b nckc nekane rli wataqc ok rkunwtifc tulih xifovkunemkwsen Nhesus.
/p néke ni·k·a·ní·i é·li-wwa·tá·k·we, ɔ́·k e·k·əno·t·ínke, tə́li-=č -xinkɔhkəni·mkwə́s·i·n nčí·sas.
/t back then when he knew it ahead of time and said that Jesus would be glorified.
/k when he saw his glory, and spake of him.

Jn 12.42
/b Jwq amunhei aluntc krkyimvrhek wlamvetaowao;
/p šúkw amənčí·i a·lə́nte ke·kayəmhé·č·i·k o·la·mhitaɔwwá·ɔ,
/t But nevertheless some of the rulers believed him,
/k Nevertheless among the chief rulers also many believed on him;

/b   jwq mutu krkw lwreok
/p   šúkw máta kéku luwe·í·ɔk,
/t   but they did not say anything,
/k   but because of the Pharisees they did not confess him,   [i.e., 'acknowledge him']

/b   rli a Paluseok ktuskaovtet wunhi cvcntu macvluf.
/p   é·li-=á· †pa·ləsi·í·ɔk -ktəskaóhti·t wə́nči ehə́nta-ma·éhəlank.
/t   because the Pharisees would drive them out of the synagogue ('meeting place').
/k   lest they should be put out of the synagogue:

Jn 12.43   /b   Rli alwrluntamevtet wlukuvnemkwsen b tali cntu lawsif   [⟨ukuvn|⟩ for ⟨ukun|⟩]
/p   é·li-aləwe·ləntamíhti·t wəlak·əni·mkwə́s·i·n yú táli entalá·wsink,
/t   As they prize most of all for one to be praised in this world,
/k   For they loved the praise of men

/b   wunwntarluntumunro wlukuneman Krtanitwet.
/p   wənuntae·ləntaməné·ɔ wəlak·əní·ma·n ke·tanət·ó·wi·t.
/t   and they think little of God being praised.
/k   more than the praise of God.

Chapter 90 (p. 154). (No new section in L.) (John 12.44-50; Mark 11.11; Matthew 21.17)

Jn 12.44   /b   Nhesus amufexsw rlwrtc,
/p   nčí·sas amankí·xsu e·ləwé·t·e,
/t   Jesus used a loud voice when he said,
/k   Jesus cried and said,
/l   But Jesus [*as he went away*] cried and said,

/b   awrn wrlamvetaet, takw ne; nrkuma tu prtalwkalet;
/p   "awé·n we·la·mhítai·t, takó· ní·, né·k·əma=tá pe·t·alo·ká·li·t.
/t   "Anyone who believes me doesn't (believe) *me*, but him who sent me.
/k   He that believeth on me, believeth not on me, but on him that sent me.

Jn 12.45   /b   awrn nret wunroo prtalwkalelehi.
/p   awé·n né·i·t wəne·ó·ɔ pe·t·alo·ka·li·lí·č·i.
/t   Anyone who sees me sees him who sent me.
/k   And he that seeth me seeth him that sent me.

Jn 12.46   /b   Preau b cntu lawsif noxrkumun;
/p   pe·á·a, yú entalá·wsink nɔ·x·é·kamən,
/t   When I came, I lit up this world with light,
/k   I am come a light into the world,

/b tulih awrn wlamvetaetc taa cntu peskrk avpewun.
/p tə́li-=č awé·n wəla·mhitaí·t·e tá=á· énta-pí·ske·k -ahpí·wən.
/t so that if anyone believes me they will not be in darkness.
/k that whosoever believeth on me should not abide in darkness.

Jn 12.47 /b Awrn puntufc ntaptwnakun jwq mutu wulamvetufc;
/p awé·n pəntánke nta·pto·ná·k·an, šúkw máta wəla·mhitánke,
/t If anyone hears my words but does not believe them,
/k And if any man hear my words, and believe not,

/b taa ne futumakevai;
/p tá=á· ní· nkət·əma·k·i·há·i,
/t I will not condemn them,
/k I judge him not:

/b rli mutu wunhi pau ntuli a ktumakevan b cntu lawset.
/p é·li- máta -wə́nči-pá·a, ntə́li-=á· -ktəma·k·í·ha·n yú entalá·wsi·t.
/t for I did not come to condemn mankind.
/k for I came not to judge the world, but to save the world.

Jn 12.48 /b Awrn mrtrlumet, ok ntaptwnakun mutu wifsituf,
/p awé·n me·t·é·ləmi·t, ó·k nta·pto·ná·k·an máta winksə́t·ank,
/t Anyone who thinks little of me and does not like hearing my words,
/k He that rejecteth me, and receiveth not my words,

/b avpwv tu krtumakevath;   [⟨avpwv⟩ for ⟨avpw⟩]
/p ahpú=tá ke·t·əma·k·í·ha·t=č:
/t for them there is one who will condemn them:
/k hath one that judgeth him:

/b aptwnakun rlaptwnreu,
/p a·pto·ná·k·an e·la·pto·né·a.
/t the words that I have spoken.
/k the word that I have spoken,

/b nunulh nuni qwtumakevkwn mukuni-kejqekc.
/p nánal=č nə́ni kwət·əma·k·íhko·n məkə́ni-ki·škwí·k·e.
/t That is what will condemn them on the last day.
/k the same shall judge him in the last day.

Jn 12.49 /b Rli mutu nevlahi aptwnru.
/p é·li- máta nihəláči -a·pto·né·a.
/t Because I do not speak on my own.
/k For I have not spoken of myself;

/b   Jwq Wrtwxumunt prtalwkalet nmelkwp aptwnakun,
/p   šúkw we·t·ó·x·əmənt pe·t·alo·ká·li·t nəmí·lko·p a·pto·ná·k·an,
/t   But the father who sent me gave me words,
/k   but the Father which sent me, he gave me a commandment,

/b   krkwh rlwreu ok wuntamaseu.
/p   kéku=č e·ləwé·a ɔ́·k wəntamá·s·ia.
/t   the things I was to say and explain.
/k   what I should say, and what I should speak.

Jn 12.50 /b Ok nwatwn toptwnakun rvalumakumek a wcnhi pumawseif.   [⟨-seif⟩ for ⟨-sif⟩]
/p   ɔ́·k no·wá·to·n tɔ·pto·ná·k·an ehaləmá·kami·k=á· wénči-pəmá·wsink.
/t   And I know his words would be a source of eternal life for people.
/k   And I know that his commandment is life everlasting:

/b   Puna krkw rlwranc, myai rlet nanc ntulwrn.
/p   pənáh, kéku e·ləwe·á·ne, mayá·i é·li·t ná=nə ntə́ləwe·n."
/t   Now, when I said things, exactly what he said to me is what I said."
/k   whatsoever I speak therefore, even as the Father said unto me, so I speak.

[Section 90 in L.1 and L.2.]

Mk 11.11 /b   Mrhi loqekc
/p   mé·či lɔ·k·wí·k·e,
/t   After evening had come,
/kl And now the eventide was come,

Mt 21.17, Mk 11.11
/b   wunukulao, khe eku wunhi, wtrnif Pctuneuf rp,
/p   wənək·alá·ɔ, kčí· íka wə́nči o·t·é·nink, †petəní·yunk é·p,
/t   he left them and went out from the town, and he went to Bethany,
/l   he left them, and went out of the city unto Bethany

/b   ok nrl atux neju,
/p   ɔ́·k né·l átax ní·š·a.
/t   and with him the twelve.
/l   with the twelve.

Mt 21.17 /b   nanc moekrnro. ‖
/p   ná=nə mɔi·k·e·né·ɔ.
/t   And there they (all) spent the night.
/kl and he lodged there.

L. has here: [Lk 21.37] In the day-time he was teaching in the temple; and at night he went out, and abode in the mount that is called the mount of Olives. [Lk 21.38] And all

the people came early in the morning to him in the temple, for to hear him.
[For Lk 21.37, see below after Mk 11.19. For Lk 21.38, see after Mk 11.15.]

Chapter 91 (p. 155). (L. section 91.) (Matthew 21.13, 16, 19; Mark 11.12-18; Luke 19.47-48, 21.37-38)

Mt 21.16, Mk 11.12
- /b Rluvparkc qrtketc wunhi Pctuni li wtrnif kavtwpwp,
- /p e·lahpa·é·k·e, kwe·tkí·t·e wə́nči †pétəni lí o·t·é·nink, kahtó·p·o·p.
- /t The next morning, when he returned from Bethany to the town, he was hungry.
- /l Now on the morrow, in the morning, as he returned from Bethany into the city, he hungered.

Mk 11.13, Mt 21.19
- /b nrr vetkov li joexkunac. Kumpavkw nu vetwq. Eku r;   [⟨vetkov⟩ for /hítkɔ/]
- /p né·e· hítkɔ lí šɔi·xkanáe. kə́mpahku ná hít·ukw. íka é·.
- /t He saw a tree by the side of the road. The tree had leaves, and he went to it.
- /l And seeing a fig-tree afar off in the way having leaves, he came to it,

- /b letrvr kaxunch apulijuk eku avpwuk.
- /p li·t·é·he·, "ká·xəne=č a·p·ələ́š·ak íka ahpúwak.
- /t He thought, "I wonder whether there will be any apples on it."
- /l if haply he might find any thing thereon:

- /b Jwk eku preatc mutu krkw muxkamwi kumpavko jwq
- /p šúkw íka pe·á·t·e, máta kéku maxkamó·wi, kə́mpahkɔ šúkw,
- /t But when he got there, he found nothing but leaves,
- /l and when he came to it, he found nothing thereon but leaves only;

- /b rli nrlumu tpisqevlak.
- /p é·li- né·ləma -tpəskwíhəla·k.
- /t because it was not yet the season.
- /l for the time of figs was not yet.

Mt 21.19, Mk 11.14
- /b Nhesus tulao, Bqc wunhi alu krkw kejekifch.
- /p nčí·sas təlá·ɔ, "yúkwe wə́nči ála- kéku -ki·š·i·k·ínkeč.
- /t Jesus said to it, "From now on let fruit (lit., things) cease to grow.
- /l And Jesus answered and said unto it, Let no fruit grow on thee henceforward:

Mk 11.14
- /b Mutuh vuji awrn krkw b wunhi mehewun.
- /p máta=č háši awé·n kéku yú wwə́nči-mi·č·í·wən."
- /t No one shall ever eat anything from this."
- /kl No man eat fruit of thee hereafter for ever.

/b   Ok rkrkematpani pwuntamulenrp.
/p   ó·k e·k·e·ki·ma·tpáni pwəntaməlí·ne·p.
/t   And his disciples heard it.
/kl And his disciples heard it.

Mt 21.19 /b   Nu vetwq jac jaoskswp.
/p   ná hít·ukw šá·e šaóskso·p.
/t   Then it immediately withered away.
/k   And presently the fig tree withered away.

Mk 11.15 /b   Nhelwsulumif prpanek.
/p   †nči·lo·sələmink pé·p·ani·k.
/t   They came to Jerusalem.
/k   And they come to Jerusalem:

Lk 21.38 (in L. at the end of sect. 90)
/b   Wrmi awrn eku macvlrp alupae patamwrekaonif;
/p   wé·mi awé·n íka ma·éhəle·p alap·a·í·i pa·tamwe·i·k·á·ɔnink,
/t   Everyone gathered in the temple early in the morning,
/kl And all the people came early in the morning to [him in] the temple,

/b   tuli a puntaonro.
/p   tóli-=á· -pəntaɔ·né·ɔ.
/t   in order to hear him.
/kl for to hear him.

Mk 11.15 /b   Nu Nhesus eku tcli tumekrn patamwrekaonif;
/p   ná nčí·sas íka tóli-təmí·k·e·n pa·tamwe·i·k·á·ɔnink.
/t   Then Jesus entered the temple.
/kl ... and Jesus went into the temple,

/b   qwtskaoo eku cntu mcmvalumwntelehi ok mclamoselehi,
/p   kwətskaó·ɔ íka énta-memhalamunti·lí·č·i ó·k mehəlamɔ·s·i·lí·č·i,
/t   He drove out those that were merchants there and those buying,
/kl and began to cast out them that sold and bought in the temple,

/b   ok tomunevenu cvcntu ajwntrnasik moniu,
/p   ó·k tɔ·manihí·na ehənta-a·š·unte·ná·s·i·k mónia,
/t   and he knocked over the (tables) where coins were exchanged,
/kl and overthrew the tables of the moneychangers,

/b   ok wulclumutuvpifumwao mcvmrtvakrmwu mcmvalumwnhek;
/p   ó·k wəlehələmatahpinkəmawá·ɔ mehəme·thake·mó·wa memhalamúnči·k.
/t   and the seats ('chairs') of those that sold doves.
/kl and the seats of them that sold doves;

Mk 11.16 /b ok mutu tulrlumaeo awrni qwnumulen tuk tu rlenako lokcns tali lamekwavmc.
/p ɔ́·k máta tələ·ləma·í·ɔ awé·ni kwənnəmə́li·n tákta e·li·ná·k·ɔ lɔ́·k·ens táli la·mi·k·əwáhəme.
/t And he did not allow anyone to carry any kind of dish inside the building.
/kl And would not suffer that any man should carry any vessel through the temple.

Mt 21.13 /b Tulao, Lrkvasw tu,
/p təlá·ɔ, "le·khá·s·u=tá,
/t He said to them, "It is written,
/k And said unto them, It is written,
/l And he taught, saying unto them, Is it not written, (Mk 11.17)

Mt 21.13, Mk 11.17
/b Wrmih cntxakret tulwcntamunh, wekeu patamwrekaon.
/p 'wé·mi=č entxa·ké·i·t, tələwéntamən=č wí·k·ia pa·tamwe·i·k·á·ɔn',
/t 'All nations shall call my house a house of prayer.'
/l My house shall be called of all nations the house of prayer;

/b Jwq kelwu ktuletwnro wcnhi krvkumwtkrsekaonek.
/p šúkw ki·ló·wa ktəli·to·né·ɔ wénči-kehkəmo·tke·s·i·k·á·ɔni·k."
/t But *you* have made it into a house of thieves." [*lit.*, 'made that by which it is']
/kl but ye have made it a den of thieves.

Lk 19.47 /b Cji kejqek eku tali pumitwnrp. [⟨-twnrp⟩ for ⟨-twnvrp⟩]
/p éši-kí·škwi·k íka táli-pəmət·ó·nhe·p.
/t Every day he preached there.
/k And he taught daily in the temple. (Cf. Lk 21.37; see end of sect. 90.)

Mk 11.18 /b Rvlrkvekrhek ok wcvevwfrhek nekanexifek puntamevtetc,
/p ehəle·khi·k·é·č·i·k ɔ́·k wehi·hunké·č·i·k ni·k·a·ni·x·ínki·k pəntamihtí·t·e,
/t When the scribes and head priests heard about it,
/k And the scribes and chief priests heard it,

/b notwnamunro wcnhi a nvelavtet,
/p nɔt·o·naməné·ɔ wénči-=á· -nhiláhti·t.
/t they looked for a way that they might kill him.
/k and sought how they might destroy him:

Lk 19.48 /b jwq qelumunro.
/p šúkw kkwi·laməné·ɔ.
/t But they could not find one.
/k And could not find what they might do: ...

Mk 11.18 /b   Koxawapani,
          /p   kɔx·awwá·p·ani,
          /t   They feared him,
          /k   for they feared him,

Lk 19.48 /b   rli wrmi awrn ave kulustaotup,
          /p   é·li- wé·mi awé·n -áhi-kələstaó·t·əp,
          /t   because all the people listened to him attentively
          /k   for all the people were very attentive to hear him.

Mk 11.18 /b   ok kanjrluntufup wunhi rlavkrkifrtwp.   [⟨-twp⟩ for /-t·əp/]
          /p   ó·k -kanše·ləntánkəp wə́nči e·lahke·kinké·t·əp.
          /t   and were astonished at his teachings.
          /k   because all the people was astonished at his doctrine.

Mk 11.19 /b   Mrhi loqekc lupi khep eku wunhi wtrnif,
          /p   mé·či lɔ·k·wí·k·e, lápi kčí·p íka wə́nči o·t·é·nink.
          /t   After evening had come, he again went out of the town.
          /k   And when even was come, he went out of the city.

Lk 21.37 (in L. at the end of sect. 90)
          /b   eku rp ovhwf Olipe rlwcntasek, na nc moekrn.
          /p   íka é·p ɔhčúnk †ɔlipí·i e·ləwentá·s·i·k, ná=nə mɔí·k·e·n.
          /t   He went to the mountain called 'of Olives', and there he spent the night.
          /k   ... and abode in the mount that is called the mount of Olives.

Chapter 92 (pp. 155-156). (L. section 92.) (Mark 11.20-26; Matthew 21.20-21)

Mk 11.20 /b   Rlavparkc eku prmskavtetc
          /p   e·lahpa·é·k·e, íka pe·mskahtí·t·e,
          /t   Early the next morning, when they passed by the place,
          /k   And in the morning, as they passed by,

          /b   wunrowapani nrl vetko tuli xwaqelen eku pchi hwpvikif.
          /p   wəne·ɔwwá·p·ani né·l hítkɔ, təli-xuwa·kwí·li·n íka péči čəphíkink.
          /t   they saw the tree, and that it was dead down to the roots.
          /k   they saw the fig tree dried up from the roots.

Mt 21.20 /b   Rkrkemunhek nc rlenamevtetc kanjrluntamwpanek.   [⟨Rkrke-‖munhek⟩]
          /p   e·k·e·ki·mə́nči·k nə́ e·li·namihtí·t·e, kanše·ləntamó·p·ani·k.
          /t   When the disciples saw that, they were astonished.
          /k   And when the disciples saw it, they marvelled,

(p. 156) /b   Lwrpanek, Jr tulkeqi jac kaxksen wu vetwq.
          /p   luwé·p·ani·k, "šé· təlkí·kwi- šá·e -ká·xksi·n wá hít·ukw."

/t They said, "See how quickly this tree has dried up."
/k saying, How soon is the fig tree withered away!

Mk 11.21 /b Petul tulao. Nrvlaleun,
/p †pí·təl təlá·ɔ, "nehəlá·lian,
/t Peter said to him, "Master,
/k And Peter ... saith unto him, Master,

/b punaw wu vetwq kuntrlumutup, mrhi kaxksw.
/p pənáw wá hít·ukw kənte·ləmát·əp; mé·či ká·xksu."
/t Look at this tree that you condemned; it has dried up."
/k behold, the fig tree which thou cursedst is withered away.

Mk 11.22 /b Nhesus tulao, Nvakalw Krtanitwet.
/p nčí·sas təlá·ɔ, "nhaká·lo· ke·tanət·ó·wi·t.
/t Jesus said to them, "Have faith in God.
/k And Jesus answering saith unto them, Have faith in God.

Mk 11.23 /b Rli kvehei ktulwvmw,
/p é·li khičí·i ktəllúhəmɔ,
/t For truly I say to you,
/k For verily I say unto you, ...

Mt 21.21 /b nvakrwserqch ok mutu jwrlumwerqc;
/p nhake·wsié·k·we=č, ɔ́·k máta šhwe·ləmwié·k·we,
/t If you have faith, and if you do not have doubts,
/k ... If ye have faith, and doubt not,

/b taa jwq nuni kuski lusewunro rlevuk wu vetwq;
/p tá=á· šúkw nəni kkáski-ləs·i·wəné·ɔ e·lí·hak wá hít·ukw,
/t you will not only be able to do what I did to this tree,
/k ye shall not only do this which is done to the fig tree,

/b jwq a ok, lrqc wuni ovhwv.
/p šúkw=á· ɔ́·k, lé·k·we wáni ɔhčú,
/t but also, if you say to this mountain,
/k but also if ye shall say unto this mountain,

/b Paleal, munwprkwf levlu,
/p 'palí·i á·l, mənəp·é·k·unk líhəla,'
/t 'Go away and jump into the sea,'
/k Be thou removed, and be thou cast into the sea;

/b   nu a nc lrw.
/p   ná=á·=nə lé·w.
/t   that's what will happen.
/k   it shall be done.

Mk 11.23 /b   Awrnh vwtrvif tali mutu jwrlumwetc,
/p   awé·n=č wté·hink táli máta šhwe·ləmwí·t·e,
/t   If anyone does not have doubts in their heart
/k   That whosoever ... shall not doubt in his heart,

/b   ave wretrluntufc lih lr krkw lwrtc,
/p   áhi-we·i·t·e·ləntánke, lí-=č -lé· kéku luwé·t·e,
/t   and if they firmly expect that something will happen if they say so,
/k   but shall believe that those things which he saith shall come to pass;

/b   tulenamunh rletrvat.
/p   təlí·namən=č e·li·t·é·ha·t.
/t   they will have happen what they want to happen.
/k   he shall have whatsoever he saith.

Mk 11.24 /b   Nuni wcnhi lilrq,
/p   nəni wénči-ləle·kw,
/t   That's why I say to you,
/k   Therefore I say unto you,

/b   Wrmih cntxi krkw wenwrrq patamarqc,
/p   wé·mi=č éntxi- kéku -wi·nəwé·e·kw pa·tama·é·k·we,
/t   everything you ask for when you pray,
/k   What things soever ye desire, when ye pray,

/b   ave wretrluntumrqc ktulih mujinumunro,
/p   áhi-we·i·t·e·ləntamé·k·we ktəli-=č -məšənəməné·ɔ,
/t   if you firmly expect that you will obtain it,
/k   believe that ye receive them,

/b   nuh nc ktulenamunro.
/p   ná=č nə́ ktəli·naməné·ɔ.
/t   that's what you will have happen.
/k   and ye shall have them.

Mk 11.25 /b   Nepaerqc patumarqc, pavketatumwmoc, avpetc hrnelavqrq;   [⟨lav⟩ for ⟨lacv⟩]
/p   ni·p·aié·k·we, pa·tama·é·k·we, pahki·t·a·t·amo·mɔ́·e, ahpí·t·e če·ni·laéhkwe·kw,
/t   When you stand and pray, if there is anyone who has wronged you, forgive them,
/k   And when ye stand praying, forgive, if ye have ought against any:

	/b	wunhih Kwxwu osavkamc rpet pavketatumaqrq khunawswakunwu.
	/p	wə́nči-=č kó·x·əwa ɔ·s·áhkame é·p·i·t -pahki·t·a·t·amá·k·we·kw kčana·wsəwa·k·anúwa.
	/t	so that your father who is in heaven will forgive you your sins.
	/k	that your Father also which is in heaven may forgive you your trespasses.

Mk 11.26	/b	Kahi mutu pavketatumarqc,
	/p	káč·i máta pahki·t·a·t·amaé·k·we,
	/t	But if you do not forgive them,
	/k	But if ye do not forgive,

	/b	Kwxwu osavkamc rpet taa kpuketatumakwunro khanawswakunwu.
	/p	kó·x·əwa ɔ·s·áhkame é·p·i·t tá=á· kpak·i·t·a·t·ama·k·o·wəné·ɔ kčana·wsəwa·k·anúwa.
	/t	your father who is in heaven will not forgive you your sins.
	/k	neither will your Father which is in heaven forgive your trespasses.

Chapter 93 (pp. 156-157). (L. section 93.) (Mark 11.27-30; Matthew 21.23-25)

Mk 11.27	/b	Lupi eku prpanek Nhelwsulumif,
	/p	lápi íka pé·p·ani·k †nči·lo·sələ́mink.
	/t	They came again to Jerusalem.
	/k	And they come again to Jerusalem:

Mk 11.27, Mt 21.23, Lk 20.1

	/b	Nrli patamwrekaonif avpamskat ok avkunwtif wrlvik aptwnakun,
	/p	né·li- pa·tamwe·i·k·á·ɔnink -ahpá·mska·t ɔ́·k -ahkənó·t·ink wé·lhik a·pto·ná·k·an,
	/t	And while he was walking in the temple and telling about the good word,
	/l	and it came to pass, that as he was walking and taught the people in the temple, and preached the gospel,

	/b	nekanexifek wcvevwfrhek ok rvlrkvekrhek ok kvekwenwuk, wtxawao;
	/p	ni·k·a·ni·x·ínki·k wehi·hunké·č·i·k, ɔ́·k ehəle·khi·k·é·č·i·k, ɔ́·k khikəwinnúwak o·txawwá·ɔ,
	/t	the head priests and scribes and elders came to him,
	/l	the chief priests and the Scribes came upon him with the elders of the people,

Mk 11.28	/b	tulawao.
	/p	təlawwá·ɔ,
	/t	and they said to him,
	/k	And say unto him,
	/l	and spake unto him, saying,

Mk 11.28 /b   Lenrn rlenako lenwavkuswakun wcnhi b lyvoseun?
         /p   "lí·ne·n e·li·ná·k·ɔ linnuwahkəs·əwá·k·an wénči- yú -laehɔ́·s·ian.
         /t   "Tell us the (kind of) authority by ('from') which you do this.
         /l   Tell us, by what authority doest thou these things?

         /b   awrn vuh ktuli melkwn nc lenwavkuswakun wcnhi b lyvoseun?
         /p   awé·n=háč ktə́li-mí·lko·n nə́ linnuwahkəs·əwá·k·an wénči- yú -laehɔ́·s·ian?"
         /t   Who is it that gave you the authority by which you do this?"
         /l   and who is he that gave thee this authority to do these things?

Mt 21.24 /b   Nhesus tulao, Nrpc kwtrnaovki krkw knatwtumwlvwmw,
         /p   nčí·sas təlá·ɔ, "né·pe kwət·ennáɔhki kéku kənat·o·t·əmo·lhúmɔ.
         /t   Jesus said to them, "I also ask you one thing.
         /k   And Jesus answered and said unto them, I also will ask you one thing,

         /b   ahemwlxerqch,
         /p   a·č·i·mo·lxié·k·we=č,
         /t   If you tell me,
         /k   which if ye tell me,

         /b   nrpch ktulunro wcnheyek nc lenwavkuswakun wcnhi b lyvoseu.
         /p   né·pe=č ktəlləné·ɔ wenčí·ai·k nə́ linnuwahkəs·əwá·k·an wénči- yú -laehɔ́·s·ia.
         /t   I, too, will tell you the source of the authority by which I do this.
         /k   I in like wise will tell you by what authority I do these things.

Mt 21.25 /b   Nhanu vwhovopwununtwakun, ta vuh wunheyb,
         /p   nčá·na wčɔhɔ·pwənəntəwá·k·an, tá=háč wənčí·ayu?
         /t   John's baptism, where was it from?
         /k   The baptism of John, whence was it?

         /b   osavkamc, ji vuh b cntu lawsif?
         /p   ɔ·s·áhkame, ší=háč yú entalá·wsink?
         /t   Heaven or this world?
         /k   from heaven, or of men?

Mk 11.30 /b   Ahemwlxeq.
         /p   a·č·i·mó·lxi·kw.
         /t   Tell me.
         /k   answer me.

Mt 21.25 /b   Nu pwunarluntamunro lutwuk;   [⟨lutw-‖uk⟩]
         /p   ná pwəna·eləntaməné·ɔ, lə́t·əwak,
         /t   Then they considered it, saying to each other,
         /k   And they reasoned with themselves, saying,

(p. 157) /b Lufwc a, osavkamc tu;
/p "lánkwe=á·, 'ɔ·s·áhkame=tá,'
/t "If we tell him, 'It's heaven,'
/k If we shall say, From heaven;

/b ktclkwnu a, Krkw vuh wcnhi mutu wulamvetaorkup?
/p ktəlkó·na=á·, 'kéku=háč wénči- máta -wəla·mhitaɔ·é·k·əp?'
/t he would tell us, 'How come you didn't believe him?'
/k he will say unto us, Why did ye not then believe him?

Mt 21.26 /b Ok a lufwc nutu b cntu lawsif, ajitc koxawunanuk rlufwmufwek
/p ɔ́·k=á· lánkwe, 'ná=tá yú entalá·wsink,' a·šíte kkɔx·a·wəná·nak e·lanko·mánkwi·k,
/t And if we tell him, 'It's this world,' we instead fear our own people,
/k But if we shall say, Of men; we fear the people; ...

Lk 20.6 /b rli a avsunu puvpakumkofq, [⟨puvpakum⟩ for ⟨pupavkum⟩]
/p é·li-=á· ahsəna -pəpahkámkɔnkw,
/t because they would throw stones at us,
/kl ... all the people will stone us: ...

Mt 21.26 /b rli wrmi awrn letrvat xifwi wrlrli lusetpanu Nhanu. [⟨wrlrli⟩ for ⟨wrlrlumi⟩]
/p é·li- wé·mi awé·n -li·t·é·ha·t, xínkwi we·lé·ləmi-ləs·i·tpána nčá·na."
/t since everyone thinks John was a great worker of wonders."
/kl ... for all hold John as a prophet.
/k ... for all men counted John, that he was a prophet indeed. (Mk 11.32)

Mk 11.33, Luke 20.7
/b Nu tulanro Nhesusu; Taa kuski lulwvvwmnu nu tu wunheyb.
/p ná təla·né·ɔ nči·sás·a, "tá=á· kkáski-ləlo·húmə na, 'ná=tá wənčí·ayu.'"
/t Then they said to Jesus, "We cannot tell you where it was from."
/l And they answered and said unto Jesus, We cannot tell whence it was.

Mk 11.33, Lk 20.8
/b Nhesus tulao,
/p nčí·sas təlá·ɔ,
/t And Jesus said to them,
/k And Jesus answering saith unto them,
/l And he said unto them,

/b Nrpc taa ktulwunro
/p "né·pe tá=á· ktəllo·wəné·ɔ
/t "And I also will not tell you
/k Neither do I tell you
/l Neither tell I you

/b   rlenako lenwavkuswakun wcnhi b lyvoseu.
/p   e·li·ná·k·ɔ linnuwahkəs·əwá·k·an wénči- yú -laehɔ́·s·ia."
/t   what the authority is by which I do this."
/l   by what authority I do these things.

Chapter 94 (p. 157). (L. section 94.) (Mark 12.1; Matthew 21.28-32)

Mk 12.1   /b   Nu tolumi rnwntvakrn, Tulao,
          /p   ná tɔ́ləmi-e·nuntháke·n, təlá·ɔ,
          /t   Then he began telling a parable, saying to them,
          /kl And he began to speak unto them by parables.

Mt 21.28 /b   Krkw vuh ktetrvavmw?
          /p   "kéku=háč kti·t·e·háhəmɔ?
          /t   "What do you think?
          /k   But what think ye?

          /b   Linwu mu nejelwpani qesul.
          /p   lɔ́nəwa=máh ni·š·i·lɔ́·p·ani kkwí·s·al.
          /t   There once was a man who had two sons.
          /k   A certain man had two sons;

          /b   Tamsc nu krkaelehi tulan, Fwes My mekumosi ntakevakunif bqc kejqek.
          /p   tá·mse ná ke·kai·lí·č·i tɔ́la·n, "nkwí·s, mái-mi·kəmɔ́·s·i nta·ki·há·k·anink yúkwe kí·škwi·k."
          /t   Then at some point he said to the older one, "Son, go work in my field today."
          /k   and he came to the first, and said, Son, go work to day in my vineyard.

Mt 21.29 /b   Tulkw, Kahi.
          /p   tɔ́lku, "káči."
          /t   The other said to him, "No, I won't."
          /k   He answered and said, I will not:

          /b   Nakarkc pwunarluntumun, nu eku ton.
          /p   na·k·a·é·k·e pwəna·elɔ́ntamən, ná íka tɔ́·n.
          /t   But after a while he thought about it, and then he went there.
          /k   but afterward he repented, and went.

Mt 21.30 /b   Ok nrl trfseselehi, nanc tulan.
          /p   ɔ́·k né·l tenksi·si·lí·č·i, ná=nə tɔ́la·n.
          /t   And to the younger one he said the same thing.
          /k   And he came to the second, and said likewise.

          /b   Tulkw, Nwxa nanc ntulsen;
          /p   tɔ́lku, "núxa·, ná=nə ntɔ́lsi·n."

Text, Transcription, and Translation

/t The other said to him, "Father, I'll do that."
/k And he answered and said, I go, sir:

/b jwq mutu eku ri.
/p šúkw máta íka é·i.
/t But he did not go there.
/k and went not.

Mt 21.31
/b Ta vuh ct rlenaqset wlelarvao wxo?
/p tá=háč=ét e·li·ná·kwsi·t o·li·lae·há·ɔ ó·x·ɔ?"
/t Which one do you think pleased his father?"
/k Whether of them twain did the will of his father?

/b Tulawao, Krkaet kct.
/p təlawwá·ɔ, "ké·kai·t=k=ét."
/t They said to him, "Well, presumably the older one."
/k They say unto him, The first.

/b Nhesus tulao, Kvehei ktulwvmw,
/p nčí·sas təlá·ɔ, "khičí·i ktəllúhəmɔ,
/t Jesus said to them, "I tell you truly,
/k Jesus saith unto them, Verily I say unto you,

/b moni mcmarnifek ok neskawsehek xqrok kunaomwkwaokh,
/p móni mehəma·e·nínki·k ó·k ni·ska·wsí·č·i·k xkwé·ok kənaomuk·əwá·ok=č.
/t the tax collectors and degenerate ('foul-living') women will get ahead of you.
/k That the publicans and the harlots

/b vetamih eku prok Krtanitwet sokemaokunif.
/p hítami=č íka pé·ɔk ke·tanət·ó·wi·t sɔ·k·i·ma·ɔ́·k·anink.
/t They shall get to God's kingdom before you.
/k go into the kingdom of God before you.

Mt 21.32
/b Rli Nhanu pchi my watulwqrkup jaxakawswakun,
/p é·li- nčá·n -péči-mái-wwa·təluk·wé·k·əp šaxahka·wsəwá·k·an,
/t For John came to teach you about righteousness,
/k For John came unto you in the way of righteousness,

/b jwq mutu kwlamvetaoewap.
/p šúkw máta ko·la·mhitaɔ·íwwa·p.
/t but you did not believe him.
/k and ye believed him not:

537

/b   Moni mcmarnifek ok neskawsehek xqrok wlamvetaowapani;
/p   móni mehəma·e·nínki·k ɔ́·k ni·ska·wsí·č·i·k xkwé·ɔk o·la·mhitaɔwwá·p·ani,
/t   The tax collectors and degenerate women believed him,
/k   but the publicans and the harlots believed him:

/b   ok nc rlenamrqc amunhei mutu qwlpevwmwp,
/p   ɔ́·k nə́ e·li·namé·k·we, amənčí·i máta kkwəlpi·húmɔ·p,
/t   and when you saw it, despite that, you did not repent,
/k   and ye, when ye had seen it, repented not afterward,

/b   ktuli a wlamvetaonrop.
/p   ktə́li-=á· -wəla·mhitaɔ·né·ɔ·p.
/t   so that you would have believed him.
/k   that ye might believe him.

Chapter 95 (p. 157-159). (L. section 95.) (Matthew 21.33-46; Mark 12.1- 12; Luke 20.9-18)

Mt 21.33 /b   Lupi klistamwq rnwntvakrokun.
/p   "lápi kələstámo·kw e·nunthake·ɔ́·k·an.
/t   "Listen to another parable.
/k   Hear another parable:

/b   Avpwp linw evakevrt,
/p   ahpó·p lə́nu ehhakí·he·t.
/t   There was a man who was a farmer.
/k   There was a certain householder,

/b   nul nu xkumap wesavkemwnjeu, wokamrnxkvumun,
/p   nál ná xkə́ma·p wisahki·múnšia, wɔ·ka·me·nxkhámən.
/t   And he it was who planted grapevines and made a fence around them.
/k   which planted a vineyard, and hedged it round about,

/b   Nanc lamamrnxkc tuntu olvrn manetw cntuh sulukakvof wesavkem,
/p   ná=nə la·mamé·nxke tə́nta-ɔ́·lhe·n, manní·to· énta-=č -sələk·á·khɔnk wísahki·m.
/t   Inside that fence he dug a hole and made a place where he would press grapes.
/k   and digged a winepress in it,

/b   ok wekwam eku tali manetw;   [⟨wekw-‖am⟩]
/p   ɔ́·k wí·k·əwam íka táli-manní·to·.
/t   And he built a structure ('house') there.
/k   and built a tower,

(p. 158)
- /b nu nokvekaevan tokevakun cvakevrlehi.
- /p ná nɔkhikaí·ha·n tɔ·ki·há·k·an ehhaki·he·lí·č·i.
- /t Then he lent out his farm to farmers.
- /k and let it out to husbandmen,

- /b Nu ovlumi ton,
- /p ná óhələmi tó·n.
- /t Then he went far away,
- /kl and went into a far country

Lk 20.9
- /b kavtu qwnakr.
- /p káhta-kwəná·ke·.
- /t intending to stay away a long time.
- /kl for a long time.

Mt 21.34, Mk 12.2, Lk 20.10
- /b Mrhi kavti tpisqevlakc cvlukveqi krkw kejekif,
- /p mé·či káhti-tpəskwihəlá·k·e ehələkhíkwi- kéku -ki·š·í·k·ink,
- /t And when the time when things ripen had almost come,
- /l And at the season, when the time of the fruit drew near,

- /b eku tulalwkalao tolwkakunu,
- /p íka təlalo·ka·lá·ɔ tɔlo·ká·k·ana
- /t he sent his servant there,
- /l he sent to the husbandmen a servant,

- /b tuli a evakevrsekri wunhi mujinamun krkw kejekif tali tokevakunif.
- /p táli-=á· ehhaki·he·s·i·ké·i wónči -məšánəmən kéku ki·š·í·k·ink táli tɔ·ki·há·k·anink.
- /t so that he might receive from the farmers the things that had grown in his field.
- /l that he might receive from the husbandmen of the fruit of the vineyard.

Lk 20.10, Mk 12.3
- /b Jwq nrk cvakevrsuk qevlwtaowao
- /p šúkw né·k ehhaki·hé·s·ak kkwihəlo·t·aɔwwá·ɔ,
- /t But the farmers chased him,
- /l But the husbandmen caught him,

- /b pwvpavkumawao pale tulskaowao,   [⟨pwvp-⟩ for ⟨pwp-⟩]
- /p pupahkamawwá·ɔ, palí·i təlskaɔwwá·ɔ.
- /t and beat him, and drove him away.
- /l and beat him, and sent him away

- /b takw krkw mwelaewao.
- /p takó· kéku mwi·la·iwwá·ɔ.
- /t They did not give him anything.
- /l empty.

Mk 12.4, Lk 20.11
- /b Nu lupi peli eku tulalwkalan.
- /p ná lápi pí·li íka təlalo·ká·la·n.
- /t Then he sent another one there.
- /l And again he sent unto them another servant;

- /b Ajitc nrl avsunu pwvpavkumawao, ok vwsrsrkycvowao [⟨pwvp-⟩ for ⟨pwp-⟩]
- /p a·šíte né·l ahsə́na pupahkamawwá·ɔ, ɔ́·k wse·s·e·k·ayehɔwwá·ɔ.
- /t Him, instead, they threw stones at and whipped.
- /l and at him they cast stones, and they beat him also,

- /b tovi mexanelevawao kokjetcvowao welelet tolumskaowao,
- /p tóhi-mi·x·aní·i-li·hawwá·ɔ, kɔkši·tehɔwwá·ɔ wi·lí·li·t, tɔləmskaɔwwá·ɔ.
- /t They treated him very shamefully, wounding his head, and drove him away.
- /l and wounded him in the head, and entreated him shamefully,

- /b takw krkw mwelaewao.
- /p takó· kéku mwi·la·iwwá·ɔ.
- /t They did not give him anything.
- /l and sent him away empty.

Lk 20.12
- /b Amanhei lupi peli eku lalwkalr.
- /p aməncí·i lápi pí·li íka lalo·ká·le·
- /t He persisted and sent yet another.
- /kl And again he sent a third:

- /b Lupi nrl kokjetrvowao, sokvanevenroi,
- /p lápi né·l kɔkši·tehɔwwá·ɔ, sɔ·khanihi·ne·ɔ́·i.
- /t Him, again, they wounded and threw out.
- /kl and they wounded him also, and cast him out,

Mk 12.5
- /b nu tuli nvelanro.
- /p ná tə́li-nhila·né·ɔ.
- /t And they proceeded to kill him.
- /kl and him they killed,

Mt 21.36
- /b Nu krxu eku tvlalwkalan, jwq amunhei nc tulsenro. [⟨tv-|l⟩ for ⟨tu-|l⟩]
- /p ná ké·x·a íka təlalo·ká·la·n, šúkw aməncí·i nə́ təlsi·né·ɔ.
- /t Then he sent several there, but they persisted in doing that.
- /kl Again, he sent other servants more than the first: and they did unto them likewise.
- /k and many others; (Mk 12.5)

Mk 12.6, Mt 21.37, Lk 20.13
- /b Nu wrtvakevakunet mawselw qesu, tovi avolao.
- /p ná we·thaki·há·k·ani·t ma·wsí·lu kkwí·s·a, tóhi-ahɔ·lá·ɔ.

/t That property-owner had one son, and he loved him dearly.
/l Then the lord of the vineyard having yet therefore one son, his well-beloved,

/b Lwr tuh vuh ntulsen?
/p lúwe·, "tá=č=háč ntə́lsi·n?
/t He said, "What shall I do?
/l he said, What shall I do?

/b qeluvlr ntalwkaluh fwes,
/p kwí·la-lé·, ntalo·ká·la=č nkwí·s.
/t I guess I have to send my son.
/l I will send my beloved son:

/b tamsc a tu nrl nrovtetc moxifwrlumawao.
/p tá·mse=á·=tá né·l ne·ohtí·t·e, mɔx·inkwe·ləmawwá·ɔ."
/t Maybe when they see him they will respect him."
/l it may be they will reverence him when they see him.   [RSV "respect" 3x]

Mk 12.6 /b Nu nrl mukuni vwtcf wunhi eku lalwkalan.
/p ná né·l məkə́ni-wténk wwə́nči- íka -lalo·ká·la·n.
/t Then he sent him to them last of all.
/l He sent him also last of all unto them.

Lk 20.14 /b Cvakevrhek nrovtetc,
/p ehhaki·hé·č·i·k ne·ohtí·t·e,
/t When the farmers saw him,
/k But when the husbandmen saw him, ...
/l But when the husbandmen saw the son,

Mt 21.38 /b lutwpanek.
/p lət·ó·p·ani·k.
/t they said to each other,
/k they said among themselves,
/l they reasoned among themselves, saying,

Lk 20.14, Mt 21.38
/b Jr wu krtu nevlatuf,
/p "šé· wá ké·t·a-nihəlá·t·ank.
/t "This is the one who is going to own it ("the heir").
/l This is the heir:

/b bv tu, nvelatumwq,
/p yúh=tá nhilá·t·amo·kw.
/t Come on, let's kill him.
/l come, let us kill him,

/b jeqetaotum,
/p ši·k·wi·taɔ́·t·am.
/t Let's take it away from him.
/l and let us seize on his inheritance,

/b nuh puna knevlatumunrn.
/p ná=č pənáh kənihəla·t·amə́ne·n.
/t See, then we will own it."
/l and [*it*] shall be ours.

Mt 21.39, Mk 12.8, Luke 20.15
/b Nu qevlwtaonro, sokvanevenro wunhi vakevakunif
/p ná kkwihəlo·t·aɔ·né·ɔ, sɔ·khanihi·né·ɔ wə́nči haki·há·k·anink.
/t Then they chased him and threw him out of the property ('field').
/l And they caught him, and cast him out of the vineyard,

/b nu tuli nvelanro.
/p ná tə́li-nhila·né·ɔ.
/t And they proceeded to kill him.
/l and slew him.

Mt 21.40 /b Bqc patc wrtvakevakunct,
/p "yúkwe pá·t·e we·thaki·ha·k·ani·t,
/t "Now when the property-owner comes,
/kl When the lord therefore of the vineyard cometh,

/b krkwh vuh tulevao nrl cvakevrlehi?
/p kéku=č=háč təli·há·ɔ né·l ehhaki·he·lí·č·i?"
/t what will he do to those farmers?"
/kl what will he do unto those husbandmen?

Mt 21.41 /b Tulawao,
/p təlawwá·ɔ,
/t They said to him,
/kl They say unto him,

Mt 21.41, Mk 12.9
/b Tovih ktumaki wrmevao patc,
/p "tóhi-č -ktəmáki-we·mi·há·ɔ pá·t·e,
/t "He will kill them all very miserably when he comes.
/l He will come and miserably destroy those wicked men,

/b pelih cvakevrlehi nokvekaevan tokevakun,
/p pí·li=č ehhaki·he·lí·č·i nɔkhikaí·ha·n tɔ·ki·há·k·an,
/t He will lend his farm to other farmers,
/l and will let out his vineyard to other husbandmen,

/b nrkh wifi melahek cntxun tpisqevlak krkw kejekun.
/p nék=č wínki-mi·lá·č·i·k éntxən-tpəskwíhəla·k kéku ki·š·í·k·ən."
/t those who will willingly give things to him every time they ripen."
/l which shall render him the fruits in their seasons.

(L. adds)
/b Nhesus lwrp,
/p nčí·sas lúwe·p,
/t Jesus said,
/l [*Jesus saith,*]

Mk 12.9
/b Kvcheh tu pr,
/p "khičí·i=č=tá pé·.
/t "Truly he will come.
/kl he will come

/b okh wrmevao nrl cvakevrlehi,
/p ɔ́·k=č wwe·mi·há·ɔ né·l ehhaki·he·lí·č·i.
/t And he will kill all those farmers.
/kl and destroy the husbandmen,

/b pelih awrni mwelan tokevakun.
/p pí·li=č awé·ni mwí·la·n tɔ·ki·há·k·an."
/t He will give his property to others."
/kl and will give the vineyard unto others.

Lk 20.16
/b Mrhi nrnwstamevtetc lwrok, Taa somi nc lri.
/p mé·či ne·no·stamihtí·t·e, luwé·ɔk, "tá=á· sɔ́·mi nɔ́ lé·i."
/t After they had understood it, they said, "That absolutely wouldn't happen!"
/kl ... And when they heard it, they said, God forbid.

Lk 20.17
/b Kokulifomao, tulao,
/p kɔ·k·əlinkɔ·má·ɔ, təlá·ɔ,
/t He fixed his gaze on them and said to them,
/kl And he beheld them, and said, ...

Mt 21.42
/b Mutu vuh vuji ktukuntamwunro xwi lrkvekunif.
/p "máta=háč háši ktak·əntamo·wəné·ɔ xúwi-le·khí·k·anink?
/t "Have you never read it in the old writing?
/kl Did ye never read in the scriptures,

Lk 20.17
/b Nc avsun wekvrhek prketwvtet, nul nuni bqc sifekameku vatr. ‖
/p 'nɔ́ ahsɔ́n wi·khé·č·i·k pe·k·i·t·úhti·t, nál nɔ́ni yúkwe sinki·k·amí·k·a hát·e·.
/t 'The very stone that the builders cast aside is now the corner of the building.
/kl The stone which the builders rejected, the same is become the head of the corner:

Mk 12.11 /b Nrvlakofq tuletwn wcnhi nc lrk, [⟨Nrvlakofq⟩ for ⟨Nrvlalkofq⟩]
(p. 159) /p nehəláˑlkɔnkw təlíˑtoˑn wénči- nə́ -léˑk.
/t Our lord caused this to happen.
/k this was the Lord's doing,

/b ok krvlu kanjelackwnu.
/p ɔ́ˑk kéhəla kkanšiˑlaehkóˑna.'
/t And he really astonished us.'
/k and it is marvellous in our eyes?

Mt 21.43 /b Nuni kwnhi lulunro,
/p nə́ni kúnči-lələnéˑɔ,
/t That's why I say to you,
/kl Therefore say I unto you,

/b Sokemaokunh Krtanitwet kwrtunumakrnro,
/p 'sɔˑkˑiˑmaˑɔ́ˑkˑan=č keˑtanətˑóˑwiˑt kəweˑtˑənəmaˑkˑeˑnéˑɔ.
/t 'God's kingdom will be taken from you.
/kl The kingdom of God shall be taken from you,

/b pelih rlvakrehek melanro nrvqwsehek tuli a kavtu lapcntamunro.
/p píˑli=č eˑlhakeˑíˑčˑiˑk miˑlaˑnéˑɔ neˑykwəsˑíˑčˑiˑk, tə́li-=áˑ -káhta-laˑpˑentamənéˑɔ.
/t It will be given to another nation that is seen to want to make good use of it.
/kl and given to a nation bringing forth the fruits thereof.

Lk 20.18 /b Awrn bni avsunif mavtrxifc jqeskvetrxenh.
/p awéˑn yóˑni ahsə́nink mahteˑxˑínke, škwiˑskhitéˑxˑiˑn=č.
/t If anyone falls on this stone, they will be smashed to pieces.
/kl Whosoever shall fall upon that stone shall be broken;

/b Okh awrn b avsun kuluvwqkc pwfqvetcvwkwnh.
/p ɔ́ˑk=č awéˑn yú ahsɔ́n kəlahóˑkwke, ppunkhwitehóˑkˑoˑn=č."
/t And if this stone falls on anyone, it will grind them to dust."
/kl but on whomsoever it shall fall, it will grind him to powder.

Mt 21.45, Mk 12.12, Lk 20.19
/b Wcvevwfrhek ok cvlrkvekrhek, ok Paluseok puntumevtetc nc rnwntvakrokun,
/p wehiˑhunkéˑčˑiˑk ɔ́ˑk ehəleˑkhiˑkˑéˑčˑiˑk ɔ́ˑk †paˑləsiˑíˑɔk pəntamihtíˑtˑe nə́ eˑnunthakeˑɔ́ˑkˑan,
/t When the priests and scribes and Pharisees heard that parable,
/l And when the chief priests and the Scribes and Pharisees had heard his parables,
/k ... the parable (Mk 12.12); ... this parable (Lk 20.19).

/b wunrmunro li vokybaif muvtrxun.
/p wəneˑmənéˑɔ líˑ- hɔkˑayəwáˑink -mahtéˑxˑən.

/t they saw that it pertained squarely to (*lit.*, landed on) themselves.
/l they perceived that he spake of them;

Mt 21.46, Mk 12.12, Lk 20.19
/b Nu jac notwnamunrop wcnhi a tvwnavtet.
/p ná šá·e nɔt·o·namǝné·ɔ·p wénči-=á· -thwǝnáhti·t.
/t Then they immediately sought a means to seize him.
/l and the same hour they sought to lay hands on him;

/b Jwq koxawao rlufwmavtehi,
/p šúkw kɔx·awwá·ɔ e·lanko·mahtí·č·i,
/t But they feared their own people,
/l but they feared the multitude,

/b rli letrvalet ncnekane ct wrwset.
/p é·li-li·t·e·há·li·t, "nehǝni·k·a·nɨ́·i-=ét -wé·wsi·t."
/t as *they* thought he must be a prophet.
/l because they took him for a prophet.

Chapter 96 (pp. 159-160). (L. section 96.) (Matthew 22.1-14)

Mt 22.1 /b Nhesus lupi trnwnvakaopani, lwrp, [⟨trnwnv-⟩ for ⟨trnwntv-⟩]
/p nčɨ́·sas lápi te·nunthakaɔ́·p·ani, lúwe·p,
/t Jesus again told them a parable, saying,
/kl And Jesus answered and spake unto them again by parables, and said,

Mt 22.2 /b Osavkamri sakemaokun tpisqi lr,
/p "ɔ·s·ahkamé·i-sa·k·i·ma·ɔ́·k·an tpǝ́skwi-lé·,
/t "The kingdom of heaven is like
/kl The kingdom of heaven is like unto

/b rlsetup sakemao krtu wekifrwvrtc qesul.
/p e·lsɨ́·t·ǝp sa·k·i·má·ɔ ké·t·a-wi·k·inke·whé·t·e kkwɨ́·s·al.
/t what happened to a king of old when he wanted to have a wedding for his son.
/kl a certain king, which made a marriage for his son,

Mt 22.3 /b Tolwkalao tolwkakunu,
/p tɔlo·ka·lá·ɔ tɔlo·ká·k·ana,
/t He sent out his servants,
/kl And sent forth his servants

/b tulao my lw wcnhemukpanek
/p tǝlá·ɔ, "mái-ló· wenči·makpáni·k.
/t telling them, "Go tell the ones I have invited.
/kl to call them that were bidden

/b   pavtetch b cntu kavtu tavkopwvultif.   [⟨vul⟩ for ⟨val⟩, for /há·l/]
/p   pahtí·t·eč yú énta-káhta-tahkɔp·o·há·ltink."
/t   Let them come to this wedding."
/kl to the wedding:

/b   Jwq mutu wifi preok.
/p   šúkw máta wínki-pe·í·ɔk.
/t   But they were unwilling to come.
/kl and they would not come.

Mt 22.4 /b   Nu krxu eku tulalwkalan,
/p   ná ké·x·a íka təlalo·ká·la·n,
/t   Then he sent several others to them,
/kl Again, he sent forth other servants, saying,

/b   tulao my lw, wcnhemukpanek;
/p   təlá·ɔ, "mái-ló· wenči·makpáni·k.
/t   telling them, "Go tell the ones I have invited.
/kl Tell them which are bidden,

/b   Mrhi fejextwn nmehwakun,
/p   'mé·či nki·š·í·xto·n nəmi·č·əwá·k·an.
/t   'I have prepared my food.
/kl Behold, I have prepared my dinner:

/b   ntaksunumuk ok weswkcfek mrhi keji nvelaok;
/p   nta·ksənəmak ɔ́·k wi·s·o·kénki·k mé·či kíši-nhilá·ɔk.
/t   My oxen and my fattened (calves) have been killed.
/kl my oxen and my fatlings are killed,

/b   wrmi krkw kejexun;
/p   wé·mi kéku ki·š·í·x·ən.
/t   Everything is ready.
/kl and all things are ready:

/b   paq cntu tuvkopwvaltif.
/p   pá·kw énta-tahkɔp·o·há·ltink.'"
/t   Come to the wedding.'"
/kl come unto the marriage.

Mt 22.5 /b   Jwq popwrluntamunro,
/p   šúkw pɔ·pəwe·ləntaməné·ɔ.
/t   But they made light of it.
/kl But they made light of it,

/b kseni musi rok,
/p ksíˑni mə́si-éˑɔk,
/t Unconcernedly they went all different ways,
/kl and went their ways,

/b aluntc tokevakunwaif, ok aluntc cntu mcmvalumwntevtet,
/p aˑlə́nte tɔˑkiˑhaˑkˑanəwáˑink, ɔ́ˑk aˑlə́nte énta-memhalamuntíhtiˑt,
/t some to their farms, and some to where they were merchants,
/kl one to his farm, another to his merchandise:

Mt 22.6
/b ok aluntc tovwunawao, wowesavkevawao, ok wunevlawao.
/p ɔ́ˑk aˑlə́nte tɔhwənawwáˑɔ, wɔwisahkiˑhawwáˑɔ, ɔ́ˑk wənihəlawwáˑɔ.
/t and some seized them, and tormented them, and killed them.
/kl And the remnant took his servants, and entreated them spitefully, and slew them.

Mt 22.7
/b Nu sakema puntufc, ave manwfsw,
/p ná saˑkˑíˑma pəntánke, áhi-manúnksu.
/t When the king heard about it, he was very angry.
/kl But when the king heard thereof, he was wroth:

/b eku tulalwkalao vwtelabmu
/p íka təlaloˑkaˑláˑɔ wtiˑláˑyəma.
/t He sent his warriors there.   ['there': or 'to them']
/kl and he sent forth his armies,

/b wrqevawao nrl ncvlwrlehi
/p wweˑkwiˑhawwáˑɔ néˑl nehəlaweˑlíˑčˑi,
/t And they killed every one of those murderers,
/kl and destroyed those murderers,

/b ok wulwsumunro vwtwtrnaelet.
/p ɔ́ˑk wəloˑsˑəmənéˑɔ wtoˑtˑeˑnaíˑliˑt.
/t and they burned their town.
/kl and burned up their city.

Mt 22.8
/b Nu tulan tolwkakunu;
/p ná tə́laˑn tɔloˑkáˑkˑana,
/t Then he said to his servants,
/kl Then saith he to his servants,

/b Kejexun piji nmehwakun,
/p 'kiˑšˑíˑxˑən píši nəmiˑčˑəwáˑkˑan,
/t 'My feast *is* ready,
/kl The wedding is ready,

/b jwq wcnhemukpanek somi mutu wuli luseibfu;
/p šúkw wenči·makpáni·k só·mi máta wǝ́li-lǝs·i·i·yúnka.
/t but the ones I invited did not at all do right.
/kl but they which were bidden were not worthy.

Mt 22.9
/b eku aq tumakunekri,
/p íka á·kw tǝma·k·ani·ké·i.
/t Go to the streets and roads.
/k Go ye therefore into the highways,

/b cntxih nrrq awrn, kprjwawu b cntu tavkopwvaltif.
/p éntxi-=č -né·e·kw awé·n kpe·š·ǝwáwwa yú énta-tahkɔp·o·há·ltink.'
/t As many people as you see you shall bring to this wedding.'
/k and as many as ye shall find, bid to the marriage.

Mt 22.10
/b Nu alwkakunuk eku tonro tumakunekri; ‖
/p ná alo·ká·k·anak íka tɔ·né·ɔ tǝma·k·ani·ké·i.
/t Then the servants went to the streets and roads.
/k So those servants went out into the highways,

(p. 160)
/b mocvowao cntxi nrovtet wrlselehi, ok mutu wrlselehi;
/p mɔ·ehɔwwá·ɔ éntxi-ne·ɔ́hti·t, we·lsi·lí·č·i ɔ́·k máta we·lsi·lí·č·i.
/t They gathered together as many as they saw, good and bad.
/k and gathered together all as many as they found, both bad and good:

/b nu kcnh cntu tavkopwvaltif krtu wepwmahek topenro.
/p ná kǝ́nč énta-tahkɔp·o·há·ltink ké·t·a-wi·po·má·č·i·k tɔp·i·né·ɔ.
/t Only then were there guests ('ones expecting to eat with him') at the wedding.
/k and the wedding was furnished with guests.

Mt 22.11
/b Sakemu eku rli tumekrtc mri punaotc krtu wepwmkwki,
/p sa·k·í·ma íka ć·li-tǝmi·k·é·t·e, mé·i-pǝnaɔ́·t·e ké·t·a-wi·po·mkúk·i,
/t And when the king came in to see his guests ('ones expecting to eat with him'),
/k And when the king came in to see the guests,

/b nr linwu, mutu rlavqelet trkopwvaltifc rvluqif.   [⟨nr⟩ for /né·e·/]
/p né·e· lǝ́nǝwa máta e·lahkwí·li·t tekɔhpo·ha·ltínke ehǝlák·wink.
/t he saw a man who was not wearing what one customarily wears at a wedding.
/k he saw there a man which had not on a wedding garment:

Mt 22.12
/b Tulao, nhwtec, Krkw vuh wcnhi b avpeun
/p tǝlá·ɔ, 'nčó·t·ie, kéku=háč wénči- yú -ahpían
/t And he said to him, 'Friend, how come you are here
/k And he saith unto him, Friend, how camest thou in hither

/b   nrli mutu tavkopwvaltwe lahrswakun avqeun.
/p   né·li- máta tahkɔp·o·ha·ltəwí·i-lač·e·s·əwá·k·an -ahkwían.'
/t   when you're not wearing wedding garments?'
/k   not having a wedding garment?

/b   Jwq qelu krkw lwr.
/p   šúkw kwí·la- kéku -lúwe·.
/t   But he didn't know what to say.
/k   And he was speechless.

Mt 22.13 /b   Nu sakema tulan tolwkakunu,
/p   ná sa·k·í·ma tə́la·n tɔlo·ká·k·ana,
/t   Then the king said to his servants,
/k   Then said the king to the servants,

/b   Kaxpelw wunuxkif ok vwekatif,
/p   'kaxpí·lo· wənáxkink ɔ́·k hwiká·t·ink,
/t   'Tie him by his hands and his feet,
/k   Bind him hand and foot,

/b   ok eku laneveq cntu ave peskrk
/p   ɔ́·k íka laníhi·kw énta-áhi-pí·ske·k,
/t   and throw him into utter darkness,
/k   and take him away, and cast him into outer darkness;

/b   cntuh salamwif ok kukumwkuntasek wepetu.
/p   énta-=č -salá·mwink ɔ́·k -kək·amo·kantá·s·i·k wi·p·í·t·a.'
/t   where there shall be loud weeping and teeth being "gnashed."'
/k   there shall be weeping and gnashing of teeth.

Mt 22.14 /b   Jr xrli wcnhemunhek, jwq tutxetwuk wrtununhek.
/p   "šé· xé·li wenči·mə́nči·k, šúkw ta·txí·t·əwak we·t·ənə́nči·k."
/t   "See, many are summoned, but few are accepted."
/k   For many are called, but few are chosen.

Chapter 97 (pp. 160-161). (L. section 97.) (Matthew 22.15-21; Mark 12.13-15; Luke 20.20-26)

Mt 22.15 /b   Nu Paluseok moi ahemwlsenro,
/p   ná †pa·ləsi·í·ok mɔ́i-a·č·i·mo·lsi·né·ɔ,
/t   Then the Pharisees went to hold a council,
/k   Then went the Pharisees, and took counsel

/b kotu muxkamunro krkw a tu rlavtet, cntu a okrkamevtet rlwrlet.
/p kót·a-maxkaməné·ɔ kéku=á·=tá e·láhti·t, énta-=á· -ɔ·ke·kamíhti·t e·ləwé·li·t.
/t desiring to find something they would say to him where they would circumscribe what he said.
/k how they might entangle him in his talk.

Mt 22.16, Mk 12.13, Lk 20.20
/b Qrnavkevawao,
/p kwe·nahki·hawwá·ɔ,
/t They watched him.
/l And they watched him,

/b ok aluntc rkrkemavtehi eku tulalwkalawao tuli a krnavkevanro;
/p ó·k a·lə́nte e·k·e·ki·mahtí·č·i íka təlalo·ka·lawwá·ɔ, tə́li-=á· -ke·nahki·ha·né·ɔ,
/t And they sent some of their disciples to him, for them to watch him,
/l and sent forth spies, certain of their disciples

/b ok wehi Vclute linwuk;
/p ó·k wíči †helat·í·i-lə́nəwak.
/t and with them Herod's men.
/l with the Herodians,

Lk 20.20 /b moi wularvosetaowao mulaji jaxavkaprehek,
/p mói-wəlaehɔ·s·i·taɔwwá·ɔ, málahši šaxahka·p·e·í·č·i·k,
/t They went and acted nicely towards him, as if upright men,
/l which should feign themselves just men,

/b rli kavtu puntaovtet krkw a tu wcnhi muvtukunemavtet tali krkybmvrsif.
/p é·li-káhta-pəntaóhti·t kéku=á·=tá wénči-mahtak·əni·máhti·t táli ke·kayəmhé·s·ink.
/t as they wanted to hear from him something that would be a basis for accusing him before the ruler.   [lit., 'by means of which they would accuse him']
/l that they might take hold of his words, that so they might deliver him unto the power and authority of the governor.

Mt 22.16, Mk 12.14, Lk 20.21
/b Eku preavtetc, tulawao;
/p íka pe·ahtí·t·e, təlawwá·ɔ,
/t When they got there, they said to him,
/l And when they were come, they asked him, saying,

Mt 22.16 /b Nrvlalerf nwatwnrn ktuli wulamwrn;
/p "nehəlá·lienk, no·wa·tó·ne·n ktə́li-wəlá·məwe·n,
/t "Master, we know that you tell the truth,
/l Master, we know that thou art true,

/k (Mt 22.16) ... Master, we know that thou art true, ...
/k (Mk 12.14) "Teacher, we know that you are true,...
/k (Lk 20.21) ... "Teacher, we know ...
/k ... that you speak and teach rightly, ..
/k (Mt 22.16) ... and teachest the way of God in truth,
/k ... neither carest thou for any man:
/k (Mk 12.14) ... and care for no man;

Lk 20.21 /b ok kwlaptwnc ok kwlavkrkifc,
/p ɔ́·k ko·la·ptó·ne ɔ́·k ko·lahke·kínke.
/t and you speak and teach correctly.
/l that thou sayest and teachest rightly,

Mt 22.16 /b ok mutu awrn krkw ktulrlumai;
/p ɔ́·k máta awé·n kéku ktəle·ləmá·i,
/t And you have no special regard for anyone,
/l neither carest thou for any man,

/b rli mutu kpunarluntamwun rlenaqset awrn,
/p é·li máta kpəna·eləntamó·wən e·li·ná·kwsi·t awé·n,
/t as you do not consider the kind of person someone is,
/l for thou regardest not the person of men,

/b tcxi jwq myai rli wulrluntuf Krtanitwet ktulavkrkifrn.
/p téxi šúkw mayá·i é·li-wəle·ĺɔntank ke·tanət·ó·wi·t ktəlahke·kínke·n.
/t And you teach nothing at all but exactly what is pleasing to God.
/l but teachest the way of God in truth.

Mt 22.17 /b Nuni wunhi lenrn. Krkw vuh ktetc?
/p nəni wɔ́nči lí·ne·n: kéku=háč ktíte?
/t Therefore, tell us: what do you think?
/kl Tell us therefore, What thinkest thou?

Lk 20.22 /b Wuleuxun vuh nmevmelanrn moni Sesul, ji vuh mutu?   [⟨-euxun⟩ for ⟨-exun⟩]
/p wəlí·x·ən=háč nəmihəmi·lá·ne·n móni †sí·sal, ší=háč máta?"
/t Is it lawful for us to be giving money to Caesar, or not?
/k Is it lawful for us to give tribute to Caesar, or not?"
/l Is it lawful to give tribute unto Caesar, or not?
[B. omits: /l shall we give, or shall we not give?]

Mt 22.18, Mk 12.15, Lk 20.23
/b Jwq watwn rlkeqi muvtawselet, ok rlkeqi lupolet,
/p šúkw o·wá·to·n e·lkí·kwi-mahta·wsí·li·t, ɔ́·k e·lkí·kwi-ləpó·li·t,
/t But he knew how wicked they were, and how clever,
/l But he knowing their wickedness, craftiness,

          /b ok rlkeqi evakevokrlet.
          /p ɔ́·k e·lkí·kwi-ihahki·hɔké·li·t.
          /t and how hypocritical ('habitually deceptive').
          /l and hypocrisy,

Mt 22.18 /b Tulao, Krkw vuh wcnhi uvqrhiverq? rvavkevokrhek.   [⟨hiv⟩ for ⟨hev⟩]
          /p təlá·ɔ, "kéku=háč wénči-ahkwe·č·í·hie·kw, ehahki·hɔké·č·i·k.
          /t He said to them, "Why do you test me, you hypocrites?"
          /l said unto them, Why tempt ye me, ye hypocrites?
          /r Why put me to the test?   (Mt 22.18, Mk 12.15, RSV).

Mt 22.19 /b Punwntuleq rlenako mcmrkrq.
          /p pənúntəli·kw e·li·ná·k·ɔ mehəmé·k·e·kw."
          /t Show me the kind of thing you give."
          /kl Shew me the tribute money.   (L. adds: "that I may see it" [Mk 12.15].)

          /b Nu pwunwntulanro monetut.
          /p ná pwənuntəla·né·ɔ mɔní·t·ət.
          /t Then they showed him a small coin.
          /kl And they brought unto him a penny.

Mt 22.20 /b Tulao, Awrn vuh nc ‖ tulenaqsen
          /p təlá·ɔ, "awé·n=háč nə́ təli·ná·kwsi·n,
          /t He said to them, "Whose likeness is that,
          /kl And he saith unto them, Whose is this image

(p. 161)   /b ok nc srkuntprxif krkw vuh lrkvasw?
          /p ɔ́·k nə́ se·kantpé·x·ink, kéku=háč le·khá·s·u?
          /t and above his head, what is written?"
          /kl and superscription?

Mt 22.21 /b Tulawaʋ, Sesul.
          /p təlawwá·ɔ, "†sí·sal."
          /t They said to him, "Caesar."
          /k They say unto him, Caesar's.
          /l And they answered and said unto him, Caesar's.

          /b Nu tulan, Melw. Sesul krkw nrvlatuf;
          /p ná təla·n, "mí·lo· †sí·sal kéku nehəlá·t·ank.
          /t Then he said to them, "Give Caesar the things that belong to him.
          /kl Then saith he unto them, Render therefore unto Caesar the things which are Caesar's;

          /b ok melw Krtanitwet nrvlatuf.
          /p ɔ́·k mí·lo· ke·tanət·ó·wi·t nehəlá·t·ank.

	/t	and give God what is *his*.
	/kl	and unto God the things that are God's.

Lk 20.26 /b Nu qelalusenro xrli awrn eku lifwrxen.
/p ná kwí·la-ləs·i·né·ɔ; xé·li awé·n íka linkwé·x·i·n.
/t Then they were at a loss what to do; many people were looking on.
/l And they could not take hold of his words before the people:
/r And they were not able ... to catch him by what he said;   (RSV)

/b Hitquswuk tcxi jwq kanjrluntamwk wunhi rlqivtet,   [⟨lu̯⟩: ⟨u⟩ imperfect]
/p či·tkwə́s·əwak; téxi šúkw kanše·lə́ntamo·k wə́nči e·lkwíhti·t.
/t They fell silent; they could do nothing but marvel at what he said to them.
/l and they marvelled at his answer, held their peace,

Mt 22.22 /b nu pwnemanro palerok.
/p ná ppo·ni·ma·né·ɔ, palí·i é·ɔk.
/t Then they left him alone and went away.
/l left him, and went their way.

Chapter 98 (pp. 161-162). (L. section 98.) (Matthew 22.23-33. Mark 12.18-27, Luke 20.27-39.)

Mt 22.23, Mk 12.18, Lk 20.27
/b Na nckc kejqek ok aluntc Sutuseok wtxawapani
/p ná-néke kí·škwi·k ɔ́·k a·lə́nte †satasí·ɔk o·txawwá·p·ani,
/t That same day some Sadducees also came to him,
/l The same day came to him certain of the Sadducees,

/b cvlwrtpanek awrn ufulukc taa vuji amwei.
/p ehələwe·tpáni·k, awé·n ankələ́k·e, tá=á· háši a·mwí·i.
/t ones who used to say that when someone died they would never rise (again).
/l which say that there is no resurrection, and they asked him, saying,

Mt 22.24, Mk 12.19
/b Tulawao Nrvlalerf, Mwjiju lrkvekrp,   [⟨-erf⟩]
/p təlawwá·ɔ, "nehəlá·lienk, †mo·šə́š·a le·khí·k·e·p,
/t They said to him, "Master, Moses wrote,
/l Saying, Master, Moses wrote unto us,

Mt 22.24, Mk 12.19, Lk 20.28
/b Linwh ufulukc falatc wehrohi mutu wnehanevtetc
/p 'lə́nu=č ankələ́k·e, nkalá·t·e wi·č·e·ɔ́·č·i, máta wəni·č·a·nihtí·t·e,
/t 'If a man dies, leaving behind his wife, and if they have no children,
/l If any man's brother die, and leave his wife behind him, and leave no children,

/b wremavtetuph ajitc wehroo
/p we·i·mahtí·t·əp=č a·šíte wwi·č·e·ɔ́·ɔ,
/t one who had been his brother must marry her instead,
/l that his brother should take his wife,

/b memunsuh qejekwvatumaoo wematifu.
/p mi·mə́nsa=č kwi·š·i·k·o·ha·t·amaɔ́·ɔ wi·mahtínka.'
/t and raise children for his late brother.'
/l and raise up seed unto his brother.

Mt 22.25 /b B tali lrp, nejaj mu wremuvtuntetpanek;
/p yú táli lé·p, ní·š·a·š=máh we·i·mahtənti·tpáni·k.
/t It happened here, that there were seven (men) who were brothers.
/kl Now there were with us seven brethren:

Lk 20.29 /b krkaetpanu vwjelintamwp nu tofulun, takw wunehaneep.
/p ke·kai·tpána wši·lə́ntamo·p, ná tɔ́nkələn; takó· wəni·č·a·ní·i·p.
/t The eldest got married, and then he died; and he had no children.
/k and the first took a wife, and died without children.
Mt 22.25 /l and the first, when he had married a wife, deceased, and having no issue, left his wife unto his brother:

Lk 20.30 /b Nu wrxanset ajitc wehron, ok nu jac uful;
/p ná we·x·ánsi·t a·šíte wwi·č·é·ɔ·n, ɔ́·k ná šá·e ánkəl.
/t Then his (next) younger brother in turn married her, and he then promptly died.
/kl And the second took her to wife, and he died childless.

Mk 12.21, Lk 20.31
/b nu lupi peli wrxansetup ajitc wehron, ok nu nanc tulenumun
/p ná lápi pí·li we·x·ansí·t·əp a·šíte wwi·č·é·ɔ·n, ɔ́·k ná=nə təlí·namən.
/t Then again another younger brother in turn married her, and the same thing happened to him.
/l and the third took her likewise;

Lk 20.31 /b kxunki wrmi nukavkc nejaj takw nuxpunc kwti wunehaneepanek,
/p kxántki wé·mi nəkáhke ní·š·a·š takó· náxpəne kwə́t·i wəni·č·a·ni·í·p·ani·k.
/t In the end all seven of them did not even have one child.
/l and in like manner the seven also had her; and they left no children, and died:

Mk 12.22 /b mukuni vwtcf wunhi nuku xqro ufulwp.
/p məkə́ni-wténk wə́nči náka xkwé·ɔ ánkəlo·p.
/t And last of all that woman died.
/kl last of all the woman died also.

Mk 12.23 /b Amwevtetc a
/p a·mwihtí·t·e=á·,

/t When they rise (again),
/kl In the resurrection therefore, when they shall rise,

Mt 22.28 /b tu vuh a rlenaqset wlvalao nrl xqro
/p tá=háč=á· e·li·ná·kwsi·t o·lhalá·ɔ né·l xkwé·ɔ,
/t which one will have that woman (as wife),
/kl whose wife shall she be of the seven?

/b rli wrmi wehrovtetup.
/p é·li- wé·mi -wi·č·e·ɔhtí·t·əp."
/t as they all were married to her?"
/kl for they all had her.
/k for the seven had her to wife.   (Mk 12.23)

Mk 12.24 /b Nhesus tulao,
/p nčí·sas təlá·ɔ,
/t Jesus said to them,
/kl And Jesus answering said unto them,

/b mutu vuh nc kwnhi hanilusewunro
/p "máta=háč nɔ́ kúnči-čáni-ləs·i·wəné·ɔ
/t "Are you not going wrong because
/kl Do ye not therefore err,

/b rli mutu wavarq nrk xwi lrkvekunuk, ok rlset Krtanitwet.
/p é·li- máta -wwa·há·e·kw né·k xúwi-le·khí·k·anak, ɔ́·k é·lsi·t ke·tanət·ó·wi·t?
/t you do not know the old writings or the nature of God?
/kl because ye know not the scriptures, neither the power of God?

Lk 20.34 /b B tali cntu lawsif wewvjeluntamun.
/p yú táli entalá·wsink wiwši·ləntamən.
/t Here in this world people marry.
/k The children of this world marry, and are given in marriage:

Lk 20.35 /b Jwqh cntxi tcpi eku pahek takok cntu lawsif,
/p šúkw=č éntxi-tépi- íka -pá·č·i·k tákɔ·k entalá·wsink.
/t But as many as shall succeed in getting to the other world,
/k But they which shall be accounted worthy to obtain that world,

/b amwevtetc wunhi ufulwakunif
/p a·mwihtí·t·e wə́nči ankələwá·k·anink,
/t when they rise from death,
/k and the resurrection from the dead, ...

/b   taa nuxpunc kavtu vwjeluntamweok,
/p   tá=á· náxpəne káhta-wši·ləntamo·wí·ɔk.
/t   will not even want to marry.
/k   neither marry, nor are given in marriage:

Lk 20.36 /b   ok taa kuski heh ufulweok,
/p   ɔ́·k tá=á· káski- čí·č -ankəlo·wí·ɔk,
/t   And they would no longer be able to die.
/kl Neither can they die any more:

Mt 22.30, Mk 12.25, Lk 20.36
/b   rli tulsenroh rlsevtet rvalwkalunhek osavkamc rpehek.
/p   é·li təlsi·né·ɔ=č e·lsíhti·t ehalo·ka·lənči·k ɔ·s·áhkame e·p·í·č·i·k.
/t   For they will be the way the angels ('messengers') in heaven are.
/l   for they are like the angels which are in heaven;   [B. omits two clauses in L.]

/b   Mwjiju rlwrtup tcpi wunhi nrvkot tulih rfulukek amwenro.
/p   †mo·šə́š·a e·ləwé·t·əp tépi wə́nči-né·ykɔt tə́li-=č enkələ́k·i·k -a·mwi·né·ɔ.
/t   It can be seen from what Moses said that the dead shall rise.
/l   that the dead are raised, even Moses shewed.

Mk 12.26 /b   Mutu vuh vuji ktukuntamwunro Mwjiju tulrkvekunif
/p   máta=háč háši ktak·əntamo·wəné·ɔ †mo·šə́š·a təle·khí·k·anink
/t   Have you never read in Moses's writings
/kl have ye not read in the book of Moses,

/b   rlatup Krtanitwet wunhi vetkwf,
/p   e·lá·t·əp ke·tanət·ó·wi·t wə́nči hítkunk?
/t   what God said to him from the bush ('tree')?
/kl how in the bush God spake unto him,

/b   nrvlalkwki ‖ Rplivcmu, ok nrvlalkwki Ysuku, ok nrvlalkwki Nhrkupu?
/p   nehəla·lkúk·i †e·pəlihéma, ɔ́·k nehəla·lkúk·i †aisák·a, ɔ́·k nehəla·lkúk·i †nče·kə́pɑ?
/t   The lord of Abraham, and the lord of Isaac, and the lord of Jacob.
/kl saying, I am the God of Abraham, and the God of Isaac, and the God of Jacob?

Lk 20.38, Mt 22.32
(p. 162) /b   Punu Krtanitwet mutu a nevlalri rfululehi, lclrxrlehi ktav;
/p   pənáh, ke·tanət·ó·wi·t máta=á· nihəla·lé·i enkələlí·č·i, lehəle·x·e·lí·č·i=ktá,
/t   Now, God would not be a lord of dead people, but of living ones,
/l   For God is not a God of the dead, but of the living:

Lk 20.38 /b   rli nrku wunhi pumawsif.
/p   é·li- né·k·a -wə́nči-pəmá·wsink.
/t   as people are alive because of him.
/kl for all live unto him.

Mk 12.27 /b Krvlu kmuxifwi hanustamwvmw.
/p kéhəla kəmax·ínkwi-čanəstamúhəmɔ."
/t You really greatly misunderstand."
/kl ye therefore do greatly err.

Mt 22.33 /b Marvlatpanek kanjrluntamwpanek rli lupot.
/p ma·ehəla·tpáni·k kanše·ləntamó·p·ani·k é·li-ləpɔ́·t.
/t The crowd was astonished because he was wise.
/kl And when the multitude heard this, they were astonished at his doctrine.

Lk 20.39 /b Nu aluntc rvlrkvekrsuk tulanro, Nrvlalerf; krvlu wulexun rlwrun.
/p ná a·lə́nte ehəle·khi·k·é·s·ak təla·né·ɔ, "nehəlá·lienk, kéhəla wəlí·x·ən e·ləwé·an."
/t Then some of the scribes said to him, "Master, what you say is truly correct."
/kl Then certain of the scribes answering said, Master, thou hast well said.

Chapter 99 (pp. 162-163). (L. section 99.) (Matthew 22.34-46; Mark 12.28-37; Luke 20:4--44.)

Mt 22.34 /b Paluseok puntamevtetc tuli wrevwkoman Satusesu,
/p †pa·ləsi·í·ɔk pəntamihtí·t·e †tɔ́li-we·yhukɔ·ma·n †sa·tasí·s·a,
/t When the Pharisees heard that he had refuted the Sadducees,
/kl But when the Pharisees had heard that he had put the Sadducees to silence,

/b nu lupi eku mocvlanro,
/p ná lápi íka mɔ·ehəla·né·ɔ.
/t they again gathered there.
/l they also were gathered together.

Mt 22.35 /b mawsw ave lupwrenw eku avpw,
/p má·wsu áhi-ləpwe·ínnu íka ahpú,
/t One very wise man was there
/l Then one of them, which was a lawyer, came

Mk 12.28 /b qwlsitao cntu krkw lutelet,
/p kwəlsət·aɔ́·ɔ énta- kéku -lət·í·li·t,
/t listening to them where they were talking together,
/kl and having heard them reasoning together,

/b nrotc tuli vetu krkw lwrlen,
/p ne·ɔ́·t·e tɔ́li-híta·- kéku -luwé·li·n,
/t and when he saw that he was skilled at talking,
/kl and perceiving that he had answered them well,

Mt 22.35 /b nu notwtumaon kotu avqrhevao, tulao
/p ná nɔt·o·t·əmáɔ·n, kɔ́t·a-ahkwe·č·i·há·ɔ, təlá·ɔ,
/t he then asked him a question, desiring to test him, saying to him,
/kl asked him a question, tempting him, and saying,

Mt 22.36 /b Nrvlaleun, Qvetulutwakunif, tu vuh rlenako aptwnakun alwe lr?
/p "nehəlá·lian, khwitələt·əwá·k·anink, tá=háč e·li·ná·k·ɔ a·pto·ná·k·an aləwí·i lé·?"
/t "Master, in the law, which commandment is the greatest?"
/k Master, which is the great commandment in the law?
/l "Master, which is the first and the great commandment of all in the law?

Mk 12.29 /b Nhesus tulao, Vetumexun tavpuntwakun,
/p nčí·sas təlá·ɔ, "hitamí·x·ən tahpantəwá·k·an:
/t Jesus said to him, "The first commandment is:
/l Jesus [answered him, and] said unto him, The first of all the commandments is,

/b Puntamwq O Isuluk, Nrvlalkofq Krtanitwet mawsw. [⟨Isuluk⟩ for ⟨Isluluk⟩]
/p 'pəntamo·kw, ó· †isəlálak: nehəlá·lkɔnkw ke·tanət·ó·wi·t má·wsu.
/t 'Listen, O Israelites, our lord God is one.
/kl Hear, O Israel; The Lord our God is one Lord:

Mk 12.30 /b Ktavoluh Nrvlalkon Krtanitwet wunhi msithri ktrvif,
/p ktahó·la=č nehəlá·lkɔn ke·tanət·ó·wi·t wə́nči məsəč·é·i kté·hink,
/t You must love your lord (or master), God, with all your heart,
/kl And thou shalt love the Lord thy God with all thy heart,

/b ok wunhi msithri ktunaprokunif,
/p ó·k wə́nči məsəč·é·i ktənna·p·e·ó·k·anink,
/t and with all your soul,
/kl and with all thy soul,

/b ok wunhi msithri kwatamwrokunif,
/p ó·k wə́nči məsəč·é·i ko·wa·t·amwe·ó·k·anink,
/t and with all your mind,
/kl and with all thy mind,

/b ok msithri wunhi khetanuswakunif.
/p ó·k məsəč·é·i wə́nči kči·t·anəs·əwá·k·anink.'
/t and with all your strength.'
/kl and with all thy strength:

/b Jr nuni vetamexun xifwi tavpuntwakun.
/p šé· nə́ni hitamí·x·ən xínkwi-tahpantəwá·k·an,
/t That is the first great commandment.
/l this is the first and great commandment.

Mk 12.31 /b   Ok nc eku wcntavqexif nanc lenakot, jr bv,
/p   ɔ́·k nə́ íka wentahkwí·x·ink ná=nə li·ná·k·ɔt, šé· yúh:
/t   And the next one to it is of the same kind; it is this:
/l   And the second is like unto it, namely this,   (adds from Mt 22.39)

/b   Ktuvoluh wetawswmut rlkeqi avolut kvaky.
/p   'ktahɔ́·la=č wi·t·a·wsɔ́mat e·lkí·kwi-ahɔ́·lat khák·ay.'
/t   'You must love your neighbor as much as you love yourself.'
/kl   Thou shalt love thy neighbour as thyself.

/b   Takw vatri rlwe lrk tavpuntwakun.
/p   takó· hat·é·i e·ləwí·i-lé·k tahpantəwá·k·an.
/t   There is no greater commandment.
/kl   There is none other commandment greater than these.

Mt 22.40 /b   Nunuli bl neju tavpuntwakunu wuntamr wrmi qvetulitwakunu
/p   nanáli yó·l ní·š·a tahpantəwá·k·ana wəntá·me· wé·mi khwitələt·əwá·k·ana
/t   It is these two commandments that are the source of all the laws
/kl   On these two commandments hang all the law

/b   ok ncnekanewrwsetpanifu toptwnakunwu.
/p   ɔ́·k nehəni·k·a·ní·i-we·wsi·tpanínka tɔ·pto·na·k·anúwa."
/t   and the words of the ancient prophets."
/kl   and the prophets.

Mk 12.32 /b   Nu rvlrkvekrs tulan, Nrvlaleun, krvlu nc rlwrun kwlamwc,
/p   ná ehəle·khí·k·e·s tɔ́la·n, "nehəlá·lian, kéhəla nə́ e·ləwé·an ko·lá·məwe.
/t   Then the scribe said to him, "Master, you really speak the truth in what you say.
/kl   And the scribe said unto him, Well, Master, thou hast said the truth:

/b   rli avpwv Krtanitwet, ok takw peli avpei nrkumu jwq.
/p   é·li ahpú ke·tanət·ó·wi·t, ɔ́·k takó· pí·li ahpí·i né·k·əma šúkw.
/t   For God exists, and there is no other except for him.
/kl   for there is one God; and there is none other but he:

Mk 12.33 /b   Nunule a nrl awrn tovolao wunhi msithri vwtrvif,
/p   nanáli=á· né·l awé·n tɔhɔ·lá·ɔ wə́nči məsəč·é·i wté·hink,
/t   He is who a person should love with alltheir heart,
/k   And to love him with all the heart,

/b   ok wunhi msithri watamwrokunif,
/p   ɔ́·k wə́nči məsəč·é·i o·wa·t·amwe·ɔ́·k·anink,
/t   and with all their mind,
/k   and with all the understanding,

/b   ok wunhi msithri tunaprokunif,
/p   ɔ·k wə́nči məsəč·é·i tənna·p·e·ɔ́·k·anink,
/t   and with all their soul,
/k   and with all the soul,

/b   ok wunhi msithri vwhetaniswakunif;
/p   ɔ́·k məsəč·é·i wə́nči wči·t·anəs·əwá·k·anink.
/t   and with all their strength.
/k   and with all the strength,

/b   ok avolan wetawswmahi ‖ rlkeqi avolat vokyu.
/p   ɔ́·k ahɔ́·la·n wi·t·a·wso·má·č·i e·lkí·kwi-ahɔ́·la·t hɔ́kaya,
/t   And for one to love their neighbor as much as they love themself,
/k   and to love his neighbour as himself,

(p. 163) /b   Nul bv alwe lr rlkeqi lrk wrmi cntxif wevwfrokun
/p   nál yúh aləwí·i e·lkí·kwi-lé·k wé·mi éntxink wi·hunke·ɔ́·k·an
/t   this is something greater than are all the sacrifices there are
/k   is more than all whole burnt-offerings and sacrifices.

/b   ok wrmi rvlarvosif patumufc.
/p   ɔ́·k wé·mi ehəlaehɔ́·s·ink pa·tamánke."
/t   and all the acts one performs when one prays."

Mk 12.34 /b   Nhesus nrfc rlkeqi wulaptwnrlet, tulao,
/p   nčí·sas nénke e·lkí·kwi-wəla·pto·né·li·t, təlá·ɔ,
/t   When Jesus saw how well he spoke, he said to him,
/kl And when Jesus saw that he answered discreetly, he said unto him,

/b   Takw kovlumupei wunhi Krtanitwet sokemaokunif.
/p   "takó· kəhələmap·í·i wə́nči ke·tanət·ó·wi·t sɔ·k·i·ma·ɔ́·k·anink."
/t   "You are not far from God's kingdom."
/kl Thou art not far from the kingdom of God.

Mt 22.41 /b   Nrli Paluseok, patumwrekaonif uvpevtet
/p   né·li- †pa·ləsi·í·ɔk pa·tamwe·i·k·á·ɔnink -ahpíhti·t,
/t   While the Pharisees were in the temple,
/kl While the Pharisees were gathered together,

Mt 22.41-42, Mk 12.35   [B. puts the end of Mk 12.35 below.]
/b   Nhesus cntu avkrkifrt notwtumaopani, tulapani.
/p   nčí·sas, énta-ahke·kínke·t, nɔt·o·t·əmaɔ́·p·ani, təlá·p·ani,
/t   Jesus, when he was teaching, asked them, saying to them,
/l   Jesus asked them, while he taught in the temple,

Mt 22.42 /b Krkw vuh kelwu ktulrlumawu Klyst?
/p "kéku=háč ki·ló·wa ktəle·ləmáwwa kəláist?
/t "What do you think of Christ?
/kl What think ye of Christ?

/b awrn vuh qesul?
/p awé·n=háč kkwí·s·al?"
/t Whose son is he?"
/kl whose son is he?

/b Lwrok Ntrpitu.
/p luwé·ɔk, "†nte·pít·a."
/t They said, "David's."
/kl They say unto him, The Son of David.

Mk 12.35 /b Tulao, Tu vuh wunhi rvlrkvekrsuk lwrnro,
/p təlá·ɔ, "tá=háč wwə́nči- ehəle·khi·k·é·s·ak -luwe·né·ɔ,
/t And he said to them, "Why do the scribes say,
/l He saith unto them, ... How say the scribes   [rearranged]

/b Klyst, Ntrpitu wqesumwkw?
/p 'kəláist †nte·pít·a o·k·wi·s·əmúk·u'?
/t 'Christ is the son of David'?
/kl that Christ is the Son of David?

Mt 22.43 /b Tu vuh wunhi Ntrpitu lwivlan nrvlalet
/p tá=háč wwə́nči- †nte·pít·a -luwíhəla·n, 'nehəlá·li·t',
/t Why does David name him 'my lord',
/kl ... How then doth David in spirit call him, ... Lord,

Mk 12.36, Mt 22.43
/b aswrkvekunif tali cntu pelset manntw alrpomatc, cntu lwrtup,
/p †a·s·uwwe·khí·k·anink táli, énta- pí·lsi·t manə́t·u -ale·p·ɔ·má·t·e, énta-luwé·t·əp,
/t in the psalms, when the holy spirit inspired his words, where he said,
/l in the book of Psalms, ... saying by the Holy Ghost,

Mk 12.36 /b Nrvlalwrt tulapani Nrvlalelehi,
/p 'nehəlá·ləwe·t təlá·p·ani nehəla·li·lí·č·i,
/t 'The lord said to my lord,
/kl ... The Lord said to my Lord,

/b Lumutavpel ntunavaonif, svaki jifalkonek vulukc rqei ksetif?
/p "ləmátahpi·l ntənna·há·ɔnink, sháki- šinka·lkɔ́ni·k -halák·e e·k·wí·i ksí·t·ink.'"?
/t "Sit on my right until I shall put your enemies under your feet.'"?
/kl Sit thou on my right hand, till I make thine enemies thy footstool.

Mk 12.37 /b Punu Ntrpitu nevlahi tulwevlapani Nrvlalwrt,
/p pənáh, †nte·pít·a nihəláči tələwihəláp·ani 'nehəlá·ləwe·t.'
/t Now, David himself called him [= Christ] lord.
/kl David therefore himself calleth him Lord;

Mt 22.45 /b tu vuh wunhi qesen?
/p tá=háč wwə́nči-kkwí·s·i·n?"
/t Why is he [= Christ] his son?" [*lit*., 'why does he have him [= Christ] as son?']
/l [If David then call him Lord,] how is he his son?
/k and whence is he then his son?

Mt 22.46 /b Jwq mutu awrn avpei krski eli kwtaptwnalat.
/p šúkw máta awé·n ahpí·i ké·ski- ílli -kwət·a·pto·ná·la·t.
/t But there was no one who was able to say even one word to him.
/kl (1) And no man was able to answer him a word, [numbers = sequence in L.]

Mt 22.46, Mk 12.34
/b Nu nckc kejqek wunhi qvetuealawapani
/p ná-néke kí·škwi·k wwə́nči-khwitaya·lawwáp·ani.
/t Then from that day on they avoided approaching him.
/l (3) ... from that day forth ...

/b mutu heh awrn wifi krkw ntwtumaoepani;
/p máta čí·č awé·n wwínki- kéku -nto·t·əmaɔ·í·p·ani.
/t No one cared to ask him anything anymore.
/kl (2) neither durst any man ... (4) ask him any more questions.

Mk 12.37 /b jwq xrli awrn wifsitaopani.
/p šúkw xé·li awé·n wwinksət·aɔ́·p·ani.
/t But many people liked to hear him.
/kl And the common people heard him gladly.

Chapter 100 (pp. 163-167). (L. section 100.) (Matthew 23.1-39; Mark 12.38; Luke 20.46)

Mt 23.1, Lk 20.45
/b Nrli xrli awrn kavtu klistaot, tulao rkrkemahi ok krtu klistaqki,
/p né·li- xé·li awé·n -káhta-kələstáɔ·t, təlá·ɔ e·k·e·ki·má·č·i ɔ́·k két·a-kələstá·kwki,
/t With many wanting to hear him, he said to his disciples and the ones wanting to hear him,
/l Then in the audience of all the people spake Jesus to the multitude, and to his disciples, [and said unto them in his doctrine,]

Mt 23.2 /b Rvlrkvekrsuk ok Paluseok topavpenro Mwjiju wulclumatuvpifum.
/p "ehəle·khi·k·é·s·ak ɔ́·k †pa·ləsi·í·ɔk tɔ·pahpi·né·ɔ †mo·šə́š·a wəlehələmatahpínkəm.

/t "The scribes and Pharisees sit in Moses's seat.
/kl The scribes and the Pharisees sit in Moses' seat:

Mt 23.3
/b Cntxih krkw eku wunhi lwqrq, kulrluntamwmoc ok nanc lusemoc;
/p éntxi-=č kéku íka -wə́nči-lúk·we·kw, kəle·ləntamo·mɔ́·e, ɔ́·k ná=nə ləs·i·mɔ́·e.
/t Everything they shall tell you from there to do, take it to heart and do the same.
/kl All therefore whatsoever they bid you observe, that observe and do;

/b jwq kahi lusevrq rlsevtet
/p šúkw káči ləs·í·he·kw e·lsíhti·t.
/t But do not do what they do.
/kl but do not ye after their works:

/b rli krkw rlwcvtet, mutu tulsewunro.
/p é·li kéku e·ləwéhti·t máta təlsi·wəné·ɔ.
/t For they do not do the things they say to do.
/kl for they say, and do not.

Mk 12.38
/b Nuxalw rvlrkvekrsuk.
/p naxá·lo· ehəle·khi·k·é·s·ak.
/t Watch out for the scribes.
/k Beware of the scribes, ...   (Also Lk 20.46; L. adds "[*therefore*]".)

Mt 23.4
/b Rli qwskwalrwvrnroi b cntu lawselehi;
/p é·li kkwəskuwale·whe·ne·ɔ́·i yú entala·wsi·lí·č·i,
/t For they put heavy loads on the backs of mankind,
/kl For they bind heavy burdens and grievous to be borne, and lay them on men's shoulders;

/b jwq nrkumao mutu nuxpunc kavtu eku lenxkreok.
/p šúkw ne·k·əmá·ɔ máta náxpəne káhta- íka -li·nxke·í·ok.
/t but they themselves are not even willing to reach out their hand to them.
/kl but they themselves will not move them with one of their fingers.

Mt 23.5
/b Wrmi cntxi krkw larvosevtet
/p wé·mi éntxi- kéku -laehɔ·s·íhti·t,
/t Everything they do,
/kl But all their works

/b jwq wunhi nc lusenro kavtu nrook rlarvosevtet.
/p šúkw wwə́nči- nə́ -ləs·i·né·ɔ, káhta-ne·ɔ́·ok e·laehɔ·s·íhti·t.
/t they only do it because they want what they do to be seen.
/kl they do for to be seen of men: ...

Mk 12.38, Lk 20.46

	/b	Wifi avpamskrok qrnevlaki rqevtetc,
	/p	wínki-ahpa·mské·ɔk kwe·nihəlá·k·i e·k·wihtí·t·e,
	/t	They like to walk around when wearing long clothing,
	/l	They love to go in long robes,

Mt 23.5 /b ok moxifwetwnro puluktulumwao   [⟨moxifwetwn-‖ro⟩]
         /p ɔ́·k mɔx·inkwi·to·né·ɔ †pwəlaktələməwá·ɔ,   [⟨pul-⟩ presumably for /pwəl-/]
         /t and they make their phylacteries large,
         /kl ... they make broad their phylacteries,

(p. 164) /b ok tonhi xifwrlunswetonroi jokvwqeunwao;
         /p ɔ́·k tónči-xinkwe·lənsəwi·to·né·ɔ šɔ·khuk·wi·ɔnəwá·ɔ.
         /t and they make their coats more ostentatious.
         /kl and enlarge the borders of their garments,

Mt 23.6 /b ok cntu wepwntif ok cntu marif
         /p ɔ́·k énta-wi·púntink ɔ́·k énta-ma·é·ink,
         /t And at a feast and in a synagogue
         /kl (1) And ... (3) at feasts, and ... (5) in the synagogues,   [numbers = sequence in L.]

         /b wifi vufq lumutavpenro tutu wcnhi a xifwrlumwqsevtet,
         /p wwínki-=hánkw -ləmatahpi·né·ɔ tətá wénči-=á· -xinkwe·ləmúkwsíhti·t.
         /t they always like to sit in any place by which they would be honored.
         /kl ... (2) love the uppermost rooms ... (4) the chief seats ...

Lk 20.46 /b ok vufq wifi oofwmkwswuk tali cntu xrlif
         /p ɔ́·k=hánkw wínki-ɔɔnko·mkwə́s·əwak táli énta-xé·link.
         /t And they always like to be greeted in a crowd.
         /kl and love greetings in the markets,

Mt 23.7 /b ok wifatumunro lanro rkrkemerf, rkrkemerf.
         /p ɔ́·k wwinka·t·aməné·ɔ la·né·ɔ 'e·k·e·kí·mienk, e·k·e·kí·mienk'.
         /t And they like to be called 'our teacher, our teacher'.
         /kl and to be called of men, Rabbi, Rabbi.

Mt 23.8 /b Kahi kelwu kavtatufvrq ktulkrnro rkrkemerf,
         /p "káči ki·ló·wa kahta·t·ánkhe·kw ktəlke·né·ɔ 'e·k·e·kí·mienk,'
         /t "Don't *you* desire to be called 'our teacher',
         /kl But be not ye called Rabbi:

         /b rli avpw Rkrkemqrq, nul nu Klyst.
         /p é·li ahpú e·k·e·kí·mkwe·kw; nál ná kəláist.
         /t for your teacher exists; he is Christ.
         /kl for one is your Master, even Christ;

	/b	Kelwu wrmi kwemavtuntevmwv.	[⟨-vmwv⟩ for /-həmɔ/]
	/p	ki·ló·wa wé·mi ko·wi·mahtəntíhəmɔ.	
	/t	*You* are all brothers.	
	/kl	and all ye are brethren.	

Mt 23.9 /b Ok kahi awrn lwrvrq kwxunu b tali cntu lawsif;
/p ɔ́·k káči awé·n luwé·he·kw 'kó·x·əna' yú táli entalá·wsink.
/t And do not say of anyone in this world 'our (inc.) father'.
/kl And call no man your father upon the earth:

/b rli mawsw Kwxwu nu rpet osavkamc.
/p é·li má·wsu kó·x·əwa, ná é·p·i·t ɔ·s·áhkame.
/t For there is one father of yours, the one in heaven.
/kl for one is your Father, which is in heaven.

Mt 23.10 /b Ok kahi lwevlavrq Nrvlalwrt,
/p ɔ́·k káči luwihəlá·he·kw 'nehəlá·ləwe·t.'
/t And don't call them 'master'.
/kl Neither be ye called masters:

/b rli mawsw Nrvlalqrq nul nu Klyst.
/p é·li má·wsu nehəlá·lkwe·kw; nál ná kəláist.
/t For there is only one who is your master; he is Christ.
/kl for one is your Master, even Christ.

Mt 23.11 /b Kelwu awrn xifwrlumwqsetc kwtalwkakanenroh.
/p ki·ló·wa awé·n xinkwe·ləmukwsí·t·e, ko·t·alo·ka·k·ani·né·ɔ=č.
/t If anyone of you is considered great, they shall be your servant.
/kl But he that is greatest among you shall be your servant.

Mt 23.12 /b Okh awrn xifwrlumatc vokyu, tufrlumwqswh.
/p ɔ́·k=č awé·n xinkwe·ləmá·t·e hókaya, tanke·ləmúkwsu=č.
/t And if anyone thinks highly of themselves, they will be thought little of.
/kl And whosoever shall exalt himself shall be abased;

/b Jwqh awrn tufrluntufc voky xifwrlumwqswh.
/p šúkw=č awé·n tanke·ləntánke hók·ay, xinkwe·ləmúkwsu=č.
/t But if anyone thinks little of themselves, they will be thought highly of.
/kl and he that shall humble himself shall be exalted.

Mt 23.13 /b Krvlu kutumakawsevmw kelwu lrporq ok Paluseok,
/p "kéhəla kkət·əma·k·a·wsíhəmɔ, ki·ló·wa le·p·ɔ́·e·kw ɔ́·k †pa·ləsi·í·ɔk;
/t "You really are miserable wretches, you wise ones and Pharisees;
/kl But woe unto you, scribes and Pharisees,

/b   kevakevokcvmwv,
/p   †kkihahki·hɔkéhəmɔ.
/t   you are hypocrites (deceivers).
/kl hypocrites!

/b   kelwu rli kpavmarq b cntu lawset osavkamre sakemaokun;
/p   ki·ló·wa é·li-kpahəmáe·kw yú entalá·wsi·t ɔ·s·ahkame·í·i-sa·k·i·ma·ɔ́·k·an.
/t   As *you* shut mankind out of the kingdom of heaven.
/kl for ye shut up the kingdom of heaven against men:

/b   takw kelwu kutu ekali tumekrvwmw,
/p   takó· ki·ló·wa kkát·a- íkali -təmi·k·e·húmɔ,
/t   *You* do not want to enter there yourselves,
/kl for ye neither go in yourselves,

/b   ok kupvekamaonro krtu tumekrhek.
/p   ɔ́·k kkəphikamaɔ·né·ɔ ké·t·a-təmi·k·é·č·i·k.
/t   and you shut it off from those that *do* want to enter.
/kl neither suffer ye them that are entering to go in.

Mt 23.14 /b   Krvlu kutumakawsevmw kelwu lrporq ok Paluseok,
/p   "kéhəla kkət·əma·k·a·wsíhəmɔ, ki·ló·wa le·p·ɔ́·e·kw ɔ́·k †pa·ləsi·í·ɔk;
/t   "You really are miserable wretches, you wise ones and Pharisees;
/kl Woe unto you, scribes and Pharisees,

/b   kevakevokcvmwv,
/p   †kkihahki·hɔkéhəmɔ.
/t   you are hypocrites (deceivers).
/kl hypocrites!

/b   rli khehequnanro kotvwxqrok wcntawsevtet,   [⟨qun⟩ for /k·ən/]
/p   é·li kči·či·k·əna·né·ɔ kɔ·tho·xkwé·ɔk wenta·wsíhti·t,
/t   For you take away from widows what they live on,
/kl for ye devour widows' houses,

/b   ok rli kavtu wulrlumwqserq kukoni vufq patamavmwv;
/p   ɔ́·k é·li-káhta-wəle·ləmukwsíe·kw, kkək·ɔ́·ni·=hánkw -pa·tamáhəmɔ.
/t   and because you want to be well liked, you always say long prayers.
/kl and for a pretence make long prayer:

/b   nunih kwnhi alwei ktumakswakun lenumunro.
/p   nə́ni=č kúnči- aləwí·i-ktəma·ksəwá·k·an -li·naməné·ɔ.
/t   For that reason you shall experience greater misery.
/kl therefore ye shall receive the greater damnation.

Mt 23.15 /b   Krvlu kutumakawsevmw kelwu lrporq ok Paluseok,
/p   "kéhəla kkət·əma·k·a·wsíhəmɔ, ki·ló·wa le·p·ɔ́·e·kw ɔ́·k †pa·ləsi·í·ɔk;
/t   "You really are miserable wretches, you wise ones and Pharisees;
/kl Woe unto you, scribes and Pharisees,

/b   kevakevokcvmwv,
/p   †kkihahki·hɔkéhəmɔ.
/t   you are hypocrites (deceivers),.
/kl hypocrites!

/b   rli qewunwxwrnro vake ok mpi   [⟨q-⟩ for /kəw-/]
/p   é·li kəwi·wəno·x·we·né·ɔ hák·i ɔ́·k mpí,
/t   For you travel the circuit of land and sea ('water'),
/kl for ye compass sea and land

/b   ktuli a kwti awrn kuntwrvalanro li rli patamarq,
/p   ktə́li-=á· kwə́t·i awé·n -kəntəwe·ha·la·né·ɔ lí é·li-pa·tamá·e·kw,
/t   in order to make one person a convert to how you pray,
/kl to make one proselyte,

/b   nuni rlsetc nu nejun ktunhi amemunsvrnro
/p   nə́ni e·lsí·t·e, ná ní·š·ən ktánči-ami·mənshe·né·ɔ
/t   and when he does that, then you make him two times more the child (of the devil)
/kl and when he is made, ye make him twofold more the child of hell

/b   rlkeqi kelwu mavtuntwameminserq.
/p   e·lkí·kwi- ki·ló·wa -mahtant·o·wami·mə́nsie·kw.
/t   than how much *you* are the children of the devil.
/kl than yourselves.

Mt 23.16 /b   Krvlu kutumakawsevmw kelwu krkrpiforq mrawxwrrq;
/p   "kéhəla kkət·əma·k·a·wsíhəmɔ ki·ló·wa ke·k·e·p·inkɔ́·e·kw, me·a·wxwé·e·kw.
/t   "You really are miserable wretches, you blind guides.
/kl Woe unto you, ye blind guides,

/b   ktulwcvmw, takw krkw lri awrn motaptwnatamun patamwrekaon
/p   ktələwéhəmɔ, takó· kéku lé·i, awé·n mot·a·pto·ná·t·amən pa·tamwe·i·k·á·ɔn,
/t   You say, it is no problem for someone to say bad things about the temple,   [!! →]
/kl which say, Whosoever shall swear by the temple, it is nothing;

/b   jwq awrn muvtaptwnatufc nc fwl patamwrekaonif rtrk hanilusw.   [⟨muv‖tapt-⟩]
/p   šúkw awé·n mahta·pto·na·t·ánke nə́ nkó·l pa·tamwe·i·k·á·ɔnink é·te·k, čáni-lə́s·u.
/t   but if someone says bad things about the gold that is in the temple, he does wrong.
/kl but whosoever shall swear by the gold of the temple, he is a debtor!

Mt 23.17   /b   Kwphavmwv, ok kukrpifovmw.
(p. 165)   /p   kkəpčáhəmɔ ɔ́·k kkak·e·p·inkɔ́həmɔ.
            /t   You are foolish and blind.
            /kl Ye fools and blind:

            /b   Tu vuh nc alwe lr fwl, ok nc patamwrekaon wcnhi peltuk nc fwl?
            /p   tá=háč nə́ aləwí·i-lé·, nkó·l ɔ́·k nə́ pa·tamwe·i·k·á·ɔn wénči-pí·ltək nə́ nkó·l?
            /t   Which is greater, the gold or the temple because of which the gold is holy?
            /kl for whether is greater, the gold, or the temple that sanctifieth the gold?

Mt 23.18   /b   Ok ktulwcvmw,
            /p   ɔ́·k ktələwéhəmɔ,
            /t   You also say,
            /l   [*Ye also say*]

            /b   awrn muvtaptwnatufc cvcntu krkw wifemaqviksasek
            /p   awé·n mahta·pto·na·t·ánke ehə́nta- kéku -winki·ma·khwiksá·s·i·k,
            /t   if someone says bad things about the altar,
            /kl Whosoever shall swear by the altar,

            /b   ta a krkw lri;
            /p   tá=á· kéku lé·i.
            /t   it would be no problem.
            /kl it is nothing;

            /b   jwq awrn muvtaptwnatufc nc nuxpufwntwakan eku rtrk, hanih lusw.
            /p   šúkw awé·n mahta·pto·na·t·ánke nə́ naxpankuntəwá·k·an íka é·te·k, čáni-=č -lə́s·u.
            /t   But if someone says bad things about the gift that is on it, he will do wrong.
            /kl but whosoever sweareth by the gift that is upon it, he is guilty.

Mt 23.19   /b   Kuphavmw ok kukrpifovmwv.
            /p   kkəpčáhəmɔ ɔ́·k kkak·e·p·inkɔ́həmɔ.
            /t   You are foolish and blind.
            /kl Ye fools and blind:

            /b   Tu vuh nc alwe lr nuxpufwntwakun.
            /p   tá=háč nə́ aləwí·i-lé·, naxpankuntəwá·k·an
            /t   Which is greater, the gift
            /kl for whether is greater, the gift,

            /b   ok nc cvcntu wifemaqviksasek krkw, wcnhi pelvik nc nuxpufwntwakun?
            /p   ɔ́·k nə́ ehə́nta-winki·ma·khwiksá·s·i·k kéku, wénči-pí·lhik nə́ naxpankuntəwá·k·an?
            /t   or the altar because of which the gift is holy?
            /kl or the altar that sanctifieth the gift?

Mt 23.20 /b Lrw awrn muvtaptwnatufc cvcntu krkw wifemaqviksasek
/p lé·w, awé·n mahta·pto·na·t·ánke ehə́nta- kéku -winki·ma·khwiksá·s·i·k,
/t The truth is, if someone says bad things about the altar,
/kl Whoso therefore shall swear by the altar,

/b takw nc jwq motaptwnatamwun, wrmi tu krkw eku rtrk.
/p takó· nə́ šúkw mɔt·a·pto·na·t·amó·wən, wé·mi=tá kéku íka é·te·k.
/t he does not say bad things about only that, but about everything on it.
/kl sweareth by it, and by all things thereon.

Mt 23.21 /b Ok awrn muvtapwnatufc patamwrekaon,
/p ɔ́·k awé·n mahta·pto·na·t·ánke pa·tamwe·i·k·á·ɔn,
/t And if someone says bad things about the temple,
/kl And whoso shall swear by the temple,

/b takw nc jwq motapwnatumwun, vupi tu wrekelehi.
/p takó· nə́ šúkw mɔt·a·pto·na·t·amó·wən, hápi=tá we·i·k·i·lí·č·i.
/t he does not say bad things about only that, but about the one dwelling there also.
/kl sweareth by it, and by him that dwelleth therein.

Mt 23.22 /b Ok awrn muvtaptwnatufc osavkamc
/p ɔ́·k awé·n mahta·pto·na·t·ánke ɔ·s·áhkame,
/t And if someone says bad things about heaven,
/kl And he that shall swear by heaven,

/b motaptwnatumun Krtanitwet tulcvlumutavpifum, ok vupi eku rpelehi.
/p mɔt·a·pto·ná·t·amən ke·tanət·ó·wi·t wəlehəlmatahpínkəm, ɔ́·k hápi íka e·p·i·lí·č·i.
/t he says bad things about God's throne and the one who sits there as well.
/kl sweareth by the throne of God, and by him that sitteth thereon.

Mt 23.23 /b Krvlu kutumakwsevmw kelwu lrporq ok Paluseok, [⟨kw⟩ for ⟨kaw⟩]
/p "kéhəla kkət·əma·k·a·wsíhəmɔ, ki·ló·wa le·p·ɔ́·e·kw ɔ́·k †pa·ləsi·í·ɔk;
/t "You really are miserable wretches, you wise ones and Pharisees;
/kl Woe unto you, scribes and Pharisees,

/b kevakevokcvmw,
/p †kkihahki·hɔkéhəmɔ.
/t you are hypocrites (deceivers).
/kl hypocrites!

/b ktulsenro eli vufq wifemakvoki skeko ok wifufi
/p ktəlsi·né·ɔ, ílli=hánkw winki·ma·khɔ́ki skí·kɔ ɔ́·k winkánki,
/t You are ones who, even with sweet-smelling herbs and sweet-tasting ones,
/kl for ye pay tithe of mint and anise and cummin,

/b knuxpi vufq krnamwenro,
/p kənáxpi-=hánkw -ke·na·mwi·né·ɔ,
/t give thanks,
/l —

/b nu wrnu nc mutu ktulsewunro maeai rlexif tavpuntwakun;
/p ná wé·na nə́ máta ktəlsi·wəné·ɔ mayá·i e·lí·x·ink tahpantəwá·k·an,
/t but still you do not do that with the main commandments,
/kl and have omitted the weightier matters of the law,

/b punu jaxukawswakun, ktumakrlwakun ok nvakrwswakun.
/p pənáh, šaxahka·wsəwá·k·an, ktəma·k·e·ləwá·k·an[?], ɔ́·k nhake·wsəwá·k·an.
/t even righteousness, mercy, and faith.
/kl judgment, mercy, and faith:

/b Nuni a mu luserqkpanc wlexunwp a nc rlumekuntamrq. [⟨luserq-|kpanc⟩]
/p nə́ni=á·=máh ləs·ie·kwpáne, wəlí·x·əno·p=á· nə́ e·lami·kə́ntame·kw.
/t If you had done that, what you accomplished would have been the right thing.
/kl these ought ye to have done, and not to leave the other undone.

Mt 23.24 /b Krkrpiforq mreawxwrrq.
/p ke·k·e·p·inkɔ́·e·kw, me·a·wxwé·e·kw,
/t You blind guides,
/kl Ye blind guides,

/b Kjekwxkpcvmunro vufq mrnrrq rli qvetu qvelrq mwxrtut,
/p †kši·k·o·xkpehəməné·ɔ=hánkw me·né·e·kw é·li-khwíta-khwíle·kw mo·x·wé·t·ət,
/t you strain what you drink because you're afraid to swallow a little bug,
/kl which strain at a gnat,

/b nu wrnu kcmuluk kmumsithri qvelawaok.
/p ná wé·na kémələk kəməmsəč·é·ɪ-khwilawwá·ɔk.
/t but still you swallow camels whole.
/kl and swallow a camel.

Mt 23.25 /b Krvlu kutumakawsevmw kelwuw lrporq ok Paluseok, [⟨kelwuw⟩ for ⟨kelwu⟩]
/p "kéhəla kkət·əma·k·a·wsíhəmɔ, ki·ló·wa le·p·ɔ́·e·kw ɔ́·k †pa·ləsi·í·ɔk;
/t "You really are miserable wretches, you wise ones and Pharisees;
/kl Woe unto you, scribes and Pharisees,

/b kevakevokcvmw,
/p †kkihahki·hɔkéhəmɔ.
/t you are hypocrites (deceivers).
/kl hypocrites!

	/b	ktulsenro kpeletwnro kpyntwao ok kwlakcnswao xqihi wunhi,
	/p	ktəlsi·né·ɔ, kpi·li·to·né·ɔ kpaintəwá·ɔ ɔ́·k ko·la·k·ensəwá·ɔ xkwíči wə́nči,
	/t	you are ones who clean your cups and your dishes on the outside,
	/kl	for ye make clean the outside of the cup and of the platter,

	/b	nu wrnu hwvotreov neskenako krkw.
	/p	ná wé·na čuhɔté·ɔ ni·ski·ná·k·ɔ kéku.
	/t	but still they are full of filthy things.
	/kl	but within they are full of extortion and excess.

Mt 23.26	/b	Kukrpifov Paluse; ‖
	/p	kkak·e·p·ínkɔ, †pá·lasi.
	/t	You are blind, you Pharisee.
	/kl	Thou blind Pharisee,

(p. 166)	/b	Vetami peletwl lamwfwc kpyntum ok kwlakcns
	/p	hítami pi·lí·to·l la·múnkwe kpaíntəm ɔ́·k ko·lá·k·ens,
	/t	First clean the inside of your cup and your dish,
	/kl	cleanse first that which is within the cup and platter,

	/b	wcnhih xqihi ok wunhi peltuk.
	/p	wénči-=č xkwíči ɔ́·k -wə́nči-pí·ltək.
	/t	so that they will also be clean on the outside.
	/kl	that the outside of them may be clean also.

Mt 23.27	/b	Krvlu kutumakawsevmw kelwu lrporq ok Paluseok,
	/p	"kéhəla kkət·əma·k·a·wsíhəmɔ, ki·ló·wa le·p·ɔ́·e·kw ɔ́·k †pa·ləsi·í·ɔk;
	/t	"You really are miserable wretches, you wise ones and Pharisees;
	/kl	Woe unto you, scribes and Pharisees, hypocrites!

	/b	kevakevokcvmw,
	/p	†kkihahki·hɔkéhəmɔ.
	/t	you are hypocrites (deceivers).
	/kl	hypocrites!

	/b	tpsiqi ktulsenro mavhekamekov rlrk [⟨tpsiqi⟩ for ⟨tpisqi⟩]
	/p	tpə́skwi ktəlsi·né·ɔ mahči·k·amí·k·ɔ é·le·k.
	/t	You are like how tombs ('graves') are.
	/kl	for ye are like unto whited sepulchres,

	/b	xqihi wunhi opulrxunw;
	/p	xkwíči wə́nči-ɔ·p·əlé·x·ənu,
	/t	They are solid white on the outside,

/b xqihi krvlu wulenakovtw,
/p xkwíči kéhəla wəli·nákɔhtu,
/t and on the outside look really nice,
/kl which indeed appear beautiful outward,

/b jwq lamwfwc rfulukei xkunu ok neskenakot.
/p šúkw la·múnkwe enkələk·í·i-xkána, ɔ́·k ni·ski·ná·k·ɔt.
/t but inside are the bones of the dead, and it looks filthy.
/kl but are within full of dead men's bones, and of all uncleanness.

Mt 23.28
/b Jr nuni tpisqi ktulsenro,
/p šé· ná=ní tpəskwi ktəlsi·né·ɔ.
/t That's what you are like.
/kl Even so

/b kwlawswenaqsevmw b tali cntu lawsif
/p ko·la·wsəwi·na·kwsíhəmɔ yú táli entalá·wsink,
/t You appear to be righteous out in the world,
/kl ye also outwardly appear righteous unto men,

/b jwq ktrvwaif tcxi jwq kevokrokun ok muvtawswakun.
/p šúkw ktehəwá·ink téxi šúkw ki·hɔke·ɔ́·k·an ɔ́·k mahta·wsəwá·k·an.
/t but in your hearts is nothing but hypocrisy ('deception') and sinfulness.
/kl but within ye are full of hypocrisy and iniquity.

Mt 23.29
/b Krvlu kutumakawsevmw kelwu lrporq ok Paluseok,
/p "kéhəla kkət·əma·k·a·wsíhəmɔ, ki·ló·wa le·p·ɔ́·e·kw ɔ́·k †pa·ləsi·í·ɔk;
/t "You really are miserable wretches, you wise ones and Pharisees;
/kl Woe unto you, scribes and Pharisees, hypocrites!

/b kevakevokcvmw,
/p †kkihahki hɔkćhəmɔ.
/t you are hypocrites (deceivers).
/kl hypocrites!

/b kwletwnro ncnekanewrwsetpanifu pwrkvakcvasevtet,
/p ko·li·to·né·ɔ nehəni·k·a·ní·i-we·wsi·tpanínka pwe·khakeha·s·íhti·t,
/t You fix up the tombs of the ancient prophets,
/kl because ye build the tombs of the prophets,

/b ok jaxukawsetpanifu pwrkvakcvasevtet;
/p ɔ́·k šaxahka·wsi·tpanínka pwe·khakeha·s·íhti·t,
/t and the tombs of the righteous of old,
/kl and garnish the sepulchres of the righteous,

Mt 23.30 /b ok ktulwcvmw; Kelwnu a lclrxreufqpanc kmwxwmsunanifu lclrxrvtetc,
/p ktələwéhəmɔ, 'ki·ló·na=á· lehəle·x·e·ankwpáne kəmux·o·msəna·nínka lehəle·x·ehtí·t·e,
/t and you say, 'If *we* (incl.) had been alive when our grandfathers lived,
/kl And say, If we had been in the days of our fathers,

/b taa kwehi mavhetwunrnap mwkumwu ncnekanewrwsetpanek.
/p tá=á· kəwíči-mahči·to·wəné·na·p mmo·kəmúwa nehəni·k·a·ní·i-we·wsi·tpáni·k.'
/t we would not have joined in defiling the blood of the prophets of old.'
/kl we would not have been partakers with them in the blood of the prophets.

Mt 23.31 /b Kpunwntvekrnro
/p kpənunthike·né·ɔ
/t And you reveal to everyone
/kl Wherefore ye be witnesses unto yourselves,

/b ktuli vwtwxwenro nukavkc nrvlatpanek ncnekancwrwseletpani.
/p ktə́li-wto·x·wi·né·ɔ nəkáhke nehəla·tpáni·k nehəni·k·a·ní·i-we·wsi·li·tpáni.
/t that you are the offspring of those that killed the prophets.
/kl that ye are the children of them which killed the prophets.

Mt 23.32 /b Pavkunhextwq kwxwawfu motyvoswakunwu.
/p pahkančí·xto·kw ko·x·əwa·únka mɔt·aehɔ·s·əwa·k·anúwa.
/t Complete the evil deeds of your fathers.
/kl Fill ye up then the measure of your fathers.

Mt 23.33 /b Kelwu ktuxkwkevmw, qejkomwrbf, kwnhekemw,
/p ki·ló·wa ktaxko·k·íhəmɔ; kwi·škaməwé·yunk kunči·k·íhəmɔ.
/t You are snakes; you are born from copperheads.
/kl Ye serpents, ye generation of vipers,

/b tu vuh a ktunimunro wcnhi a mutu avperq mavtuntwf?
/p tá=háč=á· ktənnəməné·ɔ wénči-=á· máta -ahpíe·kw mahtánt·unk?
/t What would you do so that you would not be in hell?
/kl how can ye escape the damnation of hell?

Mt 23.34 /b Mprtalwkalapanek nrvekanewrwsehek ok lupwrenwuk,
/p "mpe·t·alo·ka·lá·p·ani·k nehəni·k·a·ní·i-we·wsí·č·i·k ɔ́·k ləpwe·innúwak.
/t "I have sent you the prophets and wise men.
/kl Wherefore, behold, I send unto you prophets, and wise men, and scribes:

/b nukavkc nevlapanek aluntc psuqvetcvopanek,   [⟨nevl-⟩ for ⟨nvel-⟩]
/p nəkáhke nhilá·p·ani·k, a·lə́nte psakhwitehɔ́·p·ani·k,
/t They have been killed, and some have been crucified,
/kl and some of them ye shall kill and crucify;

/b   ok aluntc musi tali qevlwtaopanek,
/p   ó·k a·lə́nte mə́si táli kwihəlo·t·aó·p·ani·k,
/t   and some were chased all over,
/kl and some of them shall ye [scourge in your synagogues, and] persecute [them] from city to city: [rearranged in B.]

/b   ok aluntc srsrkaecvopanek tali cvcntumarif, bqc pchi,   [for ⟨cvcntu marif⟩]
/p   ó·k a·lə́nte se·s·e·k·ayehó·p·ani·k táli ehə́nta-ma·é·ink, yúkwe péči.
/t   and some have been whipped in the synagogues, down to the present time.
/kl and some of them shall ye scourge in your synagogues, ...

Mt 23.35 /b   kxunkih kvakybaif muvtrxun wrmi juxukawsetpanek mwkumwu
/p   kxántki=č khak·ayəwá·ink mahté·x·ən wé·mi šaxahka·wsi·tpáni·k mmo·kəmúwa,
/t   In the end all the blood of the righteous shall fall upon you,
/kl That upon you may come all the righteous blood

/b   rli swkuvlakup wewuntvakameq
/p   é·li-so·k·ahəlá·k·əp wi·wənthákami·kw:
/t   the way it has been shed since the world began:
/kl shed upon the earth,

/b   Rpulu vetami, kxunki Sakulyusu Pelukyusu qesu
/p   †é·pəla hítami, kxántki †sa·kalayás·a, †pi·lakayás·a kkwí·s·a,
/t   first of Abel, and finally of Zacharias, the son of Barachias,
/kl from the blood of righteous Abel unto the blood of Zacharias son of Barachias,

/b   nrvlrkup tali patamwrekaonif ok cvcntu wifemaqviksumatup trtaei.
/p   nehəlé·k·əp táli pa·tamwe·i·k·á·ɔnink ó·k ehə́nta-winki·ma·khwiksəmá·t·əp te·t·aí·i.
/t   who you killed between the temple and his incense altar.
/k   whom ye slew between the temple and the altar.

Mt 23.36 /b   Kvehe ktulwvmw, kvakywaifh muvtrxun nrli lclrxrrq.
/p   khičí·i ktəllúhəmɔ, khak·ayəwá·ink=č mahté·x·ən né·li-lehəle·x·é·e·kw.
/t   I tell you truly, it shall fall upon you in your lifetimes.
/k   Verily I say unto you, All these things shall come upon this generation.

Mt 23.37 /b   O Nhelwsulum Nhelwsulum! nrvnekane wrwsetpanifu ncnvelut
/p   "ó· †nči·ló·sələm, †nči·ló·sələm! nehəni·k·a·ní·i-we·wsi·tpanínka nenhílat,
/t   "O Jerusalem, Jerusalem! You who used to to kill the ancient prophets,
/k   O Jerusalem, Jerusalem, thou that killest the prophets,

/b   ok rvalwkalunhek yerve pwpavkumat avsunu!   [⟨yerve⟩ for ⟨yeave⟩; ⟨pwpa-‖vku⟩]
/p   ó·k ehalo·ka·lə́nči·k a·yáhi-pəpahkámat ahsə́na.
/t   and who formerly threw stones at messengers.
/k   and stonest them which are sent unto thee,

(p. 167) /b Tumeki vufq nmacvook ktumemensumuk; (Cf. Lk 13.34; ⟨mens⟩ for ⟨muns⟩.)
/p təmí·ki=hánkw nəma·ehɔ́·ɔk ktami·mə́nsəmak,
/t I have often gathered your children together,
/k how often would I have gathered thy children together,

/b mulaji tepas clukveqi macvot wnehanu li rqulwfonc
/p málahši típa·s ehələkhíkwi-ma·éhɔ·t wəni·č·á·na lí e·k·wəlúnkɔne,
/t like a hen at the times she gathers her chicks (*lit.*, children) under her wings,
/k even as a hen gathereth her chickens under her wings,

/b jwq kjifi lrlumi.
/p šúkw kšínki-lé·ləmi.
/t but you refused to let me.
/k and ye would not!

Mt 23.38 /b Punu, wekerqih xwvrtro.
/p pənáh, wi·k·ié·k·wi=č xo·he·té·ɔ.
/t See, your houses will be abandoned.
/k Behold, your house is left unto you desolate.

Mt 23.39 /b Rli ktulwvmw,
/p é·li ktəllúhəmɔ,
/t For I say to you,
/k For I say unto you,

/b bqc wunhi taa heh knrevwmw
/p yúkwe wə́nči, tá=á· čí·č kəne·i·húmɔ,
/t from here on you shall not see me again,
/k Ye shall not see me henceforth,

/b kcnh tpisqevlakc ktulih lwrnro
/p kə́nč tpəskwihəlá·k·e, ktə́li-=č -luwe·né·ɔ,
/t until the time comes that you will say,
/k till ye shall say,

/b nwlapcnswvalwq, nu pchi nuxpwxrt tulswakun Krtanitwet.
/p 'no·la·p·enso·há·lukw ná péči-naxpó·x·we·t təlsəwá·k·an ke·tanət·ó·wi·t.'"
/t 'I am blessed by the one who comes with the power of God.'"
/k Blessed is he that cometh in the name of the Lord.

Chapter 101 (p. 167). [L. section 101.] (Mark 12.41-44; Lk 21.1-4)

Mk 12.41 /b   Nhesus lumutuvpwp, rlvwqrpet tpusqei
/p   nčí·sas ləmátahpo·p, e·lhukwé·p·i·t tpəskwí·i
/t   Jesus sat, and directly in front of him
/kl   And Jesus sat over against

/b   vatr mcvmarnasek moni cvatrk,
/p   hát·e· mehəma·e·ná·s·i·k móni ehháte·k.
/t   was the treasury (*lit.*, the place where money that was collected was always put).
/kl   the treasury,

Lk 21.1 /b   apvwqrtc
/p   a·phukwé·t·e,
/t   When he looked up,
/kl   And he looked up,

Mk 12.41 /b   nrwr moni li eku laneven.
/p   néwwe· móni lí- íka -laníhi·n.
/t   he saw people tossing money into it.
/kl   and beheld how the people cast money into the treasury:

/b   Xrli rvoprehek umufrli eku laniveok.
/p   xé·li ehɔ·p·e·í·č·i·k amanké·li íka laníhí·ɔk.
/t   Many rich people each tossed in a lot.
/kl   and many that were rich cast in much.

Lk 21.2 /b   Ekali nrr krtumakselehi kotvwxqreo,
/p   íkali né·e· ke·t·əma·ksi·lí·č·i kɔ·thoːxkwé·ɔ,
/t   And he saw a poor widow go there,
/kl   And he saw also a certain poor widow ...

Mk 12.42 /b   eku lanevelw neju monetutu mutu nuxpunc kwti scns rlaovteki.
/p   íka laníhi·lu ní·š·a mɔni·t·ə́t·a máta náxpəne kwə́t·i séns e·la·ɔhtí·k·i.
/t   and she tossed in two small coins that were not even worth one cent.
/kl   and she threw in two mites, which make a farthing.

Mk 12.43 /b   Nu tulan rkrkemahi kvehe ktulwvrnw   [⟨-wvrnw⟩ for ⟨-wvmw⟩]
/p   ná tə́la·n e·k·e·ki·má·č·i, "khičí·i ktəllúhəmɔ,
/t   The he said to his disciples, "I tell you truly,
/kl   And he called unto him his disciples, and saith unto them, Verily I say unto you,

/b   nuni krtumakset kotvwxqc alwe txi eku lanive
/p   náni ke·t·əmá·ksi·t kɔ·thó·xkwe aləwí·i txí íka laníhi·,
/t   that poor widow tossed in more
/kl   That this poor widow hath cast more in,

	/b	wrmi tavqei cntxi eku lanevif;
	/p	wé·mi tahkwí·i éntxi- íka -laníhink,
	/t	than all that has been tossed in together,
	/kl	than all they which have cast into the treasury:

Lk 21.4 /b rli bk tovoprokunwaif wunhi eku vatwvtet rtrk Krtanitwet nrxpufwmunt;
 /p é·li- yó·k tɔhɔ·p·e·ɔ·k·anəwá·ink -wə́nči- íka -hatúhti·t é·te·k ke·tanət·ó·wi·t ne·xpankó·mənt,
 /t because it is out of their riches that these (others) put it in the place where what is offered to God is put,
 /kl For all these have of their abundance cast in unto the offerings of God:

Mk 12.44, Luke 21.4
 /b ajitc nrkumu qwtumakswakunif wunhi eku vatwn
 /p a·šíte né·k·əma kwət·əma·ksəwá·k·anink wwə́nči- íka -hát·o·n
 /t while in her case, in contrast, it is out of her poverty that she puts there
 /l but she of her penury did cast in

 /b jevkunh cntxi wcntawset.   [⟨wcnt-⟩ for /wənt-/]
 /p šíhkanč éntxi-wəntá·wsi·t,
 /t the entire amount that she lives on.
 /l all that she had, even all her living.

Chapter 102 (pp. 167-172). [L. section 102.] (Mt 24.1-51; Mark 13.1-37; Lk 21.5-36)

Mt 24.1 /b Nu Nhesus qwthen eku wunhi patamwrekaonif,   [⟨th⟩ for /č·/, as often]
 /p ná nčí·sas kwə́č·i·n íka wə́nči pa·tamwe·i·k·á·ɔnink.
 /t Then Jesus went out of the temple.
 /kl And Jesus went out, and departed from the temple:

 /b rkrkemahi tulao punamwq b wekwam.
 /p e·k·e·ki·má·č·i təlá·ɔ, "pənámo·kw yú wí·k·əwam."
 /t He said to his disciples, "Look at this building."
 /kl and his disciples came to him, for to shew him the buildings of the temple;

Lk 21.5 /b Aluntc tokunwtumunro rlkeqi amrmuntvetrvasek avsunu
 /p a·lə́nte tɔk·əno·t·əməné·ɔ †e·lkí·kwi-ame·manthitehá·s·i·k ahsə́na,
 /t And some talked about how marvelously hewn the stones were,
 /k And as some spake of the temple, how it was adorned with goodly stones and gifts,
 /l and some spake, how it was adorned with goodly stones, and gifts,

/b rlkeqi wulexif;
/p eˑlkíˑkwi-wəlíˑxˑink.
/t and how fine they were.
/k —

Mk 13.1 /b mawsw rkrkemunt tulao, Nrvlaleun punu rlenako bl avsunu
/p máˑwsu eˑkˑeˑkíˑmənt təláˑɔ, "nehəláˑlian, pənáh eˑliˑnáˑkˑɔ yóˑl ahsə́na
/t One of the disciples said to him, "Master, look at the kind of stones these are,
/l And one of his disciples saith unto him, Master, see what manner of stones,

/b ok rlkeqi wulexif.
/p ɔ́ˑk eˑlkíˑkwi-wəlíˑxˑink."
/t and how fine they are."
/k and what buildings are here

Mk 13.2 /b Jwq Nhesus tulao,
/p šúkw nčíˑsas təláˑɔ,
/t But Jesus said to him (or them),
/kl And Jesus answering said unto him,
/k And Jesus said unto them, (Matthew 24.2)

Mt 24.2 /b knrmunro vuh wrmi bl krkwni?
/p "kəneˑmənéˑɔ=háč wéˑmi yóˑl keˑkˑóˑni?
/t "Do you see all these things?
/kl See ye not all these things?

Mk 13.2 /b ok bl amufi wekwavmu?
/p ɔ́ˑk yóˑl amánki-wiˑkˑəwáhəma?
/t And these great buildings?
/kl these great buildings?

Mt 24.2 /b Kvehei ktulwvmw,
/p khičíˑi ktəllúhəmɔ.
/t I tell you truly,
/l Verily I say unto you,

Lk 21.6 /b tpisqevlrh lih mutu nuxpunc kwti bl avsinu petyexunwi. ‖
/p tpəskwíhəle-=č líˑ=č máta náxpəne kwə́tˑi yóˑl ahsə́na -piˑtaiˑxˑənóˑwi."
/t The time shall come that not even one of these stones will lie atop another."
/kl .. the days will come, in the which there shall not be left one stone upon another,..

Mk 13.3 /b Eku lrmuvtupetc Olipe ovhwf, wcnhi nrvkotuk patumwrekaon,
(p. 168) /p íka leˑmahtapíˑtˑe †ɔlipíˑi-ɔhčúnk, wénčiˑneˑykɔ́tˑək paˑtamweˑiˑkˑáˑɔn,
/t As he sat on Olive Mountain, from which the temple could be seen,
/kl And as he sat upon the mount of Olives, over against the temple,

/b   rkrkemunhek Petul ok Nhim ck Nhan ok Antlws wtxawapani,
/p   e·k·e·ki·mə́nči·k †pí·təl, ɔ́·k nčím, ɔ́·k nčá·n, ɔ́·k †ántəlo·s o·txawwá·p·ani,
/t   the disciples Peter and James ("Jim") and John and Andrew came to him
/l   the disciples, Peter, and James, and John, and Andrew came unto him privately,

/b   keme tulawapani,
/p   ki·mí·i təlawwá·p·ani,
/t   and said to him secretly,
/l   and asked him, saying,

Mk 13.4 /b   Nrvlalerf, myai lenrn rlkeqih nc lrk.
/p   "nehəlá·lienk, mayá·i lí·ne·n e·lkí·kwi-=č nə́ -lé·k.
/t   "Master, tell us exactly when that will happen.
/l   Master, but tell us, when shall these things be?

Mt 24.3 /b   Ok krkwh vuh nrvkot lupi kavtu paanc,
/p   ɔ́·k kéku=č=háč né·ykɔt lápi káhta-pá·ane,
/t   And what will be seen when you are about to come again,
/kl and what shall be the sign of thy coming,

/b   ok kavtu alumi alu vatrkc vuki?
/p   ɔ́·k káhta-áləmi-ála-hat·é·k·e hák·i?"
/t   and when the world is about to cease to exist?"
/kl and of the end of the world?

Mt 24.4 /b   Nhesus tulao, Trku tu, kahi awrn keolwqvrq,
/p   nčí·sas təlá·ɔ, "té·ka=tá, káči awé·n ki·ɔlúkhwe·kw.
/t   Jesus said to them, "Take care that you not let anyone deceive you.
/k   And Jesus answered and said unto them, Take heed that no man deceive you.

Mt 24.5 /b   rli xrlih awrnek prok ntulswakunif rlwrthekh, Ne tu Klyst:
/p   é·li xé·li=č awé·ni·k pé·ɔk ntəlsəwá·k·anink, e·ləwé·č·i·k=č, 'ní·=tá kəláist,'
/t   For many will come acting for me ('in my power'), who will say, 'I am Christ,'
/kl For many shall come in my name, saying, I am Christ;

Lk 21.8 /b   ok krvlu prxwhevlr.
/p   ɔ́·k, 'kéhəla pe·x·o·č·íhəle·.'
/t   and, 'The time is really near.'
/kl and, the time draweth near:

Mt 24.5 /b   Xrlih keolrok;
/p   xé·li=č ki·ɔlé·ɔk.
/t   They will deceive many.
/kl and shall deceive many.

Lk 21.8 /b kahi kulistufvrq.
/p káči kələstánkhe·kw.
/t Don't listen to it.
/kl go ye not therefore after them.

Mt 24.6 /b Kpuntamunroh li muvtakrn ok li navkonaluten.
/p kpəntaməné·ɔ=č lí-mahtá·ke·n, ɔ́·k lí-nahkɔ·nalət·i·n.   [See *Glossary*.]
/t You will hear that there is war and random conflict(?).
/l And ye shall hear of wars, and rumours of wars:
/k But when ye shall hear of wars and commotions,   (Luke 21.9)

Mk 13.7 /b Puntamrqc muvtakrokunu ok li hihpi lr wrmi b tali.
/p pəntamé·k·we mahta·ke·ɔ́·k·ana, ɔ́·k lí-čə́čpi-lé· wé·mi yú táli,
/t When you hear of wars, and that things are happening in all different places here,
/l And when ye shall hear of wars, and rumours of wars, and commotions,

Lk 21.9, Mk 13.7
/b Trku tu kahi wejasevrq ok sukwrluntufvrq.
/p té·ka=tá, káči wi·š·a·s·í·he·kw, ɔ́·k sak·we·ləntánkhe·kw.
/t take care that you not be frightened or distressed.
/l See that ye be not terrified and troubled:

Lk 21.9 /b Rli wrmih nuni vetami lr, jwq nrsko rlu vatrk.   [⟨rlu⟩ for ⟨alu⟩]
/p é·li wé·mi=č nəni hítami lé·, šúkw né·skɔ ála-hát·e·k.
/t For all of that must happen first, but before it ends.
/l for all these things must (first) come to pass, but the end shall not be yet.
/k for these things must first come to pass; but the end is not by and by.

Mt 24.7 /b Rkvokrehekh kavtwnalutwuk, okh sakemaokunuk kavtwnalitwuk,
/p e·khɔke·í·č·i·k=č kahto·nalət·əwak, ɔ́·k=č sa·k·i·ma·ɔ́·k·anak kahto·nalət·əwak.
/t Nations shall attack each other, and kingdoms shall attack each other.
/k For nation shall rise against nation, and kingdom against kingdom: ...
/l Then said he unto them, Nation shall rise against nation, and kingdom against kingdom:

Lk 21.11, Mt 24.7, Mk 13.8
/b okh xrlrnaovki tali avi qhwqevlr vaki, okh kavtwpvoten,
/p ɔ́·k=č xe·lennáɔhki táli áhi-kwčuk·wíhəle· hák·i, ɔ́·k=č kahto·phóti·n,
/t And there will be great earthquakes in many places, and there will be famine,
/l And great earthquakes shall be in divers places, and there shall be famines,

/b okh wrmevtwakun, ok sukqelarvtwakunu,   [⟨kq⟩ for /k·w/]
/p ɔ́·k=č we·mihtəwá·k·an, ɔ́·k sak·wi·laehtəwá·k·ana.
/t and there will be massacres and persecutions.
/l and pestilences, and troubles,

/b okh nrvkot wcnhih wejasvatif
/p ó·k=č né·ykɔt wénči-=č -wi·š·a·shátink,
/t And sights will be seen that will cause terror,
/l and fearful sights,

/b okh xifwenako krkw, nrvkot li vwqrbf;
/p ó·k=č xinkwi·ná·k·ɔ kéku né·ykɔt lí hukwé·yunk.
/t and great sights will be seen in heaven.
/l and great signs shall there be from heaven:

Mt 24.8 /b nunuli bl wunhi alumexun jerluntumwakun.
/p nanáli yó·l wə́nči-aləmí·x·ən ši·e·ləntaməwá·k·an.
/t From these does sorrow begin.
/l all these are the beginnings of sorrows.

Mk 13.9 /b Jwq bqc b mjatamwq,
/p šúkw yúkwe yú məšá·t·amo·kw:
/t But remember this:
/kl But take heed to yourselves:

Lk 21.12 /b Vetamih ktavwunwkwaok, okh kowesavkevkwaok,
/p hítami=č ktahwənuk·əwá·ɔk, ó·k=č kɔwisahkihkəwá·ɔk.
/t First they will seize you and torment you.
/l for before all these, they shall lay their hands on you, and persecute you,

Mk 13.9, Lk 21.12
/b okh cntu ahemwlsif ktulwxolukcvmw, okh cvcntu macvluf,
/p ó·k=č énta-a·č·i·mó·lsink ktəlo·x·ɔlək·éhəmɔ, ó·k=č ehə́nta-ma·éhəlank,
/t And you will be taken to councils and synagogues,
/l and deliver you up to councils, and to the synagogues,

Lk 21.12, Mt 24.9
/b okh cvcntu kpavwtif ktuntu avelenamwvmw   [⟨avele-⟩ for ⟨ave le-⟩]
/p ó·k=č ehə́nta-kpahó·t·ink ktə́nta-áhi-li·namúhəmɔ.
/t and in prisons you will suffer severely.
/l and into prisons to be afflicted;

Mt 24.10 /b wrmih awrnek kjifalkwaok, wunhi ne;
/p wé·mi=č awé·ni·k kšinka·lkəwá·ɔk, wə́nči ní·.
/t Everyone will hate you because of me.   [numbers = sequence in L.]
/k (4) and ye shall be hated of all nations for my name's sake.

Mk 13.9 /b okh cvcntu macvluf ktuntu srsrkacvwkcvmw,
/p ó·k=č ehə́nta-ma·éhəlank ktə́nta-se·s·e·k·ayeho·k·éhəmɔ.
/t And you will be whipped in the synagogues.
/l (1) and in the synagogues ye shall be beaten:

Mk 13.9 /b okh kprjwkrnro krkabmvrsekri ok sakemaekri, wunhi ne,
/p ó·k=č kpe·š·o·k·e·né·ɔ ke·kayəmhe·s·i·ké·i ó·k sa·k·i·ma·i·ké·i, wə́nči ní·.
/t And you will be brought among rulers and kings because of me.
/l (2) and ye shall be brought before rulers and kings for my name's sake;

Mt 24.9 /b nrkumaoh knelkwaok.
/p ne·k·əmá·ɔ=č kənilkəwá·ɔk.
/t And *they* will kill you.
/l (3) and they shall kill you:

Lk 21.13, Mk 13.9
/b Nuh myai nulwxun ktuli a punwnvekrnro. [⟨nv⟩ for ⟨ntv⟩]
/p ná=č mayá·i-naló·x·ən ktəli-=á· -pənunthike·né·ɔ.
/t Then it will be the perfect time for you to bear witness.
/l And it shall turn to you for a testimony against them.

Mk 13.11 /b Nrli alumwxolukrrq,
/p né·li-aləmo·x·ɔlək·é·e·kw,
/t As you are being led away,
/kl But when they shall lead you, and deliver you up,

/b kahi punarluntufvrq krkw a tu rlwrrq ok kahi sukqrluntufvrq,
/p káči pəna·eləntánkhe·kw kéku=á·=tá e·ləwé·e·kw, ó·k káči sak·we·ləntánkhe·kw.
/t don't think about what you might say, and don't be distressed.
/kl take no thought before-hand what ye shall speak, neither do ye premeditate:

/b rlih melkwserq ktulaptwnrnro.
/p é·li-=č -mi·lkwə́s·ie·kw ktəla·pto·ne·né·ɔ.
/t You shall speak the words that you will be given (by a higher power) to speak.
/kl but whatsoever shall be given you in that hour, that speak ye:

/b rli mutu a kelwu nevlahi ktaptwnrvwmw, jwqh nu Pelset Manitw.
/p é·li máta=á· ki·ló·wa nihəláči kta·pto·ne·húmɔ, šúkw=č ná pí·lsi·t manət·u.
/t For it would not be *you* speaking yourselves, but the holy spirit.
/kl for it is not ye that speak, but the Holy Ghost.

Lk 21.15 /b Rli kmelwvmwh ktwnwaif lupwrokun [⟨lup-‖wrokun⟩]
/p é·li kəmillúhəmɔ=č kto·nəwá·ink ləpwe·ó·k·an,
/t For I shall give you wisdom in your mouths,
/kl For I will give you a mouth and wisdom,

(p. 169) /b wcnhih eli wrmi jifalqrqek taa tcxi wrevwkomkwrq.
/p wénči-=č illi wé·mi šinka·lkwé·k·wi·k tá=á· téxi †-we·yhukɔ·mkó·we·kw.
/t because of which even all your enemies will not at all be able to refute you.
/kl which all your adversaries shall not be able to gainsay nor resist.

Mt 24.10 /b   Xrlih awrn lwkavlr, okh amuntavkununtw, okh jifaltwuk.
/p   "xé·li=č awé·n lo·káhəle·, ɔ́·k=č amətahkənə́ntu, ɔ́·k=č šinka·ltúwak.
/t   "Many will fall away and betray each other, and they will hate each other.
/kl   And then shall many be offended, and shall betray one another, and shall hate one another.   [KJV "be offended": RSV "fall away"]

Mk 13.12 /b   Wemavtuh motavkunemao tuli a ufululen,
/p   wí·mahta=č mɔtahkəni·má·ɔ, tə́li-=á· -ankələ́li·n.
/t   Their ("his") brother will denounce them, so that they would die.   (Cf. Mt 10.21.)
/kl   Now the brother shall betray the brother to death,

/b   okh linw nanc tulevan qesu,
/p   ɔ́·k=č lə́nu ná=nə təlí·ha·n kkwí·s·a.
/t   and a man will do the same to his son.
/kl   and the father the son;

/b   okh meminsuk pavswqeok tuli a ufululen qekybbmwao.
/p   ɔ́·k=č mi·mə́nsak pahsuk·wí·ɔk, tə́li-=á· -ankələ́li·n kwi·kayo·yəməwá·ɔ.
/t   And children will stand up (as in a trial) so that their parents would die.
/kl   and children shall rise up against their parents, and shall cause them to be put to death.

Lk 21.16 /b   Okh kelwu, kmutavkunemkwaok kekybbmwaok, ok kemavtwaok,
/p   ɔ́·k=č ki·ló·wa kəmatahkəni·mkəwá·ok kki·kayo·yəməwá·ɔk, ɔ́·k ki·mahtəwá·ɔk,
/t   And *you* will be denounced by your parents, and your brothers,
/kl   And ye shall be betrayed, both by parents, and brethren,

/b   ok rlafwmrqek, ok keteswaok;
/p   ɔ́·k e·lanko·mé·k·wi·k, ɔ́·k ki·t·i·s·əwá·ɔk.
/t   and your relatives, and your friends.
/kl   and kinsfolks, and friends;

/b   aluntrmerqh kwnhi nvelkrnro,
/p   a·lənté·mie·kw=č kúnči-nhilke·né·ɔ.
/t   Some of you will be killed because of it.
/kl   and some of you shall they cause to be put to death.

Lk 21.18 /b   Jwq taa kwti melaxk kelwaif pale lri.   [⟨kwti melaxk⟩: minimal space]
/p   šúkw tá=á· kwə́t·i mí·laxk ki·ləwá·ink palí·i lé·i.
/t   But not one hair on your heads will be destroyed.
/k   But there shall not an hair of your head perish.

Lk 21.19 /b   Nvakrwserqch ktunaprokunwuh wuliavpwv.
/p   nhake·wsié·k·we=č, ktənna·p·e·ɔ·k·anúwa=č wə́li-ahpú.
/t   If you have faith, your souls will be well.
/k   In your patience possess ye your souls.

Mt 24.11 /b Xrlih krkulwnrhek mrmrmuntsehek pavswqeok,
        /p xé·li=č ke·k·əlo·né·č·i·k me·me·mantsí·č·i·k pahsuk·wí·ɔk,
        /t Many lying soothsayers will rise up,
        /k And many false prophets shall rise,

        /b xrlih awrni keolrok.
        /p xé·li=č awé·ni ki·ɔlé·ɔk.
        /t and they will deceive many people.
        /k and shall deceive many.

Mt 24.12 /b Rlih ave xrltuk muvtawswakun, xrlih awrn tovoltwakun klumevlr.
        /p é·li-=č -áhi-xé·ltək mahta·wsəwá·k·an, xé·li=č awé·n tɔhɔ·ltəwá·k·an kəlamíhəle·.
        /t Because there will be much sinfulness, many people's love will go still.
        /k And because iniquity shall abound, the love of many shall wax cold.

Mt 24.13 /b Jwq awrn kvetrluntufc li wrlvikif srki lclrxrt,
        /p šúkw awé·n khite·ləntánke lí we·lhíkink sé·ki-lehəlé·x·e·t,
        /t But if anyone is serious towards the good way all their life,
        /k But he that shall endure unto the end,

        /b nrkuh lclrxrmvala.
        /p né·k·a=č lehəle·x·e·mhá·la·.
        /t *they* will be saved.
        /k the same shall be saved.

Mt 24.14 /b Bqc b ntaptwnakun vetamih wuntamasen wrmi b tali
        /p yúkwe yú nta·pto·ná·k·an, hítami=č wəntamá·s·i·n wé·mi yú táli,
        /t And this word of mine first shall be taught all over here,
        /k And this gospel of the kingdom shall be preached in all the world

        /b wunhih wrmi cntxakret puntuf;
        /p wənči-=č wé·mi entxa ké·i·t -pəntank.
        /t so that all nations shall hear it.
        /k for a witness unto all nations;

        /b nu kcnh tpisqevlr.
        /p ná kə́nč tpəskwíhəle·.
        /t Only then will the time come.
        /k and then shall the end come.

Lk 21.20 /b Nrrqch muvtakrenwuk tuli okrkamunro Nhelwsulum,
        /p "ne·é·k·we=č mahta·ke·innúwak táli-ɔ·ke·kaməné·ɔ †nči·ló·sələm,
        /t "When you see soldiers surrounding Jerusalem,
        /kl And when ye shall see Jerusalem compassed with armies,   (L. adds "therefore".)

	/b	nuh kwatwnro lih xoluneti pale lr.
	/p	ná=č ko·wa·to·né·ɔ lí=č xɔləníti palí·i -lé·.
	/t	then you will know that it very soon will be destroyed.
	/kl	then know that the desolation thereof is nigh,

Mt 24.15	/b	Lenamrqc rlwrtup nrvnekanewrwsetpanu Ntanilu;
	/p	li·namé·k·we e·ləwé·t·əp nehəni·k·a·ní·i-we·wsi·tpána †ntánəla:
	/t	When you see what the prophet Daniel said:
	/k	When ye therefore shall see what was spoken of by Daniel the prophet,
	/l	[*that is,*] the abomination of desolation, spoken of by Daniel the prophet,

	/b	neskenakqset eku nepw cntu ave peltuk,
	/p	ni·ski·ná·kwsi·t íka ní·p·o· énta-áhi-pí·ltək,
	/t	the foul one stands in the very holy place,
	/k	... the abomination of desolation ... stand in the holy place,
	/l	standing where it ought not, in the holy place,

	/b	(awrn nuni avkuntufc nunwstufch)
	/p	—awé·n nə́ni ahkəntánke nəno·stánkeč—
	/t	—if anyone reads that let them understand it—
	/kl	(whoso readeth, let him understand:)

Mt 24.16	/b	nuni lukveqi awrn Nhwe vakif avpetc kvetavtunwf lujemwetch;
	/p	nə́ni ləkhíkwi awé·n nčo·wí·i-hák·ink ahpí·t·e, khitahtə́nunk ləš·i·mwí·t·eč.
	/t	at that time if anyone is in the Jews' land, let them flee to the mountains.
	/kl	Then let them which be in Judaea flee into the mountains;

Lk 21.21	/b	ok taoni lrlai awrn avpetc khetch;
	/p	ɔ́·k tá·ɔni le·lá·i awé·n ahpí·t·e, kči·t·eč,
	/t	And even if someone is in the middle of it, let them leave.
	/l	and let them which are in the midst of it depart out;

	/b	ok pale awrnek avpevtetc kahi ekali tumekrvteveh;
	/p	ɔ́·k palí·i awé·ni·k ahpihtí·t·e, káči íkali təmi·k·ehtí·hi·č.
	/t	And if people are elsewhere, let them not enter it.
	/k	and let not them that are in the countries enter thereinto.

Mt 24.17	/b	ok awrn xqetakc avpetc
	/p	ɔ́·k awé·n xkwi·tá·k·e ahpí·t·e,
	/t	And if someone is on top of a house,
	/l	and let him which is on the house-top

	/b	kahi luvupu krkw natifveh li wekwavmif;
	/p	káči lahápa kéku na·t·ínkhi·č lí wi·k·əwáhəmink.
	/t	let them not take the time to go and get things from the house.
	/kl	not come down ... to take any thing out of his house: [omission in L.]

Mk 13.15 /b ok awrn kohumif avpetc, kahi luvupu natifveh cvavqehi.
/p ɔ́·k awé·n kɔ́čəmink ahpí·t·e, káči lahápa na·t·ínkhi·č ehahkwí·č·i.
/t And if someone is outside, let them not take the time to go and get their clothes.
/kl And let him that is in the field, not turn back again for to take up his garment.

Lk 21.22 /b Rli nunulih nrl manwfswe kejkwul
/p é·li nanáli=č né·l manunksəwí·i-ki·škúwal,
/t For those will be the days of anger,
/k For these be the days of vengeance,

/b lih pavkunhe lr wrmi krkw rlrkvasek.
/p lí-=č -pahkánči-lé· wé·mi kéku e·le·khá·s·i·k.
/t for everything that was written to come true.
/k that all things which are written may be fulfilled.

Mt 24.19 /b Krvluh nuni lukveqi ktumakswuk mrxujqhahek xqreok ok nwvlasehek;
[⟨jqh⟩ for /skwč/; ⟨las⟩ for /la·ɔhs/]
/p kéhəla=č nə́ni lǝkhíkwi ktəma·ksúwak me·x·askwčá·č·i·k xkwé·ok ɔ́·k
nuhəla·ɔhsí·č·i·k.
/t And at that time women that are big with child or nursing will be really miserable.
/k And woe unto them that are with child, and to them that give suck in those days!

Mt 24.20 /b Wenwrq ktulih mutu lwune vwjemwewunro
/p wí·nəwe·kw ktə́li-=č máta lo·waní·i -wši·mwi·wəné·ɔ,
/t Pray that you do not flee in winter,
/l And pray ye that your flight be not in the winter,

/b jita alaxemwe kejqek.
/p ší=tá ala·x·i·məwí·i-kí·škwi·k.
/t or on the day of rest.
/kl neither on the sabbath day:

Mt 24.21 /b Rli avih wejasvaten, ‖
/p é·li áhi-=č -wi·š·a·sháti·n,
/t For there shall be great terror,
/l For in those days shall be great tribulation,

(p. 170) /b mutu elrk wewuntvakameq,
/p máta ílle·k wi·wənthákami·kw,
/t which has never been since the beginning of the world,
/k such as was not since the beginning of the world to this time,
/l such as was not from the beginning of the creation which God created unto this time,
(addition from Mk 13.19)

/b ok taa heh vuji rlrk.
/p ɔ́·k tá=á· čí·č háši é·le·k.

	/t	and which will never be again.
	/kl	no, nor ever shall be.

Lk 21.23	/b	Somih ave ktumaksavten, avih lenamwk,
	/p	só·mi=č áhi-ktəma·ksáhti·n, áhi-=č -lí·namo·k.
	/t	There will be very great misery, and bad things will happen to them.
	/k	... for there shall be great distress in the land,
	/l	For there shall be great distress in the land, affliction

	/b	manwfswakunh mujekakwk b rpehek.
	/p	manunksəwá·k·an=č məši·ká·k·o·k yú e·p·í·č·i·k.
	/t	Anger will fall upon those who are here,
	/kl	and wrath upon this people.

Lk 21.24	/b	Vakifh lanevenuk wunhi xifwi kjekun
	/p	hákink=č lanihí·nak wə́nči xínkwi-kší·k·an.
	/t	and they will be thrown down by means of a sword ('big knife'),
	/k	And they shall fall by the edge of the sword,

	/b	okh vusri lwxolaok. [⟨vusr-⟩ 2x for ⟨uvsr-⟩ 1x]
	/p	ó·k=č ahsé·i lo·x·ɔlá·ɔk.
	/t	and they will be led away to scattered places.
	/k	and shall be led away captive into all nations:

	/b	Nhelwsulumh topvekakw Lomunsu
	/p	†nči·ló·sələm=č tɔ·phiká·k·u lo·mánsa
	/t	Jerusalem will be trod down by the Romans
	/k	and Jerusalem shall be trodden down of the Gentiles,

	/b	srki nevlatumalet.
	/p	sé·ki-nihəla·t·amá·li·t.
	/t	for as long as they are in charge.
	/k	until the times of the Gentiles be fulfilled.

Mt 24.22	/b	Nrvlalwrt a mav mutu tvaqetakpanc nrl kejkwu
	/p	nehəlá·ləwe·t=á·=máh máta thakwi·ta·kpáne né·l ki·škúwa,
	/t	If the lord had not shortened those days,
	/l	And except that the Lord had shortened those days,

	/b	taa awrn lclrxri.
	/p	tá=á· awé·n lehəle·x·é·i.
	/t	no one would live.
	/l	there should no flesh be saved:

/b Jwq rkrkvohi wunhi nrl kejkwu tvaqetwn.
/p šúkw e·k·e·khɔ́·č·i wwə́nči- né·l ki·škúwa -thakwí·to·n.
/t But because of the ones he chose he shortened those days.
/l but for the elect's sake, whom he hath chosen, those days shall be shortened.

Mt 24.23 /b Awrn lwqrqc, Jr nu Klyst, jitu wulc avqwv,   [⟨vq⟩ for ⟨vp⟩]
/p awé·n luk·wé·k·we, 'šé· ná kəláist,' ší·=tá, 'wəlé ahpú,'
/t If anyone says to you, 'Here is Christ,' or 'He's over there,'
/l Then if any man shall say unto you, Lo, here is Christ, or, lo, he is there;

/b kahi wulamvetawerkrq.
/p káči wəla·mhitawié·k·e·kw.
/t do not believe him.
/l believe him not.

/b Rli avpwukh rlwrhekh, ne tu Klyst,
/p é·li ahpúwak=č e·ləwé·č·i·k=č, 'ní·=tá kəláist,'
/t For there will be ones who will say, 'I am Christ,'
/l For there shall arise false Christs,   (Mt 24.24; Mk 13.22)

/b okh rlwrhek, ne tu nrvenekanewrwset,
/p ɔ́·k=č e·ləwé·č·i·k, 'ní·=tá nehəni·k·a·ní·i-wé·wsi·t.'
/t and who will say, 'I am a prophet.'
/l and false prophets,

/b xifwenakoh krkw punwntvekrok ok kanjenakov,
/p xinkwi·ná·k·ɔ=č kéku pənunthiké·ɔk ɔ́·k kanši·ná·k·ɔ.
/t They will show people great signs ('things') and wonders.
/l and will shew great signs and wonders,

/b kuski a lrkc keolaok a pepenwnhek.
/p káski·=á· -lé·k·c, ki·ɔlá·ɔk=á· pi·p·i·núnči·k.
/t If it is possible, the chosen ones would be deceived.
/l insomuch that (if it were possible) they shall deceive the very elect.

Mk 13.23 /b Trku kulrluntamwq,
/p té·ka kəle·lə́ntamo·kw.
/t Take care that you take it to heart.
/l But take ye heed:

/b Puna wrmi krkw nekane kwntamwlunro.
/p pənáh, wé·mi kéku ni·k·a·ní·i kuntamo·lə́né·ɔ.
/t Now, I have foretold everything to you.
/l behold I have foretold you all things.

Mt 24.26
/b Nuni wunhi lwqrqc,
/p nə́ni wə́nči, luk·wé·k·we,
/t For that reason, if they say to you,
/kl Wherefore if they shall say unto you,

/b Jr, nu tu ekali trkunu topen,
/p 'šé·, ná=tá íkali té·kəna tóp·i·n,'
/t 'Listen, he's out in the desert!
/kl Behold, he is in the desert;

/b kahi eku avrq.
/p káči íka á·he·kw.
/t don't go there.
/kl go not forth:

/b Jitu lwqrqc,
/p ší=tá luk·wé·k·we,
/t Or if they say to you,   (Not in L.)
/k —

/b Jr wekwavmif cntu mutu nrvkwset topen;
/p 'šé·, wi·k·əwáhəmink énta- máta -ne·ykwə́s·i·t tóp·i·n,'
/t 'Listen, he's in the house in a place where he can't be seen,'
/kl behold, he is in the secret chambers;

/b kahi wulamvetawerkrq.
/p káči wəla·mhitawié·k·e·kw.
/t don't believe them.
/kl believe it not.

Mt 24.27
/b Sasapulrvlakc vufq wcvcnhi khifwcvlak
/p sa·sa·p·əlehəlá·k·e=hánkw wehə́nči-kčinkwéhəla·k,
/t When lightning flashes in the east,
/kl For as the lightning cometh out of the east,

/b oxclr vufq pchi cli vwsekak.
/p ɔ·x·éhəle·=hánkw péči éhəli-wsí·ka·k.
/t it shines all the way to the west.
/kl and shineth even unto the west;

/b Nunih tpisqi lr linw Wrqesif lupi patc.
/p nə́ni=č tpə́skwi lé· lə́nu we·k·wí·s·ink lápi pá·t·e.
/t That is what it will be like when the man who is the Son comes again.
/kl so shall also the coming of the Son of man be.

Mt 24.28 /b Webs vufq tutu jcfexifc,
/p wióˑs=hánkw tǝtá šenkiˑxˑínke,
/t If flesh is lying somewhere,
/kl For wheresoever the carcase is,

/b opulanrok rufq eku marvlrok.   [⟨rufq⟩ for ⟨vufq⟩]
/p ɔˑpˑalanéˑɔk=hánkw íka maˑehǝléˑɔk.
/t bald eagles gather there.
/kl there will the eagles be gathered together.

Mt 24.29 /b Lwwxwrekc nrl rvotuki kejqeki,
/p "loˑoˑxˑweˑíˑkˑe néˑl ehɔhtǝkˑi kiˑškwíˑkˑi,
/t "After those difficult days go by,
/kl But immediately after the tribulation of those days,

Lk 21.25 /b wexkaohih kanjenaqswuk kejwxok ok alufok.
/p wiˑxkaɔ́čiˑ=č kanšiˑnaˑkwsúwak kiˑšˑóˑxˑɔk ɔ́ˑk alánkɔk.
/t then immediately the sun, the moon, and the stars will be marvelous to behold.
/l there shall be signs in the sun, and in the moon, and in the stars.

Mt 24.29 /b Peskuntqrvlrokh kejwxok,
/p piˑskǝntkwehǝléˑɔk=č kiˑšˑóˑxˑɔk,
/t The sun and the moon will go dark,
/l The sun shall be darkened,

/b taa oxrri,
/p tá=áˑ ɔˑxˑeˑéˑi.
/t and there will be no light.
/kl and the moon shall not give her light,

/b okh punevlrok alufok wunhi vwqrbf;
/p ɔ́ˑk=č pǝnihǝléˑɔk alánkɔk wǝ́nči hukwéˑyunk.
/t And the stars will fall from the sky.
/kl and the stars shall fall from heaven;

Lk 21.25 /b kahih b cntu lawsif ktumukih wejasvaten,
/p káčˑi=č yú entaláˑwsink ktǝmáki-=č -wiˑšˑaˑshátiˑn.
/t But in the world there will be the torment of terror.
/kl and upon the earth shall be distress of nations, with perplexity;

/b munwprkoh ok cntu tkwek kanjvetakovtwv,
/p mǝnǝpˑéˑkˑɔ=č ɔ́ˑk énta-tkóˑwiˑk kanšhitákɔhtu.
/t The seas and ocean waves will roar.
/kl the sea and the waves roaring;

Lk 21.26 /b   bh cntu lawsehek ktumakexenululw vwtrvwao, rlih wejasevtet,
/p   yú=č entala·wsí·č·i·k ktəma·k·i·x·i·nələ́lu(?) wtehəwá·ɔ, é·li-=č -wi·š·a·s·íhti·t,
/t   People's hearts will falter, because they will be afraid,
/kl men's hearts failing them for fear,

/b   rlih nrmvetet krtu lrk b xqetvakameqc.
/p   é·li-=č -ne·mhíti·t ké·t·a-lé·k yú xkwi·thakamí·k·we.
/t   because they will see what is going to happen on this earth.
/kl and for looking after those things which are coming on the earth:

/b   Qhwqevlrh vwqrbf cntu hetanrk.
/p   kwčuk·wíhəle·=č hukwé·yunk énta-čí·t·ane·k.
/t   The firmament of heaven will shake.
/kl for the powers of heaven shall be shaken.

Mt 24.30 /b   Nuh nrvkot krkw li vwqrbf
/p   ná=č né·ykɔt kéku lí hukwé·yunk
/t   Then something will be seen in heaven
/kl And then shall appear the sign of the Son of man in heaven:

/b   wunhih wavkwset linw Wrqesif;
/p   wə́nči-=č -wwahkwə́s·i·t lə́nu we·k·wí·s·ink.
/t   by which the man who is the Son will be known.
/k   —

/b   nuh wrmi cntxakret b cntu lawset vwsusalamwen,
/p   ná=č wé·mi entxa·ké·i·t yú entalá·wsi·t wsəsalá·mwi·n.
/t   Then all nations in the world will cry out.
/kl and then shall all the tribes of the earth mourn,

/b   wunrowaoh Wrqesifi linwu prat li kwmvokwf,
/p   wəne·ɔwwá·ɔ=č we·k·wi·s·ínki lə́nəwa pé·a·t lí kəmhɔ́kunk
/t   They will see the man who is the Son coming in the clouds
/kl and they shall see the Son of man coming in the clouds of heaven

/b   nuxpi tolweluswakun ok moxifwrlumwqswakun.   [⟨tolweluswa-‖kun⟩]
/p   náxpi tɔləwí·i-ləs·əwá·k·an ɔ́·k mɔx·inkwe·ləmukwsəwá·k·an.
/t   with his power and his glory.
/kl with power and great glory.

Mt 24.31 /b   Nuh mcmufwrk pwtahekun kunhemww,
(p. 171) /p   ná=č memmánkəwe·k po·t·a·č·í·k·an kənči·mó·u.
/t   Then a trumpet will sound.
/kl And ... with a great sound of a trumpet, ...

/b   nuh tolwkalan rvalwkalahi,
/p   ná=č tɔlo·ká·la·n ehalo·ka·lá·č·i,
/t   Then he will send his angels ('messengers'),
/kl And he shall send his angels ...

/b   tulih macvolen pepenaohi,
/p   táli-=č -ma·ehɔ́·li·n pi·p·i·naɔ́·č·i.
/t   to gather together the ones he selects,
/kl ... and they shall gather together his elect ...

Mk 13.27 /b   wunhi wrmi rlkekvokumekrk.
/p   wə́nči wé·mi e·lki·khɔkamí·k·e·k.
/t   from the whole extent of the earth.
/kl from the uttermost part of the earth ...   [B. condenses]

Lk 21.28 /b   Mrhih alumi nuni lrkc
/p   mé·či=č áləmi- nə́ni -lé·k·e,
/t   And when that has started to happen,
/kl And when these things begin to come to pass,

/b   ktapvwqcmwh vwqrbhf ktulifwrxenvwmw;
/p   kta·phukwéhəmɔ=č, hukwé·yunk ktəlinkwe·x·i·nhúmɔ,
/t   you must look up and lift your gaze to the sky,
/kl then look up, and lift up your heads;

/b   rli prxwhevlrh kuthwvalkrnro.
/p   é·li pe·x·o·č·íhəle·=č kkəč·o·ha·lke·né·ɔ."
/t   for the time will be near for you to be saved."
/kl for your redemption draweth nigh.

Lk 21.29 /b   Rnwntvakrokun tulao, Lwr
/p   e·nunthake·ɔ́·k an təlá·ɔ, lúwe·,
/t   And he told them a parable, saying.
/l   And he spake unto them a parable, [*saying*]

Mt 24.32 /b   nunwstamwq vetwq rli rnwntvakrf;
/p   "nəno·stámo·kw hít·ukw é·li-e·nunthákenk.
/t   "Understand the parable of a tree.
/kl Now learn a parable of the fig tree,

Lk 21.29 /b   Jr vufq wrmi vetkwk,
/p   šé·=hánkw wé·mi hítko·k,
/t   Now, for all trees,
/kl Behold the fig-tree, and all the trees.

Mt 24.32 /b   twvnututu vufq onuxqei tokevlro krtu alumi kumpavqevlakc,   [⟨evlro⟩: B. ⟨ev ro⟩]
/p   tuhənət·ə́t·a=hánkw ɔnaxkwí·i tɔk·ihəlé·ɔ ké·t·a-áləmi-kəmpahkwihəlá·k·e.
/t   the twigs become tender at the tip when they are going to start growing leaves.
/kl   When their branch is yet tender, and putteth forth leaves,

Lk 21.30 /b   nuni vufq rlenamrqc,
/p   nə́ni=hánkw e·li·namé·k·we,
/t   When you see that,
/kl   ye see

/b   nevlahi vufq kwatwnro li prxwhivlr nepun.
/p   nihəláči=hánkw ko·wa·to·né·ɔ lí-pe·x·o·č·íhəle· ní·p·ən.
/t   you know on your own that summer is approaching.
/kl   and know of your own selves that summer is now nigh at hand.

Lk 21.31 /b   Nunih ok ktulsenro,
/p   nə́ni=č ɔ́·k ktəlsi·né·ɔ,
/t   That is what you will also do,
/l   So likewise ye,

/b   nuni lenamrqc,
/p   nə́ni li·namé·k·we.
/t   when you see that.
/l   when ye shall see all these things come to pass,
/k   (Mk 13.28; Mt 24.33; Lk 21.31)

/b   kwatwnroh li Krtanutwet sokemaokun ave prxwtvatr.
/p   ko·wa·to·né·ɔ=č lí- ke·tanət·ó·wi·t sɔ·k·i·ma·ɔ́·k·an -áhi-pe·x·o·tháte·.
/t   You will know that God's kingdom is very near.
/kl   know ye that the kingdom of God is nigh at hand.

Lk 21.32 /b   Kvehei ktulwvmw,
/p   khičí·i ktəllúhəmɔ,
/t   I tell you truly,
/k   Verily I say unto you,

/b   bqe lclrxrhek nrskoh wrmi ufulevtet
/p   yúkwe lehəle·x·é·č·i·k, né·skɔ=č wé·mi ankəlíhti·t,
/t   of those living today, before all of them shall die,
/l   that this generation shall not pass away,

/b   nuh pavkunhi lr.
/p   ná=č pahkánči-lé·,
/t   it will be realized,
/l   till all these things be fulfilled.

Lk 21.33 /b Prmapanekh ok prmvakumekrk lwih lr.
/p pe·má·p·ani·k=č ɔ́·k pe·mhakamí·k·e·k, ló·wi-=č -lé·.
/t and heaven and earth will pass away.
/kl Heaven and earth shall pass away:

/b Jwq ne ntaptwnakun taa.
/p "šúkw ní· nta·pto·ná·k·an, tá=á·.
/t "But my words will not.
/kl but my words shall not pass away.

Mt 24.36 /b Jwq nuni kejqek rlkeqih nc lrk, takw awrn b cntu lawset watwun
/p šúkw nə́ni kí·škwi·k, e·lkí·kwi-=č nɔ́ -lé·k, takó· awé·n yú entalá·wsi·t o·wa·tó·wən,
/t But that day, the time when that will happen, no one on earth knows,
/l But of that day and that hour knoweth no man,
/k (Mt 24.36; Mk 13.32)

/b takw nuxpunc rvalwkalunhek osavkamc rpehek ok Wrqesif mutu,
/p takó· náxpəne ehalo·ka·lə́nči·k ɔ·s·áhkame e·p·í·č·i·k, ɔ́·k we·k·wí·s·ink máta,
/t not even the angels in heaven, and not the Son,
/l no not the angels which are in heaven, neither the Son,

/b xwvu jwq Nwx.
/p xó·ha šúkw nó·x.
/t but only my father.
/kl but my Father only.

Lk 21.34 /b Trku krnavketwq kvakybu,
/p "té·ka, ke·nahkí·to·kw khak·ayúwa,
/t "Take care that you watch yourselves,
/kl And take heed to yourselves,

/b wcnhih mutu alwrluntamwrq mehwakun, ok munrokun,
/p wénči-=č máta -aləwe·ləntamó·we·kw mi·č·əwá·k·an ɔ́·k məne·ó·k·an,
/t so that you do not have too high a regard for food or drink
/kl lest at any time your hearts be over-charged with surfeiting, and drunkenness,

/b ok mutu na b avpametrvarq,
/p ɔ́·k máta ná=yú -ahpa·mi·t·e·há·e·kw,
/t and are not preoccupied with the here and now,
/kl and cares of this life,

/b wcnhih nc kejqek mutu wexkwlkwrq.
/p wénči-=č nɔ́ kí·škwi·k máta -wi·xko·lkó·we·kw.
/t lest that day take you by surprise.
/kl and so that day come upon you unawares.

Lk 21.35
- /b Rlih lr mulaji kuluvekun,
- /p é·li=č lé· málahši kəlahí·k·an,
- /t For it will happen as if a trap
- /kl For as a snare

- /b kuluvwkwk wrmi xqetvakameqc rpehek.
- /p kəlahó·k·o·k wé·mi xkwi·thakamí·k·we e·p·í·č·i·k.
- /t falls on all those that are on the face of the earth.
- /kl shall it come on all them that dwell on the face of the whole earth.

Mt 24.37
- /b Rlrkup Norsu rpetc, lrwh patc linw Wrqesif.
- /p e·lé·k·əp †no·wé·s·a e·p·í·t·e, lé·w=č pá·t·e lə́nu we·k·wí·s·ink.
- /t What happened when Noah was around will happen when the man who is the Son comes.
- /kl But as the days of Noe were, so shall also the coming of the Son of man be.

Mt 24.38
- /b Puna lrp nrlumu prsuntprkc vake,
- /p pənáh, lé·p né·ləma pe·s·əntpé·k·e hák·i.
- /t Now, it happened before the earth was flooded.
- /kl For as in the days that were before the flood

- /b metsavtwpanek, ok munavtwpanek
- /p mi·tsahtó·p·ani·k ó·k mənahtó·p·ani·k,
- /t They were all eating and drinking,
- /kl they were eating and drinking,

- /b ok owvjeluntumpwpanek, ok owvjeluntumwrvaltwpanek,   [⟨mpwp⟩ for ⟨mwp⟩]
- /p ó·k ɔwši·ləntamó·p·ani·k, ó·k ɔwši·ləntamwe·ha·ltó·p·ani·k.
- /t and marrying and giving each other in marriage.
- /kl marrying, and giving in marriage,

- /b eku pchi nc kejqek Norsu pwsetc li mwxwlif,
- /p íka péči nə́ kí·škwi·k †no·wé·s·a po·s·í·t·e lí mux·ó·link,
- /t Up until the day when Noah entered the boat,
- /kl until the day that Noe entered into the ark,

Mt 24.39
- /b takw watwunro,
- /p takó· o·wa·to·wəné·ɔ.
- /t they did not know it.
- /kl and knew not

- /b nu prtaqexunwp wrmi aptwprpanek.
- /p ná pe·t·a·kwí·x·əno·p, wé·mi a·ptəp·é·p·ani·k.
- /t Then the water rose, and all were drowned.
- /kl until the flood came, and took them all away;

/b Nunih ok lrw patc linw wrqesif.
/p nə́ni=č ɔ́·k lé·w pá·t·e lə́nu we·k·wí·s·ink.
/t That is also how it will be when the man who is the Son comes.
/kl so shall also the coming of the Son of man be.

Mt 24.40 /b Nejuh mvehi avpwuk,
/p ní·š·a=č mhičí·i ahpúwak.
/t There will be two out in the open.
/kl Then shall two be in the field;

/b mawswh wrtuna, kuhih mawsw pewuna,
/p má·wsu=č wé·t·əna·, káč·i=č má·wsu pí·wəna·.
/t One will be taken, but the other will be left behind.
/kl the one shall be taken and the other left.

/b okh neju kovokrok ||
/p ɔ́·k=č ní·š·a kɔhɔ·k·é·ɔk.
/t And there will be two pounding corn.
/kl two *women shall be* grinding at the mill;

(p. 172) /b mawswh wrtuna okh nu mawsw pewuna.
/p má·wsu=č wé·t·əna·, ɔ́·k=č ná má·wsu pí·wəna·.
/t One will be taken, and the other one will be left behind.
/kl the one shall be taken and the other left.

Lk 21.36 /b Nuni wunhi qrxseq fumri patumaq,
/p nə́ni wə́nči kwé·xsi·kw, nkəmé·i pá·tama·kw,
/t Therefore be on guard and pray always,
/l Take ye heed; watch therefore and pray always, (Lk + Mk 13.33)

/b ktulih lrlumukrnro kpalavpenro nc krtu lrk,
/p ktə́li-=č -le·ləmək e né·ɔ kpalahpi·né·ɔ nó ké·t·a-lé·k,
/t so that you will be allowed to escape what is going to happen,
/kl that ye may be accounted worthy to escape all these things that shall come to pass,

/b ktulih kuski nepyenro rlifwrxif linw Wrqesif.
/p ktə́li-=č -káski-ni·p·ai·né·ɔ e·linkwé·x·ink lə́nu we·k·wí·s·ink.
/t and so that you will be able to stand before the man who is the Son.
/kl and to stand before the Son of man.

Mt 24.43 /b Rli mutu kwatwunro rlkeqih pat Nrvlalqrq.
/p é·li máta ko·wa·to·wəné·ɔ e·lkí·kwi-=č -pá·t nehəlá·lkwe·kw.
/t For you do not know the time when your lord (master) will come.
/kl For ye know not what hour your Lord doth come.

Mk 13.34 /b Mulaji linwu, ovlumi krtu atc;
/p málahši lə́nəwa ɔ́hələmi ké·t·a-á·t·e,
/t Like a man of old when he was intending to go far away,
/kl *For the Son of man is* as a man taking a far journey,

/b mrhi krtu alumskatc wunhi weket,
/p mé·či ké·t·a-aləmská·t·e wə́nči wí·k·i·t
/t and when he was about to depart from his house,
/kl who left his house,

/b tolwkakunu wrmi mwelao rlumekumoseleth,
/p tɔlo·ká·k·ana wé·mi mwi·lá·ɔ e·lami·kəmɔ·s·í·li·t=č,
/t he gave all his servants the tasks they were to perform,
/kl and gave authority to his servants, and to every man his work,

/b ok tulao nwheskontarlehi, Trku tu wejuksi.
/p ɔ́·k təlá·ɔ no·č·i·skɔntae·lí·č·i, 'té·ka=tá wi·šə́ksi.'
/t and he said to the door-keeper, 'Take care and do your best.'
/kl and commanded the porter to watch.

Mk 13.35 /b Krpwu krnavketwq.
/p ké·pəwa ke·nahkí·to·kw.
/t All of you also, take care.
/kl Watch ye therefore.

Mt 24.43 /b Kwatwnro
/p ko·wa·to·né·ɔ,
/t You know,
/kl But know this,

/b awrn vufq wreket, wrotaqc tuli krvkumwtkrsu kavtu toxkwn
/p awé·n=hánkw we·í·k·i·t we·ɔ·tá·k·we, tə́li- kehkəmo·tké·s·a -káhta-tóxko·n
/t that when anyone who has a house knows that a thief is going to come to him,
/kl that if the goodman of the house had known in what watch the thief would come,

/b wli vufq krnavketwn weket wcnhi vufq mutu palelrk.
/p ó·li-=hánkw -ke·nahkí·to·n wí·k·i·t wénči-=hánkw máta palí·i -lé·k.
/t he always watches his house well so that it is not destroyed.
/kl he would have watched, and would not have suffered his house to be broken up.

Mt 24.44 /b Krpwu kavtu kejenaqseq; [⟨-jen-⟩ 1x (⟨-jan-⟩ 1x) for ⟨-jun-⟩ 2x]
/p ké·pəwa káhta-ki·š·əná·kwsi·kw.
/t You also must be keen to be ready.
/kl Therefore be ye also ready:

/b   rli nrlih mutu prvarq nuh wexkaohi pon linw Wrqesif.
/p   é·li né·li-=č máta -pe·há·e·kw, ná=č wi·xkaɔ́či pɔ́·n lə́nu we·k·wí·s·ink.
/t   For while you do not expect him, then the man who is the Son will suddenly come.
/kl for in such an hour as ye think not, the Son of man cometh.

Mt 24.45
/b   Awrn vuh wulilusw ok lupwr alwkakun
/p   awé·n=háč wə́li-lə́s·u ɔ́·k ləpwé· alo·ká·k·an,
/t   Who is a good and wise servant,
/kl Who then is a faithful and wise servant,

/b   Nrvlalkwki kejemkwk tulih krnavketwn wekelet
/p   nehəla·lkúk·i ki·š·í·mkuk tə́li-=č -ke·nahkí·to·n wi·k·í·li·t,
/t   who his master assigned to watch his house,
/kl whom his lord hath made ruler over his household,

/b   ok tulih melan mcmehif cji tpisqevlak?
/p   ɔ́·k tə́li-=č -mí·la·n mehəmí·č·ink éši-tpəskwíhəla·k.
/t   and to give them food whenever the time is right?
/kl to give them meat in due season?

Mt 24.46
/b   Wlapcnswh nuni rlset alwkakun,
/p   wəla·p·énsu=č nə́ni é·lsi·t alo·ká·k·an,
/t   Blessed will be the servant who does that,
/kl Blessed is that servant,

/b   paletc Nrvlalkwki nrvkwkc tcli myai lusen.
/p   pa·lí·t·e nehəla·lkúk·i, ne·ykúk·e tə́li-mayá·i-lə́s·i·n.
/t   when his master comes back and sees him doing what he is supposed to do,.
/kl whom his lord when he cometh shall find so doing.

Mt 24.47
/b   Kvehei ktulwvmw,
/p   khičí·i ktəllúhəmɔ,
/t   I tell you truly,
/kl Verily I say unto you,

/b   qejemkwh tulih krnavketwn wrmi tulavhrswakunelet.
/p   kwi·š·í·mku=č, tə́li-=č -ke·nahkí·to·n wé·mi təlahče·s·əwa·k·aní·li·t.
/t   he will assign him to watch all his possessions.
/kl that he shall make him ruler over all his goods.

Mt 24.48
/b   Jwq a mavhilusetc nu alwkakun, vwtrvif lwrtc,
/p   šúkw=á· máhči-ləs·í·t·e ná alo·ká·k·an, wté·hink luwé·t·e,
/t   But if that servant is evil and says in his heart,
/kl But and if that evil servant shall say in his heart,

	/b	Nrvlalet taa jac pri,
	/p	"nehəlá·li·t tá=á· šá·e pé·i,"
	/t	"My master won't come back right away,"
	/kl	My lord delayeth his coming,

Mt 24.49 /b alumi pwpavkumatc wihialwkakunu,
/p áləmi-pəpahkamá·t·e wíči-alo·ká·k·ana,
/t and if he starts beatting his fellow servants,
/kl and shall begin to smite *his* fellowservants,

/b ok wepwmatc krkewselehi ok wetwsumwematc.
/p ɔ́·k wi·po·má·t·e ke·k·i·wsi·lí·č·i, ɔ́·k wi·t·o·s·əmwi·má·t·e,
/t and if he eats with drunks and drinks with them,
/kl and to eat and drink with the drunken;

Mt 24.50 /b Nrvlalwki nu alwkakun wexkaohih prlw,   [⟨-lwki⟩ for ⟨-lkwki⟩]
/p nehəla·lkúk·i ná alo·ká·k·an, wi·xkaɔ́či=č pé·lu,
/t that servant's master will suddenly come,
/kl The lord of that servant shall come

/b nrli mutu prvat, ok nrli mutu puṇarlumat,
/p né·li- máta -pé·ha·t, ɔ́·k né·li- máta -pənaé·ləma·t.
/t when he is not expecting him and not thinking of him.
/kl in a day when he looketh not for him, and in an hour that he is not aware of,

Mt 24.51 /b nuh qeskhujwkwn, okh krvakevokrsekri li melten,
/p ná=č kwi·skčaš·ó·k·o·n, ɔ́·k=č kehahki·hɔke·s·i·ké·i lí-mí·lti·n,
/t Then (his master) will cut him up, and he will be turned over to the hypocrites,
/kl and shall cut him asunder, and appoint him his portion with the hypocrites:
         [RSV: and will punish him (or cut him in pieces), and put him with ...]

/b cntuh salamwevtet, ok kukumwkuntamevtet wepetwao.
/p énta-=č -sala·mwíhti·t ɔ́·k -kək·amo·kantamíhti·t wi·p·i·t·əwá·ɔ.
/t where they will cry out and 'gnash' their teeth.
/kl there shall be weeping and gnashing of teeth.

Mk 13.35 /b Qrxseq wunhi rli mutu watwrq rlkeqih pat wreket,
/p kwé·xsi·kw wə́nči, é·li- máta -wwa·tó·we·kw e·lkí·kwi-=č -pá·t we·í·k·i·t—
/t Be on guard therefore, as you don't know when the house-owner will come—
/kl Watch ye therefore: for ye know not when the master of the house cometh,

/b loqune, jitu lai tpwqune, jitu cvlukveqi tepasuk kunhemwevtet,
/p lɔ·k·wəní·i, ší=tá lá·i-tpo·kwəní·i, ší=tá ehələkhíkwi- tipá·s·ak -kənči·mwíhti·t,
/t in the evening, or at midnight, or at the time roosters ('chickens') crow,
/kl at even, or at midnight, or at the cock-crowing,

/b   jitu alupae—
/p   ší=tá alap·a·í·i—
/t   or in the morning.
/k   or in the morning:

Mk 13.36 /b   wcnhih wexkaohi patc mutu nrvkwrq ktuli kaenro.
/p   wénči-=č, wi·xkaóči pá·t·e, máta -ne·ykó·we·kw któli-kai·né·ɔ.
/t   so that if he comes suddenly he won't see you sleeping.
/kl   Lest coming suddenly he find you sleeping.

Mk 13.37 /b   Nuni rlrq, Qrxseq wrmi awrn ntulan.
/p   nóni élle·kw ('kwé·xsi·kw!') wé·mi awé·n ntóla·n.
/t   What I tell you to do ('Be on guard!') I tell everyone to do.
/kl   And what I say unto you I say unto all, Watch.

Chapter 103 (pp. 173-176). [L. section 103.] (Matthew 25.1-46, 26.1-5; Mark 14.1-2, Luke 22.1-2)

Mt 25.1   /b   Nch osavkamri sakemaokun prtaqek
(p. 173)   /p   "nó=č ɔ·s·ahkamé·i-sa·k·i·ma·ó·k·an pe·tá·k·wi·k
/t   "Those who wait for the kingdom of heaven
/kl   Then shall the kingdom of heaven be likened unto

/b   tulsenroh, rlsevtetup tclcn mreai lusetpanek skexqrbfu,
/p   tólsi·né·ɔ=č e·lsihtí·t·əp télən me·á·i-ləs·i·tpáni·k ski·xkwe·yúnka,
/t   will do what was done by ten properly behaved young women of old,
/kl   ten virgins,

/b   wrtunuvtetc wosulrnekunwao,
/p   we·t·ənahtí·t·e wɔ·s·əle·ni·k·anəwá·ɔ,
/t   when they took their lamps,
/kl   which took their lamps,

/b   apvesvekaovtetc krtu vwjeluntumulchi.   [⟨-lchi⟩ for ⟨-lehi⟩]
/p   a·phishikaɔhtí·t·e ké·t·a-wši·ləntaməlí·č·i.
/t   and went to meet one who was going to be married.
/kl   and went forth to meet the bridegroom.

Mt 25.2   /b   Palrnuxk wli watwnro, ok palrnuxk mutu watwunro.
/p   palé·naxk ó·li-wwa·to·né·ɔ, ó·k palé·naxk máta o·wa·to·wəné·ɔ.
/t   Five knew about it well, and five didn't know about it.
/kl   And five of them were wise, and five were foolish.

Mt 25.3   /b   Nrk mutu wrotaqpanek kulunrpanek osulrnekunu,
/p   né·k máta we·ɔ·ta·kwpáni·k kələné·p·ani·k ɔ·s·əle·ní·k·ana,

/t Those that did not know about it carried lamps,
/kl They that were foolish took their lamps,

/b jwq mutu pumi kulunumwepanek.
/p šúkw máta pəmí kələnəmo·wí·p·ani·k.
/t but they did not carry any oil.
/kl and took no oil with them:

Mt 25.4 /b Nrk wrotaqkpanek kulunrpanek osulrnekunu ok vupi pumi.   [⟨qkp⟩ for /kwp/]
/p né·k we·ɔ·ta·kwpáni·k kələné·p·ani·k ɔ·s·əle·ní·k·ana ɔ́·k hápi pəmí.
/t Those that did know about it carried lamps and along with them oil.
/kl But the wise took oil in their vessels with their lamps.

Mt 25.5 /b Jwq nrli kulumavpet nu krtu vwjeluntuf, nu wrmi koenro.
/p šúkw né·li-kəlámahpi·t ná ké·t·a-wši·lə́ntank, ná wé·mi kɔi·né·ɔ.
/t But while the one who was going to be married sat quietly, they all slept.
/kl While the bridegroom tarried, they all slumbered and slept. [RSV "was delayed"]

Mt 25.6 /b Mrhi lai tpwqekc, lwrn
/p mé·či lá·i-tpo·kwí·k·e, lúwe·n,
/t At midnight a voice said,
/kl And at midnight there was a cry made,

/b Jr nu prat krtu vwjeluntuf, apvesvekw.
/p 'šé· ná pé·a·t ké·t·a-wši·lə́ntank; a·phishíko·.'
/t 'Here comes the one that's going to be married; go to meet him.'
/kl Behold, the bridegroom cometh; go ye out to meet him.

Mt 25.7 /b Nu wrmi nrk skexqrok tomwenro,
/p ná wé·mi né·k ski·xkwé·ɔk tɔ·mwi·né·ɔ,
/t Then all the young women got up,
/kl Then all those virgins arose,

/b ok wlulrwvrnroi wosulrnekunwao.
/p ɔ́·k o·ləle·whe·ne·ɔ́·i wɔ·s·əle·ni·k·anəwá·ɔ.
/t and they adjusted the flame on their lamps.
/kl and trimmed their lamps.

Mt 25.8 /b Nrk mutu wrotaqkpanek tulaowao wrotwlehi,   [⟨qkp⟩ for /kwp/]
/p né·k máta we·ɔ·ta·kwpáni·k təlawwá·ɔ we·ɔ·to·lí·č·i,
/t Those that did not know about it said to those that did know about it,
/kl And the foolish said unto the wise,

/b   Melenrn pumi, rli atrok nosulrnekununanuk.
/p   'mi·lí·ne·n pəmí, é·li a·té·ɔk nɔ·s·əle·ni·k·anəná·nak.'
/t   'Give us some oil, for our lamps have gone out.'
/kl Give us of your oil; for our lamps are gone out.

Mt 25.9
/b   Jwq wrotaqkpanek tulawapani.   [⟨qkp⟩ for /kwp/]
/p   šúkw we·ɔ·ta·kwpáni·k təlawwá·p·ani,
/t   But the ones that knew about it said to them,
/kl But the wise answered, saying,

/b   Kahi, tamsc a pcxw nwntcvlavnu;
/p   'káči; tá·mse=á· péxu nnuntehəláhəna.   [exc. for explicit inc. in L.]
/t   'No, we won't; maybe we (exc.) would soon run out.
/kl Not so; lest there be not enough for us and you:

/b   alwei wulexun eku ktanro cvctu mvalumaovtif   [⟨cvctu⟩ for ⟨cvcntu⟩]
/p   aləwí·i wəlí·x·ən, íka kta·né·ɔ ehə́nta-mhalamá·ɔhtink,
/t   It is better that you go to the marketplace,
/kl but go ye rather to them that sell,

/b   nevlahi kmavlamunro.
/p   nihəláči kəmahəlaməné·ɔ.'
/t   and that you buy some for yourselves.'
/kl and buy for yourselves.

Mt 25.10
/b   Wrtami my mvalumosevtct, eku pr nu krtu vwjeluntuf,
/p   wé·t·ami-mái-mhalamɔ·s·íhti·t, íka pé· ná ké·t·a-wši·ló́ntank,
/t   While they were occupied with going to buy, the one who was going to be married came there,
/kl And while they went to buy, the bridegroom came;

/b   ok cntxi kejunaqsetpanek wihi ekali tumekrpanek
/p   ó·k éntxi-ki·š·əna·kwsi·tpáni·k wíči- íkali -təmi·k·é·p·ani·k
/t   and all those that were ready entered along with him
/kl and they that were ready went in with him

/b   cntu kavtu tavkopwvaltif,
/p   énta-káhta-tahkɔp·o·há·ltink.
/t   to where the wedding was going to take place.
/kl to the marriage:

/b   nuli hemvasw nc wekwam.   [⟨nuli⟩ for ⟨nu li⟩]
/p   ná lí·či·mhá·s·u nə́ wí·k·əwam.
/t   And at that the house was shut up tight.
/kl and the door was shut.

Mt 25.11 /b Nu kcnh ok nrk takokek skexqrok eku ponro, tulawao,
/p ná kə́nč ó·k né·k takó·ki·k ski·xkwé·ok íka pɔ·né·ɔ, təlawwá·ɔ,
/t Only then did those other young women also come there, and they said to them,
/k Afterward came also the other virgins, saying,

/b Nrvlatamun, nrvlatamun, twfjrnumaenrn.
/p 'nehəlá·t·aman, nehəlá·t·aman, tunkše·nəmaí·ne·n.'
/t 'You who are the owner of it, open the door for us.'
/k Lord, Lord, open to us.

Mt 25.12 /b Jwq tulapani, Ktulwvmwv kvehei mutu kwavlwvwmwv.
/p šúkw təlá·p·ani, 'ktəllúhəmɔ khiči·i, máta ko·wahəlo·húmɔ.'
/t But he said to them, 'I tell you truly, I do not know you.'
/k But he answered and said, Verily I say unto you, I know you not.

Mt 25.13 /b Qrxseq wunhi
/p kwé·xsi·kw wə́nči,
/t Be on guard therefore,
/k Watch therefore,

/b rli mutu watwrq rlkeqih pat linw Wrqesif.
/p é·li- máta -wwa·tó·we·kw e·lkí·kwi·=č -pá·t lə́nu we·k·wí·s·ink.
/t as you do not know when the man who is the Son will come.
/k for ye know neither the day nor the hour wherein the Son of man cometh.

Mt 25.14 /b Rli osavkamre sakemaokun lrw,
/p "é·li ɔ·s·ahkame·í·i-sa·k·i·ma·ó·k·an lé·w,
/t "For the kingdom of heaven is like
/k For the kingdom of heaven is

/b rlsetup linwu ovlumi krvtu atc. [⟨krvtu⟩ for ⟨krtu⟩]
/p e·lsí·t·əp lə́nəwa óhəlɔmi ké·t·a-á·t·e.
/t what a man did when he was going to go far away.
/k as a man travelling into a far country,

/b nevlahi tolwkakunu wcnhemapani, totavlanrp ncvlatufi;
/p nihəláči tɔlo·ká·k·ana wwenči·má·p·ani, tɔ·tahəlá·ne·p nehəla·t·ánki.
/t He called in his own servants and turned over to them the things he owned,
/k who called his own servants, and delivered unto them his goods.

Mt 25.15 /b mawselw mwelao, palrnaxk rvoovteki moneu,
/p ma·wsí·lu mwi·lá·ɔ palé·naxk ehɔ·ɔhtí·k·i mónia,
/t To one he gave five high-value coins;
/k And unto one he gave five talents,

```
          /b  kahi mawselw neju kahi mawselw kwti,
          /p  káč·i ma·wsí·lu ní·š·a, káč·i ma·wsí·lu kwə́t·i.
          /t  to another, two; and to another, one.    [lit., 'but (to) one, two; but (to) one, one']
          /k  to another two, and to another one;

          /b  wrmi cvcntxi melanro cntxi ‖ a tcpi krnavketwvtet.
          /p  wé·mi ehə́ntxi mi·la·né·ɔ éntxi-=á· -tépi-ke·nahki·túhti·t.
          /t  Every one of them was given as much as he would be capable of taking care of.
          /k  to every man according to his several ability;

(p. 174)  /b  Nu tolumskan.
          /p  ná tɔlə́mska·n.
          /t  Then he departed.
          /k  and straightway took his journey.

Mt 25.16  /b  Nu palrnaxk mrjinifup, tolumi nvakatamunrpani,
          /p  ná palé·naxk me·š·ənínkəp tólə̇mi-nhaka·t·amə̇né·p·ani,
          /t  The one who got five set about putting them to use,
          /k  Then he that had received the five talents went and traded with the same,

          /b  palrnaxk eku wunhi patatw.
          /p  palé·naxk íka wə́nči-pa·tá·to·.
          /t  and he earned five from them.
          /k  and made them other five talents.

Mt 25.17  /b  Ok nu neju mrjinifup, neju eku wunhi patatw.
          /p  ó·k ná ní·š·a me·š·ənínkəp ní·š·a íka wə́nči-pa·tá·to·.
          /t  And the one that got two earned two from them.
          /k  And likewise he that had received two, he also gained other two.

Mt 25.18  /b  Jwq nu kwti mrjinifup moi pvokvakcvmunrp Nrvlalkwki moneum.
          /p  šúkw ná kwót·i me·š·ənínkəp mói-phɔkhakehəmə́ne·p nehəla·lkúk·i mmɔní·yəm.
          /t  But the one that got one went and buried his master's money.
          /k  But he that had received one went and digged in the earth, and hid his lord's money.

Mt 25.19  /b  Ameku praletc nrvlalqevtehi kotu watwlen rlsevtet.
          /p  amí·ka pe·a·lí·t·e nehəla·lkwihtí·č·i, kót·a-wwa·tó·li·n e·lsíhti·t.
          /t  Much later, when their master came back, he wanted to know what they had done.
          /k  After a long time the lord of those servants cometh, and reckoneth with them.

Mt 25.20  /b  Nu mrjinifup palrnaxk unhi palrnaxk eku prtw,
          /p  ná me·š·ənínkəp palé·naxk ánči- palé·naxk íka -pé·t·o·,
          /t  The one that had gotten five brought an additional five,
          /k  And so he that had received five talents came and brought other five talents,
```

	/b	tulao, Nrvlaleun ktatavlevwmp palanuxk moneu,	[⟨palanuxk⟩ for ⟨palrnuxk⟩]
	/p	təláːɔ, 'nehəláːlian, †ktaˑtahəlíˑhəmp paléˑnaxk mónia.	
	/t	and he said to him, 'Master, you let me have five coins.	
	/k	saying, Lord, thou deliveredst unto me five talents:	

/b jr palrnaxk eku nwnhi patatw.
/p šéˑ, paléˑnaxk íka núnči-paˑtáˑtu.'
/t Here, I have earned five from them.'
/k behold, I have gained beside them five talents more.

Mt 25.21 /b Nrvlalkwki tulkw,
/p nehəlaˑlkúkˑi tə́lku,
/t His master said to him,
/k His lord said unto him,

/b Wulut, wrliluseun mraopreun alwkakun.
/p 'wələt, wéˑli-lə́sˑian, meˑaˑɔˑpˑéˑian aloˑkáˑkˑan.
/t 'It is good, you who did well and were a reliable servant.
/k Well done, thou good and faithful servant:

	/b	Kmyai lusi cntu krnavketaon tutxiti,	[⟨tutxiti⟩ for ⟨tatxiti⟩]
	/p	kəmayáˑi-lə́sˑi énta-keˑnahkíˑtaɔn taˑtxíti.	
	/t	You did just what you were supposed to when you took care of a little.	
	/k	thou hast been faithful over a few things,	

	/b	kejemulh ktulih xrli kakw krnavketon.	[⟨kakw⟩ for ⟨krkw⟩]
	/p	kkiˑšˑíˑməl=č ktə́li=č xéˑli kéku -keˑnahkíˑtoˑn.	
	/t	I will appoint you to take care of many things.	
	/k	I will make thee ruler over many things:	

/b ekali tumekrl cntu wifawset Nrvlalkon.
/p íkali təmíˑkˑeˑl énta-winkáˑwsiˑt nehəláˑlkɔn.'
/t Enter the place where your master is living joyfully.'
/k enter thou into the joy of thy lord.

Mt 25.22 /b Nu ok nu neju mrjinifup, eku pon,
/p ná ɔ́ˑk ná níˑšˑa meˑšˑənínkəp íka pɔ́ˑn,
/t Then the one who had gotten two came there,
/k He also that had received two talents came

	/b	tulao, Nrlaleun ktatuvalevwmp neju moneu,	[⟨tuval⟩ for /tahəl/]
	/p	təláˑɔ, 'nehəláˑlian, ktaˑtahəlíˑhəmp níˑšˑa mónia.	
	/t	and he said to him, 'Master, you let me have two coins.	
	/k	and said, Lord, thou deliveredst unto me two talents:	

        /b   jr neju eku nwnhi patatw.
        /p   šé·, ní·š·a íka núnči-pa·tá·tu.'
        /t   Here, I have earned two from them.'
        /k   behold, I have gained two other talents beside them.

Mt 25.23 /b   Nrvlalkwki tulkw,   [repeats Mt 25.21]
               /p   nehəla·lkúk·i tə́lku,
               /t   His master said to him,
               /k   His lord said unto him,

               /b   Wulut, wrli luseun mraopreun alwkakun.
               /p   'wələ́t, wé·li-lə́s·ian, me·a·ɔ·p·é·ian alo·ká·k·an.
               /t   'It is good, you who did well and were a reliable servant.
               /k   Well done, thou good and faithful servant:

               /b   Kmyai lusi cntu krnavketaon tatxiti,
               /p   kəmayá·i-lə́s·i énta-ke·nahkí·taɔn ta·txíti.
               /t   You did just what you were supposed to when you took care of a little.
               /k   thou hast been faithful over a few things,

               /b   kejemulh ktulih xrli krnavketwn,
               /p   kki·š·í·məl=č ktə́li-=č xé·li -ke·nahkí·to·n.
               /t   I will assign you to take care of a lot.
               /k   I will make thee ruler over many things:

               /b   ekali tumekrl cntu wifawset Nrvlalkon.
               /p   íkali təmí·k·e·l énta-winká·wsi·t nehəlá·lkɔn.'
               /t   Enter the place where your master is living joyfully.'
               /k   enter thou into the joy of thy lord.

Mt 25.24 /b   Nu ok nu kwti mrjinifup eku pon,
               /p   ná ɔ́·k ná kwə́t·i me·š·əninkəp ika pɔ́·n,
               /t   Then the one who had gotten one also came there,
               /k   Then he which had received the one talent came

               /b   tulao Nrvlaleun, kwavul ktuli amuntapren.
               /p   təlá·ɔ, 'nehəlá·lian, ko·wá·həl ktə́li-amənta·p·é·i·n,
               /t   and he said to him, 'Master, I know that you are a high-handed man.
               /k   and said, Lord, I knew thee that thou art an hard man,

               /b   Ktumjimun mutu vuji rkevron,
               /p   ktəmšə́mən máta háši e·ki·hé·ɔn,
               /t   You reap what you never planted,
               /k   reaping where thou hast not sown,

/b   ok kmacvmun mutu vuji jepvamwun,
/p   ɔ́·k kəma·éhəmən máta háši ši·phamó·wan.
/t   and you gather what you never spread out.
/k   and gathering where thou hast not strawed:

Mt 25.25 /b   Koxulwvwmp numai pvokvakcvmunrp kmoneum;
/p   kkɔx·əlúhump, nəmái-phɔkhakehəmɔ́ne·p kəmɔní·yəm.
/t   I was afraid of you, and I went and buried your coin.
/k   And I was afraid, and went and hid thy talent in the earth:

/b   jr b nrvlatamun.
/p   šé· yú nehəlá·t·aman.'
/t   Here, this is what is yours.'
/k   lo, there thou hast that is thine.

Mt 25.26 /b   Nrvlalkwki tulkw,
/p   nehəla·lkúk·i tɔ́lku,
/t   His master said to him,
/k   His lord answered and said unto him,

/b   Kmutapri nwlvuntuk alwkakun;
/p   'kəmat·a·p·é·i, no·lhántək alo·ká·k·an.
/t   'You are wicked, you lazy servant.
/k   Thou wicked and slothful servant,

/b   kwatwn ntcli tumijimun mutu vuji rkevro,
/p   ko·wá·to·n, ntɔ́li-təmɔ́š·əmən máta háši e·ki·hé·ɔ,
/t   You know that I reap what I never planted,
/k   thou knewest that I reap where I sowed not,

/b   ok ntuli macvmun mutu vuji jepvamwu.
/p   ɔ́·k ntɔ́li-ma·éhəmən máta háši ši·phamó·wa.
/t   and that I gather what I never spread out.
/k   and gather where I have not strawed:

Mt 25.27 /b   Nuni a mav wcnhi nmoneum eku vataonup cvcntu moni patatwf,
/p   nɔ́ni=á·=máh wénči- nəmɔní·yəm íka -hataónəp ehə́nta- mɔ́ni -pa·tá·tunk,
/t   That should have been a reason for you to put my money where money is earned,
/k   Thou oughtest therefore to have put my money to the exchangers,

/b   wcnhi a mav mujinamanc nmoneum alwe txi mujinumanup.   [⟨nam⟩ for /nəm/]
/p   wénči-=á·=máh, məšənəmá·ne nəmɔní·yəm, aləwí·i txí -məšənəmá·nəp.
/t   so that when I got my money, I would have gotten a greater amount.
/k   and then at my coming I should have received mine own with usury.

Mt 25.28 /b Hekunw nc moni, melw nu tclcn wrlvataq.
/p čí·k·əno· nə́ móni, mí·lo· ná télən we·lháta·kw.
/t Take the coin from him, and give it to the one who has ten.
/k Take therefore the talent from him, and give it unto him which hath ten talents.

Mt 25.29 /b Rli cntxili awrn wulataq. melah
/p é·li éntxi-=lí awé·n -wəlá·ta·kw, mí·la·=č,
/t For to everyone who has some shall be given some,
/k For unto every one that hath shall be given,

/b weukih wulatw,
/p wiáki-=č -wəlá·to·.
/t and he shall have enough and to spare.
/k and he shall have abundance:

/b Jwq awrn mutu wulataqc hekunanh cntxi wulataq.
/p šúkw awé·n máta wəla·tá·k·we, čí·k·əna·n=č éntxi-wəlá·ta·kw.
/t But if anyone does not have any, as much as they have will be taken from them.
/k but from him that hath not shall be taken away even that which he hath.

Mt 25.30 /b Mutu krkw ‖ rlaprmkwset alwkakun eku laniveq cntu ave peskrk,
/p máta kéku e·la·p·e·mkwə́s·i·t alo·ká·k·an íka laníhi·kw énta-áhi-pí·ske·k,
/t Throw the worthless servant into utter darkness,
/k And cast ye the unprofitable servant into outer darkness:

(p. 175) /b cntuh lupukvatif ok kukumwkuntasek wepetu.
/p énta-=č -ləpakhátink, ó·k -kək·amo·kantá·s·i·k wi·p·í·t·a.
/t where there shall be much weeping and the 'gnashing' of teeth.
/k there shall be weeping and gnashing of teeth.

Mt 25.31 /b Linwh Wrqsesif patc nuxpi moxifwrlumwqswakun,
/p "lənu=č we·k·wí·s·ink pá·t·e náxpi mɔx·inkwc·ləmukwsəwá·k·an,
/t "When the man who is the Son comes with his glory,
/k When the Son of man shall come in his glory,

/b ok wrmi pelselehi rvulwkalahi pchi wehrotc,
/p ó·k wé·mi pi·lsi·lí·č·i ehalo·ka·lá·č·i péči-wi·č·e·ó·t·e,
/t and when he comes with all his holy angels,
/k and all the holy angels with him,

/b nch wulumutupen cntu xifwrlumwqset.
/p nə́=č wələmahtáp·i·n énta-xinkwe·ləmúkwsi·t.
/t he shall sit in his place of honor.
/k then shall he sit upon the throne of his glory:

Mt 25.32 /b Wrmih cntxakret awrn macvo li rlifwrxif;
/p wé·mi=č entxa·ké·i·t awé·n ma·éhɔ· lí e·linkwé·x·ink.
/t All nations of people shall be gathered before him.
/k And before him shall be gathered all nations:

/b tokrkvooh
/p tɔk·e·khɔ́·ɔ=č,
/t And he shall separate and select them,
/k and he shall separate them one from another,

/b mulaji nrvnwtumat mrkesu hrpavlatc wunhi fotsekri.
/p málahši nehɔnó·t·ɔma·t mekí·s·a če·p·ahɔlá·t·e wɔ́nči nkɔ·tsi·ké·i.
/t like a shepherd when he separates sheep from goats.
/k as a shepherd divideth his sheep from the goats:

Mt 25.33 /b Tunavaonifh tovlao mwrkesumu, kuhih fotsu mwununheonif. [⟨nheon⟩]
/p tɔnna·há·ɔnink=č tɔhɔlá·ɔ mwekí·s·ɔma, káč·i=č nkɔ́·tsa mwɔnančí·ɔnink.
/t He shall put his sheep on his right but the goats on his left.
/k And he shall set the sheep on his right hand, but the goats on the left.

Mt 25.34 /b Nunuh na Sakema tulan rpelehi tunavaonif,
/p nána=č ná sa·k·í·ma tɔ́la·n e·p·i·lí·č·i tɔnna·há·ɔnink,
/t Then the king shall say to those on his right,
/k Then shall the King say unto them on his right hand,

/b Nuprv, wrlapcnswvalqrq Nwx,
/p 'nɔ́pe·h, we·la·p·enso·há·lkwe·kw nó·x,
/t 'Alright, you who my father blessed,
/k Come, ye blessed of my Father,

/b mai nevlatamwq nc wulumalswakun
/p mái-nihɔlá·t·amo·kw nɔ́ wɔlamalsɔwá·k·an
/t go and take possession of the happiness
/k inherit the kingdom

/b kejextakrrkup ckc nwhi vatrkc vaki. [⟨ckc⟩ for ⟨nckc⟩]
/p ki·š·i·xta·k·e·é·k·ɔp néke núči-hat·é·k·e hák·i.
/t that was prepared for you at the beginning of the world.
/k prepared for you from the foundation of the world:

Mt 25.35 /b Rli futwpwevwmp, ktaxamevmwp,
/p é·li nkat·o·p·wí·hɔmp, ktax·amíhɔmɔ·p.
/t For I was hungry and you fed me.
/k For I was an hungred, and ye gave me meat:

	/b	futwsumwevwmp kmunvimwp;	[⟨-nvimwp⟩ for ⟨-nvivmwp⟩]
	/p	nkat·o·s·əmwí·həmp, kəmənhíhəmɔ·p	
	/t	I was thirsty, and you gave me to drink.	
	/k	I was thirsty, and ye gave me drink:	

	/b	nhupswevwmp, jwq ktumekalevmwp;
	/p	nčəpso·wí·həmp, šúkw ktəmi·k·alíhəmɔ·p.
	/t	I was a stranger, but you took me in.
	/k	I was a stranger, and ye took me in:

Mt 25.36	/b	nswpsevwmp, ktukonevmwp;
	/p	nso·psí·həmp, ktak·ɔníhəmɔ·p.
	/t	I was naked, and you clothed me.
	/k	Naked, and ye clothed me:

	/b	mpalsevwmp, kekalevmwp;
	/p	mpa·lsí·həmp, kki·k·a·líhəmɔ·p.
	/t	I was sick, and you came to see about me.
	/k	I was sick, and ye visited me:

	/b	fupvasevwmp kwtxevmwp.
	/p	nkəpha·s·í·həmp, ko·txíhəmɔ·p.'
	/t	I was in prison, and you came to me.'
	/k	I was in prison, and ye came unto me.

Mt 25.37	/b	Nuh nrk jaxukawsehek tulananro,	[⟨tulananro⟩ for ⟨tulanro⟩]
	/p	ná=č né·k šaxahka·wsí·č·i·k təla·né·ɔ,	
	/t	Then the righteous will say to him,	
	/k	Then shall the righteous answer him, saying,	

	/b	Nrvlalerf, hifc vuh ktuli kavtwpwenrp ok ktuli xamulunrnap?
	/p	'nehəlá·lienk, čínke=háč ktəli-kahto·p·wí·ne·p ó·k ktəli-xamələné·na·p?
	/t	'Master, when was it that you were you hungry and we fed you?
	/k	Lord, when saw we thee an hungred, and fed thee?

	/b	ok kavtwsumwerp, ok ktuli munrvlunrnap?	[⟨-werp⟩ for ⟨-wenrp⟩; ⟨nrv⟩ for ⟨niv⟩]
	/p	ó·k -kahto·s·əmwí·ne·p, ó·k ktəli-mənihələné·na·p?	
	/t	Or thirsty, and we gave you to drink?	
	/k	or thirsty, and gave thee drink?	

Mt 25.38	/b	Hifc vuh knrwulwvnap ktuli hpuswen, ok ktumekalulvwmnap?
	/p	čínke=háč kəne·wəlúhəna·p, ktəli-čpəs·ó·wi·n, ó·k ktəmi·k·alǝlhúmǝna·p?
	/t	When did we see you to be a stranger and bring you inside?
	/k	When saw we thee a stranger, and took thee in?

```
        /b  ok swpsen ok avkonulunrn?
        /p  ɔ·k -só·psi·n, ɔ́·k -ahkɔnəlә́ne·n?
        /t  Or to be naked, and clothed you?
        /k  or naked, and clothed thee?
```

```
Mt 25.39 /b  Hifc vuh kwtxulvwmnap nrli palseun ok nrli kpuvaseun?
        /p  čínke=háč ko·txәlhúmәna·p né·li-pa·lsían, ɔ́·k né·li-kpahá·s·ian?'
        /t  When did we come to you while you were sick or in prison?'
        /k  Or when saw we thee sick, or in prison, and came unto thee?
```

```
Mt 25.40 /b  Nuh nu Sakema tulan. Kvehei ktulwvvmw;        [⟨ktulwv-|vmw⟩ for ⟨ktulwvmw⟩]
        /p  ná=č ná sa·k·í·ma tә́la·n, 'khičí·i, ktәllúhәmɔ,
        /t  Then the king will say to them, 'Truly I say to you,
        /k  And the King shall answer and say unto them, Verily I say unto you,
```

```
        /b  Nckc nc rlevrqc eli kwti bk trfsesehek nuxesumusuk,
        /p  néke nә́ e·li·hé·k·we ílli kwә́t·i yó·k tenksi·sí·č·i·k naxi·s·әmә́s·ak,
        /t  When you did that for even one of these smallest brothers and sisters of mine,
        /k  Inasmuch as ye have done it unto one of the least of these my brethren,
```

```
        /b  tpusqi lr ne ktulevenrop.
        /p  tpә́skwi-lé· ní· ktәli·hi·né·ɔ·p.'
        /t  it was like you did it for *me*.'
        /k  ye have done it unto me.
```

```
Mt 25.41 /b     Nuh nrl mwununheonif rpelehi tulan.
        /p     "ná=č né·l mwәnančí·onink e·p·i·lí·č·i tә́la·n,
        /t     "Then he will say to those on his left,
        /k     Then shall he say also unto them on the left hand,
```

```
        /b  Pale aq b wunhi qeluluserq,
        /p  'palí·i á·kw yú wә́nči, kwí·la-lә́s·ie·kw.
        /t  'Go away from here, you hopeless ones.
        /k  Depart from me, ye cursed,
```

```
        /b  ekali hwpweq mutu a eatrk tuntrbf;
        /p  íkali čә́p·wi·kw máta=á· i·á·te·k tәnté·yunk,
        /t  and disappear into fire that will never go out,
        /k  into everlasting fire,
```

```
        /b  nu mavtuntw mrnetwntup ok rvalwkalahi.
        /p  ná mahtánt·u menni·túntәp, ɔ́·k ehalo·ka·lá·č·i.'
        /t  which was made for the devil and his angels.'
        /k  prepared for the devil and his angels:
```

Mt 25.42 /b Rli futwpwevwmp, takw ktaxamevwmwp;
/p é·li nkat·o·p·wí·həmp, takó· ktax·ami·húmɔ·p,
/t For I was hungry, and you did not feed me;
/k For I was an hungred, and ye gave me no meat:

/b futwsumwevwmp, takw kmunvevwmwp;
/p nkat·o·s·əmwí·həmp, takó· kəmənhi·húmɔ·p;
/t I was thirsty, and you did not give me to drink;
/k I was thirsty, and ye gave me no drink:

Mt 25.43 /b nhwpswevwmp, takw ktumekalevwmwp
/p nčəpso·wí·həmp, takó· ktəmi·k·ali·húmɔ·p;
/t I was a stranger, and you did not bring me inside;
/k I was a stranger, and ye took me not in:

/b nswpsevwmp, takw ktukonevwmwp;   [⟨nsw-‖psevwmp⟩]
/p nso·psí·həmp, takó· ktak·ɔni·húmɔ·p;
/t I was naked, and you did not clothe me;
/k naked, and ye clothed me not:

(p. 176) /b mpalsevwmp fupvasevwmp takw kekalevwmwp.
/p mpa·lsí·həmp, nkəpha·s·í·həmp, takó· kki·k·a·li·húmɔ·p.'
/t I was sick, and I was in prison, and you did not come to see about me.'
/k sick, and in prison, and ye visited me not.

Mt 25.44 /b Tulawaouh, Nrvlalerf,   [⟨Tulawao-|uh⟩ for ⟨Tulawaoh⟩]
/p təlawwá·ɔ=č, 'nehəlá·lienk,
/t They will say to him, 'Lord (Master),
/k Then shall they also answer him, saying, Lord,

/b Hifc vuh kunrwulwvnap ktuli kavtwpwen, ok ktuli kavtwsumwen,
/p čínke=háč kəne·wəlúhəna·p, ktə́li-kalıtú·p·wi·n, ɔ́·k ktə́li kahtó·s·ɔmwi·n,
/t when did we see you hungry, or thirsty,
/k when saw we thee an hungred, or athirst,

/b ok ktuli hpuswen, ok ktuli swpsen ok ktuli kpavasen;
/p ɔ́·k ktə́li-čpəs·ó·wi·n, ɔ́·k ktə́li-só·psi·n, ɔ́·k ktə́li-kpahá·s·i·n,
/t or a stranger, or naked, or in prison,
/k or a stranger, or naked, or sick, or in prison,

/b ok ktuli mutu wetavrmulwunrnap?'
/p ɔ́·k ktə́li- máta -wi·t·a·he·məlo·wəné·na·p?'
/t and we did not help you?'

Mt 25.45 /b Tulaoh Kvehei ktulwvmw,
/p təlá·ɔ=č, 'khičí·i ktəllúhəmɔ,

	/t	He will say to them, 'Truly I say to you,
	/k	Then shall he answer them, saying, Verily I say unto you,

/b nckc mutu nc rlevarqc mrawset bk mukuni trfsesehek,
/p né·ke máta nə́ e·li·ha·é·k·we me·á·wsi·t yó·k məkə́ni tenksi·sí·č·i·k,
/t In the past when you did not do that for one of these smallest ones,
/k Inasmuch as ye did it not to one of the least of these,

/b tpisqi lr mutu ne ktulevewunrop.
/p tpə́skwi-lé·, máta ní· ktəli·hi·wəné·ɔ·p.'
/t it's like you didn't do it for *me*.'
/k ye did it not to me.

Mt 25.46
/b Nrkih eku rok cntu a mutu vuji alu amuxavrluntamevtet;
/p né·ki=č íka é·ɔk énta-=á· máta háši -ála-amax·ahe·ləntamíhti·t,
/t Those will go to where they will never cease to suffer greatly,
/k And these shall go away into everlasting punishment:

/b kahih nrk juxavkawsehek eku, cntu taa vuji alu wulamalsevtet.
/p káč·i=č né·k šaxahka·wsí·č·i·k íka énta- tá=á· háši -ála-wəlamalsíhti·t."
/t but the righteous to where they will never cease to be blissful."
/k but the righteous into life eternal.

Mt 26.1
/b Nhesus mrhi keji nc lwrtc, nu tulan rkrkemahi,
/p nčí·sas mé·či kíši- nə́ -luwé·t·e, ná tə́la·n e·k·e·ki·má·č·i,
/t After Jesus had said that, then he said to his disciples,
/kl ... when Jesus had finished all these sayings, he said unto his disciples,

Mt 26.2
/b kwatwnro heh nejwqunakvakc, metsavtif rlwcntasek Lwif.
/p "ko·wa·to·né·ɔ, čí·č ni·š·o·k·wənakháke, mi·tsáhtink e·ləwentá·s·i·k 'ló·wink'.
/t "You know that in two more days is the feast called Passover,
/k Ye know that after two days is the feast of the passover,

/b Nunih lukveqi linw Wrqesif melten lih psuqvetcvon.
/p nə́ni=č ləkhíkwi lə́nu we·k·wí·s·ink mí·lti·n lí-=č -psakhwitého·n."
/t That will be the time the man who is the Son will be delivered to be crucified."
/k and the Son of man is betrayed to be crucified.

Mt 26.3
/b Nu ncke lukveqi, maclrpanek wcvevwfrhek
/p ná-néke ləkhíkwi ma·ehəlé·p·ani·k wehi·hunké·č·i·k,
/t At that time there gathered the priests,
/k Then assembled together the chief priests,

/b   ok rvlrkvekrhek ok krkyimvrhek,
/p   ɔ́·k ehəle·khi·k·é·č·i·k, ɔ́·k ke·kayəmhé·č·i·k,
/t   and the scribes, and the rulers,
/k   and the scribes, and the elders of the people,

/b   tali nekanexif patamwrokun krnavketaq weket, rlwcnsetup Krupus,
/p   táli ni·k·a·ní·x·ink pa·tamwe·ɔ́·k·an ke·nahkí·ta·kw wí·k·i·t, e·ləwensí·t·əp †ke·ápas.
/t   at the house of the leading priest ('prayer guardian'), whose name was Caiaphas.
/kl   unto the palace of the high priest, who was called Caiaphas,

Mt 26.4 /b   tokunwtumunro wcnhi a tvwnavtet ok nvelavtet.
         /p   tɔk·əno·t·əməné·ɔ wénči·=á· -thwənáhti·t ɔ́·k -nhiláhti·t.
         /t   They talked about how they might arrest him and kill him.
         /l   and consulted and sought how they might take Jesus by subtilty, and kill him.

Mt 26.5 /b   Jwq lwrok, Konah mutu metsavtifei kejqekc
         /p   šúkw luwé·ɔk, "kɔ́na=č máta mi·tsahtinkí·i·ki·škwí·k·e,
         /t   But they said, "Let it not be on the feast day,
         /kl   But they said, Not on the feast-*day*,

         /b   rli a tamsc xrli awrn nesktwnvrt.
         /p   é·li·=á· tá·mse xé·li awé·n -ni·sktó·nhe·t."
         /t   because there would maybe be an uproar from many people."
         /kl   lest there be an uproar among the people.

Lk 22.2 /b   Rli kxwrpanek.
         /p   é·li kxuwé·p·ani·k.
         /t   For they were in fear of the people.
         /kl   For they feared the people.

Chapter 104 (pp. 176-178). [L. section 104.] (John 13.1-30)

Jn 13.1 /b   Jwq nrlumu tpisqevlak li xifwi metsavten;
         /p   šúkw né·ləma tpəskwíhəla·k lí-xínkwi-mi·tsáhti·n,
         /t   But before the time came for the big feast,
         /k   Now before the feast of the passover,

         /b   Nhesus watwn li tpisqevlr tulih alumskan b wunhi cntu lawsif
         /p   nčí·sas o·wá·to·n lí-tpəskwíhəle·, tɔ́li-=č -alɔ́mska·n yú wə́nči entalá·wsink
         /t   Jesus knew that the time had come for him to depart from this world
         /k   when Jesus knew that his hour was come that he should depart out of this world

         /b   li Wxwf.
         /p   lí ó·x·unk,

Text, Transcription, and Translation

/t to his father,
/k unto the Father,

/b Elukveqi avolatup nrvlalahi b cntu lawselehi, eku pchi.
/p illəkhíkwi-ahɔ·lá·t·əp nehəla·lá·č·i yú entala·wsi·lí·č·i, íka péči.
/t as much as he had loved those in this world whose master he was, up to then.
/kl having loved his own, which were in the world, he loved them unto the end.

Jn 13.2
/b Loqekc mrhi keji metsevtetc,
/p lɔ·k·wí·k·e, mé·či kíši-mi·tsihtí·t·e,
/t In the evening, after they had finished eating,
/kl And supper being ended

/b nu Mavtuntw tulextaon pwunarluntumwakunelet Nhwtus Iskaleutu,
/p ná mahtánt·u təli·xtáɔ·n pwəna·eləntaməwa·k·aní·li·t †nčó·tas-iska·liát·a,
/t then the devil put it into the thoughts of Judas Iscariot,
/kl (the devil having now put into the heart of Judas Iscariot,

/b Symun qesu li a mvalumaolen.
/p †sáiman kkwí·s·a, lí-=á· -mhalamaɔ́·li·n.
/t the son of Simon, to sell him out.
/kl Simon's son, to betray him)

Jn 13.3
/b Nhesus watwn
/p nčí·sas o·wá·to·n,
/t Jesus knew
/kl Jesus knowing [that the Father had given all things into his hands, and]

/b tuli Krtanitwetif wcnheken   [⟨wcnh-⟩ for /wənč-/]
/p tə́li- ke·tanət·o·wí·t·ink -wənčí·k·i·n,
/t that he came from God,
/kl that he was come from God,

/b ok tulih eku an wcnheket.
/p ɔ́·k tə́li-=č íka -á·n wenčí·k·i·t.
/t and that he would go to where he came from.
/kl and went to God;

Jn 13.4
/b Puvswqe eku wunhi cntu metsetup, ok khelasw;
/p pahsúk·wi· íka wə́nči énta-mi·tsí·t·əp, ɔ́·k kčílahsu.
/t He got up from where he had eaten and took his clothes off.
/kl he riseth from supper, and laid aside his garments;

	/b	ok wrtunum hchesktulifqvif vcmpus; qwlumampeswlan vokyu. [⟨wrtun-‖um⟩]
	/p	ó·k wé·tənəm čehči·sktəlínkhwink hémpəs, kwəlamampi·s·ó·la·n hókaya.
	/t	And he took a towel and tied it around himself as a belt.
	/kl	and took a towel, and girded himself.

Jn 13.5
(p. 177)
/b Nu tuli mpi lokcnsif laniven,
/p ná tə́li- mpí lɔ·k·énsink -laníhi·n.
/t Then he proceeded to put water into a dish.
/k After that he poureth water into a bason,

/b nu tolumi kjextaon vwsetelet rkrkemahi,
/p ná tə́ləmi-kši·xtáɔ·n wsi·tí·li·t e·k·e·ki·má·č·i,
/t And then he began to wash his disciples feet,
/k and began to wash the disciples' feet,

/b ok vwheskvamaon krlumumpeset torkrn.
/p ó·k wči·skhamáɔ·n, ke·lamampí·s·i·t tɔé·ke·n.
/t and he wiped them for them using what he was wearing as a belt.
/k and to wipe them with the towel wherewith he was girded.

Jn 13.6
/b Symun Petulu rlumi kavtu nc levatc, tulkw,
/p †sáiman-pí·təla é·ləmi-káhta- nə́ -li·há·t·e, tə́lku,
/t Simon Peter, when he began to be about to do that for him, said to him,
/k Then cometh he to Simon Peter: and Peter saith unto him,

/b Nrvlaleun, katu vuh kjextwnu?
/p "nehəlá·lian, kkát·a-=háč -kši·xtó·na?"
/t "Master, are you intending to wash them?"
/k Lord, dost thou wash my feet?

Jn 13.7
/b Nhesus tulao, Takw bqc kwatwun rlumekintamu;
/p nči·sas təlá·ɔ, "takó· yúkwe ko·wa·tó·wən e·lami·kə́ntama.
/t Jesus said to him, "You don't know now what work I do.
/k Jesus answered and said unto him, What I do thou knowest not now;

/b jwq oerih kwatwn.
/p šúkw ɔ·wié·i=č ko·wá·to·n."
/t But you will know it by and by."
/k but thou shalt know hereafter.

Jn 13.8
/b Petul tulao, Taa vuji kujextaewunu nsetu.
/p †pí·təl təlá·ɔ, "tá=á· háši kkəš·i·xtaí·wəna nsí·t·a."
/t Peter said to him, "You shall never wash my feet,"
/k Peter saith unto him, Thou shalt never wash my feet.

Text, Transcription, and Translation

/b Nhesus tulao Mutuh kjextwlwunc taa nvakrf kwnheyei.
/p nčí·sas təlá·ɔ, "máta=č kši·xto·ló·wane, tá=á· nhák·enk kunči·aí·i."
/t Jesus said to him, "If I don't wash them for you, you won't be part of me."
/k Jesus answered him, If I wash thee not, thou hast no part with me. [RSV "in me"]

Jn 13.9
/b Symun Petul tulao,
/p †sáiman-pí·təl təlá·ɔ,
/t Simon Peter said to him,
/k Simon Peter saith unto him,

/b Mutuh jwq nsetul, nuxkulh, ok nel.
/p "máta=č šúkw nsí·t·al, nnáxkal=č ó·k ní·l."
/t "It must be not only my feet; it must be my hands and my head."
/k Lord, not my feet only, but also my hands and my head.

Jn 13.10
/b Nhesus tulao, Awrn krjexumuntup, nwhqc a;
/p nčí·sas təlá·ɔ, "awé·n ke·š·i·x·əmɔ́ntəp, nó·čkwe=á·.
/t Jesus said to him, "For someone that has been washed, it would be pointless.
/k Jesus saith to him, He that is washed needeth not

/b vwestu a jwq, rli msuthri pelset.   [⟨vwestu⟩ for ⟨vwsetu⟩]
/p wsí·t·a=á· šúkw, é·li- məsəč·é·i -pí·lsi·t.
/t It would only (need to) be their feet, as they are clean all over.
/k save to wash his feet, but is clean every whit:

/b Kelwu kpelsevmw, jwq mutu wrmi.
/p ki·ló·wa kpi·lsíhəmɔ, šúkw máta wé·mi."
/t *You* are clean, but not all (of you)."
/k and ye are clean, but not all.

Jn 13.11
/b Rli wavapani awrnh mclamwnt,
/p é·li o·wa·há·p·ani, awé·n=č méhəlamunt.
/t For he knew who was going to sell him out.
/k For he knew who should betray him;

/b nuni wunhi lwrn, Takw wrmi kpelsevwmw.
/p nə́ni wwə́nči-lúwe·n, "takó· wé·mi kpi·lsi·húmɔ."
/t That was why he said, "You are not all clean."
/k therefore said he, Ye are not all clean.

Jn 13.12
/b Mrhi keji kjextaotc vwsetelet, ok wrtunifc cvavqehi
/p mé·či kíši-kši·xtaɔ́·t·e wsi·t·í·li·t, ɔ́·k we·t·ənínke ehahkwí·č·i,
/t After he finished washing their feet, and he picked up his clothing,
/k So after he had washed their feet, and had taken his garments,

/b lupi lumutuvpwp.
/p lápi ləmátahpo·p.
/t he sat down again.
/k and was set down again,

/b Nu tulan, Kwatwnro vuh rlevlrq?
/p ná tə́la·n, "ko·wa·to·né·ɔ=háč e·líhəle·kw?
/t Then he said to them, "Do you know what I did to you?
/k he said unto them, Know ye what I have done to you?

Jn 13.13 /b Ktclwevlevmw, Rkrkemerf, ok Nrvlalerf; kwlamwcvmw,
/p ktələwihəlíhəmɔ 'e·k·e·kí·mienk' ɔ́·k 'nehəlá·lienk'; ko·la·məwéhəmɔ.
/t You address me as 'our teacher;' and 'our master'; you are right.
/k Ye call me Master and Lord: and ye say well;

/b nanc ntclsen.
/p ná=nə ntə́lsi·n.
/t That's what I am.
/k for so I am.

Jn 13.14 /b Punu ne, nrvlalqrq ok Rkrkemqrq, kjextaonc ksetwao;
/p pənáh, ní·, nehəlá·lkwe·kw ɔ́·k e·k·e·kí·mkwe·kw, kši·xtaɔ́·ne ksi·t·əwá·ɔ,
/t Now, if *I*, your teacher and master, washed your feet,
/k If I then, your Lord and Master, have washed your feet;

/b kelwu a wlavu kujextaovtenroi.
/p ki·ló·wa=á· wəláha kkəš·i·xta·ɔhti·ne·ɔ́·i.
/t *you* should all the more wash them for each other.
/k ye also ought to wash one another's feet.

Jn 13.15 /b Nwnhi nuni lusen, futatumun, nuni ktulevtenro.
/p núnči- nə́ni -lə́s·i·n, nkat·á·t·amən, nə́ni ktəlihti·né·ɔ.
/t I did that because I wanted you to do that for each other.
/k For I have given you an example, that ye should do as I have done to you.

Jn 13.16 /b Kvehei, kvehei ktclwvmw.
/p khičí·i, khičí·i, ktəllúhəmɔ,
/t Truly, truly, I say to you,
/k Verily, verily, I say unto you,

/b Rkrkemunt, takw tolwe lusewunu rkrkemkwki;
/p e·k·e·kí·mənt takó· tɔləwí·i-lə́s·í·wəna e·k·e·ki·mkúk·i,
/t The one instructed is not greater than the one who instructs him,
/k The servant is not greater than his lord;

/b ok rlwkalunt, takw tolwe lusewunu rlwkalkwki.
/p ɔ́·k e·lo·ká·lənt takó· tɔləwí·i-ləs·í·wəna e·lo·ka·lkúk·i.
/t and the one sent is not greater than the one that sent him.
/k neither he that is sent greater than he that sent him.

Jn 13.17
/b Nuni wuli watarqc ok luserqc, kwlvatrnumevmwh.
/p nə́ni wə́li-wwa·taék·we ɔ́·k ləs·iék·we, ko·lhate·namíhəmɔ=č.
/t If you know that well and do it, you will be happy.
/k If ye know these things, happy are ye if ye do them.

Jn 13.18
/b Takw wrmi cntxerq nwnhi nc lwrwun, nwavaok pepenaokek;
/p takó· wémi entxíe·kw núnči- nə́ -luwé·wən (no·wa·há·ɔk pi·p·i·naɔ́k·i·k),
/t It is not about all of you that I say that (I know who I have chosen),
/k I speak not of you all: I know whom I have chosen:

/b jwq lih pavkunhi lr rlrkvaset xwi lrkvekun, cntu lwrf,
/p šúkw lí-=č -pahkánči-lé· e·le·khá·s·i·t xúwi-le·khí·k·an, énta-lúwenk:
/t but so that what is written in the old writings may be fulfilled, where it is said:
/k but that the scripture may be fulfilled,

/b Wepwmet avpon tospunao wufonu ntcli a pulevkwn.
/p wi·pó·mi·t ahpɔ́·n tɔspəná·ɔ wánkona ntə́li-=á· -palíhko·n.
/t 'One who ate bread with me raised his heel to destroy me.'
/k He that eateth bread with me hath lifted up his heel against me.
[RSV "has lifted his heel"]

Jn 13.19
/b Bqc kwntamwlunro nrsko nc rlrk;
/p yúkwe kuntamo·ləné·ɔ né·skɔ nə́ é·le·k,
/t I'm telling you now before it happens,
/k Now I tell you before it come,

/b wunhih keji nc lrkc nrmrq ntcli ne nrkumu.   [⟨wunhi⟩ not ⟨wcnhi⟩]
/p wə́nči-=č kíši- nə́ -lé·k·e -né·me·kw, ntə́li ní· né·k·əma.
/t so that, after it happens, you will see that I am him.
/k that, when it is come to pass, ye may believe that I am he.

Jn 13.20
/b Kvehei kvehei ktclwvmw,
/p khičí·i, khičí·i, ktəllúhəmɔ,
/t Truly, truly, I tell you,
/k Verily, verily, I say unto you,

/b Awrn wulamvetaotc ntalwkakunu ne nwlamvetaq,   [⟨wul-‖amvetaotc⟩]
/p awé·n wəla·mhitaɔ́·t·e ntalo·ká·k·ana, ní· no·la·mhíta·kw,
/t if someone believes my messenger he believes *me*,
/k He that receiveth whomsoever I send receiveth me;

(p. 178) /b ok prtalwkalelehi.
/p ó·k pe·t·alo·ka·li·lí·č·i."
/t and the one that sent me."
/k and he that receiveth me receiveth him that sent me.

Jn 13.21 /b Nhesus nc keji lwrtc, suqrluntumwp tali vwtrvif,
/p nčí·sas nə́ kíši-luwé·t·e, sak·we·ləntamo·p táli wté·hink.
/t After Jesus finished saying that, he was troubled in his heart.
/k When Jesus had thus said, he was troubled in spirit,

/b myaohemwp, tulao Kvehei ktulwvmw,
/p maya·ɔ·č·í·mo·p, təlá·ɔ, "khičí·i, ktəllúhəmɔ,
/t And he made a declaration, saying to them, "Truly, I tell you,
/k and testified, and said, Verily, verily, I say unto you,

/b mrawset cntxerq, mvalumaonh nvaky.
/p me·á·wsi·t entxíe·kw mhalamáɔ·n=č nhák·ay.
/t one from among you will sell me out.
/k that one of you shall betray me.

Jn 13.22 /b Nu rkrkemunhek pwunaovtenro,
/p ná e·k·e·ki·mə́nči·k pwəna·ɔhti·né·ɔ,
/t Then the disciples looked at each other,
/k Then the disciples looked one on another,

/b rli qelulrluntumevtet awrni tu wcnhi nc lwrt.
/p é·li-kwí·la-le·ləntamíhti·t, awé·ni=tá wénči- nə́ -lúwe·t.
/t as they couldn't imagine who it was that he was speaking about.
/k doubting of whom he spake.

Jn 13.23 /b Nu nckc kwti rkrkemuntup, ekali apavtaexenwp vwtwlvrbf Nhesus;
/p ná-néke kwə́t·i e·k·e·ki·mə́ntəp íkali apahtai·x·í·no·p wto·lhé·yunk nčí·sas.
/t At that time one disciple lay against Jesus's chest.
/k Now there was leaning on Jesus' bosom one of his disciples,

/b nunuli rvolatpani.
/p nanáli ehɔ·la·tpáni.
/t He was the one he loved.
/k whom Jesus loved.

Jn 13.24 /b Nu Symun Petul tutpetaon, tuli a ntwtumaon,
/p ná †sáiman-pí·təl tətpí·tao·n, tə́li-=á· -nto·t·əmáɔ·n,
/t Then Simon Peter gestured to him to ask him
/k Simon Peter therefore beckoned to him, that he should ask

	/b	awrni tu wcnhi nc lwrt.
	/p	awé·ni=tá wénči- nə́ -lúwe·t.
	/t	who it was that he was speaking about.
	/k	who it should be of whom he spake.

Jn 13.25 /b Nu nu eku rli apavtaexefup vwtwlvrbf Nhesus, tulan,
/p ná ná íka é·li-apahtai·x·ínkəp wto·lhé·yunk nčí·sas tə́la·n,
/t Then the one who lay against Jesus's chest said to him,
/k He then lying on Jesus' breast saith unto him,

	/b	Nrvlaleun, awrn vuh?
	/p	"nehəlá·lian, awé·n=háč?"
	/t	"Master, who is it?"
	/k	Lord, who is it?

Jn 13.26 /b Nhesus tulao, Nul nu melukh b avpontut,
/p nčí·sas təlá·ɔ, "nál ná mí·lak=č yú ahpɔ́·nt·ət
/t Jesus said to him, "He is the one I will give this piece of bread to
/k Jesus answered, He it is, to whom I shall give a sop,

	/b	keji hvopwnumanc li prmetrkif.
	/p	kíši-čhɔ·pwənəmá·ne lí pe·mi·t·é·k·ink.
	/t	after I have dipped it in the grease.
	/k	when I have dipped it.

	/b	Mrhi keji hvopwunifc, nu toxaman Nhwtus Iskaleutu, Symun qesu.
	/p	mé·či kíši-čhɔ·pwənínke, ná tɔ́x·ama·n †nčó·tas-iska·liát·a, †sáiman kkwí·s·a.
	/t	After he had dipped it, then he gave it to Judas Iscariot, Simon's son.
	/k	And when he had dipped the sop, he gave it to Judas Iscariot, the son of Simon.

Jn 13.27 /b Keji nc methetc, mavtuntw ekali punhep,
/p kíši- nə́ -mi·č·í·t·e, mahtánt·u íkali pə́nči·p,
/t After he ate that, the devil entered him,
/k And after the sop Satan entered into him.

Lk 22.3 /b taoni nrkumu mawsw nrk atux neju.
/p tá·ɔni né·k·əma má·wsu né·k átax ní·š·a.
/t even though he was one of the twelve.
/kl being of the number of the twelve.

Jn 13.27 /b Nu Nhesus tulan, krtu luseun, jac lusel.
/p ná nčí·sas tə́la·n, "ké·t·a-lə́s·ian šá·e lə́s·i·l."
/t Then Jesus said to him, "What you intend to do, do right away."
/k Then said Jesus unto him, That thou doest, do quickly.

Jn 13.28 /b Jwq wepwmatpanek mutu watwunrop wcnhi nc lat;
          /p šúkw wi·po·ma·tpáni·k máta o·wa·to·wəné·ɔ·p wénči- nə́ -lá·t.
          /t But the ones who ate with him did not know why he said that to him.
          /k Now no man at the table knew for what intent he spake this unto him.

Jn 13.29 /b aluntc letrvrok rli ct Nhwtus kulunif monie nwtrs
          /p a·lə́nte li·t·e·hé·ɔk, é·li-=ét †nčó·tas -kələnink mɔnií·i-nó·t·e·s,
          /t Some thought, that because, it seems, Judas carried the money bag
          /k For some of them thought, because Judas had the bag,

          /b wunhi nc lan,
          /p wwə́nči- nə́ -lá·n,
          /t he said that to him,
          /k that Jesus had said unto him,

          /b tuli a mvalumulen krkw a nrkatumrf tali cntu xifwi metsavtif;   [⟨-mrf⟩ for /-mink/]
          /p tə́li-=á· -mhalamə́li·n kéku=á· ne·ká·t·amink táli énta-xínkwi-mi·tsáhtink,
          /t so that he would buy things that would be made use of at the big feast,
          /k Buy those things that we have need of against the feast;

          /b jitu tuli a melan krkw krtumakselehi.
          /p ší=tá tə́li-=á· -mí·la·n kéku ke·t·əma·ksi·lí·č·i.
          /t or that he would give things to the poor.
          /k or, that he should give something to the poor.

Jn 13.30 /b Mrhi wrtunifc nc avpontut, nu jac quthen;
          /p mé·či we·t·ənínke nə́ ahpɔ́·nt·ət, ná šá·e kwə́č·i·n.
          /t After he took the piece of bread, then he immediately went out.
          /k He then having received the sop went immediately out:

          /b nu nckc peskrk.
          /p ná-néke pí·ske·k.
          /t It was that same night.
          /kl and it was night.

Chapter 105 (pp. 178-179). [L. section =105.] (Luke 22.4-6; Matthew 26.14-16, Mark 14.10-11)

Lk 22.4   /b Eku rp wrvevwfrsekri ok krkyimvrsekri,
          /p íka é·p wehi·hunke·s·i·ké·i ɔ́·k ke·kayəmhe·s·i·ké·i,
          /t He went to the priests and rulers,
          /l And he went his way unto the chief priests and captains,
          /k And he went his way, and communed with the chief priests and captains,

          /b watulan tuli a kuski eku lwxolan.
          /p o·wá·təla·n, tə́li-=á· -káski- íka -ló·x·ɔla·n.

Text, Transcription, and Translation 623

/t and he made it known to them that he would be able to deliver him to them.
/l and communed with them, how he might betray him unto them.
/k how he might betray him unto them.

Lk 22.5 /b Nc rlsitaovtetc; ave wulrluntamwpanek,
/p nə́ e·lsət·aɔhtí·t·e, áhi-wəle·ləntamó·p·ani·k.
/t When they heard him say that, they were very glad.
/l And when they heard it, they were glad,

/b tulawao monih kmelwvnu.
/p təlawwá·ɔ, "móni=č kəmillúhəna."
/t They said to him, "We'll give you money,"
/l and promised to give him money.

/b Tulao Tuh vuh ktuntxi melenro, patwlrqc?   [⟨patwlrqc⟩ for ⟨prtwlrqc⟩]
/p təlá·ɔ, "tá=č=háč ktə́ntxi-mi·li·né·ɔ, pe·t·o·lé·k·we?"
/t He said to them, "How much will you give me, if I bring him to you?"
/l And he said unto them, What will ye give me, and I will deliver him unto you;

/b Tulawao, Xenxkc pvakc moni.
/p təlawwá·ɔ, "xí·nxke pháke móni."
/t They said to him, "Thirty pieces of money."
/l and they covenanted with him for thirty pieces of silver.

Lk 22.6 /b Nu noxkwmun. ‖   [⟨noxkwmun⟩ for ⟨noxkwman⟩]
/p ná nɔxkó·ma·n.
/t Then he gave them his agreement.
/l And he promised,

(p. 179) /b Nu wunwhi fumri punarluntumun
/p nə́ wənúči- nkəmé·i -pəna·elə́ntamən,
/t And starting then, he was always thinking,
/l and from that time, he sought opportunity

/b cji alu cntu xrlif avpevtet
/p éši-ála- énta-xé·link -ahpíhti·t,
/t whenever they were no longer in a crowd,
/l (2) in the absence of the multitude   [numbers = sequence in L.]

/b rnif a wunhi a apwi nc luset.
/p énnink=á·, wə́nči-=á· -á·p·əwi- nə́ -lə́s·i·t.
/t about what he could do in order to easily do that.
/l (1) how he might conveniently betray him unto them.

Chapter 106 (p. 179). [L. section 106.] (Mark 14.12-16)

Mk 14.12 /b   Nrtami kejqekc cvlukveqi mutu mehevtet pastrk avpon
/p   né·tami-ki·škwí·k·e ehələkhíkwi- máta -mi·č·íhti·t pá·ste·k ahpɔ́·n,
/t   On the first day when they do not eat bread that has risen (from fermentation),
/l   Now the first day of the feast of unleavened bread,
/k   And the first day of unleavened bread,

/b   ok cvlakveqi Lwife mrketut nvelunt;   [⟨cvlak-⟩ for ⟨cvluk-⟩]
/p   ɔ́·k ehələkhíkwi- lo·winkí·i-mekí·t·ət -nhílənt,
/t   and when the Passover lamb is always killed,
/l   when the passover must be killed,
/k   when they killed the passover,

/b   rkrkemunhek tulawao Nhesusu;
/p   e·k·e·ki·mə́nči·k təlawwá·ɔ nči·sás·a,
/t   the disciples said to Jesus,
/l   the disciples came to Jesus, saying unto him,

/b   Ta vuh ktuli wulrluntamun ntuntu wuletwnrn
/p   "tá=háč ktə́li-wəle·ləntamən ntə́nta-wəli·tó·ne·n
/t   "Where are you pleased that we prepare
/l   Where wilt thou that we go, and prepare for thee
/k   Where wilt thou that we go and prepare that thou mayest eat the passover?

/b   cntu a mvot lwife mrketut?
/p   énta-=á· -mhɔ́t lo·winkí·i-mekí·t·ət?"
/t   the place where you would eat the Passover lamb?"
/l   that thou mayest eat the passover?

Mk 14.13 /b   Nu tolwkalan neju rkrkemahi Petul ok Nhan tulao,
/p   ná tɔlo·ká·la·n ní·š a e·k·c·ki·má·č·i (†pí·təl ɔ́·k nčá·n) təlá·ɔ,
/t   Then he sent two of his disciples (it was Peter and John), saying to them.
/l   And he sendeth forth two of his disciples, Peter and John, and saith unto them,
/k   (Mk 14.13 and Lk 22.8)

/b   Eku aq wtrnif;
/p   "íka á·kw o·t·é·nink.
/t   "Go to the town.
/l   Go ye into the city,

Lk 22.10 /b   ekuh parqc, knrovmw linw
/p   íka=č pa·é·k·we, kəne·ɔ́həmɔ lə́nu
/t   When you get there, you will see a man
/kl   and behold, when ye are entered into the city, there shall a man meet you,

/b   seskwunhwf mpi prmwxovtaq.
/p   si·skəwə́nčunk mpí pe·múxɔhta·kw.
/t   who is taking a clay vessel of water somewhere.
/kl   bearing a pitcher of water;

/b   Knaolawuh li tutu rli tumekrt;
/p   kəna·ɔláwwa=č lí tətá é·li-təmí·k·e·t.
/t   You must follow him to wherever he goes in.
/kl   follow him into the house where he entereth in ;

Mk 14.14 /b   tumekrtc ktulawuh wreket;
/p   təmi·k·é·t·e, ktəláwwa=č we·í·k·i·t,
/t   When he goes in, you must say to the house-owner,
/l   and wheresoever he shall go in, say ye to the good man of the house:
/k   (Mt 26.18, Mk 14.14)

/b   Nrvlalwrt kpchi lwq, Mrhi ntupsqelavtu
/p   'nehəlá·ləwe·t kpéči-lúkw, "mé·či ntəpskwílahta.
/t   'The master sends you this message, "My time has now come.
/l   The Master saith unto thee, My time is at hand,

/b   wekeun futu tuli lwife metsi navle rkrkemukek,
/p   wí·k·ian nkát·a-táli-lo·winkí·i-mí·tsi, nahəlí·i e·k·e·ki·mák·i·k.
/t   I want to eat the Passover meal in your house, along with my disciples.
/l   I will keep the passover at thy house;

/b   tu vuh ktevcntu nc lusen?
/p   tá=háč ktihə́nta- nə́ -lə́s·i·n?'"
/t   Where do you do that?'"
/l   where is the guest-chamber where I shall eat the passover with my disciples.

Mk 14.15 /b   Kpunwntulwkwnroh vwqrbf cntu kputuk cntu wrmi krkw wulexif.
/p   kpənuntəluk·o·né·ɔ=č hukwé·yunk énta-kpát·ək, énta- wé·mi kéku -wəlí·x·ink.
/t   He will show you an upper room where everything is in good order.
/kl   And he will shew you a large upper room furnished and prepared:

/b   Nuh nc ktuntu wulextaenrn.
/p   ná=č nə́ ktə́nta-wəli·xtaí·ne·n.
/t   That's where you must make it ready for us.
/kl   there make ready for us.

Mk 14.16 /b   Na rkrkemahi tolumskalen,
/p   ná e·k·e·ki·má·č·i tɔləmská·li·n.
/t   Then his dsciples left.
/l   And his disciples went forth,

/b   eku prok wtrnif,
/p   íka pé·ɔk o·t·é·nink.
/t   And they got to the town.
/kl and came into the city,

/b   na nc tulenumunro rluntup;
/p   ná nə təli·naməné·ɔ e·lə́ntəp.
/t   Then they saw what they had been told (they would).
/kl and found as he had said unto them,

/b   ok nanc tulsenro rlat,
/p   ɔ́·k ná=nə təlsi·né·ɔ é·la·t.
/t   And they did just what he told them to.
/kl and they did as he had appointed them,

/b   ok qejextwnro nc lwife.
/p   ɔ́·k kwi·š·i·xto·né·ɔ nə́ lo·winkí·i.
/t   And they prepared the Passover meal.
/kl and they made ready the passover.

Chapter 107 (pp. 179-182). [L. section 107.] (John 13.31- 38; John 14.1-31)

Jn 13.31 /b   Apaheletc, Nhesus lwr,
          /p   a·p·a·č·i·lí·t·e, nčí·sas lúwe·,
          /t   When they got back, Jesus said,
          /l   And [*when they were returned*] Jesus said,

          /b   Bqc mrhi linw Wrqesif xifovkunemkwsw;
          /p   "yúkwe mé·či lə́nu we·k·wí·s·ink xinkɔhkəni·mkwə́s·u,
          /t   "Now the man who is the Son is glorified,
          /kl Now is the Son of man glorified,

          /b   ok Krtanitwet xifovkunemkwsw vokyelet wunhi.
          /p   ɔ́·k ke·tanət·ó·wi·t xinkɔhkəni·mkwə́s·u hɔk·aí·li·t wə́nči.
          /t   and God is glorified from him.
          /kl and God is glorified in him.

Jn 13.32 /b   Krtanitwet xifovkunemkwsetc vokyclet wunhi,
          /p   ke·tanət·ó·wi·t xinkɔhkəni·mkwəs·í·t·e hɔk·aí·li·t wə́nči,
          /t   If God is glorified from him,
          /kl If God be glorified in him,

          /b   Krtanitwet ok vokrf wunhi xifovkunemkwselw,
          /p   ke·tanət·ó·wi·t ɔ́·k hɔ́k·enk wə́nči-xinkɔhkəni·mkwəs·í·lu.

/t he is glorified also from God.
/kl God shall also glorify him in himself,

/b nu jac moxefovkunemkwsen.
/p ná šá·e mɔx·inkɔhkəni·mkwə́s·i·n.
/t Then he is glorified immediately.
/kl and shall straightway glorify him.

Jn 13.33
/b Tufamemuntutuk, heh tvakiti qetavpemulwvmw.
/p tankami·məntət·ak, čí·č thakíti kəwitahpi·məlúhəmɔ.
/t Little children, I am with you a little while yet.
/kl Little children, yet a little while I am with you.

/b Knatwnaevmwh;
/p kənat·o·naíhəmɔ=č.
/t You will look for me.
/kl Ye shall seek me:

/b rlukwp Nhwuk, tutu reau taa kpawunro;
/p e·lák·əp nčó·wak, tətá e·á·a, tá=á· kpa·wəné·ɔ.
/t As I told the Jews, where I go, you will not come.
/kl and as I said unto the Jews, whither I go, ye cannot come;

/b ok krpwu nc ktulunro.
/p ó·k ké·pəwa nə́ ktəlləné·ɔ.
/t And I tell *you* that also.
/kl so now I say unto you.

Jn 13.34
/b Wuskif tavpuntwakun kmelwvmw; Avolteq,
/p wə́skink tahpantəwá·k·an kəmillúhəmɔ: ahɔ́·lti·kw.
/t I give you a new commandment: Love each other.
/kl A new commandment I give unto you, that ye love one another;

/b rlkeqi ne avolrq lukveqi avolteq.   [⟨nẹ⟩]
/p e·lkí·kwi- ní· -ahɔ́lle·kw, ləkhíkwi-ahɔ́·lti·kw.
/t Love each other as much as *I* love *you*.
/kl as I have loved you, that ye also love one another.

Jn 13.35
/b Avolterqc, wunhih wrmi awrn watwn ktcli wulamvetaenro.   [⟨wun-‖hih⟩]
/p ahɔ·ltié·k·we, wwə́nči-=č wé·mi awé·n -wwá·to·n ktə́li-wəla·mhitai·né·ɔ."
/t If you love each other, everyone will know from that that you believe me."
/kl By this shall all men know that ye are my disciples, if ye have love one to another.

Jn 13.36
(p. 180)

/b   Symun Petul tulao, Nrvlaleun, tuh vuh ktav?
/p   †sáiman-pí·təl təlá·ɔ, "nehəlá·lian, tá=č=háč ktá?"
/t   Simon Peter said to him "Master, where will you go?"
/kl Simon Peter said unto him, Lord, whither goest thou?

/b   Nhesus tulao, Reau taa kuski bqc li naolewun,
/p   nčí·sas təlá·ɔ, "e·á·a, tá=á· kkáski- yúkwe -lí-na·olí·wən.
/t   Jesus said to him, "Where I go you (sg.) will not be able to follow me now.
/kl Jesus answered him, Whither I go, thou canst not follow me now;

/b   jwqh oeri knaoli.
/p   šúkw=č ɔ·wié·i kəná·ɔli."
/t   But by and by you will follow me."
/kl but thou shalt follow me afterwards.

Jn 13.37

/b   Petul tulao, Nrvlaleun koh vuh mutu kuski bqc naolulwun?
/p   †pí·təl təlá·ɔ, "nehəlá·lian, kóč=háč máta káski- yúkwe -na·ɔləló·wan?
/t   Peter said to him, "Master, why can't I follow you now?
/kl Peter said unto him, Lord, why cannot I follow thee now?

/b   Nwifi a tu wuntufulun kvaky.
/p   nəwínki-=á·=tá -wəntánkələn khák·ay."
/t   I would willingly die for you."
/kl I will lay down my life for thy sake.

Jn 13.38

/b   Nhesus tulao Kwefi vuh a wunhi ufulun ne?
/p   nčí·sas təlá·ɔ, "kəwínki-=háč=á· -wónči-ánkələn ní·?
/t   Jesus said to him, "Would you be willing to die for me?
/kl Jesus answered him, Wilt thou lay down thy life for my sake?

/b   Kvehei, kvehei ktulul,
/p   khičí·i, khičí·i, ktələl,
/t   Truly, truly, I tell you,
/kl Verily, verily, I say unto thee,

/b   Tepas taa kunhemwei, kcnh nuxun keji pavswranc nvaky.
/p   típa·s tá=á· kənči·mwí·i, kónč naxən kíši-pahsəwé·ane nhák·ay."
/t   The rooster ('chicken') will not crow until you have denied me three times."
/kl the cock shall not crow, till thou hast denied me thrice.

Jn 14.1

/b   Kahi suqrluntufvrq tali ktrvwaif.
/p   "káči sak·we·ləntánkhe·kw táli ktehəwá·ink.
/t   "Don't be troubled in your hearts.
/kl Let not your heart be troubled:

/b Nvakalw Krtanitwet ok nrpc nvakaleq.
/p nhaká·lo· ke·tanət·ó·wi·t, ɔ́·k né·pe nhaká·li·kw.
/t Trust in God, and trust in me, also.
/kl ye believe in God, believe also in me.

Jn 14.2 /b Nwx wekct xrli petawuntr;
/p nó·x wí·k·i·t xé·li pi·tawə́nte·.
/t My father's house has many rooms.
/kl In my Father's house are many mansions:

/b mutu a nc lrkc, ktulunrop a.
/p máta=á· nə́ lé·k·e, ktəlləné·ɔ·p=á·.
/t If that were not so, I would have told you.
/kl if it were not so, I would have told you.

/b Numy wuletwn rperqh.
/p nəmái-wəlí·to·n é·p·ie·kw=č.
/t I go to make a place for you to be.
/kl I go to prepare a place for you.

Jn 14.3 /b Kejextwlrqc rperqh, lupih mpav,
/p ki·š·i·xto·lé·k·we é·p·ie·kw=č, lápi=č mpá.
/t When I prepare a place for you to be, I will come back again.
/kl And if I go and prepare a place for you, I will come again,

/b ktalumwxolulvwmwh,
/p ktaləmo·x·ɔləlhúmɔ=č.
/t I will take you away.
/k and receive you unto myself;

/b rpeuh krpwu ktupenro.
/p é·p·ia=č ké·pəwa ktap·i·né·ɔ.
/t And you, too, will be where I am.
/k that where I am, there ye may be also.

Jn 14.4 /b Reauh, kwatwnro, ok kwatwnro rlih aav.
/p e·á·a=č ko·wa·to·né·ɔ, ɔ́·k ko·wa·to·né·ɔ é·li=č -á·a."
/t You know where I will go, and you know how I will go there."
/kl And whither I go ye know, and the way ye know.

Jn 14.5 /b Tamus tulao, Nrvlaleun takw nwatwunrn tutuh reaan,
/p táməs təlá·ɔ, "nehəlá·lian, takó· no·wa·tó·wəne·n tətá=č e·á·an.
/t Thomas said to him, "Master, we don't know where you will go.
/kl Thomas saith unto him, Lord, we know not whither thou goest;

	/b	tu vuh nwnhi watwnrn rlih aan?
	/p	tá=háč núnči-wwa·tó·ne·n é·li-=č -á·an?"
	/t	How do we know how you will go there?"
	/kl	and how can we know the way?

Jn 14.6
/b Tulkw ne tu reuf ok wulamwrokun, ok lclrxrokun.
/p tə́lku, "ní·=tá é·ank ɔ́·k wəla·məwe·ɔ́·k·an, ɔ́·k lehəle·x·e·ɔ́·k·an.
/t Jesus said to him, "I am the way ('where one goes'), and the truth, and the life.
/kl Jesus saith unto him, I am the way, the truth, and the life:

/b Taa awrn Wrtwxifif pri jwq ne wunhi.
/p tá=á· awé·n we·t·o·x·ínkink pé·i, šúkw ní· wə́nči.
/t No one will come to the father except by me.
/kl no man cometh unto the Father, but by me.

Jn 14.7
/b Waverqc a, kwavawu a ok Nwx;
/p wwa·hié·k·we=á·, ko·wa·háwwa=á· ɔ́·k nó·x.
/t If you know me, you would know my father also.
/kl If ye had known me, ye should have known my Father also:

/b bqc kwavawu, ok knrowu.
/p yúkwe ko·wa·háwwa, ɔ́·k kəne·ɔ́wwa."
/t Now you know him and you see him."
/kl and from henceforth ye know him, and have seen him.

Jn 14.8
/b Pilups tulao, Nrvlaleun, Punwntulenrn Wrtwxif
/p †pílaps təlá·ɔ, "nehəlá·lian, pənuntəlí·ne·n we·t·ó·x·ink.
/t Philip said to him, "Master, show us the father.
/kl Philip saith unto him, Lord, shew us the Father,

/b nuh norluntumunrn.
/p ná=č †nɔ·e·ləntamə́ne·n.
/t Then we will be convinced.
/kl and it sufficeth us.

Jn 14.9
/b Nhesus tulao, Bqc vuh svaki kwetavpemulwvmw,
/p nčí·sas təlá·ɔ, "yúkwe=háč sháki kəwitahpi·məlúhəmɔ,
/t Jesus said to him, "Have I been with you up to now,
/kl Jesus saith unto him, Have I been so long time with you,

/b ok mutu kwavei, Pilup?
/p ɔ́·k máta ko·wa·hí·i, †pílap?
/t and you don't know me, Philip?
/kl and yet hast thou not known me, Philip?

/b Awrn nretc, wnroo Wrtwxifi;
/p awé·n ne·í·t·e, wəne·ó·ɔ we·t·o·x·ínki.
/t If anyone sees me, he sees the father.
/kl he that hath seen me hath seen the Father;

/b tu vuh kwnhi len punwntulenrn Wrtwxif?
/p tá=háč kúnči-lí·n, 'pənuntəlí·ne·n we·t·ó·x·ink'?
/t How is it that you say to me, 'Show us the father'?
/k and how sayest thou then, Shew us the Father?

Jn 14.10 /b Mutu vuh kwlamvetamwun ntcli Wrtwxif avpetaon
/p máta=háč ko·la·mhitamó·wən ntə́li- we·t·ó·x·ink -ahpí·taɔ·n,
/t Don't you believe that I am in the father,
/kl Believest thou not that I am in the Father,

/b ok ntcli Wrtwxif avpetakwn?
/p ó·k ntə́li- we·t·ó·x·ink -ahpi·tá·k·o·n?
/t and the father is in me?
/kl and the Father in me?

/b Nrl aptwnakunul rvlapwnalrq, takw ne nevluhi,
/p né·l a·pto·ná·k·anal ehəla·pto·nálle·kw takó· ní· nihəláči.
/t The words I speak to you are not of myself.
/kl the words that I speak unto you I speak not of myself:

/b Wrtwxumunt tu rpetaet, mwekumoswakun.
/p we·t·ó·x·əmənt=tá e·p·í·tai·t mwi·kəmɔ·s·əwá·k·an.
/t It's the deed of the father who is in me.
/kl but the Father that dwelleth in me, he doeth the works.

Jn 14.11 /b Wulamvetael, ntuli Wrtwxumunt avpetaon
/p wəla·mhítai·l, ntə́li- we·t·ó·x·əmənt -ahpí·taɔ·n,
/t Believe me, that I am in the father,
/kl Believe me that I am in the Father,

/b ok ntcli Wrtwxumunt ‖ avpetakwn;
/p ó·k ntə́li- we·t·ó·x·əmənt -ahpi·tá·k·o·n.
/t and that the father is in me.
/kl and the Father in me:

(p. 181) /b vupi nc mekumoswakun wunhi wulamvetael.
/p hápi nə́ mi·kəmɔ·s·əwá·k·an wə́nči-wəla·mhítai·l.
/t Also believe me because of those deeds.
/kl or else believe me for the very works' sake.

Jn 14.12 /b Kvehei, kvehei ktclwvmw, Awrn nvakaletc
/p khičí·i, khičí·i, ktəllúhəmɔ: awé·n nhaka·lí·t·e,
/t Truly, truly, I tell you: if anyone has faith in me,
/kl Verily, verily, I say unto you, He that believeth on me,

/b nrkuh nc tulumekuntamun ne rlu nekuntamu,   [⟨rlu nekunt-⟩ for ⟨rlumekunt-⟩]
/p né·k·a=č nə́ təlami·kə́ntamən ní· e·lami·kə́ntama.
/t *he* shall do the deeds that *I* do.
/kl the works that I do, shall he do also;

/b okh alwe larvosw,
/p ɔ́·k=č aləwí·i-laehɔ́·s·u.
/t And he shall do greater ones.
/kl and greater works than these shall he do;

/b rli Nwxifh ntav.
/p é·li nó·x·ink=č ntá.
/t For I will go to my father.
/kl because I go unto my Father.

Jn 14.13 /b Tuk tu krkw wenwrrqc wunhi ne, nuh nc ktulenumunro;
/p tákta kéku wi·nəwe·é·k·we wə́nči ní·, ná=č nə́ ktəli·naməné·ɔ.
/t If you ask for anything by means of me, that will happen for you.
/kl And whatsoever ye shall ask in my name, that will I do,

/b Wrqesifh wunhi xifovkunemkwsen Wrtwxumunt.
/p we·k·wí·s·ink=č wwə́nči-xinkɔhkəni·mkwə́s·i·n we·t·ó·x·əmənt.
/t The father will be glorified because of the son.
/kl that the Father may be glorified in the Son.

Jn 14.14 /b Tuktu krkw wenwumerqc qenwrlxulunro,
/p tákta kéku wi·nəwamié·k·we, kəwi·nəwe·lxələné·ɔ;
/t If you ask me for anything, I ask for it *for* you.
/kl If ye shall ask any thing in my name,

/b nuh nc ntclsen.
/p ná=č nə́ ntə́lsi·n.
/t That's what I will do.
/kl I will do it.

Jn 14.15 /b Avolerqc, ktulsenroh rlexif ntupuntwakun.
/p "ahɔ·lié·k·we, ktəlsi·né·ɔ=č e·lí·x·ink ntap·antəwá·k·an.
/t "If you love me, you must act according to my commandments.
/kl If ye love me, keep my commandments.

Jn 14.16
/b   Nc luserqc nwenwumuh Wrtwxumunt,
/p   nə́ ləs·ié·k·we, nəwi·nəwáma=č we·t·ó·x·əmənt.
/t   If you do that, I will ask the father.
/kl And I will pray the Father,

/b   kmelkwuh peli wcvwlatrnamwvalwrsu,
/p   kəmi·lkúwa=č pí·li wehwəla·te·namo·ha·ləwé·s·a.
/t   He will give you another "comforter."
/kl and he shall give you another Comforter,

/b   nanih heme qetavpemkwu,
/p   náni=č či·mí·i kəwitahpi·mkúwa.
/t   He shall be with you always.
/kl that he may abide with you for ever;

Jn 14.17
/b   nul nu wrlamwrokunet Manutw,
/p   nál ná we·la·məwe·ó·k·ani·t manɔ́t·u.
/t   He is the spirit who is truth.
/kl Even the Spirit of truth;

/b   b cntu lawsehek taa kotalaewao,
/p   yú entala·wsí·č·i·k tá=á· kɔt·a·la·iwwá·ɔ,
/t   The people of the world will not want him,
/kl whom the world cannot receive,

/b   rli taa nrovtet, ok rli taa wavavtet;
/p   é·li- tá=á· -ne·óhti·t, ɔ́·k é·li- tá=á· -wwa·háhti·t.
/t   because they will not see him, and because they will not know him.
/kl because it seeth him not, neither knoweth him:

/b   jwq kelwu kwavawu, rli avpetaqrq
/p   šúkw ki·ló·wa ko·wa·háwwa, é·li-ahpi·tá·k·we·kw.
/t   But *you* know him, because he is in you.
/kl but ye know him; for he dwelleth with you,

/b   okh hemei kvakywaif avpw.
/p   ɔ́·k=č či·mí·i khak·ayəwá·ink ahpú.
/t   And he will be in you always.
/kl and shall be in you.

Jn 14.18
/b   Taa navlei kunukalulwvwmw, kcnh vatrkc wulatrnumwakun,
/p   tá=á· nahəlí·i kənək·aləlo·húmɔ, kə́nč hat·é·k·e wəla·te·naməwá·k·an.
/t   I will not leave you in any case until there is happiness.
/kl I will not leave you comfortless:

/b kwtxulvwmwh.
/p ko·txəlhúmɔ=č.
/t I will come to you.
/kl I will come to you.

Jn 14.19 /b Heh tvaketi, nuh b cntu lawsehek mutu heh nrvkwunro,
/p čí·č thakíti, ná=č yú entala·wsí·č·i·k máta čí·č nne·yko·wəné·ɔ.
/t A little while yet, and then the people of the world will see me no more.
/kl Yet a little while, and the world seeth me no more;

/b jwqh kelwu knrevmw; rli lclrxru,
/p šúkw=č ki·ló·wa kəne·íhəmɔ, é·li-lehəle·x·é·a.
/t But you will see me because I live.
/kl but ye see me: because I live,

/b krpwuh klclrxrvmw.
/p ké·pəwa=č kəlehəle·x·éhəmɔ.
/t And you also shall live.
/kl ye shall live also.

Jn 14.20 /b Nunih lukveqi kwatwnroh ntuli Nwx vokrf avpen,
/p nə́ni=č ləkhíkwi ko·wa·to·né·ɔ=č ntə́li- nó·x hók·enk -ahpí·n,
/t At that time you will know that I am in my Father's body,
/kl At that day ye shall know that I am in my Father,

/b ok krpwu ktcli nvakrf avpenro, ok ne ntuli kvakybaif avpen.
/p ɔ́·k ké·pəwa ktə́li- nhák·enk -ahpi·né·ɔ, ɔ́·k ní· ntə́li- khak·ayəwá·ink -ahpí·n.
/t and that you also are in my body, and that *I* am in *your* bodies.
/kl and you in me, and I in you.

Jn 14.21 /b Awrnh wulvataqc ntupuntwakun, ok nunc lusetc,   [⟨wulvataqc⟩ for ⟨wulataqc⟩]
/p awé·n=č wəla·tá·k·we ntap·antəwá·k·an, ɔ́·k ná=nə ləs·í·t·e,
/t If anyone has my commandments, and if that is what they do,
/kl He that hath my commandments, and keepeth them,

/b nunul nu ntavolwq.
/p nánal ná ntahɔ́·lukw.
/t they are the one that loves me.
/kl he it is that loveth me:

/b Awrnh avoletc, Nwxoh tovolkw,
/p awé·n=č ahɔ·lí·t·e, nó·x·ɔ=č təhɔ́·lku.
/t If anyone loves me, they will be loved by my father.
/kl and he that loveth me shall be loved of my Father,

/b okh nrpc ntavolu,
/p ó·k=č né·pe ntahó·la.
/t And I will love them, too.
/kl and I will love him,

/b okh mpunwntulan nvaky.
/p ó·k=č mpənúntəla·n nhák·ay.
/t And I will show myself to them.
/kl and will manifest myself to him.

Jn 14.22 /b Nhwtus tulao (mutu xun tu nu Iskrliut rlwcnset,)
/p †nčó·tas təlá·ɔ (máta=xán=tá ná '†iská·liat' e·ləwénsi·t),
/t Judas said to him (not, however, the one called Iscariot),
/kl Judas saith unto him, not Iscariot,

/b Nrvlaleun, tuh vuh ktunumun wunhih nelwnu jwq punwntulerf kvaky?
/p "nehəlá·lian, tá·=č=háč ktənnə́mən, wə́nči-=č ni·ló·na šúkw -pənuntəlíenk khák·ay?"
/t "Master, what will you do in order to show yourself only to us?"
/kl Lord, how is it that thou wilt manifest thyself unto us, and not unto the world?

Jn 14.23 /b Nhesus tulao, Awrnh avoletc qwlrluntumunh ntaptwnakun;
/p nčí·sas təlá·ɔ, "awé·n=č ahɔ·lí·t·e, kwəle·ló́ntamən=č nta·pto·ná·k·an.
/t Jesus said to him, "If anyone loves me, they will take my words to heart.
/kl Jesus answered and said unto him, If a man love me, he will keep my words:

/b Nwxoh tovolkw,
/p nó·x·ɔ=č tɔhó·lku.
/t And they will be loved by my father.
/kl and my Father will love him,

/b nwtxawunuh, okh nwetarmawunu,
/p no·txá·wəna=č, ó·k=č nəwi·t·ae·má·wəna.
/t And we will come to them, and we will live with them.
/kl and we will come unto him, and make our abode with him.

Jn 14.24 /b Awrn mutu rvolet takw tulsewun rlwru.
/p awé·n máta ehó·li·t takó· təlsí·wən e·ləwé·a.
/t Anyone who does not love me does not do what I say.
/kl He that loveth me not keepeth not my sayings:

/b Aptwnakun puntamrq, takw ne ntaptwnakun,
/p a·pto·ná·k·an pɔ́ntame·kw takó· ní· nta·pto·ná·k·an,
/t The words that you hear are not *my* words,
/kl and the word which ye hear is not mine,

/b nrku ‖ Wrtwxumunt prtalwkalet.
/p né·k·a, we·t·ó·x·əmənt pe·t·alo·ká·li·t.
/t but *his*, the father who sent me.
/kl but the Father's which sent me.

Jn 14.25 /b Nrli aptwnakunu rlrq srki wetarmulrq.
(p. 182) /p né·li a·pto·ná·k·ana élle·kw sé·ki-wi·t·aé·məle·kw.
/t Those words are what I said to you while I was living with you.
/kl These things have I spoken unto you, being yet present with you.

Jn 14.26 /b Jwq Wcvwlatrnumwvalwrt nul nu Pelset Manutw,
/p šúkw wehwəla·te·namo·há·ləwe·t, nál ná pí·lsi·t manət·u.
/t But the "comforter," he is the holy spirit.
/kl But the Comforter, which is the Holy Ghost,

/b Wrtwxifi pwrtalwkalkwh ntclswakunif;
/p we·t·o·x·ínki pwe·t·alo·ká·lku=č ntəlsəwá·k·anink.
/t He will be sent by the father to act for me (*lit.*, 'in my power').
/kl whom the Father will send in my name,

/b nrkuh nu wrmi krkw ktulalrpomkwu,
/p né·k·a=č ná wé·mi kéku ktəlale·p·ɔ·mkúwa.
/t It is *he* that will teach you to do everything.
/kl he shall teach you all things,

/b okh wrmi cntxi lulrq kmekwmkwnro.
/p ɔ́·k=č wé·mi éntxi-ləle·kw kəmi·ko·mko·né·ɔ.
/t And he will remind you of everything I tell you.
/kl and bring all things to your remembrance, whatsoever I have said unto you.

Jn 14.27 /b Wulufwntwakun knukavtumwlvwmw;
/p wəlankuntəwá·k·an kənəkahtəmo·lhúmɔ.
/t I leave behind peace for you.
/kl Peace I leave with you,

/b nwlufwntwakun kmelunro
/p no·lankuntəwá·k·an kəmilləné·ɔ,
/t I give you my peace,
/k my peace I give unto you:

/b takw wunhi wcvcnhi nuxpufwntet b cntu lawset.
/p takó· wə́nči wehə́nči-naxpankúnti·t yú entalá·wsi·t.
/t but not because of the reasons why people give presents to each other.
/k not as the world giveth, give I unto you.

Text, Transcription, and Translation

        /b   Kahi suqrluntufvrq ktrvwaif, ok kahi alumevrq.
        /p   káči sak·we·ləntánkhe·kw ktehəwá·ink, ɔ́·k káči a·ləmí·he·kw.
        /t   Don't be troubled in your hearts, and don't be afraid.
        /k   Let not your heart be troubled, neither let it be afraid.

Jn 14.28   /b   Kpuntaevmw, ntcli lwrn, paleh ntav, ok lupih mpav.
        /p   kpəntaíhəmɔ, ntɔ́li-lúwe·n, 'palí·i=č ntá, ɔ́·k lápi=č mpá.'
        /t   You have heard me say, 'I will go away, and I will come back.'
        /kl   Ye have heard how I said unto you, I go away, and come again unto you.

        /b   Avolerqch kwlrluntamwvmw rli lulrq Wrtwxumuntifh ntav;
        /p   ahɔ·lié·k·we=č, ko·le·ləntamúhəmɔ é·li-lɔ́le·kw, 'we·t·o·x·əmɔ́ntink=č ntá',
        /t   If you love me, you will be happy that I told you I was going to the father,
        /kl   If ye loved me, ye would rejoice, because I said, I go unto the Father:

        /b   rli Nwx alwei luset ne rlkeqi luseu.
        /p   é·li- nó·x -aləwí·i-lɔ́s·i·t ní· e·lkí·kwi-lɔ́s·ia.
        /t   as my father is greater than *I* am.
        /k   for my Father is greater than I.

Jn 14.29   /b   Bqc mrhi ktulunro nrlumu nc rlrk,
        /p   yúkwe mé·či ktəlləné·ɔ né·ləma nə́ é·le·k,
        /t   Now I have told you before it happened,
        /kl   And now I have told you before it come to pass,

        /b   wunhih keji lrkc wulamvetamrq.
        /p   wə́nči-=č kíši-lé·k·e -wəla·mhítame·kw.
        /t   so that, after it happens, you will believe it.
        /k   that, when it is come to pass, ye might believe.

Jn 14.30   /b   Bqc wunhi taa xrli krkw ktulwvwmw;
        /p   "yúkwe wə́nči tá=á· xé·li kéku ktəllúhəmɔ,
        /t   "From now on I won't say very much to you,
        /kl   Hereafter I will not talk much with you:

        /b   rli wuntu xat myai nekanexif tali cntu lawsif,
        /p   é·li- wə́ntax -á·t mayá·i-ni·k·a·ní·x·ink táli entalá·wsink.
        /t   as the true leader in the world is coming here,
        /kl   for the prince of this world cometh,

        /b   takw tcxi vatri nvakrf krkw nrvlatuf;
        /p   takó· téxi hat·é·i nhák·enk kéku nehəlá·t·ank.
        /t   and the things he is master of are not at all in me.
        /kl   and hath nothing in me.

Jn 14.31 /b jwq wunhih b cntu lawset watwn ntcli avolan Wrtwxumunt
          /p šúkw wwə́nči-=č yú entalá·wsi·t -wwá·to·n ntə́li-ahó·la·n we·t·ó·x·əmənt,
          /t But because of it the world will know that I love the father,
          /kl But that the world may know that I love the Father;

          /b ok ntcli myai lusen rletup Wrtwxumunt.
          /p ɔ́·k ntə́li-mayá·i-lə́s·i·n e·lí·t·əp we·t·ó·x·əmənt.
          /t and that I do exactly what the father told me.
          /kl and as the Father gave me commandment, even so I do.

          /b Pavswqeq alumskatumwq b wunhi.
          /p pahsúk·wi·kw; aləmská·t·amo·kw yú wə́nči."
          /t Get up; let us depart from here."
          /kl Arise, let us go hence.

Chapter 108 (pp. 182-183). [L. section 108.] (Mark 14.17; Luke 22.14-18, 21-23; Mark 14.18-
     26; Matthew 24.22-30.

Mk 14.17 /b Mrhi loqekc ekali tumekrp nc wekwavmif, ok nrk atux neju.
         /p mé·či lɔ·k·wí·k·e íkali təmí·k·e·p nə́ wi·k·əwáhəmink, ɔ́·k né·k átax ní·š·a.
         /t After evening came, he went into that house, and also the twelve.
         /l And in the evening he cometh with the twelve [*into that house*].

Lk 22.14 /b Mrhi tpusqevlakc,
         /p mé·či tpəskwihəlá·k·e,
         /t When the time had come,
         /l And when the hour was come [*to eat the passover*]

         /b ekali mujakrp cvcntu metsif, ok atux neju rlwkalunhek.
         /p íkali məšá·ke·p ehə́nta-mí·tsink, ɔ́·k átax ní·š·a e·lo·ka·lə́nči·k
         /t he sat on the floor in the eating area, and also the twelve apostles ('messengers').
         /l he sat down, and the twelve apostles with him.

Lk 22.15 /b Nu tulan, Nenwhi ntrvif tali aeuntaman
         /p ná tə́la·n, "nni·núči- nté·hink -táli-a·yántamən,
         /t Then he said to them, "I have long desired it in my heart,
         /kl And he said unto them, With desire I have desired

         /b ok uskrluntum qepwmulunro bqc bni,
         /p ɔ́·k -aske·lə́ntam kəwi·po·mələné·ɔ yúkwe yó·ni,
         /t and been impatient to eat this with you,
         /kl to eat this passover with you

         /b nrlumu amuxavrluntamwu.
         /p né·ləma amax·ahe·ləntamó·wa.

	/t	before my great suffering.
	/kl	before I suffer.

Lk 22.16
- /b Rli ktulwvmw, ta heh numehewun,
- /p é·li ktəllúhəmɔ, tá=á· čí·č nəmi·č·í·wən,
- /t For I say to you, I will not eat it again,
- /kl For I say unto you, I will not any more eat thereof,

- /b kunh pavkunhi lrkc tali Krtanutwet sokemaokunif.
- /p kə́nč pahkánči-lék·e táli ke·tanət·ó·wi·t sɔ·k·i·ma·ɔ́·k·anink."
- /t until it is fulfilled in God's kingdom."
- /kl until it be fulfilled in the kingdom of God.

Lk 22.17
- /b Nu wrtunimun munrokun nu tuli krnamwen;
- /p ná wwe·t·ənə́mən məne·ɔ́·k·an, ná tə́li-ke·ná·mwi·n.
- /t Then he took some drink in his hand and proceeded to give thanks.
- /kl And he took the cup, and gave thanks,

- /b tulao, Wrtunumwq b avkavmaovteq.
- /p təlá·ɔ, "we·t·ənə́mo·kw yú, ahkahəmá·ɔhti·kw.
- /t And he said to them, "Take this and share it among yourselves.
- /kl and said, Take this, and divide it among yourselves:

Lk 22.18
- /b Rli ‖ ktulwvmw, taa nmunrwun b wesavkemenapw,
- /p é·li ktəllúhəmɔ, tá=á· nəməné·wən yú wisahki·mi·ná·p·u,
- /t For I say to you, I will not drink this wine
- /kl For I say unto you, I will not drink of the fruit of the vine,

(p. 183)
- /b kunh prerekc sokemaokun Krtanitwet,
- /p kə́nč pe·ye·í·k·e sɔ·k·i·ma·ɔ́·k·an ke·tanət·ó·wi·t."
- /t until God's kingdom comes."
- /k until the kingdom of God shall come.

Mk 14.18
- /b Nrli lumutavpevtet ok metsevtet, Nhesus tulao, Kvehei ktulwvmw,
- /p né·li-ləmatahpíhti·t ɔ́·k -mi·tsíhti·t, nčí·sas təlá·ɔ, "khičí·i ktəllúhəmɔ,
- /t As they sat and ate, Jesus said to them, "I say to you truly,
- /kl And as they sat and did eat, Jesus said, Verily I say unto you,

- /b mrawset kelwu wepwmerq, mvalumaonh nvaky.
- /p me·á·wsi·t ki·ló·wa wi·pó·mie·kw mhalamáɔ·n=č nhák·ay.
- /t one of you who are eating with me shall sell me out.
- /kl One of you which eateth with me shall betray me.

Lk 22.21 /b Jr mclamwnth nvaky wunaxk wihi cvcntulepwifif vatr.
/p šé·, méhəlamunt=č nhák·ay wənáxk wíči ehəntali·p·wínkink hát·e·."
/t See, the hand of the one who will sell me out is here on the table with the others."
/kl ... behold, the hand of him that betrayeth me is with me on the table.

Lk 22.23 /b Nu tolumi nevlahi ntwtumaotenro
/p ná tólǝmi- nihəláči -nto·t·əma·ɔhti·né·ɔ,
/t Then they began to ask each *other*
/kl And they began to enquire among themselves,

/b awrnh tu nu rlset.
/p awé·n=č=tá ná é·lsi·t.
/t who would be the one to do it.
/kl which of them it was that should do this thing.

Mk 14.19 /b Alumi avi jerluntumwk;
/p áləmi-áhi-ši·e·lə́ntamo·k.
/t And they began to be very sad.
/k And they began to be sorrowful, ...
/kl And they were exceeding sorrowful,   (Matthew 26.22)

/b ok nanvkwti tulawao, Ne vuh Nrvlaleun?
/p ɔ́·k †nənk·wə́ti təlawwá·ɔ, "ní·=háč, nehəlá·lian?"
/t And one by one they said to him, "Is it me, master?"
/l and began to say unto him one by one, Lord, is it I? and another said, Is it I?
/k ... and to say unto him one by one, Is it I? and another said, Is it I?

Mk 14.20 /b Tulao, kelwu mrawset atux neju cntxerq
/p təlá·ɔ, "ki·ló·wa me·á·wsi·t átax ní·š·a entxíe·kw,
/t He said to them, "One of *you* twelve,
/kl And he answered and said unto them, It is one of the twelve,

/b wihi amuxkrmet li lokcnsif,
/p wíči-amaxké·mi·t lí lɔ·k·énsink,
/t who sops up food with me in the dish,
/kl that dippeth with me in the dish,

Mt 26.23 /b nulh nu li mvalumaon nvaky.
/p nál=č ná lí-mhalamáɔ·n nhák·ay.
/t *he* will be the one to sell me out.
/kl the same shall betray me.

Mk 14.21 /b Piji alumskr Linw Wrqesif li rlrkvasek wunhi voky;
/p píši alə́mske· lə́nu we·k·wí·s·ink lí e·le·khá·s·i·k wə́nči hó·k·ay.
/t The man who is the Son indeed departs in the way that was written about him.
/l The Son of man indeed goeth, as it was determined, *and* is written of him:

/b   Jwqh ktumaki lenum nu linw mrvlamwnth Wrqeselifi linwu;
/p   šúkw=č ktəmáki-lí·nam ná lə́nu méhəlamunt=č we·k·wi·s·i·línki lə́nəwa.
/t   But a miserable fate will befall the man who sells out the man who is the Son.
/kl   but woe unto that man by whom the Son of man is betrayed!   (= Mt 26.24)

/b   jeki a mav mutu vuji qejekewunrp.
/p   ší·ki=á·=máh máta háši kwi·š·i·k·í·wəne·p."
/t   It would have been better for him never to have been born."
/kl   good were it for that man if he had never been born.   (Cf. Mt 26.24.)

Mt 26.25 /b   Nu nu Nhwtus krtu mvalumwnt, tulan, Nrvlaleun, ne vuh?
/p   ná ná †nčó·tas ké·t·a-mhálamunt tóla·n, "nehəlá·lian, ní·=háč?"
/t   Then the Judas who was intending to sell him out said to him, "Master, is it me?"
/kl   Then Judas, which betrayed him, answered and said, Master, is it I?

/b   Tulkw, Nanc lr rlwrun.
/p   tə́lku, "ná=nə lé· e·ləwé·an."
/t   He replied to him, "What you say is so."
/k   He said unto him, Thou hast said.

Mt 26.26 /b   Nrli metsevtet, Nhesus wrtunum avpon, wlapcntamwvatamun,
/p   né·li-mi·tsíhti·t, nčí·sas wé·t·ənəm ahpó·n, o·la·p·entamo·há·t·amən.
/t   While they were eating, Jesus took some bread and blessed it.
/kl   And as they were eating, Jesus took bread, and blessed it,

/b   nu pwpvakrnumun, ok mwelan rkrkemahi;
/p   ná puphaké·nəmən, ó·k mwí·la·n e·k·e·ki·má·č·i.
/t   Then he tore off pieces and gave them to his diciples.
/kl   and brake it, and gave it to his disciples,

/b   tulao wrtunumwq, meheq;
/p   təlá·ɔ, "we·t·ənə́mo·kw, mí·č·i·kw.
/t   He said to them, "Take it and eat it.
/kl   and said, Take, eat;

Lk 22.19 /b   nunul bni navtwvrpi meltif wunhi kelwu;
/p   nánal yó·ni nahtuhé·p·i, mí·ltink wə́nči ki·ló·wa.
/t   This is my body, which is given for you.
/kl   This is my body which is given for you:

/b   nunih ktevlunumunro ktulih mijalenro.
/p   nə́ni=č ktihələnəməné·ɔ, ktə́li-=č -məša·li·né·ɔ."
/t   That's what you must always do in order to remember me."
/k   this do in remembrance of me.

Mt 26.27 /b Keji mehetetc, nu ok nc wrtunumun wesavkemenapw, krnamw,
/p kíši-mi·č·ihtí·t·e, ná ɔ́·k nə́ wwe·t·ənə́mən wisahki·mi·ná·p·u, ke·ná·mu.
/t After they had eaten it, then he also took the wine, and he gave thanks.
/l Likewise also after supper, he took the cup, and gave thanks,
/k (Lk 22.20) Likewise also the cup after supper, saying, ...
(Mt 26.27) And he took the cup, and gave thanks, ...
(Mk 14.23) And he took the cup, and when he had given thanks, ...

/b ok mwelan, tulao; Wrmi cntxerq munrq
/p ɔ́·k mwí·la·n, təlá·ɔ, "wé·mi entxíe·kw, məné·kw."
/t And he gave it to them, saying to them, "All of you, drink some."
/l and gave it to them, saying, Drink ye all of it;
/k (Lk 22.20)... saying, This cup is the new testament in my blood, which is shed for you.
(Mt 26.27) ... and gave it to them, saying, Drink ye all of it;
(Mk 14.23) ... he gave it to them: ...

Mk 14.23 /b wrmi mwunrnro.
/p wé·mi mwəne·né·ɔ.
/t And they all drank it.
/kl and they all drank of it.

Mt 26.28 /b Nunul bni nmwkwm; swkavlak wunhi wuski nuxkwntwakun
/p "nánal yó·ni nəmó·kəm, so·k·áhəla·k wə́nči wə́ski-naxkuntəwá·k·an,
/t "This is my blood, which was shed for the new covenant,
/l This is my blood, (the blood) of the new testament,

/b wunhih kelwu, ok xrli awrn pavketatumwnt honawswakun.
/p wə́nči-=č ki·ló·wa ɔ́·k xé·li awé·n -pahki·t·á·t·amunt čɔna·wsəwá·k·an.
/t so that you and many people will have their sins forgiven.
/k which is shed for you, and for many, for the remission of sins.

1 Corinthians 11.25
/b Nunih ktevlunumunro,
/p nə́ni=č ktihələnəməné·ɔ.
/t That's what you must make a practice of doing.
/l This do ye,

/b cjih nc lunumrq, kmujalevmw.
/p éši=č nə́ -lə́nəme·kw, kəməš·a·líhəmɔ.
/t Whenever you do that, you will remember me.
/l as oft as ye drink it, in remembrance of me.

Mt 26.29 /b Kvehei ktulwvmw, Ta lupi nmunrwun b wesavkemenapwv,
/p khičí·i ktəllúhəmɔ, tá=á· lápi nəməné·wən yú wisahki·mi·ná·p·u,
/t I tell you truly, I will not drink this wine again,

/l Verily I say unto you, I will not drink henceforth of this fruit of the vine,
/k (Mk 14.25) Verily I say unto you, I will drink no more of the fruit of the vine,
/k (Mt 26.29) But I say unto you, I will not drink henceforth of this fruit of the vine,

Mt 26.29 /b svaki nc kejqek, rlkeqi wuskif munrufq tali Nwx sokemaokunif.
/p sháki nə́ kí·škwi·k, e·lkí·kwi- wə́skink -məné·ankw táli nó·x sɔ·k·i·ma·ɔ́·k·anink.
/t up until the day when we drink the new (wine) in my father's kingdom."
/kl until that day when I drink it new with you in my Father's kingdom.

(L. sect. 108 ends here.)

Mt 26.30 /b Nu toswenro,
/p ná tɔ·s·o·wi·né·ɔ.
/t Then they sang,
/k —

/b keji naxkwvmavtetc, eku wunhi kheok, eku rok olipe ovhwf. ‖
/p kíši-naxkuhəmahtí·t·e, íka wə́nči-kčí·ɔk, íka é·ɔk †ɔlipí·i-ɔhčúnk.
/t and after singing (a hymn?), they went out from there and went to Olive Mountain.
/k (Mt 26.30 and Mk 14.26) And when they had sung an hymn, they went out into the mount of Olives. (Verse not in L.)

Chapter 109 (pp. 184-185). [L. section 109.] (Luke 22.24-38)

Lk 22.24   /b Nrlwxwctet pumencvwtvatwuk,
(p. 184) /p ne·lo·x·wéhti·t, pəmi·neho·thátəwak
/t As they walked, they all argued with each other,
/kl And there was also a strife among them,

/b wunhi rli a mawsw xifwrlumwqset.
/p wə́nči é·li-=á· má·wsu -xinkwe·ləmúkwsi·t.
/t about how one of them would be considered great.
/k/ which of them should be accounted the greatest.

Lk 22.25 /b Jwq, tulao, Sakemaok b cntu lawsif pwunwntvekrnro rlkeqi lusevtet,
/p šúkw təlá·ɔ, "sa·k·i·má·ɔk yú entalá·wsink pwənunthike·né·ɔ e·lkí·kwi-ləs·íhti·t.
/t But he said to them, "The kings of the world show people how much they do,
/kl And he said unto them, The kings of the Gentiles exercise lordship over them;

/b ok mrxifwi lusehek lwivlaok wetavrfrhek.
/p ɔ́·k me·x·ínkwi-ləs·í·č·i·k luwihəlá·ɔk wi·t·a·henké·č·i·k.
/t and those that do great things are called helpers of the people.
/kl and they that exercise authority upon them are called benefactors.

Lk 22.26 /b Jwq kelwu kahi nc lusevrq;
          /p šúkw ki·ló·wa, káči nə́ ləs·í·he·kw.
          /t But *you*, don't be that way.
          /kl But ye shall not be so:

          /b kelwu cntxerq, awrn rlwe luset, lrlumw trfsesetif;
          /p ki·ló·wa entxíe·kw awé·n e·ləwí·i-lə́s·i·t, lé·ləmo· tenksi·sí·t·ink,
          /t Anyone of all of you that is the greatest, consider him like the most junior,
          /kl but he that is greatest among you, let him be as the younger;

          /b ok nekanexif lusetch alwkakun rlset.
          /p ɔ́·k ni·k·a·ní·x·ink, ləs·í·t·e=č alo·ka·k·an é·lsi·t.
          /t and (consider him) as the the leading one, if he does as a servant does.   [reversed]
          /kl and he that is chief, as he that doth serve.

Lk 22.27 /b Tu vuh rlenaqset alwe lusw,
          /p tá=háč e·li·ná·kwsi·t aləwí·i-ləs·u,
          /t Which one is greater,
          /kl For whether is greater,

          /b cntu wepwntif lrmuvtupet, ok eku cntu mekumoset?
          /p énta-wi·púntink le·mahtáp·i·t, ɔ́·k íka énta-mi·kəmɔ́·s·i·t?
          /t one who sits at the meal, or one who works there?
          /kl he that sitteth at meat, or he that serveth?

          /b mutu vuh nu metset?
          /p máta=háč ná mí·tsi·t?
          /t Isn't it the one who eats?
          /kl is not he that sitteth at meat?

          /b Jwq ne cntu wetavpemulrq ntulsen alwkakun rlset.
          /p šúkw ní· énta-witahpí·məle·kw ntə́lsi·n alo·ká·k·an é·lsi·t.
          /t But *I*, when I am with you, am as a servant is.
          /kl but I am among you as he that serveth.

Lk 22.28 /b Kelwu amunhei kwetavpemivmw taoni ntaeavi lenum.
          /p ki·ló·wa amənčí·i kəwitahpi·míhəmɔ, tá·ɔni nta·yáhi·lí·nam.
          /t *You* persevere with me despite my tribulations.
          /kl Ye are they which have continued with me in my temptations.

Lk 22.29 /b Sakemaokunh kmelwvmw mulaji Nwx rli meletup;
          /p sa·k·i·ma·ɔ́·k·an=č kəmillúhəmɔ, málahši nó·x é·li·mi·lí·t·əp,
          /t I will give you a kingdom, the way my father has given one to me,
          /kl And I appoint unto you a kingdom, as my Father hath appointed unto me;

Lk 22.30 /b   ktulih wepwmenro, tali nsakemaokunif,
/p   ktə́li-=č -wi·po·mi·né·ɔ táli nsa·k·i·ma·ɔ́·k·anink
/t   so that you will eat with me in my kingdom
/kl   That ye may eat and drink at my table in my kingdom,

/b   ok lumutavpenro sakemae lrvlumutuvpifif,
/p   ɔ́·k -ləmatahpi·né·ɔ sa·k·i·ma·í·i-lehələmatahpínkink,
/t   and sit on thrones,
/kl   and sit on thrones

/b   ktulih krnavkevanro nrk tclcn ok neju cntxakrehek Isluluk.
/p   ktə́li-=č -ke·nahki·ha·né·ɔ né·k télən ɔ́·k ní·š·a entxa·ke·í·č·i·k †isəlɔ́lak."
/t   in order to take care of the twelve tribes of Israel."
/kl   judging the twelve tribes of Israel.

Lk 22.31 /b   Ok Nhesus lwr Symun, Symun, mavtuntw kutalwq,
/p   ɔ́·k nčí·sas lúwe·, "†sáiman, †sáiman, mahtánt·u kkat·á·lukw,
/t   And Jesus said, "Simon, Simon, the devil desires you,
/kl   And the Lord said, Simon, Simon, behold, Satan hath desired to have you,

/b   ktuli a pawunvkwn, mulaji vwet cvlukveqi wuli pawunasek;
/p   ktə́li-=á· -pawə́nk·o·n, málahši hwí·t ehələkhíkwi-wə́li-pawəná·s·i·k.
/t   so that he can sift you, like wheat at the times when it is well sifted.
/kl   that he may sift you as wheat:

Lk 22.32 /b   jwq kpatamwrlxul, li a knakatamwrokun mutu txilri;
/p   šúkw kpa·tamwé·lxəl, lí-=á· kəna·ka·t·amwe·ɔ́·k·an máta -txihəlé·i.
/t   But I have prayed for you, so that your faith would not dissipate.
/kl   But I have prayed for thee, that thy faith fail not:

/b   qwlupeunc hetanelarmwmc kemavtusuk.
/p   kwələp·iáne, či·t·ani·lae·mó·me ki·mahtə́s·ak."
/t   And after you are converted, strengthen the hearts of your brothers."
/kl   and when thou art converted, strengthen thy brethren.

Lk 22.33 /b   Tulkw, Nrvlaleun, fejunaqsi ktulih wehrwulun,
/p   tə́lku, "nehəlá·lian, nki·š·əná·kwsi, ktə́li-=č -wi·č·é·wələn,
/t   He relpied to him, "Master, I am ready to go with you,
/kl   And he said unto him, Lord, I am ready to go with thee,

/b   li cventu kpavwtif, ok cvctu nveltif.   [⟨cvctu⟩ for ⟨cventu⟩]
/p   lí ehənta-kpahó·t·ink, ɔ́·k ehənta-nhíltink."
/t   to prison and the place of execution."
/k   both into prison, and to death.

Lk 22.34 /b Tulao, kvehei ktulul Petul,
/p təláꞏɔ, "khičíꞏi ktə́ləl, †píꞏtəl,
/t And he said to him, "I tell you truly, Peter,
/kl And he said, I tell thee, Peter,

/b Tepas ta kunhemwei
/p típaꞏs tá=áꞏ kənčiꞏmwíꞏi,
/t The rooster ('chicken') will not crow
/kl the cock shall not crow this day,

/b kcnh nuxun keji pavswranc ktuli waven!
/p kə́nč naxə́n kíši-pahsəwéꞏane ktə́li-wwáꞏhiꞏn."
/t until you have denied that you know me three times."
/kl before that thou shalt thrice deny that thou knowest me.

Lk 22.35 /b Nu tulan, nckc rlwkalrqc,
/p ná təlaꞏn, "néke eꞏloꞏkalléꞏkꞏwe,
/t Then he said to them, "When I sent you forth,
/kl And he said unto them, When I sent you

/b mutu krnumwrqc moni rvatrk ok mnwtrs, krkw rvatwf, ok hepavko,
/p máta kennəmoꞏwéꞏkꞏwe móni ehháteꞏk, ɔ́ꞏk mənóꞏtꞏeꞏs kéku ehhátunk, ɔ́ꞏk čípahkɔ,
/t and you didn't have a purse for money, or a bag to put things in, or shoes,
/kl without purse, and scrip, and shoes,

/b knwntcvlavmwp vuh krkw?
/p kənuntehəláhəmɔꞏp=háč kéku?"
/t did you lack anything?"
/k lacked ye any thing?

/b Lwrok takw.
/p luwéꞏɔk, "takóꞏ."
/t They said, "No."
/k And they said, Nothing.

Lk 22.36 /b Tulao, Jwq bqc wulataqc moni cvatrk, qwnumunh,
/p təláꞏɔ, "šúkw yúkwe, [awéꞏn] wəlaꞏtáꞏkꞏwe móni ehháteꞏk, kwənnə́mən=č,
/t He said to them, "But now, if [anyone] has a purse for money, he must carry it,
/kl Then said he unto them, But now, he that hath a purse, let him take it,

/b ok mnwtrs, ok awrn mutu wulataqc ‖ xifonjekun
/p ɔ́ꞏk mənóꞏtꞏeꞏs; ɔ́ꞏk awéꞏn máta wəlaꞏtáꞏkꞏwe xinkɔnšíꞏkꞏan,
/t and a bag; and if anyone does not have a sword,
/k and likewise his scrip: and he that hath no sword,

(p. 185) /b mvalumwntch cvavqehi wunhih mvaluf;
/p mhalamúnteč ehahkwí·č·i, wə́nči-=č -mhálank.
/t let him sell his clothing in order to buy one.
/kl let him sell his garment, and buy one.

Lk 22.37 /b rli ktulwvmw. Elih nc pavkunhi lr nvakrf rlwrfup,
/p é·li ktəllúhəmɔ, ílli=č nə́ pahkánči-lé· nhák·enk e·ləwénkəp:
/t For I say to you, what was said must even be fulfilled in me:
/kl For I say unto you, that this that is written must yet be accomplished in me,

/b Wetavkemkwsw mrtawsetekri.
/p 'witahki·mkwə́s·u me·t·a·wsi·t·i·ké·i.'
/t 'He was counted in among the sinners.'
/k And he was reckoned among the transgressors:

Lk 22.38 /b Rli wrmi rlrkvasek wunhi nvaky alumi pavkunhi lr.
/p é·li wé·mi e·le·khá·s·i·k wə́nči nhák·ay áləmi-pahkánči-lé·."
/t For everything written about me is beginning to be fulfilled."
/k for the things concerning me have an end.

/b Tulawao Nrvlalerf, jr bl neju amufunjekunu.
/p təlawwá·ɔ, "nehəlá·lienk, šé· yó·l ní·š·a amankanší·k·ana."
/t They said to him, "Master, here are two swords."
/kl And they said, Lord, behold, here are two swords.

/b Tulao, Trpi tu.
/p təlá·ɔ, "tépi=tá."
/t He said to them, "It's enough."
/k And he said unto them, It is enough.

Chapter 110 (pp. 185-191). [L. section 110.] (John 15.1-27, 16.1-33, 17.1-26)

Jn 15.1 /b Nhesus tulao, Ne, tu myai wesavkemwnji, Nwx rkevrt,
/p nčí·sas təlá·ɔ, "ní·=tá mayá·i-wisahki·múnši, nó·x e·kí·he·t.
/t Jesus said to them, "I am the true vine, and my father is the grower.
/kl Jesus said: I am the true vine, and my Father is the husbandman.

Jn 15.2 /b Wrmi cntxif twvnututu nvakrf cntxi mutu krkw eku tali kejekif,
/p wé·mi éntxink tuhənət·ə́t·a nhák·enk, éntxi- máta kéku íka -táli-ki·š·í·k·ink,
/t Every branch that is in me and that has nothing growing on it,
/k Every branch in me that beareth not fruit

/b poketwnuh.
/p pɔk·í·t·o·n=č.
/t he will discard.
/k he taketh away:

/b Ok twvnututu cntxi krkw eku tali kejekif; pweletwnu
/p ɔ́·k tuhənət·ɔ́t·a éntxi- kéku íka -táli-ki·š·í·k·ink, pwi·li·tó·na,
/t And as many branches as have something growing on them, he prunes,
/k and every branch that beareth fruit, he purgeth it, [RSV "he prunes"]

/b wcnhih avalwe eku tali kejekif.
/p wénči-=č ahaləwí·i íka -táli-ki·š·í·k·ink.
/t so that even more will grow there.
/k that it may bring forth more fruit.

Jn 15.3
/b Bqc kpelsevmw wunhi ntaptwnakunu rlaptwnalrq.
/p yúkwe kpi·lsíhəmɔ wə́nči nta·pto·ná·k·ana e·la·pto·nálle·kw.
/t Now you are clean by means of my words that I have spoken to you.
/k Now ye are clean through the word which I have spoken unto you.

Jn 15.4
/b Avpetaeq, nrpch ktupetwlvwmw.
/p ahpí·tai·kw, né·pe=č ktap·i·to·lhúmɔ.
/t Be in me, and I will also be in you.
/k Abide in me, and I in you.

/b Wesavkemwnjei twvnutut, ta nevlahi krkw eku wunhi kejekunwi
/p wisahki·munšíí·i-tuhənə́t·ət, tá=á· nihəláči kéku íka wə́nči-ki·š·i·k·ənó·wi,
/t As for the branch of the vine, nothing will grow from it by itself,
/k As the branch cannot bear fruit of itself,

/b kunh wesavkemwnjif li kletakr; [⟨-kr⟩ for ⟨-kc⟩]
/p kə́nč wisahki·múnšink lí-kəli·tá·k·c.
/t unless it remains attached to the vine.
/k except it abide in the vine;

/b krpwu nanc tpusqi, mutu avpetaerqc.
/p ké·pəwa ná=nə tpə́skwi, máta ahpi·taié·k·we.
/t You also are like that if you are not in me.
/k no more can ye, except ye abide in me.

Jn 15.5
/b Ne wesavkemwnji, kuhi kelwu twvnututu.
/p ní· wisahki·múnši, káč·i ki·ló·wa tuhənət·ɔ́t·a.
/t I am the vine, while you are the branches.
/k I am the vine, ye are the branches:

	/b	Awrn avpetaetc, ok nrpc avpetaokc,
	/p	awé·n ahpi·taí·t·e, ɔ́·k né·pe ahpi·taɔ́k·e,
	/t	If anyone is in me, and I am in them, too,
	/k	He that abideth in me, and I in him,

	/b	nulh nuni vokrf xrli krkw wunhekun;
	/p	nál=č náni hɔ́k·enk xé·li kéku wənčí·k·ən.
	/t	it will be from *them* that many things grow.
	/k	the same bringeth forth much fruit:

	/b	mutu nvakalerqc, ta kuski krkw lusevwmw.
	/p	máta nhaka·lié·k·we, tá=á· kkáski- kéku -ləs·i·húmɔ.
	/t	If you do not rely on me, you will not be able to do anything.
	/k	for without me ye can do nothing.

Jn 15.6	/b	Awrn mutu avpetaetc, puvkelkwswh mulajih twvnutut, jaoskswh,
	/p	awé·n máta ahpi·taí·t·e, pahki·lkwə́s·u=č, málahši=č tuhənə́t·ət, šaɔ́sksu=č.
	/t	If anyone is not in me, he will be cast aside like a branch and will wither.
	/k	If a man abide not in me, he is cast forth as a branch, and is withered;

	/b	marvookh cntxi nc lusehek, tuntrbfh lanevenuk,
	/p	ma·ehɔ́·ɔk=č éntxi- nə́ -ləs·í·č·i·k, tənté·yunk=č lanihí·nak,
	/t	As many as there are like that will be gathered up and thrown into the fire,
	/k	and men gather them, and cast them into the fire,

	/b	cntuh lwsevtet.
	/p	énta-=č -lo·s·íhti·t.
	/t	where they will be burned.
	/k	and they are burned.

Jn 15.7	/b	Avpetaerqc, ok ntaptwnakunul avpetaqrqc,
	/p	ahpi·taié·k·we, nta·pto·ná·k·anal ahpi·ta·k·wé·k·we,
	/t	If you are in me, and my words are in you,
	/k	If ye abide in me, and my words abide in you,

	/b	tuk tu krkw wenwrrqc, nuh nc ktulevkrnro.
	/p	tákta kéku wi·nəwe·é·k·we, ná=č nə́ ktəlihke·né·ɔ.
	/t	whatever you ask for, that will be done for you.
	/k	ye shall ask what ye will, and it shall be done unto you.

Jn 15.8	/b	Xrli krkw kejekifc kvaywaif wunhi,	[⟨kvaywaif⟩ for ⟨kvakywaif⟩]
	/p	xé·li kéku ki·š·i·k·ínke khak·ayəwá·ink wə́nči,	
	/t	If many things grow from you,	
	/k	Herein is my Father glorified, that ye bear much fruit;	[Clauses reversed in B.]

/b wunhih xifovkunemkwsen Nwx;
/p wwə́nči-=č -xinkɔhkəni·mkwə́s·i·n nó·x,
/t my father will be glorified thereby,
/k —   [On the line above.]

/b okh rkrkemukek kvakybu.
/p ɔ́·k=č e·k·e·ki·mák·i·k khak·ayúwa.
/t and you will be my disciples.
/k so shall ye be my disciples.

Jn 15.9   /b Rlkeqi avolet, Wrtwxumunt, ktulkeqi avolunro;
          /p e·lkí·kwi-ahɔ́·li·t we·t·ó·x·əmənt, ktəlkí·kwi-ahɔlləné·ɔ.
          /t I love you as much as the father loves me.
          /k As the Father hath loved me, so have I loved you:

/b ntavoltwakunif heme avpeq.
/p ntahɔ·ltəwá·k·anink či·mí·i ahpí·kw.
/t Be forever in my love.
/k continue ye in my love.

Jn 15.10 /b Luserqc rlwru, nuh nc ktupenro ntavoltwakunif:
          /p ləs·ié·k·we e·ləwé·a, ná=č nə́ ktap·i·né·ɔ ntahɔ·ltəwá·k·anink,
          /t If you do what I say, in my love is where you will be,
          /k If ye keep my commandments, ye shall abide in my love;

/b rlkeqi ne luseu Nwx rlwrt, ok avpetamu tovolwakun. ‖   [⟨-lw-⟩ for ⟨-ltw-⟩]
/p e·lkí·kwi- ní· -ləs·ia nó·x é·ləwe·t, ɔ́·k -ahpí·tama tɔhɔ·ltəwá·k·an.
/t as much as *I* do what my father says and am in his love.
/k even as I have kept my Father's commandments, and abide in his love.

Jn 15.11   /b Kwnhi nc lulunro ktuli a avpetakwnro nwlvatrnumwakun,
(p. 186)   /p "kúnči- nə́ -lələné·ɔ, ktə́li-=á· -ahpi·ta·k·o·né·ɔ no·lhate·naməwá·k·an.
           /t "I say this to you, so that my joy will be in you,
           /k These things have I spoken unto you, that my joy might remain in you,

/b wcnhih pavkunji wulatrnamerq.
/p wénči-=č -pahkánči-wəla·te·namíe·kw.
/t in order that your joy will be complete.
/k and that your joy might be full.

Jn 15.12 /b Jr b ntapuntwakun. Lukveqi avolteq rlkeqi ne avolrq.
          /p šé· yú ntap·antəwá·k·an: ləkhkíwi-ahɔ́·lti·kw, e·lkí·kwi- ní· -ahɔ́lle·kw.
          /t This is my commandment: love each other as much as *I* love you.
          /k This is my commandment, That ye love one another, as I have loved you.

Text, Transcription, and Translation 651

Jn 15.13 /b Takw awrn alwe lukveqi avpetakwi avoltwakun
/p takó· awé·n aləwí·i-ləkhíkwi-ahpi·ta·k·ó·wi ahɔ·ltəwá·k·an
/t No one has more love in them
/k Greater love hath no man than this,

/b rlkeqi avpetakwk awrn mrkuk wulclrxrokun wunhi wetesu.
/p e·lkí·kwi-ahpi·tá·k·uk awé·n mé·k·ək wəlehəle·x·e·ɔ́·k·an wə́nči wi·t·í·s·a.
/t than what someone has in them who gives their life for their friends.
/k that a man lay down his life for his friends.

Jn 15.14 /b Kelwuh netesuk kvakybu, luserqc wrmi cntxi lulrq.
/p ki·ló·wa=č ni·t·í·s·ak khak·ayúwa, ləs·ié·k·we wé·mi éntxi-lɔ́le·kw.
/t *You* will be my friends, if you do everything I tell you to.
/k Ye are my friends, if ye do whatsoever I command you.

Jn 15.15 /b Bqc wunhi ta heh ktulwevlwvmw alwkakununk;   [⟨ktulwevl-⟩ for /ktələwill-/]
/p yúkwe wə́nči tá=á· čí·č ktələwillo·húmɔ 'alo·ká·k·anak'.
/t From now on I won't call you 'servants' anymore.
/k Henceforth I call you not servants;

/b rli alwkakun mutu vufq watwun rlumekuntamulet nrvlalkwki;
/p é·li alo·ká·k·an máta=hánkw o·wa·tó·wən e·lami·kəntamə́li·t nehəla·lkúk·i.
/t For a servant does not know what his master does.
/k for the servant knoweth not what his lord doeth:

/b ktulwevlwvmw netesuk,   [⟨ktulwevl-⟩ for /ktələwill-/]
/p ktələwillúhəmɔ 'ni·t·í·s·ak',
/t I call you 'my friends',
/k but I have called you friends;

/b rli wrmi cntxi lustaok Nwx watululrq.
/p é·li- wé·mi éntxi-ləstáɔk nó·x -wwa·təlɔ́le·kw.
/t as I have made known to you everything I heard from my father.
/k for all things that I have heard of my Father I have made known unto you.

Jn 15.16 /b Takw kelwu kpepenaevwmw, jwq ne kpepenwlvwmw,
/p takó· ki·ló·wa kpi·p·i·nai·húmɔ, šúkw ní· kpi·p·i·no·lhúmɔ.
/t *You* did not choose *me*, but *I* chose *you*.
/k Ye have not chosen me, but I have chosen you,

/b ok kejemulwvmw, ktulih my kejekunumunro,
/p ɔ́·k kki·š·i·məlúhəmɔ, któli-=č -mái-ki·š·i·k·ənəməné·ɔ,
/t And I declared a plan to you, that you go and raise crops,
/k and ordained you, that ye should go and bring forth fruit,

/b okh li kejekunumrq aphi vatr,
/p ó·k=č lí- ki·š·i·k·ənə́me·kw á·pči -hát·e·,
/t and that what you raised would always exist,
/k and that your fruit should remain: [RSV "abide"]

/b okh wcnhi tuktu krkw wenwumrqc Wrtwxumunt wunhi ntulswakun, melqrq.
/p ó·k=č wénči- tákta kéku wi·nəwamé·k·we we·t·ó·x·əmənt
   wə́nči ntəlsəwá·k·an -mí·lkwe·kw.
/t and it was so that whatever you ask the father for by my power he will give you.
/k that whatsoever ye shall ask of the Father in my name, he may give it you.

Jn 15.17 /b Bni ktavi lulunro, ktuli a avoltenro.
/p "yó·ni ktáhi-lələné·ɔ: ktə́li-=á· -ahɔ·lti·né·ɔ.
/t "This I tell you firmly: that you love each other.
/k These things I command you, that ye love one another.

Jn 15.18 /b B cntu lawsehek jifalqrqc, watwq ntcli ne vetami jifalkwn.
/p yú entala·wsí·č·i·k šinka·lkwé·k·we, wwá·to·kw, ntə́li- ní· hítami -šinká·lko·n.
/t If the world hates you, know that they hated *me* first.
/k If the world hate you, ye know that it hated me before it hated you.

Jn 15.19 /b B cntu lawsif wunheyerqc, ktavolkwaok a b cntu lawsehek;
/p yú entalá·wsink wənči·aié·k·we, ktahɔ·lkuwá·ɔk=á· yú entala·wsí·č·i·k.
/t If you were of ('belonged in') the world, mankind would love you.
/k If ye were of the world, the world would love his own:

/b jwq rli mutu wunheyerq b cntu lawsif, rli pepenwlrq b wunhi;
/p šúkw é·li- máta -wənči·aíe·kw yú entalá·wsink, é·li-pi·p·i·nó·le·kw yú wə́nči,
/t But because you are not of the world, because I selected you from it,
/k but because ye are not of the world, but I have chosen you out of the world,

/b nunih kwnhi jifalkwnro b cntu lawsehek.
/p nə́ni=č kúnči-šinka·lko·né·ɔ yú entala·wsí·č·i·k.
/t that is why mankind will hate you.
/k therefore the world hateth you.

Jn 15.20 /b Kulrluntamwq rlrkwp, takw alwkakun tolwe lusewun nrvlalkwki.
/p kəle·lə́ntamo·kw ellé·k·əp: takó· alo·ká·k·an tɔləwí·i-ləs·í·wən nehəla·lkúk·i.
/t Keep in mind what I said to you: the servant is not greater than his master.
/k Remember the word that I said unto you, The servant is not greater than his lord.

/b Avpevtetc mrhevehek, krpwuh avpwuk mrhevqrqek;
/p ahpihtí·t·e me·č·i·hí·č·i·k, ké·pəwa=č ahpúwak me·č·ihkwé·k·wi·k.
/t If there are those that treat me badly, there will be those that treat you badly, too.
/k If they have persecuted me, they will also persecute you;

	/b	ok avpevtetc wrlamvetufek ntaptwnakun,
	/p	ó·k ahpihtí·t·e we·la·mhitánki·k nta·pto·ná·k·an,
	/t	And if there are those that believe my words,
	/k	if they have kept my saying,

	/b	krpwuh avpwuk wrlamvetufek ktaptwnakunwu.
	/p	ké·pəwa=č ahpúwak we·la·mhitánki·k kta·pto·na·k·anúwa.
	/t	there will be those that believe your words, too.
	/k	they will keep yours also.

Jn 15.21	/b	Nunih ktulevkwnro wunhi ne,
	/p	nə́ni=č ktəlihko·né·ɔ wə́nči ní·,
	/t	They will do that to you because of me,
	/k	But all these things will they do unto you for my name's sake,

	/b	rli mutu wavavtet prtalwkalelehi.
	/p	é·li- máta -wwa·háhti·t pe·t·alo·ka·li·lí·č·i.
	/t	as they do not know the one that sent me.
	/k	because they know not him that sent me.

Jn 15.22	/b	Ne a mutu paapanc my krkw laokpanc taa ave muvtawseepanek;
	/p	ní·=á· máta pa·á·p·ane, mái- kéku -la·ɔkpáne, tá=á· áhi-mahta·wsi·í·p·ani·k.
	/t	If *I* had not come and spoken to them, they would not have been so very sinful.
	/k	If I had not come and spoken unto them, they had not had sin:

	/b	jwq bqc mutu vatri wcnhi a mutukvomevtet motawswakunwu.
	/p	šúkw yúkwe máta hat·é·i wénči·=á· -mətakhɔmíhti·t mɔt·a·wsəwa·k·anúwa.
	/t	But now they have nothing to conceal their sin. [*lit.*, 'there is not the means (to)']
	/k	but now they have no cloke for their sin.

Jn 15.23	/b	Awrn jifaletc, vwjifalao ok Nwxo.
	/p	awé·n šinka·lí·t·e, wšinka·lá·ɔ ó·k nó·x·ɔ.
	/t	If anyone hates me, he also hates my father.
	/k	He that hateth me hateth my Father also.

Jn 15.24	/b	Ne a mu mutu luseopanc tali rlifwrxenvetet, ta peli awrn krski luset,
	/p	ní·=á·=máh máta ləs·i·ɔ́·p·ane táli e·linkwe·x·i·nhíti·t,
		tá=á· pí·li awé·n ké·ski-ləs·i·t,
	/t	If *I* had not done before their eyes what no one else would be able to do,
	/k	If I had not done among them the works which none other man did,

	/b	taa tulkeqi muvtawsewunrop; [⟨muvtawsewun-‖rop⟩]
	/p	tá=á· təlkí·kwi-mahta·wsi·wəné·ɔp.
	/t	they would not have been so sinful.
	/k	they had not had sin:

(p. 187) /b jwq bqc rlei nrvkwnanuk ok rlei njifalkwnanuk ne ok Nwx.
          /p šúkw yúkwe ellí·i nne·yko·ná·nak, ɔ́·k ellí·i nšinka·lko·ná·nak, ní· ɔ́·k nó·x.
          /t But now they see us both, and they hate us both, me and my father.
          /k but now have they both seen and hated both me and my Father.

Jn 15.25 /b Jwq bqc rlrk
          /p šúkw yúkwe é·le·k
          /t But with what is happening now,
          /k But this cometh to pass,

          /b pavkunhi lr rlrkvasek aptwnakun tulrkekunwaif,   [⟨kek⟩ for /khi·k·/]
          /p pahkánči-lé· e·le·khá·s·i·k a·pto·ná·k·an tǝle·khi·k·anǝwá·ink:
          /t the words that were written in their writings are fulfilled:
          /k that the word might be fulfilled that is written in their law,

          /b Njifalkwk nwhqc.
          /p 'nšinká·lko·k nó·čkwe.'
          /t 'They hated me for no reason.'
          /k They hated me without a cause.

Jn 15.26 /b Jwq patc wcvwlatrnamwvalwrs,
          /p šúkw pá·t·e wehwǝla·te·namo·há·lǝwe·s,
          /t But when the 'comforter' comes,
          /k But when the Comforter is come,

          /b prtalwkalukh kvakywaif wunhi Wrtwxumuntif,
          /p pe·t·alo·ká·lak=č khak·ayǝwá·ink [lí] wǝ́nči we·t·o·x·ǝmǝ́ntink,   [lí missing?]
          /t who I will send to you from the father,
          /k whom I will send unto you from the Father,

          /b nu wulamwrokunei manutw, Wrtwxumuntif wcnhi khet,
          /p ná wǝla·mǝwe·ɔ·k·aní·i-manǝ́t·u, we·t·o·x·ǝmǝ́ntink wénči-kčí·t,
          /t the truth spirit that issues forth from the father,
          /k even the Spirit of truth, which proceedeth from the Father,

          /b nulh nu ntukunemwq.
          /p nál=č ná ntak·ǝní·mukw.
          /t *he's* the one who will tell of me.
          /k he shall testify of me:

Jn 15.27 /b Okh kelwu ktukunemevmw, rli jac nwhi wehrerq.
          /p ɔ́·k=č ki·ló·wa ktak·ǝni·míhǝmɔ, é·li- šá·e núči -wi·č·é·ie·kw.
          /t And *you* will tell about me, too, as you have been with me right from the start.
          /k And ye also shall bear witness, because ye have been with me from the beginning.

Jn 16.1
/b Nuni ktulunro, wcnhih mutu hanrluntumwrq.
/p "nə́ni ktəlləné·ɔ, wénči-=č máta -čane·ləntamó·we·kw.
/t "I tell you that so that you will not be reluctant.
/k These things have I spoken unto you, that ye should not be offended.

[RSV "to keep you from falling away"]

Jn 16.2
/b Paleih ktclskakwaok wunhi cvcntu macvluf;
/p palí·i=č ktəlska·k·əwá·ɔk wə́nči ehə́nta-ma·éhəlank.
/t They will drive you away from the synagogues.
/k They shall put you out of the synagogues:

/b kveheih lr
/p khičí·i=č lé·
/t Truly it will happen that,
/k yea, the time cometh, that

/b awrn nvelqrqc letrvrwh Krtanutwet nmekumosuntamao.
/p awé·n nhilkwé·k·we, li·t·é·he·w=č, 'ke·tanət·ó·wi·t nəmi·kəmɔ·s·əntamáɔ.'
/t if someone kills you, they will think, 'I am serving God.'
/k whosoever killeth you will think that he doeth God service.

Jn 16.3
/b Nunih ktulevkwnro,
/p nə́ni=č ktəlihko·né·ɔ,
/t That's what they will do to you,
/k And these things will they do unto you,

/b rli mutu wavavtet Wrtwxifi, ok ne.
/p é·li- máta -wwa·háhti·t we·t·o·x·ínki ɔ́·k ní·.
/t because they do not know the father or me.
/k because they have not known the Father, nor me.

Jn 16.4
/b Jwq mrhi ktulunro, alumi nc lrkc,
/p šúkw mé·či ktəlləné·ɔ, áləmi- nə́ -lé·k·e,
/t But I have told you, when that is beginning to happen,
/k But these things have I told you, that when the time shall come,

/b wcnhih mujatumrq, ktuli lulunro,
/p wénči-=č -məšá·t·ame·kw, ktə́li-lələné·ɔ.
/t so that you will remember that I told you.
/k ye may remember that I told you of them.

/b Kwnhi mutu vetami nuni lulwunrop,
/p kúnči- máta hítami nə́ni -ləlo·wəné·ɔ·p,
/t The reason I didn't tell you that in the beginning
/k And these things I said not unto you at the beginning,

    /b   rli wetawswmulrkup.
    /p   é·li-wi·t·a·wso·məlé·k·əp.
    /t   is because I was living among you.
    /k   because I was with you.

Jn 16.5   /b   Jwq bqc nmy toxav prtalwkaletup;
    /p   šúkw yúkwe nəmái-tóx·a pe·t·alo·ka·lí·t·əp.
    /t   But now I go to the one that sent me here.
    /k   But now I go my way to him that sent me;

    /b   takw ktulevwmw, Tu vuh ktav?
    /p   takó· ktəli·húmɔ, 'tá=háč ktá?'
    /t   You do not ask me, 'Where are you going?'
    /k   and none of you asketh me, Whither goest thou?

Jn 16.6   /b   Rli nuni lulrq wunhi jerluntamwakun hwexun ktrvwaif.
    /p   é·li- nə́ni -lə́le·kw wə́nči- ši·e·ləntaməwá·k·an -čuwí·x·ən ktehəwá·ink.
    /t   Because I told you that, sorrow fills your hearts.
    /k   But because I have said these things unto you, sorrow hath filled your heart.

Jn 16.7   /b   Jwq krvlu, wulamwrokun ktulwvmw,
    /p   šúkw kéhəla wəla·məwe·ó·k·an ktəllúhəmɔ.
    /t   But really I tell you truth.
    /k   Nevertheless I tell you the truth;

    /b   ktulapcntumunroh alumskaanc;
    /p   ktəla·p·entaməné·ɔ=č, aləmska·á·ne.
    /t   You will benefit from it if I depart.
    /k   It is expedient for you that I go away:

    /b   rli mutu alumskaanc, taa kwtxwkwewa Wcvwlatrnamwvalwrs;
    /p   é·li, máta aləmska·á·ne, tá=á· ko·txuk·o·wíwwa wehwəla·te·namo·há·ləwe·s,
    /t   For if I do not depart, the "comforter" will not come to you,
    /k   for if I go not away, the Comforter will not come unto you;

    /b   jwq alumskaanc, mprtalwkaluh wcnhih toxqrq.
    /p   šúkw aləmska·á·ne, mpe·t·alo·ká·la=č, wénči-=č -tóxkwe·kw.
    /t   but if I depart, I will send him, so that he will come to you.
    /k   but if I depart, I will send him unto you.

Jn 16.8   /b   Ok nuni patc pwunwntulanh b cntu lawselehi rli muvtawselet
    /p   ó·k náni pá·t·e, pwənúntəla·n=č yú entala·wsi·lí·č·i é·li-mahta·wsí·li·t,
    /t   And when *he* comes, he will show mankind how they are sinful,
    /k   And when he is come, he will reprove the world of sin,

/b ok jaxavkawswakun, ok kuntrlumwqswakun;
/p ɔ́·k šaxahka·wsəwá·k·an ɔ́·k kənte·ləmukwsəwá·k·an.
/t and righteousness and condemnation.
/k and of righteousness, and of judgment:

Jn 16.9
/b mavtawswakun, wunhi rli mutu wulamvetaevtet;
/p mahta·wsəwá·k·an, wə́nči é·li- máta -wəla·mhitaíhti·t;
/t Sin, because of the way they do not believe me;
/k Of sin, because they believe not on me;

Jn 16.10
/b jaxavkawswakunh wunhi rli Nwxif au ok mutu heh nrebf;
/p šaxahka·wsəwá·k·an=č, wə́nči é·li- nó·x·ink -á·a, ɔ́·k máta čí·č -ne·í·yunk;
/t righteousness, because of how I go to my father and will not be seen any more;
/k Of righteousness, because I go to my Father, and ye see me no more;

Jn 16.11
/b kuntrlumwqswakunh,
/p kənte·ləmukwsəwá·k·an=č,
/t and condemnation,
/k Of judgment,

/b wunhi rli b cntu lawsif sakemu kuntrlumwqset.
/p wə́nči é·li- yú entalá·wsink sa·k·í·ma -kənte·ləmúkwsi·t.
/t because of how the king of this world is condemned.
/k because the prince of this world is judged.

Jn 16.12
/b Piji xrli krkw katu lulvwmw, jwq taa bqc ktrpi hetanetrvavwmw.
/p "píši xé·li kéku kkát·a-ləlhúmɔ, šúkw tá=á· yúkwe ktépi-či·t·ani·t·e·ha·húmɔ.
/t "I *want* to tell you many things, but you would not be strong-minded enough now.
/k I have yet many things to say unto you, but ye cannot bear them now.

Jn 16.13
/b Jwqh rlkeqi pat wulamwrokune Manutw,
/p šúkw=č e·lkí·kwi-pá·t wəla·məwe·ɔ·k·aní·i-manə́t·u,
/t But at the time when the truth spirit shall come,
/k Howbeit when he, the Spirit of truth, is come,

/b ksukaqwnwkwuh wrmi li ‖ wulamwrokunif.
/p ksak·a·kwənúk·əwa=č wé·mi lí wəla·məwe·ɔ́·k·anink.
/t he will lead you to all truth.
/k he will guide you into all truth:

(p. 188)
/b Rlih nrkumu taa nevlahi krkw lwri,
/p é·li=č né·k·əma tá=á· nihəláči kéku luwé·i.
/t For *he* will not speak on his own.
/k for he shall not speak of himself;

	/b	Jwqh krkw puntuf tulahemwen;
	/p	šúkw=č kéku pə́ntank təla·č·í·mwi·n,
	/t	But he will tell the things he hears,
	/k	but whatsoever he shall hear, that shall he speak:

	/b	okh kwrvomakwu krkw kavtu lrkc;
	/p	ɔ́·k=č kəwe·hɔmá·k·əwa kéku káhta-lé·k·e.
	/t	and he will let you know when things are going to happen.
	/k	and he will shew you things to come.

Jn 16.14	/b	numuxifovkunemwqh;
	/p	nəmax·inkɔhkəní·mukw=č.
	/t	He will glorify me.
	/k	He shall glorify me:

	/b	rli mujinumh eku wunhi nrvlatumu, okh kpunwntulwkwnro.
	/p	é·li məšə́nəm=č íka wə́nči nehəlá·t·ama, ɔ́·k=č kpənuntəluk·o·né·ɔ.
	/t	For he will receive from what is mine, and he will show it to you.
	/k	for he shall receive of mine, and shall shew it unto you.

Jn 16.15	/b	Wrmi cntxi nevlatuf Wrtwxumunt, nrpc nevlatumun.	[Wrmi: ⟨W mi⟩]
	/p	wé·mi éntxi-nihəlá·t·ank we·t·ó·x·əmənt, né·pe nnihəlá·t·amən.	
	/t	Everything the father owns is also mine.	
	/k	All things that the Father hath are mine:	

	/b	Nuni wunhi lwrn,	[⟨wunhi⟩ for ⟨nwnhi⟩]
	/p	nə́ni núnči-lúwe·n,	
	/t	That's why I said,	
	/k	therefore said I,	

	/b	wrtunumh eku wunhi nrvlatumu, okh kpunwntulwkwnro.
	/p	wé·t·ənəm=č íka wə́nči nehəlá·t·ama, ɔ́·k=č kpənuntəluk·o·né·ɔ.
	/t	he will take from what is mine, and he will show it to you.
	/k	that he shall take of mine, and shall shew it unto you.

Jn 16.16	/b	Tvakitih mutu knrevwmw,
	/p	thakíti=č máta kəne·i·húmɔ.
	/t	In a little while you will not see me.
	/k	A little while, and ye shall not see me:

	/b	okh tvakiti lupi knrevmw,
	/p	ɔ́·k=č thakíti lápi kəne·íhəmɔ.
	/t	And you will see me in a little while again.
	/k	and again, a little while, and ye shall see me,

/b rli Wrtwxumuntifh ntav.
/p é·li we·t·o·x·əmə́ntink=č ntá."
/t For I shall go to the father."
/k because I go to the Father.

Jn 16.17
/b Nu aluntc rkrkemunhek, tultenro,
/p ná a·lə́nte e·k·e·ki·mə́nči·k təlti·né·ɔ,
/t Then some of the disciples said to each other,
/k Then said some of his disciples among themselves,

/b Krkw vuh ct nc rlkofq Tvakitih mutu knrevwmw,
/p "kéku=háč=ét nə́ é·lkɔnkw, 'thakíti=č máta kəne·i·húmɔ.
/t "I wonder what he means saying to us, 'In a little while you will not see me.
/k What is this that he saith unto us, A little while, and ye shall not see me:

/b okh tvakiti lupi knrevmw, rli Wrtwxumuntifh ntav?
/p ó·k=č thakíti lápi kəne·íhəmɔ. é·li we·t·o·x·əmə́ntink=č ntá'?"
/t And you will see me in a little while again. For I shall go to the father'?"
/k and again, a little while, and ye shall see me: and, Because I go to the Father?

Jn 16.18
/b Lwrok, Krkw nc vct wcnhi lwrt, tvakitih?
/p luwé·ɔk, "kéku=néh=ét wénči-lúwe·t, 'thakíti=č'?
/t They said, "What could possibly be the reason he said, 'In a little while'?
/k They said therefore, What is this that he saith, A little while?

/b takw kwatwunrn wcnhi nc lwrt.
/p takó· ko·wa·tó·wəne·n wénči- nə́ -lúwe·t."
/t We don't know why he said that."
/k we cannot tell what he saith.

Jn 16.19
/b Nu Nhesus watwn tuli kavtu ntwtumakwn, tulao,
/p ná nčí·sas o·wá·to·n, tə́li-káhta-nto·t·əmá·k·o·n, təlá·ɔ,
/t Then Jesus knew that they wanted to ask him a question, and said to them,
/k Now Jesus knew that they were desirous to ask him, and said unto them,

/b Knutwtumaovtenro vuh rlrq,
/p "kənat·o·t·əma·ɔhti·né·ɔ=háč élle·kw,
/t "Are you asking each other what I meant by saying to you,
/k Do ye enquire among yourselves of that I said,

/b Tvakitih mutu knrevwmw,
/p 'thakíti=č máta kəne·i·húmɔ.
/t 'In a little while you will not see me.
/k A little while, and ye shall not see me:

/b okh tvakiti lupi knrevmw?
/p ó·k=č thakíti lápi kəne·íhəmɔ'?
/t And you will see me in a little while again'?
/k and again, a little while, and ye shall see me?

Jn 16.20 /b Kvehei, kvehei ktulwvmw, klupuvkwvmwh, okh ksalamwivmw,
/p khičí·i, khičí·i, ktəllúhəmɔ, kələpahkúhəmɔ=č, ó·k=č ksala·mwíhəmɔ,
/t Truly, truly, I tell you, you will weep and you will wail,
/k Verily, verily, I say unto you, That ye shall weep and lament,

/b jwqh b cntu lawsehek wulrluntamwk;
/p šúkw=č yú entala·wsí·č·i·k wəle·ləntamo·k.
/t but mankind will be glad.
/k but the world shall rejoice:

/b ktavih jerluntamwvmw,
/p ktáhi-=č -ši·e·ləntamúhəmɔ,
/t You will be very sad,
/k and ye shall be sorrowful,

/b jwqh kjerluntamwakunwu kwnhi wulrluntumunro.
/p šúkw=č kši·e·ləntaməwa·k·anúwa kúnči-wəle·ləntaməné·ɔ.
/t but by means of your sadness you will be glad.
/k but your sorrow shall be turned into joy.

Jn 16.21 /b Xqr vufq mrhi tpusqevlakc tulih wunehanen
/p "xkwé·=hánkw mé·či tpəskwihəlá·k·e, táli-=č -wəni·č·á·ni·n,
/t "When a woman's time has come for her to have a child,
/k (1) A woman when she is in travail .. (3) because her hour is come:
                                   [numbers = sequence in L.]

/b ave vufq avrluntum
/p áhi-=hánkw -ahe·ləntam.
/t she feels a lot of pain.
/k (2) hath sorrow, ..

/b jwq vufq mrhi memuntut kejeketc,
/p šúkw=hánkw mé·či mi·mə́ntət ki·š·i·k·í·t·e,
/t But after the baby has been born,
/k but as soon as she is delivered of the child,

/b jac vufq mutu heh mwujatumwun tuli avrluntumun,
/p šá·e=hánkw máta čí·č mwəš·a·t·amó·wən táli-ahe·ləntamən,
/t she immediately no longer remembers that she felt pain,
/k she remembereth no more the anguish,

/b rli vufq wulrluntuf tuli memuntut lupi kejeken tali cntu lawsif.
/p é·li-=hánkw -wəle·lə́ntank, tə́li- mi·mə́ntət lápi -ki·š·í·k·i·n táli entalá·wsink.
/t because she is glad that another baby has been born in the world.
/k for joy that a man is born into the world.

Jn 16.22 /b Krpwu bqc ktavrluntumwvmwh, jwqh lupi knrwulwvmw,
/p ké·pəwa yúkwe ktahe·ləntamúhəmɔ, šúkw=č lápi kəne·wəlúhəmɔ,
/t You also now feel anguish, but I will see you again,
/k And ye now therefore have sorrow: but I will see you again,

/b okh kwlrluntamwvmw tali ktrvwaif,
/p ó·k=č ko·le·ləntamúhəmɔ táli ktehəwá·ink,
/t and you will be joyful in your hearts,
/k and your heart shall rejoice,

/b okh kwlrluntumwakunwu ta awrn khekunwkwunro.
/p ó·k=č ko·le·ləntaməwa·k·anúwa, tá=á· awé·n kči·k·ənuk·o·wəné·ɔ.
/t and your joy no one will take from you.
/k and your joy no man taketh from you.

Jn 16.23 /b Nunih kejqek taa krkw knatwxtaevwmw.
/p nə́ni=č kí·škwi·k tá=á· kéku kənat·o·xtai·húmɔ.
/t That day, you will ask me nothing.
/k And in that day ye shall ask me nothing.

/b Kvehei, kvehei ktclwvmw,
/p khičí·i, khičí·i, ktəllúhəmɔ,
/t Truly, truly, I tell you,
/k Verily, verily, I say unto you,

/b tuktu krkw wenwumrqc Wrtwxumunt wcnhi ne, kmelkwnroh.
    [⟨Wrtwxum-‖unt⟩; ⟨wcnhi⟩ for /wə́nči/]
/p tákta kéku wi·nəwamé·k·we we·t·ó·x·əmənt wə́nči ní·, kəmi·lko·né·ɔ=č.
/t If you ask the father for anything through me, he will give it to you.
/k Whatsoever ye shall ask the Father in my name, he will give it you.

Jn 16.24 /b Bqc pchi takw vuji krkw kwenwrvwmw wunhi ne.
(p. 189) /p yúkwe péči takó· háši kéku kəwi·nəwe·húmɔ wə́nči ní·.
/t Up to now you have never asked for anything through me.
/k Hitherto have ye asked nothing in my name:

/b Wenwrq kmujinumunroh wcnhih pavkunhi wulrluntamrq.
/p wí·nəwe·kw, kəməš·ənəməné·ɔ=č wénči·=č -pahkánči-wəle·lə́ntame·kw.
/t Ask, and you will receive what will make you utterly joyful.
/k ask, and ye shall receive, that your joy may be full.

Jn 16.25 /b Rnwntvakrakun vufq ktulwvmw, [⟨-krakun⟩ for ⟨-krokun⟩]
 /p eˑnunthakeˑóˑkˑan=hánkw ktəllúhəmɔ.
 /t I tell you parables,
 /k These things have I spoken unto you in proverbs:

 /b jwq tpusqevlrh, ktulih mutu heh rnwntvakrokun lulwunro,
 /p šúkw tpəskwíhəleˑ=č, ktəli-=č máta číˑč eˑnunthakeˑóˑkˑan -ləloˑwənéˑɔ,
 /t but the time will come for me not to tell you any more parables,
 /k but the time cometh, when I shall no more speak unto you in proverbs,

 /b jwqh maeai ktukunwtumwlunro Wrtwxumunt.
 /p šúkw=č mayáˑi ktakˑənoˑtˑəmoˑlənéˑɔ weˑtˑóˑxˑəmənt.
 /t but I will tell you plainly about the father.
 /k but I shall shew you plainly of the Father.

Jn 16.26 /b Nuni kejqek wenwrmoc wunhi ne;
 /p nə́ni kíˑškwiˑk, wiˑnəweˑmɔ́ˑe wə́nči níˑ.
 /t That day, ask through me.
 /k At that day ye shall ask in my name:

 /b ok takw ktulwvmw kpatamwrlxulvwmwh,
 /p ɔ́ˑk takóˑ ktəlloˑhúmɔ, 'kpaˑtamweˑlxəlhúmɔ=č',
 /t I'm not telling you that I will pray for you,
 /k and I say not unto you, that I will pray the Father for you:

Jn 16.27 /b rli Wrtwxumunt nevlahi avolqrq, [⟨Wrtwx̣umunt⟩]
 /p éˑli- weˑtˑóˑxˑəmənt nihəláči -ahóˑlkweˑkw,
 /t because the father loves you himself,
 /k For the Father himself loveth you,

 /b rli avolerq, ok wulamvetaerq ntcli Krtanutwetif wunheken.
 /p éˑli-ahóˑlieˑkw óˑk -wəlaˑmhitaíeˑkw ntəli- keˑtanətˑoˑwíˑtˑink -wənčíˑkˑiˑn.
 /t because you love me and believe that I was born from God.
 /k because ye have loved me, and have believed that I came out from God.

Jn 16.28 /b Wrtwxumuntif nwnhi khen, b cntu lawsif mpan;
 /p weˑtˑoˑxˑəmə́ntink núnči-kčíˑn, yú entaláˑwsink mpáˑn.
 /t I issued forth from the father and came to the world.
 /k I came forth from the Father, and am come into the world:

 /b lupi, nukavtumun b cntu lawsif Wrtwxumuntif ntav.
 /p lápi nnəkahtə́mən yú entaláˑwsink, weˑtˑoˑxˑəmə́ntink ntá."
 /t And I leave the world again and go to the father."
 /k again, I leave the world, and go to the Father.

Jn 16.29
/b Nu rkrkemahi tulkwn, krvlu bqc kmyai lwr,
/p ná e·k·e·ki·má·č·i tálko·n, "kéhəla yúkwe kəmayá·i-lúwe.
/t Then his disciples said to him, "Now you really speak plainly.
/k His disciples said unto him, Lo, now speakest thou plainly,

/b takw tufiti ktrnwnvakri.
/p takó· tankíti kte·nunthaké·i.
/t You do not talk even a little in parables.
/k and speakest no proverb.

Jn 16.30
/b Bqc krvlu nwatwnrn ktuli wrmi krkw watwn,
/p yúkwe kéhəla no·wa·tó·ne·n, ktáli- wé·mi kéku -wwá·to·n.
/t Now we know for sure that you know everything.
/k Now are we sure that thou knowest all things,

/b ok mutu kutatumwun, kcnh awrn ntwtumakonc.
/p ó·k máta kkat·a·t·amó·wən, kánč awé·n nto·t·əmá·k·one. [unclear]
/t And you do not want to, except if someone asks you.
/k and needest not that any man should ask thee:

/b Nuni nwnhi wulamvetumunrn, ktuli Krtanutwetif wunhi khen.
/p náni núnči-wəla·mhitamáne·n, ktáli- ke·tanət·o·wí·t·ink -wánči-kčí·n."
/t That's why we believe that you came out of God.
/k by this we believe that thou camest forth from God.

Jn 16.31
/b Nhesus tulao, Kvehei vuh bqc kwlamvetumunro?
/p nčí·sas təlá·ɔ, "khičí·i=háč yúkwe ko·la·mhitamáné·ɔ?
/t Jesus said to them, "Do you now truly believe it?
/k Jesus answered them, Do ye now believe?

Jn 16.32
/b Tpusqevlrh, kovun mrhi bqc,
/p tpəskwíhəle·=č, kɔhán mé·či yúkwe,
/t The time will come, indeed it is already now,
/k Behold, the hour cometh, yea, is now come,

/b ktclih avsrvlanro wrmi cntxerq li cntu nevlatamrq,
/p ktáli-=č -ahsehəla·né·ɔ, wé·mi entxíe·kw lí énta-nihəlá·t·ame·kw,
/t that you will scatter, every one of you to your own property,
/k that ye shall be scattered, every man to his own,

/b xwvuh ne knukalevmw;
/p xó·ha=č ní· kənək·alíhəmɔ.
/t and you will leave *me* alone (by myself).
/k and shall leave me alone:

/b   jwq amunhei, ta ne xwvu, rli Wrtwxumunt wetavpemet.
/p   šúkw amənčí·i, tá=á· ní· xó·ha, é·li- we·t·ó·x·əmənt -witahpí·mi·t.
/t   But regardless, I would not be alone, as the father is with me.
/k   and yet I am not alone, because the Father is with me.

Jn 16.33
/b   Bqc cntxi lulrq, kwnhi lulunro, ktuli a wulufwntenro.
/p   yúkwe éntxi-ləle·kw kúnči-lələné·ɔ, ktə́li-=á· -wəlankunti·né·ɔ.
/t   I tell you everything I'm now telling you so that you will be at peace.
/k   These things I have spoken unto you, that in me ye might have peace.

/b   B cntu lawsehek ksukwevkwaokh,
/p   yú entala·wsí·č·i·k ksak·wihkəwá·ɔk=č,
/t   Mankind will torment you,
/k   In the world ye shall have tribulation:

/b   jwq nvakrrluntamwq, rli ne ntalwvekamun b cntu lawsif.
/p   šúkw nhake·e·lə́ntamo·kw, é·li ní· ntaluhíkamən yú entalá·wsink."
/t   but have hope, for *I* overcame the world."
/k   but be of good cheer; I have overcome the world.

Jn 17.1
/b   Nhesus keji nc lwrtc, uspvwqr li osavkamc, ok lwr,
/p   nčí·sas kíši- nə́ -luwé·t·e, asphúkwe· lí ɔ·s·áhkame, ɔ́·k lúwe·,
/t   After Jesus said that, he looked up to heaven and said,
/k   These words spake Jesus, and lifted up his eyes to heaven, and said,

/b   Nwxa, mrhi tpisqevlr;
/p   "núxa·, mé·či tpəskwíhəle·.
/t   "Father, the time has come.
/k   Father, the hour is come;

/b   xifovkunem Qes, wcnhih krpc Qes xifovkunemkon;
/p   xinkɔhkə́ni·m kkwí·s, wénči·=č ké·pc kkwí·s -xinkɔhkəní·mkɔn.
/t   Glorify your son, so that you, too, may be glorified by your son.
/k   glorify thy Son, that thy Son also may glorify thee:

Jn 17.2
/b   rli kmelap alwe luswakun wcnhi nevlalat wrmi b cntu lawselehi,
/p   é·li kəmí·la·p aləwí·i-ləs·əwá·k·an, wénči-nihəlá·la·t wé·mi yú entala·wsi·lí·č·i,
/t   For you have given him power, by which he is master of all mankind,
/k   As thou hast given him power over all flesh,

/b   tulih melan mutaa vuji weqrk pumawswakun wrmi cntxi meluhi.
/p   tə́li-=č -mí·la·n máta=á· háši wí·kwe·k pəma·wsəwá·k·an wé·mi éntxi-mi·láč·i.
/t   so that he would give never-ending life to all those you have given to him.
/k   that he should give eternal life to as many as thou hast given him.

Jn 17.3 /b Nunul bni mutaa weqrk pumawswakun,
/p nánal yó·ni máta=á· wí·kwe·k pəma·wsəwá·k·an:
/t This is unending life:
/k And this is life eternal,

/b ktuli a kuski wavkwnro, xwva wrlamwrun Krtanutweun,
/p ktə́li-=á· -káski-wwahko·né·ɔ, xó·ha we·la·məwé·an ke·tanət·ó·wian,
/t so that they would be able to know you as the only truthful god,
/k that they might know thee the only true God,

/b ok Nhesus ‖ Klyst prtalwkalut.
/p ó·k nčí·sas kəláist pe·t·alo·ká·lat.
/t and Jesus Christ, who you sent.
/k and Jesus Christ, whom thou hast sent.

Jn 17.4 /b Kmuxifovkunemul bqc svaki b tali cntu lawsif;
(p. 190) /p kəmax·inkɔhkəní·məl yúkwe sháki yú táli entalá·wsink.
/t I have glorified you until now in this world.
/k I have glorified thee on the earth:

/b mrhi feji lusen rlalwkaleun.
/p mé·či nkíši-lə́s·i·n e·lalo·ká·lian.
/t I have finished what you sent me to do.
/k I have finished the work which thou gavest me to do.

Jn 17.5 /b Bqc, O Nwxa xifovkunemel wunhi nevlahi kvakrf,
/p yúkwe, ó· núxa·, xinkɔhkəní·mi·l wə́nči nihəláči khák·enk,
/t Now, O father, glorify me by means of your own self,
/k And now, O Father, glorify thou me with thine own self

/b nuxpi nc xifovkunemkwswakun, nenwhi nrvlatamanup kvakrf,
/p náxpi nə́ xinkɔhkəni·mkwəs·əwá·k·an ni·núči nehəla·t·amá·nəp khák·enk,
/t with the glory that I had a long time ago in you,
/k with the glory which I had with thee

/b nrsko rtrkc b vaki.
/p né·skɔ e·té·k·e yú hák·i.
/t before the earth existed.
/k before the world was.

Jn 17.6 /b Mpunwntulanrop ktulswakun b cntu lawsehek cntxi meleunek.
/p "mpənuntəla·né·ɔ·p ktəlsəwá·k·an yú entala·wsí·č·i·k éntxi-mi·liáni·k.
/t "I showed your power to as many of mankind as you gave me.
/k I have manifested thy name unto the men which thou gavest me out of the world:

	/b	Knevlalapanek, ok kmelenrpanek, ok qwlrluntumunro ktaptwnakunu.
	/p	kənihəla·láˑp·ani·k, ɔ́·k kəmi·li·néˑp·ani·k, ɔ́·k kwəle·ləntaməné·ɔ kta·pto·ná·k·an.
	/t	They were yours, and you gave them to me, and they kept your word.
	/k	thine they were, and thou gavest them me; and they have kept thy word.

Jn 17.7 /b Bqc mrhi watwnro li wrmi cntxi meleunup, kvakrf wunheyb.
        /p yúkwe méˑči o·wa·to·néˑɔ, lí- wé·mi éntxi-mi·liánəp khák·enk -wənčíˑayu.
        /t Now they know that everything you gave me is from you.
        /k Now they have known that all things whatsoever thou hast given me are of thee.

Jn 17.8 /b Rli nmelanro nrl aptwnakunul, meleunpani,
        /p é·li nəmi·la·néˑɔ né·l a·pto·ná·k·anal mi·lianpáni,
        /t For I gave them the words you gave me,
        /k For I have given unto them the words which thou gavest me;

        /b wrtunumunropani,   [Two clauses in KJV and L. are not in B.]
        /p wwe·t·ənəməne·ɔ́·p·ani,
        /t and they received them,
        /kl and they have received them, [and have known surely that I came out from thee,]

        /b ok wlamvetamunro ktuli prtalwkalen.
        /p ɔ́·k o·la·mhitaməné·ɔ, ktə́li-pe·t·alo·káˑli·n.
        /t and they believe that you sent me.
        /k and they have believed that thou didst send me.

Jn 17.9 /b Mpatamwrlxaok;
        /p "mpa·tamwe·lxáˑɔk.
        /t "I pray for them.
        /k I pray for them:

        /b takw mpatamwrlxaeok wrmi b cntu lawsehek, jwq cntxi meleunek;
        /p takóˑ mpa·tamwe·lxa·íˑɔk wé·mi yú entala·wsíˑčˑi·k, šúkw éntxi-mi·liáni·k.
        /t I do not pray for all mankind, but only for as many as you gave me.
        /k I pray not for the world, but for them which thou hast given me;

        /b rli knevlalaok.
        /p é·li kənihəla·láˑɔk.
        /t For they are yours.
        /k for they are thine.

Jn 17.10 /b Wrmi nrvlalukek krpc knevlalaok,
         /p wé·mi nehəla·lák·i·k ké·pe kənihəla·láˑɔk,
         /t All that are mine are yours, too,
         /k And all mine are thine,

/b ok nrvlaluhek nrpc nevlalaok.
/p ó·k nehəla·láč·i·k né·pe nnihəla·lá·ɔk.
/t and the ones that are yours are also mine.
/k and thine are mine;

/b Ok nmuxifovkunemkwswvalkwk.
/p ó·k nəmax·inkɔhkəni·mkwəs·o·há·lko·k.
/t And they cause me to be glorified.
/k and I am glorified in them.

Jn 17.11
/b Bqc, takw heh b cntu lawsif ntupewun,
/p yúkwe takó· čí·č yú entalá·wsink ntap·í·wən,
/t Now I am no longer in the world,
/k And now I am no more in the world,

/b jwq bk b cntu lawsif avpwuk, ne natu ntav.
/p šúkw yó·k yú entalá·wsink ahpúwak, ní· ná·ta ntá.
/t but these are in the world, and I go to you.
/k but these are in the world, and I come to thee.

/b Pelseun Nwxa, krnavke meleunvpanek nuxpi ktulswakun,
/p pi·lsían núxa·, ké·nahki· mi·lianpáni·k náxpi ktəlsəwá·k·an,
/t Holy father, with your power take care of those you gave me,
/k Holy Father, keep through thine own name those whom thou hast given me,

/b tuli a mawswenro, muluji kelwnu.
/p tə́li-=á· -ma·wso·wi·né·ɔ, málahši ki·ló·na.
/t so that they may be as one, like us.
/k that they may be one, as we are.

Jn 17.12
/b Srki wetavpemukup b tali cntu lawsif frnavkevapanek ktulswakunif.
/p sé·ki-witahpi·mák·əp yú táli entalá·wsink nke·nahki·há·p·ani·k ktəlsəwá·k·anink.
/t While I was with them in the world, I took care of them acting for you.
/k While I was with them in the world, I kept them in thy name:

/b Meleunvpanek, frnavkevaok bqc pchi.
/p mi·lianpáni·k nke·nahki·há·ok yúkwe péči.
/t The ones you gave me I have taken care of up to now.
/k those that thou gavest me I have kept,

/b Takw kwti taofulwi, jwq ktumakswakun qesu;
/p takó· kwə́t·i taɔnkəló·wi, šúkw ktəma·ksəwá·k·an kkwí·s·a,
/t Not one was lost, except the son of wretchedness,
/k and none of them is lost, but the son of perdition;

/b wcnhih pavkunhi lrk xwi aptwnakunu.
/p wénči-=č -pahkánči-lé·k xúwi-a·pto·ná·k·ana.
/t so that the ancient sayings would be fulfilled.
/k that the scripture might be fulfilled.

Jn 17.13
/b Bqc nata ntav,
/p yúkwe ná·ta ntá.
/t Now I go to you.
/k And now come I to thee;

/b bni ntulwrn tali cntu lawsif,
/p yó·ni ntə́ləwe·n táli entalá·wsink,
/t I say this in the world
/k and these things I speak in the world,

/b wcnhih nwlrluntumwakun vokywaif pavkuntvatrk.
/p wénči-=č no·le·ləntaməwá·k·an hɔk·ayəwá·ink -pahkantháte·k.
/t so that my joy will be fulfilled in them.
/k that they might have my joy fulfilled in themselves.

Jn 17.14
/b Nmelanrop ktaptwnakun;
/p nəmi·la·né·ɔ·p kta·pto·ná·k·an,
/t I have given them your word,
/k I have given them thy word;

/b b cntu lawsehek vwjifalawao,
/p yú entala·wsí·č·i·k wšinka·lawwá·ɔ,
/t and mankind hated them,
/k and the world hath hated them,

/b rli mutu b cntu lawsif wunheyelet,
/p é·li- máta yú entalá·wsink -wənči·aí·li·t,
/t because they do not belong in this world,
/k because they are not of the world,

/b rlkeqi nrpc mutu b wunheyeo cntu lawsif.
/p e·lkí·kwi- né·pe máta yú -wənči·aí·ɔ entalá·wsink.
/t to the same degree that I, also, am not of this world.
/k even as I am not of the world.

Jn 17.15
/b Takw kwenwumulwi ktuli a wrtunan li cntu lawsif,
/p takó· kəwi·nəwaməló·wi ktəli-=á· -wé·t·əna·n lí entalá·wsink,
/t I do not ask you to take them from (*lit.*, 'in') the world,
/k I pray not that thou shouldest take them out of the world,

	/b	jwq ktulih nwtuman wcnhih mutu mrtvekif avtet.
	/p	šúkw ktə́li-=č -nó·t·əma·n wénči-=č máta me·thíkink -áhti·t.
	/t	but that you watch over them so they do not go to what is evil.
	/k	but that thou shouldest keep them from the evil.

Jn 17.16 /b Takw b cntu lawsif wunheyewunro, [⟨wun-‖heyewunro⟩]
/p takó· yú entalá·wsink wwənči·ai·wəné·ɔ,
/t They are not of the world,
/k They are not of the world,

(p. 191) /b rlkeqi nrpc mutu b cntu lawsif wunheyeo.
/p e·lkí·kwi- né·pe máta yú entalá·wsink -wənči·aí·ɔ.
/t any more than I, also, am not of the world.
/k even as I am not of the world.

Jn 17.17 /b Pelawswvrl wunhi kwlamwrokun;
/p pi·la·wsó·he·l wənči ko·la·məwe·ɔ́·k·an.
/t Make them holy by your truth.
/k Sanctify them through thy truth:

/b ktaptwnakun wlamwrokun.
/p kta·pto·ná·k·an wəla·məwe·ɔ́·k·an.
/t Your word is truth.
/k thy word is truth.

Jn 17.18 /b Ke rlkeqi alwkaleun li cntu lawsif,
/p "kí· e·lkí·kwi-alo·ká·lian lí entalá·wsink
/t "In the same way that *you* sent *me* into the world,
/k As thou hast sent me into the world,

/b nrpc ntulkeqi lalwkalan cntu lawsif.
/p né·pe ntəlkí·kwi-lalo·ká·la·n entalá·wsink.
/t *I*, too, sent *them* into the world.
/k even so have I also sent them into the world.

Jn 17.19 /b Nevluhi mpelawswvala nvaky wunhi nrkumao,
/p nihəláči mpi·la·wso·há·la nhák·ay wə́nči ne·k·əmá·ɔ,
/t I make my own self holy because of them,
/k And for their sakes I sanctify myself,

/b tuli a ok nrkumao kuski pelawsenro wunhi wlamwrokun.
/p tə́li-=á· ɔ́·k ne·k·əmá·ɔ -káski-pi·la·wsi·né·ɔ wə́nči wəla·məwe·ɔ́·k·an.
/t so that *they* would also be able to become holy by means of the truth.
/k that they also might be sanctified through the truth.

Jn 17.20 /b Ok takw bk jwq mpatamwrlxaeok,
/p "ɔ·k takó· yó·k šúkw mpa·tamwe·lxa·í·ɔk,
/t "And I do not pray only for these,
/k Neither pray I for these alone,

/b jwq ok nrk wrlsitaehekh wunhi bk toptwnakunwu,
/p šúkw ɔ·k né·k we·lsət·aí·č·i·k=č wənči yó·k tɔ·pto·na·k·anúwa,
/t but also for those who will be my adherents because of the words of these,
/k but for them also which shall believe on me through their word;

Jn 17.21 /b tulih tavqei mawswenro;
/p tə́li-=č tahkwí·i -ma·wso·wi·né·ɔ,
/t so that they may be one together,
/k That they all may be one;

/b rlkeqi ke, Nwxa, avpetaeun, ok ne, avpetwlun,
/p e·lkí·kwi- kí·, núxa·, -ahpi·taían, ɔ·k ní· -ahpi·tó·lan,
/t in the same way that *you*, father, are in me, and *I* am in you,
/k as thou, Father, art in me, and I in thee,

/b ktuli a ok nrkumao tavqei mawswenrn;
/p ktə́li-=á· ɔ·k ne·k·əmá·ɔ tahkwí·i -ma·wso·wí·ne·n,
/t so that we and they would be one together,
/k that they also may be one in us:

/b wcnhi a b cntu lawsehek wulamvetamevtet ktuli prtalwkalen.
/p wénči-=á· yú entala·wsí·č·i·k -wəla·mhitamíhti·t, ktə́li-pe·t·alo·ká·li·n.
/t in order that the world would believe that you sent me.
/k that the world may believe that thou hast sent me.

Jn 17.22 /b Nc xifovkunemwkwswakun meleunup, nmelanro,   [⟨mwk⟩ for ⟨mvk⟩]
/p nə́ xinkɔhkəni·mkwəs·əwá·k·an mi·liánəp nəmi·la·né·ɔ.
/t The glory you gave me I have given them.
/k And the glory which thou gavest me I have given them;

/b tuli a mawswenro, lukveqi kelwnu rlkeqi mawsweufq.
/p tə́li-=á· -ma·wso·wi·né·ɔ ləkhíkwi, ki·ló·na e·lkí·kwi-ma·wsó·wiankw.
/t so that they would be one, in the same way that *we* are one.
/k that they may be one, even as we are one:

Jn 17.23 /b Ne ntupetaook, ok krpc ktupetai
/p ní· ntap·i·taɔ́·ɔk, ɔ·k ké·pe ktap·í·tai,
/t *I* am in them, and *you*, too, are in me,
/k I in them, and thou in me,

/b wcnhih pavkunhi mawswevtet,
/p wénči-=č -pahkánči-ma·wso·wíhti·t,
/t so that they will perfectly be one,
/k that they may be made perfect in one;

/b wcnhih b cntu lawsehek watwvtet ktuli prtalwkalen,
/p wénči-=č yú entala·wsí·č·i·k -wwa·túhti·t, ktə́li-pe·t·alo·ká·li·n,
/t and so that mankind will know that you sent me,
/k and that the world may know that thou hast sent me,

/b ok ktuli lukveqi avolan nrk, rlkeqi ne avoleun.
/p ó·k ktə́li-ləkhíkwi-ahɔ́·la·n né·k, e·lkí·kwi-ahɔ́·lian.
/t and that you love them as much as you love me.
/k and hast loved them, as thou hast loved me.

Jn 17.24 /b Nwxa, futatumun tutu rpeun ntuntu wetarmkwn nrk meleunvpanek,
/p "núxa·, nkat·á·t·amən, tətá é·p·ian ntə́nta-wi·t·aé·mko·n né·k mi·lianpáni·k,
/t "Father, I want those you gave me to live with me wherever you are,
/k Father, I will that they also, whom thou hast given me, be with me where I am;

/b wcnhi a kuski nrmvetet nmuxifovkunemwkwswakun meleunup,
                                        [⟨mwk⟩ for ⟨mvk⟩]
/p wénči-=á· -káski-ne·mhíti·t nəmax·inkɔhkəni·mkwəs·əwá·k·an mi·liánəp.
/t in order that they may see my glory, which you gave me.
/k that they may behold my glory, which thou hast given me:

/b rli nenwhi ktavolevwmp nrlumu rlumi vatrkc vaki.
/p é·li ni·núči ktahɔ·lí·həmp, né·ləma é·ləmi-hat·é·k·e hák·i.
/t For you loved me long ago, before the world began.
/k for thou lovedst me before the foundation of the world.

Jn 17.25 /b O jaxavkapreun Nwxa, b cntu lawsehek mutu kwavkweok;
/p "ó· šaxahka·p·é·ian núxa·, yú entala·wsí·č·i·k máta ko·wahko·wí·ɔk,
/t "O righteous father, mankind does not know you,
/k O righteous Father, the world hath not known thee:

/b jwq ne kwavul, ok bk watwnro ktuli prtalwkalen.
/p šúkw ní· ko·wá·həl, ó·k yó·k o·wa·to·né·ɔ ktə́li-pe·t·alo·ká·li·n.
/t but *I* know you, and these know that you sent me.
/k but I have known thee, and these have known that thou hast sent me.

Jn 17.26 /b Ntukunwtumaonrop rlseun, jwq qeaqih ntukunwtumun;
/p ntak·əno·t·əmaɔ·né·ɔ·p e·lsían, šúkw kwiá·kwi=č ntak·ənó·t·əmən,
/t I have talked to them about your power, but I will still talk about it more,
/k And I have declared unto them thy name, and will declare it:

/b tuli a avpetakwnro ktavoltwakun, ne rpetyekup, ok ne avpetaon.
/p tə́li-=á· -ahpi·ta·k·o·né·ɔ ktahɔ·ltəwá·k·an ní· e·p·i·taí·k·əp, ɔ́·k ní· -ahpí·taɔ·n.
/t so that your love that was in *me* may be in them, and *I* may be in them.
/k that the love wherewith thou hast loved me may be in them, and I in them.

Chapter 111 (pp. 191-192). [L. section 111.] (Matthew 26.30-35; Mark 14.26-31; Luke 22.39; John 18.1)

Jn 18.1 /b Nhesus keji nc lwrtc, nu koxkavkan Ketlun,
/p nčí·sas kíši- nə́ -luwé·t·e, ná kɔ́xkahka·n †ki·təlan.
/t After he had said that, Jesus then crossed over the stream Cedron,
/l When Jesus had spoken these words, he went forth [*out of the city*] over the brook Cedron,
/k When Jesus had spoken these words, he went forth with his disciples over the brook Cedron, ...

Lk 22.39 /b eku r Olipe ovhwf cvcntu maekrt,
/p íka é· †ɔlipí·i-ɔhčúnk, ehə́nta-maí·k·e·t,
/t He went to Olive mountain, where he was accustomed to spend the night,
/l and went, as he was wont, to the mount of Olives;
/k And he came out, and went, as he was wont, to the mount of Olives;

/b ok rkrkemahi.   [⟨rkrkema-‖hi⟩]
/p ɔ́·k e·k·e·ki·má·č·i.
/t and his disciples also.
/l and his disciples also followed him.
/k and his disciples also followed him.

Mk 14.27 /b Nhesus tulao, Wrmi cntxerq bqch trpvwqek kjuvwrlumwimw.
(p. 192) /p nčí·sas təlá·ɔ, "wé·mi entxíe·kw yúkwe=č te·phúkwi·k kšahwe·ləmwíhəmɔ.
/t Jesus said to them, "This night all of you will lose your will.   [RSV "fall away"]
/kl And Jesus saith unto them, All ye shall be offended because of me this night:

/b Rli lrkvasw mpulpetcvoh ncvnwtumat mrkesu,
/p é·li le·khá·s·u, 'mpəlpi·téhɔ=č nehənó·t·əma·t mekí·s·a,
/t For it is written, 'I shall slay the shepherd (*lit.*, one who watches over sheep),'
/kl for it is written, I will smite the shepherd,

/b wrmih nwtumunhek uvsrvlrok.
/p wé·mi=č no·t·əmə́nči·k ahsehəlé·ɔk.'
/t and all the flock (*lit.*, ones watched over) will scatter.'
/k and the sheep shall be scattered.

Mk 14.28 /b Jwq amweanc nekanih li Falulebf.
/p šúkw a·mwiá·ne, nni·k·á·ni=č lí †nka·lalí·yunk."

	/t	But when I rise (again), I shall go in the lead to Galilee."	
	/l	But after that I am risen again, I will go before you into Galilee.	
	/k	But after that I am risen, I will go before you into Galilee.	(Mk 14.28)
	/k	But after I am risen again, I will go before you into Galilee.	(Mt 26.32)

Mt 26.33 /b Jwq Petul tulao, Elih wrmi awrn lwkavlatc,
/p šúkw †pí·təl təlá·ɔ, "ílli=č wé·mi awé·n lo·kahəlá·t·e,
/t But Peter said to him, "Even if everyone (else) loses their will,
/kl But Peter answered and said unto him, Though all men shall be offended because of thee, [RSV "fall away"]
/k But Peter said unto him, Although all shall be offended, (Mk 14.29)

/b amunheih ne ta vuji lwkavlai.
/p amənčí·i=č ní· tá=á· háši llo·kahəlá·i."
/t nevertheless I will never lose my will."
/kl yet will I never be offended. [RSV "fall away"]
/k yet will not I. (Mk 14.29)

Mk 14.30 /b Nhesus tulao Kvehei ktulul,
/p nčí·sas təlá·ɔ, "khičí·i, ktə́ləl,
/t Jesus said to him, "Truly, I say to you,
/kl And Jesus saith unto him, Verily I say unto thee,

/b myai bqc trpvwqek, nrskoh nejun kunhemwet tepas,
/p mayá·i yúkwe te·phúkwi·k, né·skɔ=č ní·š·ən kənčí·mwi·t típa·s,
/t this very night, before the rooster ('chicken') crows twice,
/kl That this day, even in this night, before the cock crow twice,
/k That this night, before the cock crow ... (Matthew 26.34)

/b nuxunh kpuswrn nvaky.
/p naxə́n=č kpás·əwe·n nhák·ay."
/t you will deny me three times."
/kl thou shalt deny me thrice.

Mk 14.31 /b Jwq alwe hetanaptwnr, lwr,
/p šúkw aləwí·i-či·t·ana·ptó·ne·, lúwe·,
/t But he spoke even more strongly, saying,
/kl But he spake the more vehemently,

/b Taoni a kwimpunrmul, ta tcxi nuni ntclsewun.
/p "tá·ɔni=á· kəwimpəné·məl, tá=á· téxi nə́ni ntəlsí·wən."
/t "Even though I would die with you, I would absolutely not do that."
/kl If I should die with thee, I will not deny thee in any wise.

Mt 26.35 /b Nu ok wrmi rkrkemahi nc tulwrlen.
/p ná ɔ́·k wé·mi e·k·e·ki·má·č·i nɔ́ tələwé·li·n.
/t Then all his disciples said the same thing.
/kl Likewise also said all the disciples.

Chapter 112 (pp. 192-193). [L. section 112.] (Matthew 26.36-35; Mark 14.32-42; Luke, 22.40-46; John 18.1-2)

Mt 26.36 /b Nhesus eku prok cntu lwcntasek Krtsemrni
/p nčí·sas íka pé·ɔk énta-luwentá·s·i·k †ke·tsi·mé·ni,
/t Jesus and the others came to a place named Gethsemane,
/kl Then cometh Jesus with them unto a place called Gethsemane,
/k And they came to a place which was named Gethsemane: ... (Mk 14.32)

Jn 18.1 /b cntu mrnxkvasek, ekali tumekrok.
/p énta-me·nxkhá·s·i·k, íkali təmi·k·é·ɔk.
/t where there was an enclosed garden, and they went in there.
/kl ... where was a garden, into the which he entered, and his disciples.

Jn 18.2 /b Jwq Nhwtus mrvlamwnt, ok watwn,
/p šúkw †nčó·tas méhəlamunt ɔ́·k o·wá·to·n,
/t But Judas, who sold him out, also knew the place,
/kl And Judas also, which betrayed him, knew the place:

/b rli Nhesus tevtumeki nc tali alaxemwet, ok rkrkemahi.
/p é·li- nčí·sas tihtəmí·ki nɔ́ -táli-ala·x·í·mwi·t, ɔ́·k e·k·e·ki·má·č·i.
/t as Jesus often used to rest there, and also his disciples.
/kl for Jesus ofttimes resorted thither with his disciples.

Lk 22.40 /b Nc pravtetc, tulao,
/p nɔ́ pe·ahtí·t·e, təlá·ɔ,
/t When they got there, he said to them,
/kl And when he was at the place, he said unto them, ...

Mt 26.36 /b Nuh b klumuvtupenro srki my patamau.
/p "ná=č yú kələmahtap·i·né·ɔ, sé·ki-mái-pa·tamá·a."
/t "You must sit here while I go and pray."
/kl ... Sit ye here, while I go and pray yonder.

Mt 26.37 /b Tolumwxolao. Petulu, ok Nhimu ok Nhanu Srputesu qesul;
/p tələmo·x·ɔlá·ɔ †pí·təla, ɔ́·k nčíma ɔ́·k nčá·na, †se·patí·s·a kkwí·s·al,
/t He took along Peter, and Jim and John, Zebedee's sons,
/l And he took with him Peter, and James and John, the two sons of Zebedee,
/k And he took with him Peter and the two sons of Zebedee, ... (Mt 26.37)
/k And he taketh with him Peter and James and John, ... (Mk 14.33)

Text, Transcription, and Translation 675

/b alumi jerluntum ok nufevlr, ok qswkomalsw.
/p áləmi-ši·e·lə́ntam, ɔ́·k -nankíhəle·, ɔ́·k -kwsuk·ɔmálsu.
/t and he began to be sorrowful, and to tremble, and to feel heavy.
/l and he began to be sorrowful, sore amazed, and very heavy.
/k and began to be sorrowful and very heavy. (Mt 26.37)
/k and began to be sore amazed, and to be very heavy; (Mk 14.33)

Mt 26.38
/b Nu Nhesus tulao,
/p ná nčí·sas təlá·ɔ,
/t Then Jesus said to them,
/l Then saith Jesus unto them,
/k Then saith he unto them, ... (Matthew 26.38)

/b Ntunaprokun somi ave sukwrluntum, ntrpih nvelkwn,
/p "ntənna·p·e·ɔ́·k·an sɔ́·mi áhi-sak·we·lə́ntam, ntépi-=č -nhílko·n.
/t "My soul is extremely troubled, enough that it will kill me.
/kl My soul is exceeding sorrowful, even unto death:

/b ny b avpeq, krpwu ntaopeq.
/p ná=yú ahpí·kw; ké·pəwa ntaɔ́·p·i·kw."
/t Stay here, and you keep watch, too."
/kl tarry ye here, and watch with me.

Mt 26.39
/b Unhi r trpi a avsun prtavrf lukveqi
/p ánči-é·, tépi-=á· ahsə́n -pe·t·á·henk ləkhíkwi,
/t He went on further, the distance that a stone could be thrown to,
/l And he went a little farther, and was withdrawn from them about a stone's cast,
/k And he went a little farther, and fell on his face, and prayed, saying, O my Father, if it be possible, let this cup pass from me: nevertheless not as I will, but as thou wilt. (Matt 26.39)
/k And he went forward a little, and fell on the ground, and prayed that, if it were possible, the hour might pass from him. (Mk 14.35)
/k And he was withdrawn from them about a stone's cast, and kneeled down, and prayed, (Lk 22.41)

/b nejetqevlr, ok alwlavtclr li vakif,
/p ni·š·i·tkwíhəle·, ɔ́·k a·lo·lahtéhəle· lí hák·ink,
/t and he knelt down and threw himself face-down on the ground,
/l and kneeled down, fell on his face on the ground,

/b patama, li a pale lwxwrb tpusqevlak kuski lrkc.
/p pá·tama·, lí-=á· palí·i -lo·x·wé·yu tpəskwíhəla·k, káski-lé·k·e.
/t and he prayed that the time ("hour") might pass away, if it were possible.
/l and prayed that, if it were possible, the hour might pass from him.

Mk 14.36 /b   Lwr Wrtwxumulun, O Nwxa,
/p   lúwe·, "we·t·o·x·əmə́lan, ó· núxa·,
/t   And he said, "Father of mine, O father,
/l   And he said, Abba, O my Father,
/k   And he said, Abba, Father, all things are possible unto thee; take away this cup from me: nevertheless not what I will, but what thou wilt.   (Mk 14.36)
/k   ... saying, O my Father, if it be possible, let this cup pass from me: nevertheless not as I will, but as thou wilt.   (Mt 26.39)
/k   Saying, Father, if thou be willing, remove this cup from me: nevertheless not my will, but thine, be done.   (Lk 22.42)

/b   kuski a lrkc, krvlu wrmi krkw kuski lusi,
/p   káski-=á· -lé·k·e (kéhəla wé·mi kéku kkáski-lə́s·i),
/t   if it would be possible (and you can indeed do everything),
/l   if it be possible, and all things are possible unto thee,

/b   pale lunumael b paent;
/p   palí·i lənəmái·l yú páint.
/t   remove this cup from me.
/l   take away this cup from me:

/b   jwq mutu ne rli wulrlumtumu, ke jwq rli wulrluntumun, lrkch.
/p   šúkw, máta ní· é·li-wəle·lə́ntama, kí· šúkw é·li-wəle·lə́ntaman, lé·k·eč."
/t   But let, not what pleases *me*, but what pleases *you*, be done."
/l   nevertheless not my will, but thine, be done.

Mt 26.40 /b   Nu wtxan rkrkemahi,
/p   ná ó·txa·n e·k·e·ki·má·č·i,
/t   Then he came to his disciples,
/kl   And he cometh unto the disciples,

Mk 14.37 /b   wunroo tuli kaelen,
/p   wəne·ɔ́·ɔ tə́li-kaí·li·n.
/t   and he saw them sleeping.
/kl   and findeth them sleeping,

/b   tulao Petulu, Symun, kawi vuh ke?
/p   təlá·ɔ †pí·təla, "†sáiman, kkáwi=háč kí·?
/t   And he said to Peter, "Simon, are *you* (sg.) sleeping?
/kl   and saith unto Peter, Simon, sleepest thou?

/b   mutu vuh kuski eli kwti awlif svaki ntaopevwmw?
/p   máta=háč kkáski- ílli kwə́t·i á·wəlink -sháki-ntaɔ·p·i·húmɔ?
/t   Could you (pl.) not even keep watch for one hour?
/k   couldest not thou watch one hour?   (Mk 14.37)
/kl   What, could ye not watch with me one hour?   (Mt 26.40)

Mt 26.41 /b Ntaopeq ‖ ok patamwq,
/p ntaóꞏpꞏiꞏkw óꞏk páꞏtamoꞏkw,
/t Keep watch and pray (pl.),
/kl Watch and pray,

(p. 193) /b wunhih mutu alwvekakwrq avqrhevtwakun;
/p wə́nči-=č máta -aluhikaꞏkꞏóꞏweꞏkw ahkweꞏčꞏihtəwáꞏkꞏan.
/t so that temptation will not overcome you.
/kl that ye enter not into temptation:

/b lunaprokun vufq piji wifi, jwq wavtwvrpi jawusw.   [⟨-w⟩ for ⟨-ww⟩]
/p lənaꞏpꞏeꞏóꞏkꞏan=hánkw píši wínki, šúkw wahtuhéꞏpꞏi šawəsꞏóꞏu."
/t The soul is indeed willing, but the body is weak."
/kl the spirit indeed is willing, but the flesh is weak.

Mt 26.42 /b Nu lupi pale ton my patama;
/p ná lápi palíꞏi tóꞏn, mái-páꞏtamaꞏ.
/t Then he went away again, going to pray.
/kl He went away again the second time, and prayed,

/b lwr O Nuxa,
/p lúweꞏ, "óꞏ núxaꞏ,
/t He said, "O father,
/kl saying, O my Father,

/b bni paent mutu kuski pale vatrkc wunhi nvakrf, kcnh wrqetumanc,
/p yóꞏni páint máta káski- palíꞏi -hatéꞏkꞏe wə́nči nhákꞏenk, kə́nč weꞏkwiꞏtamáꞏne,
/t if this cup cannot be set away from me, unless I drink it up,
/kl if this cup may not pass away from me, except I drink it,

/b ke rli wulrluntumunh lrkc.
/p kíꞏ éꞏliꞏwəleꞏlə́ntaman=č léꞏkꞏe."
/t let what pleases *you* be done."
/kl thy will be done.

Mk 14.40 /b Apahetc lupi wnroo tuli kaelen,
/p aꞏpꞏaꞏčꞏíꞏtꞏe, lápi wəneꞏóꞏɔ, tə́li-kaíꞏliꞏn,
/t When he came back, he again saw them sleeping,
/kl And when he returned, he found them asleep again,

/b rli avi kavtwfomulet, ok qelu krkw lavtet.
/p éꞏli-áhi-kahtunkóꞏməliꞏt, óꞏk -kwíꞏla- kéku -láhtiꞏt. [PV gapped (misconstruing K.)]
/t as they were very sleepy and were at a loss what to say to him.
/kl for their eyes were heavy, neither wist they what to answer him.

Mt 26.44 /b Wnukalao lupi pale r my patama,
         /p wənəkˑaláˑɔ, lápi palíˑi éˑ, máiˑpáˑtamaˑ.
         /t And he left them and went away again, going to pray.
         /kl And he left them, and went away again, and prayed the third time,

         /b nunc lupi tulwrn.
         /p ná=nə lápi tə́ləweˑn.
         /t He said the same thing again.
         /kl saying the same words.

Lk 22.43 /b Nu wtxwkwn osavkamri cvalwkalunhi, vwhetanelarmkw.
         /p ná oˑtxúkˑoˑn ɔˑsˑahkaméˑi-ehaloˑkaˑlə́nči, wčiˑtˑaniˑlaéˑmku.
         /t Then an angel ('messenger') of heaven came to him and gave him inner stength.
         /kl And there appeared an angel unto him from heaven, strengthening him.

Lk 22.44 /b Somi avi amuxavrluntum, avalwe avi patuma,
         /p sɔ́ˑmi áhi-amaxˑaheˑlə́ntam, ahaləwíˑi áhi-páˑtamaˑ.
         /t He was in extreme agony and prayed harder and harder.
         /kl And being in an agony, he prayed more earnestly: [omits Heb 5.7 addition in L.]

         /b toptekswakun amufpcvlr li vakif, mulaji mvwq lenakot.
         /p tɔˑptiˑksəwáˑkˑan amankpéhələˑ lí hákˑink, málahši mhúkw liˑnáˑkˑɔt.
         /t His sweat fell to the ground in large drops, looking like blood.
         /kl and his sweat was as it were great drops of blood falling down to the ground.

Lk 22.45 /b Mrhi amwetc wunhi cntu patamat wtxao rkrkemahi,
         /p méˑči aˑmwíˑtˑe wə́nči énta-páˑtamaˑt, oˑtxáˑɔ eˑkˑeˑkiˑmáˑčˑi,
         /t After he got up from where he was praying, he came to his disciples,
         /k And when he rose up from prayer, and was come to his disciples,
         /l And when he arose up from prayer, and was come the third time to his disciples,

         /b wnro tuli kaelen rli jerluntumulet,
         /p wəneˑɔ́ˑɔ tə́li-kaíˑliˑn, éˑliˑšiˑeˑləntamə́liˑt.
         /t and he saw them sleeping, as they were sorrowful.
         /kl he found them sleeping for sorrow,

Mt 26.45 /b tulao, Kaeq, [[letrvanro]] ok alaxemweq,   [[..]] does not belong here, PV missing]
         /p təláˑɔ, "kaíˑkw, [[error]] ɔ́ˑk alaˑxˑíˑmwiˑkw;   [[..]]: '(you pl. or they) think']
         /t And he said to them, "Sleep and rest;
         /k and saith unto them, Sleep on now, and take your rest: [RSV: "Are you still ..?"]
         /l and said unto them, Why sleep ye now, and take your rest?

         /b mrhi lwi lr, mrhi trpi;
         /p méˑči lóˑwi-léˑ; méˑči tépi.

	/t	it's over now; it's enough.	
	/l	it is enough;	
	/k	it is enough,	(Mk 14.41)

—	/b	paswqeq alumskatamwq.	[apparently a correction added in the wrong place]
[Cf.	/b	Paswqeq, alumsktamwq;	(= Mk 14.42, next below).]

—	/b	[No B. translation of L.; presumably it was displaced by the preceding.]
	/l	rise and pray, lest ye enter into temptation.
	/k	Watch ye and pray, lest ye enter into temptation. (Mk 14.38; cf. Mt 26.41 above)

	/b	Jr mrhi tpusqevlr,
	/p	šé·, mé·či tpəskwíhəle·,
	/t	Look, the time has come,
	/l	Behold the hour is come,
	/k	behold, the hour is at hand, (Mt 26.45)
	/k	the hour is come; (Mk 14.41)

	/b	li Wrqesifi linwu melanro mrtawsehek.
	/p	lí- we·k·wi·s·ínki lə́nəwa -mi·la·né·ɔ me·t·a·wsí·č·i·k.
	/t	for the man who is the Son to be turned over to ('given to') sinners.
	/kl	and the Son of man is betrayed into the hands of sinners. (Mt 26.45)
	/k	behold, the Son of man is betrayed into the hands of sinners. (Mk 14.41)

Mk 14.42	/b	Paswqeq, alumsktamwq; [⟨alumsktamwq⟩ for ⟨alumskatamwq⟩ (see above)]
	/p	pahsúk·wi·kw, alǝmská·t·amo·kw.
	/t	Get up; let's go.
	/kl	Rise up, let us go;

	/b	jr mrvlamwnt nvaky mrhi prxwtavpw.
	/p	šé·, méhəlamunt nhák·ay pe·x·útahpu.
	/t	See, the one who is selling me out is near at hand.
	/kl	lo, he that betrayeth me is at hand.

Chapter 113 (pp. 193-195). [L. section 113.] (Mt 26.47-56, Mk 14.43-52, Luke 22.47-54, John 18.3-12.)

Mk 14.43, Mt 26.47, Jn 18.3

	/b	Nrli krkw lwrt wexkaohi Nhwtus mawsw atux neju cntxehek eku pr,
	/p	né·li- kéku -lúwe·t, wi·xkaɔ́či †nčó·tas, má·wsu átax ní·š·a entxí·č·i·k, íka pé·,
	/t	While he was speaking, suddenly Judas, one of the twelve, came there,
	/l	And immediately, while he yet spake, lo, Judas, one of the twelve, came,
	/k	And immediately, while he yet spake, cometh Judas, one of the twelve, and with him a great multitude with swords and staves, from the chief priest and the scribes and the elders. (Mk 14.43)

/k   And while he yet spake, lo, Judas, one of the twelve, came, and with him a great multitude with swords and staves, from the chief priests and elders of the people.
(Mt 26.47)

/k   Judas then, having received a band of men and officers from the chief priests and Pharisees, cometh thither with lanterns and torches and weapons.   (Jn 18.3)

/b   pchi wehrr xrli linwul,
/p   péči-wi·č·é·e· xé·li lə́nəwal.
/t   He came with many men.
/l   and with him a great multitude

/b   amufunjekunu ok alavonu kulunumwk,
/p   amankanší·k·ana ɔ́·k ala·hó·na kələ́nəmo·k,
/t   And they carried swords and canes,
/l   with swords and staves,

/b   patamwrokun krnavketaqek sohulumwao ok telabmwao,
/p   pa·tamwe·ɔ́·k·an ke·nahki·tá·k·wi·k sɔ·čələməwá·ɔ ɔ́·k ti·la·yəməwá·ɔ,
/t   being the soldiers and captains ('warriors') of the high priests ('prayer guardians'),
/l   having received a band of men and officers from the chief priests

/b   ok Paluseekri ok rvlrkvekrsekri, ok krkyimvrsekri wcnheyehek,
/p   ɔ́·k †pa·ləsi·i·ké·i, ɔ́·k ehəle·khi·k·e·s·i·ké·i, ɔ́·k ke·kayəmhe·s·i·ké·i wenči·aí·č·i·k.
/t   and coming from the Pharisees, and scribes, and rulers.
/l   and Pharisees, Scribes, and elders of the people,

/b   krxrnaoki osulrnekunu kulunrok, ok nrnvelwrtwfi.
/p   ke·x·ennáɔhki ɔ·s·əle·ní·k·ana kələné·ɔk, ɔ́·k nenhiləwe·túnki.
/t   And they carried several kinds of portable lights, and also deadly weapons.
/l   with lanterns and torches and weapons.

Jn 18.4   /b   Nhesus rli wataq krtu lenuf, xwvu tolumi apvesvekaoo,
/p   nčí·sas, é·li-wwá·ta·kw ké·t·a-lí·nank, xó·ha tɔ́ləmi-a·phishikaɔ́·ɔ,
/t   Jesus, as he knew what was going to happen to him, went alone to meet them,
/kl   Jesus therefore, knowing all things that should come upon him, went forth,

/b   tulao, Awrn vuh knatwnaovmw?
/p   təlá·ɔ, "awé·n=háč kənat·o·naɔ́həmɔ?"
/t   and he said to them, "Who are you looking for?"
/kl   and said unto them, Whom seek ye?

Jn 18.5   /b   Tulkw, Nhesus Nasulutif wcnheyet.
/p   tə́lku, "nčí·sas, †nasəlát·ink wenčí·ai·t."
/t   And they replied to him, "Jesus from Nazareth."
/kl   They answered him, Jesus of Nazareth.

Text, Transcription, and Translation

/b Nhesus tulao, Ne tu.
/p nčí·sas təlá·ɔ, "ní·=tá."
/t And Jesus said to them, "That's me."
/kl Jesus saith unto them, I am he.

/b Nhwtus mrvlamwnt wihi eku nepw.
/p †nčó·tas méhəlamunt wíči- íka -ní·p·o·.
/t And Judas, who sold him out, was standing there with the others.
/kl And Judas also, which betrayed him, stood with them.

Jn 18.6
/b Nu rli lat, Ne tu,
/p ná é·li-lá·t, "ní·=tá,"
/t And as soon as he said to them, "That's me,"
/kl As soon then as he had said unto them, I am he,

/b jac avjakhclrok ok vakif levlrok.
/p šá·e ahša·kčehəlé·ɔk, ó·k hák·ink lihəlé·ɔk.   [or hákink 'down']
/t they went over backwards and fell to the ground.
/kl they went backward, and fell to the ground.

Jn 18.7
/b Lupi ‖ tulao, Awrn vuh knatwnaovmw?
/p lápi təlá·ɔ, "awé·n=háč kənat·o·naóhəmɔ?"
/t And he asked them again, "Who are you looking for?"
/kl Then asked he them again, Whom seek ye?

(p. 194)
/b Tulkw, Nhesus Nasulutif wcnheyet.
/p tə́lku, "nčí·sas, †nasəlát·ink wenčí·ai·t."
/t And they replied to him, "Jesus from Nazareth."
/kl And they said, Jesus of Nazareth.

Jn 18.8
/b Nhesus tulao, Mrhi ktulwvmwp, Ne tu;
/p nčí·sas təlá·ɔ, "mé·či ktəllúhəmɔ·p, 'ní·=tá.'
/t And Jesus said to them, "I have told you that that's me.
/kl Jesus answered, I have told you that I am he:

/b ne ntwnaerqc konu lenw bk pale tonro;
/p ní· nto·naié·k·we, kóna lí·no· yó·k palí·i tɔ·né·ɔ,"
/t If you're looking for *me*, let these people go elsewhere,"
/kl if therefore ye seek me, let these go their way:

Jn 18.9
/b wcnhi myai lrk rlwrtup,
/p wénči-mayá·i-lé·k e·ləwé·t·əp,
/t so that it would happen exactly as he had said,
/kl That the saying might be fulfilled, which he spake,

	/b	meleunvpanek takw kwti ntafvelai.
	/p	"mi·lianpáni·k takó· kwə́t·i ntankhilá·i."
	/t	"Of those that you gave me I have not lost one."
	/kl	Of them which thou gavest me have I lost none.

Mk 14.44 /b Mrvlamwnt mrhi tulapani,
/p méhəlamunt mé·či təlá·p·ani,
/t The one who sold him out had said to them,
/l Now he that betrayed him had given them a token, saying,
/k Now ... (Mt 26.48)

/b Awrnh mwstwnamuk, nulh nu,
/p "awé·n=č mo·sto·ná·mak, nál=č ná.
/t "The one who I shall kiss, that will be him.
/l Whomsoever I shall kiss, that same is he;

/b ktavwunawu, khetanunawuh, kwlih alumwxolawu.
/p ktahwənáwwa, kči·t·anənáwwa=č, kó·li-=č -aləmo·x·ɔláwwa."
/t You seize him, and you must hold him firmly and lead him away safely."
/l take him, hold him fast, and lead him away safely.
/k hold him fast. (Mt 26.48)

Lk 22.47 /b Nekane avpwp.
/p ni·k·a·ní·i ahpó·p.
/t And he was in the lead.
/l And he went before them.
/k Judas, one of the twelve, went before them,

Mt 26.49 /b Wexkaohi eku r, tulao kofwmul Nrvlaleun, Nrvlaleun,
/p wi·xkaɔ́či íka é·, təlá·ɔ, "kɔnkó·məl, nehəlá·lian, nehəlá·lian,"
/t All at once he went to him and said to him, "I greet you, my master, my master."
/l And forthwith he came to Jesus, and said, Hail, Master, Master;
/k Master, master; (Mk 14.45)

/b ok mwstwnamao.
/p ɔ́·k mmo·sto·na·má·ɔ.
/t And he kissed him.
/kl and kissed him.

Mt 26.50 /b Nhesus tulao, Krkw vuh nhwtec kwnhi pav?
/p nčí·sas təlá·ɔ, "kéku=háč, nčó·t·ie, kúnči-pá?
/t And Jesus said to him, "Why have you come, friend?
/kl And Jesus said unto him, Friend, wherefore art thou come?

Lk 22.48 /b Nhwtus, kukeolu vuh linw Wrqesif rli mwstwnamut?
/p †nčó·tas, kkak·í·ɔla=háč lənu we·k·wí·s·ink é·li-mo·sto·ná·mat?"

/t Judas, are you deceiving the man who is the Son in kissing him?"
/kl Judas, betrayest thou the Son of man with a kiss?

Mt 26.50
/b Nu eku tonanro Nhesusu
/p ná íka tɔnna·né·ɔ nči·sás·a,
/t Then they laid hands on Jesus
/kl Then came they, and laid hands on Jesus,

/b tovwunawao.
/p tɔhwənawwá·ɔ.
/t and seized him.
/kl and took him.

Lk 22.49
/b Wehrvkwki nrmuletc krtu lrk, tulkw
/p wi·č·e·ykúk·i ne·məlí·t·e ké·t·a-lé·k, tə́lku,
/t When those with him saw what was going to happen, they said to him,
/kl When they which were about him saw what would follow, they said unto him,

/b Nrvlalerf, Xifonjekunh vuh ntartulawunanuk.
/p "nehəlá·lienk, xinkɔnší·k·an=č=háč ntae·t·əla·wəná·nak?"
/t "Master, shall we use a sword on them?"
/kl Lord, shall we smite with the sword?

Jn 18.10
/b Symun Petul, rli wlataq xifonjekun, qwthelavtwn,
/p †sáiman-pí·təl, é·li-wəlá·ta·kw xinkɔnší·k·an, kwəč·ílahto·n,
/t Simon Peter, since he had a sword, quickly drew it,
/k Then Simon Peter having a sword drew it,
/l [And behold, one of them which were with Jesus,] Simon Peter, having a sword, [stretched out his hand,] drew it,
/k And, behold, one of them which were with Jesus stretched out his hand, and drew his sword, and struck a servant of the high priest's, and smote off his ear. (Mt 26.51)

/b pokaman patamwrokun krnavketaq tolwkakunu,
/p pók·ama·n pa·tamwe·ɔ́·k·an ke·nahkí·ta·kw tɔlo·ká·k·ana,
/t and he struck the servant of the high priest ('prayer guardian') with it,
/kl and smote the high priest's servant,

/b povotvetcmaon vwetaokelet vwtunavaonelet wunhi.
/p pɔhɔthitehəmáɔ·n hwitaɔk·í·li·t, wtənna·ha·ɔní·li·t wə́nči.
/t and he chopped off his ear on the right side.
/kl and cut off his right ear.

/b   Nu alwkakun lwcnsw Malkus.
/p   (ná alo·ká·k·an luwénsu †má·lkəs.)
/t   (The servant's name was Malchus.)
/kl The servant's name was Malchus.

Lk 22.51

/b   Nhesus tulao, Mrhi trpi.
/p   nčí·sas təlá·ɔ, "mé·či tépi."
/t   And Jesus said to them, "That's enough, now."
/k   And Jesus answered and said, Suffer ye thus far.
/r   But Jesus said, "No more of this!"   (RSV)

/b   Nu eku tonan vwetaokelet qekrvao.
/p   ná íka tónna·n hwitaɔk·í·li·t, kwi·k·e·há·ɔ.
/t   Then he touched him on his ear and healed him.
/k   And he touched his ear, and healed him.

Mt 26.52, Jn 18.11

/b   Tulao Petulu kjakvuntekunif vatwl nc kpuxkjekun;
/p   təlá·ɔ †pí·təla, "kša·khantí·k·anink hát·o·l kpaxkší·k·an.
/t   He said to Peter, "Put your sword ('your knife') into your scabbard.
/l   Then said Jesus unto Peter, Put up again thy sword into the sheath;

/b   rli cntxih awrn wrtunif xifonjekun, ufulh wunhi xifonjekun.
/p   é·li éntxi-=č awé·n -wé·t·ənink xinkɔnší·k·an, ánkəl=č wə́nči xinkɔnší·k·an.
/t   For as many people as shall take up the sword shall die by the sword.
/kl for all they that take the sword shall perish with the sword.

Mt 26.53

/b   Ktitc vuh ta fuski bqc patamaoi Nwx,
/p   ktíte=háč, tá=á· nkáski- yúkwe -pa·tamaɔ́·i nó·x,
/t   Do you think that I wouldn't be able to pray to my father now
/kl Thinkest thou that I cannot now pray to my Father,

/b   tuli a prtalwkalan xavrlapxki rvalwkalahi?
/p   təli-=á· -pe·t·alo·ká·la·n xahe·lá·pxki ehalo·ka·lá·č·i?
/t   for him to send many hundreds of his angels?
/kl and he shall presently give me more than twelve legions of angels?

Mt 26.54

/b   Jwq tu vuh a wunhi lrw, rlwrf nunih lrw?
/p   šúkw tá=háč=á· wə́nči-lé·w, é·ləwenk, 'nə́ni=č lé·w'?
/t   But how would what was said will happen, happen?
/kl But how then shall the scriptures be fulfilled, that thus it must be?

Jn 18.11

/b   Nc paentif Nwx meletup, mutuh vuh nwrqetamwun?
/p   nə́ páintink nó·x mi·lí·t·əp, máta=č=háč nəwe·kwi·tamó·wən?"
/t   In the cup my father has given me, will I not drink it all?"
/kl The cup which my Father hath given me, shall I not drink it?

Mt 26.55-56, Mk 14.48-49, Lk 22.52-53

/b   Nu Nhesus tulan wrmi trvwnwqki;
/p   ná nčí·sas tə́la·n wé·mi tehwənúkwki,
/t   Then Jesus said to all those that seized him,
/l   In that same hour said Jesus unto the chief priests, and captains of the temple, and the elders, which were come to him,
/k   In that same hour said Jesus to the multitudes   (Mt 26.55)

/b   Mulaji vuh krvkumwtkrs knapunalavmw,
/p   "málahši=háč kehkəmó·tke·s kəna·pənaláhəmɔ,
/t   "Did you come out as if to seize a thief,
/l   Are ye come out as against a thief,

/b   amufunjekunu ok alavwnu kunumwvmw, cntu my tvwnerq?
/p   amankanší·k·ana ɔ́·k ala·hó·na kkənnəmúhəmɔ, énta-mái-thwə́nie·kw?
/t   carrying swords and canes, when you came to arrest me?
/k   with swords and with staves to take me?

Lk 22.53 /b   Hifc nckc cji kejqek kwetavpemulwvmwp tali patamwrekaonif
/p   čínke néke éši-kí·škwi·k kəwitahpi·məlúhəmɔ·p táli pa·tamwe·i·k·á·ɔnink,
/t   At times before, I was with you in the temple every day,
/l   When I was daily with you in the temple,

Mk 14.49 /b   cntu avkrkifranc,
/p   énta-ahke·kinke·á·ne,
/t   when I was teaching,
/k   teaching,

Lk 22.53 /b   takw vuji wunux ktulenxkrvwmw, tuli a twnenro;   [⟨wunux⟩ for ⟨wuntux⟩]
/p   takó· háši wə́ntax ktəli·nxkéhəmɔ, təli-=á· -thwəni·né·ɔ.
/t   and you never reached out your hands to me to arrest me.
/l   ye stretched forth no hands against me:

/b   jwq bqc ‖ ktupsqelavtavmw ok peskrk tolweluswakun.
/p   šúkw yúkwe ktəpskwilahtáhəmɔ, ɔ́·k pí·ske·k tɔləwí·i-ləs·əwá·k·an.
/t   But now your time has come, and the power of darkness.
/l   but this is your hour, and the power of darkness.

Mt 26.56 /b   Wrmi bqc rlrk
(p. 195) /p   wé·mi yúkwe é·le·k
/t   By everything that is happening now
/kl   But all this was done,

	/b	wunhi pavkunhi lr rlrkvekcvtetup nrvnekanewrwsepanek.	[⟨epa⟩ for ⟨etpa⟩]
	/p	wə́nči-pahkánči-lé· e·le·khi·k·ehtí·t·əp nehəni·k·a·ní·i-we·wsi·tpáni·k."	
	/t	what the ancient prophets wrote is fulfilled."	
	/kl	that the scriptures of the prophets might be fulfilled.	

Mt 26.56 /b Nu wrmi rkrkemahi wnukulwkwn vwjemwelw.
/p ná wé·mi e·k·e·ki·má·č·i wənək·alúk·o·n, wši·mwí·lu.
/t Then all his disciples left him and fled.
/kl Then all the disciples forsook him, and fled.

Mk 14.51 /b Kwti skenw tolumi vwtrkao Nhesusu
/p kwə́t·i skínnu tóləmi-wte·kaó·ɔ nči·sás·a.
/t And a certain young man began to follow behind Jesus.
/kl And there followed him a certain young man,

/b hetanu vcmpus eark jwq avkwv,
/p či·t·anahémpəs yá·e·k šúkw ahkú.
/t He wore only a piece of thick cloth.
/kl having a linen cloth cast about his naked body;

/b skenwuk tovwunawao.
/p skinnúwak tɔhwənawwá·ɔ.
/t The young men seized him.
/kl and the young men laid hold on him:

Mk 14.52 /b Wnukavtujemwen nc hetanu vcmpus,
/p wənəkahtəš·í·mwi·n nə́ či·t·anahémpəs,
/t And he fled leaving behind the thick cloth,
/kl And he left the linen cloth,

	/b	alumi supjemw.	[⟨sup-⟩ for ⟨swp-⟩]
	/p	áləmi-so·pší·mu.	
	/t	running away naked.	
	/kl	and fled from them naked.	

Chapter 114 (p. 195-197). [L. section 114.] (Matthew 26.57-68; Mark 14.53-65; Luke 22:54-55, 63-65; John 18.12-24)

Jn 18.12 /b Nu nrk sohuluk, ok lenwavkusehek, ok Nhwe elaok,
/p ná né·k só·čəlak ó·k linnuwahkəs·í·č·i·k ó·k nčo·wí·i-i·lá·ɔk
/t Then the soldiers and officers and the Jewish captains
/kl Then the band and the captain and officers of the Jews

/b koxpelanro Nhesusu,
/p kɔxpi·la·né·ɔ nči·sás·a.

	/t	tied Jesus up.
	/kl	took Jesus, and bound him,

Jn 18.13
- /b   vetami Anus weket tulwxolawao,
- /p   hítami †á·nas wí·k·i·t təlo·x·ɔlawwá·ɔ,
- /t   They took him first to Annas's house,
- /kl   and led him away to Annas first;

- /b   rli vwjelumatup Krupus, krnavketakup patamwrokun nckc lukveqi.
- /p   é·li-wši·ləmá·t·əp †ke·ápas, ke·nahki·tá·k·əp pa·tamwe·ɔ́·k·an néke ləkhíkwi.
- /t   since he was the father-in-law of Caiaphas, the high priest at that time.
- /kl   for he was father-in-law to Caiaphas, which was the high priest that same year.

Jn 18.14
- /b   Nul nu Krupus latup rlafwmahi,   [⟨latup⟩ for ⟨rlatup⟩]
- /p   nál ná †ke·ápas e·lá·t·əp e·lanko·má·č·i,
- /t   It was Caiaphas who had told his people,
- /kl   Now Caiaphas was he, which gave counsel to the Jews,

- /b   Wulexun tu kwti linw tufulun wunhi wrmi awrni.   [⟨tuf-⟩ for /tɔnk-/]
- /p   wəlí·x·ən=tá kwə́t·i lə́nu tɔ́nkələn wə́nči wé·mi awé·n.
- /t   'It is a good thing for one man to die for all.'
- /kl   that it was expedient that one man should die for the people.

Jn 18.24
- /b   Anus anvwqi mwelan Krupusu patamwrokun krnavketwlet
- /p   †á·nas a·nhúkwi mwí·la·n †ke·apás·a pa·tamwe·ɔ́·k·an ke·nahki·tó·li·t
- /t   Anas turned him over ('gave him') in turn to Caiaphas, the high priest,
- /l   And Annas sent him bound unto Caiaphas the high priest.
- /kl   Now Annas had sent him bound unto Caiaphas the high priest:

- /b   nrli kaxpeselet;
- /p   né·li-kaxpi·s·í·li·t.
- /t   still tied up.
- /kl   ("bound")

Mk 14.53
- /b   nenwhi eku maclrpanek wrmi wcvevwfrhek ok kvekwenwuk ok rvlrkvekrhek   [⟨rvlrk vekrhek⟩]
- /p   ni·núči íka ma·ehəlé·p·ani·k wé·mi wehi·hunké·č·i·k, ɔ́·k khikəwinnúwak, ɔ́·k ehəle·khi·k·é·č·i·k
- /t   Long before, all the priests, and elders, and scribes had gathered
- /kl   and with him were assembled all the chief priests, and the elders, and the scribes.
- /k   ... to Caiaphas the high priest, where the scribes and the elders were assembled.

                                                                                            (Mt 26.57)

- /b   Krupus weket.
- /p   †ke·ápas wí·k·i·t.
- /t   at the house of Caiaphas.   [from Mt 26.57]

Jn 18.15 /b   Symun Petul navokr, jwq ovlumi vwtcfwm
          /p   †sáiman-pí·təl na·hóke·, šúkw ɔ́həlǝmi wténk úm,
          /t   Simon Peter followed, but he kept far behind,
          /l   And Simon Peter followed Jesus afar off,
          /k   And Simon Peter followed Jesus, and so did another disciple: that disciple was known unto the high priest, and went in with Jesus into the palace of the high priest.
          /k   But Peter followed him afar off unto the high priest's palace, and went in, (Matthew 26.58)

          /b   pchi weket patamwrokun krnavketaq,
          /p   péči wí·k·i·t pa·tamwe·ɔ́·k·an ke·nahkí·ta·kw,
          /t   as far as the high priest's house,
          /l   unto the high priest's palace,

          /b   ok peli rkrkemkwset.
          /p   ɔ́·k pí·li e·k·e·ki·mkwǝ́s·i·t.
          /t   and also another disciple.
          /kl and so did another disciple.

          /b   Nunuli nrl Krupus wnunaoo.
          /p   nanáli né·l †ke·ápas wǝnǝnaɔ́·ɔ.
          /t   He was one that Caiaphas knew,
          /kl That disciple was known unto the high priest,

          /b   wihi ekali tumekr;
          /p   wíči- íkali -təmí·k·e·.
          /t   and he went in with the others.
          /kl and went in with Jesus into the palace of the high-priest;

Jn 18.16 /b   kahi Petul, kohumif joei skontc nepw.
          /p   káč·i †pí·təl kɔ́čəmink šɔí·i skɔ́nte ní·p·o·.
          /t   But Peter stood outside beside the door.
          /kl but Peter stood at the door without.

Jn 18.17 /b   Nunu qwthen rkrkemkwset wrovkwk Krupusu,
          /p   ná ná kwɔ́č·i·n e·k·e·ki·mkwǝ́s·i·t we·ɔ́hkuk †ke·apás·a,
          /t   Then the disciple that Caiaphas knew went out,
          /kl Then went out that other disciple, which was known unto the high priest,

          /b   krkw tulao xqro nwtheskontyrlehi, tumekulao Petulu.
          /p   kéku təlá·ɔ xkwé·ɔ no·č·i·skɔntae·lí·č·i, təmi·k·alá·ɔ †pí·təla.
          /t   and he spoke to the woman who was the door-keeper and brought Peter in.
          /kl and spake unto her that kept the door, and brought in Peter.

Jn 18.18 /b Alwkakunuk, ok elaok tuntrwvrok
/p alo·ká·k·anak ó·k i·lá·ɔk tənte·whé·ɔk
/t The servants and captains made a fire
/l And the servants and officers had made a fire of coals
/k And the servants and officers .. had made a fire of coals;

Lk 22.55 /b tali lawuntc,
/p táli la·wə́nte,
/t in the middle of the room,
/l in the midst of the hall
/k .. in the midst of the hall, ..

Jn 18.18 /b rli tvrk,
/p é·li-thé·k.
/t as it was cold.
/l (for it was cold)
/k for it was cold:

Lk 22.55 /b lrmutuvpevtetc
/p le·matahpihtí·t·e,
/t When they sat down
/l and were set down together,

Jn 18.18 /b rovsevtetc,
/p e·ɔhsihtí·t·e,
/t and warmed themselves,
/l and they warmed themselves,

Lk 22.55 /b Petul ekali mujakr,
/p †pí·təl íkali məšá·ke·,
/t Peter sat on the ground there,
/l and Peter sat among them
/k Peter sat down among them.

Mt 26.58 /b kotu watwn krkwh rlrk,
/p kɔ́t·a-wwá·to·n kéku=č é·le·k,
/t wanting to know what would happen,
/kl to see the end:

Mk 14.54 /b wihi aosw.
/p wíči-aɔ́s·u.
/t and warmed himself with the others.
/kl and warmed himself at the fire.
/k and Peter stood with them, and warmed himself. (Jn 18.18)

Jn 18.19 /b   Nu patamwrokun krnaxketaq notwtumaon Nhesusu, [⟨naxk⟩ for /nahk/]
          /p   ná pa·tamwe·ó·k·an ke·nahkí·ta·kw nɔt·o·t·əmáɔ·n nči·sás·a
          /t   Then the high priest asked Jesus
          /kl The high priest then asked Jesus

          /b   wunhi rkrkemahi, ok alutwnvrt.
          /p   wə́nči e·k·e·ki·má·č·i ɔ́·k allət·ó·nhe·t.
          /t   about his disciples and his preaching.
          /kl of his disciples, and of his doctrine.

Jn 18.20 /b   Nhesus tulao, cntu a puntyrf ‖ ntuntu vuf krkw lwr; [⟨-yrf⟩ for /-aink/]
          /p   nčí·sas təlá·ɔ, "énta-=á· -pɔ́ntaink ntə́nta-=hánkw kéku -lúwe.
          /t   Jesus said to him, "I always spoke where people would hear me.
          /kl Jesus answered him, I spake openly to the world;

(p. 196) /b   aphi vuf cvcntu macvluf ntuntu pumutwnvc. Nhwuk pcvpavtet,
          /p   á·pči=hánkw ehə́nta-ma·éhəlank ntə́nta-pəmət·ó·nhe, nčó·wak pehpáhti·t.
          /t   I always preached in synagogues, where the Jews come.
          /kl I ever taught in the synagogue, and in the temple, whither the Jews always resort;

          /b   takw vuji kemei krkw ntclwri.
          /p   takó· háši ki·mí·i kéku ntələwé·i.
          /t   I never spoke in secret.
          /kl and in secret have I said nothing.

Jn 18.21 /b   Krkw vuh wcnhi ne ntwtumaeun?
          /p   kéku=háč wénči- ní· -nto·t·əmaían?
          /t   Why do you ask *me*?
          /kl Why askest thou me?

          /b   ntwtumaw nrk puntyehek, krkw rluk;
          /p   ntó·t·əmaw né·k pəntaí·č·i·k, kéku é·lak.
          /t   Ask those that heard me what I said to them.
          /kl ask them which heard me, what I have said unto them:

          /b   rli watwnro krkw rluk.
          /p   é·li o·wa·to·né·ɔ kéku é·lak."
          /t   For they know what I said to them."
          /k   behold, they know what I said.

Jn 18.22 /b   Keji nc lwrtc, mawsw elu kexki nepyet pokamao Nhesusu
          /p   kíši- nə́ -luwé·t·e, má·wsu í·la kí·xki ní·p·ai·t pɔk·amá·ɔ nči·sás·a,
          /t   After he said that, one captain who was standing nearby struck Jesus,
          /kl And when he had thus spoken, one of the officers which stood by struck Jesus

/b   pukulinhrxen,
/p   pak·ələnčé·x·i·n,
/t   using the palm of his hand,
/k   with the palm of his hand,

/b   tulao, Nuni vuh ktulan Patamwrokun krnavketaq?
/p   təlá·ɔ, "nəni=háč ktəla·n pa·tamwe·ɔ́·k·an ke·nahkí·ta·kw?"
/t   and he said to him, "Is that what you say to the high priest?"
/k   saying, Answerest thou the high priest so?

Jn 18.23 /b   Nhesus tulao, muvtaptwnranc ahemwel ntcli muvtaptwnrn,
/p   nčí·sas təlá·ɔ, "mahta·pto·ne·á·ne, a·č·í·mwi·l ntóli-mahta·ptó·ne·n.
/t   Jesus said to him, "If I have said evil things, report that I have said evil things.
/kl   Jesus answered him, If I have spoken evil, bear witness of the evil:

/b   jwq wulaptwnranc, krkw vuh wcnhi pavkumeun?
/p   šúkw wəla·pto·ne·á·ne, kéku=háč wénči-pahkámian?"
/t   But if I have said good things, why did you hit me?"
/kl   but if well, why smitest thou me?

Mt 26.59 /b   Nu wcvevwfrhek ok krkybmvrhek ok wrmi cvahemwlsehek,
/p   ná wehi·hunké·č·i·k ɔ́·k ke·kayəmhé·č·i·k ɔ́·k wé·mi eha·č·i·mo·lsí·č·i·k
/t   Then the priests and the rulers ("elders") and all the council members
/kl   Now the chief priests, and elders, and all the council,

/b   ntwnamwk kulwnrokunu wcnhi a Nhesusu nvelavtet;
/p   ntó·namo·k kəlo·ne·ɔ́·k·ana wénči-=á· nči·sás·a -nhiláhti·t.
/t   searched for lies by means of which they could kill Jesus.
/kl   sought false witness against Jesus, to put him to death;

Mt 26.60 /b   jwq mutu muxkamweok;
/p   šúkw máta maxkamo·wí·ɔk.
/t   But they did not find any.
/kl   But found none:

/b   piji xrli krkwlwnrhek eku prok,   [⟨krkwlwn-⟩ for ⟨krkulwn-⟩]
/p   píši xé·li ke·k·əlo·né·č·i·k íka pé·ɔk,
/t   Many liars *did* come there,
/k   yea, though many false witnesses came, yet found they none.
/l   yea, though many false witnesses came and bare false witness against him, yet found they none.

Mk 14.56 /b   jwq hihpi lwrok.
/p   šúkw čə́čpi-luwé·ɔk.
/t   but they gave differing accounts.
/l   for their witness agreed not together.

Mt 26.60 /b Vwtcf wunhi eku prok neju krkulwnrhek.
/p wténk wə́nči íka pé·ɔk ní·š·a ke·k·əlo·né·č·i·k,
/t After the others, two liars came there,
/kl At the last came two false witnesses,

Mk 14.58 /b lwrok, mpuntaowunap wu lunw tuli lwrn.
/p luwé·ɔk, "mpəntaɔ́·wəna·p wá lə́nu tə́li-lúwe·n,
/t and they said, "We heard this man say,
/l And said, We heard this fellow say,
/k And said, This fellow said, (Mt 26.61); We heard him say, (Mk 14.58)

Mk 14.58 /b Mpaletwnh b patamwrekaon kejetwf wunhi wunaxku,
/p "mpalí·to·n=č yú pa·tamwe·i·k·á·ɔn, ki·š·í·tunk wə́nči wənáxka,
/t "I shall destroy this temple, that was made by hands,
/kl I will destroy this temple that is made with hands,

/b nuxih kejqc nuh peli fejetwn, mutu wunhi wunaxku.
/p náxi-=č -kí·škwe, ná=č pí·li nki·š·í·to·n, máta wə́nči wənáxka."
/t and in three days, then I shall make another, not by hands."
/kl and in three days I will build another made without hands.   [in: Mk "within"]

Mk 14.59 /b Jwq amunhei mutu trpi kwtrnaovki lwreok.
/p šúkw amənčí·i máta tépi kwət·ennáɔhki luwe·í·ɔk.
/t But despite that they could not agree on a single account.
/kl But neither so did their witness agree together.

Mk 14.60 /b Nu patamwrokun krnavketaq posqen laountc nepw,
/p ná pa·tamwe·ɔ́·k·an ke·nahkí·ta·kw pɔ́skwi·n, la·wə́nte ní·p·o·,
/t Then the high priest got up and stood in the middle of the room,
/kl And the high priest stood up in the midst,

/b tulao Nhesusu,
/p təlá·ɔ nči·sás·a,
/t and he said to Jesus,
/kl and asked Jesus, saying,

/b Mutu vuh krkw ktulwri wunhi nc rlavkunemkrun?
/p "máta=háč kéku ktələwé·i wə́nči nə́ e·lahkəni·mké·an?"
/t "Don't you have anything to say about the testimony against you?"
/kl Answerest thou nothing? what is it which these witness against thee?

Mk 14.61 /b Jwq Nhesus hetkwsw, takw krkw lwri.
/p šúkw nčí·sas či·tkwə́s·u, takó· kéku luwé·i.
/t But Jesus kept quiet and said nothing.
/l But Jesus held his peace, and answered nothing.
/k But he held his peace, and answered nothing.

	/b	Lupi patamwrokun krnuvketaq tulao,
	/p	lápi pa·tamwe·ó·k·an ke·nahkí·ta·kw təlá·ɔ,
	/t	And again the high priest said to him,
	/kl	Again the high priest asked him, and said unto him,

Mt 26.63	/b	Ktulul bqc b tali rlifwrxif Prmawswvalwrt Krtanutwet,
	/p	"ktələl yúkwe yú táli e·linkwé·x·ink pe·ma·wso·há·ləwe·t ke·tanət·ó·wi·t,
	/t	"I say to you here before God, the giver of life,
	/kl	I adjure thee by the living God,

	/b	maeai lenrn,
	/p	mayá·i lí·ne·n,
	/t	tell us truly,
	/kl	that thou tell us

	/b	ktuli Klysten qesumwkwn Krtanutwet, Wrlapenswvalwrt.
	/p	ktəli-kəláisti·n, -kkwi·s·əmúk·o·n ke·tanət·ó·wi·t, we·la·p·enso·há·ləwe·t."
	/t	that you are Christ, the son of God, the giver of blessings?"
	/l	whether thou be the Christ, the Son of God the blessed?
	/k	whether thou be the Christ, the Son of God. (Mt 26.63)
	/k	Art thou the Christ, the Son of the Blessed? (Mk 14.61)

Mk 14.62	/b	Nhesus tulao, Netu.
	/p	nčí·sas təlá·ɔ, "ní·=tá.
	/t	And Jesus said to him, "I am.
	/l	Jesus saith unto him, [Thou hast said. And Jesus said,] I am:
	/k	And Jesus said, I am: (Mk 14.62)
	/k	Jesus saith unto him, Thou hast said: (Mt 26:64)

	/b	Ok ktulwvmw, knrowuh linw Wrqesif lrmuvtupet tunavaonif xifwi luswakun
	/p	ó·k ktəllúhəmɔ, kəne·ówwa=č lónu we·k·wí·s·ink le·mahtáp·i·t tənna·há·ɔnink xínkwi-ləs·əwá·k·an,
	/t	And I say to you all, you will see the man who is the Son sitting on the right of the great power,
	/kl	nevertheless I say unto you, Hereafter shall ye see the Son of man sitting on the right hand of power,
	/k	nevertheless I say unto you, (Mt 26.64)
	/k	and ye shall see the Son of man sitting on the right hand of power, (Mk 14.62)

	/b	kumvwkwf xqihi pchi punet.
	/p	kəmhókunk xkwíči péči-pəní·t.
	/t	and coming down on top of a cloud (or clouds).
	/kl	and coming in the clouds of heaven. (Mk 14.62)

Mt 26.65 /b Nu patamwrokun krnavketaq vwtwxkunumun rqet, lwr,
/p ná pa·tamwe·ɔ́·k·an ke·nahkí·ta·kw wto·xkənə́mən é·k·wi·t, lúwe·,
/t Then the high priest tore his clothing and said,
/kl Then the high priest rent his clothes, saying,

/b Mrhi tu motapwnalao Krtanutwelehi; [⟨tapw⟩ for ⟨taptw⟩]
/p "mé·či=tá mɔt·a·pto·na·lá·ɔ ke·tanət·o·wi·lí·č·i.
/t "He has said bad things about God.
/kl He hath spoken blasphemy;

/b krkw ‖ vuh a wcnhi qeaqi nvakalufq mrtavkunemahek?
/p kéku=háč=á· wénči- kwiá·kwi -nhaká·lankw metahkəni·má·č·i·k?
/t Why should we rely any more on ones who accuse him?
/kl what further need have we of witnesses?

(p. 197) /b jr kpuntaowunu tuli mavtukuneman Krtauntwelehi.
/p šé· kpəntaɔ́·wəna tɔ́li-mahtak·əní·ma·n ke·tanət·o·wi·lí·č·i.
/t Here we all heard him say bad things about God.
/kl behold, now ye have heard his blasphemy.

Mt 26.66 /b Krkw vuh ktetrvavmw?
/p kéku=háč kti·t·e·háhəmɔ?"
/t What do you think?"
/kl What think ye? (= Mk 14.64)

/b Nu wrmi qwntrlumanro, lwrok, Trpi wunhi nvelan.
/p ná wé·mi kwənte·ləma·né·ɔ, luwé·ɔk, "tépi wə́nči-nhíla·n."
/t Then they all condemned him, saying, "It's enough reason for him to be killed."
/l And they all answered and condemned him and said, He is guilty of death.
/k They answered and said, He is guilty of death. (Mt 26.66)
/k And they all condemned him to be guilty of death. (Mk 14.64)

Mt 26.67 /b Nu vwsuswkvolanro wujkifwelet, ok welelet pwpavkamawao,
/p ná wsəs·ukhɔ·la·né·ɔ wəškinkwí·li·t, ɔ́·k wi·lí·li·t pupahkamawwá·ɔ.
/t Then they all spat in his face, and they smacked him on the head.
/kl Then did they spit in his face, and buffeted him; [RSV "and struck him"]

Lk 22.63 /b nrk lunwuk krnavkevahek wunwhqrvawao,
/p né·k lə́nəwak ke·nahki·há·č·i·k wəno·čkwe·hawwá·ɔ,
/t The men in charge of him hit him unprovoked,
/l and the men that held Jesus mocked him,
/k And the men that held Jesus mocked him, and smote him.

Mk 14.65 /b mwtavqifwrvowao,
/p mwətahkwinkwehɔwwá·ɔ.
/t and they covered his face.

	/l	covered his face,
	/k	and to cover his face,

Lk 22.64 /b keji nc levavtetc wujkifwelet pwpuvkumawao,
/p kíši- nə́ -li·hahtí·t·e, wəškinkwí·li·t pupahkamawwá·ɔ.
/t After they had done that to him, they smacked him on the face,
/kl and when they had blindfolded him, they struck him on the face,

/b tulaowao lenrn ke Klyst, awrn vuh ktuli pavkumkwn?
/p təlawwá·ɔ, "lí·ne·n, kí· kəláist, awé·n=háč ktəli-pahkámko·n?"
/t and said to him, "Tell us, you Christ, who is it that hit you?"
/l and asked him, saying, Prophesy, unto us, thou Christ, Who is he that smote thee?
/k thou Christ,   (Matthew 26.68)

Lk 22.65 /b Xrlrnaovki ok peli krkw tuli mavhi lawao;
/p xe·lennáɔhki ɔ́·k pí·li kéku təli-máhči-lawwá·ɔ.
/t There were also many other kinds of bad things that they said to him.
/kl And many other things blasphemously spake they against him.

Mk 14.65 /b ok alwkakunuk pwpavkumaowao pukulunhrxenwk.
/p ɔ́·k alo·ká·k·anak pupahkamawwá·ɔ, pak·ələnče·x·í·no·k.
/t And the servants struck him with the palms of their hands.
/kl and the servants did strike him with the palms of their hands.

Chapter 115 (pp. 197-198). [L. section 115.] (Mt 26.69-75, Mk 14.66-72, Lk 22.56-57, Jn 18.17, 25-27)

Lk 22.56-57, Mt 26.69-70, Mk 14.66-68, Jn 18.17
/b Nrli Petul paleihi lumutavpet
/p né·li- †pí·təl pali·íči -ləmátahpi·t,
/t While Peter was sitting a little ways off,
/kl Now Peter sat without in the palace: (Mt 26.69)
/k And as Peter was beneath in the palace,   (Mk 15.66)

/b eku pr patamwrokun krnavketaq wskexqrbmw,   [⟨-mw⟩ for ⟨-mu⟩]
/p íka pé· pa·tamwe·ɔ́·k·an ke·nahkí·ta·kw o·ski·xkwé·yəma,
/t one of the high priest's unmarried young women came there,
/k there cometh one of the maids of the high priest,

/b nunul nu nwheskontart.
/p nánal ná no·č·i·skɔ́ntae·t.
/t She was the door-keeper.
/k the damsel that kept the door.

/b Nrotc Petulu pr aoselet,
/p ne·ó·t·e †pí·tǝla pé·-aɔs·í·li·t,
/t When she saw Peter as he warmed himself by the fire,
/l And when she saw Peter as he sat by the fire, warming himself,

/b tovi kulifomao,
/p tóhi-kǝlinkɔ·má·ɔ,
/t she looked at him intensely
/k she earnestly looked upon him,

/b tulao, Mutu vuh ke mawsw wu linw rkrkemahi?
/p tǝlá·ɔ, "máta=háč kí· má·wsu wá lǝnu e·k·e·ki·má·č·i?
/t and said to him, "Aren't you one of this man's disciples?
/l and said, Art not thou also one of this man's disciples?

/b kwehrop mu wu Nhesus Falulebf wcnheyet.
/p kǝwi·č·é·ɔ·p=máh wá nčí·sas †nka·lalí·yunk wenčí·ai·t."
/t You were with this Jesus from Galilee."
/l Thou also wast with Jesus of Galilee.

/b Jwq paswr wrmi rlifwrxenulet tali, lwr,
/p šúkw pahsúwe· e·linkwe·x·í·nǝli·t táli, lúwe·,
/t But he denied it before them all, saying,
/l But he denied before them all, saying,

/b Xqr, takw ne, takw ne nwavai,
/p "xkwé·, takó· ní·; takó· ní· no·wa·há·i.
/t "Woman, I am not; *I* don't know him.
/l Woman, I am not, I know him not.

/b takw nunwstamwun rlwrun.
/p takó· nnǝno·stamó·wǝn e·lǝwé·an."
/t I don't understand what you're saying."
/l I know not neither understand what thou sayest.

/b Nu rli anvwquntrk ton,
/p ná é·li-a·nhukwǝnte·k tó·n.
/t Then he went into the porch.
/l And he went out into the porch,

/b nu tepas qunhemwen.
/p ná típa·s kwǝnčí·mwi·n.
/t Then the rooster ('chicken') crowed.
/l and the cock crew.

Lk 22.58, Mt 26.71-72, Mk 14.69-70, Jn 18.25

    /b Nrli nc rli anvwquntrk avpet,
/p né·li- nə́ é·li-a·nhukwə́nte·k -ahpí·t,
/t While he was sitting on the porch,
/l And when he was gone out into the porch,

    /b nul nu skexqr lupi wunroo, ok peli,
/p nál ná skí·xkwe lápi wəne·ɔ́·ɔ, ɔ́·k pí·li.
/t the same young woman saw him again, and another one.
/k this maid saw him again, and another,

    /b tulawao eku rpelehi,
/p təlawwá·ɔ íka e·p·i·lí·č·i,
/t And they said to those sitting there,
/l and said unto them that were there,

    /b wuni wehropani Nhesusu Nhesulutif wcnheyelehi.   [⟨Nhesulutif⟩ for ⟨Nasulutif⟩]
/p "wáni wwi·č·e·ɔ́·p·ani nči·sás·a †nasəlát·ink wenči·ai·lí·č·i."   [emended]
/t "This man was with Jesus from Nazareth."   [*man* supplied]
/l This fellow was also with Jesus of Nazareth.

    /b Nuni wunhi lan, mutu vuh ke mawsw nu rkrkemahi?
/p nə́ni wə́nči-lá·n, "máta=háč kí· má·wsu ná e·k·e·ki·má·č·i?"
/t He was therefore asked, "Aren't you one of his disciples?"
/l They said therefore unto him, Art not thou also one of his disciples?

    /b Lupi paswr kvetaptwnr, lwr, Mutu nwavai nu lunw.
/p lápi pahsúwe·, khita·ptó·ne·, lúwe·, "máta no·wa·há·i ná lə́nu."
/t And again he denied it and insisted, saying, "I don't know that man."
/l And again he denied with an oath, I am not, I do not know the man.

Lk 22.59-60, Mt 26.73-74, Mk 14.70-72, Jn 18.26-27

    /b Nakarkc, avpami ct kwti awlif
/p na·k·a·é·k·e, ahpá·mi=ét kwə́t·i á·wəlink,
/t A while later, perhaps by about one hour,
/l And after a while, about the space of one hour after,

    /b mawsw alwkakun patamwrokun krnavketaq tolwkakunu,
/p má·wsu alo·ká·k·an pa·tamwe·ɔ́·k·an ke·nahkí·ta·kw tɔlo·ká·k·ana—
/t one servant of the high priest's servants—
/l one of the servants of the high priest,

    /b (nul nu rlafwmat Petul pvotvetcvmaot vwetaokelet,)
/p nál ná e·lankó·ma·t †pí·təl phɔthitehəmáɔ·t hwitaɔk·í·li·t—
/t he was a relative of the one whose ear Peter chopped off—
/l (being his kinsman whose ear Peter cut off)   (Jn 18.26)

/b ave lwr kvehei tu wu wehropani, rli Falulebf wunheyb.
/p áhi-lúwe·, "khičí·i=tá wá wwi·č·e·ɔ́·p·ani, é·li †nka·lalí·yunk wənčí·ayu.
/t said insistently, "Truly this (man) was with him, for he is from Galilee."
/l confidently affirmed, saying, Of a truth this fellow also was with him: for he is a Galilaean.

/b Nu tulan Petulu, Mutu vuh kunrwulwevwmp ‖
/p ná tə́la·n †pí·təla, "máta=háč kəne·wəlo·wí·həmp
/t Then he said to Peter, "Didn't I see you
/l And he said to Peter, Did not I see thee

(p. 198)
/b tali cntu twkomrnxkvasek ktuli wehron?
/p táli énta-tuk·ome·nxkhá·s·i·k ktə́li-wi·č·é·ɔ·n?"
/t in the garden with him?"
/l in the garden with him?   (Jn 18.26)

/b Ok kexki, nepaehek tulawao, kvehei tu ke nuni kwnheyen, rli Faluleeu, [⟨-n⟩ om.]
/p ɔ́·k kí·xki ni·p·aí·č·i·k təlawwá·ɔ, "khičí·i=tá nə́ni kunčí·ai·n, é·li-†nka·lalí·ian.
/t And those standing nearby said to him, "Surely you are from there, as you are a Galilean.
/l And they that stood by said unto Peter, Surely thou art one of them; for thou art a Galilaean,

/b rlexseun kuthevlalwkwn.
/p e·li·xsían kkəč·ihəlalúk·o·n."
/t Your speech exposes you."
/l for thy speech bewrayeth thee.   (Mt 26.73; RSV "your accent betrays you")

/b Petul lupi paaswr, alumi muvtaptwnr, ok kvetaptwnr lwr,   ⟨paas-⟩ for [⟨pavs-⟩]
/p †pí·təl lápi pahsúwe·, áləmi-mahta·ptó·ne·, ɔ́·k khita·ptó·ne·, lúwe·,
/t And Peter denied it again and began to swear, and he insisted, saying,
/l Peter then denied again, and began to curse and to swear, and said,

/b Linw, takw nwatwun rlwreun,
/p "lə́nu, takó· no·wá·to·wən e·ləwé·an.
/t "Man, I don't know what you're saying.
/l Man, I know not what thou sayest.

/b takw nwavai nu linw rkunemrq.
/p takó· no·wa·há·i ná lə́nu e·k·əní·me·kw."
/t I don't know that man you people are talking about."
/l I know not this man of whom ye speak.

/b Nu jac nrli nc lwrt, tepas lupi qwnhemwen.
/p ná šá·e, né·li- nə́ -lúwe·t, típa·s lápi kwənčí·mwi·n.

/t Then immediately, while he was saying that, a rooster ('chicken') crowed again.
/l And immediately, while he yet spake, the second time the cock crew.

Lk 22.61 /b Nu Nrvlalwrt eku tulvwqrn pwunaoo Petulu;
/p ná nehəláˑləweˑt íka təlhúkweˑn, pwənaɔ́ˑɔ †píˑtəla.
/t Then the Lord turned to Peter and looked at him.
/l And the Lord turned, and looked upon Peter.

/b nu Petul mwjatumun rlkwkup Nrvlalwrlehi,
/p ná †píˑtəl mwəšˑáˑtˑamən eˑlkúkˑəp nehəlaˑləweˑlíˑčˑi,
/t Then Peter remembered what the Lord had said to him,
/l And Peter remembered the word of the Lord,

/b rlkwkup, nrskoh tepas nejun kunhemwet,
/p eˑlkúkˑəp, "néˑskɔ=č típaˑs níˑšˑən kənčíˑmwiˑt,
/t when he said to him, "Before the rooster ('chicken') crows twice,
/l how he had said unto him, Before the cock crow twice,   (*twice* from Mk 14.72)

/b nuxunh keji pavswrn nvaky;
/p naxən=č kkíši-pahsúweˑn nhákˑay."
/t you will have denied me three times."
/k thou shalt deny me thrice.

Mk 14.72 /b mrjatufc khe, ok ave lupuq.
/p meˑšˑaˑtˑánke, kčíˑ, ɔ́ˑk áhi-ləpákw.
/t When he remembered it, he went out and wept bitterly.
/l And when he thought thereon, he went out, and wept bitterly.   (Mk + Lk 22.62)

Chapter 116 (p. 198). [L. section 116.] (Matthew 27.1-2; Mark 15.1; Luke 22.66-71, 23.1: John 18.28)

Lk 22.66 /b Jac alupae
/p šáˑe alapˑaˑíˑi,
/t First thing early in the morning,
/l And straightway in the morning, as soon as it was day,

/b macvlrok cvahemwlsehek ok wrmi wcvevwfrhek ok rvlrkvekrhek,
/p maˑehəléˑɔk ehaˑčˑiˑmoˑlsíˑčˑiˑk ɔ́ˑk wéˑmi wehiˑhunkéˑčˑiˑk ɔ́ˑk ehəleˑkhiˑkˑéˑčˑiˑk,
/t the councillors and all the priests and scribes gathered together,
/l the elders of the people and all the chief priests and the scribes came together,
/k [= Luke + *all* (Matthew 27.1), + *and the whole council* (Mk 15.1).]

Mt 27.1   /b   tokunwtumunro tuli a nvelanro Nhesusu;
          /p   tɔk·əno·t·əməné·ɔ táli-=á· -nhila·né·ɔ nči·sás·a.
          /t   and they discussed killing Jesus.   [*lit.*, 'that they would']
          /kl took counsel against Jesus to put him to death:

Lk 22.66 /b   ok eku pwrjwawao, cvcntu ahemwlsevtet, tulawao,
          /p   ó·k íka pwe·š·əwawwá·ɔ ehə́nta-a·č·i·mo·lsíhti·t, təlawwá·ɔ,
          /t   And they took him to where they had their councils and said to him,
          /kl and led him into their council, saying,

Lk 22.67 /b   Ke vuh kvehei Klyst? lenrn.
          /p   "kí·=háč khičí·i kəláist? lí·ne·n.
          /t   "Are you truly the Christ? Tell us."
          /kl Art thou the Christ? tell us.

          /b   Tulao, lulrqc a ta kwlamvetyevmw.
          /p   təlá·ɔ, "ləlé·k·we=á·, tá=á· ko·la·mhitai·húmɔ.
          /t   And he said to them, "If I tell you, you will not believe me.
          /kl And he said unto them, If I tell you, ye will not believe:

Lk 22.68 /b   Ok a ntwtumwlrqc, taa ktapahi krkw levmw, ok taa kpwnunevwmw.
                                                                    [⟨-vmw⟩ for ⟨-vwmw⟩]
          /p   ó·k=á· nto·t·əmo·lé·k·we, tá=á· kta·p·a·č·i- kéku -li·húmɔ, ó·k tá=á· kpo·nəni·húmɔ.
          /t   And if I ask you, you won't speak to me in return, and you won't release me.
          /kl And if I also ask you, ye will not answer me, nor let me go.

Lk 22.69 /b   Jwq knrowuh linw Wrqesif
          /p   šúkw kəne·ówwa=č lə́nu we·k·wí·s·ink
          /t   But you shall see the man who is the Son
          /kl Hereafter shall the Son of man
          /k   and ye shall see the Son of man sitting ...   (Mk 14.62)

          /b   lrmuvtupet tunavaanif Krtanutwet tolwe luswakun.   [⟨-vaan-⟩ for /-há·ɔn-/]
          /p   le·mahtáp·i·t tənna·há·ɔnink ke·tanət·ó·wi·t tɔləwí·i-ləs·əwá·k·an."
          /t   sitting on the right hand of God's power."
          /kl sit on the right hand of the power of God.   (Lk 22.69)

Lk 22.70 /b   Nu wrmi tulanro, Ke vuh nu Krtanutwet Qesu?
          /p   ná wé·mi təla·né·ɔ, "kí·=háč ná ke·tanət·ó·wi·t kkwí·s·a?"
          /t   Then they all said to him, "Are you God's son?"
          /kl Then said they all, Art thou then the Son of God?

          /b   Tulao, Ne tu.
          /p   təlá·ɔ, "ní·=tá."
          /t   And he said to them, "I am."

| | /kl | And he said unto them, Ye say that I am. |
| | /k | And Jesus said, I am. (Mk 14.62) |

Lk 22.71 /b Lwrok, Krkw vuh a wcnhi unhi krkw ntwnamufq;
/p luwé·ɔk, "kéku=háč=á· wénči-ánči- kéku -ntó·namankw?
/t And they said, "Why should we ask anything more?
/k And they said, What need we any further witness?

/b rli nevlahi kpuntaowunu, wunhi nevlahi vwtwnif.
/p é·li nihəláči kpəntaó·wəna wə́nči nihəláči wtó·nink."
/t For we have heard him ourselves out of his own mouth."
/k for we ourselves have heard of his own mouth.

Lk 23.1 /b Nu wrmi posqenro;
/p ná wé·mi pɔskwi·né·ɔ.
/t Then they all stood up.
/kl And the whole multitude of them arose,

Mt 27.2, Jn 18.28
/b ok tonhi kaxpelawao Nhesusu, ok tolumwxolawao wunhi Krupusif,
/p ɔ́·k tónči-kaxpi·lawwá·ɔ nči·sás·a, ɔ́·k tɔləmo·x·ɔlawwá·ɔ wə́nči †ke·apás·ink,
/t And they tied Jesus up again, and they led him away from Caiaphas,
/l And when they had bound Jesus, they led him away from Caiaphas,

Jn 18.28 /b eku tulwxolawao wekwavmif cvcntu awrn kejavkunemunt,
/p íka təlo·x·ɔlawwá·ɔ wi·k·əwáhəmink ehə́nta- awé·n -kišahkəní·mənt.
/t leading him to the building where people were judged and sentenced.
/kl unto the hall of judgment,

Mt 27.2 /b mwelanro fopunulu Pontius Pylutu;
/p mwi·la·né·ɔ †nkapənála, "Pontius" †pailát·a.
/t And they turned him over (*lit.*, 'gave him') to the governor, Pontius Pilate.
/kl and delivered him to Pontius Pilate the governor;

Jn 18.28 /b ave alupae.
/p áhi-alap·a·í·i.
/t It was very early in the morning.
/kl and it was early.

Chapter 117 (p.199). [L. section 117.] (Matthew 27.3-10; Acts 1.18)

Mt 27.3 /b Nhwtus mrvlumwntup nrfc li kuntrlumalen,
/p †nčó·tas, mehəlamúntəp, nénke lí-kənte·ləmá·li·n,
/t Judas, the one who had sold him out, when he saw that he was condemned,
/kl Then Judas, which had betrayed him, when he saw that he was condemned,

	/b	nevlahi jerluntum;
	/p	nihəláči ši·e·lə́ntam.
	/t	felt sorry for his part.
	/kl	repented himself,

	/b	eku pwrtaon nc xenxkc pvakc moni wcvevwfrsu ok cvahemwlselehi,
	/p	íka pwé·t·aɔ·n nə́ xí·nxke pháke móni wehi·hunké·s·a ɔ́·k eha·č·i·mo·lsi·lí·č·i.
	/t	And he brought the thirty pieces of money to the priests and councillors.
	/kl	and brought again the thirty pieces of silver to the chief priests and elders,

Mt 27.4 /b lwr, nhani lusi, rli mvalumaif nc peltuk mvwq.
/p lúwe·, "nčáni-lə́s·i, é·li-mhalamáink nə́ pí·ltək mhúkw.
/t And he said, "I have done wrong by selling the innocent ('clean, pure') blood."
/kl Saying, I have sinned in that I have betrayed the innocent blood.

/b Tulawao krkw vuh a wcnhi nelwnu nc punarluntumrf?
/p təlawwá·ɔ, "kéku=háč=á· wénči- ni·ló·na nə́ -pəna·elə́ntamenk?
/t They said to him, "Why should *we* give thought to that?
/kl And they said, What is that to us?

/b Ke a wulava.
/p kí·=á· wəláha."
/t It should rather be *you*."
/kl see thou to that.

Mt 27.5 /b Nu patamwrekaonif tulaneven nrl moniu;
/p ná pa·tamwe·i·k·á·ɔnink təlaníhi·n né·l mónia.
/t Then he threw the coins in the temple.
/k And he cast down the pieces of silver in the temple,

/b nu pale ton, ok vwjcvlalao vokyu.
/p ná palí·i tɔ́·n, ɔ́·k wšehəlalá·ɔ hókaya.
/t Then he went away and hanged himself.
/k and departed, and went and hanged himself.

Acts 1.18 /b Punevlr avhehkolevlr, pvokhrxen,
/p pəníhəle·, ahči·čkɔlíhəle·, phɔkčé·x·i·n,
/t He fell, falling headfirst, and his body burst open when he landed,
/kl (and falling headlong, he burst asunder in the midst,

[RSV: "burst open in the middle"]

/b wrmi wlukjeu ktetrxunw.
/p wé·mi wəlakšía kti·té·x·ənu.
/t and all the intestines fell out on impact.
/kl and all his bowels gushed out.)

Mt 27.6
/b Wcvevwfrhek wrtunumunroi nrl moniu;
/p wehi·hunké·č·i·k wwe·t·ənəmənе·ó·i né·l mónia,
/t And the priests took those coins,
/kl And the chief priests took the silver pieces,

/b ok lwrok, Takw wulexunwi, bl moniu vatwn, cvatrk mcmarnasek,
/p ó·k luwé·ɔk, "takó· wəli·x·ənó·wi yó·l mónia hát·o·n ehháte·k mehəma·e·ná·s·i·k,
/t and they said, "It is not right for these coins to be put where the collection is,
/kl and said, It is not lawful for to put them into the treasury,

/b rli mvwq wunhi mvalasek.
/p é·li- mhúkw -wə́nči-mhalá·s·i·k."
/t as they were bought with blood."
/kl because it is the price of blood.

Mt 27.7
/b Rkunwtumevtetc, vaki wunhi mvalumunro,
/p e·k·əno·t·əmihtí·t·e, hák·i wwə́nči-mhalaməné·ɔ,
/t After they talked about it, they used them to buy land
/kl And they took counsel, and bought with them

/b cvcntu manevuntup seskwe vwsuk,
/p ehə́nta-manni·hə́ntəp si·skəwí·i-hó·s·ak,
/t where clay pots used to be made,
/kl the potter's field,

/b cvcntuh qtaowununt pale wcnheyehek.   [⟨qtaow-⟩ for ⟨qtaw-⟩]
/p ehə́nta-=č -kwtáwənənt palí·i wenči·aí·č·i·k.
/t as a place where people from elsewhere would be buried.
/kl to bury strangers in.

Mt 27.8
/b Nuni wunhi vaki lwcntasek, mvwqei-vaki bqc pchi.
/p nə́ni wə́nči- hák·i -luwentá·s·i·k mhukwí·i-hák·i yúkwe péči.
/t That is why the land is called the land of blood to the present time.
/kl Wherefore that field was called, The field of blood, unto this day.

Mt 27.9
/b Nu pavkunhi lrp rlwrtup, Nhclemyusu ncvnekanewrwsetpanu,
/p ná pahkánči-lé·p e·ləwé·t·əp †nčeli·mayás·a nehəni·k·a·ní·i-we·wsi·tpána,
/t Then was fulfilled what the ancient prophet Jeremiah had said,
/kl Then was fulfilled that which was spoken by Jeremy the prophet,

/b rlwrtup, Wrtunumunro nc xenxkc pvakc moni,
/p e·ləwé·t·əp, "wwe·t·ənəməné·ɔ nə́ xí·nxke pháke móni,
/t when he said, "They took the thirty pieces of money,
/kl saying, And they took the thirty pieces of silver,

/b   rlaovtet nu linw Nhwok mrvlumwnhi;
/p   e·lá·ɔhti·t ná lə́nu, nčó·wak mehəlamúnči,
/t   the price ('value') of the man that the Jews sold,
/kl the price of him that was valued, whom they of the children of Israel did value;

Mt 27.10 /b   mwrkunro wunhi vaki scseskwuvwsvrs nrlatuf, [⟨nrl-⟩ for ⟨nrvl-⟩]
/p   mwe·k·əné·ɔ wə́nči hák·i sehsi·skəwahó·she·s nehəlá·t·ank,
/t   and they gave them for land that a clay-pot-maker owned,
/kl And gave them for the potter's field,

/b   Nrvlalwrt rletup ntulwrn.
/p   nehəlá·ləwe·t e·lí·t·əp ntə́ləwe·n."
/t   as the Lord told me to say."
/kl as the Lord appointed me.

Chapter 118 (p. 199-200). [L. section 118.] (John 18.28-32)

Jn 18.28 /b   Jwq nrkumao takw ekali tumekreok cvcntu awrn kejavkunemunt,
/p   šúkw ne·k·əmá·ɔ takó· íkali təmi·k·e·í·ɔk ehə́nta- awé·n -kišahkəní·mənt,
/t   But *they* did not enter the place where people are judged and sentenced,
/kl And they themselves went not into the judgment hall,

/b   rli a nesketwvtetc vokybu,
/p   é·li=á·, ni·ski·tuhtí·t·e hɔk·ayúwa,
/t   for if they defiled themselves,
/kl lest they should be defiled;

/b   wunhi a mutu kuski mehewunro lwif e. [⟨lwif e⟩ for ⟨lwife⟩]
/p   wwə́nči-=á· máta -káski-mi·č·i·wəné·ɔ lo·winkí·i.
/k   they would not be able to eat the passover meal because of it.
/t   but that they might eat the passover.

Jn 18.29 /b   Pylut ekali khe, tulao, Krkw vuh, ktulavkunemawu, nu linw?
/p   †páilat íkali kčí·, təlá·ɔ, "kéku=háč ktəlahkəni·máwwa ná lə́nu."
/t   Pilate went out to them and said to them, "What are you saying about that man?"
/kl Pilate then went out unto them, and said, What accusation bring ye against this man?

Jn 18.30 /b   Tulawao, Mutu a muxifwi avhifxatc,
/p   təlawwá·ɔ, "máta=á· maxínkwi-ahčinkxá·t·e,
/t   And they said to him, "If he were not disobedient in a major way,
/kl They answered and said unto him, If he were not a malefactor,

/b   ta kprtwlwunrn.
/p   tá=á· kpe·t·o·ló·wəne·n."

	/t	we wouldn't bring him to you."
	/k	we would not have delivered him up unto thee.
Jn 18.31	/b	Pylut tulao, Alumwxolw, levw nevlahi rlexif qetulutwakunwu.
	/p	†páilat təlá·ɔ, "aləmó·x·ɔlo·, lí·ho· nihəláči e·lí·x·ink kkwi·tələt·əwa·k·anúwa."
	/t	Pilate said to them, "Take him away and treat him according to your own law."
	/kl	Then said Pilate unto them, Take ye him, and judge him according to your law.

	/b	Nhwak tulawao, Takw nelwnu nevlatumwunrn li a awrn ‖ nvelan;
	/p	nčó·wak təlawwá·ɔ, "takó· ni·ló·na nnihəla·t·amó·wəne·n lí·=á· awé·n -nhíla·n."
	/t	The Jews said to him, "*We* don't have the say over anyone being killed."
	/kl	The Jews therefore said unto him, It is not lawful for us to put any man to death:

Jn 18.32	/b	nuni lrw, pavkunhi lr Nhesus rlwrtup, rlufulkh.	[⟨rlufulkh⟩ for ⟨rlufulukh⟩]
(p. 200)	/p	nə́ni lé·w, pahkánči-lé· nčí·sas e·ləwé·t·əp e·lánkələk=č.	
	/t	That happened, and what Jesus had said about how he would die was fulfilled.	
	/kl	That the saying of Jesus might be fulfilled, which he spake, signifying what death he should die.	

Chapter 119 (p. 200-201). [L. section 119.] (Matthew 27.11-14, Mark 15.2-5, Luke 23.2-12, John 18.33-38.)

Lk 23.2	/b	Nu tolumi muvtukunemanro, lwrok,
	/p	ná tɔ́ləmi-mahtak·əni·ma·né·ɔ, luwé·ɔk,
	/t	Then they began to say bad things about him, saying,
	/kl	And they began to accuse him, saying,

	/b	numuxkaowunu nu lunw tuli avhifxrwvrn rlafwmalerfi,
	/p	"nəmaxkaɔ́·wəna ná lə́nu, tɔ́li-ahčinkxé·whe·n e·lanko·ma·liénki,
	/t	"We found that man making our people (*lit.*, relatives) disobedient,
	/kl	We found this fellow perverting the nation,

	/b	ok qetvekrn mevmarnumaon moni Sesul,
	/p	ɔ́·k -khwithíke·n mihəma·e·nəmáɔ·n mɔ́ni †sí·sal.
	/t	and forbidding people to collect money for Caesar.
	/kl	and forbidding to give tribute to Caesar,

	/b	ok evlwr, ne Klyst, sakema nvaky.
	/p	ɔ́·k ihəlúwe·, 'ní· kəláist; sa·k·í·ma nhák·ay.'"
	/t	And he's always saying, 'I am Christ; I am a king.'"
	/kl	saying that he himself is Christ a King.

Jn 18.33	/b	Nu Pylut vwtumekrn cvcntu awrn kejavkunemunt,
	/p	ná †páilat wtəmí·k·e·n ehə́nta- awé·n -kišahkəní·mənt,
	/t	Then Pilate went into the place where people are judged and sentenced,
	/kl	Then Pilate entered into the judgment hall again,

	/b	notwmao Nhesusu.
	/p	nɔt·o·má·ɔ nči·sás·a,
	/t	and he called Jesus to come.
	/kl	and called Jesus,

Mt 27.11	/b	Nhesus eku my nepw rlifwrxenulet fopunulu.
	/p	nčí·sas íka mái-ní·p·o· e·linkwe·x·í·nəli·t †nkapənála.
	/t	Jesus went and stood before the governor.
	/kl	And Jesus stood before the governor:

Jn 18.33	/b	Tulao ke vuh Nhwe sakema?
	/p	təlá·ɔ, "kí·=háč nčo·wí·i-sa·k·í·ma?"
	/t	And he said to him, "Are you the king of the Jews?"
	/kl	and the governor asked him, saying, Art thou the King of the Jews?

Jn 18.34	/b	Nhesus tulao, nevlahi vuh nc ktulen;
	/p	nčí·sas təlá·ɔ, "nihəláči=háč nə́ ktə́li·n,
	/t	Jesus said to him, "Do you ask me that on your own,
	/kl	Jesus answered him, Sayest thou this thing of thyself,

	/b	ji vuh mutu?
	/p	ší=háč máta?"
	/t	or not?"
	/kl	or did others tell it thee of me?

Jn 18.35	/b	Pylut tulao, Nhw vuh nvaky?
	/p	†páilat təlá·ɔ, "nčó·=háč nhák·ay?
	/t	Pilate said to him, "Am I a Jew?
	/kl	Pilate answered, Am I a Jew?

	/b	Ketvakrok, wcvevwfrhek, mprtakwnro kvaky;
	/p	ki·thaké·ɔk, wehi·hunké·č·i·k, mpe·t·a·k·o·né·ɔ khák·ay.
	/t	Your own nation, the priests, brought you to me.
	/kl	Thine own nation and the chief priests have delivered thee unto me:

	/b	krkw vuh ktulacvosi?
	/p	kéku=háč ktəlaehɔ́·s·i?"
	/t	What did you do?"
	/kl	what hast thou done?

Jn 18.36
- /b Nhesus tulao; Nsakemaokun takw b wunheyei cntu lawsif;
- /p nčí·sas təlá·ɔ, "nsa·k·i·ma·ɔ́·k·an takó· yú wənči·aí·i entalá·wsink.
- /t Jesus said to him. "My kingdom does not belong to this world.
- /kl Jesus answered, My kingdom is not of this world:

- /b nsakemaokun a b wunheyekc cntu lawsif,
- /p nsa·k·i·ma·ɔ́·k·an=á· yú wənči·aí·k·e entalá·wsink,
- /t If my kingdom did belong to this world,
- /kl if my kingdom were of this world,

- /b ntalwkakunuk a muvtakrok wcnhi a Nhwuk mutu tvwnevtet.
- /p ntalo·ká·k·anak=á· mahta·ké·ɔk, wénči·=á· nčó·wak máta -thwəníhti·t.
- /t my servants would fight, so that the Jews would not seize me.
- /kl then would my servants fight, that I should not be delivered to the Jews:

- /b Jwq nsakemaokun pale wunheyb.
- /p šúkw nsa·k·i·ma·ɔ́·k·an palí·i wənčí·ayu."
- /t But my kingdom belongs to another place."
- /kl but now is my kingdom not from hence.

Jn 18.37
- /b Pylut tulao, Sakemaunt kvaky?
- /p †páilat təlá·ɔ, "sa·k·í·ma=ɔ́nt khák·ay?"
- /t Pilate said to him, "Are you, nevertheless, a king?"
- /kl Pilate therefore said unto him, Art thou a king then?

- /b Nhesus tulao, Kvehei tu sakema nvaky.
- /p nčí·sas təlá·ɔ, "khičí·i=tá sa·k·í·ma nhák·ay.
- /t Jesus said to him, "I am truly a king.
- /kl Jesus answered, Thou sayest that I am a king.

- /b Jr b nwnhi b tuli kejeken, ok nwnhi pan cntu lawsif,
- /p šé· yú núnči- yú -táli-ki·š·í·k·i·n ɔ́·k núnči-pá·n entalá·wsink:
- /t This is why I was born in the world and why I came here:
- /kl To this end was I born, and for this cause came I into the world,

- /b ntulih watvekrn wulamwrokun.
- /p ntə́li-=č -wwa·thíke·n wəla·məwe·ɔ́·k·an.
- /t to make known the truth.
- /kl that I should bear witness unto the truth.

- /b Wrmi cntxi wulamwrokunif wunheyet, pwuntamun rlwru.
- /p wé·mi éntxi- wəla·məwe·ɔ́·k·anink -wənčí·ai·t pwɔ́ntamən e·ləwé·a."
- /t Everyone that belongs to the truth hears what I say."
- /kl Every one that is of the truth heareth my voice.

Jn 18.38 /b   Pylut tulao, Krkw vuh wulamrokun?
         /p   †páilat təlá·ɔ, "kéku=háč wəla·məwe·ɔ́·k·an?"
         /t   Pilate said to him, "What is truth?"
         /kl Pilate saith unto him, What is truth?

         /b   keji nc lwrtc lupi khe li Nhwekri,
         /p   kíši- nə́ -luwé·t·e, lápi kčí· lí nčo·wi·ké·i.
         /t   After saying that, he went out again to the Jews.
         /kl And when he had said this, he went out again unto the Jews,

         /b   tulao, Takw tcxi nmuxkamwun krkw rli mavhiluset.
         /p   təlá·ɔ, "takó· téxi nəmaxkamó·wən kéku é·li-máhči-lə́s·i·t."
         /t   And he said to them, "I have not found anything bad in him at all."
         /kl and saith unto them, I find in him no fault at all.

Mk 15.3 /b   Nu wcvevufrhek ok rvahemwlsehek
         /p   ná wehi·hunké·č·i·k ɔ́·k eha·č·i·mo·lsí·č·i·k
         /t   Then the priests and councillors
         /kl And the chief priests and elders   [*and elders* from Mt 27.12]

         /b   xrlrnaovki krkw tuli mavtukunemanro;
         /p   xe·lennáɔhki kéku tə́li-mahtak·əni·ma·né·ɔ.
         /t   accused him of many kinds of things,
         /kl accused him of many things:

         /b   jwq mutu krkw tulaeo.
         /p   šúkw máta kéku təla·í·ɔ.
         /t   but he said nothing to them.
         /kl but he answered nothing.

Mk 15.4 /b   Pylut lupi notwtumaoo, tulao, Mutu vuh kutu krkw laeok?
         /p   †páilat lápi nɔt·o·t·əmaɔ́·ɔ, təlá·ɔ, "máta=háč kkát·a- kéku -la·í·ɔk?
         /t   Pilate asked him again, saying to him, "Don't you want to say anything to them?
         /kl And Pilate asked him again, saying, Answerest thou nothing?

         /b   krvlu xrlrnaovki ktuli muvtukunemkc.
         /p   kéhəla xe·lennáɔhki ktə́li-mahtak·əní·mke."
         /t   You are accused of a great many things."
         /kl behold how many things they witness against thee.

Mt 27.14 /b   Jwq mutu tcxi krkw tulaeo.
         /p   šúkw máta téxi kéku təla·í·ɔ.
         /t   But he said nothing at all to him.
         /kl And he answered him to never a word;

	/b	Nuni wunhi avi kanjrluntumun nu fopunul.
	/p	nəni wwə́nči-áhi-kanše·lə́ntamən ná †nkápənal.
	/t	And the governor was greatly astonished by that.
	/kl	insomuch that the governor marvelled greatly.

Lk 23.5 /b Jwq ‖ alwe manwfvetaqswuk, lwrok,
/p šúkw aləwí·i manunkhita·kwsúwak, luwé·ɔk,
/t But their shouts grew angrier, and they said,
/kl And they were the more fierce, saying,

(p. 201) /b Honrluntumwvrnu wrmi awrni, wrmi Nhwekri pwpami avkrkifrn,
/p "čɔne·lə́ntamo·hé·na wé·mi awé·ni, wé·mi nčo·wi·ké·i pup·á·mi-ahke·kínke·n,
/t "He makes everyone discontented, going around teaching among all the Jews,
/kl He stirreth up the people, teaching throughout all Jewry,

/b vetami puna Falulebf kxunki ny b pchi.
/p hítami pənáh †nka·lalí·yunk, kxántki ná=yú péči."
/t beginning even in Galilee, and eventually as far as here."
/kl beginning from Galilee to this place.

Lk 23.6 /b Pylut puntufc li lwrn Frlule;   [⟨Frlule⟩: ⟨Fclule⟩ [Jn 7.1] (cf. ⟨Falule-⟩)]
/p †páilat pəntánke lí-lúwe·n "†nké·lali·,"   [or †nkélali·]
/t When Pilate heard Galilee mentioned,
/kl When Pilate heard of Galilee,

/b lwr Falulebf vuh wunhyb wu linw?   [⟨wunhyb⟩ for ⟨wunheyb⟩]
/p lúwe·, "†nka·lalí·yunk=háč wənčí·ayu wá lə́nu?"
/t he said, "Is this man from Galilee?"
/kl he asked whether the man were a Galilaean.

Lk 23.7 /b nu rli puntuf tuli wunheyelen Vclut cntu kvekybmvrt,
/p ná é·li-pə́ntank tə́li-wənči·aí·li·n †hélat énta-khikayə́mhe·t,
/t And as soon as he heard that he was from the place where Herod ruled,
/kl And as soon as he knew that he belonged unto Herod's jurisdiction,

/b jac lwr Vclutif lwxolw;
/p šá·e lúwe·, "†helát·ink ló·x·ɔlo·."
/t he said, "Take him to Herod."
/kl he sent him to Herod,

/b nckc lukveqi Nhelwsulumif avpelwp.
/p (néke ləkhíkwi †nči·lo·sələ́mink ahpí·lo·p.)
/t (At that time he was in Jerusalem,)
/kl who himself also was at Jerusalem at that time.

Lk 23.8 /b Vclut nrotc Nhesusu avi wulrluntum,
/p hélat ne·ó·t·e nči·sás·a, áhi-wəle·lə́ntam.
/t When Herod saw Jesus he was very glad.
/kl And when Herod saw Jesus, he was exceeding glad:

/b rli wunenwhi kavtu nropani,
/p é·li wəni·núči-káhta-ne·ó·p·ani.
/t For he had wanted to see him for a long time.
/kl for he was desirous to see him of a long season,

/b rli xrlrnaovki krkw tevlustumunrpani;
/p é·li xe·lennáɔhki kéku tihələstəməné·p·ani,
/t For he had been hearing many different things,
/kl because he had heard many things of him;

/b ok letrvr nroh tuli kanjyvosen.
/p ó·k li·t·é·he·, "nné·ɔ=č tə́li-kanšaehó·s·i·n."
/t and he thought he would see him perform a miracle.
/kl and he hoped to have seen some miracle done by him.

Lk 23.9 /b Xrli krkw notwtumaoo, jwq mutu krkw tulkweo.
/p xé·li kéku nɔt·o·t·əmaɔ́·ɔ, šúkw máta kéku təlko·wí·ɔ.
/t He asked him many things, but he said nothing to him in reply.
/kl Then he questioned with him in many words; but he answered him nothing.

Lk 23.10 /b Wcvevwfrhek ok rvlrkvekrhek eku nepwuk
/p wehi·hunké·č·i·k ó·k ehəle·khi·k·é·č·i·k íka ni·p·ó·wak,
/t The priests and scribes stood there
/kl And the chief priests and scribes stood

/b vwsku tovi muvtukunemawao;
/p hwə́ska tóhi-mahtak·əni·mawwá·ɔ.
/t and vehemently accused him.
/kl and vehemently accused him.

Lk 23.11 /b Vclut ok telabmu, motrlumawao, wowesavkevawao,
/p hélat ó·k ti·lá·yəma mɔt·e·ləmawwá·ɔ, wɔwisahki·hawwá·ɔ,
/t Herod and his captains felt contempt for him and mocked him,
/kl And Herod with his men of war set him at nought, and mocked him,

/b totanwao wrli opulrxif jakvwqeun; [⟨totanwao⟩ for ⟨totaowao⟩]
/p tɔ·taɔwwá·ɔ wé·li-ɔ·p·əlé·x·ink ša·khuk·wí·ɔn.
/t and they put on him a fine shiny-white coat.
/kl and arrayed him in a gorgeous robe,

/b   nu Pylutif tuli kunhhunan.
/p   ná †pailát·ink tə́li-kənččə́na·n.
/t   Then he sent him to Pilate.
/kl and sent him again to Pilate.

Lk 23.12 /b   Na nckc kejqek Pylut ok Vclut wulafwntwuk,
/p   ná-néke kí·škwi·k †páilat ɔ́·k †hélat wəlankúntəwak.
/t   And that same day Pilate and Herod became reconciled as friends.
/kl And the same day Pilate and Herod were made friends together:

/b   ekali wunhi jifaltwpanek.
/p   íkali wə́nči-šinka·ltó·p·ani·k.
/t   They had been enemies before.
/kl for before they were at enmity between themselves.

Chapter 120 (pp. 201-202). [L. section 120.] (Matthew 27.15-28; Mark 15.6-14; Luke 23.13-23; John 18.39-40.)

Lk 23.13 /b   Pylut mormapani wevevwfrlehi, ok krkybmvrlehi, ok navkoi awrni;
/p   †páilat mɔ·e·má·p·ani wehi·hunke·lí·č·i ɔ́·k ke·kayəmhe·lí·č·i ɔ́·k nahkɔ́·i awé·ni,
/t   Pilate called together the priests and the rulers and ordinary people,
/kl And Pilate, when he had called together the chief priests and the rulers and the people,

Lk 23.14 /b   tulao, Kprtaenro wu linw, mulaji hrnrluntumwvalwrt.
/p   təlá·ɔ, "kpe·t·ai·né·ɔ wá lə́nu málahši če·ne·ləntamo·há·ləwe·t.
/t   and he said to them, "You brought me this man as one who spreads discontent.
/kl Said unto them, Ye have brought this man unto me, as one that perverteth the people:

/b   Mrhi feji wavav tali rlifwrxenrq,
/p   mé·či nkíši-wwá·ha táli e·linkwe·x·í·ne·kw,
/t   I have now come to know him in your presence,
/kl and, behold, I, having examined him before you,

/b   jwq takw nmuxkamwi vokrf nc rlavkunemrq
/p   šúkw takó· nəmaxkamó·wi hɔ́k·enk nə́ e·lahkəní·me·kw.
/t   but I did not find in him any of what you accuse him of.
/kl have found no fault in this man touching those things whereof ye accuse him:

Lk 23.15 /b   takw wuluki, ok Vclut mutu;
/p   takó· wəláki, ɔ́·k †hélat máta.
/t   I just didn't, and also Herod did not.
/kl No, nor yet Herod:

/b rli punu eku ntuli kunhhinap,
/p é·li pənáh íka ntə́li-kənččə́na·p
/t For I even sent him to him.
/kl for I sent you to him; [RSV "for he sent him back to us"]

/b jr takw krkw muxkamwi wcnhi a ufululet.
/p šé· takó· kéku maxkamó·wi wénči-=á· -ankələ́li·t.
/t And here he found nothing he should die for.
/kl and, lo, nothing worthy of death is done unto him. [RSV "has been done by him"]

Lk 23.16 /b Bv tu luvupu nsrsrkycvon, nuh kcnh mpwnunan.
/p yúh=tá, lahápa nse·s·e·k·ayéhɔ·n, ná=č kə́nč mpó·nəna·n."
/t Alright, I'll whip him first, and then I'll release him."
/kl I will therefore chastise him, and release him.

Mt 27.15 /b Nuni rli tavqepwifc,
/p nə́ni é·li-tahkwi·p·wínke,
/t When that feast was held,
/kl Now at that feast

/b aphi vufq fopunul pwnunr kwti krpvaselehi
/p á·pči=hánkw †nkápənal pó·nəne· kwə́t·i ke·pha·s·i·lí·č·i.
/t the governor would always release one prisoner.
/kl the governor was wont to release unto the people a prisoner,

/b tuk tu rlenaqselehi trqepwelehi rletrvalet nuni a.
/p tákta e·li·na·kwsi·lí·č·i te·k·wi·p·wi·lí·č·i e·li·t·e·há·li·t, náni=á·.
/t Whichever one the feast-goers wanted, that would be the one.
/kl whom they would.

Mt 27.16 /b Nckc lukveqi kpavaswp kwti wrovkwset tuli palalwkasen,
/p néke ləkhíkwi kpahá·s·o·p kwə́t·i we·ɔhkwə́s·i·t tə́li-palalo·ká·ɜ·i·n,
/t At that time a certain well-known criminal had been imprisoned,
/kl And they had then a notable prisoner,

/b lwcnswp Mpalupus,
/p luwénso·p †mpalápas.
/t who was named Barabbas.
/kl called Barabbas,

Mk 15.7 /b nul nu nvelwrp cntu palalwkaset;
/p nál ná nhíləwe·p énta-palalo·ká·ɜ·i·t,
/t He was one who had murdered someone in committing a crime,
/kl (2) ... who had committed murder in the insurrection. [numbers = sequence in L.]

/b   ok ‖ wehi kaxpeswpanek wehumatpanek prlalwkaseletc.
/p   ó·k wíči-kaxpi·s·ó·p·ani·k wi·č·əma·tpáni·k pe·lalo·ka·s·i·lí·t·e.
/t   and those that helped him in his crime were tied up with him.
/kl (1) which lay bound with them that had made insurrection with him, ...

Mk 15.8 /b Nu macvlahek tolumi xawvetaqsenro, tulawao, Levenrn cvlevirf.
(p. 202) /p ná ma·ehəlá·č·i·k tóləmi-xa·whita·kwsi·né·ɔ, təlawwá·ɔ, "li·hí·ne·n ehəlí·hienk."
/t Then the crowd began shouting, saying to him, "Do for us what you always do."
/kl And the multitude crying aloud began to desire him to do as he had ever done unto them.

Mt 27.17 /b Mrhi wrmi krlumuvpeletc, Pylut tulao,
/p mé·či wé·mi ke·lamahpi·lí·t·e, †páilat təlá·ɔ,
/t After they were all seated quietly, Pilate said to them,
/kl Therefore when they were gathered together, Pilate said unto them,

Jn 18.39 /b Lexun kwti vufq kmelwvmw krpvaset bqc lukveqi.
/p "lí·x·ən: kwə́t·i=hánkw kəmillúhəmɔ ke·phá·s·i·t yúkwe ləkhíkwi.
/t "There is a custom: I always turn over to you one prisoner at this time.
/kl But ye have a custom, that I should release unto you one at the passover:

Mt 27.17 /b Ta vuh rlenaqset ktuli wulrluntumunro bqc kmelunro?
/p tá=háč e·li·ná·kwsi·t ktə́li-wəle·ləntaməné·ɔ, yúkwe kəmilləné·ɔ,
/t Which one is it that you would like me to turn over to you now,
/kl Whom will ye that I release unto you?

/b Mpalupus, ji vuh Nhesus rlwevlunt Klyst?
/p †mpalápas, ší=háč nčí·sas, e·ləwíhələnt kəláist?
/t Barabbas, or Jesus, who is called Christ?
/k Barabbas, or Jesus which is called Christ?

Mk 15.9 /b Ktuli vuh wulrluntumunro kmelunro Nhwe sakema?
/p ktə́li-=háč -wəle·ləntaməné·ɔ, kəmilləné·ɔ nčo·wí·i-sa·k·í·ma?"
/t Is it that you'd like me to turn over to you the king of the Jews?"
/kl Will ye that I release unto you the King of the Jews?

Mk 15.10 /b Rli watwn tuli wcvevwfrhek wunhi eku prjwanro
/p é·li o·wá·to·n tə́li- wehi·hunké·č·i·k -wə́nči- íka -pe·š·əwa·né·ɔ,
/t For he knew that the priests brought him there because of
/kl For he knew that the chief priests had delivered him

/b rli kufwelavtet xifwrlumwqswakun.
/p é·li-kankwi·láhti·t xinkwe·ləmukwsəwá·k·an.
/t how they were jealous of him because of the fame.
/k for envy.

Mt 27.19 /b Pylut mrhi lrmuvtupetc, cntu xifwrlumwqset,
/p †páilat mé·či le·mahtap·í·t·e énta-xinkwe·ləmúkwsi·t,
/t After Pilate had sat down in the place of honor,
/kl When he was set down on the judgment seat,

/b wehrohi eku prtalwkrmwelw, tulkw;
/p wi·č·e·ó·č·i íka pe·t·alo·ke·mwí·lu, tə́lku,
/t his wife sent him a message, saying to him,
/kl his wife sent unto him, saying,

/b Kahi naheverkuh nu jaxukawset linw;
/p "káči na·či·hié·k·ač ná šaxahká·wsi·t lə́nu.
/t "Don't have anything to do with that righteous man.
/kl Have thou nothing to do with that just man:

/b rli srki opuf xrlrnaovki nwnhi avrluntum rlajemweu wunhi nrkumu.
/p é·li sé·ki·ó·p·ank xe·lennáɔhki núnči-ahe·lə́ntam e·la·š·í·mwia wə́nči né·k·əma."
/t For I suffered during the morning from many things in a dream because of him."
/kl for I have suffered many things this day in a dream because of him.

Mt 27.20 /b Jwq wcvevwfrhek ok wcvetahemwlsehek tulevanro
/p šúkw wehi·hunké·č·i·k ɔ́·k wehi·t·a·č·i·mo·lsí·č·i·k təli·ha·né·ɔ
/t But the priests and councillors got them
/kl But the chief priests and elders persuaded the multitude

/b wunhi a lwrlet, Mpalupus a; kuhih Nhesus nvela.
/p wə́nči-=á· -luwé·li·t, "†mpalápas=á·; káč·i=č nčí·sas nhíla·,"
/t to say it should be Barabbas, but Jesus must be killed.
/kl that they should ask Barabbas, and destroy Jesus.

Mt 27.21 /b Fopunul tulao;
/p †nkápənal təlá·ɔ,
/t The governor said to them,
/kl The governor answered and said unto them,

/b Ta vuh rlenaqset nrk neju, kutatumunro kmelunro?
/p "tá=háč e·li·ná·kwsi·t né·k ní·š·a kkat·a·t·amən·é·ɔ, kəmillən·é·ɔ?"
/t "Which of those two do you want me to turn over to you?"
/kl Whether of the twain will ye that I release unto you?

Lk 23.18 /b Kwtun alumi lwrok Alumwxol wu;
/p kwə́t·ən áləmi-luwé·ɔk, "aləmó·x·ɔl wá.
/t All at the same time they said, "Take this one away.
/k And they cried out all at once, saying, Away with this man,
/l And the multitude cried out all at once, saying, Away with this man,

/b Mpalupus melenrn.
/p †mpalápas mi·lí·ne·n."
/t Give us Barabbas."
/kl and release unto us Barabbas:

Jn 18.40 /b Kevkumwtkrp nu Mpalupus.
/p kihkəmó·tke·p ná †mpalápas.
/t This Barabbas had been a thief.
/kl Now Barabbas was a robber.

Lk 23.20 /b Rli Pylut wifi a luxunat Nhesusu, lupi notwtumaoo, tulao,
/p é·li- †páilat -wínki-=á· -laxəna·t nči·sás·a, lápi nɔt·o·t·əmaɔ́·ɔ, təlá·ɔ,
/t As Pilate would be willing to release Jesus, he asked them again, saying to them,
/l Pilate therefore, willing to release Jesus, spake again to them, saying,

Mt 27.22 /b Krkwh vuh ntcleva Nhesus, rlwevlunt Klyst,
/p "kéku=č=háč ntəlí·ha nčí·sas, e·ləwíhələnt 'kəláist,'
/t "What shall I do with Jesus, who is called 'Christ,'
/kl What shall I do then with Jesus, which is called Christ,

Mk 15.12 /b rlwevlrq Nhwe sakema?
/p e·ləwíhəle·kw 'nčo·wí·i-sa·k·í·ma'?"
/t who you call the king of the Jews?"
/kl him whom you call king of the Jews?

Mk 15.13 /b Wrmalamwuk lwrok, Psuqvetcvov, psuqvetcvov.
/p we·malá·məwak, luwé·ɔk, "psakhwitéhɔw, psakhwitéhɔw."
/t And they all shouted, saying, "Crucify him, crucify him."
/l And they all cried out again, saying, Crucify him, crucify him.
/k And they cried out again, Crucify him. (Mk 15.13)
/k Crucify him, crucify him. (Lk 23.21, Jn 19.6)

Lk 23.22 /b Pylut lupi tulao, Koh, krkw vuh li muvtarvosw?
/p †páilat lápi təlá·ɔ, "kɔ́č? kéku=háč lí-mahtaehɔ́·s·u?
/t Pilate again said to them, "Why? What evil has he done?
/l And Pilate said unto them the third time, Why, what evil hath he done?

/b takw ne nmuxkamwi wcnhi a nvelunt.
/p takó· ní· nəmaxkamó·wi wénči-=á· -nhílənt.
/t *I* have not found any reason why he should be killed.
/l I have found no cause of death in him:

/b Bv tu luvupu nsrsrkacvon nuh kcnh mpwnunan. [= Lk 23.16, above]
/p yúh=tá, lahápa nse·s·e·k·ayéhɔ·n, ná·č kə́nč mpó·nəna·n."
/t Alright, I'll whip him first, and then I'll release him."
/l I will therefore chastise him, and let him go.

Mk 15.14 /b Jwq avalwei amufalamwuk,
/p šúkw ahaləwí·i amankalá·məwak,
/t But they shouted with even louder voices,
/l And they cried out the more exceedingly,

Lk 23.23 /b li a psuqvetcvolen.
/p lí-=á· -psakhwitehó·li·n.
/t that he should be crucified.
/l [they were instant with loud voices, requiring] that he might be crucified.

/b Ok wcveufrhek kxunki patavelswuk.
/p ó·k wehi·hunké·č·i·k kxántki pa·tahi·lsúwak.
/t And eventually the priests won out.
/l And the voices of them and of the chief priests prevailed.

Chapter 121 (pp. 202-203). [L. section 121.] (Matthew 27.24-30; Mark 15.15-19; Luke 23.25; John 19.1-3.)

Mt 27.24 /b Pylut nrfc tuli mutu krkw patatwun,
/p †páilat nénke, təli- máta kéku -pa·ta·tó·wən,
/t When Pilate saw that he gained nothing,
/kl When Pilate saw that he could prevail nothing,

/b tuli jwq ‖ wunhi avalwei xawvetaqselen,
/p təli- šúkw -wənči- ahaləwí·i -xa·whita·kwsí·li·n,
/t and that they only shouted all the more because of it,
/kl but that rather a tumult was made,

(p. 203) /b wrtunum mpi kjelunhr tali rlifwrxenulet;
/p wé·t·ənəm mpí, kši·lənče· táli e·linkwe·x·í·nəli·t,
/t he took some water and washed his hands before them,
/kl he took water, and washed his hands before the multitude,

/b tulao, Mpalavpen wu jaxukawset mwkum;
/p təlá·ɔ, "mpálahpi·n wá šaxahká·wsi·t mmó·kəm.
/t saying to them, "I am innocent of the blood of this righteous person.
/kl saying, I am innocent of the blood of this just person:

/b kelwu nevlahi punarluntamwq.
/p ki·ló·wa nihəláči pəna·eləntamo·kw."
/t *You* take care of it yourselves."
/kl see ye to it.

Mt 27.25 /b Nu wrmi tulwrnro, nelwnuh nvakynanif muvtrxun mwkum
/p ná wé·mi tələwe·né·ɔ, "ni·ló·na=č nhak·ayəná·nink mahté·x·ən mmó·kəm,

/t   Then they all said, "His blood will fall on *ourselves*,
/kl Then answered all the people, and said, His blood be on us,

/b   ok avanvwqi nehanunanuk.
/p   ɔ́·k aha·nhúkwi nni·č·a·nəná·nak."
/t   and on the succeeding generations of our children."
/kl and on our children.

Mk 15.15 /b Nu Pylut rli kavtu wulelarmat
/p   ná †páilat, é·li-káhta-wəli·laé·ma·t,
/t   Then Pilate, as he wanted to say something to please them,
/kl And so Pilate, willing to content the people,

Lk 23.24 /b tulao, bv tu nanc lrkch rlwrrq.
/p   təlá·ɔ, "yúh=tá, ná=nə lé·k·eč e·ləwé·e·kw."
/t   said to them, "Alright, let that be done as you say."
/kl gave sentence that it should be as they required.

Mk 15.15 /b Loxunao Mpalupusu,
/p   lɔx·əná·ɔ †mpalapás·a,
/t   And he released Barabbas,
/kl And he released Barabbas unto them,

Lk 23.25 /b krtalalifi, nani rli palalwkasetup, ok nvelwrtup wunhi kpavonrp.
/p   ke·t·a·la·línki. (náni é·li-palalo·ka·s·í·t·əp ɔ́·k -nhiləwé·t·əp wə́nči-kpahɔ́·ne·p.)
/t   the one who was desired. (He was one who had been imprisoned because he had been a criminal and a murderer.)
/kl that for sedition and murder was cast into prison, whom they had desired,

Mk 15.15 /b Kuhi Nhesusu keji srsrkycvotc nu mwrkun lih psuqvetcvolen.
/p   káč·i nči·sás·a, kíši-se·s·e·k·ayehɔ́·t·e, ná mwé·k·ən lí·=č -psakhwitehɔ́·li·n.
/t   But Jesus, after he whipped him, he then handed over to be crucified.
/kl and delivered Jesus, when he had scourged him, to be crucified. (Cf. Matt 27.26.)

Mt 27.27 /b Nu fopunul vwsohulumu tolumwxalanro Nhesusu   [⟨xal⟩ for /x·ɔl/]
/p   ná †nkápənal wsɔ·čələma tɔləmo·x·ola·né·ɔ nči·sás·a
/t   Then the governor's soldiers took Jesus
/kl Then the soldiers of the governor took Jesus

/b   li cvcntu lahemwlsif.
/p   lí ehəntala·č·i·mó·lsink.
/t   to where councils were held.
/kl into the common hall, (/l) called Pretorium;   (Mk 15.16: Praetorium)

Mt 27.27 /b Prkunhi marvwntc sohuluk.
/p peˑkˑánči-maˑehúnte sɔ́ˑčəlak,
/t After the whole band of soldiers was assembled,
/kl and gathered unto him the whole band of soldiers.
/k and they call together the whole band. (Mk 15.16)

Mt 27.28 /b Nu qwthelavswlanro, ok muxkrk xifokvwqeun tokonawao.
/p ná kwəčˑilahsoˑlaˑnéˑɔ, ɔ́ˑk máxkeˑk xinkɔˑkhukˑwíˑɔn tɔkˑɔnawwáˑɔ.
/t they then stripped him and dressed him in a large red coat.
/kl And they stripped him, and put on him a scarlet robe. (Cf. Lk 23.11.)

Mt 27.29 /b Kejetwvtetc kawunjei alwqrpi, eku totaonro,
/p kiˑšˑiˑtuhtíˑtˑe kaˑwənšíˑi-aˑloˑkwéˑpˑi, íka tɔˑtaɔˑnéˑɔ.
/t And after making a headdress of thorns, they put it on him.
/kl And when they had platted a crown of thorns, they put it upon his head,

/b ok vwtunavaonelet totawao wekunusq.
/p ɔ́ˑk wtənnaˑhaˑɔníˑliˑt tɔˑtaɔwwáˑɔ wíˑkənaskw.
/t And they put a reed in his right hand.
/kl and a reed in his right hand:

/b Nu tolumi nejetqivlanro li rlifwrxenulet, wowesavkevawao,
/p ná tɔ́ləmi-niˑšˑiˑtkwihəlaˑnéˑɔ lí eˑlinkweˑxˑíˑnəliˑt, wɔwisahkiˑhawwáˑɔ,
/t Then they began kneeling down before him, and they mocked him,
/kl and they bowed the knee before him, and mocked him,

/b lwrok kofwmulwvnw, Nhwe sakema; [⟨w-|vnw⟩ for ⟨w-|vnu⟩]
/p luwéˑɔk, "kɔnkɔˑməlúhəna, nčoˑwíˑi-saˑkˑíˑma."
/t saying, "We greet you, king of the Jews."
/kl saying, Hail, King of the Jews!

Mt 27.30 /b vwsuswkvolawao,
/p wsəsˑukhɔˑlawwáˑɔ,
/t And they spat on him
/kl And they spit upon him,

Jn 19.3 /b ok pwpavkumawao
/p ɔ́ˑk pupahkamawwáˑɔ,
/t and struck him,
/l and smote him with their hands, (KJV has "they")

Mt 27.30 /b ok nu wekunusq wrtunumunro pwpavkumanro welelet.
/p ɔ́ˑk ná wíˑkənaskw wweˑtˑənəmənéˑɔ, pupahkamaˑnéˑɔ wiˑlíˑliˑt.
/t And then they took the reed and struck him on the head with it.
/kl and took the reed, and smote him on the head.

Chapter 122 (pp. 203-204). [L. section 122.] (John, 19.4-16)

Jn 19.4 /b   Nuni wunhi Pylut lupi khen tulao,
/p   nə́ni wwə́nči- †páilat lápi -kčí·n, təlá·ɔ,
/t   For that reason, Pilate again went out, and he said to them,
/kl   Pilate therefore went forth again, and saith unto them,

/b   Punu kprtwlunro,
/p   "pənáh, kpe·t·o·lənéɔ,
/t   "Here, I bring him to you,
/kl   Behold, I bring him forth to you,

/b   ktuli a watwnro ntcli mutu muxkamwun krkw rli haneluset.   [⟨hane⟩ for ⟨hani⟩]
/p   ktə́li-=á· -wwa·to·né·ɔ, ntə́li- máta -maxkamó·wən kéku é·li-čáni-ləs·i·t."
/t   for you to know that I do not find anything that he has done wrong."
/kl   that ye may know that I find no fault in him.

Jn 19.5 /b   Nu Nhesus eku tuli khen,
/p   ná nčí·sas íka tə́li-kčí·n.
/t   Then Jesus came out to him.
/kl   Then came Jesus forth,

/b   tolwqrpesenu nrl kaounju, ok nc muxkrk xifokvwqeun toqen.
/p   tɔ·lo·kwe·p·i·s·í·na ka·wə́nša, ɔ́·k nə́ máxke·k xinkɔ·khuk·wí·ɔn tɔ́k·wi·n.
/t   He was wearing the thorns as a headdress, and he wore the large red coat.
/kl   wearing the crown of thorns, and the purple robe.   (Cf. Lk 23.11.)

/b   Pylut tulao, Jr wu linw!
/p   †páilat təlá·ɔ, "šé· wá lə́nu!"
/t   Pilate said to them, "Here is the man."
/kl   And Pilate saith unto them, Behold the man!

Jn 19.6 /b   Wcvevwfrhek ok elaok nrovtetc, amufalamwuk,
/p   wehi·hunké·č·i·k ɔ́·k i·lá·ɔk ne·ɔhtí·t·e, amankalá·məwak,
/t   When the priests and captains saw him, they shouted with loud voices,
/kl   When the chief priests therefore and officers saw him, they cried out,

/b   lwrok, Psuqvetcvw, psuqvetcvw!
/p   luwé·ɔk, "psakhwitého·, psakhwitého·."
/t   saying, "Crucify him, crucify him."
/kl   saying, Crucify him, crucify him.

/b   Pylut tulao, Wrtunw, my psuqvetcvw,
/p   †páilat təlá·ɔ, "wé·t·əno·, mái-psakhwitého·,
/t   Pilate said to them, "Take him and go and crucify him,
/kl   Pilate saith unto them, Take ye him, and crucify him:

| | /b | rli ne, mutu muxkamwu krkw rli haniluset.
| | /p | é·li- ní· máta -maxkamó·wa kéku é·li-čáni-lə́s·i·t."
| | /t | for *I* do not find anything that he has done wrong."
| | /kl | for I find no fault in him.

Jn 19.7   /b Nhwok tulawao, Qvetulutwakun nwlvatwvnu, wunhih ufulun,   [⟨Qve-‖tul⟩]
           /p nčó·wak təlawwá·ɔ, "khwitələt·əwá·k·an no·lhatúhəna, wwə́nči-=č -ánkələn,
           /t The Jews said to him, "We have a law, and because of it he must die,
           /kl The Jews answered him, We have a law, and by our law he ought to die,

(p. 204)   /b rli nrkumu nevlahi lwevlat vokyu Krtanutwet qesu.
           /p é·li- né·k·əma nihəláči -luwíhəla·t hɔ́kaya ke·tanət·ó·wi·t kkwí·s·a."
           /t as *he* of his *own* accord called himself God's son."
           /l because he made himself the Son of God.

Jn 19.8   /b Pylut nc rlsitufc ekalisi wejasw.
           /p †páilat nə́ e·lsət·ánke, ikalísi wi·š·á·s·u.
           /t When Pilate heard that, he was even more afraid.
           /kl When Pilate therefore heard that saying, he was the more afraid;

Jn 19.9   /b Lupi ekali tumekr cvcntu awrn kejavkunemunt,
           /p lápi íkali təmí·k·e· ehə́nta- awé·n -kišahkəní·mənt,
           /t He went again into the place where people are judged and sentenced,
           /kl And went again into the judgment hall,

           /b tulao Nhesusu, Ta vuh kwnheyi?
           /p təlá·ɔ nči·sás·a, "tá=háč kunčí·ai?"
           /t and he said to Jesus, "Where are you from?"
           /kl and saith unto Jesus, Whence art thou?

           /b Jwq Nhesus mutu krkw tulaeo.
           /p šúkw nčí·sas máta kéku təla·í·ɔ.
           /t But Jesus did not say anything to him.
           /kl But Jesus gave him no answer.

Jn 19.10   /b Pylut tulao, Mutu vuh krkw ktulei?
           /p †páilat təlá·ɔ, "máta=háč kéku ktəlí·i?
           /t And Pilate said to him, "Aren't you speaking to me?
           /kl Then saith Pilate unto him, Speakest thou not unto me?

           /b mutu vuh kwatwun ntcli trpi lusen kpusavqvetrvwlun?   [⟨vqv⟩ for ⟨vq⟩ (Jn 19.15)]
           /p máta=háč ko·wa·tó·wən, ntə́li-tépi-lə́s·i·n, kpəsahkwi·tehó·lən?
           /t Don't you know that I have the power to crucify you?
           /kl knowest thou not that I have power to crucify thee,

/b ok ntcli trpi lusen kpwnunulun?
/p ɔ́·k ntə́li-tépi-lə́s·i·n kpo·nənə́lən?"
/t And that I have the power to release you?"
/kl and have power to release thee?

Jn 19.11 /b Nhesus tulao, Taa tcxi kuski lisei,
/p nčí·sas təlá·ɔ, "tá=á· téxi kkáski-ləs·í·i,
/t And Jesus said to him, "You would have no power at all,
/kl Jesus answered, Thou couldest have no power at all against me,

/b mutu lextakronc wunhi vokwf.
/p máta li·xta·k·é·ɔne wə́nči hɔ́kunk.
/t if it were not established for you from on high.
/kl except it were given thee from above:

/b Nuni wunhi melkon nvaky alwei muvtawsw.
/p nə́ni wə́nči, mí·lkɔn nhák·ay aləwí·i mahtá·wsu."
/t Therefore, the one that turned me over to you commits more of a sin."
/kl therefore he that delivered me unto thee hath the greater sin.

Jn 19.12 /b Nu wunwhi Pylut punarluntumun tuli a pwnunan;
/p nə́ wənúči- †páilat -pəna·elə́ntamən tə́li·=á· -pó·nəna·n.
/t And starting then Pilate considered releasing him.
/kl And from thenceforth Pilate sought to release him:

/b jwk Nhwok amufexswuk, lwrok,
/p šúkw nčó·wak amanki·xsúwak, luwé·ɔk,
/t But the Jews shouted with loud voices, saying,
/kl but the Jews cried out, saying,

/b pwnunatc wu lunw, ta kwetesewun Sesul;
/p "po·nənát·e wá lə́nu, tá=á· ko·wi·t·i·s·í·wən †sí·sal.
/t "If you release this man, you will not be a friend of Caesar's.
/kl If thou let this man go, thou art not Caesar's friend:

/b rli awrn sakemawvrtc vokyu, mataptwnalao Sesulu.   [⟨mat-⟩ for /mɔt·-/]
/p é·li awé·n sa·k·i·ma·whé·t·e hɔ́kaya, mɔt·a·pto·na·lá·ɔ †sí·sala."
/t For if anyone makes himself a king, he maligns Caesar."
/kl whosoever maketh himself a king speaketh against Caesar.

Jn 19.13 /b Pylut nc rlsitaotc kohumif tulwxolao Nhesusu,
/p †páilat nə́ e·lsət·aɔ́·t·e, kɔ́čəmink təlo·x·ɔlá·ɔ nči·sás·a,
/t When Pilate heard that from him, he brought Jesus outside,
/kl When Pilate therefore heard that saying, he brought Jesus forth,

/b   ekali mujakr cntu xifwrlumwqset, cntu lwcntasek cntu avsunvasek.
/p   íkali məšá·ke· énta-xinkwe·ləmúkwsi·t, énta-luwentá·s·i·k 'énta-ahsənhá·s·i·k'.
/t   and he sat down on the ground in a place of honor in a place called "the Pavement" ('where it's paved (*lit.*, made like rock)').
/kl and sat down in the judgment seat in a place that is called the Pavement,

/b   Kuhi Nhwok tulwuntamunro cntu twkovtif.   [⟨lwunt⟩ for ⟨lwcnt⟩]
/p   káč·i nčó·wak tələwentaməné·ɔ 'énta-túkɔhtink'.
/t   But the Jews call it 'Round Hill'.
/kl but in the Hebrew, Gabbatha.   [*lit.* 'raised', interpreted as 'the temple-mound']

Jn 19.14 /b   Nu nckc kejqek wcnhavkwuk tulih tavqepwenro peskrkc;
/p   ná-néke kí·škwi·k wenčahkúwak tə́li-=č -tahkwi·p·wi·né·ɔ pi·ské·k·e.
/t   That same day they prepared to have the feast after nightfall.
/kl And it was the preparation of the passover,

/b   avpamc ct paxuqr;   [⟨avpamc|ct⟩ for ⟨avpami|ct⟩]
/p   ahpá·mi=ét pa·xhákwe·.
/t   And it was about noontime.
/kl and about the sixth hour:

/b   tulao Nhwu, Punw, ksakemabmwu.
/p   təlá·ɔ nčó·wa, "pənó· ksa·k·i·ma·yəmúwa."
/t   And he said to the Jews, "Look at your king."
/kl and he saith unto the Jews, Behold your King!

Jn 19.15 /b   Jwq amufexswuk, tulawao, Alumwxol, alumwxol, psuqvetcvov.   [⟨-ov⟩ for /-ow/]
/p   šúkw amanki·xsúwak, təlawwá·ɔ, "aləmó·x·ɔl, aləmó·x·ɔl, psakhwitéhɔw,"
/t   But they cried out with loud voices, saying to him, "Take him away! Take him away! Crucify him!"
/kl But they cried out, Away with him, away with him, crucify him.

/b   Pylut tulao, mpusavqetcvoh vuh ksakemabmwu?
/p   †páilat təlá·ɔ, "mpəsahkwi·téhɔ=č=háč ksa·k·i·ma·yəmúwa?"
/t   Pilate said to them, "Shall I crucify your king?"
/kl Pilate saith unto them, Shall I crucify your King?

/b   Wevevwfrhek tulawao,   [⟨We-⟩ for ⟨Wc-⟩]
/p   wehi·hunké·č·i·k təlawwá·ɔ,
/t   The priests said to him,
/kl The chief priests answered,

/b   Takw peli nwsakemabmevwmnu Sesul jwq.
/p   "takó· pí·li no·s·a·k·i·ma·yəmi·húməna †sí·sal šúkw."
/t   "We have no other king except Caesar."
/kl We have no king but Caesar.

Jn 19.16 /b Nu mwrkun lih psuqvetcvolen.
/p ná mwé·k·ən lí-=č -psakhwitehó·li·n.
/t Then he handed him over to be crucified.
/kl Then delivered he him therefore unto them to be crucified. ...

Chapter 123 (pp. 204-205). [L. section 123.] (Matthew 27.31-34; Mark 15. 20-23; Luke 23.26-34; John 19.16-18)

Mt 27.31, Mk 15.20
/b Sohuluk mrhi keji owesavkevavtetc, qwthelavswlanro nc muxkrk,
/p só·čəlak mé·či kíši-ɔwisahki·hahtí·t·e, kwəč·ilahso·la·né·ɔ nə́ máxke·k,
/t After the soldiers had mocked him, they took the red (garment) off of him,
/l And the soldiers, after they had mocked him, took off the purple from him,
/k And after that they had mocked him, they took the robe off from him, (Mt 27.31)
/k And when they had mocked him, they took off the purple from him, (Mk 15.20)

Mt 27.31 /b nevlahi rvavqelet pwunhelavswlanro,
/p nihəláči ehahkwí·li·t pwənčilahso·la·né·ɔ.
/t and they put his own clothes on him.
/kl and put his own raiment on him,

/b nu eku tulwxolanro cntu kavtu psuqvetcvovtet.
/p ná íka təlo·x·ɔla·né·ɔ énta-káhta-psakhwitehóhti·t.
/t Then they led him to the place where they intended to crucify him.
/kl and led him out to crucify him.

Jn 19.17 /b Kheok eku wunhi wtrnif,
/p kčí·ɔk íka wə́nči o·t·é·nink.
/t They went out of the city.
/kl (1) And he ... (3) went forth   [numbers = sequence in L.]

/b wtkivwen ajwaqvetcvasek
/p o·tkíhhwi·n a·š·əwa·khwitehá·s·i·k
/t And he carried the cross on his shoulder
/kl ... (2) bearing his cross ...

/b li cntu lwcntasek xkununtpif.   [⟨xkunt-‖pif.⟩]
/p lí énta-luwentá·s·i·k xkanántpink.
/t to a place called Skull Place (*lit.*, 'at the skull').
/kl into a place called the place of a skull, [which is called in the Hebrew Golgotha:]

Mt 27.32, Mk 15.21, Lk 23.26

(p. 205) /b Nrlwxolavtet pumeskarok linwu Sylen wcnheyelehi,   [⟨pumesk-⟩ for ⟨pumusk-⟩?;
/p ne·lo·x·ɔláhti·t, †pəməskaé·ɔk lə́nəwa †sáili·n wenči·ai·lí·č·i.   [but see *Glossary*.]
/t As they were leading him there, they passed a man from Cyrene.
/l And as they led him away, they laid hold upon a man of Cyrene, Simon by name, who passed by,

/b lwcnsw Symun, rlekvatif owm Rleksantul ok Lwpus wxwao;
/p luwénsu †sáiman, e·li·khátink wúm, †e·li·ksántəl ɔ́·k †lɔ́·pəs o·x·əwá·ɔ.
/t His name was Simon, and he was coming from the country, the father of Alexander and Rufus.
/l coming out of the country, the father of Alexander and Rufus;

/b tovwunawao, tomunhevawao wehuman Nhesusu
/p tɔhwənawwá·ɔ, tɔmənči·hawwá·ɔ wwí·č·əma·n nči·sás·a.
/t They laid hold of him and compelled him to help Jesus.
/l on him they laid the cross, and compelled him to bear it after Jesus.

/b wtrkaoo nrkanr wtkivwen nc ajwaqvetcvasek.
/p o·t·e·kaɔ́·ɔ, né·k·a né· o·tkíhhwi·n nə́ a·š·əwa·khwitehá·s·i·k.
/t And he followed behind him bearing the cross on *his* shoulder, also.

Lk 23.27 /b Xuvrli awrn wtrkaoo, aluntc xqrok,
/p xahé·li awé·n o·t·e·kaɔ́·ɔ, a·lə́nte xkwé·ɔk.
/t Many people followed after him, some of them woman.
/kl And there followed him a great company of people, and of women,

/b nrk moemawao tovi jerlumawao.
/p né·k mɔi·mawwá·ɔ, tɔ́hi-ši·e·ləmawwá·ɔ.
/t And those wept over him and grieved very much for him.
/kl which also bewailed and lamented him.

Lk 23.28 /b Nhesus qtukifwrxen tulao.
/p nčí·sas kwtək·inkwé·x·i·n, təlá·ɔ,
/t Jesus looked back and said to them,
/kl But Jesus turning unto them said,

/b Nhelwsulum tonenu, kahi maemevrq,
/p "†nči·lo·sələm tɔ·ní·na, káči mai·mí·he·kw,
/t "Daughters of Jerusalem, don't weep for me,
/kl Daughters of Jerusalem, weep not for me,

/b jwq mawuntamwq kvakybu, ok knehanwaok.
/p šúkw mawə́ntamo·kw khak·ayúwa ɔ́·k kəni·č·a·nəwá·ɔk.
/t but weep for yourselves and your children.
/kl but weep for yourselves, and for your children.

Lk 23.29 /b Rli prerekch kejqeki, lwrokh,
/p é·li pe·ye·í·k·e=č ki·škwí·k·i, luwé·ɔk=č,
/t For, when the days come, they will say,
/kl For, behold, the days are coming, in the which they shall say,

/b Wulapcnsw, mutu vuji wrnehanet, ok mutu vuji awrni nwvlahek;
/p 'wəla·p·énsu máta háši we·ni·č·á·ni·t, ɔ́·k máta háši awé·ni nuhəlá·č·i·k.'
/t 'Blessed is one who never had children, and those who never nursed one.'
/kl Blessed are the barren, and the wombs that never bare, and the paps which never gave suck.

Lk 23.30 /b nuh ok tulanro amufi ovhwu, vupvekaenrn,
/p ná=č ɔ́·k təla·né·ɔ amánki-ɔhčúwa, 'haphikaí·ne·n,'
/t Then also they will say to the mountains, 'Fall on top of us,'
/kl Then shall they begin to say to the mountains, Fall on us;

/b psuntvekaenrn ovhwuk.
/p 'psənthikaí·ne·n,' ɔhčúwak.
/t and to the hills, 'Cover us.'
/l and to the hills, Cover us.

Lk 23.31 /b Bni levavtetc uskako vetko, krkw vuh a tulevawao Xwaqeletc?
/p yó·ni li·hahtí·t·e aská·kɔ hítkɔ, kéku=háč=á· təli·hawwá·ɔ xuwa·kwi·lí·t·e?"
/t If this is what they do to a green tree, what would they do to one when it's dead?"
/kl For if they do these things in a green tree, what shall be done in the dry?

Lk 23.32 /b Ok neju prlalwkesetpanek wihi eku lwxolaok lih ok nrk nvelanro. [⟨ke⟩ for ⟨ka⟩]
/p ɔ́·k ní·š·a pe·lalo·ka·s·i·tpáni·k wíči- íka -lo·x·ɔlá·ɔk, lí-=č ɔ́·k né·k -nhila·né·ɔ.
/t And two criminals were taken there with him, for them to be put to death also.
/l And there were also two other malefactors led with him to be put to death.
/k And there were also two others, malefactors, led with him to be put to death.

Lk 23.33 /b Eku pravtetc cntu lwcntasek Kclpuli,
/p íka pe·ahtí·t·e énta-luwentá·s·i·k †kélpəli
/t When they came to the place named Calvary
/k And when they were come to the place, which is called Calvary,
/l And when they were come to the place called Golgotha,

Mt 27.34 /b myai lwrn xkununtpif,
/p (mayá·i lúwe·n: xkanántpink),
/t (plainly said: Skull Place),
/l that is to say, a place of a skull,

Mt 27.34 /b mwelawao jwapwv krkw avi wesavkuf weumxki, tuli a munrn;
/p mwi·lawwá·ɔ šəwá·p·u, kéku áhi-wísahkank wiámxki, təli-=á· -məné·n.
/t They gave him vinegar mixed with something very bitter, for him to drink.
/kl they gave him vinegar to drink, mingled with gall:

/b mrhi qrtuntufc, takw wifi munrwun.
/p mé·či kwe·t·antánke, takó· wwínki-məné·wən.
/t After he had tasted it, he did not want to drink it.
/kl and when he had tasted thereof, he would not drink.

Lk 23.33, Jn 19.18
/b Nanc tuntu psuqvetcvonro, ok nrl neju pcpalalwkaseletpani,
/p ná=nə tə́nta-psakhwitehɔ·né·ɔ, ɔ́·k né·l ní·š·a pehpalalo·ka·s·i·li·tpáni,
/t That's where they crucified him, and those two who had been criminals,
/l There they crucified him, and the two malefactors with him;

/b mawsw vwtunavaonelet, ok mawsw mwununheonelet,
/p má·wsu wtənna·ha·oní·li·t, ɔ́·k má·wsu mwənanči·oní·li·t,
/t one on his right, and the other on his left,
/l one on the right hand, and the other on the left,

/b Nhesus lrlai avpwv.
/p nčí·sas le·lá·i ahpú.
/t with Jesus being in between.
/l and Jesus in the midst.

Mk 15.28 /b Nanc tali pavkunhi lrp rlrkvasek xwi lrkvekunif,
/p ná=nə táli-pahkánči-lé·p e·le·khá·s·i·k xúwi-le·khí·k·anink:
/t That is where what is written in the old writings was fulfilled:
/kl And the scripture was fulfilled, which saith,

/b Pcpalalwkasetekri wetavkema.
/p pehpalalo·ka·s·i·t·i·ké·i witahkí·ma·.
/t "He was counted in among the criminals."
/kl He was numbered with the transgressors.

Lk 23.34 /b Nu Nhesus tulwrn, Nuxa, pavketatamaw, rli mutu watwvtet, rlsevtet.
/p ná nčí·sas tə́ləwe·n, "núxa·, pahki·t·á·t·amaw, é·li- máta -wwa·túhti·t e·lsíhti·t."
/t Then Jesus said, "Father, forgive them, as they don't know what they're doing."
/kl Then said Jesus, Father, forgive them; for they know not what they do.

Chapter 124 (pp. 205-207). [L. section 124.] (Matthew 27.35-37, 39-50; Mark 15.24-26, 29-37; Luke 23.34-46; John 19.19-30.)

Jn 19.23 /b   Sohuluk mrhi kiji psuqvetcvovtetc, wrtunumunro rvavqelet
            /p   só·čəlak mé·či kíši-psakhwitehɔhtí·t·e, wwe·t·ənəməné·ɔ ehahkwí·li·t.
            /t   The soldiers, after they had crucified him, took his clothing.
            /kl   Then the soldiers, when they had crucified Jesus, took his garments,

            /b   wunrwrnaovkunumunro, tobmunro;
            /p   wəne·wennaɔhkənəməné·ɔ, tɔyəməné·ɔ.
            /t   They made four parts of it, and each picked one.   [*lit.*, 'they picked them out']
            /kl   and made four parts, to every soldier a part;

            /b   xifokvwqeon musut,
            /p   xinkɔ·khuk·wí·ɔn məsát.
            /t   The large coat was in one piece.
            /kl   [and also his coat:] now the coat was without seam,

            /b   tukw kulexasei.
            /p   takó· kəli·x·a·s·í·i.
            /t   It was not sewn together.
            /kl   woven from the top throughout.

Jn 19.24 /b   Nuni wunhi lutenro,
            /p   nə́ni wwə́nči-lət·i·né·ɔ,
            /t   For that reason they said to each other,
            /kl   They said therefore among themselves,

            /b   Keskunekunuk arkrtumwq awrnh tu nevlatuf.   [⟨wqaw-‖rnh⟩; ⟨nevl-⟩ for ⟨ncvl-⟩]
            /p   "ki·skəní·k·anak ae·ké·t·amo·kw, awé·n=č=tá nihəlá·t·ank."
            /t   "Let's 'cast lots' for who will be the one to have it."   [*lit.*, 'use broken-off sticks']
            /kl   Let us not rend it, but cast lots for it, whose it shall be:

Lk 23.34 /b   Nu qeskunekunavrnro.
(p. 206) /p   ná kwi·skəni·k·anahe·né·ɔ.
            /t   Then they "cast lots."
            /l   and they cast lots:
            /k   And they parted his raiment, and cast lots.

Jn 19.24 /b   Nu pavkunhi lr lrkvekun rlwrt;
            /p   ná pahkánči-lé· le·khí·k·an é·ləwe·t:
            /t   Then what the book (or writing) says was fulfilled:
            /kl   that the scripture might be fulfilled, which saith,

       /b   tokvamaovtenro rvavqeani,
       /p   "tɔkhama·ɔhti·né·ɔ ehahkwiá·ni,
       /t   "They distributed my garments to each other,
       /kl They parted my raiment among them,

       /b   ok numuxifokvwqeon wunhi keskunekunuvrok.
       /p   ɔ́·k nəmax·inkɔ·khuk·wí·ɔn wə́nči ki·skəni·k·anahé·ɔk."
       /t   and they "cast lots" for my large coat."
       /kl and for my vesture they did cast lots.

       /b   Jr nuni tulsenrop sohuluk.
       /p   šé· nə́ni təlsi·né·ɔ·p sɔ́·čəlak.
       /t   And *that* is what the soldiers did.
       /kl These things therefore the soldiers did.

Mt 27.36 /b   Nanc wulumuvtupenro, qrnavkevaoao.
       /p   ná=nə wələmahtap·i·né·ɔ, kwe·nahki·hawwá·ɔ.
       /t   They sat down there and watched him.
       /kl And sitting down they watched over him there;

(Omitted: /l   And it was the third hour, when they crucified him.)

Jn 19.19 /b   Nu Pylut tulrkvamun rlavkunemkwselet;
       /p   ná †páilat təle·khámən e·lahkəni·mkwəs·í·li·t,
       /t   Then Pilate wrote what the accusation against him (Jesus) was,
       /l   And Pilate wrote a title, what his accusation was,   (+ Mk 15.26)

       /b   srkuntprxenulet pwsavqextwn.
       /p   se·kantpe·x·í·nəli·t pwəsahkwí·xto·n.
       /t   and he affixed it above his (obv.) head.
       /l   and put it on the cross over his head,   (+ Mt 27.37)

       /b   Lrkvasw, NHESUS NASULUTIF WCNHEYET, NHWE SAKEMA.
       /p   le·khá·s·u: nčí·sas †nasəlát·ink wenčí·ai·t, nčo·wí·i-sa·k·í·ma.
       /t   What was written was: Jesus of Nazareth, king of the Jews.
       /l   And the writing was, JESUS OF NAZARETH THE KING OF THE JEWS.

Jn 19.20 /b   Nhwexsen cntu lrkvasek ok Fulekexsen, ok Lwmunsexsen.
       /p   nčo·wí·xsi·n entale·khá·s·i·k, ɔ́·k nkəli·kí·xsi·n, ɔ́·k lo·mansí·xsi·n.
       /t   The writing there was in the Jewish language, and in Greek, and in Latin.
            [*lit.*, 'the Jewish language was spoken where it was written, ..']
       /kl (3) and it was written in Hebrew, and Greek, and Latin.   [numbers = order in L.]

       /b   Nu xrli Nhwok tokuntamunro rlrkvasek,
       /p   ná xé·li nčó·wak tɔk·əntaməné·ɔ e·le·khá·s·i·k.

| | /t | Then many Jews read what was written, |
| | /l | (1) This title then read many of the Jews: |

	/b	rli joei wtrnif tali psuqvetcvwnt.
	/p	é·li- šɔí·i o·t·é·nink -táli-psakhwitéhunt.
	/t	since he was crucified at the edge of the city.
	/l	(2) for the place where Jesus was crucified was nigh to the city:

Jn 19.21 /b Wcvevwfrhek tulaoao Pylutu, Kahi lrkvekrvun, Nhwe sakema,
　　　　 /p wehi·hunké·č·i·k təlawwá·ɔ †pailát·a, "káči le·khi·k·é·han 'nčo·wí·i-sa·k·í·ma,'
　　　　 /t And the priests said to Pilate, "Don't write 'king of the Jews,'
　　　　 /kl Then said the chief priests of the Jews to Pilate, Write not, The King of the Jews;

　　　　 /b jwq a rli lwrt sakema nvaky.
　　　　 /p šúkw=á· é·li-lúwe·t, 'sa·k·í·ma nhák·ay.'"
　　　　 /t but it should be the way he said: 'I am king.'"
　　　　 /kl but that he said, I am King of the Jews.

Jn 19.22 /b Pylut tulao, Nuni rlrkvekru, ne ntulrkvekrn.
　　　　 /p †páilat təlá·ɔ, "nə́ni e·le·khi·k·é·a, ní· ntəle·khí·k·e·n."
　　　　 /t And Pilate said to them, "What I wrote, *I* wrote."
　　　　 /kl Pilate answered, What I have written I have written.

Mt 27.39 /b Eku pcpamskahek, wcvrmwalaoao,
　　　　 /p íka pep·a·mská·č·i·k wwehe·məwa·lawwá·ɔ,
　　　　 /t Those that passed by there made fun of him
　　　　 /kl And they that passed by reviled him,

Mk 15.29 /b ok kokulwlawao, tutuntavkwqcvlrok,　　　　　　　　　[⟨kokulwl-⟩: B. ⟨kokul|lwl-⟩]
　　　　 /p ó·k kɔk·əlo·lawwá·ɔ, tət·antahko·kwehəlé·ɔk,
　　　　 /t and cursed at him, shaking their heads,
　　　　 /kl and railed on him, wagging their heads,

　　　　 /b lwrok, Kevsav, krtu paletaon patamwrekaon,
　　　　 /p luwé·ɔk, "kihsáh! ké·t·a-palí·taɔn pa·tamwe·i·k·á·ɔn,
　　　　 /t and saying, "For shame! You who were going to destroy the temple
　　　　 /kl and saying, Ah, thou that destroyest the temple,

　　　　 /b ok nuxi kejqc peli krtu kejetaon,
　　　　 /p ó·k náxi-kí·škwe pí·li ké·t·a-ki·š·í·taɔn,
　　　　 /t and were going to build another in three days,
　　　　 /kl and buildest it in three days,

Mk 15.30 /b lclrxmvrl kvaky;
/p lehəle·x·é·mhe·l khák·ay.
/t save yourself.
/kl save thyself.

Mt 27.40 /b ke qesumwkonc Krtanutwet, cntu psuqvetcvaseun wunhi lexi.
/p kí· kkwi·s·əmúk·ɔne ke·tanət·ó·wi·t, énta-psakhwitehá·s·ian wɔ́nči-lí·x·i."
/t If you are the son of God, come down from your cross."
/kl If thou be the Son of God, come down from the cross.

Lk 23.35 /b Eku cntu marvlahek tcxi jwq punaswuk.
/p íka énta-ma·ehəlá·č·i·k téxi šúkw pəná·s·əwak.
/t The people gathered there did nothing but look on.
/kl And the people stood beholding.

Mt 27.41 /b Patamwrokun krnavketaq, ok wcvevwfrhek, ok rvlrkvekrliek,
/p pa·tamwe·ɔ́·k·an ke·nahkí·ta·kw, ɔ́·k wehi·hunké·č·i·k, ɔ́·k ehəle·khi·k·é·č·i·k,
/t The high priest, and the priests, and the scribes,
/l Likewise also the chief priests mocking him, said among themselves with the scribes and elders:
/k Likewise also the chief priests mocking him, with the scribes and elders, said,

/b ok wcvetahemwlsehek, wcvrmwalaoao nevlahi lutwuk,
/p ɔ́·k wehi·t·a·č·i·mo·lsí·č·i·k wwehe·məwa·lawwá·ɔ, nihəláči lɔ́t·əwak,
/t and the councillors made fun of him, saying among themselves,
/k —

Mt 27.42 /b Peli vufq awrni lclrxrmvr,
/p "pí·li=hánkw awé·ni lehəle·x·é·mhe·,
/t "He saves other people,
/kl He saved others;

/b jwq mutu koski lclrxmvalaeo vokyu.
/p šúkw máta kɔ́ski-lehəle·x·e·mha·la·í·ɔ hɔ́kaya.
/t but he cannot save himself.
/kl himself he cannot save.

Mt 27.42 /b Klystetc, Islule sakematc Krtanutwet pepenaotc;
/p kəlaistí·t·e, †isələlí·i-sa·k·i·má·t·e, ke·tanət·ó·wi·t pi·p·i·naɔ́·t·e,
/t If he is Christ, if he is the King of Israel, and if God chose him,
/l If he be Christ, the King of Israel, the chosen of God,
/k If he be the King of Israel,
/k if he be Christ, the chosen of God. (Lk 23.35)

Mt 27.42 /b lexetc a eku wunhi cntu ajwaqvetcvasek
/p li·x·í·t·e=á· íka wɔ́nči énta-a·š·əwa·khwitehá·s·i·k,

| | /t | if he comes down from the cross, |
| | /kl | let him now come down from the cross, |

	/b	kwlamvetaounu a.
	/p	ko·la·mhitaɔ́·wəna=á·.
	/t	we would believe him.
	/kl	and we will believe him.

Mt 27.43 /b Nokalapani Krtanutwelehi,
/p nɔ·ka·lá·p·ani ke·tanət·o·wi·lí·č·i,
/t He trusted in God.
/kl He trusted in God;

/b bqc a loxunwkw wifalkwkc;
/p yúkwe=á· lɔx·ənúk·u, winka·lkúk·e,
/t He (God) would release him now, if he likes him,
/kl let him deliver him now, if he will have him:

/b rli evlwrt, ne Krtanutwet qesu.
/p é·li-ihəlúwe·t, 'ní· ke·tanət·ó·wi·t kkwí·s·a.'"
/t as he always says, 'I am the son of God.'"
/kl for he said, I am the Son of God.

(Omitted: /kl The thieves also, which were crucified with him, cast the same in his teeth. ...
[= Mt 27.44])

Lk 23.36 /b Ok sohuluk wcvrmwalaoao, lupi eku tunumaonro nc jwapw,
/p ɔ́·k sɔ́·čəlak wwehe·məwa·lawwá·ɔ, lápi íka tənnəmaɔ·né·ɔ nɔ́ šəwá·p·u,
/t And the soldiers made fun of him, again reaching the vinegar up to him.
/kl And the soldiers also mocked him, coming to him, and offering him vinegar,

Lk 23.37 /b tulaoao, Ke Nhwe sakemaeunc, lclrxrmval kvaky.
/p təlawwá·ɔ, "kí· nčo·wí·i-sa·k·i·ma·iáne, lehəle·x·é·mha·l khák·ay.
/t and saying to him, "If you are the king of the Jews, save yourself."
/kl And saying, If thou be the king of the Jews, save thyself.

Lk 23.39 /b Ok nu mawsw pcpalalwkaset wihi psuqvetcvaset wcvrmwalao,   [⟨tcv-‖aset⟩]
/p ɔ́·k ná má·wsu pehpalalo·ká·s·i·t wiči-psakhwitehá·s·i·t wwehe·məwa·lá·ɔ,
/t And one of the criminals who was crucified with him made fun of him,
/kl And one of the malefactors, which were hanged, railed on him,

(p. 207) /b tulao, Ke Klysteunc, lclrxrmval kvaky, ok nrpunu.
/p təlá·ɔ, "kí· kəlaistiáne, lehəle·x·é·mha·l khák·ay, ɔ́·k né·pəna."
/t saying to him, "If you are Christ, save yourself, and us, too."
/kl saying, If thou be Christ, save thyself and us.

Lk 23.40 /b Jwq nu mawsw qetulao; tulao,
/p šúkw ná má·wsu kkwi·təláˑɔ, təláˑɔ,
/t But the other one admonished him, saying to him,
/kl But the other answering, rebuked him, saying,

/b Mutu vuh koxai Krtanutwet jr krpc kwehi amuxavelarvkwsi?
/p "máta=háč kkɔx·á·i ke·tanət·ó·wi·t, šéˑ ké·pe kəwíči-amax·ahi·laehkwə́s·i?
/t "Don't you fear God, and here you, too, are in torment with him?
/kl Dost not thou fear God, seeing thou art in the same condemnation?

Lk 23.41 /b Kelwnu wuli; rli kpatatwnrn wcnhi nc lenumufq.
/p ki·ló·na wə́li, é·li kpa·ta·tó·ne·n wénči- nə́ -lí·namankw.
/t For *us* it's right, for we earned why that is happening to us.
/kl And we indeed justly; for we receive the due reward of our deeds:

/b Kuhi wuni takw krkw li hanilusei.
/p káč·i wáni takóˑ kéku lí-čáni-ləs·í·i."
/t But this (man) has not done wrong in any way."
/kl but this man hath done nothing amiss.

Lk 23.42 /b Ok tulao Nhesusu, Nrvlaleun, [⟨Nrvl⟩: B. ⟨Nrv-|vl⟩]
/p ɔ́·k təláˑɔ nči·sás·a, "nehəlá·lian,
/t And he said to Jesus, "My lord,
/kl And he said unto Jesus, Lord,

/b mujalemc eku paanc ksakemaokunif.
/p məša·lí·me, íka pá·ane ksa·k·i·ma·ɔ́·k·anink."
/t remember me when you arrive in your kingdom."
/kl remember me when thou comest into thy kingdom.

Lk 23.43 /b Nhesus tulao, Kvehei ktulul,
/p nčí·sas təláˑɔ, "khičí·i ktə́ləl,
/t And Jesus said to him, "Truly, I say to you,
/kl And Jesus said unto him, Verily I say unto thee,

/b rlumih kejqek kwetavpemi tali wifawswakunif.
/p é·ləmi-=č -kí·škwi·k kəwitahpí·mi táli winka·wsəwá·k·anink."
/t Later today you will be with me in 'paradise'."
/kl To-day shalt thou be with me in paradise.

Chapter 125 (pp. 207-208). [L. section 125.] (Matthew 27.51-56; Mark 15.38-41; John 23.47-49.)

Jn 19.25 /b Kexki cntu ajwaqvetcvasek, Nhesus kovrsu nepw
/p kí·xki énta-a·š·əwa·khwitehá·s·i·k nčí·sas kɔhé·s·a ní·p·o·,

/t   Next to the cross stood Jesus's mother,
/kl Now there stood by the cross of Jesus his mother,

/b   ok wetkwxkov, Mrlesu Kleopus wehrohi ok Mrles Maktulen.   [⟨-ov⟩ for /-ɔ/]
/p   ɔ·k wi·tkúxkɔ, me·lí·s·a, †kəliɔ́·pəs wi·č·e·ɔ́·č·i, ɔ́·k mé·li·s-†má·ktali·n.
/t   and her sister, Mary, Cleophas's wife, and Mary Magdalene.
/kl and his mother's sister, Mary the wife of Cleophas, and Mary Magdalene.

Jn 19.26 /b   Nhesus nrotc kovrsu
/p   nčí·sas ne·ɔ́·t·e kɔhé·s·a,
/t   When Jesus saw his mother,
/kl When Jesus therefore saw his mother,

/b   ok rvolahi rkrkemahi, eku nepyelehi,
/p   ɔ́·k ehɔ·lá·č·i e·k·e·ki·má·č·i íka ni·p·ai·lí·č·i,
/t   and his disciple, the one he loved, standing there,
/kl and the disciple standing by, whom he loved,

/b   tulao kovrsu, Xrqr, nanih kwqesen.   [⟨Xrqr⟩ for ⟨Xqr⟩]
/p   təlá·ɔ kɔhé·s·a, "xkwé·, náni=č ko·k·wí·s·i·n."
/t   he said to his mother, "Woman, he will be your son."
/kl he saith unto his mother, Woman, behold thy son!

Jn 19.27 /b   Ok nrl tulao rkrkemahi, punw kavrs.   [⟨punw⟩ 2p–3 for ⟨punaw⟩ 2s–3]
/p   ɔ́·k né·l təlá·ɔ e·k·e·ki·má·č·i, "pənáw kkáhe·s."
/t   And he said to his disciple, "Look at your mother."
/kl Then saith he to the disciple, Behold thy mother!

/b   Nu wunwhi krnavkevan tali weket.
/p   nɔ́ wənúči-ke·nahkí·ha·n táli wí·k·i·t.
/t   And from that time on he took care of her in his house.
/kl And from that hour that disciple took her unto his own home.

Mk 15.33, Mt 27.45, Lk 23.44
/b   Paxukqrkc peskutqcvlr wrmi rlkekvokumekrk, [⟨peskutqcvlr⟩: s.b. ⟨peskaqevlr⟩]
/p   pa·xhakwé·k·e, pi·ska·kwíhəle· wé·mi e·lki·khɔkamí·k·e·k.   [emended]
/t   At noon, it got dark over the whole length and breadth of the land.
/l   And when the sixth hour was come, there was darkness over all the land

/b   peskutqcvlr kejwx lrlai tuntan svaki.   [⟨peskutqcvlr⟩ for ⟨peskuntqcvlr⟩]
/p   pi·skəntkwéhəle· kí·š·o·x, le·lá·i tɔ́nta·n sháki.
/t   The sun went dark until it stood halfway (down).
/l   unto the ninth hour.

Mk 15.34 /b Mrhi lrlai cntakc, Nhesus amufexsw lwr
/p mé·či le·lá·i entá·k·e, nčí·sas amankí·xsu, lúwe·,
/t After the sun stood halfway (down), Jesus cried out with a loud voice, saying,
/kl And at the ninth hour Jesus cried with a loud voice, saying,

/b Elac, Elac, lama sapaktanc?
/p "†í·lae, í·lae, láma sapaktáne?"
/kl Eli, Eli, lama sabachthani?　　　　　　　　　　　　　(Mt 27.46: Eli, Eli)

/b cntu lunexsif lwr Krtanutweun, Krtanutweun, koh vuh faleun?
/p énta-laní·xsink, lúwe·, "ke·tanət·ó·wian, ke·tanət·ó·wian, kóč=háč nkálian?"
/t In Delaware, he said, "O God, O God, why have you abandoned me?"
/kl which is, being interpreted, My God, my God, why hast thou forsaken me?

Mt 27.47 /b Aluntc eku nepaehek lwrok, Jr notwmao Elyusu.
/p a·lənte íka ni·p·aí·č·i·k luwé·ɔk, "šé·, nɔt·o·má·ɔ †i·layás·a."
/t Some who were standing there said, "Here, he is calling for Elias."
/l And some of them that stood by, [when they heard that,] said, Behold, this man calleth for Elias. (Mk 15.35: Behold, he calleth Elias.)

Jn 19.28 /b Nu, Nhesus rli wataq li mrhi pavkunhi lr rlrkvasek,
/p ná nčí·sas, é·li-wwá·ta·kw lí- mé·či -pahkánči-lé· e·le·khá·s·i·k,
/t Then Jesus, as he knew that what was written was now fulfilled,
/kl After this, Jesus knowing that all things were now accomplished, that the scripture might be fulfilled,

/b lwr, futwtsumwi.　　　　　　　　　　　　　　[⟨futwtsumwi⟩ for ⟨futwsumwi⟩]
/p lúwe·, "nkat·ó·s·əmwi."
/t said, "I'm thirsty."
/kl saith, I thirst.

Jn 19.29 /b Vws eku avpw hovotr jwapw,
/p hó·s íka ahpú, čuhóte· šəwá·p·u.
/t And there was a pot there, full of vinegar.
/kl Now there was set a vessel full of vinegar:

Mt 27.48 /b mawsw linw eku jevlr,
/p má·wsu lənu íka šíhəle·.
/t And one man ran to it.
/kl And straightway one of them ran,

/b muvtavlyu wrtunr mpif cvavpelehi jwapwf tuntu skuppalao,
/p mahtáhəlaya wé·t·əne· mpínk ehahpi·lí·č·i, šəwá·p·unk tənta-skappalá·ɔ.
/t And he took a sponge (lit., moss that is (found) in water) and wet it in vinegar.
/kl and took a spunge, and filled it with vinegar,

	/b	nu tuli wekunuskwf rhkexuman, ok eku tunumaoo, tuli a munrlen.
	/p	ná tóli- wi·kənáskunk -e·čkí·x·əma·n, ó·k íka tənnəmaó·ɔ, tóli-=á· -məné·li·n.
	/t	And he proceeded to stick it on a reed, and he reached some up to him to drink.
	/kl	and put it on a reed, and gave him to drink. (Cf. Mk 15.36, Lk 23.36, Jn 19.29.)

Mt 27.49 /b Jwq aluntc lwrok, konu lenaw,
/p šúkw a·lónte luwé·ɔk, "kóna lí·naw.
/t But some said, "Leave him alone.
/kl The rest said, Let be,

/b kaxunch nuku Elyusu moi lclrxrmvalao.
/p ká·xəne=č náka †i·layás·a mói-lehəle·x·e·mha·lá·ɔ."
/t Let's see whether Elias will come and save him."
/kl let us see whether Elias will come to save him.

Jn 19.30 /b Nhesus mrhi mrjuntufc nc jwapw
/p nčí·sas mé·či me·š·antánke nó šəwá·p·u,
/t After Jesus had taken a taste of the vinegar,
/kl When Jesus therefore had received the vinegar,

/b amufexsw, lwr, Mrhi kefetwn.   [⟨kefetwn⟩ for ⟨kejetwn⟩]
/p amankí·xsu, lúwe·, "mé·či ki·š·í·to·n."
/t he cried out in a loud voice, saying, "Now it is finished."   (+ Lk 23.46)
/kl he said, It is finished:

Lk 23.46 /b Keji nc lwrtc nu tulwrn
/p kíši- nó -luwé·t·e, ná tóləwe·n,
/t After he said that, then he said,
/k And when Jesus had cried with a loud voice, he said,
/l And when Jesus had cried again with a loud voice, he said,

/b Nwxa, ‖ knuxkif ntatwn nmantwakun.
/p "núxa·, kənáxkink ntá·to·n nəmant·uwwá·k·an."
/t "Father, I put my spirit in your hands."
/kl Father, into thy hands I commend my spirit:

Jn 19.30 /b Nu tolumi pulapekoarvlan, nu tofulun.   [⟨pulap⟩ for ⟨palap⟩]
(p. 208) /p ná tóləmi-†pa·la·p·i·k·ɔaéhəla·n, ná tónkələn.
/t Then his neck began to droop, and then he died.
/k and he bowed his head, and gave up the ghost.
/l and having said thus, he bowed his head and gave up the ghost.
/k and having said thus, he gave up the ghost.   (Lk 23.46)

Mt 27.51 /b Patamwrekaonif lamekwavmc cntu kpapcvlak vcmpus pasekevlr;
/p pa·tamwe·i·k·á·ɔnink la·mi·k·əwáhəme énta-kpa·p·éhəla·k, hémpəs pahsi·k·íhəle·.
/t Inside the temple where it was curtained off, the cloth split in two lengthwise.
/l And, behold, the veil of the temple was rent in twain, in the midst, from the top to the bottom;
/k And, behold, the veil of the temple was rent in twain from the top to the bottom;
/k and the veil of the temple was rent in the midst.   (Lk 23.45)

/b ok qhwkvokcvlr, ok asunu papaxevlro,
/p ɔ́·k kwčukhɔkéhəle·, ɔ́·k ahsɔ́na pa·pa·x·ihəlé·ɔ.
/t And there was an earthquake, and rocks split in pieces.
/kl and the earth did quake, and the rocks rent;

Mt 27.52 /b ok mavhekumeko twfjcvlro,
/p ɔ́·k mahči·k·amí·k·ɔ tunkšehəlé·ɔ.
/t And graves opened.
/kl And the graves were opened;

/b ok xrli wrlilusetpanek kretpanek amweok
/p ɔ́·k xé·li wé·li-ləs·i·tpáni·k ke·i·tpáni·k a·mwí·ok
/t And many who had been good people and had been sleeping arose
/l and many bodies of saints which slept arose,   [KJV "of the saints"]

Mt 27.53 /b wunhi mavhekumeqekri.   [B. ends sentence here.]
/p wɔ́nči mahči·k·ami·k·wi·ké·i.
/t from the graves.
/kl And came out of the graves   [/k "And"; /l "and"]

/b Nhesus mrhi amwetc, ekali tumekr Nhelwsulumif,   [B. makes Jesus the subject.]
/p nčí·sas mé·či a·mwí·t·e, íkali təmí·k·e· †nči·lo·səlɔ́mink.
/t After Jesus had risen from the dead, he went into Jerusalem.
/kl after his resurrection, and went into the holy city,

/b xrli awrn wunroo.
/p xé·li awé·n wəne·ɔ́·ɔ.
/t Many people saw him.
/kl and appeared unto many.

Mt 27.54, Mk 15.39, Lk 23.47
/b Nu elu nwtumat Nhesusu ok wehrvkwki,
/p ná í·la nó·t·əma·t nči·sás·a ɔ́·k wi·č·e·ykúk·i
/t The captain watching over Jesus, and those who were with him,
/l Now when the centurion, which stood over against him, and they that were with him, watching Jesus,

	/b	nrmvetetc li qhwkvokcvlr, ok wrmi rlrk,
	/p	ne·mhití·t·e lí-kwčukhɔkéhəle·, ɔ́·k wé·mi é·le·k,
	/t	when they saw the earthquake and everything that happened,
	/l	saw the earthquake, and those things that were done,

	/b	ok rli ufuluk nrli amufexset,
	/p	ɔ́·k é·li-ánkələk né·li-amankí·xsi·t,
	/t	and how he died while crying out with a loud voice,
	/l	that he so cried out, and gave up the ghost,

	/b	ave wejaswuk,
	/p	áhi-wi·š·á·s·əwak.
	/t	they were very afraid.
	/l	they feared greatly,

	/b	ok nu elu xifoxkunemao Krtanutwelehi; lwr,	[⟨x-⟩ for expected ⟨mox-⟩]
	/p	ɔ́·k ná í·la xinkɔhkəni·má·ɔ ke·tanət·o·wi·lí·č·i, lúwe·,	[/x-/ for expected /mɔx·-/]
	/t	And that captain praised God, saying,	
	/l	and the centurion glorified God, saying,	

	/b	Kvehei lrw wuli luswp wuku linwu.
	/p	"khičí·i lé·w: wəli-lə́s·o·p wáka lə́nəwa.
	/t	"It is true: this man was good.
	/l	Certainly this was a righteous man,

	/b	Kvehei manutw qesu.
	/p	khičí·i manə́t·u kkwí·s·a."
	/t	Truly he was God's son."
	/l	Truly this man was the Son of God.

Lk 23.48	/b	Ok wrmi prnasehek nc rlenamevtetc wrmi rlrk,
	/p	ɔ́·k wé·mi pe·na·s·í·č·i·k nə́ e·li·namihtí·t·e wé·mi é·le·k,
	/t	And when all those who were looking on saw all those things that happened,
	/kl	And all the people that came together to that sight, beholding the things which were done,

	/b	pokuntamunro vwtwlvywu alumi qtukeok.
	/p	pɔk·antamənéɔ wto·lháyəwa, áləmi-kwtək·í·ɔk.
	/t	they struck their chests and began going back.
	/kl	smote their breasts, and returned.

Lk 23.49, Mt 27.55

/b Ncvnrotpanek, ok xqrok naolatpanek Falulebf wunhi
/p nehəne·ɔ·tpáni·k, ɔ́·k xkwé·ɔk na·ɔla·tpáni·k †nka·lalí·yunk wə́nči
/t And his acquaintances ('those who had regularly seen him'), and the women who had followed him from Galilee
/l And all his acquaintance, and the women that followed him from Galilee,

/b trpalatpanek ovlumihi nepwuk.
/p te·p·a·la·tpáni·k, ɔhələmíči ni·p·ó·wak.
/t and had tended to his needs, stood some distance away.
/l ministering unto him, stood afar off; [among whom was [*list*].]   [B. omits names]

Mk 15.41 /b Ok xrli peli xqrok eku nepwuk Nhelwsulumif pchi wehrotpanek,
/p ɔ́·k xé·li pí·li xkwé·ɔk íka ni·p·ó·wak †nči·lo·sələmink péči-wi·č·e·ɔ·tpáni·k,
/t And many other women stood there, who had come with him to Jerusalem,
/l and many other women were there, which came up with him unto Jerusalem;
/k and many other women which came up with him unto Jerusalem.

Lk 23.49 /b wunrmunro rlrk.
/p wəne·məné·ɔ é·le·k.
/t and they saw what happened.
/l and beheld these things.
/k beholding these things.

Chapter 126 (pp. 208-209). [L. section 126.] (John 19.31-37)

Jn 19.31 /b Nu nckc kejqek wcnhavkwuk
/p ná-néke kí·škwi·k wenčahkúwak,
/t That same day they made preparations,
/kl (2) [because] it was the preparation,   [numbers = sequence in L.]

/b rli nuh nc rlavpark alaxemwre-kejkwv.
/p é·li ná=č nɔ́ e·lahpá·e·k ala·x·i·məwe·í·i-kí·šku.
/t as the next morning was going to be the day of rest.
/kl (3) that is, the day before the sabbath,   (Mk 15.42; L.: bracketed in italics)

/b Nuni wunhi Nhwok wenwumanro Pylutu
/p nə́ni wwə́nči- nčó·wak -wi·nəwama·né·ɔ †pailát·a,
/t For that reason the Jews asked Pilate
/kl (1) The Jews therefore, (6) besought Pilate

/b tuli a pwpwqkuxkoncvonro,
/p tə́li-=á· -po·po·kwkaxkɔnehɔ·né·ɔ,
/t for them to break their legs
/kl (7) that their legs might be broken,

/b ok lexunanro,
/p ó·k -li·x·əna·né·ɔ.
/t and take them down.
/kl (8) and that they might be taken away.

/b rli takw kotatumwunro vwjcvlalen alaxemwre-kejqekc,
/p é·li takó· kɔt·a·t·amo·wəné·ɔ wšehəlá·li·n ala·x·i·məwe·í·i-ki·škwí·k·e.
/t For they did not want for them to be hanging up on the day of rest.
/kl (4) that the bodies should not remain upon the cross on the sabbath day,

/b rli tovi xifwrluntumunro nc alaxemwri kejqek.
/p é·li tóhi-xinkwe·ləntaməné·ɔ nə́ ala·x·i·məwe·í·i-kí·škwi·k.
/t For they greatly revered the day of rest.
/kl (5) (for that sabbath day was an high day,)

Jn 19.32 /b Nu sohuluk tolumi mawselw pwpwqkaxkoncvonro, ok takoki.
/p ná só·čəlak tóləmi- ma·wsí·lu -po·po·kwkaxkɔnehɔ·né·ɔ, ó·k takó·ki.
/t Then the soldiers set about breaking the legs of one of them, and then the other.
/kl Then came the soldiers, and brake the legs of the first, and of the other which was crucified with him.

Jn 19.33 /b Jwq Nhesusu prnaovtetc wunroao tuli mrhi ufulun,
/p šúkw nči·sás·a pe·naɔhtí·t·e, wəne·ɔwwá·ɔ tóli- mé·či -ánkələn.
/t But when they looked at Jesus, they saw that he was already dead.
/kl But when they came to Jesus, and saw that he was dead already,

/b nu mutu pwpwqkaxkoncvowunro.
/p ná máta ppo·po·kwkaxkɔnehɔ·wəné·ɔ.
/t Then they did not break his legs.
/kl they brake not his legs:

Jn 19.34 /b Jwq mawsw sohul tufamekun tafamao vwpxkonif;   [⟨taf-⟩ for ⟨tof-⟩]
/p šúkw má·wsu só·čəl tankamí·k·an tɔnkamá·ɔ húpxkɔnink.
/t But one soldier pierced him in the "side" (*lit.* 'back') with a spear. [as in Jn 20.20]
/kl But one of the soldiers with a spear pierced his side,

/b eku wuntpcvlr mvwq ok mpi.
/p íka wəntpéhəle· mhúkw ó·k mpí.
/t And there flowed out blood and water.
/kl and forthwith came there out blood and water.

Jn 19.35 /b Nrfup, tulahemwen, ok krvlu wulamwr rlahemwet;
(p. 209) /p nénkəp təla·č·í·mwi·n, ó·k kéhəla wəlá·məwe· e·la·č·í·mwi·t.
/t The one who saw it reported it, and he indeed told the truth in what he reported.
/kl And he that saw it bare record, and his record is true:

/b ok watwn tuli wulamwrn, wunhi a wulamvetamrq.
/p ɔ́·k o·wá·to·n tə́li-wəlá·məwe·n, wə́nči-=á· -wəla·mhítame·kw.
/t And he knew what he was saying was true, which is why you should believe it.
/kl and he knoweth that he saith true, that ye might believe.

Jn 19.36
/b Nuni rlrk, pavkunhi lr, nenwhi rlrkvasek,
/p nə́ni é·le·k, pahkánči-lé· ni·núči e·le·khá·s·i·k.
/t When that happened, what was written long before was fulfilled:
/kl For these things were done, that the scripture should be fulfilled,

/b Taa kwti wxkunum kuxkvasei.
/p "tá=á· kwə́t·i ó·xkanəm kaxkha·s·í·i."
/t "Not one bone of his shall be broken."
/kl A bone of him shall not be broken.

Jn 19.37
/b Ok lupi palei cntu lrkvasek, cntu lwrf,
/p ɔ́·k lápi palí·i entale·khá·s·i·k, énta-lúwenk,
/t And again what is written in another place, where it says,
/kl And again another scripture saith,

/b Pwunaowaoh tufamavtehi.
/p "pwənaɔwwá·ɔ=č tankamahtí·č·i."
/t "They shall look at the one they pierced."
/kl They shall look on him whom they pierced.

Chapter 127 (p. 209-210). [L. section 127.] (Matthew 27.57-61; Mark 15.42-47; Luke 23.50-56; John 19.38-42.)

Mt 27.57, Mk 15.43, Lk 23.50-51, Jn 19.38
/b Mrhi loqekc
/p mé·či lɔ·k·wí·k·e,
/t After evening had come,
/l And after this, when the even was come,

/b eku pr avoprenw Alumuteu wcnheyet, Nhwe wtrnif, lwcnsw Nhosi,
/p íka pé· ahɔ·p·e·ínnu †aləmatía wenčí·ai·t, nčo·wí·i-o·t·é·nink, luwénsu †nčɔ́·si.
/t there came there a rich man from Arimathaea, a Jewish town, named Josey.
/l behold there came a rich man of Arimathaea, a city of the Jews, named Joseph,

/b mraopret wcvetahemwlset, wuli jaxukawsw.
/p me·a·ɔ·p·é·i·t wehi·t·a·č·i·mó·lsi·t, wə́li-šaxahká·wsu.
/t An upstanding member of the council, he was good and righteous.
/l an honourable counsellor, and he was a good and just man.

/b Nuni mutu tuli wulrluntumwunrp rlyrvosevtet;
/p náni máta tə́li-wəle·ləntamó·wəne·p e·laehɔ·s·íhti·t.
/t *He* had not been pleased with what they all did.
/l The same had not consented to the counsel and deed of them,

/b Rli nokatumunrp Krtanutwet sokemaokun,
/p é·li nɔ·ka·t·amə́ne·p ke·tanət·ó·wi·t sɔ·ki·ma·ɔ́·k·an.
/t For he had put faith in the kingdom of God.
/l but also himself waited for the kingdom of God,

/b wlamvetaopani Nhesusu, alwt mulaji kemei, rli koxao Nhwu.
/p o·la·mhitaɔ́·p·ani nči·sás·a, alóˑt málahši ki·mí·i, é·li kɔx·á·ɔ nčó·wa.
/t He had believed in Jesus, although as if secretly, for he feared the Jews.
/l being a disciple of Jesus, but secretly for fear of the Jews,

Lk 23.52, Mt 27.58, Mk 15.43

/b Nani linw amunheevlr, vwtumekumao Pylutu,
/p náni lə́nu amənči·íhəle·, wtəmi·k·amá·ɔ †pailát·a,
/t That man went "boldly" (*lit.*, forcefully) and entered where Pilate was,
/l This man went in boldly unto Pilate,

/b notwxtaon nc avtwvrpi, tuli a pale lwxovtwn.
/p nɔt·o·xtáɔ·n nə́ ahtuhé·p·i, tə́li-=á· palí·i -lúxɔhto·n.
/t and he asked him for the body, so that he could take it away.
/l and begged the body of Jesus, that he might take it away.

Mk 15.44 /b Jwq Pylut takw orluntamwi tuli krvlu mrhi ufulun;
/p šúkw †páilat takó· †ɔ·e·ləntamó·wi tə́li- kéhəla mé·či -ánkələn.
/t But Pilate doubted that he was already really dead.
/kl And Pilate marvelled if he were already dead: [RSV "wondered"]

/b wcnhemao nrl elao,
/p wwenči·má·ɔ né·l i·lá·ɔ,
/t And he summoned the captain
/kl and calling unto him the centurion,

/b tulao, nakri vuh mrhi uful?
/p təlá·ɔ, "na·k·é·i=háč mé·či ánkəl?"
/t and said to him, "Has he already been dead for a while?"
/kl he asked him whether he had been any while dead. [RSV "sometime dead"]

Mk 15.45, Jn 19.38, Mt 27.58

/b Mrhi ahemwlxwqkc nrl elao;
/p mé·či a·č·i·mo·lxúkwke né·l i·lá·ɔ,
/t After the captain had reported to him,
/l And when he knew it of the centurion,

/b   nu tulan nanc lrkch,
/p   ná tə́la·n, "ná=nə lé·k·eč."
/t   then he said to him, "Let that be done."
/l   he gave him leave,

/b   ok lwr, Melw Nhosi nc avtwvrpi.
/p   ó·k lúwe·, "mí·lo· †nčɔ́·si nə́ ahtuhé·p·i."
/t   And he said, "Give Josey the body."
/l   and commanded the body to be delivered to Joseph.

Mk 15.46
/b   Nu Nhosi movlumun wrltuk vcmpus, ok wulexunao.
/p   ná †nčɔ́·si mɔ́həlamən wé·ltək hémpəs, ó·k wəli·x·əná·ɔ.
/t   Then Josey bought some fine cloth, and he took him down.
/kl   And he bought fine linen, and took him down.

Jn 19.39
/b   Nikotemus eku pr, yavi toxatup Nhesusu peskrwunei,
/p   †nikɔtí·mas íka pé·, a·yáhi-tɔx·á·t·əp nči·sás·a pi·ske·wəní·i.
/t   And Nicodemus came there, who had previously come to Jesus in the night.
/kl   And there came also Nicodemus, which at the first came to Jesus by night,

/b   eku prtw mpeswn, rlwcntasek mul ok alos tavqunaswu,
/p   íka pé·t·o· mpí·s·o·n, e·ləwentá·s·i·k †mə́l ó·k †á·lɔ·s tahkwəná·s·əwa,
/t   He brought there medicine, called myrrh and aloes mixed together,
/kl   and brought a mixture of myrrh and aloes,

/b   avpami ct kwtapxki pwntif.
/p   ahpá·mi=ét kwət·á·pxki púntink.
/t   maybe about a hundred pounds.
/kl   about an hundred pound weight.

Jn 19.40
/b   Wexqcvonro nc eark vcmpus vupi nc mpeswn,
/p   wwi·xkwehɔ·né·ɔ nə́ yá·e·k hémpəs hápi nə́ mpí·s·o·n,
/t   And they wrapped him in that piece of cloth along with that medicine,
/kl   [Then took] they [the body of Jesus and] wound it in linen clothes with the spices,

/b   rlunumevtet Nhwok pwrkvakcvwtevtetc.
/p   ehələnəmíhti·t nčó·wak pwe·khakeho·t·ihtí·t·e.
/t   the way the Jews do when they bury each other.
/kl   as the manner of the Jews is to bury.

Jn 19.41
/b   Kexki cntu psuqvetcvwnt tuli mrnxkvasw,
/p   kí·xki énta-psakhwitéhunt táli-me·nxkhá·s·u.
/t   Near the place where he was crucified there was a garden (*lit.*, 'it was fenced').
/kl   Now in the place where he was crucified there was a garden;

/b nunc lamamrnxkc vatr avsunei awrn a cvlunt,
/p ná=nə la·mamé·nxke hát·e· ahsəní·i awé·n=á· éhələnt.
/t And in that garden there was a stone tomb ('place where people would be put').
/kl and in the garden a new sepulchre,
/k in a sepulchre that was hewn in stone, (Lk 23.53)

Mt 27.60 /b Nhosi toletwnrp,
/p †nčɔ́·si təli·tó·ne·p.
/t Josey was who had made it.
/l which he [*Joseph*] had hewn out in the rock:

Jn 19.41 /b nrlumu vuji awrn eku valaep.
/p né·ləma háši awé·n íka halá·i·p.
/t And no one had ever yet been put there.
/kl wherein was never man yet laid.

Jn 19.42, Lk 23.54, Mt 27.60

/b Nunc tovlanro Nhesusu,
/p ná=nə tɔhəla·né·ɔ nči·sás·a,
/t That is where they put Jesus,
/l There laid they Jesus therefore

/b rli pcxwhevlak alaxemwre kejqek,
/p é·li-pe·x·o·č·íhəla·k ala·x·i·məwe·í·i-kí·škwi·k,
/t as the day of rest was getting close,
/l because [of the Jews' preparation day, and] the sabbath drew on;

/b ok rli nanc li kexki vatrk,
/p ɔ́·k é·li- ná=nə lí kí·xki -hát·e·k.
/t and as it was near that place.
/l for the sepulchre was nigh at hand,

/b ok xifwi avsun ekali tuphcvmwk xqihi mavhekumekwf,   [⟨av-‖sun⟩]
/p ɔ́·k xínkwi-ahsə́n íkali təpčéhəmo·k xkwíči mahči·k·amí·k·unk.
/t And they rolled a large stone in front of that tomb (*lit.*, 'on top of that grave').
/l and [*they*] rolled a great stone to the door of the sepulchre,

(p. 210) /b nu tuli pale anro.
/p ná təli- palí·i -a·né·ɔ.
/t And with that they went away.
/l and departed.

Lk 23.55, Mt 27.61, Mk 15.47
/b   Xqrok naolatpanek wunhi Falulebf
/p   xkwé·ɔk na·ɔla·tpáni·k wə́nči †nka·lalí·yunk
/t   The women who had followed him from Galilee
/l   And the women also which came with him from Galilee, followed after,

/b   punaswpanek wrlexumalifc,
/p   pəna·s·ó·p·ani·k we·li·x·əma·línke,
/t   had looked on when he was laid to rest,
/l   and beheld the sepulchre:

/b   Mrles Maktulen, ok Mrles Nhim kovrsu,
/p   mé·li·s-†má·ktali·n ɔ́·k mé·li·s, nčím kɔhé·s·a,
/t   Mary Magdalene, and Mary the mother of Jim.
/l   and there was Mary Magdalene, and the other Mary the mother of Joses,

/b   kexki lumutavpwpanek,
/p   kí·xki ləmatahpó·p·ani·k
/t   They had sat nearby
/l   sitting over against the sepulchre,

/b   pwunaowapani rlexumalif.
/p   pwənaɔwwá·p·ani e·li·x·əmá·link.
/t   and had watched how he was laid.
/l   beholding how his body was laid.

Lk 23.56 /b   Ok nrk palerpanek, wuletwpanek wifemakvoki mpeswnu, ok jrmrk;
/p   ɔ́·k né·k palí·i é·p·ani·k, wəli·tó·p·ani·k winki·ma·khɔ́ki mpi·s·ó·na ɔ́·k šé·me·k.
/t   And they went away and prepared sweet-smelling medicines and ointment.
/kl And they returned, and prepared spices and ointments;

/b   kulumavpwuk alaxemwre kejqekc, rli nc lexiſ ɥvetulutwakun.
/p   kəlamahpúwak ala·x·i·məwe·í·i-ki·škwí·k·e, é·li- nə́ -lí·x·ink khwitələt·əwá·k·an.
/t   And they sat quietly on the day of rest, because that accords with the law.
/kl and rested the sabbath day according to the commandment.

Chapter 128 (p. 210). [L. section 128.] (Matthew 27.62-66)

Mt 27.62 /b   Mrhi alaxemwre kejqekc
/p   mé·či ala·x·i·məwe·í·i-ki·škwí·k·e,
/t   When the day of rest had come,
/kl Now the next day, that followed the day of the preparation,

/b   wevevwfrhek ok paluseok Pylutif tali marxwrok   [⟨wevev-⟩ for ⟨wcvev-⟩]
/p   wehi·hunké·č·i·k ɔ́·k †pa·ləsi·í·ɔk †pailát·ink táli ma·e·x·wé·ɔk.

| | /t | the priests and Pharisees gathered at Pilate's. |
| | /kl | the chief priests and Pharisees came together unto Pilate, |

Mt 27.63 /b tulaowao, numujatumunrn tuli nuku cvakevokrtup rlwrtup,
/p təlawwá·ɔ, "nəməš·a·t·amə́ne·n, tə́li náka ehahki·hɔké·t·əp, e·ləwé·t·əp,
/t And they said to him, "We remember that he was a deceiver, who said,
/kl Saying, Sir, we remember that that deceiver said,

/b qeaqi lclrxrtc,
/p kwiá·kwi lehəle·x·é·t·e:
/t when he was still alive:
/kl while he was yet alive,

/b nuxwqwnakvakch ntamwi;
/p 'naxo·k·wənakháke=č ntá·mwi.'
/t 'In three days I shall rise (from the dead).'
/kl After three days I will rise again.

Mt 27.64 /b bv tu lwrl, Krnavketwq nc mavhekameq nuxwqunakvakc svaki;
/p yúh=tá lúwe·l, 'ke·nahkí·to·kw mahčí·k·ami·kw naxo·k·wənakháke sháki,'
/t You'd better say, 'Watch that grave for three days (*lit.* 'until in three days'),'
/kl Command therefore that the sepulchre be made sure until the third day,

/b rli a tamsc rkrkemunhek peskrwunei kumutkcvtet,   [⟨kumut⟩ for ⟨kumwt⟩[
/p é·li-=á· tá·mse e·k·e·ki·mə́nči·k pi·ske·wəní·i -kəmo·tkéhti·t.
/t as perhaps the disciples would steal him away at night,
/kl lest his disciples come by night, and steal him away,

/b lwrok a, amweo tu wunhi mavhekamekwf,
/p luwé·ɔk=á·, 'a·mwí·ɔ=tá wə́nči mahči·k·amí·k·unk,'
/t and they would say, 'He that was dead has risen from the grave,'
/kl and say unto the people, He is risen from the dead:

/b wunhi a alwei hetani lri rlavkevokrtup.   [⟨lri⟩ for ⟨lrk⟩]
/p wə́nči-=á· aləwí·i -čí·t·ani-lé·k e·lahki·hɔké·t·əp."
/t by which it would be more serious than his previous deception."
/kl so the last error shall be worse than the first.

Mt 27.65 /b Pylut tulao, Kwlvalavmw tu, ncnwtuntufek;
/p †páilat təlá·ɔ, "ko·lhaláhəmɔ=tá nehəno·t·əntánki·k.
/t Pilate said to them, "You have some guards for it.
/kl Pilate said unto them, Ye have a watch: [RSV "a guard of soldiers"]

/b   eku aq, vwusku hetanextwq.
/p   íka á·kw, hwə́ska či·t·aní·xto·kw."
/t   Go there and make it as secure as possible (*lit.* 'extremely strong')."
/kl go your way, make it as sure as ye can.

Mt 27.66 /b   Nu eku tonro,
/p   ná íka tɔ·né·ɔ.
/t   Then they went there.
/kl So they went,

/b   vwhetanextwnro mavhekameq, pwkvvamunro nc avsun
/p   wči·t·ani·xto·né·ɔ mahči·k·ami·kw, ppuk·uwhamə́né·ɔ nə́ ahsə́n,
/t   and they made the tomb ('grave') secure, sealing the stone,
/kl and made the sepulchre sure, sealing the stone,

/b   ok nwtuntamulehih eku valrok.
/p   ó·k no·t·əntaməlí·č·i=č íka halé·ɔk.
/t   and they stationed there ones who would guard it.
/kl and setting a watch.   [RSV "a guard"]

Chapter 129 (pp. 210-212). [L. section 129.] (Matthew 28.1-8; Mark 16.1-8; Luke 24.1-9, 12; John 20.1-10.)

Mk 16.1 /b   Mrhi lwwxrekc alaxemwe kejqek,
/p   mé·či lo·o·x·we·í·k·e ala·x·i·məwí·i-kí·škwi·k,
/t   After the day of rest had past,
/kl When the sabbath was past,

/b   Mrli Maktulen ok Mrles Nhim kovrsu ok Srlom,
/p   mć·li-†má·ktali·n, ó·k mé·li·s nčím kɔhé·s·a, ó·k †sé·lɔ·m
/t   Mary Magdalene, and Mary Jim's mother, and Salome
/kl Mary Magdalene and Mary the mother of James, and Salome,

/b   mvalamwpanek mpeswn jrmunavtet a.
/p   mhalamó·p·ani·k mpí·s·o·n, še·mənáhti·t=á·.
/t   had bought medicine to rub him with.
/kl had bought sweet spices, that they might come and anoint him.

Mk 16.2, Jn 20.1, Mt 28.1, Lk 24.1
(Omitted: /l (1) And very early in the morning the first day of the week,)   [nos. = order in L.]

/b   Qeaqi peskr nu eku tonro mavhekamekwf,
/p   kwiá·kwi pí·ske·, ná íka tɔ·né·ɔ mahči·k·amí·k·unk.
/t   It was still dark when they went to the tomb ('grave').   ['when': *lit.*, 'and then']
/l   (2) when it was yet dark, (4) they came to the sepulchre,

Text, Transcription, and Translation

/b   qunumunro nc mpeswn wrletwvtetup,
/p   kwənnəməné·ɔ nə́ mpí·s·o·n we·li·tuhtí·t·əp.
/t   They carried the medicine that they had prepared.
/l   (6) bringing the spices which they had prepared.

/b   krxu peli xqrok wehrowao tuli a punamunro.
/p   ké·x·a pí·li xkwé·ɔk wwi·č·e·ɔwwá·ɔ, tə́li-á· -pənəməné·ɔ.
/t   Several other women went with them to see it.
/l   (5) and certain others with them, to see it,

/b   Mrhi alumi prtapun nu eku ponro mavhekamekwf. ‖
/p   mé·či álǝmi-pe·t·á·p·an, ná íka pɔ·né·ɔ mahči·k·amí·k·unk.
/t   Dawn was already breaking when they came to the tomb. ['when': *lit.*, 'and then']
/l   (3) as it began to dawn, (4) they came to the sepulchre,   [(4) repeated in B.]

Mt 28.2   /b   Nu wexkawhi qhwqivlr vuki,
(p. 211) /p   ná wi·xkaɔ́či kwčuk·wíhəle· hák·i.
        /t   Then suddenly the earth shook.
        /kl   And, behold, there was a great earthquake:

/b   rli Nrvlalwrt cvalwkalahi pchi pune wunhi osavkamc,
/p   é·li nehəlá·ləwe·t ehalo·ka·lá·č·i péči-pəní· wə́nči o·s·áhkame.
/t   For an angel ('one that the Lord sends') came down from heaven.
/kl   for the angel of the Lord descended from heaven,

/b   eku r, pale tulhrneven nc avsun wunhi mavhekamekwf,
/p   íka é·, palí·i tǝlče·níhi·n nə́ ahsə́n wə́nči mahči·k·amí·k·unk.
/t   And he went there and rolled away the stone from the tomb.
/kl   and came and rolled back the stone from the door,

/b   nu tuli vapavpen;
/p   ná tə́li-hápahpi·n.
/t   And with that he sat on it.
/kl   and sat upon it.

Mt 28.3   /b   sasapulclakif lenaqsw ok rqet lukveqi opulrxun kwnif;
        /p   sa·sa·p·ǝlehǝlá·k·ink li·ná·kwsu, ɔ́·k é·k·wi·t lǝkhíkwi-ɔ·p·ǝlé·x·ǝn kó·nink.
        /t   His expression was like lightning, and his clothing shone as white as snow.
        /kl   His countenance was like lightning, and his raiment white as snow:
                                                [RSV "His appearance"]

Mt 28.4   /b   nwtuntufek rli kxovtet nufevlrok,
        /p   no·t·ǝntánki·k, é·li-kxɔ́hti·t, nankihǝlé·ɔk,
        /t   The guards, because they feared him, trembled,
        /kl   And for fear of him the keepers did shake,

        /b ok mulaji ufulwk tulenaqsenro,
        /p ó·k málahši ánkəlo·k təli·na·kwsi·né·ɔ.
        /t and their expressions were as if they were dead.
        /kl and became as dead men,

Mk 16.8 /b ok vwjemwuk.
        /p ó·k wší·məwak.
        /t And they ran away.
        /l [*and fled*].   (L. adds this here.)
        /k ... and fled from the sepulchre

Mk 16.3 /b Nrk xqrok lutwok,
        /p né·k xkwé·ɔk lə́t·əwak,
        /t Meanwhile, those women said to each other,
        /l And they [*the women*] said among themselves,

        /b awrnh vuh ct pale ktunumakwnrn nc avsun wunhi mavhekamekwf?
        /p "awé·n=č=háč=ét palí·i ktənnəma·k·ó·ne·n nə́ ahsə́n wə́nči mahči·k·amí·k·unk?"
        /t "Who do you think will move that stone away from the tomb ('grave') for us?"
        /kl Who shall roll us away the stone from the door of the sepulchre?

Mk 16.4 /b rli ave muxrp.
        /p é·li áhi-maxé·p.
        /t For it was very large.
        /kl for it was very great.   [L. moves this before the following]

Mk 16.4 /b Eku rlifwrxenvetetc wunrmunro, nc avsun li mrhi pale vatr.
        /p íka e·linkwe·x·i·nhití·t·e, wəne·məné·ɔ nə́ ahsə́n lí- mé·či palí·i -hát·e·.
        /t And when they looked, they saw the stone already set to one side.
        /kl And when they looked, they saw that the stone was rolled away.

Jn 20.2 /b Nu Mrli Maktulen tolumamclan,
        /p ná mé·li-†má·ktali·n tɔləma·méhəla·n.
        /t Then Mary Magdalene ran from there.
        /l Then [*Mary Magdalene*] runneth

        /b wtxao Symun Petulu ok takoki rkrkemkwselehi
        /p o·txá·ɔ †sáiman-pí·təla ó·k takó·ki e·k·e·ki·mkwəs·i·lí·č·i;
        /t She came to Simon-Peter and another disciple;
        /kl and cometh to Simon Peter, and to the other disciple

        /b nunuli nrl Nhesus rvolahi,
        /p nanáli né·l nčí·sas ehɔ·lá·č·i.
        /t he was the one Jesus loved.
        /kl whom Jesus loved,

	/b	tulao, Pale tulwxolawao Nrvlalkofwi wunhi mavhekamekwf,
	/p	təlá·ɔ, "palí·i təlo·x·ɔlawwá·ɔ nehəla·lkónkwi wə́nči mahči·k·amí·k·unk.
	/t	And she said to them, "They have taken our lord away from the tomb.
	/kl	and saith unto them, They have taken away the Lord out of the sepulchre,

	/b	takw nwatwunrn tutu cvlavtet.
	/p	takó· no·wa·tó·wəne·n tətá ehəláhti·t.
	/t	We don't know where they put him."
	/kl	and we know not where they have laid him.

Lk 24.3	/b	Kuhi nrk takokek xqrok ekali punheok mavhekamekwf,
	/p	káč·i né·k takó·ki·k xkwé·ɔk íkali pənči·ɔk mahči·k·amí·k·unk.
	/t	Meanwhile, however, those other women entered the tomb,
	/l	And [*the other women*] entered into the sepulchre,
	/k	And they entered in,

	/b	jwq mutu muxkamwunro wavtwvrpi Nhesus.	[⟨muxk-⟩ for /mɔxk-/]
	/p	šúkw máta mɔxkamo·wəné·ɔ wahtuhé·p·i nčí·sas.	
	/t	but they did not find Jesus's body.	
	/kl	and found not the body of the Lord Jesus.	

Lk 24.4	/b	Jwq nrli qelalrluntumevtet,
	/p	šúkw né·li·kwí·la·le·ləntamíhti·t,
	/t	But while they were wondering what was going on,
	/kl	And it came to pass, as they were much perplexed thereabout,

Mk 16.5	/b	nrrok skenwu lrmuvtupet vwtunrvaonwaif wuntavqi,
	/p	ne·é·ɔk skinnúwa, le·mahtáp·i·t wtənne·ha·ɔnəwá·ink wə́ntahkwi,
	/t	they saw a young man sitting to their right,
	/kl	they saw a young man sitting on the right side,

	/b	qrnevlak opulrxif avkw.
	/p	kwe·níhəla·k ɔ·p·əlé·x·ink ahkú.
	/t	and he wore a long, shiny-white garment.
	/kl	clothed in a long white garment.

Lk 24.4	/b	Nu ok peli linw osulrxunw rqehi
	/p	ná ɔ́·k pí·li lə́nu, ɔ·s·əlé·x·ənu e·k·wí·č·i.
	/t	Then there was also another man whose garments shone.
	/l	And he *with another man* in shining garments
	/k	behold, two men stood by them in shining garments:

	/b	wexkaohi kexkiti nejekapwok;
	/p	wi·xkaɔ́či ki·xkíti ni·š·i·k·a·p·ó·wak.
	/t	And suddenly the two of them were standing together even closer to them.
	/l	stood by them;

Mk 16.5, Lk 24.5
- /b nu wejasenro vukif li alwlavtrvlrok.
- /p ná wwi·š·a·s·i·né·ɔ, hák·ink lí-a·lo·lahtehəlé·ɔk.
- /t Then they were frightened, and they threw themselves face-down on the ground,
- /l and they were affrighted, and bowed down their faces to the earth.

Mt 28.5, Mk 16.6
- /b Nu cvalwkalunt tulao nrl xqro, Kahi wejasevrq,
- /p ná ehalo·ká·lənt təlá·ɔ né·l xkwé·ɔ, "káči wi·š·a·s·í·he·kw.
- /t And the angel ('messenger') said to the women, "Don't be afraid.
- /l And the angel answered, and saith unto the women, Be ye not affrighted,

- /b rli nwatwn ktuli ntwnaonro Nhesus Nasulutif wcnheyet
- /p é·li no·wá·to·n ktəli-nto·naɔ·né·ɔ nčí·sas †nasəlát·ink wenčí·ai·t,
- /t As I know that you're looking for Jesus of Nazareth
- /l for I know that ye seek Jesus of Nazareth,

- /b psuqvetcvwntup.
- /p psakhwitehúntəp.
- /t who was crucified.
- /l which was crucified.

Lk 24.5
- /b Koh vuh ntwnarq prmawset li rfulukekri?
- /p kóč=háč ntó·nae·kw pe·má·wsi·t lí enkələk·i·ké·i?
- /t Why are you looking among the dead for one who is living?
- /kl Why seek ye the living among the dead?

Mt 28.6
- /b Takw tu b topewun,
- /p takó·=tá yú tɔp·í·wən.
- /t He's not here.
- /kl He is not here;

- /b mrhi amwep,
- /p mé·či á·mwi·p.
- /t He has already risen (from the dead).
- /kl for he is risen,

- /b nuni rlwrtup.
- /p nə́ni e·ləwé·t·əp.
- /t That is as he had said.
- /kl as he said.

- /b Bv tu, punamwq jrfexifup.
- /p yúh=tá, pənámo·kw šenki·x·ínkəp.
- /t Come and see the place where he lay.
- /kl Come, see the place where the Lord lay.

Mt 28.7 /b Jac alumskaq, mai lw rkrkemahi, ok Petul,
/p šá·e aləmska·kw, mái-ló· e·k·e·ki·má·č·i, ó·k †pí·təl,
/t Go right away, and tell his disciples, including Peter,
/l And go quickly, and tell his disciples, and Peter, [*in particular*]
/k And go quickly, and tell his disciples (Mt 28.7)
/k But go your way, tell his disciples and Peter (Mk 16.7)

/b tuli mrhi amwen wunhi ufulwakunif,
/p táli- mé·či -á·mwi·n wánči ankələwá·k·anink.
/t that he has now risen from death.
/kl that he is risen from the dead;

/b ok knekanetakwu li Falulebf,
/p ó·k kəni·k·a·ni·tá·k·əwa lí †nka·lalí·yunk.
/t Also, he is going ahead of you to Galilee.
/kl and, behold, he goeth before you into Galilee;

/b nuh nc ktuntu nronro,
/p ná=č ná ktánta-ne·ɔ·né·ɔ.
/t That is where you will see him.
/kl there shall ye see him:

/b jr mrhi ktulunro.
/p šé·, mé·či ktəlləné·ɔ.
/t So, now I have told you.
/kl lo, I have told you.

Lk 24.6 /b Mujatamwq rlqrkup qeaqi rpetc Falulebf
/p məšá·t·amo·kw e·lkwé·k·əp kwiá·kwi e·p·í·t·e †nka·lalí·yunk.
/t Remember what he said to you when he was still in Galilee.
/kl Remember how he spake unto you when he was yet in Galilee,

Lk 24.7 /b lwrp, Wrqesifi linwu melanroh mrtawsehek
/p lúwe·p, 'we·k·wi·s·ínki lánəwa mi·la·né·ɔ=č me·t·a·wsí·č·i·k
/t He said, 'The Son who is a man must be turned over to evil-doers
/kl saying, The Son of man must be delivered into the hands of sinful men,

/b lih psuqvetcvon,
/p lí-=č -psakhwitého·n.
/t to be crucified.
/kl and be crucified,

/b jwqh ‖ nuxi kejqekc lupi amwe.
/p šúkw=č náxi-ki·škwí·k·e, lápi á·mwi·.'"
/t But after three days he shall rise again.'"
/kl and the third day rise again.

Lk 24.8   /b   Nu mwjatumunro rlwrletup.
(p. 212)   /p   ná mwəš·a·t·aməné·ɔ e·ləwe·lí·t·əp.
           /t   Then they remembered what he had said.
           /kl And they remembered his words,

Mt 28.8, Mk 16.8
           /b   Ok jac alumskrok eku wunhi mavhekamekwf,
           /p   ó·k šá·e aləmské·ɔk íka wə́nči mahči·k·amí·k·unk.
           /t   And right away they departed from that tomb.
           /l   And they departed quickly, and fled from the sepulchre,

           /b   wejaswuk, ok avi wulrluntamwk;
           /p   wi·š·á·s·əwak ó·k áhi-wəle·ĺəntamo·k.
           /t   They were fearful and very happy.
           /l   with fear and great joy:

           /b   somi kanjrluntamwk, qwlupuhi nufevlrok,
           /p   só·mi-kanše·ĺəntamo·k, †kwələpáči nankihəlé·ɔk.
           /t   They were so astonished they even trembled.
           /l   for they trembled and were amazed:

           /b   takw awrni krkw lreok naohei, rli wejasevtet,
           /p   takó· awé·ni kéku le·í·ɔk naɔč·í·i, é·li-wi·š·a·s·íhti·t
           /t   They did not speak to anyone on the way, as they were fearful
           /l   neither said they any thing [on the way] to any man; for they were afraid;

           /b   ok kjamcvlavtet tuli a watulanro rkrkemkwselehi.
           /p   ó·k -kša·mehəláhti·t, tə́li-=á· -wwa·təla·né·ɔ e·k·e·ki·mkwəs·i·lí·č·i.
           /t   and were running fast to take the news to the disciples.
           /l   and did run to bring his disciples word.

Jn 20.3   /b   Jwq Petul ok takok rkrkemkwset
           /p   šúkw †pí·təl ó·k tákɔ·k e·k·e·ki·mkwə́s·i·t,
           /t   But Peter and the other disciple,
           /l   Then Peter and that other disciple
           /k   (1) Peter therefore ... (3) and that other disciple,   [numbers = sequence in K.]

           /b   mrhi puntaovtetc Mrli Maktulenu, kheok
           /p   mé·či pəntaɔhtí·t·e mé·li-†ma·ktalí·na, kčí·ɔk,
           /t   having heard what Mary Magdalene said, went out
           /l   went forth [upon what Mary Magdalene had related unto them]
           /k   ... (2) went forth, ...

           /b   eku jevlrok mavhekamekwf,
           /p   íka šihəlé·ɔk mahči·k·amí·k·unk.

	/t	and ran to the tomb.
	/kl	and came to the sepulchre. (Jn 20.4) So they ran both together:

Jn 20.4
- /b jwq nu takok rkrkemkwset wunukalao Petulu,
- /p šúkw ná tákɔ·k e·k·e·ki·mkwə́s·i·t wənək·alá·ɔ †pí·təla,
- /t But the other disciple outran Peter
- /kl and the other disciple did outrun Peter,

- /b vetami eku mwxkevlr mavhekamekwf.
- /p hítami íka mo·xkíhəle· mahči·k·amí·k·unk.
- /t and was the first to arrive at the tomb.
- /kl and came first to the sepulchre.

Jn 20.5
- /b Ekali rnexen, wnrmunu vcmpsu jrfexifi,
- /p íkali e·ní·x·i·n, wəné·məna hémpsa šenki·x·ínki,
- /t He stooped down to look in and saw the pieces of cloth lying there.
- /kl And he stooping down, *and looking in*, saw the linen clothes lying; [italics in K.]

- /b jwq mutu ekali punhei.
- /p šúkw máta íkali pənčí·i.
- /t But he did not go in there.
- /kl yet went he not in.

Jn 20.6
- /b Nu kcnh Symun Petul eku mwxkevlan,
- /p ná kə́nč †sáiman-pí·təl íka mmo·xkíhəla·n,
- /t At that point Simon-Peter arrived there,
- /kl Then cometh Simon Peter following him,

- /b ekali punhe mavhekamekwf,
- /p íkali pə́nči· mahči·k·amí·k·unk,
- /t and he entered the tomb,
- /kl and went into the sepulchre,

- /b wunrmunu vcmpsu jcfexifi
- /p wəné·məna hémpsa šenki·x·ínki.
- /t and he saw the pieces of cloth lying there.
- /kl and seeth the linen clothes lie,

Jn 20.7
- /b jwq wexqrptekifup wel takw nc vatri vcmpsu rtrk   [⟨kif⟩ for /k·énk/]
- /p šúkw wi·xkwe·pti·k·énkəp wí·l takó· nə́ hat·é·i hémpsa é·te·k.
- /t But what his head had been bound up with was not where the pieces of cloth were.
- /kl And the napkin, that was about his head, not lying with the linen clothes,

/b paleihi vatr pupxkawunasw.
/p pali·íči hát·e·, †pəpxkawəná·s·u.
/t It lay a little to one side, all folded up.
/kl but wrapped together in a place by itself.

Jn 20.8
/b Na ok nu takok rkrkemkwset eku tuli punhen, nrtami eku mwxkevlatup,
/p ná ɔ·k ná tákɔ·k e·k·e·ki·mkwəs·i·t íka təli-pə́nči·n, né·tami- íka -mo·xkihəlá·t·əp,
/t Then that other disciple also went in there, the one who had arrived there first,
/kl Then went in also that other disciple, which came first to the sepulchre,

/b wunrmun, ok wlamvetamun.
/p wəné·mən ɔ́·k o·la·mhítamən.
/t and he saw it and believed it.
/k and he saw, and believed.
/l and he saw, and believed [*that the body of the Lord was not there*].

Jn 20.9
/b Nuni pchi takw wununwstamwnro rlrkvasek
/p nə́ni pə́či takó· wənəno·stamo·wəné·ɔ e·le·khá·s·i·k,
/t Up to then they did not understand what was written,
/kl For as yet they knew not the scripture,

/b tulih amwen wunhi ufulwakunif.
/p təli-=č -á·mwi·n wə́nči ankələwá·k·anink.
/t that he would rise from death.
/kl that he must rise again from the dead.

Jn 20.10
/b Nu nrk rkrkemkwsehek mohenro
/p ná né·k e·k·e·ki·mkwəs·í·č·i·k mɔ·č·i·né·ɔ.
/t Then those disciples went back home.
/kl Then the disciples went away again unto their own home,

Lk 24.12
/b kanjrluntamwk wunhi rlrk.
/p kanše·lə́ntamo·k wə́nči é·le·k.
/t They were astonished by what had happened.
/l wondering at that which was come to pass.
/k ... wondering [in himself] at that which was come to pass.

Chapter 130 (pp. 212-213). [L. section 130.] (Mark 16.9; John 20.11-17)

Mk 16.9
/b Nhesus mrhi amwetc, nunc kejqek alupae
/p nčí·sas mé·či a·mwí·t·e, ná=nə kí·škwi·k alap·a·í·i,
/t After Jesus had risen from the dead, that same day early in the morning,
/kl Now when *Jesus* was risen early the first day of the week,

/b vetami wuncnsetaoo Mrli Maktulenu,
/p hítami wənentsi·taɔ́·ɔ mé·li-†ma·ktalí·na,
/t the first one he appeared to was Mary Magdalene,
/kl he appeared first to Mary Magdalene,

/b nrl yavi nejaj mavtuntwu ktuskamaotup.
/p né·l a·yáhi- ní·š·a·š mahtant·ó·wa -ktəskamaɔ́·t·əp.
/t who he had previously driven seven devils out of.
/kl out of whom he had cast seven devils.

Jn 20.11 /b Kexki mavhekamekwf nepw avi lupuq,
/p kí·xki mahči·k·amí·k·unk ní·p·o·, áhi-ləpákw.
/t She stood near the tomb and wept very hard.
/l For [*when she came again unto the sepulchre*] she stood without weeping:
/k But Mary stood without at the sepulchre weeping: [RSV "outside the tomb"]

/b nrli lupukuk, ekali rnexen, lamwfwc mavhekamekwf.
/p né·li-ləpák·ək, íkali e·ní·x·i·n la·múnkwe mahči·k·amí·k·unk.
/t As she wept, she stooped down to look inside the tomb.
/kl and as she wept, she stooped down and looked into the sepulchre;

Jn 20.12 /b Ekali nrr neju cvalwkalunhi
/p íkali né·e· ní·š·a ehalo·ka·lə́nči.
/t And she saw two angels ('messengers') there.
/kl And seeth two angels

/b opulrxenwk,
/p ɔ·p·əle·x·í·no·k,
/t They were shiny-white,
/kl in white,

/b mawsw rlvwqrxenuletup wlumuvtupen kuhi mawsw rlsetrxenuletup;
/p má·wsu e·lhukwe·x·i·nəlí·t·əp wələmahtáp·i·n, káč·i má·wsu e·lsi·t·e·x·i·nəlí·t·əp.
/t and one sat where his head had lain, with the other where his feet had been.
/kl sitting, the one at the head, and the other at the feet, where the body of Jesus had lain:

Jn 20.13 /b Tulkw, Xqr, krkw vuh wcnhi lupukun?
/p tə́lku, "xkwé·, kéku=háč wénči-ləpák·an?"
/t And they said to her, "Woman, why are you weeping?"
/kl And they say unto her, Woman, why weepest thou?

/b Tulao rli wrtunavtet nrvlalelehi   [⟨nrvlale-‖lehi⟩]
/p təlá·ɔ, "é·li-we·t·ənáhti·t nehəla·li·lí·č·i,
/t And she said to them, "Because they took my lord,
/kl She saith unto them, Because they have taken away my Lord,

(p. 213) /b   ok rli mutu watwu tutu rvlavtet.
          /p   ɔ́·k é·li- máta -wwa·tó·wa tətá ehəláhti·t."
          /t   and because I don't know where they put him."
          /kl and I know not where they have laid him.

Jn 20.14 /b   Keji nc lwrtc qwlwpe, wunroo Nhesusu nepyet,
          /p   kíši- nə́ -luwé·t·e, kwələp·i·, wəne·ɔ́·ɔ nči·sás·a ní·p·ai·t,
          /t   After saying that, she turned and saw Jesus standing,
          /kl And when she had thus said, she turned herself back, and saw Jesus standing,

          /b   jwq mutu wununaoeo.
          /p   šúkw máta wənənaɔ·í·ɔ.
          /t   but she did not recognize him.
          /kl and knew not that it was Jesus.

Jn 20.15 /b   Nhesus tulao, Xqr, koh vuh lupukun?
          /p   nčí·sas təlá·ɔ, "xkwé·, kɔ́č=háč ləpák·an?"
          /t   And Jesus said to her, "Woman, why are you weeping?"
          /kl Jesus saith unto her, Woman, why weepest thou?

          /b   awrn vuh knatwnao?
          /p   awé·n=háč kənat·ó·naɔ?
          /t   Who are you looking for?
          /kl whom seekest thou?

          /b   Jwq letrvr nunul ct wu wrtvakevakunet, tulao,
          /p   šúkw li·t·é·he·, "nánal=ét wá we·thaki·há·k·ani·t," təlá·ɔ,
          /t   But she thought, "This must be the owner of the garden ('field')," and said to him,
          /kl She, supposing him to be the gardener, saith unto him,

          /b   Ke alumwxolutsvunc b wunhi, lel tutu cvclut,
          /p   "kí· aləmo·x·ɔlatsháne yú wə́nči, lí·l tətá éhəlat.
          /t   "If *you* have taken him from here, tell me where you put him.
          /kl Sir, if thou have borne him hence, tell me where thou hast laid him,

          /b   paleih ntulwxolu.
          /p   palí·i=č ntəló·x·ɔla."
          /t   I shall take him away."
          /kl and I will take him away.

Jn 20.16 /b   Nhesus tulao, Mrli!
          /p   nčí·sas təlá·ɔ, "mé·li."
          /t   Jesus said to her, "Mary!"
          /kl Jesus saith unto her, Mary!

/b Nu eku tulekapaen, tulao Nrvlaleun.
/p ná íka təli·k·á·p·ai·n, təlá·ɔ, "nehəlá·lian."
/t Then she came up to him and said to him, "Master."   [or 'my lord']
/kl She turned herself and saith unto him, Rabboni; which is to say, Master.

Jn 20.17 /b Nhesus tulao, Kahi mujunevun, rli nrlumu ntuspei li Nwxif;
/p nčí·sas təlá·ɔ, "káči məšəní·han, é·li né·ləma ntaspí·i lí nó·x·ink.
/t And Jesus said to her, "Don't touch me, for I have not yet gone up to my father.
/kl Jesus saith unto her, Touch me not: for I am not yet ascended to my Father:

/b eku al nemavtusekri,
/p íka á·l ni·mahtəs·i·ké·i,
/t Go to my brothers
/kl but go to my brethren,

/b lul, ntuspi li Nwxif krpwu Kwxwaif,
/p lól, ntáspi lí nó·x·ink, ké·pəwa ko·x·əwá·ink,
/t and tell them, I am going up to my father, and your father also,
/kl and say unto them, I ascend unto my Father, and your Father;

/b Frtanutwetumif krpwu Krtanutwetumwaif.
/p nke·tanət·o·wí·t·əmink, ké·pəwa kke·tanət·o·wí·t·əmink."
/t to my God, and your God also."
/kl and to my God, and your God.

Chapter 131 (p. 213). [L. section 131.] (Matthew 28.9-10.)

Mt 28.9 /b Nrlwxwrvtet nrk takokek xqrok
/p ne·lo·x·wéhti·t né·k takó·ki·k xkwé·ɔk,
/t As the other women walked along,
/l And as *the other women* went
/k And as they went

/b mrohcmwlxahek rkrkemkwselehi,
/p me·ɔ·č·i·mo·lxá·č·i·k e·k·e·ki·mkwəs·i·lí·č·i,
/t the ones going to inform the disciples,
/kl to tell his disciples,

/b nokeskaowao Nhesusu, tulkwao, wrmi koofwmulwvmw.
/p nɔk·i·skaɔwwá·ɔ nči·sás·a, təlkəwá·ɔ, "wé·mi kɔɔnko·məlúhəmɔ."
/t they met Jesus, and he said to them, "I greet you all."
/kl behold, Jesus met them, saying, All hail.

        /b   Jac eku tonaowao vwsetelet, ok moxifovkunemawao.   [⟨nao-|w⟩ for /-nnaww-/]
        /p   šá·e íka tɔnnawwá·ɔ wsi·t·í·li·t, ɔ́·k mɔx·inkɔhkəni·mawwá·ɔ.
        /t   Immediately they touched their hands to his feet and praised him.
        /kl And they came and held him by the feet, and worshipped him.

Mt 28.10 /b   Nhesus tulao, Kahi wejasevrq;
        /p   nčí·sas təlá·ɔ, "káči wi·š·a·s·í·he·kw.
        /t   Jesus said to them, "Don't be afraid.
        /kl Then said Jesus unto them, Be not afraid:

        /b   mai lw nemavtusuk, eku aq Falulebf,
        /p   mái-ló· ni·mahtəs·ak, 'íka á·kw †nka·lalí·yunk.'
        /t   Go tell my brothers to go to Galilee.
        /kl go tell my brethren that they go into Galilee,

        /b   nuh nc ntuntu nrvkwnro.
        /p   ná=č nə́ ntə́nta-ne·yko·né·ɔ."
        /t   That's where they will see me."
        /l   and there shall they see me.

[L. section 132.] (Matthew 28.11-15.)

Mt 28.11 /b   Nrlwxwrvtet nu nrk aluntc nwtuntufpanek eku ponro wtrnif,
        /p   ne·lo·x·wéhti·t, ná né·k a·lə́nte no·t·əntankpáni·k íka pɔ·né·ɔ o·t·é·nink,
        /t   As they walked along, some of those who had been guards came into the city
        /kl Now when they were going, behold, some of the watch came into the city,

        /b   tulahemwlxanro patamwrokun krnavketwlehi, wrmi rlrk.
        /p   təla·č·i·mo·lxa·né·ɔ pa·tamwe·ɔ́·k·an ke·nahki·to·lí·č·i wé·mi é·le·k.
        /t   and reported to the high priest(s) everything that happened.
        /kl and shewed unto the chief priests all the things that were done.

Mt 28.12 /b   Mrhi maclavletc wrmi cvahemwlsehek. Mrhi keji ahemwlsevtetc,   [⟨vl⟩ for ⟨vt⟩]
        /p   mé·či ma·ehəlahtí·t·e wé·mi eha·č·i·mo·lsí·č·i·k, mé·či kíši-a·č·i·mo·lsihtí·t·e,
        /t   After all the councillors had assembled, and after they had deliberated,
        /kl And when they were assembled with the elders, and had taken counsel,

        /b   xrli moni mwelawao nrl sohulu,
        /p   xé·li móni mwi·lawwá·ɔ né·l sɔ́·čəla,
        /t   they gave a lot of money to those soldiers,
        /kl they gave large money unto the soldiers,

Mt 28.13 /b   tulawao, ktulwcvmwh
        /p   təlawwá·ɔ, "ktələwéhəmɔ=č,
        /t   telling them, "You must say,
        /kl saying, Say ye,

/b rkrkemkwsehek fumwtumwkwnrnani peskrwunei nrli kaerf;
/p 'e·k·e·ki·mkwəs·í·č·i·k nkəmo·t·əmuk·o·ne·ná·ni pi·ske·wəní·i né·li-kaíenk.'
/t 'The disciples stole him from us at night while we slept.'
/kl His disciples came by night, and stole him away while we slept;

Mt 28.14 /b ok Fopunul puntufc,
/p ó·k †nkápənal pəntánke,
/t And if the governor hears about it,
/kl and if this come to the governor's ears,

/b nwlaptwnalawunuh, wcnhi mutu krkw lenamwrq.
/p no·la·pto·na·lá·wəna=č, wénči- máta kéku -li·namó·we·kw."
/t we will speak favorably to him so that nothing happens to you."
/kl we will persuade him, and secure you.

Mt 28.15 /b Nu wrtunumunro nrl moneu, ok nunc tulsenro rlunt.
/p ná wwe·t·ənəməné·ɔ né·l mónia, ó·k ná=nə təlsi·né·ɔ é·lənt.
/t Then they took the money, and they did just what they were told to do.
/kl So they took the money, and did as they were taught:

/b Nuni lwrokun aphi puntakot tali Nhwekri bqc pchi. ‖
/p nə́ni luwe·ó·k·an á·pči pəntá·k·ɔt táli nčo·wi·ké·i yúkwe péči.
/t And that tale is always heard among the Jews, down to the present.
/kl and this saying is commonly reported among the Jews until this day.

Chapter 132 (p. 214). [L. section 133.] (Mark 16.10-11; Luke 24.9-11; John 20.18.)

Mk 16.10, Jn 20.18
/b Mrli Maktulen eku wtxao rkrkemkwselehi,
/p mé·li-†má·ktali·n íka o·txá·ɔ e·k·e·ki·mkwəs·i·lí·č·i,
/t Mary Magdalene came to the disciples,
/l Mary Magdalene came to the disciples,

/b nrli jerluntumulet ok lupukulet.
/p né·li-ši·e·ləntaməli·t ó·k -ləpák·əli·t.
/t as they grieved and wept.
/l as they mourned and wept,

/b Tulahemwlxan rli nrot Nrvlalwrlehi, ok rlaptwnalkwk.
/p təla·č·i·mó·lxa·n é·li-né·ɔ·t nehəla·ləwe·lí·č·i, ó·k e·la·pto·ná·lkuk.
/t And she reported to them how she had seen the Lord, and what he said to her.
/l and told them, that she had seen the Lord, and that he had spoken these things unto her;

Mk 16.11 /b Jwq puntumevtetc tuli lclrxrn, ok rli nrnsetakwk,
/p šúkw pəntamihtí·t·e tə́li-lehəlé·x·e·n, ɔ́·k é·li-nentsi·tá·k·uk,
/t But when they heard that he was alive, and how he had appeared to her,
/kl And they, when they had heard that he was alive, and had been seen of her,

/b takw wlamvetumwnro.
/p takó· o·la·mhitamo·wəné·ɔ.
/t they did not believe it.
/kl believed not.

Lk 24.9-10
/b Nhornc, ok Mrles Nhim kovrsu, ok takokek xrok wehrotpanek,
[⟨Nhornc⟩: ⟨-nc⟩ probably for ⟨-ne⟩; ⟨xrok⟩ for ⟨xqrok⟩]
/p †nčɔ·é·ni, ɔ́·k mé·li·s, nčím kɔhé·s·a, ɔ́·k takó·ki·k xkwé·ɔk wi·č·e·ɔ·tpáni·k,
/t Joanna, and Mary, Jim's mother, and other women that had been with them,
/l It was [Mary Magdalene,] Joanna, and Mary the mother of James, and other women that were with them,

/b nunc tulahemwlxanro nrl atux kwti ok wrmi takoki.
/p ná=nə təla·č·i·mo·lxa·né·ɔ né·l átax kwə́t·i ɔ́·k wé·mi takó·ki.
/t reported that to the eleven and all the others.
/l which told these things unto the eleven, and to all the rest:

Lk 24.11 /b Jwq taptwnakunwu tulrluntumulen mulaji nwhqc, [⟨tapt-⟩ for /tɔ·pt-/]
/p šúkw tɔ·pto·na·k·anúwa təle·ləntamə́li·n málahši nó·čkwe,
/t But their account seemed to their listeners like so much foolish talk,
/l but their words seemed to them as idle tales,
/k And their words seemed to them as idle tales,

/b takw wlamvetumulewun.
/p takó· o·la·mhitamə́lí·wən.
/t and they did not believe it.
/kl and they believed them not.

1 Cor 15.5
/b Nu nckc kejqek Symun Petul ok wunropani.
/p ná-néke kí·škwi·k †sáiman-pí·təl ɔ́·k wəne·ɔ́·p·ani.
/t The same day Simon-Peter had also seen him.
/l And [*the same day*] he was seen of Cephas [*Simon Peter*].

Chapter 133 (pp. 214-215). [L. section 134.] (Mark 16.12-13; Luke 24.13-25.)

Mk 16.12 /b Nu ok nckc kejqek neju wuncnsetaopani
/p ná- ɔ́·k -néke kí·škwi·k ní·š·a wənentsi·taɔ́·p·ani,
/t That same day also he appeared to two of them,

/l   After that he appeared [in another form] unto two of them.
/k   After that he appeared [in another form] unto two of them, [as they walked, and went into the country.]

/b   peli lacvosw.
/p   pí·li laehɔ́·s·u.
/t   adopting another form.
/kl ... in another form ...

Lk 24.13 /b   neju linwuk wtrnututif rpanek cntu lwcntasek Emeus   [⟨nut⟩ for ⟨nrt⟩]
/p   ní·š·a lə́nəwak o·t·e·ne·t·ə́t·ink é·p·ani·k, énta-luwentá·s·i·k †i·mí·as,
/t   Two men went to a village, a place called Emmaus,
/k   [And, behold,] two of them went [that same day] to a village called Emmaus,
/l   *For* behold, two of them went that same day into the country, to a village called Emmaus,
/k   ... as they walked, and went into the country.   (Mk 16.12)

/b   avpami ct nejaj mylif wunhi Nhelwsulumif.
/p   ahpá·mi=ét ní·š·a·š máilink wə́nči †nči·lo·sələ́mink.
/t   about seven miles from Jerusalem.
/kl which was from Jerusalem about threescore furlongs.

Lk 24.14 /b   Nrlwxwcvtet tukunwtumunro wrmi rlrk.   [⟨tuk-⟩ for /tɔk-/]
/p   ne·lo·x·wéhti·t, tɔk·əno·t·əməné·ɔ wé·mi é·le·k.
/t   As they walked along they talked about all the things that happened.
/kl And they talked together of all these things which had happened.

Lk 24.15 /b   Nrli avkunwtumevtet, ok avi punarluntumevtet,
/p   né·li-ahkəno·t·əmíhti·t ɔ́·k -áhi-pəna·eləntamíhti·t,
/t   And as they talked about them and considered them intensely,
/kl And it came to pass, that, while they communed together, and reasoned,

/b   Nhesus pwrxwsvekaoo. tolumi wehroo;
/p   nčí·sas pwe·x·o·shikaɔ́·ɔ, tɔ́ləmi-wi·č·e·ɔ́·ɔ.
/t   Jesus approached them and began accompanying them.
/kl Jesus himself drew near, and went with them.

Lk 24.16 /b   jwq mutu wununaoewao.
/p   šúkw máta wənənaɔ·iwwá·ɔ.
/t   But they did not recognize him.
/kl But their eyes were holden that they should not know him.   [RSV "kept from"]

Lk 24.17 /b   Tulkwao, Krkw vuh, ktaeavkunwtumwvmw naohe wcnhi jerluntamrq?
/p   təlkəwá·ɔ, "kéku=háč kta·yahkəno·t·əmúhəmɔ naɔč·í·i wénči-ši·e·lə́ntame·kw?"
/t   And he said to them, "What are you talking about on the way that makes you sad?"
/kl And he said unto them, What manner of communications are these that ye have one to another, as ye walk, and are sad?

Lk 24.18 /b   Nu mawsw rlwcnswet Kleopus tulao,
/p   ná má·wsu e·ləwénsi·t †kəliɔ́·pəs təlá·ɔ,
/t   The one named Cleopus said to him,
/kl And the one of them, whose name was Cleopas, answering said unto him,

/b   Ke vuh jwq khwpswi tali Nhelwsulum,
/p   "kí·=háč šúkw kčəpsó·wi táli †nči·ló·sələm?
/t   "Are you only a stranger in Jerusalem?
/kl Art thou only a stranger in Jerusalem,   [RSV "Are you the only visitor to J. who"]

/b   eli vuh mutu kwatwun rlrk mrhi krxi kejqc?
/p   ílli=háč máta ko·wa·tó·wən é·le·k mé·či kéxi-kí·škwe?"
/t   Don't you even know what has happened the last few days?"
/kl and hast not known the things which are come to pass there in these days?

Lk 24.19 /b   Tulao krkw vuh?
/p   təlá·ɔ, "kéku=háč?"
/t   And he said to them, "What?"
/kl And he said unto them, What things?

/b   Tulawao, Wunhi Nhesusu wcnheyetup Nasulutif
/p   təlawwá·ɔ, "wə́nči nči·sás·a, wenči·aí·t·əp †nasəlát·ink,
/t   And they said to him, "Concerning Jesus who came from Nazareth,
/kl And they said unto him, Concerning Jesus of Nazareth,

/b   nrnekanewrwsetup, kanji lusetup,
/p   nehəni·k·a·ní·i-we·wsí·t·əp, kánši-ləs·í·t·əp,
/t   who was a prophet and did marvelous things,
/kl which was a prophet mighty in deed

/b   ok prmtwnvrtup tali rlifwrxif Krtanutwet, ok wrmi awrn;
/p   ɔ́·k pe·mto·nhé·t·əp táli e·linkwé·x·ink ke·tanət·ó·wi·t, ɔ́·k wé·mi awé·n.
/t   and who preached before God and everyone.
/kl and word before God and all the people:

Lk 24.20 /b   ok rli wcvevwfrhek ok frkybmvrsumunanuk mwrkunropani
/p   ɔ́·k é·li wehi·hunké·č·i·k ɔ́·k nke·kayəmhe·s·əməná·nak mwe·k·əne·ɔ́·p·ani
/t   And how the priests and our rulers handed him over
/kl And how the chief priests and our rulers delivered him

	/b	li a kuntrlumalen wcnhi nvelunt ok psuqvetcvwnt.
	/p	lí-=á· -kənte·ləmá·li·n, wénči-nhílənt ɔ́·k -psakhwitéhunt.
	/t	to be condemned, in order for him to be put to death and crucified.
	/kl	to be condemned to death, and have crucified him.

Lk 24.21 /b Jwq nelwnu ntetrvavnap [⟨ntetrva-‖vnap⟩]
/p šúkw ni·ló·na nti·t·e·háhəna·p,
/t But *we* thought,
/kl But we trusted

(p. 215) /b nul nu krtu nevlatamwrwvrt netvakrwunanu;
/p 'nál=ná ké·t·a-nihəla·t·amwé·whe·t ni·thake·wəná·na.'
/t 'He is the one who is going to set our nation free.'
/kl that it had been he which should have redeemed Israel:

/b pu nu bqc mrhi nuxwqunakut li keji nc lr. [⟨pu nu⟩ for ⟨punu⟩]
/p pənáh, yúkwe mé·či naxo·k·wənák·at lí-kíši- nɔ́ -lé·.
/t Now, it has now been three days since that was done.
/kl and beside all this, to-day is the third day since these things were done.

Lk 24.22 /b Kvehei, ok fanjelarmkwnanuk rluntc ntwxqrbmnanuk,
             [⟨rluntc⟩ for ⟨aluntc⟩; ⟨bm-|n⟩ for ⟨bmun⟩]
/p khičí·i, ɔ́·k nkanši·lae·mko·ná·nak a·lə́nte ntuxkwe·yəməná·nak.
/t Truly so, and we were astonished by the report of some of our women.
/kl Yea, and certain women also of our company made us astonished,

/b jrpac eku prpanek mavhekamekwf;
/p še·p·á·e íka pé·p·ani·k mahči·k·amí·k·unk.
/t Early this morning they came to the tomb.
/kl which were early at the sepulchre;

Lk 24.23 /b qelumunro nc avtwvrpi, apahevtetc lwrok,
/p kkwi·ləməné·ɔ nɔ́ ahtuhé·p·i, a·p·a·č·ihtí·t·e, luwé·ɔk,
/t They didn't find the body, and when they came back, they said,
/kl And when they found not his body, they came, saying,

/b Fanji lenamwvnu
/p "nkanši-li·namúhəna.
/t "We had a miraculous experience.
/kl that they had also seen a vision

/b cvalwkalunhek ntclkwnu, mrhi tu lclrxr.
/p ehalo·ka·lə́nči·k ntəlkó·na, 'mé·či=tá lehəléx·e·.'
/t We were told by angels that he was now alive.
/kl of angels, which said that he was alive.

Lk 24.24 /b   Ok aluntc netesunanuk eku rpanek mavhekamekwf,
- /p   ɔ́·k a·lə́nte ni·t·i·s·əná·nak íka é·p·ani·k mahči·k·amí·k·unk.
- /t   And some of our friends went to the tomb.
- /kl And certain of them which were with us went to the sepulchre,

- /b   ok nrk nanc tulenamunro xqrok rlahemwevtet.
- /p   ɔ́·k né·k ná=nə təli·naməné·ɔ xkwé·ɔk e·la·č·i·mwíhti·t.
- /t   And *they* found ('saw') it just the way the women described.
- /kl and found it even so as the women had said:

- /b   Jwq mutu wunroewao.
- /p   šúkw máta wəne·ɔ·iwwá·ɔ."
- /t   But they did not see him."
- /kl but him they saw not.

Lk 24.25 /b   Nu tulan, Krvlu kuphavmw,
- /p   ná tə́la·n, "kéhəla kkəpčáhəmɔ.
- /t   Then he said to them, "You are truly foolish.
- /kl Then he said unto them, O fools,

- /b   jvot ktrvwaof kwlamvetumunro   [⟨-aof⟩ for /-á·unk/]
- /p   šhɔ́t ktehəwá·unk ko·la·mhitaməné·ɔ
- /t   There is a weakness (faintness) in your hearts to believe
- /kl and slow of heart to believe

- /b   wrmi ncnekanewrwsetpanek rlwcvtetup!
- /p   wé·mi nehəni·k·a·ní·i-we·wsi·tpáni·k e·ləwehtí·t·əp.
- /t   all that the prophets of old have said.
- /kl all that the prophets have spoken:

Lk 24.26 /b   Mutu ksi lexunwi tuli a Klyst nc lenamun,
- /p   máta=ksí li·x·ənó·wi, tə́li-=á· kəláist nə́ -lí·namən,
- /t   Wasn't it laid down (or set) that Christ would experience that,
- /kl Ought not Christ to have suffered these things,

- /b   ok ekali tumekri moxifwrlumwqswakunif?   [⟨tumekri⟩ for ⟨tumekrn⟩]
- /p   ɔ́·k íkali -təmí·k·e·n mɔx·inkwe·ləmukwsəwá·k·anink?"
- /t   and enter his 'glory'?"
- /kl and to enter into his glory?

Lk 24.27 /b   Nu tolumi wretavkunwtumaon Mwjiju rlwrtup
- /p   ná tɔ́ləmi-we·itahkəno·t·əmáɔ·n †mo·šəš·a e·ləwé·t·əp
- /t   Then he began to explain to them what Moses had said,
- /kl And beginning at Moses and all the prophets, he expounded unto them in all the scriptures the things concerning himself.

/b ok wrmi ncnekanewrwsetpanek rlrkvekrvtetup cntu avkunemkwk.
/p ó·k wé·mi nehəni·k·a·ní·i-we·wsi·tpáni·k e·le·khi·k·ehtí·t·əp énta-ahkəní·mkuk.
/t and what all the prophets of old had written where they told about him.
/l —

Lk 24.28
/b Kexki pravtetc nc wtrnututif ravtet, [⟨nut⟩ for ⟨nrt⟩]
/p kí·xki pe·ahtí·t·e nə́ o·t·e·ne·t·ə́t·ink e·áhti·t,
/t When they came near the village they were going to,
/kl And they drew nigh unto the village, whither they went:

/b nu tulacvosen mulaji kotu lwen;
/p ná təlaehó·s·i·n málahši kót·a-ló·wi·n.
/t then he acted as if he intended to go on by.
/kl and he made as though he would have gone further.

Lk 24.29
/b jwq tovi lawao maekrtaenrn,
/p šúkw tóhi-lawwá·ɔ, "mai·k·e·taí·ne·n.
/t But they said to him firmly, "Stay with us.
/kl But they constrained him, saying, Abide with us:

/b rli mrhi lokw xwluneti peskr.
/p é·li mé·či ló·k·u, xuləníti pí·ske·."
/t For it is already evening and will soon be dark."
/kl for it is toward evening, and the day is far spent.

/b Nu eku tuli wehron tuli a maekrtaon.
/p ná íka tə́li-wi·č·é·ɔ·n, tə́li-=á· -mai·k·é·taɔ·n.
/t Then he went there with them, to stay with them.
/kl And he went in to tarry with them.

Lk 24.30
/b Mrhi mrjvakrvtetc tuli a metsenro, wrtunum avpon,
/p mé·či me·šhakehtí·t·e, tə́li-=á· -mi·tsi·né·ɔ, wé·t·ənəm ahpɔ́·n.
/t After they had sat down (on the floor) to eat, he took some bread,
/kl And it came to pass, as he sat at meat with them, he took bread,

/b nu tuli pataman nu kcnh pwpvakrnumun, nu tuli kukuluntulan.
/p ná tə́li-pá·tama·n, ná kə́nč puphaké·nəmən, ná tə́li-kək·ələ́ntəla·n.
/t And he proceeded to pray, before breaking it into pieces and, with that, handing it out to them.
/kl and blessed it, and brake, and gave to them.

Lk 24.31
/b Nu wcxkaohi wununaonro,
/p ná wi·xkaɔ́či wənənaɔ·né·ɔ,
/t Then suddenly they recognized him,
/kl And their eyes were opened, and they knew him;

	/b	ok tolu nroao.	
	/p	ɔ́·k tɔ́·la-ne·ɔwwá·ɔ.	
	/t	and they saw him no more.	[*lit.*, 'could not see him']
	/kl	and he vanished out of their sight.	

Lk 24.32
	/b	Lutwok mutu vuh ktcvnauk kjuseeok	[⟨ktcvnauk⟩ for ⟨ktcvnanuk⟩]
	/p	lət·əwak, "máta=háč ktehəná·nak kšəs·i·í·ɔk,	
	/t	One said to the other, "Weren't our hearts warm	
	/kl	And they said one to another, Did not our heart burn within us,	

	/b	nrli krkw lwkwfq naohei, wretavkunwtumakofwc xwi aptwnakunu?
	/p	né·li- kéku -lúk·ɔnkw naɔč·í·i, -we·itahkəno·t·əma·k·ɔ́nkwe xúwi-a·pto·ná·k·ana?"
	/t	when he spoke to us on the way and explained to us the old texts?"
	/kl	while he talked with us by the way, and while he opened to us the scriptures?

Lk 24.33
	/b	Nu posqenro qtukeok li Nhelwsulumif.
	/p	ná pɔskwi·né·ɔ, kwtək·í·ɔk lí †nči·lo·sələmink.
	/t	Then they got up, and they returned to Jerusalem.
	/kl	And they rose up the same hour, and returned to Jerusalem,

	/b	Wtxawao nrl atux kwti
	/p	o·txawwá·ɔ né·l átax kwət·i.
	/t	And they came to the eleven.
	/kl	and found the eleven gathered together,

	/b	ok takokek wihi eku avpwuk.
	/p	ɔ́·k takɔ́·ki·k wíči- íka -ahpúwak,
	/t	And others were there with them
	/kl	and them that were with them,

Lk 24.34
	/b	Lwrok kvehei tu Nrvlalwrt mrhi amw,	
	/p	luwé·ɔk, "khičí·i=tá nehəlá·ləwe·t mé·či á·mu.	
	/t	and said, "Truly, the lord has now risen.	
	/kl	Saying, The Lord is risen indeed,	[RSV "who said"]

	/b	Symunu wuncnsetaoo.
	/p	†sáimana wənentsi·taɔ́·ɔ."
	/t	He appeared to Simon."
	/kl	and hath appeared to Simon.

Lk 24.35
	/b	Tohemwlxawao naohei rlenamevtet
	/p	tɔ·č·i·mo·lxawwá·ɔ naɔč·í·i e·li·namíhti·t,
	/t	And they recounted to them what had happened to them on the way,
	/kl	And they told what things were done in the way,

/b ok rli nunaovtet cntu avpon pvukrnumuletc,
/p ɔ́·k é·li-nənaɔ́hti·t énta- ahpɔ́·n -phake·nəmelí·t·e.
/t and how they recognized him when he broke the bread.
/kl and how he was known of them in breaking of bread.

Mk 16.13 /b Jwq mutu wlamvetaoewao. ‖
/p šúkw máta o·la·mhitaɔ·iwwá·ɔ.
/t But they did not believe them.
/kl Neither believed they them.

Chapter 134 (pp. 216-217). [L. section 135.] (Mark 16.14; Luke 24.36-48; John 20.19-25.)

Jn 20.19 /b Nu nckc peskrk,
(p. 216) /p ná-néke pí·ske·k,
/t That same evening,
/kl Then the same day at evening, [being the first day of the week,]

/b mrhi keji kpuvasekc skonty, cntu macvlavtet rkrkemkwsehek,
/p mé·či kíši-kpaha·s·í·k·e skɔ́ntay énta-ma·eheláhti·t e·k·e·ki·mkwəs·í·č·i·k,
/t after the door had been shut in the place where the disciples gathered,
/kl when the doors were shut, where the disciples were assembled,

/b rli kxovtet Nhwu,
/p é·li-kxɔ́hti·t nčó·wa,
/t because they feared the Jews,
/kl for fear of the Jews,

Lk 24.36, Mk 16.14
/b nrli krkw lwcvtet ok metsevtet,
/p né·li- kéku -luwéhti·t ɔ́·k -mi·tsíhti·t,
/t while they were speaking and eating,
/l (1) and as they thus spoke [*with the two disciples,*] (4) as they sat at meat,
                                                    [numbers = sequence in L.]
/k And as they thus spake (Lk 24.36), as they sat at meat (Mk 16.14)

Jn 20.19, Mk 16.14
/b Nhesus wuncnsetao nrl atux kwti,   [⟨-tao⟩ for /-taɔ́·ɔ/]
/p nčí·sas wənentsi·taɔ́·ɔ né·l átax kwə́t·i.
/t Jesus appeared to the eleven.
/l (2) came Jesus, and (3) appeared to the eleven   (Jn 20.19, Mk 16.14)

Jn 20.19 /b rlvwqrpelet nepw; tulao koofwmulwvmw.
/p e·lhukwe·p·í·li·t ní·p·o·, təlá·ɔ, "kɔɔnko·məlúhəmɔ."
/t He stood before them and said to them, "I greet you all."
/l (5) and stood in the midst of them, and saith unto them, Peace be unto you.

Lk 24.37 /b Jwq wejaswuk, letrvrok, hepy ct nrovnu;
/p šúkw wi·š·á·s·əwak, li·t·e·hé·ɔk, "čí·p·ay=ét nne·óhəna."
/t But they were afraid, thinking, "We probably see a ghost."
/kl But they were terrified and affrighted, and supposed that they had seen a spirit.

Lk 24.38 /b tulao koh vuh salavkevlarq,   [⟨vk⟩ for /xk/]
/p təlá·ɔ, "kóč=háč salaxkihəlá·e·kw
/t And he said to them, "Why are you agitated
/kl And he said unto them, Why are ye troubled?

/b ok nc letrvarq tali ktrvwaif?
/p ó·k nə́ li·t·e·há·e·kw táli ktehəwá·ink.
/t and thinking that in your hearts?
/kl and why do thoughts arise in your hearts?

Lk 24.39 /b Punamwq naxku, ok nsetu, li krvlu ne.
/p pənámo·kw nnáxka ó·k nsí·t·a, lí kéhəla ní·.
/t Look at my hands and my feet, that it is really me.
/kl Behold my hands and my feet, that it is I myself:

/b Eku aluneq, punaeq,   [⟨a luneq⟩]
/p íka aléni·kw, pənái·kw.
/t Touch me and look at me.
/kl handle me, and see;

/b rli manutw takw wewswei ok xkunwei,
/p é·li manət·u takó· wio·s·o·wí·i ó·k xkano·wí·i.
/t For a spirit doesn't have flesh and bones.
/kl for a spirit hath not flesh and bones,

/b takw tulenaqsewun ne rlenaqseu.
/p takó· təli·na·kwsí·wən ní· e·li·na·kwsía."
/t It doesn't look the way *I* look."
/kl as ye see me have.

Lk 24.40 /b Keji nc lwrtc pwunwtulan wunaxku ok vwsetu,   [⟨nwt⟩ for ⟨nwnt⟩]
/p kíši- nə́ -luwé·t·e, pwənúntəla·n wənáxka ó·k wsí·t·a
/t After saying that, he showed them his hands, and his feet,
/kl And when he had thus spoken, he shewed them his hands, and his feet,

Jn 20.20 /b ok vwpxkon.
/p ó·k húpxkɔn.
/t and his "side" (*lit.*, 'back').
/kl and his side.

	/b	Nu rkrkemkwsehek wlrluntamunro, rli nrovtet Nrvlalwrlehi.
	/p	ná e·k·e·ki·mkwəs·í·č·i·k o·le·ləntaməné·ɔ, é·li-ne·ɔ́hti·t nehəla·ləwe·lí·č·i.
	/t	Then the disciples were glad because they saw the Lord.
	/kl	Then were the disciples glad, when they saw the Lord.

Lk 24.41	/b	Nrli mutu myai wulamvetaovtet,
	/p	né·li- máta mayá·i wəla·mhitaɔ́hti·t,
	/t	While they still did not truly believe him,
	/kl	And while they yet believed not

	/b	rli somi kanjrluntumevtet ok wulrluntumevtet,
	/p	é·li-só·mi-kanše·ləntamíhti·t ɔ́·k -wəle·ləntamíhti·t,
	/t	as they were too astonished and happy,
	/kl	for joy, and wondered,

	/b	tulkwao, Kwlvatwvmw vuh mehwakun?
	/p	təlkəwá·ɔ, "ko·lhatúhəmɔ=háč mi·č·əwá·k·an?"
	/t	he said to them, "Do you have any food?"
	/kl	he said unto them, Have ye here any meat?

Lk 24.42	/b	Nu mwelanro pvakri mvakavtrpwsifi namrsu, ok ovjexybek jwkul,
	/p	ná mwi·la·né·ɔ phaké·i †mhakahte·p·o·s·ínki namé·s·a ɔ́·k ohši·x·ayó·wi·k šó·k·əl.
	/t	Then they gave him a piece of a roasted fish and a honeycomb.
	/kl	And they gave him a piece of a broiled fish, and of an honeycomb.

Lk 24.43	/b	wrtunumun ok mwehen tali rlvwqrpelet.
	/p	wwe·t·ənə́mən, ɔ́·k mwí·č·i·n táli e·lhukwe·p·í·li·t.
	/t	He took it and ate it in front of them.
	/kl	And he took it, and did eat before them.

Mk 16.14	/b	Nhesus tokunwtumaon rli mutu wulamvetumulet,
	/p	nčí·sas tɔk·əno·t·əmáɔ·n é·li- máta -wəla·mhitamə́li·t,
	/t	And Jesus talked to them about the fact that they did not believe,
	/l	And Jesus upbraided them with their unbelief,

	/b	ok rli hetanuselet vwtcvwao,
	/p	ɔ́·k é·li-či·t·anəs·í·li·t wtehəwá·ɔ,
	/t	and that their hearts were hard (*lit.*, 'strong'),
	/kl	and hardness of heart, [i.e., obtuseness]

	/b	wunhi mutu wulamvetaovtet, nrl nrtami nroletpani, mrhi amweletc.
	/p	wə́nči- máta -wəla·mhitaɔ́hti·t né·l né·tami-ne·ɔ·li·tpáni, mé·či a·mwi·lí·t·e.
	/t	because they did not believe those that had first seen him after he rose (from the dead).
	/kl	because they believed not them which had seen him after he was risen.

Lk 24.44 /b   Tulao, Jr b ktulunrop, nckc wehrwlrqc,
/p   təlá·ɔ, "šé· yú ktəlləné·ɔ·p, néke wi·č·e·wəlé·k·we,
/t   And he said to them, "This is what I told you formerly when I was with you:
/kl   And he said unto them, These are the words which I spake unto you, while I was yet with you,

/b   pavkunhih lr Mwjiju rlrkvekrtup rlenumuh
/p   pahkánči-=č -lé· †mo·šə́š·a e·le·khi·k·é·t·əp, e·lí·nama=č,
/t   There will be fulfilled what Moses of old wrote about what would happen to me,
/kl   that all things must be fulfilled, which were written in the law of Moses,

/b   ok ncnekanewrwsetpanifu ok tali aswrkvekunif.
/p   ɔ́·k nehəni·k·a·ní·i-we·wsi·tpanínka, ɔ́·k táli †a·s·uwwe·khí·k·anink."
/t   and the ancient prophets, and also in the psalms ('song writings')."
/kl   and in the prophets, and in the psalms, concerning me.

Lk 24.45 /b   Nu twfjrnumaon pwunarluntumwakunelet,
/p   ná tunkše·nəmáɔ·n pwəna·eləntaməwa·k·aní·li·t,
/t   Then he opened their understanding,
/kl   Then opened he their understanding,

/b   wunhi kuski nunwstumulet nrl xwi aptwnakunu;
/p   wə́nči-káski-nəno·stáməli·t né·l xúwi-a·pto·ná·k·ana.
/t   so that they were able to understand the ancient scriptures.
/kl   that they might understand the scriptures,

Lk 24.46 /b   tulao jr nc lrkvasw,
/p   təlá·ɔ, "šé· nə́ le·khá·s·u:
/t   And he said to them, "That is what is written:
/kl   and said unto them, Thus it is written,

/b   Klysth amuxavrluntufc
/p   kəláist=č amax·ahe·ləntánke,
/t   When (in future) Christ suffers torments,
/kl   and thus it behoved Christ to suffer,

/b   ufulwakunifh wunhi amwe mrhi nuxi kejqekc.
/p   ankələwá·k·anink=č wə́nči-á·mwi· mé·či náxi-ki·škwí·k·e,
/t   he will rise up from death after three days,
/kl   and to rise from the dead the third day.

Lk 24.47 /b   Wcnhih pumutwnvrn   [⟨Wcnhi⟩ for ⟨Wunhi⟩ /wə́nči/]
/p   wə́nči-=č -pəmət·ó·nhe·n
/t   so that it will be preached
/kl   And that repentance and remission of sins should be preached in his name among all nations,   [recast]

/b li a vokrf li qwlupevtetc, pavketatumaon motawswakunwu wrmi rkvokrehek;
/p lí-=á·, hók·enk lí-kwələp·ihtí·t·e, -pahki·t·a·t·amáɔ·n mɔt·a·wsəwa·k·anúwa wé·mi e·khɔke·í·č·i·k,
/t that the sins of all nations will be forgiven them, if they turn to him (*i.e.*, repent),
/kl —

/b Nhelwsulumifh wunhi alumi. [⟨Nh-‖elwsulumifh⟩]
/p †nči·lo·sələmink=č wə́nči álami.
/t starting from Jerusalem.
/kl beginning at Jerusalem.

Lk 24.48 /b Kelwuh kwatvekrnro, rli mrhi ktulenamunro.
(p. 217) /p ki·ló·wa=č ko·wa·thike·né·ɔ, é·li mé·či ktəli·naməné·ɔ.
/t *You* shall bear witness to it, for you have experienced it.
/kl And ye are witnesses of these things.

Jn 20.21 /b Nu Nhesus lupi tulan koofwmulwvmw;
/p ná nčí·sas lápi tə́la·n, "kɔɔnko·məlúhəmɔ.
/t Then Jesus said to them again, "I greet you all.
/k Then said Jesus to them again, Peace be unto you:
/l Then said Jesus [*at going away*] to them again, Peace be unto you:

/b Nwx rlkeqi alwkalet, nrpc ktulkeqi alwkalunro.
/p nó·x e·lkí·kwi-alo·ká·li·t, né·pe ktəlkí·kwi-alo·kalləné·ɔ."
/t In the same way that my father sent me, I, too, send you."
/kl as my Father hath sent me, even so send I you.

Jn 20.22 /b Keji nc lwrtc, wulrxalao,
/p kíši- nə́ -luwé·t·e, wəle·x·a·lá·ɔ.
/t After saying that, he breathed on them.
/kl And when he had said this, he breathed on them,

/b tulao, Nuxpawseq Pelset Manutw.
/p təlá·ɔ, "naxpá·wsi·kw pí·lsi·t manə́t·u.
/t And he said to them, "Possess the holy spirit.
/l and saith unto them, Receive ye the Holy Ghost:

Jn 20.23 /b Awrnh pavketatamarqc motawswakun, pavketatumaonh,
/p awé·n=č pahki·t·a·t·amaé·k·we mɔt·a·wsəwá·k·an, pahki·t·a·t·amáɔ·n=č.
/t If you forgive anyone their sins, they will be forgiven them.
/kl Whose soever sins ye remit, they are remitted unto them;

/b okh awrn mutu pavketatamarqc, taa pavketatamaoun.
/p ɔ́·k=č awé·n máta pahki·t·a·t·amaé·k·we, tá=á· pahki·t·a·t·amaɔ́·wən."
/t And if you do not forgive someone, they will not be forgiven them."
/kl and whose soever sins ye retain, they are retained.

Jn 20.24 /b Jwq Tamus rlwcnset Kavprs takw wihi eku avpei
/p šúkw ✝támas, e·ləwénsi·t 'kahpé·s', takó· wíči- íka -ahpí·i
/t But Thomas, who was called 'the Twin', was not there with them
/kl But Thomas, one of the twelve, called Didymus, was not with them

/b Nhesus wrtxatc.
/p nčí·sas we·txá·t·e.
/t when Jesus came to them.
/kl when Jesus came.

Jn 20.25 /b Nrk tulaoao, Mrhi nrowunu Nrvlalkofq. ⟨-aoao⟩ for /-awwá·ɔ/
/p né·k təlawwá·ɔ, "mé·či nne·ɔ́·wəna nehəlá·lkɔnkw."
/t The others said to him, "We have seen our lord."
/kl The other disciples therefore said unto him, We have seen the Lord.

/b Jwq tulkwao, ne a nrokc
/p šúkw təlkəwá·ɔ, "ní·=á· ne·ɔ́k·e,
/t But he said to them, "If *I* see him,
/kl But he said unto them,

/b nrmanc mwkwsuk rlvetcvwntup wunaxkif
/p ne·má·ne məkó·s·ak e·lhitehúntəp wənáxkink,
/t and see where the nails were hammered into his hands,
/kl Except I shall see in his hands the print of the nails,

/b ok mutu ekali punhenxkronc, ok vwpxkonif mutu li punhenxkronc,
/p ɔ́·k máta íkali pənči·nxke·ɔ́·ne, ɔ́·k húpxkɔnink máta lí-pənči·nxke·ɔ́·ne,
/t and if I do not stick my hand in there, and stick my hand in his back,
/kl and put my finger into the print of the nails, and thrust my hand into his side,

/b ta nwlamvctamwun.
/p tá=á· no·la·mhitamó·wən."
/t I will not believe it."
/kl I will not believe.

Chapter 135 (p. 217). [L. section 136.] (John 20.26-29.)

Jn 20.26 /b Lupi xaj cntxwqunakvakc, rkrkemunhek kwtrnaovki avpwuk
/p lápi xá·š entxo·k·wənakháke, e·k·e·ki·mə́nči·k kwət·ennáɔhki ahpúwak,
/t Eight days later, the disciples were in one place,
/kl And after eight days again his disciples were within,

/b Tamus wihi, kpuvasw skonty;
/p ✝támas wíči, kpahá·s·u skɔ́ntay.

| | /t | including Thomas, and the door was closed. |
| | /kl | (1) and Thomas with them: (3) the doors being shut,   [numbers = sequence in L.] |

/b wexkaohi Nhesus eku lrlai nepw,
/p wi·xkaóči nčí·sas íka le·lá·i ní·p·o·.
/t Suddenly Jesus was standing there in the middle (of the room).
/kl (2) then came Jesus, (4) and stood in the midst,

/b tulao, Koofwmulwvmw.
/p təlá·ɔ, "kɔɔnko·məlúhəmɔ."
/t He said to them, "I greet you all."
/kl (5) and said, Peace be unto you.

Jn 20.27 /b Ok tulao Tamusu, wuntax lenxkc, punu naxku;
/p ó·k təlá·ɔ †tamás·a, "wəntax lí·nxke, pənáh nnáxka.
/t And he said to Thomas, "Reach out your hand to me, and look at my hands.
/kl Then saith he to Thomas, reach hither thy finger, and behold my hands;

/b wuntax lenxkc, punhenxkc li nvwpxkonif.
/p wəntax lí·nxke, pənčí·nxke lí nhúpxkɔnink.
/t Reach out your hand to me, and stick your hand into my back.
/kl and reach hither thy hand, and thrust it into my side:

/b Kahi kulwvetufvun, wlamvetu.
/p káči kəlo·hitánkhan; wəla·mhíta."
/t Do not disbelieve it; believe it to be true."
/kl and be not faithless, but believing.

Jn 20.28 /b Tamus tulao, Nrvlaleun, Krtanutweun!
/p †támas təlá·ɔ, "nehəlá·lian, ke·tanət·ó·wian!"
/t And Thomas said to him, "My lord, O God."
/kl And Thomas answered and said unto him, My Lord and my God.

Jn 20.29 /b Nhesus tulao, Rli nrun kwlamvetumun.   [⟨nrun⟩ for ⟨nreun⟩]
/p nčí·sas təlá·ɔ, "é·li-né·ian, ko·la·mhítamən.
/t Jesus said to him, "Because you see me, you believe it to be true.
/kl Jesus saith unto him, Thomas, because thou hast seen me, thou hast believed:

/b Wlapcnswukh mutu nrehek wulamvetaevtetc.
/p wəla·p·énsəwak=č máta ne·í·č·i·k, wəla·mhitaihtí·t·e."
/t Blessed will be those who do not see me, if they believe in me."
/kl blessed are they that have not seen, and yet have believed.

Chapter 136 (p. 217-219). [L. section 137.] (John 21.1-23.)

Jn 21.1 /b   Mutu qwnei Nhesus lupi wuncnsetaoo rkrkemahi
/p   máta kwəní·i nčí·sas lápi wənentsi·taó·ɔ e·k·e·ki·má·č·i
/t   Not long after, Jesus again appeared to his disciples,
/kl   After these things Jesus shewed himself again to the disciples

/b   tali Typeleuse munwprkwf.
/p   táli †taipi·lias·í·i-mənəp·é·k·unk.
/t   at the sea of Tiberias.
/kl   at the sea of Tiberias;

/b   Jr b myai lrp.
/p   šé· yú mayá·i-lé·p.
/t   Here is what truly happened.
/kl   and on this wise shewed he himself.

Jn 21.2 /b   Kwtrnaovki avpwuk, Symun Petul, ok Tamus rlwcnset Kavprs,
/p   kwət·ennáɔhki ahpúwak †sáiman-pí·təl, ó·k ††támas e·ləwénsi·t 'kahpé·s,'
/t   Together in one place were Simon-Peter, and Thomas (called 'the Twin'),
/kl   There were together Simon Peter, and Thomas called Didymus,

/b   ok Nutanul wcnheyet Krnebf Falulebf, ok Sepute qesul,   [⟨Se⟩ for ⟨Sc⟩]
/p   ó·k †natá·nəl wenčí·ai·t ke·ní·yunk, †nka·lalí·yunk, ó·k †sépati kkwí·s·al,
/t   and Nathaniel from Cana in Galilee, and Zebedee's sons,
/kl   and Nathanael of Cana in Galilee, and the sons of Zebedee,

/b   ok peli neju ‖ rkrkemahi,
/p   ó·k pí·li ní·š·a e·k·e·ki·má·č·i.
/t   and two others of his disciples.
/kl   and two other of his disciples.

Jn 21.3 /b   Symun Petul tulao nrl nmyi nwtamunsen.   [⟨muns⟩ for /méns/]
(p. 218) /p   †sáiman-pí·təl təlá·ɔ né·l, "nəmái-no·t·aménsi·n."
/t   Simon-Peter said to the others, "I'm going fishing."
/kl   Simon Peter saith unto them, I go a fishing.

/b   Tulawao, Kwehrwulunrn.
/p   təlawwá·ɔ, "kəwi·č·e·wəlóne·n."
/t   And they said to him, "And we're going with you."
/kl   They say unto him, We also go with thee.

/b   Nu jac tolumskanro, mwxwlif li pwseok.
/p   ná š·áe tɔləmska·né·ɔ, mux·ó·link lí-po·s·í·ɔk.
/t   Then they left right away and got into a boat.
/kl   They went forth, and entered into a ship immediately;

/b Jwq kwti tpwqc mutu nvelreok.
/p šúkw kwə́ti-tpóʾkwe máta nhileʾíʾɔk.
/t But all night they caught nothing.   [*lit.*, 'did not kill any']
/kl and that night they caught nothing.

Jn 21.4
/b Mrhi opufc, Nhesus eapri nepw;
/p méʾči ɔʾpʾánke, nčíʾsas yaʾpʾéʾi níʾpʾoʾ.
/t After dawn, Jesus was standing on the shore.
/kl But when the morning was now come, Jesus stood on the shore:

/b jwq rkrkemahi mutu wununakweo.
/p šúkw eʾkʾeʾkiʾmáʾčʾi máta wənənaʾkʾoʾwíʾɔ.
/t But his disciples did not recognize him.
/kl but the disciples knew not that it was Jesus.

Jn 21.5
/b Nhesus tulao, Memunstwq, kwlvatwvmw vuh mehwakun?
/p nčíʾsas təláʾɔ, "miʾmə́nstoʾkw, koʾlhatúhəmɔ=háč miʾčʾəwáʾkʾan?
/t Jesus said to them, "Children, do you have any food?"
/kl Then Jesus saith unto them, Children, have ye any meat?

/b Tulaowao, Takw.   [⟨aow⟩ for /aww/]
/p təlawwáʾɔ, "takóʾ."
/t And they said to him, "No."
/kl They answered him, No.

Jn 21.6
/b Tulao, Ktunavaonwaif wuntavqi li hvoponeveq ktunsvekunwu,
/p təláʾɔ, "ktənnaʾhaʾɔnəwáʾink wə́ntahkwi líʾčhɔʾpɔníhiʾkw ktanshiʾkʾanúwa.
/t He said to them, "Throw your net in on your right side.
/kl And he said unto them, Cast the net on the right side of the ship,

/b kmuxkamwvmwh.
/p kəmaxkamúhəmɔ=č."
/t You will find some."
/kl and ye shall find.

/b Nu eku tulanivenro;
/p ná íka təlanihiʾnéʾɔ.
/t Then they threw it there.
/kl They cast therefore,

/b jwq tolai vwtunumunro scmi xrli ptavwrok.   [⟨scmi⟩ for ⟨somi⟩]
/p šúkw tóʾlai-wtənəməné·ɔ, sóʾmi xéʾli ptahwéʾɔk.
/t But they were unable to pull it up, they had caught so many.   [*lit.*, 'too many']
/kl and now they were not able to draw it for the multitude of fishes.

Jn 21.7 /b   Nuni wunhi rkrkemkwset Nhesus rvolatpani lan Petulu,
         /p   nə́ni wwə́nči- e·k·e·ki·mkwə́s·i·t nčí·sas ehɔ·la·tpáni -lá·n †pí·tǝla,
         /t   The disciple that Jesus loved therefore said to Peter,
         /kl Therefore that disciple whom Jesus loved saith unto Peter,

         /b   Nrvlalkofq tu nu.
         /p   "nehǝlá·lkɔnkw=tá ná."
         /t   "That's our lord."
         /kl It is the Lord.

         /b   Symun Petul nc rlsitufc,
         /p   †sáiman-pí·tǝl nə́ e·lsǝt·ánke,
         /t   When Simon-Peter heard that that was the case,
         /kl Now when Simon Peter heard that it was the Lord,

         /b   wrhelavtwn wunwtamcnswe vcmpus qwlumapelan vokyu, rli swpsw,
         /p   wwe·č·ílahto·n wǝnɔ·t·amensǝwí·i-hémpǝs, kwǝlama·pí·la·n hókaya (é·li só·psu).
         /t   he grabbed his fisherman's shirt and tied it on around him (as he was naked).
         /kl he girt his fisher's coat unto him, (for he was naked,)

         /b   nu hovopokevlun.   [⟨hov-⟩ for /wčɔh-/]
         /p   ná wčɔhɔ·pɔ·k·íhǝlǝn.
         /t   And then he jumped into the water.
         /kl and did cast himself into the sea.

Jn 21.8 /b   Kuhi nrk takokek rkrkemunhek, eku lelavtaok,
         /p   káč·i né·k takó·ki·k e·k·e·ki·mə́nči·k íka lilahtá·ɔk,
         /t   But those other disciples went there in the boat,
         /kl (1) And the other disciples came in a little ship;   [numbers = sequence in L.]

         /b   mwxwlif wuntaptwnro nc avkonekun,
         /p   mux·ó·link wwǝnta·ptɔ·né·ɔ nə́ ahkɔ·ní·k·an,
         /t   tying the net from the boat,
         /kl (3) dragging the net with fishes.

         /b   rli mutu laetunc avpevtet avpami ct kwtapxki eatif.
         /p   é·li- máta la·í·tane -ahpíhti·t, ahpá·mi=ét kwǝt·á·pxki yá·tink.
         /t   as they were not out in the middle, (but) maybe about a hundred yards.
         /kl (2) (for they were not far from land, but as it were two hundred cubits,)

Jn 21.9 /b   Mrhi mcjavkavtetc, nrmwk tunty
         /p   mé·či mešahkahtí·t·e, né·mo·k tə́ntay,
         /t   After they landed, they saw a fire,
         /kl As soon then as they were come to land, they saw a fire of coals there,

	/b	namrsuk eku, ok avpon.
	/p	namé·s·ak íka, ó·k ahpó·n.
	/t	and there were fish there, and bread.
	/kl	and fish laid thereon, and bread.

Jn 21.10 /b Nhesus tulao, Prjw aluntc namrsuk trvwnrqek.
/p nčí·sas təlá·ɔ, "pé·š·əw a·lə́nte namé·s·ak tehwəné·k·wi·k."
/t Jesus said to him, "Bring some of the fish you caught."
/kl Jesus saith unto them, Bring of the fish which ye have now caught.

Jn 21.11 /b Nu Symun Petul kopan, wtunumun nc unsvekun, kopavtwn,
/p ná †sáiman-pí·təl kóp·a·n, o·t·ənə́mən nə́ anshí·k·an, kópahto·n.
/t Then Simon-Peter got out of the water, pulled on the net, and hauled it out.
/kl Simon Peter went up, and drew the net to land

/b hwexenwk amufi namrsuk, kwtapxki ok palrnaxk txenkc ok nuxav.
/p čuwi·x·í·no·k amánki-namé·s·ak, kwət·á·pxki ó·k palé·naxk txí·nxke ó·k naxá.
/t It was full of large fish, a hundred and fifty-three of them.
/kl full of great fishes, and hundred and fifty and three:

/b Jwq taoni nc txi eku avpwuk takw palelri nc unsvekun.
/p šúkw tá·ɔni nə́ txí íka ahpúwak, takó· palí·i-lé·i nə́ anshí·k·an.
/t But even though there were that many in it, the net was not destroyed.
/kl and for all there were so many, yet was not the net broken.

Jn 21.12 /b Nhesus tulao Wuntux aq metseq.
/p nčí·sas təlá·ɔ, "wə́ntax á·kw, mí·tsi·kw."
/t Jesus said to them, "Come here and eat."
/kl Jesus saith unto them, Come and dine.

/b Jwq qetu lawao, awrn vuh ke?
/p šúkw kkwí·ta-lawwá·ɔ, "awé·n=háč kí·?"
/t But they were afraid to ask him who he was.   [lit., "Who are you?"]
/kl And none of the disciples durst ask him, Who art thou?

/b wavawao li nunul Navlalwrt.   [⟨Navl-⟩ for ⟨Nrvl-⟩]
/p o·wa·hawwá·ɔ lí nánal nehəlá·ləwe·t.
/t They knew that he was the Lord.
/kl knowing that it was the Lord.

Jn 21.13 /b Nu Nhesus wrtunumun avponu, qwkuluntulan, ok namrsu.
/p ná nčí·sas wwe·t·ənə́mən ahpó·na, kwək·ələ́ntəla·n, ó·k namé·s·a.
/t Then Jesus took the loaves and handed them out to them, and the fish also.
/kl Jesus then cometh, and taketh bread, and giveth them, and fish likewise.

Jn 21.14　/b　Nu bqc nckc mrhi nuxun Nhesus wuncnsetaon rkrkemahi,
　　　　　/p　ná=yúkwe néke mé·či naxən nčí·sas wənentsí·taɔ·n e·k·e·ki·má·č·i,
　　　　　/t　That was now three times that Jesus had appeared to his disciples,
　　　　　/k　This is now the third time that Jesus shewed himself to his disciples,
　　　　　/l　This is now the third time that Jesus shewed himself to his disciples [*either to all, or to several together*],

　　　　　/b　srki amwet.
　　　　　/p　sé·ki-á·mwi·t.
　　　　　/t　since he had risen (from the dead).
　　　　　/kl　after that he was risen from the dead.

Jn 21.15　/b　Mrhi keji metsevtetc, Nhesus tulao Symun Petulu, Symun Nhonus qesu,
　　　　　/p　mé·či kíši-mi·tsihtí·t·e, nčí·sas təlá·ɔ †sáiman-pí·təla, "†sáiman, nčɔ́·nas kkwí·s·a,
　　　　　/t　After they had eaten, Jesus said to Simon-Peter, "Simon, Jonas's son,
　　　　　/kl　So when they had dined, Jesus saith to Simon Peter, Simon, son of Jonas,

　　　　　/b　alwei vuh ktulkeqi avoli rlkeqi bk avolevtet?
　　　　　/p　aləwí·i=háč ktəlkí·kwi-ahɔ́·li e·lkí·kwi- yó·k -ahɔ·líhti·t?"
　　　　　/t　do you love me more than these others love me?"
　　　　　/kl　lovest thou me more than these?

　　　　　/b　Tulao Kvehei, ‖ Nrvlaleun, kwatwn ktuli avolun.
　　　　　/p　təlá·ɔ, "khičí·i, nehəlá·lian, ko·wá·to·n ktə́li-ahɔ́llən."
　　　　　/t　And he said to him, "Truly, my lord, you know that I love you."
　　　　　/kl　He saith unto him, Yea, Lord; thou knowest that I love thee.

(p. 219)　/b　Nhesus tulao, Xam nmrketutumuk.
　　　　　/p　nčí·sas təlá·ɔ, "xám nəmeki·t·ə́t·əmak."
　　　　　/t　And Jesus said to him, "Feed my lambs."
　　　　　/kl　He saith unto him, Feed my lambs.

Jn 21.16　/b　Lupi tulao, Symun Nhonus qesu, ktavoli vuh?
　　　　　/p　lápi təlá·ɔ, "†sáiman, nčɔ́·nas kkwí·s·a, ktahɔ́·li=háč?"
　　　　　/t　Again he said to him, "Simon, Jonas's son, do you love me?"
　　　　　/kl　He saith to him again the second time, Simon, son of Jonas, lovest thou me?

　　　　　/b　Tulao, Kvehei Nrvlaleun, kwatwn ktuli avolun.
　　　　　/p　təlá·ɔ, "khičí·i, nehəlá·lian, ko·wá·to·n ktə́li-ahɔ́llən."
　　　　　/t　And he said to him, "Truly, my lord, you know that I love you."
　　　　　/kl　He saith unto him, Yea, Lord; thou knowest that I love thee.

　　　　　/b　Tulkw, Xam nmrkesumuk.
　　　　　/p　tə́lku, "xám nəmekí·s·əmak."
　　　　　/t　And he said to him in turn, "Feed my sheep."
　　　　　/kl　He saith unto him, Feed my sheep.

Jn 21.17
/b Lupi tulao, Symun Nhonus qesu, ktavoli vuh?
/p lápi təlá·ɔ, "†sáiman, nčó·nas kkwí·s·a, ktahó·li=háč?"
/t And again he said to him, "Simon, Jonas's son, do you love me?"
/kl He saith unto him the third time, Simon, son of Jonas, lovest thou me?

/b Petul sukwrluntum rli nuxun lwkwk, Ktavoli vuh?
/p †pí·təl sak·we·ləntam é·li- naxə́n -lúk·wək, "ktahó·li=háč?"
/t Peter was distressed because he asked him three times if he loved him.
/kl Peter was grieved because he said unto him the third time, Lovest thou me?

/b Tulao, Nrvlaleun, wrmi krkw kwatwv;
/p təlá·ɔ, "nehəlá·lian, wé·mi kéku ko·wá·tu.
/t And he said to him, "My lord, you know everything.
/kl And he said unto him, Lord, thou knowest all things;

/b kwatwn ktuli avolun.
/p ko·wá·to·n któli-ahóllən."
/t You know that I love you."
/kl thou knowest that I love thee.

/b Nhesus tulao, xam nmrkesumuk.
/p nčí·sas təlá·ɔ, "xám nəmekí·s·əmak.
/t And Jesus said to him, "Feed my sheep.
/kl Jesus saith unto him, Feed my sheep.

Jn 21.18
/b Kvehei ktulul, wrskenweunc, nevlahi vufq kulumumpeswlap kvaky,
/p khičí·i któləl, we·skinnəwiáne, nihəláči=hánkw kkəlamampi·s·ó·la·p khák·ay.
/t Truly, I say to you, when you were a young man, you would put on your own belt.
/kl Verily, verily, I say unto thee, When thou wast young, thou girdedst thyself,

/b knevlatumunrp vufq raun;
/p kənihəla·t·amə́ne·p=hánkw e·á·an.
/t You would have the say over where you went.
/kl and walkedst whither thou wouldest:

/b jwqh velwseunc, kjepenxkch,
/p šúkw=č hilo·s·iáne, kši·p·í·nxke=č,
/t But when in the future you are old, you will stretch out your hands,
/kl but when thou shalt be old, thou shalt stretch forth thy hands,

/b pelih awrn kulumumpeswlwq,
/p pí·li=č awé·n kkəlamampi·s·ó·lukw,
/t and someone else will put your belt on you
/kl and another shall gird thee,

	/b	okh ktulwxolwkwn mutu krtu wxrun.	[⟨krtu wxrun⟩ for ⟨krtuwxrun⟩]
	/p	ó·k=č ktəlo·x·ɔlúk·o·n máta ke·t·ao·x·wé·an."	
	/t	and will take you where you don't want to go."	
	/kl	and carry thee whither thou wouldest not.	

Jn 21.19 /b Nuni rlat wuntamaon rlufululeth, Krtanutwet rli wulrluntuf.
/p nə́ni é·la·t, wwəntamáɔ·n, e·lankələli·t=č ke·tanət·ó·wi·t é·li-wəle·ləntank.
/t So he said to him, telling him how *he* would die in a way pleasing to God.
/kl This spake he, signifying by what death he should glorify God.

/b Keji nc lwrtc tulao, Naolel.
/p kíši- nə́ -luwé·t·e, təlá·ɔ, "ná·ɔli·l."
/t After saying that, he said to him, "Follow me."
/kl And when he had spoken this, he saith unto him, Follow me.

Jn 21.20 /b Petul qrtkifwrxifc wunroo rkrkemkwselehi
/p †pí·təl kwe·tkinkwe·x·ínke, wəne·ɔ́·ɔ e·k·e·ki·mkwəs·i·lí·č·i
/t When Peter looked back, he saw the (other) disciple
/kl (1) Then Peter, turning about, seeth the disciple   [numbers = sequence in L.]

/b nunuli nrl rvolahi Nhesus,
/p —nanáli né·l ehɔ·lá·č·i nči·sas,
/t —he was the one that Jesus loved,
/kl whom Jesus loved ...

/b yavi metsevtetc ekali apavtaovpet ok lat,
/p a·yáhi-, mi·tsihtí·t·e, íkali -apahtáɔhpi·t ó·k -lá·t,
/t who previously, when they were eating, sat leaning on him and said to him,
/kl (3) which also leaned on his breast at supper, and said,

/b awrnh vuh li mvalumaon kvaky;
/p "awé·n=č=háč lí-mhalamáɔ·n khák·ay?"—
/t "Who is it that will sell you out?"—
/kl (4) Lord, which is he that betrayeth thee?

/b tuli naolwkwnro,
/p təli-na·ɔluk·o·né·ɔ.
/t that he was following them.
/kl (2) following;

Jn 21.21 /b tulao, Nhesusu Nrvlaleun tuh vuh wu tulsen?
/p təlá·ɔ nči·sás·a, "nehəlá·lian, tá=č=háč wá tə́lsi·n?"
/t And he said to Jesus, "My lord, what will this (man) do?"
/kl Peter seeing him saith to Jesus, Lord, and what shall this man do?

Jn 21.22 /b Nhesus tulao, Ne a lrlumukc tcli a ny b avpen svaky apaheanc,
/p nčí·sas təlá·ɔ, "ní·=á· le·ləmák·e, tə́li·=á· ná=yú -ahpí·n sháki a·p·a·č·iá·ne,
/t Jesus said to him, "If *I* want him to stay here until I come back,
/kl Jesus saith unto him, If I will that he tarry till I come,

/b koh vuh a luxarlumut?
/p kóč=háč=á· laxaé·ləmat?
/t why would you worry about him?
/kl what is that to thee?

/b Naolel.
/p ná·ɔli·l."
/t Follow me."
/kl follow thou me.

Jn 21.23 /b Nuni wunhi lwrnro,
/p nə́ni wwə́nči-luwe·né·ɔ,
/t Because of that they said,
/kl Then went this saying abroad among the brethren,

/b wuni rkrkemkwset, ta ufulwi;
/p "wáni e·k·e·ki·mkwə́s·i·t, tá=á· ankəló·wi."
/t "This disciple will not die."
/kl that that disciple should not die:

/b jwq Nhesus takw lwrep ta tu ufulwi,
/p šúkw nčí·sas takó· luwé·i·p, "tá=á·=tá ankəló·wi,"
/t But Jesus did not say, "He will not die,"
/kl yet Jesus said not unto him, He shall not die;

/b jwq, ne a lrlumukc tuli a ny b avpen svaki apaheanc,
/p šúkw, "ní·=á· le·ləmák·e, tə́li·=á· ná=yú -ahpí·n sháki a·p·a·č·iá·ne,
/t but, "If I want him to stay here until I come back,
/kl but, If I will that he tarry till I come,

/b koh vuh a luxarlumut?
/p kóč=háč=á· laxaé·ləmat?"
/t why would you worry about him?"
/kl what is that to thee?

Chapter 137 (pp. 219-220). [L. section 138.] (Matthew 28.16-20; Mark 16.15-18; 1 Corinthians 15.6.)

Mt 28.16 /b   Eku rpanek nrk atux kwti Falulebf,
/p   íka é·p·ani·k né·k átax kwə́t·i †nka·lalí·yunk,
/t   The eleven went to Galilee,
/kl   Then the eleven disciples went away into Galilee,

/b   ovhwf rpanek Nhesus rlatup
/p   ɔhčúnk é·p·ani·k nčí·sas e·lá·t·əp.
/t   and went to the mountain where Jesus had told them to.
/kl   into a mountain where Jesus had appointed them:
                          [RSV "mountain to which J. had directed them"]

1 Cor 15.6
/b   ok xrli peli wemavtwao eku macvlrlw alwei ct palrnaxk txapxki.
/p   ɔ́·k xé·li pí·li wi·mahtəwá·ɔ íka ma·ehəlé·lu, aləwí·i palé·naxk txá·pxki.
/t   And many others of their "brethren" gathered there, more than five hundred.
/l   (and there were above five hundred brethren gathered together there.)

Mt 28.17 /b   Mrhi ‖ nrovtetc potumawao;   [⟨aw⟩ for /aɔww/]
/p   mé·či ne·ɔhtí·t·e, pɔ·tamaɔwwá·ɔ.
/t   After they saw him, they prayed to him.
/kl   And when they saw him, they worshipped him:

/b   jwq aluntc mutu orluntumwepanek.
/p   šúkw a·lə́nte máta †ɔ·e·ləntamo·wí·p·ani·k.
/t   But some doubted.
/kl   but some doubted.

Mt 28.18 /b   Nhesus pwcxwsvekaoa, ok tulao,   [⟨-aoa⟩ for /-aɔ́·ɔ/]
(p. 220) /p   nčí·sas pwe·x·o·shikaɔ́·ɔ, ɔ́·k təlá·ɔ,
/t   Jesus came near to them and said to them,
/kl   And Jesus came and spake unto them, saying,

/b   Mrhi nmelkc alwei luswakun,
/p   "mé·či nəmí·lke aləwí·i-ləs·əwá·k·an,
/t   "Power has been given to me.
/kl   All power is given unto me

/b   nevlatamun wrmi osavkamc ok prmvakamekrk.
/p   nnihəlá·t·amən wé·mi ɔ·s·áhkame ɔ́·k pe·mhakamí·k·e·k.
/t   I am the master of all of heaven and earth.
/kl   in heaven and in earth.

Mt 28.19, Mk 16.15
- /b Wrmi aq nc wunhi rlkevokamekrk,   [⟨rlkevok-⟩ for ⟨rlkekvok-⟩]
- /p wé·mi á·kw nə́ wə́nči e·lki·khɔkamí·k·e·k.
- /t Go therefore into the whole wide world.
- /l (1) Go ye therefore into all the world,   [numbers = sequence in L.]
- /k Go ye therefore, (Mt 28.19)
- /k Go ye into all the world, (Mk 16.15)

Mt 28.19
- /b avkrkemw wrmi cntxakret awrn,
- /p ahke·kí·mo· wé·mi entxa·ké·i·t awé·n.
- /t Teach all nations of people.
- /kl (3) and teach all nations,

Mk 16.15
- /b avkunwtumw wrlvik aptwnakun wrmi lclrxrhek,
- /p ahkənó·t·əmo· wé·lhik a·pto·ná·k·an wé·mi lehəle·x·é·č·i·k.
- /t Tell about the gospel (*lit.*, 'good word') to all living beings.
- /kl (2) and preach the gospel to every creature,

Mt 28.19
- /b hvopwunekrq tulswakunif Wrtwxumunt, ok Wrqesif, ok Pelset Manutw;
- /p čhɔ·pwəní·k·e·kw təlsəwá·k·anink we·t·ó·x·əmənt, ɔ́·k we·k·wí·s·ink, ɔ́·k pí·lsi·t manə́t·u.
- /t Baptize acting for ('in the power of') the father, and the son, and the holy spirit.
- /kl baptizing them in the name of the Father, and of the Son, and of the Holy Ghost:

Mt 28.20
- /b lukrkemw tuli lusenro wrmi cntxi lulrq.
- /p lak·e·kí·mo·, tə́li-ləs·i·né·ɔ wé·mi éntxi-lə́le·kw.
- /t Teach them to do everything I told you to do.
- /kl Teaching them to observe all things whatsoever I have commanded you: ...

Mk 16.16
- /b Awrnh wulamvetufc ok hvopununtc osavkamch lwxola.   [⟨pun⟩ for /pwən/]
- /p awé·n=č wəla·mhitánke ɔ́·k čhɔ·pwənə́nte, ɔ·s·áhkame=č ló·x·ɔla·.
- /t If anyone believes and is baptized, they will be taken to heaven.
- /kl He that believeth and is baptized shall be saved;

- /b Kuhih awrn mutu wulamvetufc, mavtuntwfh laneven.
- /p káč·i=č awé·n máta wəla·mhitánke, mahtánt·unk=č laníhi·n.
- /t But if someone does not believe, they shall be thrown to the devil (or devils).
- /kl but he that believeth not shall be damned.

Mk 16.17
- /b Jrh b tulsenro wrlamvetufek,
- /p "šé·=č yú təlsi·né·ɔ we·la·mhitánki·k:
- /t "And here's what the believers shall do:
- /kl And these signs shall follow them that believe;

/b   ntclswakunh wunhi ktuskarok mavtuntwu,
/p   ntəlsəwá·k·an=č wə́nči-ktəskaé·ɔk mahtant·ó·wa.
/t   By my power they shall drive out devils.
/kl In my name shall they cast out devils;

/b   okh peli rlexsif kuski lexswuk,
/p   ó·k=č pí·li ehəlí·xsink káski-li·xsúwak.
/t   And they will be able to speak other languages.
/kl they shall speak with new tongues;

Mk 16.18 /b   okh xkwku wrtunrok,
/p   ó·k=č xkó·k·a we·t·əné·ɔk.
/t   And they shall pick up snakes.
/kl They shall take up serpents;

/b   ok a munrvtetc rvafulif taa polevkwunro;
/p   ó·k=á· mənehtí·t·e ehánkəlink, tá=á· pɔlihko·wəné·ɔ.
/t   And if they drink what people die from, it will not cause them to perish.
/kl and if they drink any deadly thing, it shall not hurt them;

/b   palselehih eku alunavtec, wulumalselwh.   [⟨-vtec⟩ for ⟨-vtetc⟩]
/p   pa·lsi·lí·č·i=č íka alənahtí·t·e, wəlamalsí·lu=č.
/t   If they put their hands on sick people, they will be well.
/kl they shall lay hands on the sick, and they shall recover.

Mt 28.20 /b   Jr kwehrwulwvmwh, eku pchi alu vatrkc vaki.
/p   šé·, kəwi·č·e·wəlúhəmɔ=č íka péči ála-hat·é·k·e hák·i."
/t   And here, I will be with you until the world ceases to exist."
/kl And lo, I am with you alway, even unto the end of the world. ...

(B. omits L. from 1 Cor 15.7.)

Chapter 138 (pp. 220-221). [L. section 139.] (Acts 1.3-12; Mark 16.19-20; Luke 24.49-53.)

Acts 1.3 /b   Mrhi nrenxkc txwquni nrnsetaotc rlwkalahi,
/p   mé·či ne·í·nxke txó·k·wəni nentsi·taó·t·e e·lo·ka·lá·č·i,
/t   After he had appeared to his apostles for forty days,
/l   *Now Jesus*, being seen of the apostles forty days,
/k   ... being seen of them forty days,

/b   ok avkunwtumaovtc rlrk Krtanutwet sokemaokun.   [⟨-ovtc⟩ for /-ó·t·e/]
/p   ó·k ahkəno·t·əmaó·t·e é·le·k ke·tanət·ó·wi·t sɔ·k·i·ma·ó·k·an,
/t   and told them about how God's kingdom was,
/kl and speaking of the things pertaining to the kingdom of God:

Acts 1.4 /b Marvlrpanek tali Nhelwsulumif,
/p ma·ehəlé·p·ani·k táli †nči·lo·sələmink.
/t they all gathered in Jerusalem.
/l And, being [...] assembled together with them [*at Jerusalem*]
/k And, being assembled together with them,

/b tulao, kahi alumskavrq b wunhi,
/p təlá·ɔ, "káči aləmská·he·kw yú wə́nči.
/t And he said to them, "Don't leave this place.
/kl he commanded them that they should not depart from Jerusalem,

/b prtwq rlqrkup Wrtwxumunt.
/p pé·to·kw e·lkwé·k·əp we·t·ó·x·əmənt,
/t Wait for what the father told you,
/kl but wait for the promise of the Father, which, *saith he*, ye have heard of me.

Lk 24.49 /b Mprtalwkaluh kvakywaif rlqrkup Nwx.
/p "mpe·t·alo·ká·la=č khak·ayəwá·ink," e·lkwé·k·əp nó·x.
/t when my father told you, "I shall send him to you."
/l Behold (saith he) I send the promise of my Father upon you:
/k And, behold, I send the promise of my Father upon you:

/b Nhelwsulumif avpeq
/p †nči·lo·sələmink ahpí·kw
/t Stay in Jerusalem
/kl but tarry ye in the city of Jerusalem,

/b svaki vokwf wunhi nuxpufwmkrrqc alwei luswakun.
/p sháki hɔ́kunk wə́nči-naxpanko·mke·é·k·we aləwí·i-ləs·əwá·k·an.
/t until you are granted power from heaven.
/kl until ye be endued with power from on high.

Acts 1.5 /b Nhanu kvehei hihvopwunekrp li mpif,
/p nčá·na khičí·i čičhɔ·pwəní·k·e·p lí mpínk.
/t The late John indeed baptized in water.
/kl For John truly baptized with water;

/b jwqh kelwu Pelvik Manutwakunif ktcli hvopwunekcvmw,
            [Emend ⟨-ekcvmw⟩ to ⟨-ukcvmw⟩ to accord with K. and L.]
/p šúkw=č ki·ló·wa pí·lhik manət·uwwá·k·anink ktə́li-čhɔ·pwənək·éhəmɔ,
      [Reading /-ək·éhəmɔ/ 'be baptized' for the apparent /-i·k·éhəmɔ/ 'baptize' of B.]
/t But *you* shall be baptized in the power of the holy spirit,
                              [as emended; *lit.*, 'in holy spiritual-power']
/kl but ye shall be baptized with the Holy Ghost

/b   rli krxwqunuku.
/p   é·li-ke·x·o·k·wənák·a."
/t   in a few days."
/kl not many days hence.

Acts 1.6 /b   Nrli maowunupevtet notwtumaoao, tulawao,   [⟨maowun-⟩ for /ma·wən-/]
/p   né·li-ma·wənap·íhti·t, nɔt·o·t·əmaɔwwá·ɔ, təlawwá·ɔ,
/t   While they were sitting together, they asked him a question, saying to him,
/kl When they therefore were come together, they asked of him, saying,

/b   Nrvlalerf, bqc, vuh lupi kutu myaextwn Nhwe ‖ sakemaokun?
/p   "nehəlá·lienk, yúkwe=háč lápi kkát·a-maya·í·xto·n nčo·wí·i-sa·k·i·ma·ɔ́·k·an?"
/t   "Master, are you now going to set the Jewish kingdom right again?"
/kl Lord, wilt thou at this time restore again the kingdom to Israel?

[Note: Some text was missing from the copy used at the top of page 221 causing the loss of one to three characters at the beginning of seven lines; these have been restored from the 1906 reprint and confirmed from the KHS copy online.]

Acts 1.7 /b   Tulao, kelwu takw trpi lusewunro; kwatwnro krkw.
(p. 221) /p   təlá·ɔ, "ki·ló·wa takó· ktépi-ləs·i·wəné·ɔ, ko·wa·to·né·ɔ kéku.
/t   He said to them, "*You* aren't up to knowing things.
/kl And he said unto them, It is not for you to know

/b   Wrtwxumunt xwvu nrvlatuf rlkeqih tpisqevlak.
/p   we·t·ó·x·əmənt xó·ha nehəlá·t·ank e·lkí·kwi-=č -tpəskwíhəla·k.
/t   The father alone is the one in control of the time when it will happen.
/kl the times or the seasons, which the Father hath put in his own power.

Acts 1.8 /b   Jwqh kmujinumvwmw alwei luswukun
/p   šúkw=č kəməš·ənəmhúmɔ aləwí·i-ləs·əwá·k·an
/t   But you shall receive power
/kl But ye shall receive power,

/b   rlkeqi Pelset Manutw avpetaqrq;
/p   e·lkí·kwi- pí·lsi·t manə́t·u -ahpi·tá·k·we·kw.
/t   at the time when the holy spirit is in you.
/l   after that the Holy Ghost is come upon you:
/b   okh kwntamasenro nvaky,
/p   ɔ́·k=č kuntama·s·i·né·ɔ nhák·ay,
/t   And you shall bear witness to me,
/kl and ye shall be witnesses unto me

/b   tali Nhelwsulumif ok wrmi avpami Nhwe vakif, ok Sumrlebf
/p   táli †nči·lo·sələmink ɔ́·k wé·mi ahpá·mi nčo·wí·i-hák·ink ɔ́·k †same·lií·yunk,

| | /t | in Jerusalem and all about the Jewish land and Samaria, |
| | /kl | both in Jerusalem, and in all Judaea, and in Samaria, |

	/b	kxunkih rli wekvokamekrk.
	/p	kxántki=č é·li-wi·khɔkamí·k·e·k."
	/t	and eventually to the ends of the earth."
	/kl	and unto the uttermost part of the earth.

Acts 1.9 /b Keji nc lwrtc,
/p kíši- nə́ -luwé·t·e,
/t After saying that,
/kl And when he had spoken these things, ...

Lk 24.50 /b tolumwxolao svaki Pctuni;
/p tɔləmo·x·ɔlá·ɔ sháki †pétəni,
/t he led them out as far as Bethany.
/kl he led them out as far as to Bethany,

/b nunc tuntu uspenxkrn potamwrlxao.
/p ná=nə tə́nta-aspí·nxke·n, pɔ·tamwe·lxá·ɔ.
/t There he raised his hands and prayed for them.
/kl and he lifted up his hands, and blessed them.

Lk 24.51 /b Nrli patamwrlxat
/p né·li-pa·tamwé·lxa·t,
/t And as he prayed for them,
/kl [And it came to pass,] while he blessed them,

Acts 1.9 /b tali rlifwrxenulet,
/p táli e·linkwe·x·í·nəli·t,
/t in the place where they were looking,
/l *and* while they beheld
/k ... while they beheld,
(Omitted: /kl he was parted from them, [Lk 24.51])

Acts 1.9 /b alumi uspe,
/p áləmi-áspi·.
/t he began rising upwards.
/l and taken up
/k he was taken up;

/b tolu nrowao rli kwmvwq tolumwvolwkwn   [⟨mwvo⟩ for ⟨mwxo⟩]
/p tɔ́·la-ne·ɔwwá·ɔ, é·li kə́mhɔkw tɔləmo·x·ɔlúk·o·n
/t And they were unable to see him, as with that a cloud took him away
/kl and a cloud received him out of their sight.
(Omitted: /l and carried him up [Lk 24.51: and carried up].)

Mk 16.19 and Lk 24.51
/b li osavkamc,
/p lí ɔ·s·áhkame.
/t to heaven.
/kl into heaven,

/b tunavaonif Krtanutwet wulumuvtupen.
/p tənna·há·ɔnink ke·tanət·ó·wi·t wələmahtáp·i·n.
/t And he sat at God's right hand.
/kl and he sat on the right hand of God.

Acts 1.10 /b Nrli avi eku lifwrxenvetet rlet,   [⟨rlet⟩ for ⟨ralet⟩]
/p né·li·áhi- íka -linkwe·x·i·nhíti·t e·á·li·t,
/t While they were looking intently at where he was going,
/kl And while they looked stedfastly toward heaven as he went up,

/b wexkaohi neju linwuk oopavkwuk eku wihi nepwuk.
/p wi·xkaɔ́či ní·š·a lə́nəwak ɔɔpahkúwak, íka wíči-ni·p·ó·wak.
/t suddenly there were two men dressed in white standing there with them.
/kl behold, two men stood by them in white apparel;

Acts 1.11 /b Tulkwao, Falulei linwuk,
/p təlkəwá·ɔ, "†nka·lalí·i·lə́nəwak,
/t Those others said to them, "Men of Galilee,
/kl Which also said, Ye men of Galilee,
/b Krkw vuh wcnhi nepyerq uspifwrxenrq?
/p kéku=háč wénči-ni·p·aíe·kw, -aspinkwe·x·í·ne·kw?
/t why are you standing and looking up?
/kl why stand ye gazing up into heaven?

/b Nul nu Nhesus wtunumakrrq wunhi osavkamc,   [⟨wtu-⟩ for ⟨wrtu-⟩]
/p nál ná nčí·sas we·t·ənəma·k·é·e·kw wə́nči ɔ·s·áhkame,
/t That was Jesus who was taken from you into (lit., 'from') heaven.
/kl this same Jesus, which is taken up from you into heaven,

/b nuh nc lupi tunumun patc wunhi osavkamc.
/p ná=č nə́ lápi tənnə́mən, pá·t·e wə́nči ɔ·s·áhkame."
/t He will do the same thing again when he comes from heaven."
/kl shall so come in like manner as ye have seen him go into heaven.

Lk 24.52 /b Nu potamaonro, ok qtukeok li Nhelwsulum,
/p ná pɔ·tamaɔ·né·ɔ, ɔ́·k kwtək·í·ɔk lí †nči·ló·sələm.
/t Then they prayed to him and went back to Jerusalem.
/kl And they worshipped him, and returned to Jerusalem

	/b	avi wulrluntamwwxrok	[⟨-wxr-⟩ for /-o·x·wé·-/]
	/p	áhi-wəle·ləntaməwo·x·wé·ɔk	
	/t	They were extremely joyful as they walked	
	/kl	with great joy:	

Acts 1.12 /b cku wunhi Olipe ovhwf, avpami ct kwti mylif nc wunhi.
        /p íka wə́nči †ɔlipí·i-ɔhčúnk, ahpá·mi=ét kwə́t·i máilink nə́ wə́nči,
        /t from Olive mountain, maybe about one mile from there.
        /kl from the mount called Olivet, which is from Jerusalem a sabbath day's journey.

Lk 24.53 /b Aphi eku avpwpanek patamwrekaonif
        /p á·pči íka ahpó·p·ani·k pa·tamwe·i·k·á·ɔnink,
        /t And they were always in the temple,
        /kl And were continually in the temple,

        /b tuntu wulukunemanro, ok xifovkunemanro Krtanutwelehi,
        /p tə́nta-wəlak·əni·ma·né·ɔ ɔ́·k -xinkɔhkəni·ma·né·ɔ ke·tanət·o·wi·lí·č·i,
        /t praising and glorifying God there,
        /kl praising and blessing God.

L. adds /b eku pchi mrhi Pelset Manutw wrtxatc.
        /p íka péči mé·či pí·lsi·t manə́t·u we·txá·t·e.
        /t until after the holy spirit came to them.
        /l [after the outpouring of the Holy Ghost]

Mk 16.20 /b Alumskrpanek, wrmi li pumutwnvrpanek,
        /p aləmské·p·ani·k, wé·mi lí-pəmət·o·nhé·p·ani·k.
        /t And they headed out and preached everywhere.
        /kl And [*L. addition here*] they went forth, and preached every where,

        /b Nrvlalwrt wetavrmapani, ok vwhetanetwnrp nc aptwnakan,
        /p nehəlá·ləwe·t wwi·t·a·he·má·p·ani, ɔ́·k wči·t·ani·tó·ne·p nə́ a·pto·ná·k·an,
        /t And the lord helped them and strengthened the word
        /kl the Lord working with them, and confirming the word

        /b rli avkanjacvoselet.
        /p é·li-ahkanšaehɔ·s·í·li·t.
        /t by the way they did miracles.
        /kl with signs following.   [RSV "by the signs that attended it"]

[B. omits L.'s "Conclusion" from John 22.30-31 and 21.25.]

www.ingramcontent.com/pod-product-compliance
Lightning Source LLC
Chambersburg PA
CBHW060417010526

44118CB00017B/2257